# The Story of God Bible Commentary Series Endorsements

"Getting a story is about more than merely enjoying it. It means hearing it, understanding it, and above all, being impacted by it. This commentary series hopes that its readers not only hear and understand the story, but are impacted by it to live in as Christian a way as possible. The editors and contributors set that table very well and open up the biblical story in ways that move us to act with sensitivity and understanding. That makes hearing the story as these authors tell it well worth the time. Well done."

**Darrell L. Bock,** Dallas Theological Seminary

"The Story of God Bible Commentary series invites readers to probe how the message of the text relates to our situations today. Engagingly readable, it not only explores the biblical text but offers a range of applications and interesting illustrations."

**Craig S. Keener,** Asbury Theological Seminary

"I love the Story of God Bible Commentary series. It makes the text sing, and helps us hear the story afresh."

**John Ortberg,** Senior pastor of Menlo Park Presbyterian Church

"Bible study leaders, Christians searching for a devotional guide, and pastors who know the importance of expositional preaching will all benefit from this clearly written, theologically perceptive guide through Paul's letter to the Christians in Philippi. Lynn Cohick brings not only her valuable expertise in the language and culture of the New Testament to Philippians, but also her Christian experience and mature theological reflection. The result is a clear, helpful guide through this small but rich part of God's Word."

**Frank Thielman,** Beeson Divinity School

"The Story of God Bible Commentary series is unique in its approach to exploring the Bible. Its easy-to-use format and practical guidance brings God's grand story to modern-day life so anyone can understand how it applies today."

**Andy Stanley,** North Point Ministries

"I'm a storyteller. Through writing and speaking I talk and teach about understanding the Story of God throughout Scripture and about letting God reveal more of His story as I live it out. Thus I am thrilled to have a commentary series based on the Story of God—a commentary that helps me to Listen to the Story, that Explains the Story, and then encourages me to probe how to Live the Story. A perfect tool for helping every follower of Jesus to walk in the story that God is writing for them."

**Judy Douglass,** Director of Women's Resources, Cru

"The Bible is the story of God and his dealings with humanity from creation to new creation. The Bible is made up more of stories than of any other literary genre. Even the psalms, proverbs, prophecies, letters, and the Apocalypse make complete sense only when set in the context of the grand narrative of the entire Bible. This commentary series breaks new ground by taking all these observations seriously. It asks commentators to listen to the text, to explain the text, and to live the text. Some of the material in these sections overlaps with introduction, detailed textual analysis and application, respectively, but only some. The most riveting and valuable part of the commentaries are the stories that can appear in any of these sections, from any part of the globe and any part of church history, illustrating the text in any of these areas. Ideal for preaching and teaching."

**Craig L. Blomberg,** Denver Seminary

"Pastors and lay people will welcome this new series, which seeks to make the message of the Scriptures clear and to guide readers in appropriating biblical texts for life today."

**Daniel I. Block,** Wheaton College and Graduate School

"An extremely valuable, and long overdue series that includes comment on the cultural context of the text, careful exegesis, and guidance on reading the whole Bible as a unity that testifies to Christ as our Savior and Lord."

**Graeme Goldsworthy,** author of *According to Plan*

# ROMANS

# Editorial Board of The Story of God Bible Commentary

# The Story of God Bible Commentary

## ROMANS

Michael F. Bird

Tremper Longman III & Scot McKnight
*General Editors*

ZONDERVAN ACADEMIC

*Romans*


Published in Grand Rapids, Michigan, by Zondervan. Zondervan is a registered trademark of The Zondervan Corporation, L.L.C., a wholly owned subsidiary of HarperCollins Christian Publishing, Inc.

Requests for information should be addressed to customercare@harpercollins.com.

Zondervan titles may be purchased in bulk for educational, business, fundraising, or sales promotional use. For information, please email SpecialMarkets@Zondervan.com.

ISBN 978-0-310-59906-7 (ebook)

Library of Congress Cataloging-in-Publication Data
Bird, Michael F.
Romans / Michael F. Bird.
pages cm.—(Story of God Bible commentary)
Includes bibliographical references and index.
ISBN 978-0-310-32718-9 (hardcover)
1. Bible. Romans—Commentaries. I. Title.
BS2665.53.B56 2015
227'.1077—dc23 2015026775



*Cover design: Ron Huizinga*
*Cover image: iStockphoto®*
*Interior design and composition: Greg Johnson/Textbook Perfect*

*Printed in the United States of America*

24 25 26 27 28 29 30 31 32 33 34 /TRM/ 19 18 17 16 15 14 13 12 11 10 9 8 7 6 5

In gratitude to the many pastors who have shared the love of Christ with me and my family in both word and deed.

Craig Corkill

Joey Huggins†

Craig Lloyd

David D'Amour

Angus Macrae

Dan Bigg

## Old Testament series

1 ▪ Genesis—*Tremper Longman III*
2 ▪ Exodus—*Christopher J. H. Wright*
3 ▪ Leviticus—*Jerry E. Shepherd*
4 ▪ Numbers—*Jay A. Sklar*
5 ▪ Deuteronomy—*Myrto Theocharous*
6 ▪ Joshua—*Lissa M. Wray Beal*
7 ▪ Judges—*Athena E. Gorospe*
8 ▪ Ruth/Esther—*Marion Taylor*
9 ▪ 1–2 Samuel—*Paul S. Evans*
10 ▪ 1–2 Kings—*David T. Lamb*
11 ▪ 1–2 Chronicles—*Carol M. Kaminski*
12 ▪ Ezra/Nehemiah—*Douglas J. Green*
13 ▪ Job—*Martin A. Shields*
14 ▪ Psalms—*Elizabeth R. Hayes*
15 ▪ Proverbs—*Ryan P. O'Dowd*
16 ▪ Ecclesiastes/Song of Songs—*George Athas*
17 ▪ Isaiah—*Mark J. Boda*
18 ▪ Jeremiah/Lamentations—*Andrew G. Shead*
19 ▪ Ezekiel—*D. Nathan Phinney*
20 ▪ Daniel—*Wendy L. Widder*
21 ▪ Minor Prophets I—*Beth M. Stovell*
22 ▪ Minor Prophets II—*Beth M. Stovell*

## New Testament series

1 ▪ Matthew—*Rodney Reeves*
2 ▪ Mark—*Timothy G. Gombis*
3 ▪ Luke—*Kindalee Pfremmer DeLong*
4 ▪ John—*Nicholas Perrin*
5 ▪ Acts—*Dean Pinter*
6 ▪ Romans—*Michael F. Bird*
7 ▪ 1 Corinthians —*Justin K. Hardin*
8 ▪ 2 Corinthians—*Love L. Sechrest*
9 ▪ Galatians—*Nijay K. Gupta*
10 ▪ Ephesians—*Mark D. Roberts*
11 ▪ Philippians—*Lynn H. Cohick*
12 ▪ Colossians/Philemon—*Todd Wilson*
13 ▪ 1–2 Thessalonians—*John Byron*
14 ▪ 1–2 Timothy, Titus—*Marius Nel*
15 ▪ Hebrews—*Radu Gheorghita*
16 ▪ James—*Mariam J. Kamell*
17 ▪ 1 Peter—*Dennis Edwards*
18 ▪ 2 Peter, Jude—*C. Rosalee Velloso Ewell*
19 ▪ 1–3 John—*Constantine R. Campbell*
20 ▪ Revelation—*Jonathan A. Moo*
21 ▪ Sermon on the Mount —*Scot McKnight*

# Contents

*The Story of God Bible Commentary Series* . . . xi
*Author's Preface* . . . xiv
*Abbreviations* . . . xviii
Introduction to Romans . . . 1
Resources for Those Teaching or Preaching the Book of Romans . . . 15
Commentary on Romans . . . 17
*Scripture Index* . . . 543
*Extrabiblical Literature Index* . . . 565
*Subject Index* . . . 569
*Author Index* . . . 575

# The Story of God Bible Commentary Series

The Word of God may not change, but culture does. Think of what we have seen in the last twenty years: we now communicate predominantly through the internet and email; we read our news on iPads and computers; we can talk on the phone to our friends while we are driving, while we are playing golf, or while we are taking long walks; and we can get in touch with others from the middle of nowhere. We carry in our hands small devices that connect us to the world and to a myriad of sources of information. Churches have changed; the "Nones" are rising in numbers and volume, and atheists are bold to assert their views in public forums. The days of home Bible studies are waning, there is a marked rise in activist missional groups in churches, and pastors are more and more preaching topical sermons, some of which are not directly connected to the Bible. Divorce rates are not going down, marriages are more stressed, rearing children is more demanding, and civil unions and same-sex marriages are knocking at the door of the church.

Progress can be found in many directions. While church attendance numbers are waning in Europe and North America, churches are growing in the South and the East. More and more women are finding a voice in churches; the plea of the former generation of leaders that Christians be concerned not just with evangelism but with justice is being answered today in new and vigorous ways. Resources for studying the Bible are more available today than ever before, and preachers and pastors are meeting the challenge of speaking a sure word of God into shifting cultures.

Readers of the Bible change, too. These cultural shifts, our own personal developments, the progress in intellectual questions, as well as growth in biblical studies and theology and discoveries of new texts and new paradigms for understanding the contexts of the Bible—each of these elements works on an interpreter so that the person who reads the Bible today asks different questions from different angles.

Culture shifts, but the Word of God remains. That is why we as editors of The Story of God Bible Commentary series, a commentary based on the New International Version 2011 (NIV 2011), are excited to participate in this new series of commentaries on the Bible. This series is designed to address this generation with the same Word of God. We are asking the authors to explain what the Bible says to the sorts of readers who pick up commentaries so they can understand not only what Scripture says but what it means for today. The Bible does not change, but relating it to our culture changes constantly and in differing ways in different contexts.

When we, the New Testament editors, sat down in prayer and discussion to choose authors for this series, we realized we had found fertile ground. Our list of potential authors staggered in length and quality. We wanted the authors to be exceptional scholars, faithful Christians, committed evangelicals, and theologically diverse, and we wanted this series to represent the changing face of both American and world evangelicalism: ethnic and gender diversity. I believe this series has a wider diversity of authors than any commentary series in evangelical history.

The title of this series, emphasizing as it does the "Story" of the Bible, reveals the intent of the series. We want to explain each passage of the Bible in light of the Bible's grand Story. The Bible's grand Story, of course, connects this series to the classic expression *regula fidei*, the "rule of faith," which was the Bible's Story coming to fulfillment in Jesus as the Messiah, Lord, and Savior of all. In brief, we see the narrative built around the following biblical themes: creation and fall, covenant and redemption, law and prophets, and especially God's charge to humans as his image-bearers to rule under God. The theme of God as King and God's kingdom guides us to see the importance of Israel's kings as they come to fulfillment in Jesus, Lord and King over all, and the direction of history toward the new heavens and new earth, where God will be all in all. With these guiding themes, each passage is examined from three angles.

**Listen to the Story.** We believe that if the Bible is God speaking, then the most important posture of the Christian before the Bible is to listen. So our first section cites the text of Scripture and lists a selection of important biblical and sometimes noncanonical parallels; then each author introduces that passage. The introductions to the passages sometimes open up discussion to the theme of the passage while other times they tie this passage to its context in the specific book. But since the focus of this series is the Story of God in the Bible, the introduction leads the reader into reading this text in light of the Bible's Story.

**Explain the Story.** The authors follow up listening to the text by explaining each passage in light of the Bible's grand Story. This is not an academic series, so the footnotes are limited to the kinds of texts typical Bible readers and preachers readily will have on hand. Authors are given the freedom to explain the text as they read it, though you should not be surprised to find occasional listings of other options for reading the text. Authors explore biblical backgrounds, historical context, cultural codes, and theological interpretations. Authors engage in word studies and interpret unique phrases and clauses as they attempt to build a sound and living reading of the text in light of the Story of God in the Bible.

Authors will not shy away from problems in the texts. Whether one is examining the meaning of "perfect" in Matthew 5:48, the complexities with Christology in the hymn of Philippians 2:6–11, the challenge of understanding Paul in light of the swirling debates about the old, new, and post-new perspectives, the endless debates about eschatology, or the vagaries of atonement theories, the authors will dive in, discuss evidence, and do their best to sort out a reasonable and living reading of those issues for the church today.

**Live the Story.** Reading the Bible is not just about discovering what it meant back then; the intent of The Story of God Bible Commentary series is to probe how this text might be lived out today as that story continues to march on in the life of the church. At times our authors will tell stories about what this looks like; at other times they may offer some suggestions for living it out; but always you will discover the struggle involved as we seek to live out the Bible's grand Story in our world.

We are not offering suggestions for "application" so much as digging deeper; we are concerned in this section with seeking out how this text, in light of the Story of God in the Bible, compels us to live in our world so that our own story lines up with the Bible's Story.

Scot McKnight, general editor New Testament
Lynn Cohick, Joel Willitts, and Michael Bird, editors

# Author's Preface

> Paul's letter to the Romans is really the chief part of the New Testament and is truly the purest gospel. It is worthy not only that every Christian should know it word for word, by heart, but also that all believers should occupy themselves with it every day, as the daily bread of the soul. We can never read it or ponder over it too much, for the more we deal with it, the more precious it becomes and the better it tastes.[1]

> Paul's letter to the Romans is a classic ... probably without equal among New Testament texts.[2]

Why would anyone write yet another commentary on Romans? Good question! Commentaries on Romans are well served and always have been. I do not claim to have read all of them, but I do have a cohort of my favorites that I have tried to interact with during my own study of the letter.[3]

---

1. Martin Luther, "Preface to the Letter of Saint Paul to the Romans," in *Luther's Works* 35 (Saint Louis: Concordia, 1960), 365.

2. Phil Esler, *Conflict and Identity in Romans: The Social Setting of Paul's Letter* (Minneapolis: Fortress, 2003), 1.

3. Gerald L. Bray, trans. and ed., *Ambrosiaster: Commentaries on Romans and 1—2 Corinthians* (ACT; Downers Grove, IL: InterVarsity, 2009); John Chrysostom, "The Homilies of St. John Chrysostom: Epistle of St. Paul the Apostle to the Romans," in *NPNF* 11: 329–564; Theodore de Bruyn, *Pelagius's Commentary on St Paul's Epistles to the Romans* (Oxford: Clarendon, 1993); Karl Barth, *The Epistle to the Romans* (trans. E. C. Hoskyns; London: Oxford University Press, 1932); C. H. Dodd, *The Epistle to the Romans* (London: Hodder & Stoughton, 1932); C. K. Barrett, *A Commentary on the Epistle to the Romans* (New York: Harper & Row, 1957); C. E. B. Cranfield, *The Epistle to the Romans* (ICC; 2 vols.; Edinburgh: T&T Clark, 1975–79); Ernst Käsemann, *Commentary on Romans* (trans. G. W. Bromiley; Grand Rapids: Eerdmans, 1980); Leon Morris, *The Epistle to the Romans* (Pillar; Grand Rapids: Eerdmans, 1988); James D. G. Dunn, *Romans 1–8, 9–16* (WBC; 2 vols.; Dallas: Word, 1988); Joseph A. Fitzmyer, *Romans* (AB; New York: Doubleday, 1993); Peter Stuhlmacher, *Paul's Letter to the Romans: A Commentary* (trans. S. Hafemann; Louisville: Westminster John Knox, 1994); Douglas J. Moo, *The Epistle to the Romans* (NICNT; Grand Rapids: Eerdmans, 1996); Brendan Byrne, *Romans* (SP; Collegeville, MN: Liturgical, 1996); Mark D. Nanos, *The Mystery of Romans: The Jewish Context of Paul's Career* (Minneapolis: Fortress, 1996); Luke Timothy Johnson, *Reading Romans: A Literary and Theological Commentary* (New York: Crossroads, 1997); Thomas R. Schreiner, *Romans* (BECNT; Grand Rapids: Baker, 1998); Klaus Haacker, *Der Brief des Paulus an die Römer* (THKNT; Leipzig: Evangelische Verlagsanstalt, 1999); Christopher Bryan, *A Preface to Romans: Notes on the Epistle in its Literary and Cultural Setting* (Oxford: Oxford University Press, 2000); A. Katherine Grieb, *The Story of Romans: A Narrative Defense of God's Righteousness* (Louisville: Westminster John Knox, 2002); N. T. Wright, "Romans," in *New Interpreter's Bible* (ed. L. E. Keck; Nashville: Abingdon, 2002), 10:395–770; Charles H. Talbert, *Romans* (Macon, GA:

On my desk I have kept commentaries by N. T. Wright (NIB), Douglas J. Moo (NICNT), Tom Schreiner (BECNT), and Robert Jewett (Hermeneia) close by as my primary dialogue partners, with several others never far away (Leon Morris, James D. G. Dunn, Leander Keck, Charles Talbert, and Luke Timothy Johnson). Lest people think that I'm simply adding yet another volume to an already crowded library of Romans commentaries, let me add that the problem of a proliferation of Romans commentaries is not a new one. At the height of the European Reformation, for example, no less than ten Romans commentaries were written by Protestant and Catholic theologians between 1532 and 1542. In fact, John Calvin felt the need to apologize and defend his choice of writing a commentary on Romans at this time. The French Reformer wrote:

> Since so many scholars of pre-eminent learning have previously devoted their efforts to explaining this Epistle, it seems unlikely that there is any room left for others to produce something better.... It will, however, I hope be admitted that nothing has ever been so perfectly done by men that there is no room left for those who follow them to refine, adorn, or illustrate their work. I do not dare to say anything of myself, except that I thought that the present work would be of some profit, and that I have been led to undertake it for no other reason than the common good of the Church.[4]

Like Calvin, I know I haven't come up with the first word or the last word on Romans. Like Calvin too, I also believe that what I have to say in my reading of Romans might "be of some profit" to readers and for "the common good of the church"—an aim that is actually achievable thanks to the goals and format of the Story of God Bible Commentary Series (SGBC). Romans is a letter with its own narrative world and is a clear extension of the biblical story line. Romans is "big picture" theology, and it naturally lends itself to expositing the canonical narrative from which it springs. What is more, Paul's

---

Smyth & Helwys, 2002); Esler, *Conflict and Identity in Romans*; Thomas H. Tobin, *Paul's Rhetoric in its Contexts: The Argument of Romans* (Peabody, MA: Hendrickson, 2004); Ben Witherington, *Paul's Letter to the Romans: A Socio-Rhetorical Commentary* (Grand Rapids: Eerdmans, 2004); William Dumbrell, *Romans: A New Covenant Commentary* (Eugene, OR: Wipf & Stock, 2005); Leander E. Keck, *Romans* (ANTC; Nashville: Abingdon, 2005); Robert K. Jewett, *Romans: A Commentary* (Hermeneia; Minneapolis: Fortress, 2007); Craig S. Keener, *Romans* (NCCS; Eugene, OR: Cascade, 2009); Frank Matera, *Romans* (Paideia; Grand Rapids: Baker, 2010); Arland J. Hultgren, *Paul's Letter to the Romans: A Commentary* (Grand Rapids: Eerdmans, 2011); Colin G. Kruse, *Paul's Letter to the Romans* (Pillar; Grand Rapids: Eerdmans, 2012); Solomon Andria, *Romans* (ABCS; Nairobi: Hippo, 2012).

4. John Calvin, "John Calvin to Simon Grynaeus," *Calvin's Commentaries: The Epistles of Paul the Apostle to the Romans and Thessalonians* (trans. R. Mackenzie; Grand Rapids: Eerdmans, 1960), 2–3.

letter to the Romans is deeply steeped in pastoral and missional theology. Not just in the later chapters, but beginning front and center in Romans 1 we can detect the mission of God operating in the mission of the church. Thus, I was excited when asked to contribute the volume on Romans in the SGBC. For I knew that I had hit the theological jackpot in terms of writing a commentary that brings the scriptural story into the living stories of the pastors and people who cherish what is easily Paul's most magnificent letter.

Among the many parts of the Christian Bible, none has arguably been so treasured and so influential as Paul's letter to the Romans. Its impact on the great thinkers of the church like Augustine, Martin Luther, and Karl Barth testify to the letter's enduring poignancy and power. Over a span of centuries, Romans has been a powerful source for theological reformation and an inspiration for spiritual renewal. When people read Romans, big things can happen: paradigms shift, decades of compromise are called out, the superficiality of Christian culture is named and shamed, we are refreshed by a scandalous grace, joy in the gospel is rediscovered, and the evangelical mission of the church is reaffirmed.

My thesis is that Romans is the gospel at theological depth. In this letter, Paul explores how the gospel creates a community of worshipers from Jews and Gentiles who are united in the Messiah. Paul cannot be with the Roman Christians for the moment, so in the interim he "gospelizes" them, that is to say, he endeavors to cultivate a gospel-soaked faith, spirituality, unity, and mission in the Roman house churches. At ground level, Paul wrote to the Romans to solicit their support for his own mission westward, to unify their fractious house churches around a common set of gospel values, and to direct them to live obediently under the one Lord.

There are several people I need to thank for this project. First, my fellow editors, Scot McKnight, Joel Willitts, and Lynn Cohick, who have been great coworkers to construct a commentary series that will help pastors and preachers get inside the biblical story. Second, special thanks to my colleagues at Ridley College, not the least Brian Rosner, a true-blue Pauline scholar, for his encouragement. Third, to the great team at Zondervan including Katya Covrett, Jesse Hillman, Nancy Erickson, and especially Verlyn Verbrugge, who worked on this manuscript in his last days before passing away. Verlyn was a sweet Christian man, a great academic editor, and I am very grateful for having the opportunity to have worked with him. Fourth, two Ridley students, Matt Smith and Rachel Lopez, who read through a draft and offered some good advice and feedback. Fifth, personal testimonies were sent to me by Craig Lloyd, James Allman, Craig Keener, and Bob Mendelsohn, to whom I am grateful. Sixth, and of course, my family, who have continued to bless me with their love, support, and encouragement. Seventh, the assistance of the Ridley librarian Ruth Millard for finding several books for me and indulging my contempt for book return due dates. Eighth, Ben Sutton ably compiled the bibliography and the list of abbreviations.

Finally, I've been blessed by the ministry of many fine people who have pastored me and my family in the Christian faith. To them this book is dedicated. To that end, I hope this commentary enables similar men and women in the church to do what Paul set out to do, namely, to encourage a diverse and complicated group of believers to "do what leads to peace and to mutual edification" as they live and work under the auspices of the Lord Jesus Christ (Rom 14:19).

# Abbreviations

| | |
|---|---|
| AB | Anchor Bible |
| ABCS | Africa Bible Commentary Series |
| *ABD* | *Anchor Bible Dictionary* |
| ACT | Ancient Christian Texts |
| AGAJU | Arbeiten zur Geschichte des antiken Judentums und des Urchristentums |
| ANTC | Abingdon New Testament Commentary |
| *BAR* | *Biblical Archaeology Review* |
| *BBR* | *Bulletin of Biblical Research* |
| BDAG | W. Bauer, F. W. Danker, W. F. Arndt, and F. W. Gingrich. *A Greek-English Lexicon of the New Testament and Other Early Christian Literature*. 3rd ed. Chicago: University of Chicago Press, 2000. |
| BECNT | Baker Exegetical Commentary on the New Testament |
| *Bib* | *Biblica* |
| *BSac* | *Bibliotheca Sacra* |
| *BZ* | *Biblische Zeitschrift* |
| BZNW | Beihefte zur Zeitschrift für die neutestamentliche Wissenschaft |
| *CBR* | *Currents in Biblical Research* |
| CEV | Common English Version |
| *CITM* | James D. G. Dunn. *Christianity in the Making*. 2 vols. Grand Rapids: Eerdmans, 2003, 2009. |
| *CONTUOT* | Greg K. Beale, and D. A. Carson, eds. *Commentary on the New Testament Use of the Old Testament*. Grand Rapids: Baker, 2007. |
| COQG | N. T. Wright. Christian Origins and the Question of God. 4 vols. Minneapolis: Fortress, 1992–2013. |
| *CTR* | *Criswell Theological Review* |
| *DPL* | Gerald F. Hawthorne, and Ralph P. Martin, eds. *Dictionary of Paul's Letters*. Downers Grove, IL: InterVarsity, 1993. |
| *EDB* | D. N. Freedman, A. C. Myers, and A. B. Beck, eds. *Eerdmans Dictionary of the Bible*. Grand Rapids: Eerdmans, 2000. |
| *EDEJ* | *Eerdmans Dictionary of Early Judaism* |
| *EvQ* | *Evangelical Quarterly* |

| | |
|---|---|
| *ExpT* | *Expository Times* |
| FS | Festschrift |
| *HBT* | *Horizons in Biblical Theology* |
| ICC | International Critical Commentary |
| *Int* | *Interpretation* |
| *JBL* | *Journal of Biblical Literature* |
| *JBTh* | *Journal of Biblical Theology* |
| *JES* | *Journal of Ecumenical Studies* |
| *JETS* | *Journal of the Evangelical Theological Society* |
| *JSNT* | *Journal for the Study of the New Testament* |
| JSNTSup | Journal for the Study of the New Testament Supplement Series |
| *JSPL* | *Journal for the Study of Paul's Letters* |
| *Jub* | *Jubilees (Old Testament Pseudepigrapha)* |
| *LAB* | *Liber Antiquitatum Biblicarum* |
| LHJS | Library of Historical Jesus Studies |
| LN | Louw and Nida |
| LNTS | Library of New Testament Studies |
| LS | Louvain Studies |
| LSJ | Liddel, Scott, and Jones. *Greek-English Lexicon.* |
| LXX | Septuagint (Greek Old Testament) |
| *m.* | Mishnah |
| MSG | The Message |
| MT | Masoretic Text (Hebrew Bible) |
| $NA^{28}$ | Nestle-Aland Greek New Testament, 28th Edition |
| NCCS | New Covenant Commentary Series |
| *NDBT* | *New Dictionary of Biblical Theology* |
| *NDIEC* | *New Documents Illustrating Early Christianity.* 10 vols. Grand Rapids, MI: Eerdmans, 1997–2012. |
| NET | New English Translation |
| NIB | New Interpreter's Bible |
| NICNT | New International Commentary on the New Testament |
| NIV | New International Version |
| NLV | New Living Version |
| *NovT* | *Novum Testamentum* |
| *NPNF* | *Nicene and Post-Nicene Fathers* |
| NSBT | New Series in Biblical Theology |
| NTM | New Testament Monographs |
| PNTC | Pillar New Testament Commentary |
| PS | Pauline Studies |
| *RTF* | *Reformed Theological Review* |
| *Sanh.* | Sanhedrin |
| *SBJT* | *Southern Baptist Journal of Theology* |

| | |
|---|---|
| SBLDS | Society of Biblical Literature Dissertation Series |
| SBLGNT | Society of Biblical Literature Greek New Testament |
| SE | Studia Evanglica |
| SGBC | The Story of God Bible Commentary |
| Sir | Sirach |
| *SJT* | *Scottish Journal of Theology* |
| SNTSMS | Society for New Testament Studies Monograph Series |
| SP | Sacra Pagina |
| *SVTQ* | *Saint Vladimir's Theological Quarterly* |
| *TDNT* | *Theological Dictionary of the New Testament* |
| THKNT | Theologischer Handkommentar zum Neuen Testament |
| *TynBul* | *Tyndale Bulletin* |
| UBS$^5$ | United Bible Society New Testament, 5th Edition |
| *USQR* | *Union Seminary Quarterly Review* |
| WBC | Word Biblical Commentary Series |
| Wis | Wisdom of Solomon |
| *WTJ* | *Westminster Theological Journal* |
| WUNT | Wissenschaftliche Untersuchungen zum Neuen Testament |
| *ZNW* | *Zeitschrift für die neutestamentliche Wissenschaft und die Kunde der älteren Kirche* |

# Introduction to Romans

Paul's epistle to the Romans stands arguably as the apex of Pauline thought. It is the longest letter in the Pauline corpus. In addition, it is his most theologically erudite and pastorally applicable set of teachings about faith in Jesus Christ. It is a letter that has had a monumental impact in the history of Christian thought. Before we can get into the text, there are several introductory matters that we have to address.[1]

## The Story of the Roman Christians

We do not know precisely *when* Christianity came to Rome. We are told by Luke that many Jews and proselytes from Rome were present on the day of Pentecost, and they may have returned to Rome around AD 30/31 sporting a newfound faith borne of an encounter with Jesus' followers and excited by new spiritual experiences (Acts 2:10–11). Otherwise, Suetonius reports that Claudius expelled the Jews around AD 49 because they were constantly rioting about a certain figure called "Chrestus," a probable Latinism for "Christ" (Suetonius, *Claudius* 25.2).[2] This corroborates Luke's account of Priscilla and Aquila being forced out of Italy by Claudius's edict and arriving in Corinth, where they met Paul in AD 50/51 (Acts 18:2). The only other concrete piece of evidence we have is that the three men who delivered a letter from the church in Rome to the church in Corinth in AD 95 are described as "old men" who had been "blameless" since youth, and therefore probably had been believers since their childhood in the 30s or 40s (*1 Clem* 63.3; 65.1). Given this data, we can presumptively date a Christian presence in Rome no later than the early AD 40s.

In terms of *how* Christianity came to Rome, again, we simply do not know for certain. Probably correct is the fourth-century commentator Ambrosiaster,

1. See further introductions to Romans in Michael F. Bird, "The Letter to the Romans," in *All Things to All Cultures: Paul among Jews, Greeks, and Romans* (eds. M. Harding and A. Nobbs; Grand Rapids: Eerdmans, 2013), 177–204; and Gary M. Burge, Lynn H. Cohick, and Gene L. Green, *The New Testament in Antiquity: A Survey of the New Testament within Its Cultural Contexts* (Grand Rapids: Zondervan, 2009), 321–35.

2. Tacitus (*Annals* 15.44) continued the misspelling of the name with "Chrestianos" for "Christians." Confusion over the name Christos/Chrestus continued even into the second century as evidenced by Tertullian, *Apology* 3 and Justin Martyr, *Apology* 1.4.

who claimed that "the Romans embraced the faith according to the Jewish rite," which is to say that Christianity entered Rome via the Jewish synagogues. There were probably multiple streams of entry of the faith into the Roman synagogues as Christianity was carried by Jewish pilgrims returning from Jerusalem, Jewish immigrants from the east, travelling merchants, and especially the slave trade. Soon, it seems, the Christian faith was transmitted to Gentiles, since by the time Paul writes to them he assumes a significant Gentile audience (see Rom 1:5–6, 13; 11:13; 15:15–16). Debates about the Messiah and rivalry for the adherence of the growing number of God-fearers and proselytes joining this messianic group led to violent confrontations within the Jewish communities of Rome. The result of the tumults was Claudius's expulsion of many Jews from Rome, including Jewish Christian leaders like Priscilla and Aquila.[3]

The most meticulous study of Christian origins in Rome has been undertaken by Peter Lampe. After combing through literary, inscriptional, and archaeological evidences, Lampe concludes that Christianity took root and flourished in the poorest and overcrowded districts of Rome, most probably the Trastevere and the Appian Way outside of the Porta Capena, and perhaps also the Aventine Hill and Mars Field. Furthermore, given the prevalence of slave names in the greetings in Romans 16:3–16, he argues that a large number of the Roman Christians were either slaves or freedman, with many drawn from the ranks of Jewish households like "Aristobulus" and "Herodion" (16:11–12). So Christianity may well have begun in Rome as a movement among Jewish Christian slaves and ex-slaves and soon attracted increasing numbers of God-fearers to its ranks.[4]

Paul probably acquired knowledge of the recent history of the Roman churches and awareness of their ethnic diversity through colleagues like Priscilla and Aquila, who had resided in Rome for a time. Several observations about the Roman Christians can be gleaned from the letter itself. To begin with, Paul's implied audience is comprised of Gentiles (Rom 1:5–6, 13; 11:13; 16:6–15) who know the gospel, since Paul quotes traditional material that he expects them to be familiar with (1:3–4, 3:22–25; 4:25; 6:17; 10:9–11; 15:15). Reports of their faith and obedience have extended to the east (1:8, 16:19), as has their adherence to a recognizable pattern of teaching (6:17; 16:17). They know the Jewish law or "Torah" probably as former

3. The plausibility of Suetonius's account is enhanced when we remember that similar such tumults over messianic faith occurred in Jerusalem (Acts 6:9–15), Pisidian Antioch (13:45, 50), Iconium (14:2, 5), Lystra (14:19), and Corinth (18:12–17).

4. Peter Lampe, *From Paul to Valentinus: Christians at Rome in the First Two Centuries* (Minneapolis: Fortress, 1993).

God-fearers and proselytes (7:1). The Romans are full of goodness and knowledge and are able to instruct one another (15:14–15). Paul expects a positive reception from them when he arrives (15:22–24, 28–29). He knows, directly and indirectly, some twenty-six people in Rome (16:3–16).

In regard to the situation in Rome to which Paul is writing, one gets the impression from the letter that Paul is addressing a church that is factionalized along ethnic lines. According to Romans 16:3–5, it appears that many Jewish Christians returned to Rome after Claudius's death in AD 54 when his edict was rescinded. The six-year interval between 49 and 54 AD meant that Christianity began to grow in Rome with increasing number of Gentile converts and without the leadership or patronage of Jewish Christian leaders. By the time that Paul wrote his greetings, only a minority of the believers there were identifiable as Jewish Christians (Priscila and Aquila [16:3–5], Mary [16:6], Andronicus and Junia [16:7], household of Aristobulus [16:10], and Herodion [16:11]). Moreover, during this period Christianity probably moved its social center of gravity away from the Jewish communities and into house churches, tenement churches, or meeting places in workshops in the poorer suburbs of Rome. If Romans 9–11 and 14–15 are illustrative of the Roman context, Paul wrote to the Roman Gentiles after the return of the Jewish Christian exiles to Rome when rifts were beginning to open up between different factions.

Furthermore, although "Christianity" was perceived as an intra-Jewish sect in the 50s, by the time of Nero's persecution against Christ-believers in the mid-60s, it had become possible to differentiate "Jews" from "Christians." According to later tradition, it was during Nero's persecution that Paul and Peter were probably martyred. Thus, Paul was writing to the Roman churches during a time of ethnic flux when the ethnic make-up of the churches was shifting toward a Gentile majority, bringing with it cultural and theological points of contention. What is arguably implicit is that Paul thinks that the Romans have heard rumours that he is antinomian on morality (Rom 3:7–8; 6:1) and supersessionist about Israel with the church effectively replacing Israel (9:1–5), the very things that Jewish communities were most affronted by and formed part of Paul's infamous reputation (see Acts 20:20–21; 28:17; cf. Jas 2:14–26).

Personally, I wonder if some Jewish Christians and conservative Gentile Christians in Rome harbored reservations about Paul because of this reputation. I wonder too if some Gentile Christians had heard of these rumours, wholeheartedly embraced that view of Paul, and even appealed to a caricature of Paul to justify their own disregard for Torah and denigration of Israel. Paul, then, does not want misconceptions of his teaching used as a stick to bash Jewish Christians. A scenario along those lines corresponds with Paul's knowledge of divisions based on matters related to whether the Torah was still binding on believers (Rom 14:1 – 15:13). This explains why across the letter Paul walks a tight rope between affirming the Torah's goodness as well as the termination of its jurisdiction over believers.

We will explore the purpose(s) of Romans below, but for now it suffices to say that the situation in Rome, as far as we can reconstruct it, seems to assume that some kind of friction between Gentile Christians and Jewish Christians has developed. The issues could have been manifold and included in-house debates over Torah, leadership tensions caused by the expulsion and return of Jewish Christians to Rome, and divisions fostered by ethnic prejudices. Paul shows genuine concern that the Roman house churches might splinter along ethnic or theological lines. In light of that, Paul wants to work for the unity of the Roman churches by binding them together around the gospel and his vision of the church as the multi-ethnic people of God. That way Paul can return to Jerusalem with a unified Roman church behind him, and a unified Roman church is more likely to be able to support his future missionary work in Spain. Given this proposal, I invite you, as you read through Romans, to imagine what it would be like for a group of Gentile Christians meeting in a cramped apartment (called an *insula*) in the impoverished parts of the Trastevere (i.e., a suburb in Rome), led by a fictitious leather worker named Rufus (cf. Rom 16:13), to read over this letter in that setting. Imagine Paul's letter to the Romans as viewed through the eyes of Roman Gentiles.

## The Story of Paul Writing to the Romans

Paul wrote Romans after finishing an extensive period of ministry to Gentiles in the eastern part of the Mediterranean (Rom 15:15 – 23). His immediate plans were to visit Jerusalem in order to deliver the collection taken up from the Gentile churches. Thereafter, he intended to visit Rome (15:24, 28 – 29, 32) as he had longed to do (1:13; 15:22 – 23) and then proceed west to Spain (15:24, 28).

We can identify Paul's location from his commendation of his delegate Phoebe, who is a "deacon/servant" of the church in Cenchreae (Rom 16:1), and the list of persons who also send their greetings like Erastus (see Acts 19:22; 2 Tim 4:20) suggests a provenance from the Corinthian isthmus (Rom 16:21 – 23). This data can be correlated with Luke's account in Acts, which depicts Paul as leaving Macedonia and staying in Greece for three months before setting out for Troas with the collection and a cohort of delegates (Acts 20:1 – 5). It is during this three-month stay in Corinth, as he reflected on his immediate journey to Jerusalem and a future expedition to Spain, that he turned his mind to the Romans and dispatched Phoebe with his communication to them.

In other letters, Paul was usually responding to some crisis or urgent need. According to Dunn, however, Paul wrote Romans in different circumstances:

> In this case, in contrast, in the relative leisure and calm of Corinth, at the close of his successful missioning in the Aegean area, he had been able to work through in considerable detail the content and character of the gospel which had been his principal message as "apostle to the Gentiles" — and not simply for his own self-satisfaction, or even necessarily for an immediate purpose. It was rather that the challenges which had surfaced again and again in his mission and in his attempts to maintain positive relations with the home churches in Judea and Antioch had repeatedly been occasioned by the difficulties of reconciling the gospel of a *Jewish* Messiah with a vocation to preach this Messiah among the *Gentiles*. The composition of Romans gave him the opportunity to work these issues through as thoroughly as we have now seen. But having done this, there were still specific issues of which he knew in Rome, and which needed to be addressed, some a direct expression of the tensions he had laid bare particularly in his third telling of the gospel's story [i.e., Romans 12–15].[5]

Thus, Romans was written at a transitionary point in Paul's career when he had momentary respite and was at a geographical and intellectual juncture where it was time to reflect on the past and to look ahead to the future.

Dating any event in Paul's career is always difficult and usually inexact. We can safely date the letter after Claudius's edict in AD 49 (Acts 18:2), after Gallio became proconsul of Achaia in AD 51 (18:12), and after the death of Claudius in AD 54, when his edict was rescinded and Jewish Christians like Priscilla and Aquila were able to return to Rome (Acts 16:3–5). We are probably looking at a date post AD 55, when Paul is in Corinth on a three-month stay (20:2–3) and is about to set sail for Jerusalem (Rom 15:25–32). It could have been written as late as AD 59, especially if Paul's remark about taxes in Romans 13:6–7 reflects the public unrest created by the dubious practices of tax farmers that Nero clamped down on through several tax reforms in AD 58.[6] Thus, given a post-55 date and the likelihood that Paul arrived in Rome around AD 59/60, we can date Romans around AD 56/57.[7]

---

5. James D. G Dunn, *Beginning from Jerusalem* (CITM 2; Grand Rapids: Eerdmans, 2009), 919 (emphases original).

6. As reported by Tacitus, *Annals* 13.50–51, and Suetonius, *Nero* 10.

7. Cf. similarly Dunn, *Romans*, 1:xliii; idem, *Beginning from Jerusalem*, 512; Jewett, *Romans*, 18–21; Andria, *Romans*, 2.

## Why Did Paul Write Romans?

A multiplicity of proposals for the purpose of Romans have been suggested.[8]

1. **A theological treatise.** The Muratorian Canon regarded Romans as written "concerning the plan of the Scriptures showing that their foundation is Christ." Among the Reformers, Luther said in his preface to Romans that Paul "wanted to compose a summary of the whole of Christian and evangelical teaching which would also be an introduction to the whole Old Testament."[9] Luther's junior colleague, Philip Melanchthon, in his *Loci Communes Theologici*, labeled Romans a "compendium of Christian doctrine." John Calvin regarded the letter as a systematic exposition of justification by faith.[10] Not long ago, J. C. Beker suggested that Romans is "dogmatics in outline," not a timeless theological product but a "treatise."[11] More recently Douglas Campbell has claimed that, in Romans 5–8 at least, Paul "provisionally articulates a systematic theology."[12]

While Romans is Paul's most theologically loaded and logically coherent exposition of the Christian faith, it is problematic to regard it as a theological treatise for at least two reasons: (a) It fails to say much about key topics such as the Holy Spirit, church, sacraments, and eschatology. (b) Paul's letters were always situational, and Romans is no exception as evidenced by his greetings (1:1–15) and account of his missionary intentions (15:14–16:27).

2. **A summary of Pauline teaching.** Others suppose that Romans is a précis of Paul's teaching in the light of disputes that he had in Antioch, Galatia, and Corinth. That is why there are so many connections between Romans and Paul's other letters. For instance, there are similarities with Galatians and Romans 1–4 concerning justification. There are also similarities between 1 Corinthians 8 and Romans 14–15 concerning disputed matters of food and fellowship. Günther Bornkamm proposed that Romans was Paul's "Last

---

8. See esp. Paul Minear, *The Obedience of Faith: The Purposes of Paul in the Epistle to the Romans* (London: SCM, 1979); Karl P. Donfried, ed., *The Romans Debate* (rev. ed.; Peabody, MA: Hendrickson, 1991); A. J. M. Wedderburn, *The Reasons for Romans* (Minneapolis: Fortress, 1991); L. Ann Jervis, *The Purpose of Romans: A Comparative Letter Structure Investigation* (JSNTSup 55; Sheffield: JSOT Press, 1991); James C. Miller, *The Obedience of Faith, The Eschatological People of God, and the Purpose of Romans* (SBLDS 177; Atlanta: SBL, 2000); Jewett, *Romans*, 80–91; A. Andrew Das, *Solving the Romans Debate* (Minneapolis: Fortress, 2007); Richard L. Longenecker, *Introducing Romans: Critical Issues in Paul's Most Famous Letter* (Grand Rapids: Eerdmans, 2011), 43–51, 94–166.

9. Martin Luther, "Preface to the Letter of St. Paul to the Romans," *Christian Classics Ethereal Library*. http://www.ccel.org/l/luther/romans/pref_romans.html.

10. John Calvin, *Calvin's Commentaries: Romans-Galatians* (Wilmington, DE: Associated Publishing, n.d.), 12:1333.

11. J. C. Beker, *Paul the Apostle: The Triumph of God in Life and Thought* (Philadelphia: Fortress, 1980), 77.

12. Douglas A. Campbell, "Christ and the Church in Paul: A 'Post-New Perspective' Account," in *Four Views on the Apostle Paul* (ed. M. F. Bird; Grand Rapids: Zondervan, 2013), 141.

Will and Testament," a summation of his teaching as well as a rehearsal for the defense of his ministry as he prepared to go to Jerusalem to deliver the collection.[13] There is something right about this suggestion since Romans indeed reflects a mature theology of the Pauline mission.[14] James Dunn comments:

> Paul's primary objective ... was to think through his gospel in the light of the controversies which it had occasioned and to use the calm of Corinth to set out both his gospel itself and its ramifications in writing with a fullness of exposition which the previous trials and tribulations had made impossible and which would have been impossible to sustain in a single oral presentation.[15]

The problem with this summary view is: (a) It does not take into account the differences between Romans and the other Pauline letters. For a start, Paul's tone in discussing the law is very different from Galatians. Likewise, Paul's exhorations to the weak in Romans 14 cover the issues of meat, sacred days, and wine, which is not the same issue as idol-food as discussed in 1 Corinthians 8. (b) There is also a lot of material in Romans that does not appear in the other letters, such as the analogy of the olive tree (Rom 11:13–31) and his instructions about taxes and government (13:1–7). These cannot be explained as a summary of Paul's teaching or form the basis for his notes in a defense of his apostolate in Jerusalem. While Romans is undoubtedly a distillation of his missional theology, it still contains a specificity that cannot be accounted for by his reflections on his teaching or by his preparations to defend himself in Jerusalem.

3. **A letter soliciting support for the Pauline mission.** Paul says explicitly in the letter that he intends to travel west to Spain, and he evidently needed the support of the Roman churches for this journey (Rom 15:24–28). In light of that, several scholars have proposed that Paul wrote the letter principally to solicit the support of the Roman congregations for his future evangelistic efforts in Spain.[16] Luke Timothy Johnson goes so far as to call Romans, in essence, a fund-raising letter.[17]

---

13. Günther Bornkamm, "The Letter to the Romans as Paul's Last Will and Testament," in *The Romans Debate* (ed. K. P. Donfried; Peabody, MA: Hendrickson, 1991), 16–28. Jacob Jervell ("The Letter to Jerusalem," in *The Romans Debate*, 53–64) also emphasizes the role of Romans as a preparation for Paul's speech in Jerusalem.

14. N. A. Dahl, "The Missionary Theology in the Epistle to the Romans," in *Studies in Paul: Theology for the Early Christian Mission* (Minneapolis: Augsburg, 1977), 70–94.

15. Dunn, *Beginning from Jerusalem*, 867.

16. W. G. Kümmel, *Introduction to the New Testament* (trans. H. C. Kee; Nashville: Abingdon, 1975), 312–13.

17. Johnson, *Romans*, 6–9.

The problems here are as follows: (a) Would such an elaborate and lengthy letter be required to solicit funds? In Philippians, Paul renews the bonds of fraternity with the audience and asks them to provide further financial assistance to him, but Philipppians is nowhere near as dense or lengthy as Romans. Granted, in order to get the support of the Roman churches, Paul would have to lay out his gospel at length to clarify his views, thus accounting for Romans 1–8. But such a purpose hardly warrants the inclusion of Romans 9–11, which deals with the problem of Israel's rejection of the gospel and the Gentiles' acceptance of it. (b) Neither does this theory require the exhortations in Romans 12–15, which appear to have a specific context in mind. The latter half of Romans must be explained by circumstances exterior to Paul's own situation. Most likely, Paul writes such things because he has caught wind of events transpiring in Rome that he wishes to address before he arrives there. So I think "yes" to a missionary purpose, but there is something else going on in Rome that occasions Paul's letter and its specific construction, apology, and exhortations.

4. **A letter to bring unity to the Roman churches.** Many have asserted that Paul wrote Romans in order bring the fractured groups among the Roman churches together. Some perceive Paul in Romans 9–11 urging Gentile Christians not to imitate the anti-Judaism of Roman cultural elites, and some regard Paul as trying in Romans 14–15 to foster reconciliation between the "strong" and the "weak."[18] A landmark study by Wolfgang Wiefel argued that the ban on Jewish assemblies and the expulsion of the Jews from Rome under Claudius significantly impacted the shape of Christianity in Rome between AD 49 and 54. In the intervening years, the Christian movement became largely separated from the synagogues and developed a mostly Gentile leadership among house churches. The return of the Jewish Christians created internal tensions over the Jewish law and leadership of the Gentile-majority house churches. So, Paul wrote Romans to effect reconciliation between them. According to Wiefel, the situation behind the letter is that it was written to "assist the Gentile Christian majority, who are the primary addressees of the letter, to live together with the Jewish Christians in one congregation, thereby putting an end to their quarrels about status."[19] This vacuum theory has been

18. Wolfgang Wiefel, "The Jewish Community in Ancient Rome and the Origins of Roman Christianity," in *The Romans Debate* (ed. K. P. Donfried; Peabody, MA: Hendrickson, 1991), 85–101; Dunn, *Romans*, 1:lvi–lviii; idem, *Beginning from Jerusalem*, 873–74; Wright, "Romans," 10:406–8; J. P. Sampley, "The Weak and the Strong: Paul's Careful and Crafty Rhetorical Strategy in Romans 14:1–15:13," in *The Social World of the First Christians* (ed. L. M. White and L. Yarbrough; Minneapolis: Fortress, 1995), 40–52; W. L. Lane, "Social Perspectives on Roman Christianity during the Formative Years from Nero to Nerva," in *Judaism and Christianity in First-Century Rome* (ed. K. P. Donfried and P. Richardson; Grand Rapids: Eerdmans, 1998), 196–244 (esp. 199–202); Esler, *Conflict and Identity in Romans*, 133.

19. Wiefel, "Jewish Community in Ancient Rome," 96.

popular and become the predominating view in scholarship.[20] The strengths of this view are that it identifies a plausible social context for the content in Romans 9–15 and makes sense of the emotive exhortations that appear at the end, such as Paul's concern that his audience pursue the things of peace (14:19) and accept one another as Christ accepted them (15:7).

There are, however, a few problems that plague this vacuum view. (a) We cannot be certain that the "weak" were Jewish Christians and the "strong" were Gentile Christians. Paul was a Jewish Christian who considers himself to be one of the "strong" (Rom 15:1), and similar language concerning the "weak" was used in a Gentile majority church in Corinth (1 Cor 8:7, 10). There could be Gentile Christians with strong scruples about food, drink, and idolatry, just as there could be Jewish Christians who became liberal in such matters. (b) The significance of the expulsion of the Jews from Rome in AD 49 is potentially overestimated. For a start, Paul nowhere mentions the expulsion even implicitly in the letter. It is also more likely that the ring leaders or those few synagogues known to be tumultuous were penalized with expulsion, rather than exiling every single one of the 50,000-plus Jews in Rome, many of whom were Roman citizens.[21]

Though the Gentile Christians could have become slightly more independent in the absence of their Jewish-Christian colleagues, we have no firm reason to believe that Christianity became essentially Gentilized in the years immediately following Claudius's edict of expulsion. According to Peter Oaks, while Romans 14–15 exhibits signs of tension between house churches, issues that may relate to the Jewish heritage of its members, to say that the tension is a direct result of the return of Jewish Christians to Rome who had been expelled by Claudius is not demanded since other scenarios can account for this tension.[22] In fact, some scholars think that the entire letter is meant for digestion *within* Gentile churches in Rome.[23] Thus, the notion of a Jewish

20. W. B. Russell, "An Alternative Suggestion for the Purpose of Romans," *BSac* 45 (1988): 174–84; J. C. Walters, *Ethnic Issues in Paul's Letter to the Romans: Changing Self-Definition in Earliest Roman Christianity* (Valley Forge, PA: Trinity Press International, 1993); Francis Watson, "The Two Roman Congregations: Romans 14:1–15:13," in *The Romans Debate* (ed. K.P. Donfried; Peabody, MA: Hendrickson, 1991), 203–15; idem, *Paul, Judaism, and the Gentiles: Beyond the New Perspective* (2nd ed.; Grand Rapids: Eerdmans, 2007), 163–91.

21. Lampe, *From Paul to Valentinus*, 15.

22. Peter Oakes, *Reading Romans in Pompeii: Paul's Letter at Ground Level* (London: SPCK, 2009), 74–75.

23. A. Andrew Das, *Solving the Romans Debate* (Peabody, MA: Hendrickson, 2007), 202, 263–64 (a Gentile audience for Romans is also advocated by Paul Achtemeier, Neil Elliott, Stanley Stowers, and Lloyd Gaston, to name a few). The problem with Das's (*Romans Debate*, 262) proposal is that he thinks the persons greeted in Romans 16:1–16 were not part of the Roman churches Paul is writing to.

vacuum followed by a Gentile majority thereafter in the Roman churches is more assumed than demonstrable.[24]

5. **An eclectic proposal.** I suspect the reasons for Romans are multiple and complex. Moreover, we would be wise to consider that Paul may have had more than one purpose in mind when he wrote the letter.[25]

Paul's primary aim is to garner the support of the Roman Christians for his planned journey to Spain as per option 3, yet he also wants to return to Jerusalem to deliver the collection with all of the Gentile churches firmly behind him as the apostle to the Gentiles (Rom 1:13; 15:24–25). Paul writes to the Roman churches, the Gentile wing in particular—but knowing full well that Jewish Christian critics and supporters in the city will come across the letter as well—to formally introduce himself and his ministry to them. However, if Paul is to succeed in winning their support and service, he has two implied tasks.

First, he must win them over to his account of the gospel if they are to support his projected missionary plans (Rom 1:9, 15–16; 2:16; 15:15–21; 16:25).[26] Schreiner comments: "He knew that such support would not be forthcoming unless they had a firm grasp of the Pauline gospel. Thus he articulated his gospel in some detail in the letter so that the Romans would comprehend the basics of his gospel and so that they could reply to critics who distorted what Paul taught."[27] Paul does that by setting out his gospel at theological depth in order to better "establish" them in the faith (1:11, 16; 15:15; 16:25). Romans is a presentation of Paul's gospel explaining how it unveils God's saving righteousness (1:16), including its ability to bring people into moral transformation (3:5–8; 6:1–23; 14:16), its distinctiveness from the Judaism of the Pharisees (9:33–10:4), combined with continuity with the ancient Israelite religion (9:4–5; 11:25–32), and conformity to the pattern of Scripture (1:2; 3:21; 9:6; 15:8–12). In particular, Paul strives to show that his gospel is prefigured by the Torah (1:17; 3:21), is Torah-affirming (3:31; 7:12, 14; 13:8–10), and takes up the eschatological vision of the Torah for saving and unifying Jews and Gentiles in God's people (10:5–6; 15:10).[28] Paul

24. Jerome Murphy O'Connor, *Paul: A Critical Life* (New York: Oxford University Press, 1996), 333; J. Ross Wagner, *Heralds of the Good News: Isaiah and Paul "in Concert" in the Letter to the Romans* (Leiden: Brill, 2003), 33–34; John M. G. Barclay, "Is It Good News That God Is Impartial? A Response to Robert Jewett, *Romans: A Commentary*," *JSNT* 31 (2008): 91–94; Esler, *Conflict and Identity in Romans*, 102–6.

25. Cranfield, *Romans*, 2:815; Dunn, *Romans*, 1:lv; Wedderburn, *Reasons for Romans*, 5–6; Schreiner, *Romans*, 19; Longenecker, *Introducing Romans*, 157–60.

26. Cranfield, *Romans*, 2:823; Moo, *Romans*, 29–30; Schreiner, *Romans*, 20–23, 774; Dunn, *Romans*, 2.856.

27. Schreiner, *Romans*, 774.

28. Mark Reasoner, *The Strong and the Weak: Romans 14.1–15.13 in Context* (SNTSMS 103; Cambridge: Cambridge Universty Press, 1999), 234.

deploys an impressive array of scriptural and rhetorical arguments to prove that his gospel is God-honoring, Christ-centered, and valid for both Jews and Gentiles. Thus, from Paul's side, the goal of his exposition is to show that he is a divinely accredited apostle who faithfully proclaims the Jewish gospel about Israel's Messiah to the nations.

A second implied task is some preventive pastoral care. While the expulsion of Jewish Christians under Claudius can be overstated in significance, its impact on Christ-believers in Rome would hardly have been neglible. The expulsion must have had huge implications for the structure and membership of the Roman churches even if they did not suddenly evolve into an instant Gentile majority. Likewise, the return of the Jewish Christians to Rome after Claudius's death would have been equally complicated and messy as to how relations between the resident believers and former exiles would resume. Furthermore, if it is true that the Roman churches' faith had been reported over the whole world (Rom 1:8), then the letter must be dealing with issues that were "on the front burner," as it were, in Rome.[29] It seems that Paul well knows the problems that the churches in Rome were facing. This is principally the fragmentation, real or potential, of the Roman house churches over obedience to the Torah on issues that symbolize visible loyalty to the Jewish way of life.

Then there is also the need for a strategy to assist them in negotiating the hazards of living in a pagan society (Romans 12–13). Paul also is compelled to counter preemptively some Gentile Christians who were tempted to imitate the rancorous anti-Judaism of Roman cultural elites (Romans 9; 11). If unity is the aim, then Paul wisely expounds the interlocking nature of Jewish and Gentile missions (1:16; 10:14–21; 11:13–33; 15:8–9, 27) and exposits God's faithfulness to Israel and his impartiality toward Jews and Greeks in Jesus Christ (Romans 1–4; 9–10; 14:9–10). This setting also accounts for a key theological emphasis of the letter: explaining how God, in the Messiah, welcomes Gentiles into his people, and how believing Jews and Gentiles in the Messiah should equally welcome one another (4:16; 5:8–11; 15:6–7). Thus, from the Romans' side, Paul's goal is to foster a confederation of ethnically diverse house churches in Rome who constitute the renewed people of God in the new covenant age.

In brief, Romans is a word of exhortation,[30] a masterpiece of missional theology, culturally savvy apologetics, christological exegesis, pastoral care, theological exposition, and artful rhetoric—all designed to win over the

29. Ibid., 221.

30. David E. Aune, "Romans as a *Logos Protreptikos*," in *The Romans Debate* (ed. K. P. Donfried; Peabody, MA: Hendrickson, 1991), 278–96.

audience to Paul's gospel, to support his mission in Spain, to draw Jewish and Gentile Christians in Rome closer together, to strengthen them in the faith despite the perils of Roman culture, and to encourage his audience to identify with the apostle to the Gentiles as he goes to Jerusalem.

## The Story "in" Paul's Letter to the Romans

If we had to summarize what Romans is all about, we could condense it down to this: God is creating out of Jews and Gentiles a people to praise him. Paul regards the gospel as the proclamation that Israel's long-anticipated release and restoration is happening and is magnetically drawing the Gentiles into its luminous display of divine mercy. For it is by redeeming Israel that God has acted also to reconcile the Gentiles, and God has determined to include Jews and Gentiles in the one people of God, on the same basis: faith in Jesus.[31]

We might say that Romans 1–4 is the *soteriological citadel*, where Paul narrates the gospel of salvation, explaining how believers shift from wrath to righteousness, how the Torah provides the scaffolding for the future building but is not part of its permanent structure. The citadel unveils God's prized work of a renewed Abrahamic family sharing in one faith in one God by the Messiah's death and resurrection.[32] Then, Romans 5–8 is the *cosmic cathedral*, adorned with a mixture of religious artwork and echoing with choral music, which describes how believers have transferred from the reign of sin and death into the lordship of Jesus. The ambience of the cathedral is supplied by none other than the gift of the Spirit, which comes as a power to resist the flesh. Next, Romans 9–11 might be likened to an *olive garden chapel*, where believers can celebrate Israel's privileges, lament Israel's past failures, speak prayerfully into Israel's current state, and hold out an olive branch of hope for Israel's future. Thereafter, 12:1–15:13 is *Christ College, the school of faith*, where love and hope are on the syllabus, the Messiah's story is lived out in their own lives, and the church is prepared to be a people ready to worship God in faithfulness, truth, and glory. Finally, 15:14–16:27 is the *missionary panel*, where Paul locates his own apostolic labors in the domain of God's grand purposes, and he calls on believers in all places to support God's people in God's work for them.

The story of Romans obviously then stands within the larger biblical story: the story of creation fallen and creation renewed, men and women estranged in sin and then reconciled in Christ, Israel's tragic misstep before a redemptive

31. Wagner, *Heralds of the Good News*, 357.

32. I owe this image of Romans 1–4 as a citadel to Douglas Campbell, *The Deliverance of God* (Grand Rapids: Eerdmans, 2009), 313.

future, Gentile foreigners becoming adopted heirs of Israel's God, and God's people always rejoicing in the promises and provision of their Lord and Savior. To be more precise, Romans is part of the biblical story of the world condemned in Adam (1:18–32; 5:12–21), Israel's covenantal call to herald God's reign to the nations, let down by the fact that Israel too is entrenched in Adam (2:1–3:20; 9:6–10:21), and the Messiah as the goal of God's redemptive purposes to create a redeemed family for Abraham (4:1–25; 10:4; 15:7–13). The story narrated in Romans is that in the Messiah, God has been faithful to Israel and been merciful to the nations, exactly as Scripture said he would be. God's dealings with Israel and the Gentiles are not two separate or conflicting stories, but part of the one and same story climaxing in Jesus.

It is no surprise, then, that Paul's letter to the Romans pivots on biblical themes like God's righteousness, where this "righteousness" is synonymous with God's saving action (see Isaiah 51 and Psalm 51). This righteousness is cognate to God's truthfulness and faithfulness, which comes to Israel as the saving event of the Messiah's death and resurrection. It is a righteousness that will put the whole world to rights and rightens believers within that world on the basis of faith ahead of the final judgment (see Rom 1:17; 2:16; 3:21–26; 10:3).

Then there is the Spirit, the life-giving power of God, leading and guiding God's people into true covenant righteousness. One of the blessings of the new covenant that the prophets had spoken about was that God would one day pour out his Spirit in a whole new way, which would be proof that God's long-awaited day of deliverance had finally come (see Ezek 36:26–27; 37:14; Joel 2:27–28). The shocking thing is that this happened not to the politically powerful nor to the religiously scrupulous, but to the followers of Jesus, including Gentiles. The Spirit came upon a people who did not have the usual badges of belonging to God, such as circumcision, but who had experienced a circumcision of the heart, that is, faith in Israel's God and inner renewal (see Rom 2:25–29). It was the Spirit who would lead them in their struggle against the flesh and give them hope in the face of suffering (Rom 8:1–27).

Next we have to say that the theme of "Israel" is central to Paul's story of salvation. Paul is crystal clear about the goodness of Israel's inherited privileges (Rom 3:1–5; 9:1–5) and the inviolability of Israel's election (11:29). According to Scripture, Israel was the elect nation, chosen by God and put into the world to herald God's kingly power and to praise his name to the nations (see Exod 19:5–6; Isa 41:8; 44:1). While God's story included Israel, it was not strictly about Israel, as God's purposes extended back to the promises given to the patriarchs about blessing the nations through Abraham's seed. When that story is worked out in Romans, it means that salvation is based on grace and received by faith rather than restricted to ethnic kinship and or appropriated by performing deeds of the Torah (see Rom 3:27–31; 4:9–17; 10:1–4).

And we can hardly forget the Messiah as the key character in the story of Romans. While Romans does not have a christological text as extravagant as Philippians 2:5–11 or Colossians 1:15–20, even so, there is a strong affirmation of Jesus' messianic identity (Rom 1:3–4; 15:7–8), with an implicit reference to the incarnation (8:3) and later an explicit one (see 9:5). In Romans, Jesus is the Messiah, the Son of God, a new Adam, the redeemer of Israel, and rescuer of Gentiles.

So all in all, God with his gift of righteousness, the Spirit, Israel, and Messiah are vital characters in the biblical story of how God reveals his salvation to both Israel and the nations. Romans drips with citations and allusions to Scripture because Paul takes up these biblical themes and shows that they have their fulfillment in the death and resurrection of Jesus.

Delving into Romans also compels us to read the Old Testament with a hermeneutical lens which identifies Jesus as the centerpiece of Israel's redemptive history. Jesus is the "goal" or "climax" of Israel's law (Rom 10:4) so that God's purposes for Israel must be interpreted in light of him (see Acts 13:32–33; 2 Cor 1:20). The key verses that unlock this story of promise and fulfillment for us are the dramatic point in the letter where Paul says: "For I tell you that Christ has become a servant of the Jews on behalf of God's truth, so that the promises made to the patriarchs might be confirmed and, moreover, that the Gentiles might glorify God for his mercy" (Rom 15:8–9). God's action in Jesus does not set aside all that was said to Israel; rather, it confirms it and proves that God was faithful.

Yet we must not forget that God is faithful to all of his promises, those given to Israel and those made to the patriarchs, which is why God acted in his Messiah to bring the Gentiles to praise his name and to glorify him by forgiving their sins and sending the Spirit into their hearts. That is the scriptural story that Paul tethers to his gospel—a gospel promised beforehand in the prophets and fulfilled in the Lord Jesus Christ. Romans is then perfectly suited, as Martin Luther saw, to being a Christian introduction to the Old Testament. In other words, Romans shows us that the Old Testament must be read as a Jesus-story that points toward the divine saving action executed in God's messianic deliverer.

# Resources for Those Teaching or Preaching the Book of Romans

Andria, Solomon. *Romans*. ABCS. Nairobi: Hippo, 2012.

Barth, Karl. *The Epistle to the Romans*. Translated by E. C. Hoskyns. London: Oxford University Press, 1932.

Bird, Michael F. *The Saving Righteousness of God: Studies in Paul, Justification, and the New Perspective*. Milton Keynes, UK: Paternoster, 2007.

———. *A Bird's Eye-View of Paul: The Man, His Mission, and His Message*. Downers Grove, IL: InterVarsity, 2008.

———. "Justification: A Progressive Reformed View." Pages 83–111 in *Justification: Five Views*. Edited by Paul R. Eddy and J. Beilby. Downers Grove, IL: InterVarsity, 2011.

———. "'One Who Will Arise to Rule over the Nations': Paul's Letter to the Romans and the Roman Empire." Pages 146–65 in *Jesus is Lord, Caesar Is Not: Evaluating Empire in New Testament Studies*. Edited by J. Modica and S. McKnight. Downers Grove, IL: InterVarsity, 2013.

———. "The Letter to the Romans." Pages 177–204 in *All Things To All Cultures: Paul Among Jews, Greeks, and Romans*. Edited by Mark Harding and Alanna Nobbs. Grand Rapids: Eerdmans, 2013.

Burns, J. Patout, ed. and trans. *Romans: Interpreted by Early Christian Commentators*. The Church's Bible. Edited by R. L. Wilken. Grand Rapids: Eerdmans, 2012.

Calvin, John. "John Calvin to Simon Grynaeus." *Calvin's Commentaries: The Epistles of Paul the Apostle to the Romans and Thessalonians*. Translated by R. Mackenzie. Grand Rapids: Eerdmans, 1960.

Dunn, James D. G. *Romans 1–8, 9–16*. WBC; 2 vols. Dallas: Word, 1988.

———. *Beginning from Jerusalem*. CITM 2. Grand Rapids: Eerdmans, 2009.

Jewett, Robert K. *Romans: A Commentary*. Hermeneia. Minneapolis: Fortress, 2007.

Johnson, Luke Timothy. *Reading Romans: A Literary and Theological Commentary*. New York: Crossroads, 1997.

Käsemann, Ernst. *Commentary on Romans*. Translated by G. W. Bromiley. Grand Rapids: Eerdmans, 1980.

Keck, Leander E. *Romans*. ANTC. Nashville: Abingdon, 2005.

Keener, Craig S. *Romans*. NCCS. Eugene, OR: Cascade, 2009.

Longenecker, Richard N. *Introducing Romans: Critical Issues in Paul's Most Famous Letter*. Grand Rapids: Eerdmans, 2011.

McKnight, Scot. *The King Jesus Gospel: The Original Good News Revisited.* Grand Rapids: Zondervan, 2011.

Moo, Douglas J. *The Epistle to the Romans.* NICNT. Grand Rapids: Eerdmans, 1996.

Oakes, Peter. *Reading Romans in Pompeii: Paul's Letter at Ground Level.* London: SPCK, 2009.

Rosner, Brian S. *Paul and the Law: Keeping the Commandments of God.* NSBT 31. Downers Grove, IL: InterVarsity, 2013.

Schreiner, Thomas R. *Romans.* BECNT. Grand Rapids: Baker, 1998.

Sprinkle, Preston. *Paul and Judaism Revisited: A Study of Divine and Human Agency in Salvation.* Downers Grove, IL: InterVarsity, 2013.

Talbert, Charles H. *Romans.* Macon, GA: Smyth & Helwys, 2002.

Witherington, Ben. *Paul's Letter to the Romans: A Socio-Rhetorical Commentary.* Grand Rapids: Eerdmans, 2004.

Wright, N.T. "Romans." In *New Interpreter's Bible.* Edited by L. E. Keck. NIB 10. Nashville: Abingdon, 2002.

CHAPTER 1

# Romans 1:1–7

## LISTEN to the Story

[1]Paul, a servant of Christ Jesus, called to be an apostle and set apart
for the gospel of God—[2]the gospel he promised beforehand through
his prophets in the Holy Scriptures [3]regarding his Son, who as to his
earthly life was a descendant of David, [4]and who through the Spirit of
holiness was appointed the Son of God in power by his resurrection
from the dead: Jesus Christ our Lord. [5]Through him we received grace
and apostleship to call all the Gentiles to the obedience that comes from
faith for his name's sake. [6]And you also are among those Gentiles who are
called to belong to Jesus Christ.

[7]To all in Rome who are loved by God and called to be his holy
people:

Grace and peace to you from God our Father and from the Lord Jesus Christ.

*Listening to the texts in the story:* Isaiah 52:1–10; Mark 1:1–15; 1 Corinthians 15:1–8.

In the opening of the "citadel" of Romans 1–4, Paul introduces himself to the Roman churches. Paul wastes no time and hits the ground running in this letter by bringing up that which matters most: the gospel and the cause of the gospel, which he endeavours to promote as an apostle. Ultimately, Paul wants to make sure that he and the Roman Gentile Christians are singing off the same sheet of gospel music. Since Paul cannot be in Rome in person, he wants to embed the gospel in their community, to defend himself against any rumor of antinomianism or anti-Israelite sentiment, and to prevent a diverse and potentially fractious Christian community from fragmenting along ethnic lines of Jew versus Gentile. In other words, Paul wants to *gospelize* the Romans, that is, to conform them to the pattern of teaching that the gospel imparts. Paul pursues this for the sake of unity with the Roman churches and for the promotion of the gospel in a wider pan-Roman theater that reaches from Jerusalem all the way around to Spain.

This densely packed beginning to the letter touches on the biblical story in many ways. First, it calls to mind the Isaianic "glad tidings" or "gospel" about the end of Israel's exile and the launching of the new exodus found in Isaiah 52:1–10. The big rescue that Isaiah looked forward to began with the return of the Babylonian exiles under the Persian king Cyrus, but it was properly fulfilled only in the salvation wrought by the life, death, and resurrection of Jesus, which is why there are so many new exodus allusions across the letter. Second, the messianic hope of many Jews in antiquity was based on the word of the prophets that God would one day send a new David to deliver Israel (see Isa 11:1; Jer 23:5; Ezek 34:23–24; 37:24–25; Mic 5:2). For Paul, the resurrection is paramount proof that Jesus is the Messiah who is Israel's deliverer and Lord of the nations. So when Paul says that his gospel is "promised beforehand" in Scripture, he means it is the final act to the story of Isaiah's gospel and Israel's messianic hopes.

The opening verses break down with (1) Paul's self-introduction (v. 1); (2) a description of the gospel (vv. 2–4); (3) a description of his apostolic ministry (v. 5); and (4) a greeting to the Roman churches (vv. 6–7).

## EXPLAIN the Story

### Paul the Apostle (1:1)

The name "Paul" (*Paulus* in Latin, *Paulos* in Greek) was a relatively common name in the ancient world. "Paul" is either a cognomen or a nickname used because the Hebrew "Saul" (*šā'ûl*) was foreign to Greek speakers. In the prescript of the letter Paul immediately sets out his credentials to the Romans in three quick-fire descriptions of himself as "servant [slave]," "apostle," and "set apart."

Paul first describes himself as a "servant of Jesus Christ" (see "servants of the Lord" in 2 Kgs 18:12 [Moses]; Judg 2:8 [Joshua]; 2 Sam 7:5 [David]; Amos 3:7; Zech 1:6 [the prophets]). The word *doulos* has the nuance of "slave" and denotes one subject to the authority of another. Paul uses this expression of himself elsewhere in his letter openings (Phil 1:1; Titus 1:1; cf. Gal 1:10). As a "slave of Christ" Paul is expressing his solemn devotion to Jesus in terms analogous to the master-slave relationship with connotations of absolute belongingness and total submission. While all Christians are slaves of Christ (see 1 Cor 7:22–23; Eph 6:6), Paul is a *special* slave with a *special* office. The title "Jesus Christ" probably first emerged as a shorthand way of saying Jesus *is the* Christ or Jesus *is the* Messiah. In fact, "Jesus Christ" is probably an encoded reference to the status and story of Jesus as the Messiah of Israel and Lord of the cosmos.[1]

A second element that Paul introduces about himself is that he was "called to be an apostle." The call was not an invitation; instead, it was a radical summons. In the Septuagint "call" (*klētos*) is equivalent to "choose" (e.g., Isa 41:9; 42:6; 48:12). Paul did not volunteer for service, but he was chosen to be an apostle by a sovereign action of God (see Gal 1:1; 1 Cor 15:10). This arresting sense of divine call is reminiscent of the commissioning of prophets in the Old Testament like Amos, Isaiah, Jeremiah, and Ezekiel. Paul stands in a line of great prophetic figures whom God chose and utilized for his own redemptive purposes.

An "apostle" means literally "one who is sent." It is most likely indebted to the Jewish concept of a *šāliaḥ*—the sending of an envoy who represents the sender as if himself in person. In Hebrews, Jesus is called an "apostle" in the sense that he is sent from God (Heb 3:1). Titus and Epaphroditus are each designated as an *apostolos* ("messenger") of certain churches (2 Cor 8:23; Phil 2:25). At the end of Romans, Andronicus and Junia are known as "outstanding among the apostles," which probably indicates their role as missionaries sent out from a Christian community (Rom 16:7). Although Paul was not one of the twelve disciples, he encountered the risen Jesus on the road to Damascus and was called to his apostolic work to proclaim the gospel among the nations (see Acts 22:21; 26:16–18; 1 Cor 9:1; 15:8–9; Gal 1:15–16).[2]

The third aspect of Paul's self-description is that he was "set apart" for an evangelistic task. Ironically, the former Pharisee who gloried in his set-apartness from sinners is now set apart as God's messenger to the quintessential sinners, the Gentiles. A similar testimony is given by Paul in Gal 1:15, where he described how God "set me apart from my mother's womb and called me by his grace."

In the church at Antioch, the Holy Spirit led the community to "set apart" Paul and Barnabas for the work which God had called them to undertake (Acts 13:1–3). This set-apartness is also related to the priestly service of carrying the gospel to the nations that Paul undertakes (Rom 15:16).

Paul was called to be a servant and an apostle, set apart for a priestly work. These are not merely descriptions, they are tasks; Paul serves, was sent, and was consecrated for the sake of the "gospel of God" (see Rom 15:16; 2 Cor

1. Michael F. Bird, *Colossians and Philemon* (NCCS; Eugene, OR: Wipf & Stock, 2009), 34.

2. For a brief summary of the meaning of "apostle," see further Paul K. Moser, "Apostle," in *EDB* 78–79.

11:7; 1 Thess 2:2, 8–9; 1 Tim 1:11).[3] What Paul says about himself is geared toward explaining his role as a herald of the "gospel of God." No sooner has Paul mentioned the "gospel of God" than he proceeds to describe the "gospel concerning his Son" in 1:3 and the "gospel of his Son" in 1:9. Elsewhere when Paul mentions the gospel, it is usually in association with Jesus Christ as its main subject (see 1 Cor 9:12; 15:1–5; 2 Cor 2:12; 4:4; 9:13; 10:14; Phil 1:17; 1 Thess 3:2; 2 Thess 1:8; 2 Tim 2:8). The interchangeability of "Son," "Jesus," and "God" as subjects of the gospel is possible because the identity of God is bound up with the "one God" and "one Lord" who are both revealed in the gospel (see 1 Cor 8:6). That means to tell the gospel of God is to tell the story of Jesus. The gospel narrates how God breaks into the world through his Son and the Spirit in order to fulfill the promises that he made to his people.

None of this should surprise us because Romans is the most theocentric letter of the Pauline corpus, with the word *theos* ("God") occurring 153 times! Paul is the quintessential Jesus freak, but he is not a mono-Jesus adherent. In fact, God, Son, and Spirit all figure prominently in his opening narration of the gospel story in Romans 1:1–4. Theologically speaking, Romans is a discourse about God as he is known through the gospel. As the apostle called, sent, and set apart by God, Paul sets out before the Roman Christians the story of how God's plan to repossess the world for himself has now been executed in his own Son, the Lord Jesus Christ.

Before we expound Paul's gospel further, it is important to establish the background story of "gospel" in its various contexts. From Isaiah 40:9 and 52:7 we learn that the "good news" (the meaning of the two components of *eu-angelion*, "gospel") is the announcement that God's reign is coming because God himself is coming; he will at last redeem his people from exile and slavery and shepherd them; then the ends of the earth will see his salvation.[4] Also, when Jesus began his ministry in proclaiming the gospel, he did not go around simply announcing that he was about to die for the sins of the world and thereafter people will be able to get into heaven. He was picking up this prophetic story line of national sin-exile-redemption-new creation. When Jesus preached the "gospel of God" (Mark 1:14) and the "gospel of the king-

---

3. The sense of the genitive "of God" is ambiguous as it might mean a gospel *from God* or a gospel *about God*. Most likely, both senses are intended. The gospel is both a revelation *from God* (Gal 1:12) and is about what *God himself* has done in the faithfulness, death, and resurrection of Jesus the Messiah (2 Cor 5:21).

4. Cf. *Pss. Sol.* 11:1–3: "Blow in Zion on the trumpet to summon (the) holy ones. Proclaim in Jerusalem the voice of him who brings good news, for God has had pity on Israel in visiting them. Stand on the height, O Jerusalem, and behold your children. From the east and the west, gathered together by the Lord. From the north they come in the gladness of their God. From the isles afar off God has gathered them."

dom" (Matt 24:14), he was saying that these prophetic promises were coming to fruition. The shot clock had counted down to zero, the new exodus was here, God's reign was at last breaking in, and the proof of this was the healings and exorcisms he was performing (e.g., Luke 11:20).

Furthermore, we should note the usage of "gospel" (*euangelion*) in the context of the political propaganda and religion of the Roman Empire. The Romans had their own "gospel" about the accession of new emperors to the throne. In AD 69, while laying siege to Jerusalem, the Roman general Vespasian decided to press his claim to imperial power after the deaths of three emperors in a three-year span. Listen to what Josephus says about him: "When news spread of Vespasian's accession to the throne every city celebrated the *good news* and offered sacrifices on his behalf" (Josephus, *War* 4.618), and "On reaching Alexandria Vespasian was greeted by the *good news* from Rome and by embassies of congratulations from every quarter of the world, now his own ... the whole empire being now secured and the Roman state saved beyond expectation" (ibid., 4.656–57).

Given this linguistic background, it was inevitable that adherents of the "gospel of Jesus Christ" would come into conflict with political apparatus behind "the gospel of Rome" as there can only be one Lord and one Son of God in the world. It is either the Son of David or the son of Augustus (see Luke 2:1–4; Acts 17:7). Paul's gospel was not something exclusively spiritual; rather, it was theo-political, and Jews and Romans both knew it.[5]

### Paul's Gospel (1:2–4)

Returning to the prescript, Paul states that the gospel is something that God "promised beforehand through his prophets in the Holy Scriptures" (v. 2). In other words, this new announcement is prepromised in the ancient faith of Israel. Paul shows the conformity of his gospel to Israel's prophetic hopes. This is similar to 1 Corinthians 15:3–5, where Jesus' death and resurrection are "according to the Scriptures," and Galatians 3:8, where Paul says that "Scripture foresaw that God would justify the Gentiles by faith, and announced the gospel in advance to Abraham." While we tend to treasure innovation and newness, in the ancient world it was the antiquity and longevity of religious traditions that were prized. For Paul the gospel is the continuation and fulfillment of the story of Israel (see Acts 13:32–33; 2 Cor 1:20). What is more, he assumes a particular way of reading Israel's Scriptures, what we might call

---

5. On Paul and empire in Romans, see Michael F. Bird, "Paul's Letter to the Romans," in *Jesus Is Lord, Caesar Is Not: Evaluating Empire in New Testament Studies* (eds. J. Modica and S. McKnight; Downers Grove, IL: InterVarsity, 2013), 146–65.

a *christotelic* hermeneutic, as Jesus is the goal of the scriptural promises (see Rom 10:4). The content of the gospel is enumerated in vv. 3–4 as:

> regarding his Son,
> who was born
> from the seed of David
> according to the flesh
> who was appointed
> the Son of God in power
> according to the Spirit of holiness
> by resurrection from the dead:
> Jesus Christ our Lord.[6]

It is likely that this is a short summary of the gospel that Paul himself received (perhaps it was an early creed, hymn, prose, or confession of faith given the non-Pauline language). It is probably the case that this gospel summary was already known to the Roman churches so that Paul quotes it to affirm their sharing of a common gospel tradition. In these brief verses we are instantly struck by its forthright announcement about the messianic identity and sovereign name of Jesus. The gospel here is the declaration that Jesus is the climax of Israel's hopes, he is installed as God's vice-regent, and his resurrection has inaugurated the beginning of the end of the ages. Note that the gospel is not four spiritual laws, nor a logical syllogism about reconciling God's holiness and human sin. Instead, it is the announcement that Jesus is the long awaited Messiah of Israel and Lord of the world. To tell the gospel, then, is to tell the story of Jesus.[7]

To regard the gospel as a story is not, as some might think, a recent postmodern fad. Paul had just stated in v. 2 that this gospel story lines up the story of Israel's Scriptures. But if you believe not Paul, then believe Martin Luther, who said: "The gospel is a story about Christ, God's and David's Son, who died and was raised and is established as Lord. This is the gospel in a nutshell."[8]

Romans 1:3–4 is not simply a convenient collection of christological titles; rather, it tells a short story about the identity of Jesus Christ. Jesus is the preexistent "Son" who is humanly born in the line of "David" and designated

6. My own translation, which slightly amends the NIV. Note the parallelism between various portions of the text, which suggests that it was probably a piece of poetic, hymnic, or confessional pre-Pauline material. The interesting parallels are (a) Son/Lord Jesus Christ, (b) born/appointed, (c) Seed of David/Son of God, and (d) according to the flesh/according to the Spirit of holiness.

7. See esp. Scot McKnight, *The King Jesus Gospel: The Original Good News Revisited* (Grand Rapids: Zondervan, 2011).

8. Martin Luther, "A Brief Instruction on What to Look for and Expect in the Gospels," *Luther's Works* (ed. E. T. Bachmann; 55 vols.; Philadelphia: Fortress, 1960), 35:118.

as the "Son of God" through the Holy Spirit, who later raised him from the dead, and this event proleptically inaugurated the eschatological age. The one called Jesus is also the "Lord," and the claims of his sovereignty are far reaching (see Rom 12:19; 14:4–11). Toward the end of Romans we see just how sweeping the consequences of his authority are for the believing community. A Christian, whether Jew or Gentile, is one who confesses that Jesus "is Lord" (10:9–12); they are to corporately serve the Lord (12:11), to put on the Lord (13:14), and together to glorify the Father and Lord Jesus Christ (15:6). Resurrection and lordship cast a shadow over the entire epistle to the point that Jesus was *raised* to *reign*: "For this very reason, Christ died and returned to life so that he might be the Lord of both the dead and the living" (14:9). When 1:3–4 is taken with 15:8–9, 12, then, "Christ's Davidic heritage fulfills the promises and confirms God's faithfulness to the Jews; his appointment—that is, his resurrection—relates him to the Gentiles as the mode of their inclusion in the family of Abraham and the rule of the Messiah."[9]

A debate surrounds the Greek word *horizō* as to whether it means "declared," "designated," or "appointed." Generally speaking, conservative exegetes have been reluctant to accept the translation of "appointed" on the grounds that it might imply an adoptionist christology (i.e., Jesus only *became* God's Son during his baptism, resurrection, or ascension). However, the evidence strongly suggests that "appointed" is the proper translation. First of all, "appointed" is the basic lexical meaning of *horizō* (see Acts 10:42; 17:31).[10] Second, it appears that early Christians interpreted Psalm 2:7 as being typologically fulfilled in the resurrection and exaltation of Christ (see Acts 2:36; 13:33; Heb 1:5). Käsemann was correct to see the emphasis here on "becoming" rather than on "being."[11] However, this does not deny Jesus' sonship prior to the resurrection, only that the resurrection served to translate the sonship of Jesus into a new eschatological function that he did not previously discharge.[12] A further significance is that this appointment has a quasi-judicial character. Whatever the world said about Jesus, by his resurrection, God has declared him to be his Son. The resurrection marks out Jesus as the one in whom God's saving promises are made good. On top of that, we are already seeing how central "resurrection" is in Romans.[13] Paul will later argue that the same Spirit that worked to appoint Jesus as Son is now at work in believers to sanctify them,

9. Christopher G. Whitsett, "Son of God, Seed of David: Paul's Messianic Exegesis on Romans 2:3–4," *JBL* 119 (2000): 677.

10. BDAG 723.

11. Käsemann, *Romans*, 12.

12. Cf., e.g., Dunn, *Romans*, 1:14; Moo, *Romans*, 48; Schreiner, *Romans*, 38–43.

13. Cf. Peter Head, "Jesus' Resurrection in Pauline Thought: A Study in the Epistle of Romans," in *Proclaiming the Resurrection* (ed. Peter Head; Carlise, UK: Paternoster, 1998), 58–80; N. T.

to adopt them as children of God, and he will raise them up at the last day (see Rom 8:2–17).

The phrase "by [his] resurrection of the dead" can also be tricky. The preposition *ex* is perhaps causal, where it designates resurrection as the immediate cause of the Son's exalted life and elevation to lordship. The problem with this is that the personal pronoun "his" is not found in the Greek text and is inserted by translators (see NEB; NIV; ESV). More probable, *ex* is temporal (see KJV; NRSV; NASB; NET) and conforms to the early Christian belief that Jesus' resurrection was actually the beginning of the general resurrection (see Matt 27:52–53; Acts 4:2; 23:6; 1 Cor 15:20, 23; Col 1:18; Rev 1:5). This last option is validated by the fact that *anastaseōs nekrōn* is a generalizing plural that literally means the "standing up of dead corpses" and hints at the future resurrection of all persons at the end of history. Yet we should not engage in either-or exegesis. Two ideas are implied: the resurrection of Jesus marks out the beginning of the general resurrection, but in the context of disclosing Jesus' messianic identity as the Son of God.[14]

### Apostolic Grace and Gentile Obedience (1:5)

It is precisely "through" the Lord Jesus that Paul says "we received grace and apostleship" (v. 5). The picture here is of the Lord Jesus calling people to a special apostolic ministry. That evidently started during his own earthly life (see Mark 3:13–16) and continued with the calling of Paul himself (see Gal 1:15–16). In Ephesians, the exalted Christ distributes the offices of apostle, prophet, evangelist, and teaching pastor to the church in order to build it up into maturity (Eph 4:11–13). Note too that the "we" implies not only Paul but also his coworkers, who are similarly recipients of apostolic grace. This brings us to the first mention of "grace" in Romans, and it designates the benevolence and favor of God toward his servants. In fact, "grace" and "apostleship" might be intended to be taken together as something like the "grace *of* apostleship," to the effect that God's gracious purposes are being worked out through his apostolic emissaries (see Rom 15:15–16; 1 Cor 12:28; 15:10).

The purpose of apostleship is then situated toward two goals. Instrumentally, the goal of apostolic ministry is to "call all the Gentiles to the obedience that comes from faith." More literally this refers to the "obedience of faith" (*hypakoēn pisteōs*), which could designate: (a) faith and obedience; (b) faith that consists of obedience; or (c) faith that leads to obedience. I tend to prefer

---

Wright, *The Resurrection of the Son of God* (COQG 3; London: SPCK, 2003), 241–67; J. R. Daniel Kirk, *Unlocking Romans: Resurrection and the Justification of God* (Grand Rapids: Eerdmans, 2008).

14. Paul Beasley-Murray, "Romans 1:3–4: An Early Confession of Faith in the Lordship of Jesus," *TynBul* 31 (1980): 153–54.

a variation of the last option and identify faith as defining the manner and mode of obedience, i.e., an obedience produced by the gospel.[15] Faith for Paul includes assent and trust, but it also embraces faithfulness and loyalty as a way of life in Jesus Christ. Elsewhere faith and obedience are interchangeable for Paul (Rom 1:8; 10:16; 16:19). Importantly, Paul closes Romans by referring to the revelation of Jesus Christ that brings Gentiles to the "obedience that comes from faith" (16:26). It is surely significant that Paul begins and ends Romans with reference to the "obedience of faith." Elsewhere, in Paul's priestly service of the gospel, what Christ achieves through him is to enable Gentiles to "become an offering acceptable to God, sanctified by the Holy Spirit" and to lead "the Gentiles to obey God" (15:16, 18).

Thus Romans, the great epistle of justification by faith, is also the great epistle of the obedience of faith. The Protestant paranoia that a call for obedience somehow dilutes the pure gospel of justification is misplaced, as N. T. Wright comments:

> Such anxiety misses the point. When Paul thinks of Jesus as Lord, he thinks of himself as a slave and of the world as being called to obedience to Jesus' lordship. His apostolic commission is not to offer people a new religious option, but to summon them to allegiance to Jesus, which will mean abandoning other loyalties. The gospel issues a command, an imperial summons; the appropriate response is obedience.[16]

Let us not forget that faith, faithfulness, and obedience are prerequisites for "righteousness" (Rom 1:17; 4:5, 11–24; 5:17; 6:16; 9:30; 10:4–6). Paul wants Christ-believing Gentiles to exhibit a steadfast belief in God and the Lord Jesus Christ (4:1–25; 10:9–10), but also to display in their way of life an appropriate holiness, love, obedience, service, worship, unity, and the fruit of righteousness. Such an obedience visibly counters allegations that Paul's law-free gospel leads to lawless behavior (see 3:7–8; 6:1–2; cf. 1 Cor 9:20–21), and it is an obedience that shames the hypocrisy of Jewish teachers in their claims to be teachers of Gentiles (2:1–29).[17] That is possible because Christians are driven to obedience, not by the letter of the law, but by dying with Christ and living by the Spirit (see Romans 6–8). Twice Paul commends the Roman Christians for their obedience (6:17; 16:19), and in many ways

---

15. Jewett, *Romans*, 110.

16. N. T. Wright, "Romans," 10:420; cf. Moo, *Romans*, 52–53: "Paul called men and women to a faith that was always inseparable from obedience—for the Savior in whom we believe is nothing less than our Lord—and to an obedience that could never be divorced from faith—for we can obey Jesus as Lord only when we have given ourselves to him in faith."

17. Cf. "Because of the service by which you have proved yourselves, others will praise God for the obedience that accompanies your confession of the gospel of Christ" (2 Cor 9:13).

Paul is writing this letter to shore up their commitment and conformity to the apostolic "pattern of instruction" that is central to his own missionary work.

While bringing Gentiles to the "obedience of faith" is a key purpose of Paul's apostleship, it is instrumental to a final goal of bringing honor and glory for the sake of "his name" (Rom 1:5). But whose name are we talking about here? Is it God's name or Jesus Christ's name? Given the surrounding context with the mention of the gospel of the Lord Jesus Christ (v. 4), his bestowing of grace and apostleship (v. 5), and the Gentiles in Rome called to belong to Jesus Christ (v. 6), it is hard to resist the conclusion that the obedience of the Gentiles is *for the sake* of honoring Jesus' name. Switching ahead to the end of Romans again, we find Paul saying that Christ served the circumcision (i.e., Israel) to confirm the promises made to the patriarchs so that, quoting Psalm 18:49, the Gentiles would praise God's name (Rom 15:9).

Let's think on this for a moment. The goal of Paul's apostolic vocation and the purpose of Jesus' advent to Israel were to make the promises of the Abrahamic covenant a reality by drawing immoral, idol-worshiping, pork-eating Gentiles into faith, obedience, and worship toward the names of God and Jesus. The story of salvation in Romans with its polyphonic symphony of movements about Adam, Christ, Israel, wrath, justice, justification, and reconciliation lead to a redeemed humanity, a restored Israel, and a renewed creation, and these turn out to be the stunning means of the glorification of God the Father and the Lord Jesus Christ (see Rom 11:33–36; 15:6; 16:27).

### To the Gentiles in Rome (1:6–7)

Paul further locates the Romans as among the Gentiles "who are called to belong to Jesus Christ" (v. 6) in the sense that they are effectually drawn into God's saving purposes (see Rom 8:28; 1 Cor 1:1–2, 24). The repetition of "called" (*klētos*) in vv. 6–7 is far from accidental. Paul is "called" to be an apostle (v. 1), and the emphasis means that both author and audience share in a divine call that binds them together.

The formalities of the prescript are drawn to a close with the greetings "to all in Rome" (v. 7).[18] Most likely, while Paul is predominantly addressing the Gentile Christians in Rome (see Rom 1:13; 11:13; 15:15–16), he is fully mindful of the fact that what he says here will also be relayed to Jewish Christians in Rome, and so his arguments proceed with due sensitivity, unlike his somewhat uncut and unplugged outburst in Galatians. Perhaps the letter carrier Phoebe will even go around the various Christian assemblies and exhort the Roman Christians with this letter. The Roman believers are "loved

18. Oddly "in Rome" is missing from several textual witnesses either by accident or by the deliberate attempt to make the letter more general rather than local in its focus.

by God" and "called to be his holy people," expressing the privileges and responsibility of their calling. Then, with "grace and peace," Paul wishes on them a blessing of divine treasures that include a power that totally embraces them and establishes their access to God. All this because God is our Father and Jesus Christ is our Lord.[19] As Chrysostom wrote: "Strange! How mighty is the love of God! We who were enemies and disgraced, have all at once become saints and sons. For when he calls Him Father, he shows them to be sons; and when he says sons, he has unveiled the whole treasure of blessings."[20]

In the prescript Paul introduces himself to the Romans as a faithful "servant" of God. He underscores that they both partake of a special divine calling. Paul and the Romans are further bound together by a common set of shared symbols, in effect saying: "Your Christ and Lord is my Christ and Lord; your God is my God; we share the very same gospel; we accept the same Scriptures."[21] As Gentiles they are under the jurisdiction of Paul's apostolate, and yet he does not invoke the weight of his apostolic authority over them (see 2 Cor 10:8; 13:10). Instead, he gently commends himself as a faithful minister of the gospel in the hope that they will be aroused to support the gospel that he proclaims. Our cohort of Roman Christians meeting in Rufus's modest apartment might well be curious and cautious about the letter opening, knowing that Paul had a reputation for strife, but remain impressed nonetheless with his display of religious authority and rhetorical acumen.

These first seven verses kickstart Romans with a bang, and at the forefront of our meditation of this passage should be two things, the "gospel" and the "obedience of faith."

### Knowing and Living the Gospel

Paul does not even get halfway through his greeting to the Romans before he launches into a short précis about the gospel. Evidently the gospel matters to him, and so it should. The gospel drives theology, authenticates the church, and is paramount for discipleship.

When it comes to a living theology, the immediate issues are: Where do you begin and what holds the whole thing together? If Romans is anything to go by, the starting point and integrating point for Christian thought are

19. Käsemann, *Romans*, 16.
20. Chrysostom, *Rom. Hom.* 1.
21. A. B. du Toit, "Persuasion in Romans 1:1–7," *BZ* 33 (1989): 203.

apprehended in the gospel. Christian thinkers have forever debated what exactly is the starting point of theology. Is it the doctrine of natural revelation, is it the doctrine of Scripture, or is it the doctrine of the Trinity? Where do we start? It's not a purely academic matter because where you begin can determine where you finish up.

While Romans is mostly certainly not a systematic theology by any stretch of the imagination, it remains all the same the most theological of Paul's letters in terms of working out a consistent theological train of thought. But note that Paul's beginning point in Romans is the gospel. Paul does not begin this magisterial epistle with a preface trying to justify whether it is possible to talk about God; rather, he simply begins by setting out the gospel of God and Jesus Christ. It is vitally important, then, that we get the gospel right and get it early. If the Christian life is a journey, the gospel is the first information center that we come to. Moreover, any theology that claims the name "evangelical" is obligated to make the "evangel" central to its structure. The gospel thereby becomes the beginning, center, and boundary of all theological discussion.[22]

Paul proves my point. According to him, Christology is about contemplating the person and work of Christ known to us through the "gospel of Christ" (Rom 15:19; 1 Cor 9:12; 2 Cor 2:12; 9:13; 10:14; Gal 1:7; Phil 1:27; 1 Thess 3:2). Christian ethics requires living a life "worthy of the gospel" (Phil 1:27). A study of salvation prods us to unpack the polyphonic richness of the gospel of salvation (Rom 1:16; Eph 1:13). Apologetics is our attempt to offer a "defense of the gospel" (Phil 1:16). A church is in essence a community of the gospelized. The sacraments are a means of grace communicated through the symbols of the gospel: baptism and Lord's Supper. Mission is the church's strategy to "advance the gospel" (Phil 1:12).[23] Every sub-branch of Christian theology is indelibly connected to the gospel like branches drawing nutrients from a vine. Peter Jensen is bang on target when he writes:

> The gospel stands at the beginning of the story that explains why there are Christians at all, on the boundary between belief and unbelief—often, for the hearer, prior to a knowledge of the Bible itself. For the person entering from the outside, the gospel is the introduction to the faith, the starting-point for understanding. It then rightly becomes the touchstone of the faith. Since this is where faith begins, it is essential that faith continues to conform to it.[24]

22. See Michael F. Bird, *Evangelical Theology* (Grand Rapids: Zondervan, 2013).
23. Michael F. Bird, *A Bird's Eye-View of Paul* (Downers Grove, Il: InterVarsity, 2008).
24. Peter Jensen, *The Revelation of God* (Downers Grove, IL: InterVarsity, 2002), 32.

The gospel also matters ecclesiologically in the sense that it defines what the church is and marks out the boundaries of its faith. In the early church we see precisely how the gospel became the normative fixture for their thinking, their service, and their proclamation. And yet, that led to a healthy degree of diversity-in-unity rather than yielding up a supposedly watertight system of doctrine. Irenaeus considered the gospel "handed down to us in the Scriptures, to be the ground and pillar of our faith."[25] The exposition of the gospel among many Christians in the late second century took on an essentially narrative shape when they summarized their beliefs in the *regula fidei* ("rule of faith"). Hearing again from Irenaeus, his account of the "ancient tradition" consisted of the belief that,

> there is one God, the Creator of heaven and earth, and all things therein, by means of Christ Jesus, the Son of God; who, because of His surpassing love towards His creation, condescended to be born of the virgin, He Himself uniting man through Himself to God, and having suffered under Pontius Pilate, and rising again, and having been received up in splendour, shall come in glory, the Saviour of those who are saved, and the Judge of those who are judged, and sending into eternal fire those who transform the truth, and despise His Father and His advent.[26]

That statement of course is really an embryonic version of the Apostle's Creed. Let us remember that the early creeds of the church, far from being cold, stale, and dry dogma, were really a "portable story" that enabled Christian communities to tell the story of the Christian faith to disciples, new converts, and outsiders.[27]

In light of that, what I would like to see is Bible study leaders sit down with some folk and ask them to describe the main acts in the biblical story. If you do this, pay particular attention to which parts of the story persons emphasize, what precise descriptions they use, how they describe God in this story, what role does Jesus and the church have in the story, and especially what gives their particular telling of the story its momentum and cohesion. After that, look at what is unique in their narration and what they share with others in the group who described the same story line as well.

That is a useful exercise on three fronts: (1) It forces everyone to sit down and think about the big picture (which people rarely do); (2) it also shows

25. Irenaeus, *Adv. Haer.* 3.1.1.

26. Ibid., 3.4.1–2.

27. N. T. Wright, "Reading Paul, Thinking Scripture," in *Scripture's Doctrine and Theology's Bible: How the New Testament Shapes Christian Dogmatics* (ed. Markus Bockmuehl and Alan J. Torrance; Grand Rapids: Baker, 2008), 64–65.

how the subtle differences in telling the story varies from person to person based on their background; and (3) it provides an excellent way for introducing the study of a new book, whether that is Judges, Isaiah, Mark, or Hebrews. If story is the most characteristic expression of worldview, then being able to articulate the Christian story is an exercise that should widen our understanding of the acts of God in redemptive history, but it also forces us to think through what the story means to us given our own unique setting and situation. Alternatively, preaching a sermon or series of sermons on the biblical story line can also benefit a congregation in a similar way.[28]

The varied ways of narrating the *regula fidei* themselves stem from the variety of gospel presentations in the New Testament. In the Gospel of Matthew, Jesus is the Davidic Shepherd-King and the quintessential teacher of Torah who comes to restore Israel and rescues Gentiles. The Gospel of Mark portrays Jesus paradoxically as the powerful Son of God and the suffering Son of Man who brings redemption. In the Gospel of Luke and Acts, Jesus is the anointed prophet of God who inaugurated the period of messianic salvation and his exaltation brings the forgiveness of sins. The Fourth Gospel concentrates on Jesus as the Word of God made flesh who gives eternal life to his followers. Outside the Gospels, Paul's message of deliverance is heavily indebted to the motif of reconciliation, in the Johannine epistles we are confronted with the imagery of cleansing for sin, in Hebrews the priestly work of Christ comes to the fore, and in the Apocalypse of John the Seer it is Jesus' victory over the evil world that is uppermost. While there is an irreducible plurality to the message of Jesus Christ in the New Testament, we can easily find a number of common threads that weaves them all together. The unity of the New Testament is not a single doctrine like "justification by faith alone," but a constellation or cluster of shared ideas and common experiences that unified the church around one Lord, one faith, and one baptism.

The unity of Scripture, the fulcrum of the *regula fidei*, and the root of the creeds can be traced to their shared testimony about how the triune God has brought salvation to the world through Jesus Christ. The "evangelical" and "apostolic" story of the church, in its multiple tellings, remains the grounds for communion, mission, and fellowship for all times. Thus, when along comes a Marcion, a Valentinus, or any number of theological innovators, Christians are quite within their right to warn, discipline, and exclude persons who want to rewrite the story. God is no cosmic aeon, trying desperately to release our imprisoned souls from the crypt of the physical body; no, in our

28. Cf. Trevin Wax, "12 Books that Showcase the Grand Narrative of Scripture," *TGC Blog*. See http://thegospelcoalition.org/blogs/trevinwax/2014/07/28/12-books-that-showcase-the-grand-narrative-of-scripture/.

story we believe in the redemption *of* the body, not redemption *from* the body! Jesus Christ is no philosopher giving us a good moral example and teaching about God's love; no, Jesus Christ is God made flesh and he himself is the way because, as the chorus goes, "these are the facts as we have received them."

As for church life more generally, it is vitally important that we preach an authentic gospel in evangelism and that Christians receive a good dose of the gospel in their discipleship. If you preach a gospelette, you will get Christianettes. I often tell my students the story that Charlie Chaplain once entered a Charlie Chaplain look-a-like contest and came second! Sadly, even today many Christians cannot tell the difference between the authentic gospel and the flimsy imitation. Too often Christians settle for a bumper-sticker type approach to the gospel with pithy one-liners, like "God loves you and has a wonderful plan for your life." Some gospel presentations give me the impression that God is either some kind of self-help therapist who wants me to feel better about myself or else is much like the "leader" of a cult who promises to transport his adherents to the far away planet "Blisstonia" on death.

If we do not imbibe our parishioners, family, and friends with an adequate understanding of the gospel, they will naturally begin to experience the spiritual inadequacies that follow from an inadequate gospel. Whether it is dealing with the continuing struggle against sin, wrestling with a big picture of God, thinking through the implications of Jesus' lordship, living in the midst of suffering, or engaging in missionary work, none of these things can seriously happen if you are operating with a truncated idea of what the gospel is. I say, take the cheesy wrapping paper off the gospel, delete the gospel twitters, and feel your way through the fabric of Scripture's testimony to the gospel. Instead of good advice you'll get good news, big news, shocking news about the God nobody was expecting. The God of creation has not let this world wallow forever in the mire of sin, injustice, and death caused by the disobedience of his creatures. On the contrary, he has been preparing his plan to put the world to right through his people Israel and by his Son Jesus. God himself comes in the Son and through the Spirit to rescue his children, to take the curse of exile away by taking the curse of sin on himself at the cross, to bring a new creation in the midst of death, to execute justice over the seeming invincible reign of tyrants, so that God's people may once again dwell in the paradise of God's very own presence.

Let gospel-driven spirituality sink into your preaching, your prayers, your counselling, your worries, your conversation, your Bible reading, your finances, your tears, your marriage, and your occupation and see what happens! Renewal comes when the transformative power of the gospel is let loose on Christians. That is because discipleship according to Paul is the process of being *gospelized.* When you tenderize a portion of meat, the whole portion becomes tender. If you sterilize a surgical tool, the entire tool is made sterile. If you magnetize a piece of metal, the metal turns magnetic. Similarly, when you are *gospelized*, you start to reflect in the various facets of your life the realities that the gospel announces and imparts to you: life, hope, joy, peace, faith, and love. A disciple of Jesus Christ should be a walking and talking miniature of the gospel. He or she is filled with its qualities, excited about its meaning, and consumed with a passion for its announcement. Apologies for ripping off Rick Warren, but the Christian life is the gospel-driven life!

### The Only True Faith is an Obedient Faith

The objective of Paul's ministry among the nations was not to get people to make "decisions," but to bring the Gentiles to the "obedience of faith." Obedience is a major part of discipleship, which is why in the great commission of Matthew 28:19–20, the risen Jesus tells his followers to teach others to "obey everything I have commanded you." Obedience is the test of true discipleship. Yet it is probably one of the least emphasized elements of Christian preaching and Christian worship. Apart from the hymn "Trust and Obey," I have a hard time recollecting any worship songs that celebrate and exhort obedience. I am sure that others have been written, but in my experience they are seldom sung. Probably because we don't like to be reminded that we are subservient to anyone, much less enlisted into service. But obedience in the Christian life is not of the sort that is forcibly extracted from us as if we were a slave or an unwilling subordinate. It is more like the rescued following the instructions of their rescuer. It flows out of a love for the one who first loved us. It is a willing service to the Lord who served us in humility and lowliness.

Obedience is also a sign that the covenantal promises of renewal have been brought to pass. Our faith and obedience are signs that God's Spirit is at work in us and the miracle of new birth has taken place. It is faith and obedience that demonstrates our kinship with the saints of old. Paul knew that this was important for the Roman Christians. The presence of faith and obedience legitimates Gentiles as members of God's people, even though they did not have the outward symbols of Israel's election. To apply that to ourselves, it means that a desire to obey and a godly sorrow for disobeying are marks that believers have entered the promises of God.

Going further, we can even say somewhat provocatively that Paul plainly holds obedience to be the necessary condition of salvation, even though the efficient cause of salvation remains the redemptive work of Jesus Christ.[29] This

29. Cf. Thomas R. Schreiner, *Run to Win the Prize: Perseverance in the New Testament* (Nottingham, UK: Inter-Varsity, 2009).

emphasis on obedience is far from opposed to the gospel promises of salvation by grace through faith. In the Lutheran tradition there is an emphasis on salvation through *sola fide* ("faith alone"), but also on salvation as producing in believers a *nova obedientia* ("new obedience").[30] Just as faith is a gift, so too is the power unto obedience. Viewed this way, the call to obedience does not mean that we have to sacrifice our sense of assurance. For the one who calls us to obey and to work out our salvation with fear and trembling is also working in us to will and to work out his good purposes (Phil 2:12–13).

Thus, obedience is not conceived of as our independent effort to please God as if we were trying to get there on our own steam. Rather, cultivating the obedience that flows out of this God-given faith is the goal of our spiritual journey. Our obedience is never perfect; it need not be, for we rest and rely on the obedience of Jesus Christ who, as the new Adam and the true Israel, has fulfilled the roles given to humanity in his own person. Jesus was obedient where Adam and Israel failed. He was obedient to death, even death on a cross (Phil 2:8). Therefore, Jesus was vindicated and exalted by the Father for his obedience (Phil 2:9–11; 1 Tim 3:16), and because we are united to him, we share in his vindication. By faith we are justified in the justification of God's obedient Son. By faith we are reconciled through the faithfulness of Israel's Messiah. By faith we are *reckoned* to be one with him who was himself obedient. It is natural, then, that from this union we will burst forth in a passion to foster God-praising, Christ-honoring, self-denying obedience in our own lives. As Charles Spurgeon said:

> We preach the obedience of faith. Faith is the fountain, the foundation, and the fosterer of obedience. Men obey not God till they believe him. We preach faith in order that men may be brought to obedience. To disbelieve is to disobey. One of the first signs of practical obedience is found in the obedience of the mind, the understanding, and the heart; and this is expressed in believing the teaching of Christ, trusting to his work, and resting in his salvation. Faith is the morning star of obedience. If we would work the work of God, we must believe on Jesus Christ whom he hath sent. Brethren, we do not give a secondary place to obedience, as some suppose. We look upon the obedience of the heart to the will of God as salvation. The attainment of perfect obedience would mean perfect salvation. We regard sanctification, or obedience, as the great design for which the Saviour died. He shed his blood that he might cleanse us from dead works, and purify unto himself a people zealous for good works. It is for this that we were chosen: we are "elect unto holiness." We know

30. Augsburg Confession, art. 6.

> nothing of election to continue in sin. It is for this that we have been called: we are "called to be saints." Obedience is the grand object of the work of grace in the hearts of those who are chosen and called: they are to become obedient children, conformed to the image of the Elder Brother, with whom the Father is well pleased.[31]

The decision to obey is one that we make day by day and moment by moment. Whether it is lifting your eyes away from the front of a illicit magazine cover in a store, sorting out your finances on what you will give to church and charities, refusing to do something unethical in your workplace, consciously arranging your time so that you are able to serve in your local church, or committing yourself to daily Bible study—all require discipline. But obedience has its blessings and rewards as it draws us closer to our Lord. It makes us more like Christ Jesus, and through obedience we are sharpened and refined as tools in the hands of God.

If we believe this, we must get away from the dichotomy of faith and obedience. As Dietrich Bonhoeffer said, "Only the believing obey, only the obedient believe."[32] We do not want to be legalistic about it. I know people might fret about what this might do to church numbers, but it is high time that we introduced some real accountability into our church membership on the matter of obedience. We have to find creative ways to encourage and admonish people in obedience. I can suggest one way: to make it a condition of membership that every member of the church must be involved in a prayer group, Bible study group, men's/women's group, ministry, or team where they have a buddy or friend to whom they can talk about their spiritual inventory. If you do that, I guarantee that you will see the cockroaches run for darkness lest their sham faith be exposed for what it is. Let me add that there is a pastoral and transparent way of doing this as opposed to a ruthless legalistic way, but I'm sure you get the point. We need our creeds, but they are worthless without our deeds. To pursue an obedient faith in our churches means nothing more than letting our walk match our talk.

31. Charles Spurgeon, "The Obedience of Faith" (Sermon # 2195). *The Spurgeon Archive*. See www.spurgeon.org/sermons/2195.htm.

32. Dietrich Bonhoeffer, *Discipleship* (Minneapolis: Fortress, 2001), 63.

CHAPTER 2

# Romans 1:8–17

## LISTEN to the Story

[8]First, I thank my God through Jesus Christ for all of you, because your faith is being reported all over the world.

[9]God, whom I serve in my spirit in preaching the gospel of his Son, is my witness how constantly I remember you [10]in my prayers at all times; and I pray that now at last by God's will the way may be opened for me to come to you. [11]I long to see you so that I may impart to you some spiritual gift to make you strong—[12]that is, that you and I may be mutually encouraged by each other's faith. [13]I do not want you to be unaware, brothers and sisters, that I planned many times to come to you (but have been prevented from doing so until now) in order that I might have a harvest among you, just as I have had among the other Gentiles.

[14]I am obligated both to Greeks and non-Greeks, both to the wise and the foolish. [15]That is why I am so eager to preach the gospel also to you who are in Rome.

[16]For I am not ashamed of the gospel, because it is the power of God that brings salvation to everyone who believes: first to the Jew, then to the Gentile. [17]For in the gospel the righteousness of God is revealed—a righteousness that is by faith from first to last, just as it is written: "The righteous will live by faith."

*Listening to the texts in the story:* Psalm 98; Isaiah 66:19; Habakkuk 2:4; 2 Corinthians 5:21; Philippians 3:9.

In this section, Paul now intends to build further rapport with the Roman believers by underscoring how they all belong to a worldwide communion. He informs them of their constant place in his prayers and highlights the mutuality of their faith. Then, somewhat dramatically, Paul sets up his primary thesis about the gospel, which will undergird everything he has to say in the letter about sin, salvation, transformation, Torah, hope, Israel, ethics, mission, and unity. I cannot stress enough that Paul here is still pressing his gospel theme that he began with in vv. 2–4. The gospel is a story about Jesus, which has penetrated into the eastern part of the Roman Empire and is creating Christ-shaped communities all over the place, like the very ones he is now addressing. The gospel is divine power unleashed to save Jews and Greeks. The gospel unveils divine righteousness to judge and to justify. The gospel is a message from God and about God, a message that invades this world, and its proclamation creates a new people by creating faith in those who hear it. Paul sees himself as an instrument of God's saving action, an action that drives his preaching, prayers, and praxis. In these brief words, Paul is beginning to invite his readers to identify with his message and to share in the promotion of his particular apostolic mission to take the gospel to places it has not gone before.

The background story here is that Paul sees himself as playing a key role in God's plan to extend his salvation to the ends of the earth. Just as Isaiah looked ahead to a time when the returnees from exile would be sent abroad as ensigns to the nations, going as far as Greece, Libya, and Spain (see Isa 66:19–20), in a similar way, Paul may have envisioned his apostolic ministry as taking the shape of an arc that went from Jerusalem to northern Greece to Rome to Spain; then, who knows, perhaps back along the North African coast and finally to Egypt and home to Jerusalem (see Rom 15:17–24). Just as the Psalter called Israel to sing God's praises among the nations and make them seek out God's blessings (see Pss 57:9; 67:2–4; 96:10), so too Paul believed that he was sent out to the Greeks and barbarians of the world with the good news that God would bless them in Israel's Messiah. Paul was driven by the fact that in the Bible he read that God intended to make Abraham the father of many nations (see Rom 4:17–18). God's salvation reaches out to the world through the revelation of God's righteousness in the gospel, a righteousness that proves God's faithfulness to Israel and brings mercy to the nations (see Ps 98:1–3).

Paul's introductory remarks run as follows: (1) a thanksgiving for the Roman believers (v. 8); (2) spellling out his affection for the Roman believers combined with an explanation as to why he has not visited them before (vv. 9–15); and (3) a summation of his unyielding convictions about the gospel (vv. 16–17).

## EXPLAIN the Story

### Paul's Thanksgiving (1:8)

Paul begins to narrate the circumstances that led him to write the letter. He explains in particular why, if he is *the* apostle to the *Gentiles*, he has not visited the Roman Christians earlier. Like his other letters, Paul moves to a thanksgiving for his audience, nominating it as the "first" thing he wants to mention in the course of cultivating a relationship with the Roman believers (v. 8). Such a thanksgiving reflects the typical nature of the early church's worship being directed as it was *to* God the Father and *through* the Lord Jesus Christ. Reverence for Jesus is made with reference to the one God who indicates that Jesus shares in the divine identity.[1]

The occasion for Paul's thanksgiving is "because your faith is being reported all over the world" (v. 8). The "world" here is hyperbole, and Paul means that the churches in the Greco-Roman world have heard about the converts made in Rome. At the end of the letter Paul will also mention how everyone has heard about the Romans' "obedience" (Rom 16:19). The early church seemed to have possessed a clear awareness of being a worldwide network. The first Christians did not, despite all of their diversity, see themselves as isolated and introspective congregations each keeping to their own. On the contrary, there was what Michael Thompson called a "Holy Internet," with believers travelling widely, visiting each other, writing to one another, and sharing each other's literature.[2] Whereas Paul wrote Romans from the environs of Corinth around AD 56/57, some three decades later (ca. AD 90) a senior presbyter in Rome named Clement wrote to the Corinthians using what pastoral clout he had to try and solve some of the problems there.[3] Paul is thankful for the Romans because the report of their faith—a faith that has been maintained amidst external pressure and among internal clamor—had truly made its way around the Christian grapevine.

The elephant in the room, so to speak, that Paul needs to address is his absence from Rome. If he is the divinely appointed apostle to the Gentiles, then why has he not yet visited the largest Gentile city in the inhabited world? Why has Paul not attempted to correspond with the Roman Gentile believers resident there if they are, as Paul alleges, under the jurisdiction of his apostolate? By analogy, it is kind of like someone claiming to be the Anglican Archbishop of California, but failing to visit the Anglican churches in Los Angeles after twenty years in the job! People might now ask, who is this Paul guy, what's his deal, what's he got to do with us? If he is a somebody, then why hasn't he visited us yet? Moreover, with Paul's reputation being what it was, he might not have been welcomed by some folks because of his

1. Cf. Larry Hurtado, *Lord Jesus Christ: Devotion to Jesus in Earliest Christianity* (Grand Rapids: Eerdmans, 2003), 151–53.

2. Michael B. Thompson, "The Holy Internet: Communication between Churches in the First Christian Generation," in *The Gospels for All Christians: Rethinking the Gospel Audiences* (ed. R. Bauckham; Grand Rapids: Eerdmans, 1998), 49–70.

3. The letter is called *1 Clement.* See the translation in Michael Holmes, *The Apostolic Fathers: Greek Texts and English Translations* (Grand Rapids: Baker, 2007).

controversial views about the Torah (see Rom 3:8; 6:1–2; cf. Acts 20:20–21; 28:17). Whatever the Roman believers had heard or thought about Paul, Luke makes it clear that by the time Paul finally got to Rome, the believers there were grateful and encouraged by his arrival (see Acts 28:14–15).

### Paul's Concern for the Romans (1:9–15)

Paul endeavors in a number of ways to assuage any ambiguous feelings the Romans might have about his ministry or his motives.

First, Paul stresses that even while he is engaged in "preaching the gospel," God can testify as a witness to "how constantly I remember you in my prayers at all times" (vv. 9–10). Paul routinely reminded his audiences of the constancy of his prayers for them (1 Cor 1:4; Eph 1:16; Phil 1:4; Col 1:3; 1 Thess 1:2; 2 Thess 1:3; Phlm 4) and how he regularly makes petitions for their growth in the faith (Eph 1:16–19; Phil 1:9–11; Col 1:9–11; Phlm 6). These prayers are windows into the theocentric piety, Christ-centered devotion, and pastoral heart of the apostle. A model for our own prayers if there ever was one! While Paul has been away from the Romans, the Romans have never been far from Paul's prayers.

Second, Paul says he specifically prays for the opportunity to visit Rome and explains why he has not visited them to date. Paul's prayer for the Romans is that hopefully "by God's will the way may be opened for me to come to you" (v. 10). What Paul means is that visiting Rome is at the top of his apostolic agenda. Related to that, Paul explains in v. 13 that he has previously planned to visit them, but has thus far been prevented from doing so. When Paul states, "I do not want you to be unaware, brothers and sisters," he has in mind something like "Do not get the wrong impression about me." Paul uses the expression frequently in his letters for getting the right perspective on contentious matters (see Rom 11:25; 1 Cor 10:1; 12:1; 2 Cor 1:8; 1 Thess 4:13).

The reason why Paul has not yet visited them is not because of disinterest. Rather, he has thus far "been prevented from doing so until now" (v. 13). Paul mentions what these hindrances are at the end of the letter, namely, he has been busy preaching the gospel from Jerusalem all the way around to Illyricum (Rom 15:17–23). To that we can add from our knowledge of Paul's other letters and from Acts that Paul has also had to deal with church problems in Antioch, Galatia, Corinth, and Thessalonica, in addition to enduring beatings and imprisonments that also tend to tax one's time! Whatever obstacles had hitherto prevented Paul from coming to Rome, Paul now thinks that they are sufficiently cleared out of the way as to enable him to head to Spain via Rome. Sadly, the events narrated in Acts 21:28 show that Paul had no idea about the many misfortunes that were about to befall him and would yet hinder his missionary plans. He would make it to Rome several years later only after first being mobbed, arrested, enduring a lengthy imprisonment and trial, and surviving a shipwreck!

Paul gives three reasons for his intended visit to Rome. First, his "longing" to be with the Romans is so that "I may impart to you some spiritual gift to make you strong" (v. 11). The words *charisma pneumatikon* are normally translated as "spiritual gift" (NRSV, NIV, ESV, CEB, NET). Paul mentions these gifts later in Romans (Rom 12:6) and elsewhere in his letters (1 Cor 1:7; 7:7; 12:4, 9, 28–31; 1 Tim 4:14; 2 Tim 1:6). The spiritual gifts pertain to Spirit-given abilities to serve and work among the churches in various ways. Paul gives no indication that he had a particular gift in mind that he could bestow on the Romans. Later Paul will write that he wants the Romans to be "filled with joy and peace" and "overflow with hope in the power of the Holy Spirit" (Rom 15:13), which is part of the overall purpose of his ministry that all believing Gentiles would be "acceptable to God and sanctified by the Holy Spirit" (15:16). Perhaps Paul means no more than his presence among them will convey the "full measure of the blessing of Christ" (15:29).

However, this spiritual gift should be more readily connected to the purpose of the letter itself.[4] I would aver that since writing was largely a substitute for personal presence,[5] Paul was attempting to do in this letter what he could not do in person. Although Paul cannot strengthen the believers in person, he seeks to strengthen them all the same by laying out the gospel in theological depth in his letter. The Roman churches need the Pauline gospel to better understand the unity of Jews and Gentiles in Christ and the mutuality that will flow from a gospel-soaked community. Let us remember that Paul's gospel pertains not just to initial preaching but to an entire sequence of activities that results in settled and mature churches, i.e., gospelizing.[6] He writes this letter to them in the hope that his epistolary gospelizing will do what he could not do in person, namely, impart a spiritual blessing to the Roman churches based on the exposition and application of the gospel to their common life together—something the Gentile Christians who looked down on their Jewish brothers and sisters needed to hear. The unpacking of the gospel is the spiritual gift that he wants to share with them to strengthen them in their faith. It is by reminding them of the "pattern of teaching that has now claimed

4. Gordon D. Fee, *God's Empowering Presence: The Holy Spirit in the Letters of Paul* (Peabody, MA: Hendrickson 1994), 487–88.

5. Libanius (*Ep*. 37.1) wrote, "Now, it would be sweeter to be able to see each other, but neither is the second best choice trivial, namely to send and to receive a letter" and (*Ep*. 245.9) "When you look at my letter, think that you are looking at me."

6. Paul Bowers, "Fulfilling the Gospel: The Scope of the Pauline Mission," *JETS* 30 (1987): 198.

your allegiance" (Rom 6:17) that the Romans will be "filled with knowledge and [be] competent to instruct one another" (15:14).

A further purpose for Paul's projected visit to Rome is that "you and I may be mutually encouraged by each other's faith" (v. 12). Mutuality forms an essential part of Paul's exhortation in Rom 14:1–15:13. Paul's visit will encourage the Roman believers by his evangelical ministry; concurrently, their faith will also encourage Paul. The "encouragement" that Paul wants is probably their "assistance" and "refreshment" in the form of material support for his mission to Spain (Rom 15:24–32).

In keeping with the missional theme, a third purpose of Paul's intended visit to Rome is "in order that I might have a harvest among you, just as I have had among the other Gentiles" (v. 13). Rome was filled with Greeks and barbarians, the civilized and the brutish, the wise and the unlearned—at least from a Roman perspective. These are the people to whom Paul was obligated to minister as part of his apostolic call (see 1 Cor 1:22–24, 9:16–23; 10:22). That is why he is so eager to preach the gospel in Rome (vv. 14–15). Once more, this rehearses what Paul will say at the end of the letter. Paul has finished preaching in the eastern regions, so now he wants to go west, to Rome and then to Spain, to continue "to preach the gospel where Christ was not known" (15:20). The Romans are invited to partner with Paul in the task of leading the Gentiles to obey God through his evangelistic mission (1:5; 15:18; 16:26).

### The Revelation of God's Righteousness (1:16–17)

Coming to vv. 16–17, we reach the nerve center of this letter. These verses function much like a thesis statement, a central claim, the *propositio*, that Paul will expound and defend. Unfortunately several of the phrases are contested in their meaning and have to be explored at length, especially the meaning of the "righteousness of God" and the citation from Hab 2:4. For a preliminary summary, Chrysostom put it wonderfully when he said: "It is the righteousness of God that is revealed here, not yours but God's, a righteousness both abundant and easily accessible. For you do not receive it by toils and labors, but you receive it by a gift from above contributing one thing only from yourself, namely, 'believing.'"[7]

Paul's eagerness to preach the gospel in Rome provides occasion for him to affirm his pride in the gospel. The apostle asserts that "I am not ashamed of the gospel," which is a roundabout way of saying that "I am proud of the gospel." Evidently there were those who thought that he should be ashamed of his message and his ministry. It was after all "a stumbling block to Jews

---

7. Chrysostom, *Hom. Rom.* 2.

and foolishness to Gentiles" (1 Cor 1:23). Many of Paul's detractors, Jews and some Jewish Christians, thought that Paul was doing the unthinkable. He was declaring that the Gentiles are acceptable to God on the basis of faith in Jesus, apart from observing the Torah, and completely bypassing the visible emblems of Israel's election (see Acts 15:1–2; Gal 2:4–5; 5:1–12; 1 Thess 2:15).

The objection was probably along the lines that Paul was denigrating the God-given Torah by failing to insist on obedience to it. Furthermore, by dissolving the category of "God-fearer," Paul was lowering the currency of Israel's election by telling Gentiles that they had a part in something that was meant to be the exclusive property of Jews. Paul does not think the gospel is shameful; rather, it establishes the righteousness of those who believe in it. According to Mark Reasoner, "Paul's gospel itself is without shame (1.16; 3.8; 6.21). Those who follow it will not be ashamed (5.5; 9.33; 10.11). The believers in Rome should not live shamefully (12.17b; 13.1–14). Paul's gospel accounts for a ministry that is not shameful (15.17–21) and he asks his Roman readers to pray for him lest he be shamed in Jerusalem (15.30–32)."[8]

Paul is not ashamed of the gospel "because it is the power of God that brings salvation to everyone who believes: first to the Jew, then to the Gentile" (v. 16). Elsewhere Paul says that the "word of the cross" is the "power of God" (1 Cor 1:18). The gospel contains the "power of God" in the sense that God actualizes his rescuing purposes through it. The gospel is a speech-act, in that it not only announces the way of salvation, but actualizes salvation in those who hear it with faith (see Rom 10:17; 1 Thess 2:13). The same power of God manifested in raising the Son (Rom 1:4), in creation (1:20), in the divine acts of redemptive history (9:17, 22), in keeping covenant promises (4:21), and in miraculous events (15:19) is also infused into the gospel. The gospel manifests God's death-defeating, curse-reversing, evil-vanquishing, devil-crushing, sin-cleansing, life-giving, love-forming, people-uniting, super-über-mega-grace power that results in "salvation."

The Greek word *sōtēria* ("salvation") is fairly broad and connotes rescue and deliverance from peril.[9] For Paul, salvation is both "now" and "not yet." These dual concepts are evident in Romans where Paul discusses salvation as something already achieved by Jesus' death and resurrection in terms of justification by faith and peace with God (e.g., Rom 5:1; 8:1), yet he holds out hope for salvation in the future (e.g., 8:23; 13:11). Throughout Romans, Paul uses a wide array of images for salvation, including justification, redemption, reconciliation, peace, freedom, and life. At their core is the notion of sharing in life from God in Christ through the Spirit.

8. Reasoner, *The Strong and the Weak*, 225.

9. BDAG 985–86.

This "salvation" extends to everyone, Jews and Gentiles, without distinction (see Rom 3:22; 10:12). The universality of the gospel will prove to be a theme that constantly reemerges in the letter. In fact, the great mystery that Paul alludes to later is that God's saving promise for Israel and for the world finds its resolution in the gospel (see 11:25–32; 16:25–27). The order in which salvation comes is "first to the Jew" and "then to the Gentile." Such a statement does not imply that God merely offers salvation first to the Jews out of some kind of politeness, knowing that they'll reject it, so that the "real" mission to the Gentiles can begin. The priority is a redemptive-historical necessity. God's plan has always been to reach the world through Israel—hence Israel's many privileges (see 3:2; 9:4–5). That is why Israel was a "kingdom of priests" (Exod 19:5–6) and a "light to the nations" (Isa 42:6; 49:6).

God's intention has always been that a transformed Israel would transform the world. Jesus himself focused his ministry exclusively on Israel (Matt 10:5–6; 15:24), and yet his work would result in Gentiles sharing in the messianic banquet (Matt 8:11–12) and effect a worldwide mission to all nations (Matt 24:14; 28:19–20).[10] At the climax of the letter, Paul announces that the inclusion of the Gentiles in salvation was contingent on Jesus' ministry to Israel. He writes: "For I tell you that Christ has become a servant of the Jews on behalf of God's truth, so that the promises made to the patriarchs might be confirmed," promises that would result in the Gentiles glorifying God for his mercy (Rom 15:8–9). Thus, Paul proposes the interlocking destiny of Jews and Gentiles in the story of Israel's Messiah.

An additional reason for pride in the gospel is because in the gospel "the righteousness of God is revealed" (v. 17). The meaning of the "righteousness of God" (*dikaiosynē theou*) is widely disputed.[11] Since the Reformation this "righteousness" has commonly been thought to designate a legal status that believers receive from God, an imputed righteousness.[12] There is some validity to this view insofar as Paul does mention righteousness as a gift given to believers resulting in a new status before God (see Rom 4:6, 24; 5:17; 9:30; 10:3–6; 1 Cor 1:30; Gal 2:21; Phil 3:9), and righteousness has forensic qualities (se Rom 8:1, 33; 1 Cor 1:30). More recently, other interpreters have argued that the "righteousness of God" is more tantamount to God's "covenant faithfulness."[13] Again, some truth can be found here, insofar as divine

10. See Michael F. Bird, "The Historical Jesus and the Early Christian Gentile Missions," in *Jesus in Continuum* (ed. Tom Holmén; WUNT 289; Tübingen: Mohr Siebeck, 2012), 63–86.

11. See discussion in Michael F. Bird, *The Saving Righteousness of God: Studies in Paul, Justification, and the New Perspective* (Milton Keynes, UK: Paternoster, 2007), 6–39.

12. Cf., e.g., Cranfield, *Romans*, 1:97–99.

13. Dunn, *Romans*, 1:40–42; Wright, "Romans," 10:396–406. According to G. Schrenk ("δικαιοσύνη," *TDNT* 2.195): "This linking of right and salvation is most deeply grounded in the

faithfulness and divine righteousness are often set in proximity and parallel (see Deut 7:9; 32:4; Pss 25:10; 26:3; 40:10–11; 89:28, 49; 111:5–10; 143:1; Isa 11:5; 16:5; Zech 8:8). Furthermore, there is a long history extending from Ambrosiaster to Karl Barth in identifying the "righteousness of God" as God's faithfulness.

A further complicating factor is that the "righteousness of God" can be regarded as *either* an objective genitive (i.e., a righteousness *from* God) or else a subjective genitive (i.e., a righteousness that *belongs to* God or an activity *performed by* God). While the two options are not incommensurable, it is more likely that the "righteousness of God" is a subjective genitive for two reasons. (1) It makes sense of the context of Romans 1–3, which is pervaded by statements about divine qualities and activities such as God's "power" (1:16), "wrath" (1:18; 3:5), "judgment" (2:2–3, 5), "goodness" (2:4), "truthfulness" (3:7), and "faithfulness" (3:3). (2) There are multiple examples in the Old Testament where "righteousness" and "salvation" are effectively synonymous (e.g., Pss 51:14; 71:15–16; 98:2; Isa 46:13; 56:1; Mic 7:9), and usage here is also analogous to instances where God's righteousness is God's mighty actions of deliverance (e.g., Judg 5:11; 1 Sam 12:7). Hence, the "righteousness of God" is both attribute and action. The righteousness of God signifies the fidelity and justice of God's character, the demonstration of his character as the judge of all the earth, and his faithfulness toward Israel in Jesus Christ. The righteousness of God, then, is the character of God embodied and enacted in his saving actions. It is a saving event that is comprehensive, and it involves vivification, justification, and transformation.

In addition, while hearers familiar with the Old Testament might hear resonances about God's covenant faithfulness and saving power, hearers familiar with the Roman concept of *iustitia* or justice might discern in the phrase reference to God's distributive justice. This Latin term has connotations of equity and fairness so that in a Roman context it could connote the idea of God's impartial and just provision of salvation to all. For those living on the margins of Roman society or those suffering under injustice among the exploited, the good news of God's *iustitia* would be a source of solace in a society that often denied them fairness and justice.[14] The net point in "God's righteousness" is the eschatological divine action in being faithful to

---

covenant concept. הקדיש is the execution of covenant faithfulness and covenant promises. God's righteousness as His judicial reign means that in covenant faithfulness to His people He vindicates and saves them."

14. Cf. Frank Thielman, "God's Righteousness as God's Fairness in Romans 1:17," *JETS* 54 (2011): 35–48; Michael J. Gorman, "Justification and Justice in Paul, with Special Reference to the Corinthians," *JSPL* 1 (2011): 23–40.

his covenant and establishing his justice over creation through the invading story of gospel.[15]

The manner in which the saving righteousness of God is appropriated is by means of faith. Paul underscores this with a peculiar Greek construction that runs *ek pisteōs eis pistin* (lit., "from faith to faith"). But whose faith is it here? Some think it might mean from God's faithfulness to human faith, from Jewish faith to Gentile faith, or from Christ's faithfulness met with the response of human faith. Generally speaking, *ek pisteōs* is used by Paul to indicate that faith is the instrument through which the saving benefits of Christ's death and resurrection are communicated to people (see Rom 3:26, 30; 4:16; 5:1; 9:30, 32; 10:6). In light of that, Paul probably means something like salvation is received "from start to finish by faith" (NLT). As to what "faith" means in Paul's letters, David Hays says that the Pauline idea of faith "combined elements of cognitive assertion, trust, and faithfulness" and "faith, for Paul, is the mode by which Christians participate or live spiritually in Christ."[16]

To recap, Paul is stating that the apocalyptic unveiling of God's saving power in the gospel is received by faith. To underscore that faith is the instrument for salvation, and to demonstrate the conformity of his gospel to the pattern of Scripture, Paul makes a citation from Hab 2:4: "The righteous will live by faith." There are some slight but significant differences between the Hebrew, Greek, and Pauline wordings of the verse.[17] That aside, Paul's point is that Scripture supports his claim that faith is the instrument by which one stands before God as righteous and becomes a member of God's people. Just like the people in the day of Habakkuk, even now the people of God need to wait in faith for the final revelation of God's salvation.

Paul's citation of Habakkuk 2:4 is indicative of the fact that Scripture will prove to be crucial in Paul's unfolding argument because Christ and his gospel are not redemptive-historical blips divorced from the story of God, Israel, and the world. Rather, Christ is the fulfillment of Israel's hopes, and the gospel stands in accord with the scriptural promises. As Francis Watson writes: "It is scripture that shapes the contours of the Christ-event, and to discern how it does so is to uncover the true meaning of Scripture itself. Pauline theology is

15. Michael F. Bird, "Justification: A Progressive Reformed View," in *Justification: Five Views* (ed. P. Eddy and J. Beilby; Downers Grove, IL: InterVarsity, 2011), 140–42; Colin Kruse, *Paul, the Law and Justification* (Leicester: Apollos, 1996), 169–70; Schreiner, *Romans*, 65.

16. David M. Hay, "Paul's Understanding of Faith as Participation," in *Paul and His Theology* (ed. S. E. Porter; PS 3; Leiden: Brill, 2006), 46, 52.

17. MT: But the righteous one by his faith shall live.
LXX: But the righteous one shall live by my faithfulness.
Gal 3:11/Rom 1:17: But the righteous one by faith shall live.
Heb 10:38: But my righteous one by faith shall live.

thus intertextual theology: explicit scriptural citations are simply the visible manifestations of an intertextuality that is ubiquitous and fundamental to Pauline discourse."[18]

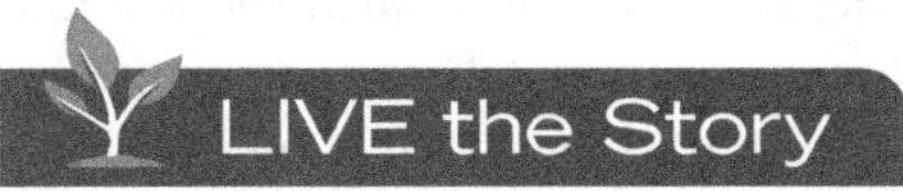


When the rubber of Romans 1:8 – 17 hits the road of Christian life, what does it look like? I want to draw the reader's attention to two things: cultivating relationships with the global church and not being ashamed of the gospel.

### Worldwide Communion

I find it interesting that Paul is quick to draw attention to the fact that the Roman churches' faith and obedience has been reported all over the world, presumably to the churches in Greece, Asia, Syria, and Palestine. Paul begins his narration with an affirmation that the Roman believers belong to a worldwide network of believers with a common faith and a common Lord. While Paul's theology takes his audience to a bigger picture of God, Paul also wants his audience to have a bigger picture of the church.

Whatever corner of the globe we inhabit — I'm typing this sentence while living in Australia — our slice of church is only a small part of a larger entity. The universal body of Christ is a multinational and multiethnic group that covers the globe. We are all one in Christ Jesus in that we share one Lord, one faith, and one baptism. Despite all our diversity, denominationally and culturally, what unites us together is infinitely stronger than anything that might drive us apart. As we bind ourselves to the Lord, so too we bind ourselves to each other irrespective of our foibbles and failings.

For me this image of one multinational church was beautifully made when I visited a church where the minister arranged a video clip about all the people in his congregation of different nationalities. Each congregant of foreign background spoke of what faith in Christ meant for them given their background and heritage. It was a medium-sized rural church, but they still had more than sixteen different nationalities represented in their parish. The climax of the event was when they brought out the sixteen flags of each nation represented in the congregation. No flag was raised above the others, no flags were bowed before another; then at the end of the service all the flags were laid at the foot of a cross. It was a beautiful image of the church as a diverse people coming from every tribe, language, and nation, joined together in a united worship of the Lord Jesus.[19]

---

18. Francis Watson, *Paul and the Hermeneutics of Faith* (London: T&T Clark, 2004), 17.
19. Bird, *Colossians and Philemon*, 45 – 46.

The twenty-first century has become a time of intense globalization with increasing movement across borders and heightened levels of economic interdependence between regions. In such a context it is important that the churches work together in gospel partnership. Obviously such cooperation between Western mission-sending churches and majority world churches has long existed. Previously this mission relationship was based on a colonial model of leadership and with a view to evangelizing the populace. Yet in many places what is needed now is not so much new Western-led missions, but support to help equip and empower these churches in evangelizing their own people and educating a new generation of leaders. The next big vista in missions is mentoring leaders, churches, and institutions to be agents of transformation in their own contexts.

I find it disconcerting when well-intentioned Western mission organizations send missionaries to plant their own brand of churches in foreign territories where flourishing churches of the same basic denominational type already exist — something I've seen even in Australia and the UK with mixed results. It is especially perplexing when the indigenous churches are robustly orthodox and energetically evangelical. Why do they need another Baptist church or another Presbyterian church on the same street as the one that is there now? Such a practice is based on paternalism, not partnership; it values control not communion, and it promotes mistrust rather than cooperative mission. The churches of Africa, Asia, and South America need more denominations to the same degree that our heads need a mild bludgeoning with a heavy object. Planting new churches in unreached areas is great thing, but to plant an Americanized or Europeanized colony among a network of already vibrant local churches seems an irresponsible use of resources and a slap in the face to existing churches. Would it not be better to send a team to work with an existing local church rather than trying to replicate it or even rival it?

Remember that Paul is not trying to plant a Pauline-friendly church in Rome filled with his own people to politely compete with the churches already there. No, Paul wants partnership with the existing churches, churches he did not plant, churches that he does not try to control, so that together they can promote a common gospel. He wants to bless them as much as be blessed by them. That is simply an outworking of the church as the body of Christ. One body with many parts, full of a diversity of gifts, and suited to a number of unique ministries.

Consider the following. Given that English is the *lingua franca* of the global village, Americans are well positioned to engage in English-language teaching ministries almost anywhere in the world where people want to learn English. In Europe, some South American missionaries have made headway among Muslim immigrants helped by the fact that they don't look European and have no history of conflict with peoples of the Middle East. Chinese Christians are among the best placed, culturally and geographically, to establish and encourage the small number of churches in Southeast Asia. Similarly, Australia and New Zealand have long been springboards for missions into the Asia Pacific. Believers in every region of the world have their own work and wisdom to contribute to the worldwide church's effort to fulfill the Great Commission.

We must keep in mind that Romans is a missional document, plotting Paul's local part in a wider movement in the Greco-Roman world and connecting his mission to the Romans' own situation. Paul knows that he is not the only Christian worker on the circuit as he has many friends who serve in similar missionary endeavours (see Rom 16:1–23). Paul does not care who preaches the gospel as long as the gospel is preached (see Phil 1:18). Paul wants the Roman believers to see themselves as part of this worldwide mission movement and how they can play a role in that mission, specifically, in his own call as the apostle to the Gentiles. In the same way, whatever missionary work we are called to carry out or support, we should pursue it with conscious regard for the global church, seeing them not just as not as objects of ministry but also as partners in ministry.

Just as Paul can pray unceasingly for these Roman churches he has not yet visited, so too we can earnestly pray for the well-being of other churches all over the world. Prayer for churches, missions, and organizations active in other countries should form a segment of our individual and corporate prayer life. During chapel in my own college, we routinely pray for various continents and countries over the course of the week. This is part of what it means to belong to the communion of saints so as to be in prayerful support for one another.

Several friends of mine were fortunate enough to attend the 2010 Lausanne Global Congress held in Capetown, South Africa. There they experienced the diverse array of the global church with people of nearly every race, ethnicity, and country in attendance. It was a time of shared worship, testimonies, Bible teaching, strategizing, and recommitment to mission. In many ways, the Lausanne Movement, with its motto "The Whole Church Taking the Whole Gospel to the Whole World," embodies the precise type of evangelical mission that Paul was trying to engender in his letter to the Romans. Paul's gospel for the Jew and the Greek is for us the same gospel for the Arab and the American, for the Zambian and the Peruvian, or for the Japanese and the Lithuanian.

**The Gospel of Shame**

When Paul says that he is not ashamed of the gospel, he's bringing to the surface a series of underlying attacks that he has experienced in his ministry. Some people thought that Paul should be ashamed of the message he was telling and the ministry he was performing. That is because the gospel of Jesus Christ was foolishness to Greeks, a stumbling block to Jews, and utter madness to Romans (see Acts 26:24; 1 Cor 1:23). A crucified Messiah? God accepts Gentiles without submission to the Law of Moses? Resurrection from the dead? A power greater than Rome and Rome's gods? How many times did synagogue leaders in Antioch, Roman officials in Ephesus, or philosophers in Athens say to Paul, "You don't really believe that nonsense, do you?"

You could make a case according to the canons of contemporary Western belief that Christians should be deeply ashamed about their gospel. For Christians believe:

- There is one triune God, not a plethora of gods, nor an impersonal consciousness at the heart of the universe.
- The single most important event in the history of the world is Jesus' crucifixion and resurrection.
- Jesus' death was atonement for human evil, not merely an example of human suffering.
- God raised Jesus from the dead and "resurrection" is no empty metaphor for God's continuing cause.
- God has placed a human being, the exalted Lord, at the helm of the universe.
- Jesus is the only way to God, not one of many ways to God.
- The gift of the Holy Spirit is a real experience, not the name we give to our religious consciousness.
- The church is a gathering of the saints for service to God, not a religious society with backward beliefs and Victorian-era morals.
- At the return of Jesus every knee will bow, including every Jew, Muslim, Hindu, atheist, and Scientologist.
- There will be a final judgment after which there will follow everlasting life or everlasting destruction for every man and woman of the world.

These beliefs are grievously offensive to inner-city Greeks as much as to barbarians out in the burbs. These beliefs are shameful because they seem entirely unjustified, morally offensive, and needlessly exclusive. How dare Christians believe that only their God is God! How dare Christians say that a hook-up culture demeans our sexuality! How dare Christians restrict marriage to heterosexual couples! How dare Christians violate the reproductive rights of women! How dare Christians keep worshiping some mad rabbi from backwater Palestine when they could worship the state or earth! How dare Christians keep on, well, being Christian![20]

In the face of accusations of shame we can do one of two things: become ashamed of the gospel or else embrace the shame of the cross.

First, on becoming ashamed of the gospel, we could capitulate to the surrounding culture and try to make our faith more palatable to others by reconfiguring it according to perceived norms. There is a long history to this approach. The second-century heretic Marcion tried to do exactly this when he attempted to turn Christianity into a Greco-Roman philosophy by excising all Jewish traits from the Christian faith. The old liberals of the late-nineteenth and early-twentieth centuries tried to bring Christianity into alignment with the spirit of the age by rethinking doctrines of salvation and incarnation through giving up on the idea of the supernatural and by reducing religion to ethics. Postmodern theologians do something similar by cherry picking theology to create new beliefs that reverberate with contemporary notions of tolerance and diversity. They do that by, ironically, being intolerant, monolithic, and exclusive toward historic Christianity in their construction of beliefs and ethics.

As a historic, orthodox, evangelical believer this is not an option I am willing to entertain. You end up with a domesticated god who looks a lot like the little god-impersonators in the prevalent culture. You end up with the type of Christianity that looks like a cross between Marcion and Dr. Phil—just a bunch of self-assuring banter dressed up in some religious grammar designed to affirm what everyone already thinks. People become ashamed of the gospel when they value the opinion of someone else other than God our Savior. Why stand up and get ridiculed for Jesus when metaphorically kneeling before a hundred-foot tall golden statue of Oprah draped in a rainbow sash will get you accepted in the public square?

This is not an option for faithful believers. To begin with, I think about the time when Bishop Polycarp of Smyrna was put on trial and was asked to swear allegiance to Caesar and to curse the Christ. The old bishop said: "Eighty and six years have I served him, and he never did me any wrong: how then can I blaspheme my King and my Savior?"[21] Amen to that! I'd rather have the deep, deep love of Jesus any day of the week and twice on Sunday than

20. To be frank, there are heaps of things in church history and the church present that we should be ashamed about. The Christian faith has been an inspiration toward beautiful goods and used to justify deplorable evils. A fear that our actions will bring shame on God should hopefully make us more discerning about the types of activities we endorse and participate in.

21. *Mart. Pol.* 9.3.

all the friends, fame, or fortune that being ashamed of Christ might afford me. I ain't gonna sell out my Lord who saved me so that a hipster dressed as a lumberjack and drinking an eighteen dollar latté with almond milk thinks I'm cool. In addition, it is so easy to kneel before cultural idols when you get tired of being called an uncultured, superstitious Neanderthal. And I do tire of it! Sometimes standing up for Jesus at college, at work, or even in your family feels like you've got one big target painted on your forehead. But you know what? I've been standing up for Jesus for so long that I've developed a cramp in my thigh, so kneeling before a hundred-foot tall golden statue of Oprah will not be forthcoming.

Second, on embracing the shame of the cross, that is the pattern that Jesus and Paul set before us. Let us remember that crucifixion was not only one of the cruelest and most torturous deaths, but it also expressed the zenith of degradation, disempowerment, and dishonor. To be crucified was to be depersonalized. According to Luke, Jesus dramatically told his disciples, "Whoever wants to be my disciple must deny themselves and take up their cross daily and follow me," and the alternative is "Whoever is ashamed of me and my words, the Son of Man will be ashamed of them when he comes in his glory and in the glory of the Father and of the holy angels" (Luke 9:23, 26). Jesus gives his disciples the choice between taking up the shame of the cross or else being ashamed of him. Paradoxically, embracing the shame of the cross will lead to glory while being ashamed of Jesus will lead to an even greater indignity.

In 1 Corinthians, Paul expounds the message of the cross by noting how God uses the message to heap shame on others: "God chose the foolish things of the world to shame the wise; God chose the weak things of the world to shame the strong. God chose the lowly things of this world and the despised things—and the things that are not—to nullify the things that are, so that no one may boast before him" (1 Cor 1:27–29). The cross becomes an instrument of reversal so that the dualities of wise-foolish, weak-powerful, and humble-great are all turned upside down. In the shame of the cross we find God's wisdom, power, righteousness, and redemption. Now one thing should be crystal clear. Following Jesus means a willingness to embrace the shame of the cross, to carry this shame, and to even boast in this shame around the public square.

That said, drifting away from orthodoxy is not the only way of being ashamed of gospel of Christ. We can be ashamed of the gospel in far more ways than drifting away from the theological fixtures that bind us to Christ. Even fully orthodox and robustly evangelical believers can find themselves ashamed of the gospel. They become ashamed of the gospel when they take greater pride in things opposed to the gospel. In fact, we can find ourselves all too often ashamed of this gospel by what we say or don't say, what we do or don't do, or by what we are afraid of. We could say:

I am ashamed of the gospel when I am afraid to tell it.
I am ashamed of the gospel when I'm too intimidated to uphold it.
I am ashamed of the gospel when I'm too lazy to teach it.
I am ashamed of the gospel when I'm too selfish to live a life worthy of it.
I am ashamed of the gospel when I make other things the center of fellowship.
I am ashamed of the gospel when I affirm any political, economic, or social position that denies what the Lord Jesus taught about the poor, the orphan, the sick, the elderly, or the homeless.
I am ashamed of the gospel when I make excuses for the unchristian behavior of my political heroes.
I am ashamed of the gospel when I spend more money on chocolate than charity.
I am ashamed of the gospel when my social life becomes more important than my church life.
I am ashamed of the gospel when I spend more time combing my hair than active in prayer.

If, like Paul, we are not ashamed of the gospel (Rom 1:16), that implies maintaining a robust evangelical faith centered on the cross and living as if the only opinion that counts is what the Lord Jesus thinks, for it is before him that we will give account of ourselves (see 2:16; 14:10).

CHAPTER 3

# Romans 1:18–32

## LISTEN to the Story

[18]The wrath of God is being revealed from heaven against all the godlessness and wickedness of people, who suppress the truth by their wickedness, [19]since what may be known about God is plain to them, because God has made it plain to them. [20]For since the creation of the world God's invisible qualities—his eternal power and divine nature—have been clearly seen, being understood from what has been made, so that people are without excuse.

[21]For although they knew God, they neither glorified him as God nor gave thanks to him, but their thinking became futile and their foolish hearts were darkened. [22]Although they claimed to be wise, they became fools [23]and exchanged the glory of the immortal God for images made to look like a mortal human being and birds and animals and reptiles.

[24]Therefore God gave them over in the sinful desires of their hearts to sexual impurity for the degrading of their bodies with one another. [25]They exchanged the truth about God for a lie, and worshiped and served created things rather than the Creator—who is forever praised. Amen.

[26]Because of this, God gave them over to shameful lusts. Even their women exchanged natural sexual relations for unnatural ones. [27]In the same way the men also abandoned natural relations with women and were inflamed with lust for one another. Men committed shameful acts with other men, and received in themselves the due penalty for their error.

[28]Furthermore, just as they did not think it worthwhile to retain the knowledge of God, so God gave them over to a depraved mind, so that they do what ought not to be done. [29]They have become filled with every kind of wickedness, evil, greed and depravity. They are full of envy, murder, strife, deceit and malice. They are gossips, [30]slanderers, God-haters, insolent, arrogant and boastful; they invent ways of doing evil; they disobey their parents; [31]they have no understanding, no fidelity, no love, no mercy. [32]Although they know God's righteous decree that those who do such things deserve death, they not only continue to do these very things but also approve of those who practice them.

*Listening to the texts in the story*: Genesis 1–3; 6–10; Psalms 19; 98; 106; Exodus 20:4–5; Leviticus 18:22; Wisdom of Solomon 13–15.

What Paul says now must be placed against the backdrop of a wider story of creation and fall. Paul knows that the world has gone horribly wrong. The intrusion of evil into the world has meant that alienation and hostility exist between God and humanity. Furthermore, as a direct result of the entrance of evil, humans themselves perpetrate the most inhumane acts toward each other. These verses thus echo the scriptural story of Adam and Eve as the impact of their "fall" is now experienced on the entire human race—a story Paul will take up again in 5:12–21. In addition, the reference to exchanging the "truth about God for a lie" in Romans 1:25 is definitely allusive to how our primeval parents were seduced by the lie of the deceiver. Romans 1:18–25 shows how pagan peoples rehearse Adam's sin in their own rebellion against God and so extend their exile from God's presence.[1] Paul is showing what the story of humanity's descent into wickedness laid out in Genesis 1–11 looks like when manifested in downtown Rome.

Paul contends that (1) human wickedness is sourced in a denial of natural knowledge of God (vv. 18–23), (2) resulting in a corruption that has infiltrated even into human sexuality (vv. 24–27), and (3) he catalogues the moral deviancy of humanity without God (vv. 28–32). Sketched out futher, Paul documents how people, when deprived of knowledge of God, enter into a depraved state that combines idolatry, immorality, impurity, and inhumanity. He sees the full plight of people in their most wretched state, where they are deliberately ignorant, darkened in reason, sexually debased, consumed with love for evil, and worthy of condemnation. Tragically, the once glorious children of Adam and Eve have become little more than brutal beasts that seek to shake off the last bridles that hold any form of constraint upon pursuing their pleasures and cultivating their carnality. God has only one response to such a disobedient and destructive creature: wrath!

### The Wrath of God and Knowledge of God (1:18)

Paul moves the discussion on with the words, "The wrath of God is being revealed from heaven against all the godlessness and wickedness of people, who suppress the truth by their wickedness" (v. 18). But how does this relate to what has gone before? How does the *revelation* of God's righteousness

1. On the role of Adam (and Eve) in Romans 1, several scholars think that 1:18–32 is at least allusive of Genesis 2–3. See Morna D. Hooker, "Adam in Romans 1," *NTS* 6 (1959–60): 297–306; idem, "A Further Note on Romans 1," *NTS* 13 (1966–67): 181–83; A. J. M. Wedderburn, "Adam in Paul's Letter to the Romans," in *Studia Biblica* 3 (ed. E.A. Livingstone; JSNTSup 3; Sheffield: JSOT Press, 1980), 413–30; Schreiner, *Romans*, 81; Grieb, *Story of Romans*, 19.

(v. 17) relate to the *revelation* of God's wrath (v. 18)?[2] The NIV obscures the connection with the preceding verses by omitting the coordinating conjunction *gar* ("for"). Better is "*For* the wrath of God is being revealed from heaven" (see ESV, NRSV, and NET). Worse is the NLT, which assumes a contrast between v. 17 and v. 18 with "But God shows his anger from heaven." It looks to me as if the proximity and parallel between the revelation of righteousness in the gospel and the revelation of wrath from heaven indicate that God's gospel determines the purpose of God's wrath. The gospel unveils the "secrets of the human heart," which Christ will judge on the appointed day (see Rom 2:16; 14:10; 1 Cor 14:25). The gospel spells out human culpability to such a shocking extent that divine justice seems not only inevitable but even morally necessary. It is under the shadow of divine wrath that the good news of God's grace, mercy, and salvation appears all the more unlikely, entirely unmerited, and even scandalous.[3]

What is more, a further connection between v. 17 and v. 18 is that the revelation of God's wrath is itself a manifestation of God's righteousness. Let us remember that the biblical background for God's righteousness refers to God's saving justice for Israel. Yet God would save Israel by entering into contention against her enemies, such as the Canaanites, the Assyrians, or the Babylonians. God's deliverance of Israel was principally through his retributive judgment of Israel's enemies, establishing justice over the earth; this was his "righteousness" (e.g., Isa 11:3–5; Pss 89:5–18; 98:1–9). Yet the Israelites also knew that God could enter into contention against them, and they would ask God to pardon them for no other reason than his covenant faithfulness toward them; this too was his "righteousness" (e.g., Pss 51:14; 143:1–3; Dan 9:2–19). God's saving righteousness and his punitive wrath are then different aspects of the one event.

Thus, God's righteousness is a duality containing both a punitive verdict and a pardoning vindication, judgment and justification, retribution and redemption. The upshot is that the shift from v. 17 to v. 18 is a shift from God's saving justice to God's retributive justice. As such, v. 18 is not introducing a new topic.[4] I would paraphrase the verse as, "In speaking of God's saving justice, we cannot forget his punitive justice against evil either. For the righteous rage of God is even now being revealed from heaven against all who act without recourse to God and who descend into utterly wicked ways."

---

2. Both verses use the verb *apokalyptō*, meaning "to cause something to be fully known" (BDAG 112).

3. Jewett, *Romans*, 150–51.

4. Mark Seifrid, *Christ, our Righteousness: Paul's Theology of Justification* (NSBT 9; Downers Grove, IL: InterVarsity, 2000), 35–47.

What Paul says about God's wrath here stands in continuity with the Old Testament's depiction of God's anger burning against those engaging in evil, whether kings, nations, or even Israel. In Paul's letters, God's wrath is normally something reserved for the judgment day (see Rom 2:5, 8; 4:15; 5:9; 9:22; 12:19), but here it is already in the process of "being revealed from heaven." Heaven is obviously the seat of God's throne, and Paul has in mind God's ongoing process of retribution against human evils.[5] Paul writes here in a prophetic role by stating God's intention to prosecute his lawsuit against humanity on account of their idolatry and wickedness. The object of God's ongoing wrath is identified as "all the godlessness and wickedness of people, who suppress the truth by their wickedness." The point is that God's anger burns against people who commit vertical sins against God (i.e., godlessness) and horizontal sins against their fellow humans (i.e., wickedness). This behavior derives from a suppression of the truth about God—a keeping down the truth that God is there and that he will treat each according to their deeds. Evidently God's existence and justice are so traumatic for people who treasure their personal evils that they are left with only one option to cope with such a predicament: denial.

## Knowledge of God Rejected (1:19–23)

The reason why people suppress the truth about God is given in v. 19 as "since what may be known about God is plain to them, because God has made it plain to them." People are universally confronted with God, and that is what they need to suppress. What this knowledge of God is and how it is apparently plain to people Paul does not precisely say, but theologians have sometimes spoken of a twofold natural knowledge of God.[6] First, an innate knowledge of God is hardwired into human existence—a sense of the divine, or an inherent awareness of God's being that connects immediately with human existence. Second, a derivative knowledge of God can be inferred from the immensity, order, and beauty of creation itself. Paul arguably refers to a knowledge of God of this order that is manifested, literally, "in them" (*en autois*) in vv. 19–20. As Schreiner comments, "God has stitched into the fabric of the human mind his existence and power, so that they are instinctively recognized when one views the created world."[7]

---

5. In 3:5, wrath is something that can be brought against Paul's Jewish interlocutor in the present time. Also, in 13:4, human governments are "agents of wrath" in their execution of justice and so represent one medium for divine wrath in the present time.

6. On natural revelation and natural theology, see further Bird, *Evangelical Theology*, 173–93.

7. Schreiner, *Romans*, 86.

Experiencing the wonder of the world around us imparts to us an awareness of a Creator who is distinct from creation and who is also sovereign over its operation. Hence Paul's words: "For since the creation of the world God's invisible qualities—his eternal power and divine nature—have been clearly seen, being understood from what has been made" (v. 20). The visible things of the world point to an invisible Creator who possesses "eternal power" (*aidios dynamis*) and a "divine nature" (*theiotēs*). Human beings have been wired up to know him and to believe in him so that when they observe nature, the theater of God's glory, they instinctively know something of God. Indeed, they may even feel, as Calvin did, ravished by God's beauty.[8]

The tragedy is that rather than appropriate this knowledge of God as their Creator with worship, human beings instead reason their way away from God. Paul identifies the human response to God's revelation of himself in nature as issuing in a refusal to either glorify him or thank him. This results in people becoming futile and foolish in their thinking, darkened in their hearts, and exchanging the glory of God for inglorious idols that resemble birds, animals, and reptiles (Rom 1:21–23). This is what it means in practice to suppress the truth about God, which Paul mentioned in 1:18. Sin turns people's minds away from God and even against God.

This is called the noetic effect of sin. Sin does not simply mess with humanity's moral compass. Sin infects the mind to such a degree that human reasoning assumes a default position that is hostile to God. People prefer to be stupefied by their sin rather than immerse themselves in God's majesty. People savor the dementia of evil over the joy of worshiping their Creator. Origen said that "those who seemed to exalt themselves as living in the light of wisdom were cast down into the deepest darkness of stupidity."[9] At the root of the problem is the idea of exchange. Humanity has "exchanged" the glory of the immortal God for inglorious things made in the image of creatures (see Deut 4:16–17). Just as Adam and Eve believed the serpent rather than God, so too has humanity "exchanged" the truth of God for a lie. Humanity has fallen into a downward spiral that progresses from disobedience, to denial, to idolatry, to degrading passions, and to a depraved mind. In this wretched state humanity has become doxologically challenged.[10]

8. See the exploration of this theme in Belden C. Lane, *Ravished by Beauty: The Surprising Legacy of Reformed Spirituality* (Oxford: Oxford University Press, 2011).

9. Cited in J. Patout Burns, ed. and trans., *Romans: Interpreted by Early Christian Commentators* (The Church's Bible; ed. R. L. Wilken; Grand Rapids: Eerdmans, 2012), 27.

10. Cf. Israel's own "exchange" in the golden calf incident in Exodus 32; in Psalm 106:20 "they exchanged their glorious God for an image of a bull, which eats grass," and in Jeremiah 2:11, "my people have exchanged their glorious God for worthless idols."

God does not shrug his shoulders at human rebellion; instead, Paul says, "Therefore God gave them over in the sinful desires of their hearts to sexual impurity for the degrading of their bodies with one another. They exchanged the truth about God for a lie, and worshiped and served created things rather than the Creator—who is forever praised. Amen" (vv. 24–25). In sequence, idolatry leads to immorality since depriving God of his glory yields people up to depraved desires. According to Wisdom of Solomon 14:27, "For the worship of idols not to be named is the source and cause and end of every evil." Or as Moo points out, the whole panopoly of people's sins that plagues humanity has its roots in the soil of idolatry.[11]

## Descent into Depravity (1:24–25)

The "therefore" in v. 24 announces the first divine response to human wickedness. God gives people over to the very desires that serve to alienate them from him. That God "gives them over" (*paredōken*) most probably means that God takes away his constriction of their depravity, and humanity is thus freed to indulge in its perverse desires. According to Ambrosiaster, "to *hand over* means to permit, not to encourage or to force."[12] The results of the unchecked gratification of sinful desires are a polluting and shaming of their own bodies.

Although there is no explicit wording to the effect that the "impurity" and "degrading" is sexual as the NIV states, sexual conduct is probably implied given the following context in vv. 26–27. On top of that, Wisdom of Solomon connects sexual immorality with idolatry; hence "the idea of making idols was the beginning of fornication, and the invention of them was the corruption of life" (Wis 14:12). Noticeably, the effects of sin are not spelled out in terms of guilt and debt, but with reference to impurity and dishonor, something familiar to the Jewish and Greco-Roman worldview. The underlying premise for Paul's remarks is that humans bear God's image, and the web of idolatry and immorality constitutes a sickening contamination of that image and an offensive misuse of something precious to God. Human sin could be likened to taking a prestigious Oscar statue, vomiting your bacteria-filled stomach over it, and then using it to clean your toilet. Sin is the defilement and dishonoring of little icons of God.

11. Moo, *Romans*, 110.

12. Bray, *Ambrosiaster*, 12. Others like Moo (*Romans*, 111) prefer to see God taking a more active role: "God does not simply let the boat go—he gives it a push downstream. Like a judge who hands over a prisoner to the punishment his crime has earned, God hands over the sinner to the terrible cycle of ever-increasing sin." The problem is that a "handing over" implies a moment of taking "hands off" the subject and leaving him or her susceptible to a power that God himself is not directly controlling, i.e., sin. Hence the idea of a withdrawal of divine restraint seems better.

In addition, humans "exchanged the truth about God for a lie, and worshiped and served created things rather than the Creator" (v. 25). Human desires are turned away from God so that the truth about God, his existence, and his attributes is exchanged for servitude to dead, inanimate objects. Humanity, with its debased desires, would rather worship things they have created themselves rather than pay homage to their Creator. Paul's critique here of pagan religion and pagan behavior is not new. In Isaiah 40, 44, Wisdom of Solomon 13–15, and throughout Philo we find similar denunciations of the folly of idolatry by Jewish authors. Speaking of these heretical acts makes Paul shudder, and he interjects a short doxology to the "God who is forever praised" as a deliberate counterpoint to human idolatry (v. 25). Paul praises the God whom pagans ignore or blaspheme. Evidently a key indicator for the spiritual and moral state of men and women can be summed up with the question: Whom do you worship?

### Bondage in Sexual Perversity (1:26–28)

Paul next provides a concrete example of the contamination and degradation of the body caused by wicked desires with particular reference to homosexual practices. Paul does not focus on sexual sins because he has some kind of fixation with sex, but because sexual immorality is a type of warning light that signals the moral chaos that follows it.[13] When Paul says in v. 26, "Because of this," the antecedent to "this" is probably God's wrath against human wickedness back in v. 18. Paul restates the point he just made that God, after observing the godlessness and impropriety of people, gave the people "over to shameful lusts." Paul now gives a precise example of these lusts with mention of homoerotic acts (vv. 26–27): "Even their women exchanged natural sexual relations for unnatural ones. In the same way the men also abandoned natural relations with women and were inflamed with lust for one another. Men committed shameful acts with other men, and received in themselves the due penalty for their error." The passage is understandably controversial, especially in light of marriage equality debates and issues pertaining to the ordination of openly gay men and women in some mainline denominations.[14] What the text says and what one should do with it are huge matters for exegetical investigation and pastoral application.

In the Greco-Roman world, generally speaking, same-sex relationships between women were routinely condemned, while homosexual acts between

---

13. Grieb, *The Story of Romans*, 29.

14. What follows is heavily indebted to Michael F. Bird and Sarah Harris, "Paul's Jewish Sexuality in Romans 1:26–27," in *Sexegesis: An Evangelical Response to Five Uneasy Pieces* (ed. Gordon D. Preece and Michael F. Bird; Sydney: Anglican Press Australia, 2012), 87–104.

men were regarded as normal under certain conditions. Ancient Greek culture had a long tradition of pederasty between older males and younger boys. In Rome, homoerotic relationships were largely about power since one sexually penetratred a social inferior, such as a freedman, a slave, or a prostitute. It was thought shameful for a citizen to allow himself to be the penetrated partner in a sexual act with a social equal as it meant adopting a position of servility and femininity. In ancient literature one can find philosophical advocates for the superiority of same-sex relationships over heterosexual relationships. Still, other Greek and Roman authors regarded homosexual acts with disdain. Juvenal mocked the drunken debauchery of women that often led to lesbian sexual acts.[15] The Socratic tradition as expressed through Plato and Xenophon condemned homosexual practices.[16]

The Old Testament resoundingly prohibits homosexual practices (Lev 18:22; 20:13), and the rejection is continued in postbiblical Jewish literature as well.[17] In keeping with Jewish tradition, Paul too censures homosexual acts in other letters (1 Cor 6:9; 1 Tim 1:10).[18] Looking at Romans 1:24–28, Paul appears to be describing Roman and Greek males who lived promiscuous lives with procreative sex at home and recreative sex with others, including prostitutes and slaves, of both genders. Paul expresses the customary Jewish revulsion at the practice as a departure from God's gift of human sexuality.

It is useful to think about Paul's remarks about homosexuality here in light of the diverse social location of his audience. First, if many of the Gentile Christians in Rome were slaves, they were open to frequent sexual abuse and exploitation by their male masters. Not only girls and women, but even young boys were captured, imported, sold, and then prostituted into sexual slavery. Christian slaves may have known all too well the degrading shame and physical violation of sexual subjection. A way that masters often teased their male slaves was by reminding them of what they could demand of them, i.e., to get down on all fours.[19] Paul's remarks represent an introduction to the plight of

15. Juvenal, *Satire* 6.306–13.

16. Plato, *Symp.* 217–19; Xenophon, *Mem.* 2.1.32.

17. Cf., e.g., Philo, *Abraham* 135–36; *Spec. Laws* 2.50; *T. Levi* 14.6; 17.11; *T. Naph.* 4.1; *2 En.* 10.4; *Sib. Or.* 3.185–87, 594–600, 763; 5.386–433; Josephus, *Against Apion* 2.25, 199.

18. Cf. the survey of literary ancient views about homosexuality and homoeroticism in Thomas K. Hubbard, *Homosexuality in Greece and Rome: A Sourcebook of Basic Documents* (Berkley, CA: University of California Press, 2003); Martti Nissinen, *Homoeroticism in the Biblical World: A Historical Perspective* (trans. K. Stjerna; Minneapolis: Fortress, 1998), 57–122. Recommended reading also includes William R. G. Loader, *Making Sense of Sex: Attitudes towards Sexuality in Early Jewish and Christian Literature* (Grand Rapids: Eerdmans, 2013); and Preston M. Sprinkle, "Romans 1 and Homosexuality: A Critical Review of James Brownson's *Bible, Gender, Sexuality*," *BBR* 24.4 (2014): 515–28.

19. Jewett, *Romans*, 180–81.

present and former slaves who resented the sexual exploitation of themselves and their children in a culture typified by an aggressive bisexuality.[20] Second, for those Christians who were slave owners and made slaves gratify their sexual lusts, who might have previously participated in *symposia* (i.e., drinking parties) with homoerotic pleasures, who used male prostitutes, or who engaged in homosexual relationships, they could see their former way of life as an experience of divine wrath, a wrath that they have now escaped by coming under the lordship of Jesus Christ.

Central to Paul's critique of homosexuality is its unnaturalness as indicated by his use of the word *physikos* for "nature/natural." Paul's phrase *para physin* is best translated as "contrary to nature" since the natural use of sex organs is exchanged for something else.[21] He says that women exchanged "the natural use [of men] for what is contrary to nature [i.e., lesbianism]," and that men left the "natural use of women [i.e., in the sexual act]" and instead became "inflamed with lust for one another." As Robert Gagnon points out, Paul, minimally, is referring to the anatomical and procreative complementarity of men and women as their sexual organs are designed for each other, something not true of gay sex.[22]

If we take Romans 1:26–28 together with other Pauline texts about the human body (e.g., 1 Cor 7:1–40; 11:1–16), it is clear that sexuality is intrinsic to human bodily existence and that heterosexuality in particular was part of the divinely created order for humanity. Departures from the norm of God's creation represent defiance against the Creator and are indicative of a state of lostness. To suppress the truth about the one God who made the heavens and the earth invariably leads to a rejection of God's design for sex as a means of partnership and procreation between men and women. As N. T. Wright comments: "homosexual behaviour is a distortion of the creator's design and ... such practices are evidence, not of the intention of any specific

---

20. Jewett, *Romans*, 181.

21. Philo and Josephus both refer to homosexual relations as "contrary to nature" (*para physin*) in several places (Josephus, *Apion* 2.273; Philo, *Spec. Laws* 3.38; *Abraham* 133–36). Josephus (*Against Apion* 2.199) even states that the marriage of a man and a woman is "according to nature" (*kata physin*) whereas a "mixing" (*mixis*) of male and male is abhorred by the law and deserving of death. The author of *T. Naph* 3.3–4 considers homosexuality a departure "from the order of nature." Ovid (*Metam.* 9.758) refers to a girl who loved another girl, yet she knew that "nature does not will it." Plato (*Laws* 1.2 [636 BC]) regarded sexual relations between same-sex couples as "contrary to nature." Chrysostom wrote: "For which is more pleasurable pray, cohabiting with women or with males? With women or with mules? Yet still we shall find many that pass over women, and cohabit with creatures void of reason, and abuse the bodies of males. Yet natural pleasures are greater than unnatural ones" (*Hom. Rom.* 9).

22. Robert A. J. Gagnon, *The Bible and Homosexual Practice: Texts and Hermeneutics* (Nashville: Abingdon, 2001), 254.

individual to indulge in such practice for its own sake, but of the tendency within an entire society for humanness to fracture when gods other than the true one are being worshipped."[23]

It is important to note that Paul is not dealing exclusively with pederasty, even though it formed a large part of homosexual practice in the ancient Mediterranean world.[24] Greek society, even more so than Roman society, accepted a variegated pattern of sexual behavior ranging from the use of male and female slaves as sexual "partners," through to pederasty, the sexual exploitation of young boys, but it must be remembered that life-long consensual homosexual relationships were not unknown and even same-sex marriages took place. According to Sprinkle, "there was a broad spectrum of sexual relationships available to Paul. We cannot assume that Paul only had nonconsensual and unhealthy relations in view and therefore condemned (only) *these* types of relations. Paul most probably was aware of at least some consensual, even marital, unions among both men and women of the same gender."[25]

Paul's specification of lesbianism alongside male homosexuality in 1:26–27 makes explicit that he is addressing same-sex practice in general and not only pederasty or any variant form.[26] Thus Paul makes a strongly egalitarian claim that both male and female same-sex relationships are judged equally even though Greco-Roman society deemed the lesbian relationship as *para physin* while the male homosexual relationship had some social acceptance. For Paul, men and women were equally at risk of idolatry and falling deeper into the path of dehumanization.

### Expressions of Immorality (1:28–32)

These verses contain a long list of vices that people in their depraved state commit, and Paul makes specific mention of God's righteous judgment against those who do such things. Paul rehearses what he has already said by adding: "Furthermore, just as they did not think it worthwhile to retain the knowledge of God, so God gave them over to a depraved mind, so that they do what ought not to be done" (v. 28). God has given people over to the desires of their hearts (v. 24), to their dishonorable passions (v. 26), and to a depraved mind (v. 28). God is allowing people to submerge themselves further into the depth of subhumanity because it is tragically what they want. The result is patterns of behavior that "ought not to be done."

23. Wright, "Romans," 10:434.
24. Keener, *Romans*, 37.
25. Sprinkle, "Romans 1," 527.
26. This is widely agreed, see Jewett, *Romans*, 177; Keener, *Romans*, 39.

The morass of immoral behaviors spelled out in vv. 29–31 is analogous to the vice lists found in other Greco-Roman, Jewish, and Christian writings.[27] Lest we think Paul is overly enthusiastic in his cataloguing of immoral behaviors, I would point out that Philo lists 147 items in one of his vice lists.[28] We might paraphrase Paul's list here as:

> And now they are like jugs of sewage filled to the brim with rank injustice, moral rot, insatiable greed, engrossed with envy, plotting murder, engaged in endless wrangling, given to open treachery, a maelstrom of malevolence, loving violence, full of false accusations, haters of anything or anyone to do with religion, resolutely insolent, utterly arrogant, completely full of themselves, architects of evil, parents of perdition. They have become a horde of senseless, untrustworthy, unfeeling, and unmerciful subhuman creatures who have divested themselves of a true humanity.

The climax of the vice list is v. 31, with the claim that people engrossed in wickedness have "no understanding, no fidelity, no love, no mercy."[29] That is illustrative of the fact that sin is fundamentally a negation of humanity; it takes away something of our ability to know, trust, love, and empathize with others. Sin at its worst erodes what is best about our humanity.

Although humans might feign ignorance of God becaue of their suppression of knowledge about him, deep down Paul says "although they know God's righteous decree that those who do such things deserve death, they not only continue to do these very things but also approve of those who practice them" (v. 32). The corruption of the human heart becomes such that it denies the fittingness of God's judgment against wickedness; but not only that, it arrogates itself to approving of what God abhors. The inversion of values is the ultimate evidence that humanity has gone rotten.

To be blunt, reading Romans 1:18–32 is like walking down the crack alley of the human soul. Paul documents the irreligious and inhumane depths that humanity descends into when alienated from the Creator God. Paul fittingly expounds the story of a world gone horribly wrong on account of human rebellion against God, and he describes what that story looks like in downtown Rome. Rufus and his house church would resonate with Paul's words as they recognized his description of moral evils and prevalent idolatry as a state that surrounded them constantly in their daily lives. According to Paul, when Adam and Eve were expelled from the garden of Eden, there was

---

27. Cf. C. G. Kruse, "Virtues and Vices," in *DPL* 962–93.

28. Philo, *Sacrifices*, 32.

29. The verse is rhetorically powerful in Greek with a dense packing together of similar sounding words (*asynetous*, *asynthetous*, *astorgous*, and *aneleçēmonas*) to create assonance.

a gradual process of corruption that infected the entire span of human existence. Now in Romans 1:18–32, we meet the depths of the Adamic condition in the immorality and idolatry of pagan peoples. Paul's declaration of the revelation of God's righteousness in the gospel surfaces as God's intention to rectify humanity, but it also unveils the vile condition of humanity and the fittingness of divine judgment against them. In sum, we see that "God insists on his rightful claim to be God against the world which denies him."[30]

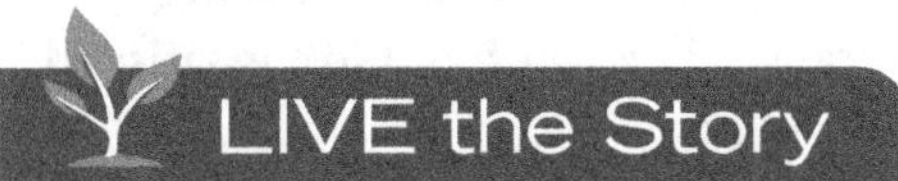

## LIVE the Story

Romans 1:18–32 holds many hot-potato topics—things like God and nature, idolatry and false religion, or the essence of sin. But two topics that I think stand out for reflection are God's wrath and Paul's teaching about homosexuality.

### The Good News of God's Wrath

The "wrath of God" is not a favorite topic of discourse, and many people much prefer instead to mediate on the love of God.[31] Yet "wrath" at this point in Romans is not meant in the sense of some kind of disproportionate and implacable fit of blind rage that God suddenly spins into because he sees people on earth doing naughty things and because people are not paying him enough attention. No, God's wrath is the response of his holiness toward moral evil. It is God's righteous indignation, his rage even, against those who seek to undermine his reign, who gratify the most debasing of desires, or who seek to abuse the most vulnerable of persons. When I lived in Scotland, I heard a shocking news story about a couple who violently beat their four-year-old daughter to death, put her body in a suitcase, and threw her into the River Ness. When I heard the story, I had only one emotion—rage—and an appropriate emotion it was considering the heinous deed. In a world of evil, God's wrath is good news, for it means he stands against wickedness!

It is unfortunate that some churches and traditions tend to deny or downplay the significance of God's wrath. The trend began early when the second-century heretic Marcion omitted the genitive "of God" in the "wrath of God" from v. 18 in his edition of Paul's letters in order to remove God from the notion of wrath. The late C. H. Dodd found the notion of God's wrath so unpalatable that he described God's wrath not as a willful action, but simply

30. Seifrid, *Christ, our Righteousness*, 44.

31. On the relationship between God's love and God's wrath, see D. A. Carson, "God's Love and God's Wrath," *BSac* 156 (1999): 387–98; idem, *The Difficult Doctrine of the Love of God* (Wheaton, IL: Crossway, 2000).

as "some process or effect in the realm of objective facts," a process that God is somewhat removed from.[32] Also, Rob Bell's recent book *Love Wins* wrestles with the question: If Jesus saves us from God's wrath, how could that God ever be good, or how could that message ever be good news? Bell's answer is that ultimately God's love and God's wrath are irreconcilable and love must win over wrath if God is to be a gracious God. A friend of mine once attended a denominational meeting where the song "In Christ Alone" was played, and he noticed how a significant number of clergy present could not bring themselves to utter the line in the song that says, "The wrath of God is satisfied." You get the point: God's wrath is not popular!

Now nobody likes the idea of an angry God. People much prefer a gentler and more sensitive deity, perhaps a friendly and benign old man who lives in the heavens, something along the lines of an Anglican version of Santa Claus. But, in the face of human evil, divine love without divine wrath yields up a "God" lacking a moral spine and incapable of dishing out justice to each as they deserve. Such a morally vacuous "God" suits the proclivity of people uncomfortable with the notion that any recompense remains for their deeds and so they can dispense with the necessity of repentance and satisfy themselves with a "God" who, while disliking sin, has not the stomach to hold anyone accountable for their deeds. The result is that we are given a picture of God that all too candidly resembles the one that H. Richard Niebuhr warned us about: a God without wrath who takes men and women without sin to a kingdom without judgment thanks to the ministrations of a Christ without a cross.[33]

In response, we can assert the biblical testimony that God burns with rage against evil; not just the evil that dictators and pedophiles commit, but evil that languishes inside each and every one of us. The human heart is, as Calvin said, a factory of idols. The human heart is, as Ezekiel saw, wicked to its core.

Now is not the time to engage in a treatise on total depravity, but if you ever want to see the evil in the human heart, just permit people the opportunity of acting anonymously. When people think no one is watching or they cannot be caught, you will see what malice people are really capable of and what sinister desires they harbor. Each of us in our own way shakes our little fist against heaven and cries out in arrogance, "I will do it my way." While we are not as evil as we can be — the goodness of the divine image still resonates within us — even so, evil is a disease that invades our soul or a beast raging inside us that we will not tame. That is why, as Paul says in Ephesians, we were once deserving of God's wrath (Eph 2:5). It is God's wrath against our evil,

32. Dodd, *Romans*, 22.

33. H. Richard Niebuhr, *The Kingdom of God in America* (New York: Harper & Row, 1937), 193.

God's contention against our self-worship, God's lawsuit against our lawlessness, that deserves judgment. Unless we accept the premise of God's anger against evil, our evil no less, the gospel loses its gravity. As Katherine Grieb writes: "An evangelist who preaches only God's love without insisting also upon God's righteousness against wickedness and evil does not really preach good news."[34]

Of course, it is equally possible to misuse the notion of divine wrath and end up with an equally distorted image of God as some type of "rage-aholic." Let us remember that wrath is not a permanent part of God's nature; rather, it is something provoked or aroused by human misconduct, not intrinsic to his person. God's justice is indeed a permanent fixture of his character, and that justice can be expressed as divine wrath when circumstances render it appropriate. Yet God is not in a perpetual state of anger, as if "wrath" was his normal state of mind. As Stephen Travis puts it: "Wrath is not a permanent attribute of God. For whereas love and holiness are part of his essential nature, wrath is contingent upon human sin: if there were no sin, there would be no wrath."[35] If love without wrath yields a morally vacuous God, to preach wrath without mercy is to turn God into a masochistic monster.

Jonathan Edwards's sermon "Sinners in the Hands of an Angry God" was a classic piece of Puritan preaching crafted to bring people to wallow in misery for their sins and to cling to God in his mercy and love. Edwards set forth a vivid image of God's wrath against sin at one point saying, "God holds you over the pit of hell, much as one holds a spider, or some loathsome insect over the fire, abhors you, and is dreadfully provoked: his wrath towards you burns like a fire; he looks upon you as worthy of nothing else, but to be cast into the fire." Yet note where Edwards takes his sermon: "And now you have an extraordinary opportunity, a day wherein Christ has thrown the door of his mercy wide open, and stands in calling and crying with a loud voice to poor sinners, a day wherein many are flocking to him, and pressing into the kingdom of God."

To preach on wrath without mercy will result either in a hatred for God or in a desperate yet ultimately futile attempt to please him with moral striving and religiosity. To preach on wrath in isolation from a well-rounded biblical theology will reduce salvation to buying fire insurance rather than seeing salvation as participating in the very life of God held forth in Christ. When one speaks of divine wrath, it should not be done with an angry voice and with fists pounding a pulpit, but with eyes welling with tears and hands wide open, as if one were begging a suicidal son or daughter to come down from a ledge,

---

34. Grieb, *Story of Romans*, 26.

35. Stephen H. Travis, "Wrath of God (NT)," *ABD* 6:997.

recalling as well that God does not delight in the destruction of the wicked but desires all people to be saved. The Lord Jesus does not seek to persuade a wrathful Father to be merciful. For if God was not merciful, he would not have sent his only Son to be a propitiation for our sins. The good news is that God satisfies his own justice and placates his own wrath by expunging our sin through drawing its deadly consequences away from us and taking us into the life of the triune God.

Finally, the message of divine wrath is not just something that explains to lost men and women why Jesus is Savior and what deeds they need to repent of. God's wrath continues to have an exhortatory function in the church. God's wrath operates in the spheres of creation and covenant as it presumes God's intent to put the world to rights and to hold his covenant partners to account. We understand the nature of God, sin, and salvation only when we realize that "all of us also lived among them at one time, gratifying the cravings of our flesh and following its desires and thoughts. Like the rest, we were by nature deserving of wrath" (Eph 2:3). Only then can we appreciate the big "but" that changes the course of cosmic history: "*But* because of his great love for us, God, who is rich in mercy, made us alive with Christ even when we were dead in transgressions — it is by grace you have been saved" (Eph 2:4–5).

Karl Barth told a story about a man who got lost on his way home one night in a blinding snowstorm. On finding his way, he was horrified when he realized that he had walked across a lake covered only by a very thin sheet of ice.[36] In the same way, reflecting on the wrath of God reminds us of the perilous disaster we once faced and how grateful we must be to our gracious God for delivering us by handing over his Son for our transgressions and raising him for our justification (Rom 4:25).

### God Is Not a Homophobe

"God hates me," Roger said. "Whenever the preacher spoke from Leviticus or Romans, that is what I was told. God hates the gays the same way that he hated Sodom and Gomorrah. And since I knew I was gay, I believed that God hated me."

Roger paused for a moment, removed his baseball cap, and rubbed his face. "I spent so many nights asking, begging, and crying for God to change me, but he never did. And that is when I realized, either he is not there, or else he doesn't care."

---

36. Karl Barth, "Saved by Grace," *Deliverance to the Captives* (trans. M. Wieser; New York: Harper & Row, 1978), 35–42, cited by Grieb, *Story of Romans*, 26–27.

Roger's story is one I've heard several times. Many men and women in the church who have same-sex desire can feel like God hates them simply for no other reason that they feel attracted to members of the same sex. It does not help when Christian people and Christian preachers talk as if God hates all sin, but he has some kind of special anger reserved for gays and lesbians.

Let me add that I've witnessed firsthand the threat of violence that homosexual men and women often face. Many years ago when I was in the army, after a week of maneuvers out in the field, I went on a boys' night on the town with my unit. Late into the night we walked across a park and passed by two gay men who were holding hands on their quiet stroll. All of a sudden one of the highest ranking soldiers in our group started yelling out all sorts of profanities against the gay couple and had to be physically restrained from attacking them. The soldier in question was not religious, just drunk and prejudiced. The gay couple scurried away in fear. The memory of that event has stayed with me and made me more sensitive to the plight of gay men and women.

So how should we teach texts like Romans 1:26–27, given that many gay folks feel unloved by God and rejected by the church, and live with the threat of violence in our streets? Some respond by saying, "Well, Paul is only talking about pederasty, Paul only censures heterosexuals who perform homosexual acts out of power or excessive lust, Paul is unaware of life-long gay relationships, or else Paul does not have the final word on what counts as 'natural.' "[37] I am not convinced by these arguments since I think Paul, as someone who lived in the Greco-Roman world, knew about the various expressions of human sexual behavior and also knew what the Jewish Scriptures taught about such things. In Romans 1:26–27, Paul demonstrates how human idolatry has resulted in a perversion of human sexuality. He documents instances where human sexuality has gone against what God originally intended.

However, as Ernst Käsemann correctly observed, for Paul sexual perversion is "the result of God's wrath, not the reason for it."[38] God does not have a special loathing for gays and lesbians. When Paul includes homosexual behavior in his vice lists, he does not make it the pinnacle of sinful behavior; rather, it is just another example of human conduct affronting to God (see 1 Cor 6:9–11). The Bible censures homosexual behavior, but it does not condemn people for having what we moderns would call a homosexual orientation. Let us remember that "all have sinned and fall short of the glory of God" (Rom 3:23), and everyone needs redeeming mercy and transforming grace that is offered us in the Lord Jesus Christ. The gospel of grace is inclusive; it is open

---

37. See James V. Brownson, *Bible, Gender, Sexuality: Reframing the Church's Debate on Same-Sex Relationships* (Grand Rapids: Eerdmans, 2013), 223–55.

38. Käsemann, *Romans*, 47.

to everyone, men and women, Jew and Greek, black or white, Arab or American, gay or straight, bisexual or transsexual, and people may come as they are. But, and this is important, no one is allowed to stay as they are. God does his transforming work in us to change our values, our character, our conduct, and even our sexuality into conformity to the image of his Son.

It can, is, and will be a struggle for Christian men and women with same-sex attraction to live faithfully with the burden that they carry. Ideally they receive the prayer and support they need from a network of family, friends, mentors, supporters, and their congregation. I would even go so far as to say that struggling with same-sex attraction is not a bar to ministry since we all struggle with sin, even sins of a sexual nature. In fact, the best evangelical preacher I've heard in the UK, Vaughan Roberts, is the rector of a parish church in Cambridge. He confesses to struggle with same-sex attraction yet still has a vibrant and faithful ministry.

I used to lead an ecumenical Bible study on an army barracks. I remember vividly the small group in question: a fiery Lutheran warrant officer, a meek Pentecostal girl from the transportation corps, a liberal Catholic logistics captain, and a softly spoken nominally Anglican lady working for the Department of Defense. When we got to the subject of the then-recent election of Rowan Williams as Archbishop of Canterbury and his views of sexuality, well, the conversation heated up like a furnace. The Lutheran warrant officer earnestly made the point that the Bible condemns homosexuality. The liberal Catholic rebutted that sexuality is genetically determined and cannot be helped, so one should not condemn homosexuals. The nominal Anglican lady said that gay people make such great friends and are great at helping you decorate your house. Meanwhile the meek Pentecostal girl just sat there quietly not saying a thing. The polite conversation quickly became a heated argument with the polemical temperature rising by the second.

Despite my best efforts to moderate the tone and to change the subject, it just got worse. It turned into a yelling match with the Bible-bashing Lutheran trying to shout down the liberal Catholic on the one side and the nominal Anglican lady adding her two-cents every so often. The poor Pentecostal girl sat there very quiet, staring at the floor catatonically, wisely avoiding the melee. Right before I was gonna yell, "Time out, children, time to go home," all of a sudden the Pentecostal girl loudly interjected with the words, "I used to be a lesbian, but Jesus saved me." Right after that there was a silence you could cut with a knife. The Lutheran, the Catholic, the Anglican, and the poor Bible study leader had nothing to say. What do you say to that? How do you follow that up? The Pentecostal girl shared her story about her former life in lesbianism. She was clear that Jesus had saved her from that lifestyle and she was happily engaged to a lovely young man from her church. Let me be clear, I'm not saying that her story will be the story of every homosexual man and woman who professes faith. The reasons why people have same-sex desires are complex and range from biology to biography. Some Christians with same-sex desires struggle with it all of their lives in the same way that heterosexuals can struggle with certain desires. I know that there are many ex-gays, but I also know that there are many ex-ex-gays too.

My point is that while we need to affirm that Romans 1:26–27 places homosexual behavior under the category of sin, we can offer all men and women, with any kind of sexual struggle, the hope laid out in the rest of Romans, namely, that Christ saves us from the penalty of sin, gradually from the power of sin, and one day from the very presence of sin. The relevance of Romans to the "gay issue" is not some kind of cliché message that sinners must "turn or burn" or even "hate the sin but love the sinner." The biblical response embodied by Paul is for all people to "believe in him who raised Jesus our Lord from the dead" (4:24), to confess that "Jesus is Lord" (10:9), to "clothe yourselves with the Lord Jesus Christ, and do not think about how to gratify the desires of the flesh" (13:14), and for the church corporately to "accept one another, then, just as Christ accepted you, in order to bring praise to God" (15:7).

CHAPTER 4

# Romans 2:1 – 29

## LISTEN to the Story

[1]You, therefore, have no excuse, you who pass judgment on someone else, for at whatever point you judge another, you are condemning yourself, because you who pass judgment do the same things. [2]Now we know that God's judgment against those who do such things is based on truth. [3]So when you, a mere human being, pass judgment on them and yet do the same things, do you think you will escape God's judgment? [4]Or do you show contempt for the riches of his kindness, forbearance and patience, not realizing that God's kindness is intended to lead you to repentance?

[5]But because of your stubbornness and your unrepentant heart, you are storing up wrath against yourself for the day of God's wrath, when his righteous judgment will be revealed. [6]God "will repay each person according to what they have done." [7]To those who by persistence in doing good seek glory, honor and immortality, he will give eternal life. [8]But for those who are self-seeking and who reject the truth and follow evil, there will be wrath and anger. [9]There will be trouble and distress for every human being who does evil: first for the Jew, then for the Gentile; [10]but glory, honor and peace for everyone who does good: first for the Jew, then for the Gentile. [11]For God does not show favoritism.

[12]All who sin apart from the law will also perish apart from the law, and all who sin under the law will be judged by the law. [13]For it is not those who hear the law who are righteous in God's sight, but it is those who obey the law who will be declared righteous. [14](Indeed, when Gentiles, who do not have the law, do by nature things required by the law, they are a law for themselves, even though they do not have the law. [15]They show that the requirements of the law are written on their hearts, their consciences also bearing witness, and their thoughts sometimes accusing them and at other times even defending them.) [16]This will take place on the day when God judges people's secrets through Jesus Christ, as my gospel declares.

[17]Now you, if you call yourself a Jew; if you rely on the law and boast
in God; [18]if you know his will and approve of what is superior because
you are instructed by the law; [19]if you are convinced that you are a guide
for the blind, a light for those who are in the dark, [20]an instructor of
the foolish, a teacher of little children, because you have in the law the
embodiment of knowledge and truth—[21]you, then, who teach others,
do you not teach yourself? You who preach against stealing, do you steal?
[22]You who say that people should not commit adultery, do you commit
adultery? You who abhor idols, do you rob temples? [23]You who boast
in the law, do you dishonor God by breaking the law? [24]As it is written:
"God's name is blasphemed among the Gentiles because of you."
[25]Circumcision has value if you observe the law, but if you break the
law, you have become as though you had not been circumcised. [26]So then,
if those who are not circumcised keep the law's requirements, will they
not be regarded as though they were circumcised? [27]The one who is not
circumcised physically and yet obeys the law will condemn you who, even
though you have the written code and circumcision, are a lawbreaker.
[28]A person is not a Jew who is one only outwardly, nor is circumcision
merely outward and physical. [29]No, a person is a Jew who is one inwardly;
and circumcision is circumcision of the heart, by the Spirit, not by the
written code. Such a person's praise is not from other people, but from
God.

*Listening to the texts in the story*: Deuteronomy 10:16; Exodus 19:5–6; Isaiah 52:5; Ezekiel 36; Jeremiah 31; Psalm 62:12; Proverbs 24:12; Wisdom of Solomon 15:1–5.

Paul argued in Romans 1:18–32 that the whole pagan world has been caught up in and corrupted by the fall of Adam and Eve. This fallen nature is visibly expressed in humanity's hostility toward God, their descent into idolatry, the futility of their thinking, and the contamination of their bodies by sexual immorality. The consequences are a rupture between God and humanity, the entrance of evil into the world, and the introduction of death. When God's righteousness is revealed to them, it is not a saving justice that is unveiled in the first instance; rather, it is the dramatic disclosure of his wrath against the immensity of human wickedness. In places like Romans 5:12–21 and 1 Corinthians 15:21–22, 56, Paul provides the framework for this "Adamic" reading of human history, that is, seeing all of humanity in light of the fall of Adam, which is the effective cause of the corruption of humanity.

Where does Israel fit into this picture? Israel was elected by divine grace (see Deut 9; Ezek 16; Dan 9). Israel in many ways recapitulated the vocation of Adam by its divine call to multiply and to fill the earth (Gen 1:28; 12:2–3; 17:2, 6, 8; 22:16–18; Exod 32:13). Israel was to be in Canaan what Adam and Eve were supposed to be in Eden: protector, custodian, and regent. God's reign over the world would be exercised through Israel and its kings (Pss 2; 89; Dan 2). Israel was supposed to be a kingdom of priests and a light to the nations (Exod 19:5–6; Isa 42:6–7; 49:6). The nation of Israel with its covenant, Torah, temple, and worship was meant to draw the nations to Zion and to Yahweh, who dwelt there (Isa 2:2–4; Mic 4:1–4; Zech 8:21–23).

This is why the sectarians at Qumran looked forward to a day when their little sect—the truest and purest part of Israel in their thinking—would recapture the "glory of Adam" (see 1QS 4.22–23; CD 3.19–20; 1QH 17.14–15). The seer who composed *4 Ezra* complained bitterly to God that the world was created as Israel's inheritance, yet the pagan nations had put their foot on Israel's neck so to speak. The seer asks why God would allow it to be so (*4 Ezra* 6.56–59). Evidently, God's solution to the problem of Adam was a project called Israel. And Israel was thus meant to be Israel-for-the-sake-of-the-world, a theme that reemerges time and time again in biblical and postbiblical literature.[1]

In Romans 2 Paul argues that Israel is not fulfilling its covenantal mandate to be a new Adam and to draw the nations to the Creator God. He drives the point home by depicting an imaginary Jewish character who believes in his own superiority over others on the basis of his inherited covenantal privileges and because he rests in the Torah.[2] The character claims to be a teacher and guide to the Gentiles since he possesses God's revelation in the Torah and even claims to perform it accordingly. But, Paul responds, this chap has not really kept the Torah, with the result that by his hypocrisy God's name is not glorified among the nations; rather, it is blasphemed! So Israel, symbolized by the imaginary opponent, has not really lived out its covenantal obligations to be a magnet to the nations. They have tragically failed in that task by not keeping the covenant that supposedly gave them the mandate to be preachers to pagans.

In fact, Israel has become the very thing it was warning about: a people immersed in sin. To state this in a different way, we might say that the beacon of light designed to warn the approaching ships of the jagged rocks of

1. See further, N. T. Wright, *The New Testament and the People of God* (COQG 1; London: SPCK, 1992), 263–68; Michael F. Bird, *Jesus and the Origins of the Gentile Mission* (LNTS 331; London: T&T Clark, 2007), 26–29, 126–43.

2. On Israel's reception of the law as proving their election, see 4 Maccabees 5:25: "We believe that the law was established by God, we know that in the nature of things the Creator of the world in giving us the law has shown sympathy toward us."

judgment is broken and is now pointing the ships in the wrong direction. The needle in the compass that was supposed to point to true north is instead spinning around like a wind-cock on a gusty day. The physician sent to cure people of the flu looks like he's suffering from plague. In the end, Israel's priority in salvation (Rom 1:16) has become a priority in judgment (2:9), and Israel might even find herself shamed by the better conduct of pagans when all things are set out impartially (2:27).

To this end, Paul constructs his argument as a "diatribe," which is a rhetorical speech made against an imaginary opponent, mimicking his voice, and anticipating his responses.[3] Paul thus argues in this chapter that there is no superiority for the Jewish opponent by (1) presiding in judgment (vv. 1–11), (2) possessing the Torah (vv. 12–16), (3) privileged ethnicity (vv. 17–24), or (4) partaking of circumcision (vv. 25–29). God is faithful, but also impartial. And how divine fidelity and divine impartiality fit together is the subject that follows. Paul's point is that the Jews have no right to boast over their pagan neighbors because, while God is faithful to Israel, he is also impartial in his judgment against Israel. So, in the end, Gentiles and Jews both stand before God "without excuse" on account of their sin (1:20; 2:1).

## EXPLAIN the Story

### The Hypocritical Teacher (2:1–5)

Some Jewish Christians who were proud of their national way of life and were listening to Romans 1:18–32 being read to them might have concluded that this Paul character does not seem so bad after all. He clearly knows the Torah and accepts the Jewish tradition that pork-eating, pantheon-worshiping, pansexual pagans are destined for the deity's dumpster of destruction. However, just as Amos listed the sins of Israel's neighbors before getting on to his main point, i.e., the sins of Israel (Amos 1–3), so too Paul now shifts from pagan wickedness to his next point, namely, that even the Jews are liable to divine judgment.[4] Paul pivots his focus from the wickedness of the pagan world (1:18–32) to the failures of the covenant people (2:1–29) in order to

3. According to David Aune (*The Westminster Dictionary of New Testament and Early Christian Literature and Rhetoric* [Lousiville: Westminster John Knox, 2003], 127), a diatribe is "a modern literary term describing an informal rhetorical mode of argumentation principally characterized by a lively dialogical style including the use of imaginary discussion partners (often addressed abruptly), to whom are attributed hypothetical objections and false conclusions." A diatribe was used mainly as a pedagogical teaching tool, not necessarily with a specific opponent in mind. It is unlikely that Paul is trying to mimic the position of a particular Jewish teacher resident in Rome whom he has heard about.

4. Cf. Dodd, *Romans*, 32; Moo, *Romans*, 128–29; Wright, "Romans," 10:445.

demonstrate that Israel too shows the symptoms of sin and is thus susceptible to divine judgment.

Paul's argument is all the more remarkable given that contemporareous Jewish writings often issued strident denunciations of Gentile idolatry and immorality and lauded the inherent superiority of the Jewish way of life. Paul's remarks in Romans 1:18–32 are aligned with Wisdom 12–16 and *Jubilees* 5 with their depiction of the wickedness of the pagan nations. However, Paul departs from Wisdom and *Jubilees* in one important regard. Whereas those two works argued that the Israelites, though rebellious in the wilderness, would escape with a reprieve if they would cling to God's law (see Wis 16:5–6, 10–11; *Jub* 5.17–18), Paul believes that the Jews are just as guilty as the pagans, so everyone—Jew and Gentile—is in the dock.[5]

In 2:1–5 Paul begins his diatribe by pointing out that this imaginary Jewish teacher,[6] who is convinced of his own rightness before God and his qualification to render judgment against the behavior of others, is in fact running the gauntlet of divine judgment. It is not entirely clear how the "therefore" of 2:1 relates back to 1:18–32. Most likely, Paul is implying something like the principle of God's judgment against sin in the pagan world can also be applied to God's judgment against sin in the Jewish world. Paul immediately introduces the problem befalling his imaginary opponent, namely, that he has "no excuse," which is to say that he is without a defense with regards to the charges laid against him.

Paul twice addresses his interlocutor with the derogatory form "mere human being"[7] to underscore his ignorance and insolence before the divine prerogatives of judgment. The reason he is without excuse is clear: this man does himself the very things he condemns in others, an observation confirmed by a comparison of the vice lists detailing Jewish sins in 2:21–23 with the earlier list of Gentile sins in 1:28–31. Paul elaborates in vv. 2–3 that since "we know" that God judges all things in accordance with the truth, everyone who does these things will fall under God's judgment. The imaginary opponent is told in no uncertain terms that taking the moral high ground is not a safe place to hide from that judgment.

---

5. Wright, "Romans," 10:429.

6. While some have insisted that the interlocutor in 2:1–16 is a Gentile (e.g., Stanley Stowers, *A Rereading of Romans* (New Haven: Yale Univ. Press, 1994), 100–104; Esler, *Conflict and Identity*, 151) or "Gentile moralist" (Rodriguez, *If You Call Yourself a Jew*, 37–38), I side with the majority in identifying the figure as a Jew (see esp. Cranfield, *Romans*, 1:137–39; Fitzmyer, *Romans*, 297). The literary similarities between Romans 2:1–6 and Wisdom of Solomon, in addition to the references to "doing the law" in 2:13–16, imply that a Jewish figure is envisaged.

7. The Greek phrase *ō anthrōpe*, comprising of an interjection and a vocative noun, is tantamount to, "You, Sir!" (Dunn, *Romans*, 1:79).

Paul then alleges that his dialogue partner is exhibiting willful contempt for divine mercy by failing to show contrition for his hypocrisy (vv. 4–5). Paul invites his imaginary opponent to acknowledge the rightfulness of his position. Paul effectively asks him, "Do you accept the facts I'm telling?" to which the alternative is Paul's rhetorical question, "Or do you show contempt for the riches of his kindness, forbearance and patience, not realizing that God's kindness is intended to lead you to repentance?" (v. 4). How God is kind to the imaginary opponent is not stated, but it probably pertains to God's common and covenantal grace and God's refusal thus far to inflict punishment on the fictitious character for his sinful behavior. The fact that he deserves judgment and that God has to date not imposed his punishments should lead such a person to repentance. Yet instead of acting so, Paul insinuates that his fictive opponent is ingrained with "stubbornness" and an "unrepentant heart," with the result that "you are storing up wrath against yourself for the day of God's wrath, when his righteous judgment will be revealed" (v. 5). The "day of wrath" is a biblical phrase for the time of final judgment.[8] Paul's point is that the pretentious teacher, whether a moral philosopher like Seneca or revered rabbi like Akiba, finds himself equally condemned before the divine tribunal.

### God's Repayment Plan (2:6–11)

Paul provides further support for his contention by claiming that God intends to hold the world to account and give each their due (vv. 6–16). A piece of scriptural evidence is adduced by way of a quotation from Psalm 62:12/Proverbs 24:12, where God "will repay each person according to what they have done" (v. 6). What such repayment looks like is laid out in vv. 7–10:

| Verse | Content | Description | Outcome |
|---|---|---|---|
| v. 7 | Behavior | To those who by persistence in doing good seek glory, honor and immortality | Positive |
| | Result | he will give eternal life | |
| v. 8 | Behavior | But for those who are self-seeking and who reject the truth and follow evil, | Negative |
| | Result | there will be wrath and anger. | |
| v. 9 | Result | There will be trouble and distress for every human being | Negative |
| | Behavior | who does evil: | |
| | *Persons* | first for the Jew, then for the Gentile | |

8. Cf., e.g., Ps 110:5; Isa 13:13; Zeph 1:14–15, 18; 2:2; Rev 6:17.

| Verse | Content | Description | Outcome |
|---|---|---|---|
| v. 10 | Result | but glory, honor and peace | Positive |
| | Behavior | for everyone who does good | |
| | *Persons* | first for the Jew, then for the Gentile | |

Paul is saying that those who do good and seek God will be rewarded in due course with a spate of benefits including immorality and divine honors. In contrast, Paul says, those who do evil and reject the truth will in turn receive a mix of human misfortune and divine rage. Importantly, Paul universalizes the principle of giving each their due by emphasizing its all-encompassing horizon. It is not just debauched pagans or hypocritical philosophers who are in the dock here, but it applies to "everyone" and "every human being," even the Jews. The principle stated in Psalm 62:12/Proverbs 24:12 means that the election of Israel establishes that the Jews will come first before the bar of divine judgment, not that they will be excused from it. The Jews come ahead of the Gentiles, yet the prospects ahead for both are salvation and judgment.

Paul defends this notion by way of reference to God's impartiality. Jews stand alongside Gentiles under the shadow of divine disfavor because "God does not show favoritism" (v. 11). Now to many Jews this was attacking the foundation of their theology of election and who they were. Surely God did have a favorite nation and was partial to the people of Israel. Surely election meant that Israel had "most favored nation" status. Paul will not deny Israel's covenantal privileges—in fact, he will celebrate them in Romans 3:2; 9:4–5. However, his point is that those inherited privileges amount to naught apart from covenantal obedience. Those covenantal privileges, Torah and circumcision, are no talisman against divine recompense.

### Justification according to Works (2:12–16)

Paul provides yet further evidence for this principle that God will judge everyone, Jews and Gentiles, according to what they have done. He states: "All who sin apart from the law will also perish apart from the law, and all who sin under the law will be judged by the law" (v. 12). Judgment will be for everyone irrespective of whether it is a Gentile who sins "apart from the law" or whether it is a Jew who sins "under the law." This is reinforced with an explanatory comment: "For it is not those who hear the law who are righteous in God's sight, but it is those who obey the law who will be declared righteous" (v. 13). Any good Jewish teacher could agree with that; indeed, even James the brother of Jesus said as much in his own letter (see Jas 2:14–26; cf. *m.'Abot* 1.17). However, the idea that Paul believed a person will be declared righteous (i.e., justified) on the basis of deeds has caused a cerebral meltdown and hermeneutical convulsions in many Protestant interpreters. How could Paul, the apostle of salvation by grace alone, through faith alone, say such a thing? Is Paul suffering from theological amnesia or experiencing a "Judaizing relapse"?[9] A few comments are in order.[10]

A common line has been to argue that Romans 2:13–14 is merely hypothetical. Paul deliberately sets up a straw man, suggesting that while it might be possible in theory for someone to fulfill the law and merit justification, the reality is that nobody ever actually measures up. Calvin believed that Paul was setting up the principle of Leviticus 18:5, "The person who obeys them will live by them," in order to remind his Jewish opponents that it is not knowledge of the law that avails before God, but only its fulfillment in perfect obedience. Calvin said: "We can prove from this passage that no one is justified by works; for if they alone are justified by the law who fulfill the law, it follows that no one is justified; for no one can be found who can boast of having fulfilled the law."[11] Calvin's perspective has been influential especially among Reformed interpreters.[12]

But there are three problems with the hypothetical view: (1) Paul does not give the impression of setting up a "let's assume for a moment" type of argument. There are no conditional clauses posed as "If ... then...." When Paul presents a theoretical perspective, he usually introduces it with the phrase, "I am speaking in human terms" (*anthrōpion legō*), as in Romans 3:5 and 6:19. There are no indications here of a hypothetical thesis being set up only to be torn down. (2) We must also point out that what Paul says here is put into the context of the final judgment (2:16). If condemnation at the final judgment on account of evil deeds is real, surely the same must be true about the prospect of a future justification on account of good deeds. (3) Finally, the notion that believers will face the final judgment and must produce good deeds to set before the Lord is not foreign to either Paul or the New Testament.[13]

At the same time, Paul cannot be arguing that that final justification is the reward for moral righteousness. Let's take a forward glimpse at the conclusion to Rom 1:18–3:20, where Paul sums up, in light of the universality of sin, that "no one will be declared righteous in God's sight by the works of the law"

9. Käsemann, *Romans*, 57.

10. See fuller argumentation about Romans 2:13–16 in Bird, *Saving Righteousness of God*, 155–78.

11. John Calvin, *Commentary on the Epistle of Paul the Apostle to the Romans* (trans. J. Owen; Bellingham, WA: Logos Bible Software), 96.

12. Cf. e.g., Moo, *Romans*, 140–42, 148.

13. Cf., e.g., Matt 12:36–37; 25:31–46; John 5:28–29; 1 Cor 3:10–15; 2 Cor 5:10; Gal 6:7–8; Col 3:25; 2 Tim 4:14; Jas 2:14–26; Rev 20:11–15.

(Rom 3:20 = Ps 143:2). Elsewhere Paul told the Galatians in no uncertain terms that "if righteousness could be gained through the law, [then] Christ died for nothing!" (Gal 2:21), and to the Ephesians he famously wrote, "For it is by grace you have been saved, through faith—and this is not from yourselves, it is the gift of God—not by works, so that no one can boast" (Eph 2:8–9). Paul does not have a Pelagian bone in his body, nor is he a closet legalist trying to smuggle in some merit theology through a rhetorical back door. So how do we solve this conundrum?

The solution, I believe, is that Paul is speaking cryptically about Christian Gentiles, who, by their obedience as enabled through the Spirit, fulfill the law and thus shame an imaginary Jewish opponent (see Rom 8:1–13). Don't read Romans 2 with the question in your head, "Am I saved by what I believe or by what I do?" That would impose a foreign issue into what Paul is addressing here. Instead, ask yourself, "How did Israel come to be like the Gentiles?" and "How is God going to get Israel and the Gentiles out of this mess?" Paul argues that everyone is condemned whether that is under Moses or without Moses (v. 12). Nevertheless, he begins to drop subtle hints about the coming AD period and the type of solution God has to get Israel and the nations back into fellowship with himself.[14]

That is why Paul adds a parenthetical remark in vv. 14–15 about Gentiles who do not have the law, yet still do the things that the law requires and become lawful in themselves. Most commentators translate v. 14 as "When the Gentiles, who do not have the law, *by nature do* the things required by the law...." But I would translate it differently, as "When the Gentiles, who do not *by nature have* the law, do the things required by the law...."[15] Paul is not talking about Gentiles who have a *natural law* inscribed on their hearts. Instead, he is talking about some Gentiles who did not have access to the law as intrinsic to their ethnic identity, or birth, and yet have the *works of the law* inscribed on their hearts.

Furthermore, the Gentiles in 2:14–15, who do not have the law by either nature or birth, but still do it, sound remarkably similarly to the Gentiles described in 2:25–29, which itself looks remarkably like Paul's description of new covenant people in Romans 8 and 2 Corinthians 3. Romans 2:25–29 describes those who are physically uncircumcised, yet keep the law's requirements; who are inwardly Jewish and are circumcised in their heart, not by the

---

14. Simon J. Gathercole, *Where Is Boasting? Early Jewish Soteriology and Paul's Response in Romans 1–5* (Grand Rapids: Eerdmans, 2002), 126–29.

15. I am assuming that the adjective *physis* modifies what precedes it rather than what follows it. See also Gathercole, *Where Is Boasting?* 127.

letter but by the Spirit. This "inward" Jew, who is circumcised in his heart by the Spirit, is a Gentile Christian, in whom the hopes of the exilic prophets for inner renewal have become a reality through God's life-creating work (Jer 31:31–34; Ezek 36:24–28). To push ahead even further, the Gentiles described in Romans 2:14–15, 25–29 look like the believers in Romans 8:1–11, who live such lives that "the righteous requirement of the law might be fully met in us, who do not live according to the flesh but according to the Spirit" (Rom 8:4; cf. 13:8–10).[16] This is a state of affairs that pertains to Christian believers, as Seifrid puts it: "True obedience to the law comes from beyond the law, in the work of the Spirit of God who is given through the gospel."[17]

If so, the justification to the doers of the law in 2:13–16 is not hypothetical, nor is it legalistic. Instead, this future justification refers to Christian Gentiles, who fulfill the law by their life in the Spirit, so that the works they do are the outworking of Christ's work in them. Their behavior accords with God's verdict declared in the present and enacted in the future. That is what justification "according to works" means.

### Hypocrisy of the Teacher Again (2:17–24)

Paul returns to some of the themes in vv. 1–11 about the privileges and pretense of his interlocutor in a series of rhetorical questions (vv. 17–24). The opponent is finally specified as someone who calls himsef a "Jew" and described as one who has come to "rely on the law and boast in God" (v. 17). This is a simple restatement of the three pillars of ancient Judaism: monotheism, election, and Torah. There is one God, who elected Israel, and he gave them the Torah. These are the inherited privileges that the Jews celebrated and to which they held fast. Since they had been "instructed by the law" and received this revelation about God, it meant that law-abiding Jews had "the full embodiment of knowledge and truth" pertaining to God. Extant Jewish literature emphasized the inviolability of Israel's election and their superiority over the nations precisely because they received and rested on the Torah.

---

16. For similar reading of Romans 2, see Cranfield, *Romans* 1:154–65; Gathercole, *Where Is Boasting?* 124–30; idem, "A Law unto Themselves: The Gentiles in Romans 2.14–15," *JSNT* 85 (2002): 27–49; N. T. Wright, *Justification: God's Plan and Paul's Vision* (Downers Grove, IL: InterVarsity, 2009), 182–97; idem, "Romans," 10:441–43; Francis Watson, *Paul, Judaism, and the Gentiles: Beyond the New Perspective* (Grand Rapids: Eerdmans, 2007), 192–216; Jewett, *Romans*, 213; Ardel B. Caneday, "Judgment, Behavior, and Justification according to Paul's Gospel in Romans 2," *JSPL* 1 (2011): 153–92.

17. Seifrid, *Christ, Our Righteousness*, 55.

| Wisdom of Solomon 15:1–5 | 2 Baruch 48:22–24 |
|---|---|
| But you, our God, are kind and true, patient, and ruling all things in mercy. For even if we sin we are yours, knowing your power; but we will not sin, because we know that you acknowledge us as yours. For to know you is complete righteousness, and to know your power is the root of immortality. For neither has the evil intent of human art misled us, nor the fruitless toil of painters, a figure stained with varied colors, whose appearance arouses yearning in fools, so that they desire the lifeless form of a dead image. | In you we have put our trust, because, behold your Law is with us, and we know that we do not fall as long as we keep your statutes. We shall always be blessed; at least, we did not mingle with the nations. For we are all a people of the Name; we, who received one Law from the One. And that Law that is among us will help us, and that excellent wisdom which is in us will support us. |

Given this narrative, the Jewish people had a special line to God, special access to divine wisdom, and special insight into the divine purposes as laid out in the Torah. Therefore, the learned Jew could claim to "know his will" and "approve of what is superior" (v. 18). With such privileges—and Paul nowhere denies them—the interlocutor is assumed to count himself needed in certain offices: a guide for the blind, a light for those in darkness, an instructor of the foolish, and a teacher of children (vv. 19–21). In a world that was cruel, brutal, and dark, the elect nation of Israel was meant to be a kingdom of priests and a light to the nations (Exod 19:5–6; Isa 42:9; 49:9). According to Wisdom of Solomon 18:4, Israelites were the ones "through whom the imperishable light of the law was to be given to the world." Whether in Canaan or in Corinth, the Jewish people were meant to do exactly the sort of thing that his Jewish opponent presumes to do, namely, to teach pagans the ways of God and how to live a life pleasing to God. In fact, this is precisely why Philo and Josephus boast about the few Gentiles who have converted to Judaism through the magnetic attraction of the Jewish way of life.[18]

Paul, however, points out that something has gone very wrong, for this Jewish instructor has not lived up to his privileged vocation. In fact, his judgment on the pagan world recoils back on himself.[19] Earlier in v. 2 Paul maintained that his opponent does the things that he condemns in others.

18. Cf. Michael F. Bird, *Crossing over Sea and Land: Jewish Missionary Activity in the Second Temple Period* (Peabody, MA: Hendrickson, 2009), 77–132; Scot McKnight, *A Light among the Gentiles: Jewish Missionary Activity in the Second Temple Period* (Minneapolis: Fortress, 1991), 90–97.

19. Dodd, *Romans*, 32.

Similarly in vv. 21–22, Paul asks how his interlocutor can presume the office of teacher when he does the same acts he teaches against. Such acts include stealing, adultery, and robbing temples. Now obviously Paul is being hyperbolic; he does not mean that all Jews everywhere are thieving, promiscuous, religious vandals. Yet the sharp barb of truth at the end of this rhetorical whip is that his opponent has not lived up to the vocation that the mandate in the Torah has placed on him. It would only take a little introspection, wrestling with his own "evil impulse" (as the rabbis called it) and meditating on the penitential psalms, for this imaginary opponent to realize that he might not be much better than his pagan neighbor.

Paul then makes a powerful indictment of his opponent: "You who boast in the law, do you dishonor God by breaking the law? As it is written: 'God's name is blasphemed among the Gentiles because of you'" (vv. 23–24). The question must be answered affirmatively since the imaginary adversary knows deep down that he transgresses the law. If so, then what right has he to boast? Obviously none! He cannot boast in his mere possession of the law if it has not been put it into practice. He cannot boast in his practice of the law if he has transgressed it.

Note the wider context. Whereas the Gentiles exchanged the glory of God for miserable idolatry (Rom 1:23), and God expects all people to seek after his glory (2:7), the Jewish teacher has brought dishonor on God by way of his transgression (2:23–24). God looks down on his people and sees that his guides are blind, the covenantal lights have gone dark, and the teachers have failed their own exams. Paul likens the current situation to the state of the Jews during the Babylonian exile, where God's name was blasphemed among the Gentiles because of them (Isa 52:5). The implication seems to be that just like Israel in exile, so now more than ever, the Jews need to hear the good news about God's kingship, so that their transgressions can be cleansed, and their shame turned to honor (52:7).

### Circumcision of the Heart and the True Jew (2:25–29)

Paul adds rhetorical insult to moral injury by alleging that circumcision cannot be relied upon to secure divine favor without obedience to the Torah. Furthermore, the covenantal blessings associated with circumcision can in some circumstances be given to those who are not circumcised (vv. 25–29). The back story here is that circumcision was given to Abraham as a sign of the covenantal promises granted to him by God (Gen 17:9–14). The Israelites circumcised their sons on the eighth day as a way of marking their bodies with the promise of the covenant (Lev 12:3). Yet this physical circumcision of the flesh was to be married to an inner circumcision of the heart (Deut 10:16), something done by God (Deut 30:6) and associated with the spiritual renewal that the exilic prophets anticipated taking root in Israel one day (Jer 4:4; 6:10; 9:25; Ezek 44:7). Paul believed that the covenantal prestige of circumcision was now true of those who were physically uncircumcised but had believed in Israel's Messiah (Phil 3:3), who had experienced the Spirit-wrought circumcision of the heart, which takes place in the miracle of new birth (Col 2:11–12), a transformation that is so amazing that physical circumcision no longer compares to it (1 Cor 7:9; Gal 6:13).

Paul drops two big theological bricks to smash a covenant theology that presumes on the efficacy of ethnic identity for divine blessings.[20] First, he says that the covenant sign of circumcision is effective *only if* accompanied by observance of the law.[21] In which case, breaking the law means that "you have become as though you had not been circumcised." That is to say, willful disobedience not only nullifies the covenant blessings, it also makes one effectively a Gentile, someone outside the covenant (v. 25). Second, the reverse also holds, "if those who are not circumcised keep the law's requirements, will they not be regarded as though they were circumcised?" (v. 26). Note something important here. Paul is introducing a category of persons who are in the covenant even though they are not circumcised. Paul does that by way of a theology of imputation, namely, by arguing that obedience can be *reckoned* as the same as circumcision.[22] Those who keep the Torah's requirements can be regarded as being full and faithful covenant partners with God. Paul's point, shocking as it would sound to many Jews, was in fact a scriptural perspective; that is, all things being equal, an obedient heart always trumps a circumcised foreskin.[23]

Paul heaps more shame on his interlocutor by stating that law-obedient Gentiles would be right to condemn law-breaking Jews: "The one who is not circumcised physically and yet obeys the law will condemn you who, even though you have the written code and circumcision, are a lawbreaker" (v. 27). In an ironic turning of the tables, the Jewish teacher who presumed to judge Gentiles now finds himself judged by them and shamed by their better behavior.

Paul justifies these controversial remarks with a claim that the privileges of Jewish identity do not derive from the ethnic marker of circumcision but

20. Cf. e.g., Wis. 15; *Pss. Sol.* 9–10; *T. Levi* 15.2; *m. Sanh.* 10.1.

21. Commentators are divided as to whether the Jews thought that the law required perfect obedience or merely a genuine intention to obey it. Paul's premise is not so much a moral perfection that the law required as much as it is the human inability to do whatever it is that the law requires.

22. Cf. similarly Romans 9:8 about persons being "reckoned" as Abraham's seed.

23. Cf. Deut 10:16; Jer 4:4; 9:25–26; Ezek 44:9.

from the interior reality of a life lived in complete devotion to God. He writes: "A person is not a Jew who is one only outwardly, nor is circumcision merely outward and physical. No, a person is a Jew who is one inwardly; and circumcision is circumcision of the heart, by the Spirit, not by the written code" (vv. 28–29). These short verses are really paving the way for Romans 9, where Paul will differentiate between an "Israel according to the flesh" and an "Israel according to the promise." It is reminiscent of what Paul taught in 2 Corinthians 3:6 concerning the ministry of the law and the ministry of the Spirit. It recalls Paul's remarks in Philippians 3:3 that "it is we who are the circumcision, we who serve God by his Spirit, who boast in Christ Jesus, and who put no confidence in the flesh."

The persons to be divinely praised, or we could just as well say justified or blessed, are those who are circumcised in the heart by the Spirit, who fulfill the law, who are inwardly Jewish, and who live in obedience to God. Such persons will later be shown to be Gentile Christians, who have died and risen with the Messiah, who live under the aegis of Jesus' lordship, and live not according to the flesh but according to the Spirit. In brief, Paul redraws the whole symbolic universe of Israel's election around the hope for a Spirit-wrought transformation of the heart.

In 2:1–29, Paul blots out in a single stroke any theology of election that presumed upon grace without obedience or clung to ethnic privileges without recourse to God's life-giving power. The sure way to divine favor—claiming Jewish identity, relying on the Torah, exegeting the minutiae of its instructions, bragging about God, wagging a finger against Gentiles—is not so sure after all. The Jews may have knowledge of the Torah, but they have not kept it. The Jews may have physical circumcision, but not necessarily a circumcision of their hearts. And that is why the Jews are without excuse, condemned by an approaching judgment and facing wrath, rage, distress, and affliction. In the end, Israel is also in Adam.

## LIVE the Story

Given the highly charged rhetoric of the passage, loaded as it is with sharp polemics and no little amount of hyperbole, how do we live out this text? Assuming that no contemporary reader of this text is a moralizing Jewish teacher with a strong sense of ethnic pride and religious zeal, what could this possibly mean for us? Well, several things! First, let's discuss the menace of hypocrisy; second, the dangers of a superiority complex; and third, the virtue of a missiological vocation.

### The Menace of Hypocrisy

Paul exposes the hypocrisy of his fictive Jewish opponent in 2:1–29. Paul's interlocutor does the same things he condemns in others, he commits the same misdeeds that he censures others for, and he therefore has no right to claim the moral high ground or to set himself on a pedestal over others. Hypocrisy is the pretentious claim to virtues that one does not really hold. Hypocrisy means saying one thing and then doing another. Hypocrisy happens when people think they can get away with inconsistencies between their beliefs and their behaviors. Hypocrisy derives from believing one is somehow immune from the rules to which others are subject.

To give a concrete example, during my time in the army, I always remember how morale crushing it was when senior ranks would threaten the enlisted men with all sorts of punishments for behavior we knew that they themselves brazenly committed. I remember one particular instance where a crusty old warrant officer nearly tore shreds off my skin for the heinous offense of walking several meters from my office to my car without wearing the appropriate military headdress for being outdoors. Yet the next day I saw the same warrant officer do exactly the same thing he accosted me for doing. How could he so condemn me for such a trivial offense when he himself did the same thing? Hypocrisy is the surest way to create distrust and anger against those who are in leadership.

The proverb, "Physician, heal thyself!" is probably one of the oldest and most well-known of proverbs. It was known in the ancient writings of Euripides and in the letters of Cicero. Jesus thought that the proverb epitomized the response of the people of Nazareth to his ministry, telling him to put up or shut up concerning evidence for the prophetic role that he was claiming for himself (Luke 4:23). The rub of the proverb is basically this: How can you presume to offer me something that you yourself so obviously need? It's like drug cheat Lance Armstrong offering advice on the importance of honesty, disgraced Illinois Governor Rod Blagojevich giving guidance on how to stem corruption in the public sector, or actor Charlie Sheen sermonizing on the need for celebrities to show some humility. In each case, we'd say, "Physician, heal thyself!" Do not lecture us on what you yourself need more than anybody else! Indeed, it is hypocritical to pontificate on a subject that one clearly needs lessons on.

The Christian tradition has always had a lot to say about hypocrisy, play acting, pretending to be a paragon of virtue when one is really a purveyor of vice. Jesus taught in the Sermon on the Mount that disciples should be sufficiently self-critical before they presume to lecture others about their moral failings. Hence his words: "Why do you look at the speck of sawdust in your brother's eye and pay no attention to the plank in your own eye? How can you say to your brother, 'Let me take the speck out of your eye,' when all the time there is a plank in your own eye? You hypocrite, first take the plank out of your own eye, and then you will see clearly to remove the speck from your brother's eye" (Matt 7:3–5).

Later in the Gospel of Matthew, Jesus violently censured the Pharisees, the recognized authorities on religion and ethics, for preaching God's law but failing to properly obey it (see Matthew 23). At the incident in Antioch, when Peter withdrew from table fellowship with Gentiles at the behest of certain men from James, Paul took Peter to task and called him a hypocrite to his face. Paul saw that Peter was not keeping in step with the truth of the gospel by insisting that Gentile believers could not have fellowship with Jewish believers unless they were circumcised. Peter knew that God accepted Gentiles as Gentiles, based on faith, not keeping the law, yet Peter folded like a card table to please the Jacobean faction (see Gal 2:11–14).

Hypocrisy is not just poor form, it is a menace because it harms the integrity of the gospel. David Garland argues that hypocrisy in religion is more than willful pretense and deceptively pretending to have more moral capital than one actually possesses. Hypocrisy in religion is a problem of both heart and hermeneutics. That is because hypocritical leaders are those who place themselves in a position of authority over others and subvert Scripture by replacing it with confidence in their own man-made traditions. That is why wherever you find legalism, you will inevitably find hypocrisy as well.[24]

If we wanted to come up with a paraphrase of Romans 2 that speaks against Christian hypocrisy, we could put it as follows:

Now you, if you call yourself a Christian; if you rely on the Spirit, and boast in the triune God; if you claim to be theologically conservative because you attend the right conferences; if you are convinced that you are a guide for lost people, a light for those who are in darkness, an instructor of Sunday school children because you went to the finest seminary for preachers—well then, you who preach on Sunday, what do you do between Monday and Saturday? You who preach against legalism, do you burden others with your own list of rules on how to curry God's favor? You who like to jump on the social justice bandwagon, do you pay a pittance of a wage to the immigrants who work your yard because you know they are not legal residents? You who claim to be pro-family, do you invest time and energy in your spouse and children? You who say that people should not commit adultery, do you watch internet porn in hotels on business trips? You who tell us to tithe till it hurts, do you

24. David E. Garland, *The Intention of Matthew 23* (NovTSup 52; Leiden: Brill, 1979), 115–16.

give to God from your own pocket? You who boast in your denomination, do you hold your denomination to account when it fails to report sex abuse or when it sucks up to politicians you know have a sham faith? As it is written: "God's name is blasphemed across the internet because of you."

Let us remember that hypocrisy is a threat to the gospel because Christians claim that God has transformed them to be a force for good and yet many of them live like Sodom and Gomorrah when they think nobody is watching. As Brennan Manning famously said: "The greatest single cause of atheism in the world today is Christians: who acknowledge Jesus with their lips, walk out the door, and deny Him by their lifestyle. That is what an unbelieving world simply finds unbelievable." Hypocrisy is what sadly turns the church into a factory of unbelief.

## The Dangers of a Superiority Complex

At the root of all hypocrisy is a smug sense of self-assured superiority. Such smugness can happen on the national, tribal, and individual levels. As much as I love America—they gave us Chick-Fil-A after all—certain quarters of the political landscape seem to believe in American exceptionalism, whereby America is somehow immune from international law when it comes to resolving international conflict. My own country, Australia, at the social level, has always found it hard to relate to Asia and has had a tendency to look down on Asia as either a military threat or as a political basket case. Although Australia was originally a British colony with a strong sense of British identity, Australia is now economically and culturally closely interconnected with Asia. Be that as it may, some Australians believe that they can act with exceptionalism when it comes to dealing with asylum seekers, negotiating the sharing of resources with neighboring countries, and often act with a degree of condescension rather than partnership when it comes to aid programs for developing countries in our region. According to Solomon Andria, some ethnic groups in Africa feel themselves superior to others based on the exploits of their ancestors. Some like the Falasha in Ethiopia claim superiority based on the Jewish roots of their ancestral lineage.[25] The tragedy is that whenever we become convinced we are better than someone else, we can be mistaken into thinking that we can treat others with disdain.

Let me add that a superiority complex is not like a sense of pride or belief in the strength of one's convictions. I'm proud of my country, my state, and my church. I'm convinced about the validity of my Christian beliefs over secular values. I believe Christian virtues are inherently better than the alternatives

25. Andria, *Romans*, 56.

when it comes to creating a society of responsibility, compassion, and human flourishing. Yet a superiority complex is what emerges when the self-perceived rightness of my beliefs and values gives me a license to trample down others who do not share them. When I use my beliefs not as a life-preserver to help others, but as a stick to beat up others, then I'm acting out of a sense of superiority. In other words, a sinful sense of superiority derives from hubris not humility, from preaching without listening, and conviction without compassion. A self-righteous superiority is what separates a virtuous saint from the moralizing legalist.

Let us keep in mind that Paul's remarks lambasting his imaginary Jewish opponent for hypocrisy and an inflated sense of self-superiority are universally applicable to other contexts. The charges do not apply exclusively to the Jews or just to moralizing pagan philosophers. Paul's arguments are applicable to Christians too. In fact, what Paul says in Romans 2 *against* hypocrisy and a superiority complex provide the premise *for* cultivating an ethic of mutual acceptance within the Roman congregations in Romans 14–15. According to Robert Jewett, Paul here has the goal of "creating an argument that provides the premise for an ethic of mutual tolerance between the competitive house and tenement churches in Rome, which could enable them to participate with integrity in the Spanish mission."[26] It seems that certain pockets of the Roman churches were divided over the question of the degree of law observance required to live faithfully in a pagan city. Factions may have developed over Jewish and Gentile approaches to ethics and interpretative disputes arisen about how the Torah should be applied to their situation. It was a setting ripe precisely for the kind of hypocrisy and judgmentalism that Paul so passionately censures in Romans 2. In the course of the letter, Paul scuttles any refuge for hypocrisy or self-righteous moralism by setting forth the equality principle of the gospel and the moral imperatives for unity. Jewett comments, "Paul opens a way to overcome cultural and religious bigotry by means of righteousness through faith in Christ crucified."[27]

### The Virtue of a Missiological Vocation

Although Paul largely takes his fictive opponent to task for hypocrisy and judgmentalism, there is still a sense in which Paul affirms a key vocation of Israel to be a guide for the blind and light for those in the dark (Rom 2:19). This is part of the first order purposes of Israel's election, to be a kingdom of priests (Exod 19:5–6) and a light to the nations (Isa 42:6; 49:6). Israel was meant to be an ark of hope amidst the flood of idolatry, immorality, and

26. Jewett, *Romans*, 197.

27. Ibid., 203.

inhumanity that existed in the ancient Near East. Israel's Torah was meant to be a beacon of justice in an unjust world. Israel's temple was supposed to be a magnet to the nations, drawing them to share in Israel's worship of the one true God. Israel's king was meant to emulate the reign of God on earth by ruling righteously.

Israel's success in this role as God's envoy to the nations has been relatively mixed. The mere continuation of the Jewish religion by the Jewish people across three millennia is proof enough of their commitment to preserve their way of life, their religious heritage, ethics, Scripture, and their God-centered worldview. Yet the prophets obviously saw Israel's failure to live up to this covenantal vocation when they indicted Israel for replicating the worst of the nations (e.g., Amos), or else they forfeited all responsibility to mediate God's blessings to the nations (e.g., Jonah). Even some contemporary Jewish thinkers have been modestly critical of the Jewish peoples' failure to live up to this covenantal calling. In fact, at the 2008 Lambeth Conference, the chief British Rabbi Jonathan Sacks spoke about how the Christian church has succeeded where the Jews had corporately failed by taking the Jewish message of God's forgiveness to the world:

> We did not take it to the world. We are few. You are many. You took it to the world. In fact, we are so few. I have the numbers of Jews from all of the countries in the world. That is part of my job now and I travel to see them. We have 5 Jews in China. You can bet that they have 6 synagogues and someone is saying that the Jews are running the country. You have taken that message of one who was a Jew to the world. Take that message as a Jewish message: forgive them Father. If there is one Jewish message we need it is the courage to forgive one another. To walk side by side in many differences of faith, but the shared experience of faith. The World is enlarged by differences. We must do what Joseph did in Genesis. We must have the courage to forgive one another.[28]

Sacks was graciously lauding one good thing about church history, that is, how Christians took the Jewish message of God's Messiah and God's forgiveness to the world. That makes perfect sense since Jesus wasn't trying to replace Israel with a new religious body made up of Gentiles; rather, he wanted his followers to be Israel and to project Israel's covenantal blessings to the nations. To put it in Pauline terms, Christ became a servant of Israel to confirm the promises made to the patriarchs about God's intention to bless the world

28. Chris Sugden and Chertie Wetzel, "Rabbi Sir Jonathan Sachs Answers Questions on Covenants, Jesus and Peace." *Virtuosity: The Voice for Global Orthodox Anglicanism.* Ed. David Virtue. See www.virtueonline.org/portal/modules/news/article.php?storyid=8753.

through Abraham's offspring (Rom 15:7–8). The gospel of Jesus Christ is the story that comes to and through Israel's covenantal history. Salvation is Israel-shaped, and the church is part of the continuing story of Israel according to the promise.

Thus, the church's mission is not to imitate Cynic philosophers and just wander around cities trying to shock people with weird antics and countercultural aphorisms in the hope of gaining notoriety and a few token followers. Nor are Christians to be like the Stoic philosophers and try to provide moral guidance and intellectual tutelage for the aristocratic class. The church's mission is to be "a guide for the blind, a light for those who are in the dark, an instructor of the foolish, a teacher of little children" (Rom 2:19–20). We, the church, are to be Israel-for-the-sake-of-the-world. We go out heralding the good news that God's faithfulness, justice, and deliverance have been demonstrated in the life, death, and resurrection of Jesus the Messiah of Israel.

For all of Paul's rhetoric against the "Jew" and despite his criticism of Israel's disobedience to God's commands, Paul offers a wholesale validation of Israel's covenantal vocation. Israel was the elect people and their calling was irrevocable. Yet their election was not an end in and of itself, but was purposed for a missional goal as part of the wider divine purposes in the *missio dei*. In other words, divine election necessitates missional vocation. Paul now sees Israel's vocation through the lens of Jesus' life, death, and resurrection. Jesus was both the servant of Israel and the messianic king of Israel who embodied Israel's mission in himself and commissioned his followers to fulfill it further. As such, in Jesus Christ we find the climactic revelation of the faithfulness of God to Israel and the transformation of Israel's vocation around the Messiah and his Spirit-empowered people. We have good reason for thinking that Paul believed his own apostolic mission to the Gentiles was a distinctively Jewish task since preaching to Gentiles about the forgiveness of sins in the Messiah's name was how the Gentiles would be reconciled to God and initiated into Abraham's family.[29]

The church, freshly released from the fetters of slavery in sin, goes into the world much like Israel went into Canaan from Egypt. The redeemed people go forth, empowered by the Spirit, declaring the Son, and inviting the nations into fellowship with God the Father. The upshot is that we cannot reduce the church's place in the world to a preservationist tendency to simply batten down the hatches and wait out the storm until the frosty winds of atheism, secularism, pluralism, and Islam have blown over. Nor can we retreat to the

29. On this see recently Lionel J. Windsor, *Paul and the Vocation of Israel: How Paul's Jewish Identity Informs His Apostolic Ministry, with Special Reference to Romans* (BZNW 205; Berlin: Walter de Gruyter, 2014).

safe obscurity of the cultural desert, climb our lofty prayer pole, and recite the prayer of Jabez over and over until Michael and his angels come down from heaven to smite our enemies. Instead we have the hard work, frustrating job, and risky business of being a light to the nations, the salt of the earth, and a city of the hill. The most powerful symbol and the most palpable expression of the church's election is their mission to the world as ambassadors of Jesus Christ. It is in the busyness of mission that we prove and confirm our election. The church is the people who know God, and they go with God as they proclaim the love of God the Father, the grace of Jesus Christ, and the fellowship of the Holy Spirit.

This missional vocation can be lived out in different ways: in the prayers for God to open doors for the gospel, in our financial sacrifice to enable mission, in the work of chaplains in the armed services, among those who plant churches in the cities, among those renewing rural congregations, with those who work in refugee camps, and among those who translate the Bible into languages in which the Word is not yet known. While it might feel that we are always fighting an uphill battle against the world to make the gospel known to the world, let us not forget the success the church has had in its global mission over the past two thousand years. Somewhere between a third and half of the world's population professes Christian faith of some kind. The reason is that men and women of church history have taken the church's missional vocation seriously and made the sacrifices necessary to preach the gospel to the ends of the earth.

I think particularly of people like John Geddie (1815–1872) and his missionary work in the New Hebrides, modern Vanuatu, in the South Pacific. He worked amidst the cannibals and tribal violence of the island to establish a church in a career filled with up and downs, highlights and setbacks, as well as joys and doldrums. Geddie worked there for twenty-four years until his death. In a church on the tiny island of Aneityum there was laid a plaque behind the pulpit in his honor. It reads so: "In memory of John Geddie, D.D., born in Scotland, 1815, minister in Prince Edward Island seven years, Missionary sent from Nova Scotia to Aneiteum for twenty-four years. When he landed in 1848, there were no Christians here, and when he left in 1872 there were no heathen."

CHAPTER 5

# Romans 3:1 – 20

## LISTEN to the Story

1What advantage, then, is there in being a Jew, or what value is there
in circumcision? 2Much in every way! First of all, the Jews have been
entrusted with the very words of God.

3What if some were unfaithful? Will their unfaithfulness nullify God's
faithfulness? 4Not at all! Let God be true, and every human being a liar.
As it is written:

> "So that you may be proved right when you speak
> and prevail when you judge."

5But if our unrighteousness brings out God's righteousness more
clearly, what shall we say? That God is unjust in bringing his wrath on us?
(I am using a human argument.) 6Certainly not! If that were so, how could
God judge the world? 7Someone might argue, "If my falsehood enhances
God's truthfulness and so increases his glory, why am I still condemned as a
sinner?" 8Why not say—as some slanderously claim that we say—"Let us
do evil that good may result"? Their condemnation is just!

9What shall we conclude then? Do we have any advantage? Not at all!
For we have already made the charge that Jews and Gentiles alike are all
under the power of sin. 10As it is written:

> "There is no one righteous, not even one;
> 11there is no one who understands;
> there is no one who seeks God.
> 12All have turned away,
> they have together become worthless;
> there is no one who does good,
> not even one."
> 13"Their throats are open graves;
> their tongues practice deceit."
> "The poison of vipers is on their lips."
> 14"Their mouths are full of cursing and bitterness."

[15]"Their feet are swift to shed blood;
[16]ruin and misery mark their ways,
[17]and the way of peace they do not know."
[18]"There is no fear of God before their eyes."

[19]Now we know that whatever the law says, it says to those who are under the law, so that every mouth may be silenced and the whole world held accountable to God. [20]Therefore no one will be declared righteous in God's sight by the works of the law; rather, through the law we become conscious of our sin.

*Listening to the texts in the story*: Deuteronomy 7:9; Psalms 5; 10; 14; 36; 51; 59; 116; 140; 143; 147; Isaiah 59:7–8; Proverbs 1:1; Ecclesiastes 7:20.

Paul now tries to anticipate the objections of his imaginary Jewish interlocutor. If it is true that the inherited privileges of the Jewish people (i.e., their monotheistic worship, divine election of the nation, and receiving the Torah) have had a null and void impact in making Israel any better than the pagan nations, then is the failure not really Israel's but actually God's failure? If Israel falters, has God failed to be faithful to his chosen people? If Paul is right, is not God's faithfulness put under a cloud of suspicion because God has reneged on his covenant promise to sustain and save Israel? Furthermore, if the logic holds that Gentiles and Jews alike are caught in evil and are justly condemned, then why bother following the Jewish way of life?

That is the issue at hand, and this is not the only place where Paul takes it up. Romans 3:1–20 is really a microcosm of the argument that Paul will rehearse later in Romans 9–11. There he will attempt to demonstrate that Israel's failure to believe in the gospel does not nullify God's faithfulness, since God's electing purposes run through Israel and are bigger than Israel. Not only that, but Israel's rejection is the mechanism that leads to Gentile inclusion, and Gentile inclusion will lead to Israel's eventual reconciliation with God. Thus, divine faithfulness to the patriarchs, to Israel, and to Christ-believers all holds firm.

It is worth remembering that 3:1–20 rehashes a familiar theme in the biblical story, namely, God's rebuking of Israel for her waywardness and his revulsion at the conduct of the nations. The culturally dominating image of God as some kind of long-bearded, benign old man with the voice of actor Morgan Freeman, who can easily have the wool pulled over his eyes and has a live-and-let-live view of things, is dismantled by a cursory reading of the Old

Testament. The totality of God's government of the universe leads inevitably to the application of his justice in terms of both vindication and judgment. God's judgment, as we saw in 1:18 – 30, is not a disproportionate feat of rage. Rather, divine wrath is the response of God's holiness toward moral evil.

Judgment in the Old Testament is always a middle term between warnings on the one hand and deliverance on the other. The preliminary phase, prophetic warning, is God's advanced notice that the nation has lost its way and must turn back immediately or risk punitive consequences. Ezekiel provides a good example when he tells the exiles, "Therefore, you Israelites, I will judge each of you according to your own ways, declares the Sovereign LORD. Repent! Turn away from all your offenses; then sin will not be your downfall" (Ezek 18:30). Paul draws on the Psalms and Isaiah to show that Israel and all humanity need to hear the divine "no" to their sin before they can receive the divine "yes" through Jesus Christ. Importantly, God's faithfulness to Israel and his mercy to the nations do not obviate the reality of God's contention against sin, for people must turn away from sin and turn to God for forgiveness if judgment is to be avoided.

The argument in 3:1 – 20 can be split up in two parts, both beginning with the question of Jewish "advantage." On that question, Paul gives a "yes and no" answer. In vv. 1 – 8, Paul answers affirmatively, upholding Israel's privileged role as custodian of divine oracles, but countenancing it with a particular qualification. God's faithfulness is not contingent on Israel's faithfulness to that vocation. What is more, it is spurious and sacrilegious to insist that God's faithfulness to Israel precludes the possibility of God's judging of Israel. Paul rejects the premise that for God to be faithful, upright, and true, he must accept Israel whether in the right or in the wrong. If that were the case, God would have no grounds to prosecute the world in its rebellion because God's own moral compass would be skewed.

Then, in vv. 9 – 18, Paul answers negatively, saying that there is no Jewish advantage, on the grounds that Jews and Gentiles are both condemned by the weight of the sin that presses on them. This point is then proved by a catena of texts from the Psalms and the prophet Isaiah. God's election of Israel entails their special relationship with God and their unique vocation as the covenant people. It does not mean that Israel will be excluded from judgment, for God will judge the entire world.

Then, in vv. 19 – 20, Paul comes to his climactic conclusion concerning the entire span of the argument set out in 1:18 – 3:20. No one will be declared righteous before God by adopting the Jewish way of life as given in the Torah. While the Torah gives knowledge of sin, it is powerless to effect liberation from sin. That in turn sets the stage for the next move in Paul's argument in Romans.

Exactly how, then, will God's righteousness be disclosed? How will God's intent to rectify creation and be faithful to Israel come to fruition? Where should one look for it and what will the result be for Israel and for the world?

## EXPLAIN the Story

### Israel's Privileges and God's Faithfulness (3:1–4)

Paul has just pointed out (1) how Jewish privileges will not provide a sure escape from God's judgment on the appointed day (see Rom 2:16–24); (2) that is because the covenant sign of circumcision is only effective in the context of covenantal obedience; in which case (3) Paul creates the possibility that Gentile obedience can be reckoned as circumcision or covenantal membership (see 2:25–29). If that is true, then someone might well ask, "What advantage, then, is there in being a Jew, or what value is there in circumcision?" (3:1). Paul's argument in Romans 2 has raised the question as to whether Jewish identity can ever be grounds for assurance. To put it bluntly, one could ask of Paul, what is the point of being Jewish then? Why not apostasize from Judaism as some aristocratic Jews did, like Tiberius Alexander or the great-grandchildren of Herod the Great?[1]

Whereas one might expect that Paul will give a negative answer to the question, he does the opposite; he provides a positive affirmation of Jewish identity: "Much in every way! First of all, the Jews have been entrusted with the very words of God" (3:2). Paul will list other benefits of Jewishness later on (see 9:4–5), but here he focuses on Israel's custodianship of the "words of God." Israel has been *entrusted* (*pisteuō*) with the *oracles of God* (*logia tou theou*). This is far more than Israel running a chain of bookstores that stock editions of the Hebrew Bible. The words in question are in fact the "promises of God," on which Paul majors—the promises made to the patriarchs about creating a one-world-family through Israel and her Messiah (see 4:12–18, 9:6–13; 11:28; esp. 15:8–12). Abraham was promised to be a father of many nations. Therefore, Israel's job description was to be kings and priests of the world, to turn Canaan into a new Eden, and to lead the nations into the worship of God.

Sadly though, Israel had mixed fortunes in fulfilling that task. As time went by, they either imitated the worst of the nations or else prided themselves in their separation from the nations—neither of which was conducive to being a kingdom of priests and a light to the nations. Israel was not faithful to this covenantal task to which God's election bound her.

1. Josephus, *Ant.* 18.141; 20.100. On Jewish apostasy more generally, see Stephen G. Wilson, *Leaving the Fold: Apostates and Defectors in Antiquity* (Minneapolis: Fortress, 2004), 23–56.

| Thematic Links between Romans 3 and 9–11 | |
|---|---|
| The question of Jewish privileges | 3:1 = 9:1–5 |
| Has God failed? | 3:3 = 9:6; 11:1–2 |
| Some Jews failed/Some Jews faithful | 3:3 = 9:27; 11:5 |
| Is God unjust? | 3:5 = 9:14 |
| Righteousness of God | 3:5 = 10:3 |
| Why does God condemn? | 3:7 = 9:19 |
| Equality between Jews and Gentiles | 3:9 = 10:12 |
| Israel's failure in the Torah | 3:9 = 9:30–10:21 |

That is why Paul adds: "What if some were unfaithful? Will their unfaithfulness nullify God's faithfulness?" (3:3). This is getting down to the real point of contention. Can Israel's failure to keep the Torah and to share the divine promises with the nations—the two go together as the former is the condition for the latter—be attributed to God's unfaithfulness to Israel?[2] Predictably Paul cannot entertain such a notion that God is unfaithful. Thus he responds in v. 4 with "Not at all!" The Greek *mē genoito* is an emphatic form of negation in Greek combining a negative particle with an optative verb to signify Paul's revulsion at the mere thought. Idiomatically we might say with the voice of a Mafia don, "Forget about it" or perhaps with the voice of a Californian surfer, "No way, dude."[3] Paul adds a proverbial thought allusive of Psalm 116:11 (LXX 115:2), "Let God be true, and every human being a liar." He also adds a citation from Psalm 51:4 (LXX Ps 50:6), "So that you may be proved right when you speak and prevail when you judge." The context of Psalm 51 is, of course, David's adultery with Bathsheba, and David recognizes how God's declaration of his wrong establishes that God is right. The net point is that God's faithfulness or "righteousness" is manifested even through the sins of his people.[4]

2. Note that Paul says that "some" (*tines*) were unfaithful, not that all Israel was unfaithful, an important point that will feed into his remnant theology later (see 9:27; 11:5).

3. See other translations "God forbid" (KJV), "By no means!" (NRSV, ESV), "Absolutely not!" (NETS, CEB), "Out of the question!" (NJB), and "May it never be!" (NASB). On the optative mood here, see Daniel B. Wallace, *Greek Grammar beyond the Basics* (Grand Rapids: Zondervan, 1996), 482; Stanley E. Porter, Jeffrey T. Reed, and Matthew Brook O'Donnell, *Fundamentals of New Testament Greek* (Grand Rapids: Eerdmans, 2010), 373–74; Stanley E. Porter, *Idioms of the Greek New Testament* (2nd ed.; Sheffield: Sheffield Academic Press, 1999), 59–61.

4. Moo, *Romans*, 179–80.

## God's Righteousness and Jewish Unrighteousness (3:5–9)

Paul seems to digress for a moment in vv. 5–8 as he takes the time to respond to some counterassertions that deny that God can be both faithful to Israel and yet simultaneously judge the nation in the eschatological future. Significantly, Paul changes perspective from talking *about* the Jews in vv. 1–4 to speaking *as one of them* in vv. 5–8. Hence his use of first person pronouns in "our unrighteousness," "wrath on us," "my falsehood," "I am condemned as a sinner," and "Let us do evil." Paul switches into a speech-in-character that identifies himself with unfaithful Jews and their national unfaithfulness, which is on par with the unrighteousness condemned in the earlier stages of the argument (see 1:18, 29: 2:8).[5] Paul brings the attributes of God's righteousness and truthfulness to the surface to see how they fair in light of some rather specious objections.

First, Paul asks as an objector, "But if our unrighteousness brings out God's righteousness more clearly, what shall we say? That God is unjust in bringing his wrath on us?" (3:5). The premise for the objection is drawn from Paul's citation of Psalm 51. If our sin proves that God is righteous, righteous in the sense that God was both the judge and the justifier of a sinner like David, then in what possible sense can God's wrath against Israel ever be total or final?[6] At the heart of the objection is the presumption that God's righteousness rests on Israel's righteousness, and if it not be so, God is not faithful. In other words, God's faithfulness is thought to imply that Israel permanently possesses a get-out-of-judgment-free-card.

The sort of attitude that Paul is correcting is reminiscent of the time of Jeremiah, when the populace thought that the temple made them immune from divine judgment. Jeremiah mocked their mantra: "This is the temple of the LORD, the temple of the LORD, the temple of the LORD!" and declared to them the divine warning that threatened them: "My anger and my wrath will be poured out on this place—on man and beast, on the trees of the field and on the crops of your land—and it will burn and not be quenched" (Jer 7:4, 20). Paul responds that such a charge is a merely "human argument," one that requires an emphatic negation, "Certainly not." Paul asserts in counterpoint

5. Dunn, *Romans*, 1:111.

6. Commentators differ on whether God's righteousness here refers to his saving justice or to his punitive justice. On the one hand, Romans 1:17 and 3:21 could indicate a reference to God's saving justice. On the other hand, the context of judgment in 3:1–20 could suggest God's punitive justice. To complicate the matter further, Psalm 51, from which Paul takes his cue in Romans 3:4, includes both God's punitive justice (Ps 51: 4) and his saving justice (Ps 51:14). Now I have to confess that tracing the logic of Paul's thought here is like trying to nail jelly to the wall and the jelly fights back UFC style. My own mind went back and forth over 3:5–8 and I wrote several different exegeses about it. In the end, the argument seems the most coherent if 3:5–8 speaks of a punitive righteousness that is juxtaposed with divine fidelity. In other words, Paul is a dialectic theologian, holding God's punitive justice and saving justice in deliberate tension.

that if that were true, "How could God judge the world?" (vv. 5b – 6). God's Word clearly promises judgment for disobedience as part of the covenant (e.g., Deut 27 – 31), and if God reneges and refuses to judge Israel, he has no grounds to judge the rest of the world either. In Paul's mind, God's faithfulness to Israel means that judgment is for the Jew first and then the Gentile, rather than excluding Israel but falling on the Gentiles (see Rom 2:9)!

Second, Paul asks again as an objector, "If my falsehood enhances God's truthfulness and so increases his glory, why am I still condemned as a sinner?" (v. 7). This reiterates the same point stated in v. 5 whereby Israel's failure serves to prove God's uprightness either as judge or as deliverer. God's faithfulness to Israel seemingly guarantees an amnesty for all sinners within Israel. But some even go further and ask, "Why not say — as some slanderously claim that we say — 'Let us do evil that good may result?' " Paul has probably heard that taunt more than once as his Torah-free gospel for Gentiles was regarded as promoting antinomianism (see Acts 21:20 – 21; Rom 6:2). If some Gentiles are seizing on Paul's alleged antinomianism to justify their own antinomian theology, Paul seeks here to shortcircuit it. Ironically, Paul's critique of Jewish presumption on God's favor dovetails with Jewish critiques of Paul's Torah-free gospel for Gentiles; both are said to cultivate indifference toward holiness and righteousness because God is faithful. In response, Paul vehemently declares that those who construct such arguments make God out to be fickle and have come to a point where "their condemnation is just!" (v. 8). Summing up vv. 1 – 8, Doug Moo is on the money when he writes:

> Taken as a whole, then, the passage both affirms the continuing faithfulness of God to his covenant people and argues that his faithfulness in no way precludes God from judging the Jews. Provoking this discussion is the Jewish tendency to interpret God's covenant faithfulness solely in terms of his salvific promises. Paul meets that conception with a broader and deeper view of God's faithfulness — his faithfulness to remain true to his character and to *all* his words: the promises of cursing for disobedience as well as blessing for obedience.[7]

Paul returns to the question of Jewish advantage, and this time sports a negative answer. "What shall we conclude then? Do we have any advantage? Not at all!" (v. 9). Paul's conclusion based on his preceding argument in 2:1 – 3:8 is that the Jewish advantages are, strangely enough, not really all that advantageous.[8] Not because God's faithfulness has failed, but because

---

7. Moo, *Romans*, 180.

8. Paul uses three different words in Rom 3:1, 9 for "advantage" or "value": *perissos* ("abundance"), *ōpheleia* ("benefit"), and *proechō* ("to be in a prominent position"). See BDAG 805, 869, 1107.

Jewish transgression of the covenant has put them on par with Gentiles. Paul provides this explanation, "For we have already made the charge that Jews and Gentiles alike are all under the power of sin" (3:9). Paul's declares that God already has an accusation to be laid against Jews and Gentiles.[9] Their behavior has occurred because both are "under sin." The Greek text does not say "power" as does the NIV, NRSV, and CEB. However, the idea of sin being a hostile power that holds the world within the vestiges of its dark grip is certainly congruent with Paul's thought. The expression anticipates what Paul will say later about the one who lives under the law, namely, that "I am unspiritual, sold as a slave to sin" (Rom 7:14).

### Catalogue of Carnality (3:10–18)

Substantiation for the claim that Jews and Gentiles are under sin is made in vv. 10–18 with a dense collection of citations from the Psalms and one from Isaiah about the depravity of the human subject. Paul launches a barrage of scriptural evidence probably of his own composition and with a degree of interpretative freedom in his wording. The effect is that humanity is without righteousness, without understanding, and without kindness; they don't seek God because they have turned away from God (Ps 14:1–3; cf. Ps 53:1–3; Eccl 7:20); their speech is full of deception and obscenity (Pss 5:9; 140:3; 10:7); people are consumed with bloodlust, wreak havoc everywhere, and do not know peace (Isa 59:7–8; cf. Prov 1:16); and humanity lacks the fear of God (Ps 36:1). This is what it means to be under sin, to act without excuse, and to shun God's glory. In fact, there is an ignoble consistency across Romans 1–3 concerning the sins perpetrated by both Jews and Gentiles, which is precisely why both are captive under sin and are facing a charge from God.

### Summary Argument (3:19–20)

The argument stretching from 1:18–3:20 now reaches its end: "Now we know that whatever the law says, it says to those who are under the law, so that every mouth may be silenced and the whole world held accountable to God. Therefore no one will be declared righteous in God's sight by the works of the law; rather, through the law we become conscious of our sin" (vv. 19–20). Paul's summary here is largely hermeneutical; it is about the proper way to understand the meaning of Torah for Jews and Gentiles. Whereas the Jewish interlocutor reads the Torah as knowledge of God's promises given to Israel and which is to be passed onto Gentiles, Paul hears in the Torah the tragic

---

9. Here the verb *proaitiaomai* means "to reach a charge of guilt prior to an implied time" or to "accuse beforehand" (BDAG 865).

| Recurring Vices in Romans 1–3 | |
|---|---|
| Unrighteousness | 1:18, 29; 2:8; 3:5, 10. |
| Wickedness | 1:30; 2:9; 3:8. |
| Denying the truth | 1:18, 25; 2:8; 3:4. |
| Without excuse | 1:20, 29; 2:1. |
| Arrogance | 1:22, 29–30; 2:1–5, 17, 21. |
| Rejecting God's glory | 1:21, 23, 30; 2:23; 3:11, 18. |
| Debased thinking | 1:21, 28, 31; 2:4; 3:11. |
| Sexual sins | 1:26–28; 2:22. |
| Sins with idolatry | 1:25; 2:22. |
| Violence | 1:29, 30; 3:15. |
| Sinful speech | 1:29; 3:7, 13–15. |
| Blasphemy | 1:30; 2:24; 3:8. |
| Unfaithfulness | 1:31; 3:3. |
| Sins in the heart | 1:21, 24; 2:5, 15. |
| Strife | 1:29; 2:8. |

news of human subjugation in sin.[10] The verdict of the Torah, echoed in the Psalms and in Isaiah, is that God's right to judge is affirmed and no reasonable grounds for a counter-retort exists. God can rightly prosecute his contention against both a rebellious world and an unfaithful Israel. In the end, all of humanity is headed for a "forensic catastrophe."[11]

Like "a piece of Galatians falling out of the sky,"[12] Paul adds that the consequence of the universality of sin, the "therefore," is that "no one will be declared righteous in God's sight by the works of the law" (v. 20). The verb *dikaioō* is forensic and is ordinarily used in a declarative act that pronounces the rightness of a particular party in some matter of dispute.[13] For Jews it meant in particular that they have a right covenantal standing before God. Paul is emphatic that no one, none of all or any flesh (*pasa sarx*), will be

10. Mark A. Seifrid, "Romans," *CONTUOT*, 617.

11. D. A. Carson, "Atonement in Romans 3:21–26," in *The Glory of the Atonement: Biblical, Theological and Practical Perspectives* (ed. C. E. Hill and F. A. James; Downers Grove, IL: InterVarsity, 2004), 120.

12. Oakes, *Reading Romans in Pompeii*, 155.

13. Cf. Bird, *Saving Righteousness of God*, 17–18; Moo, *Romans*, 79–90; Wright, *Justification*, 90–92; Stephen Westerholm, *Perspectives Old and New on Paul: The "Lutheran" Paul and His Critics* (Grand Rapids: Eerdmans, 2004), 261–84.

declared to be in the right before God on the basis of "works of the law." The phrase "works of the law" (*ex ergōn nomou*) has prompted a sway of debate as to its meaning (see Rom 2:15; 3:27–38; Gal 2:16; 3:2, 5, 10).[14] At the risk of simplicity, the main options are:

1. The ceremonial law (e.g., Jerome, Pelagius, Peter Abelard, Martin Bucer)
2. The social boundary markers of the law with specific reference to circumcision, dietary laws, and Sabbath (e.g., James Dunn, N. T. Wright)
3. Keeping the law with a legalistic spirit (e.g., Daniel Fuller, C. E. B. Cranfield)
4. The works prescribed by the law (e.g., Augustine, Luther, Calvin)

The phrase is hard to discern because it is incredibly rare in Jewish usage.[15] On the one hand, the "works of the law" seems to mean no more than the "works that the law requires" and embraces all 613 commandments of the Torah. On the other hand, the phrase cannot be divorced from its social context whereby faithful observance of the law would mean a separation from Gentile social spaces and require the maintenance of boundaries to preserve the purity of Jewish communities.[16] On a third hand (if I can borrow one), the phrase also seems to reflect Jewish sectarian disputes about *halakhah* or the precise manner in which the Torah was to be interpreted and lived. Of these three options, I prefer to describe the "works of the law" as referring to the Jewish way of life as codified in the Torah.[17]

---

14. Cf., e.g., Robert Keith Rapa, *The Meaning of "Works of the Law" in Galatians and Romans* (New York: Peter Lang, 2001); Jacqueline C. R. de Roo, *Works of the Law at Qumran and in Paul* (NTM 13; Sheffield: Sheffield Phoenix, 2006).

15. Cf., e.g., 4QMMT 31; 1QS 5.21, 6.18; *2 Bar.* 57.2.

16. Interestingly Ambrosiaster defines the "law" in 3:21 as "law of the sabbath, the circumcision, the new moon, and revenge," and in 3:28 he defines "works of the law" as "circumcision or new moons or the veneration of the sabbath" (Bray, *Ambrosiaster*, 28).

17. Watson, *Beyond the New Perspective*, 19. I've also argued elsewhere (Michael F. Bird, "What if Martin Luther Had Read the Dead Sea Scrolls? Historical Particularity and Theological Interpretation: Galatians as a Test Case," *JTI* 3 [2009]: 117) that while works of the law means "works that the law requires," it is impossible to eliminate the social and ethnic connotations of the phrase: (1) A cursory glance of Menahem Stern's *Greek and Latin Authors on Jews and Judaism* shows how pagan authors were confused and disgusted by Jewish separation from Gentiles demanded by their distinctive way of life (e.g., Tacitus, *Histories* 5.5). (2) Several pieces of literature assume a default setting of Jews separating from the Gentiles (e.g., Acts 10:28; Gal 2:11–14; *Ep. Arist.* 139). (3) It is surely interesting that in the second century when Justin Martyr discusses the Torah with Trypho the Jew, the first point Justin brings up is Jewish separation from Gentiles (*Dial. Tryph.* 10). (4) Without reducing Paul's remarks about "works" to Jewish attitudes of exclusion and superiority, it is hard to avoid the fact that in Romans and Galatians Paul addresses the question of Jewish boundary makers and rites of passages vis-à-vis Gentile Christians.

If that is the case, what Paul appears to be saying is that taking up Torah observance, in whole or in part, even to the point of proselytizing and joining a Jewish community, will not constitute a "righteousness" that avails before God. A proper reading of the Torah discloses its inability to deliver persons from the evil within themselves. Furthermore, the Torah really serves to declare God's righteous contention against all transgressors; that is, the law brings "consciousness" or "knowledge" of sin.

Let us remember that the Gentile Christians whom Paul addresses probably had at one time or other some degree of affiliation with Judaism. They perhaps once envisaged their departure from paganism to(ward) Judaism as a way of deliverance, a deliverance based on coming to knowledge of the Torah and sharing in Israel's covenantal promises. Yet Paul is telling these Gentile believers that their transference from a pagan life to a Jewish life was like running from the port side to the starboard side of a sinking ship. Paul's argument is that there is something wrong with humanity — all humanity, Jews and Gentiles — that the Torah cannot fix. The place of the Jew and the Gentile is under sin and under judgment. Yet a tension remains because that is not the sum of the story. If God is the rectifier of creation and the faithful sovereign over Israel, how will God deliver Israel and even those among the nations in order to uphold his glory? Enter stage left, the other side of God's righteousness: not the prosecution of divine wrath against humanity, but the provision of divine salvation through God's Son, the Lord Jesus Christ.

## LIVE the Story

Romans 3:1 – 20 proves that Israel has no right of reply to God's verdict against their transgression of the Torah. Indeed, Paul puts their transgression of the Torah under a microscope to show exactly what this transgression looks like and how dehumanizing it is. In a nutshell, Paul gives a most ungrand tour on the sinful nature of the human heart as exposed by God's Torah. In light of that, the topic of sin requires some further exploration as to how our understanding of sin shapes what we think about the human need and its resolution in Christ.

### Putting Sin Back in the Spotlight

The area of "hamartiology" pertains to the study of the doctrine of sin.[18] It is not the most popular doctrine for study, nor is it the most popular subject of sermons in my experience. According to Fleming Rutledge, "it is difficult,

18. See Bird, *Evangelical Theology*, 666 – 83.

nowadays, to gain a hearing for Paul. All this talk about sin! Sophisticated people in the twentieth century long since gave up talking about sin — we talk about obsessive behavior, or neurotic patterns, or deviance, or pathology, or disorder, or whatever (I do this myself), but not sin."[19] Similarly, the famous clinician Karl A. Menninger once wrote a book called *Whatever Happened to Sin?* in which he observed how the language of sin had gradually faded out of usage as a consequent of the rise of the modern therapeutic culture that had gripped Western society. Now if feeling good is your goal, then admitting your sin or even reflecting on your sin was always going to inhibit fuzzy wuzzy feelings of personal self-validation. The upshot was that modern culture shoved sin under the carpet and tried to bury feelings of guilt with self-indulgent and self-affirming mantras. The vain attempt to deal with one's own sins through a mixture of denial and hedonism was always bound to fail because, as the Bible says, "your sin will find you out" (Num 32:23 KJV) and "those who plow evil and those who sow trouble reap it" (Job 4:8 NIV).

But what exactly is sin? Paul has a lot to say about sin, its origins, its appearance, and its consequences. According to Romans, sin entered the world through the disobedience of Adam, with the result of introducing condemnation and death to all of humanity and of constituting Adam's progeny as sinners (5:12, 16, 19). As a result everyone has sinned and fallen short of God's glory (3:23). Furthermore, because humans rejected God, God gave them over to sinful desires (1:24). In this economy of sin and judgment the wages of sin is death (6:23). On either side of the Jew/Gentile divide we find sin because sin was in the world before the law (5:13), those who sin apart from law will perish, and those under the law will have their sins judged by the law (2:12) since the law brings knowledge of our sin (3:20). Sin even uses the law to arouse sinful passions and to foster lawless behavior (7:5–7). Inevitably, then, Jews and Gentiles are both under the power of sin (3:9). Finally, faith is the antithesis of sin since whatever does not come from faith is sin (14:23).

It is clear from Paul's letter to the Romans, especially in the vice lists, that sin is both horizontal and vertical. Obviously sin has terrible consequences for the individual, his or her family, and society at large. Sin corrupts our desires, infects our attitudes, ruins our speech, perverts our sexuality, and drives our conduct. Sin is manifested in theft, anger, hatred, jealousy, lust, lies, greed, gossip, selfishness, and a thousand other sordid vices. Humanity at its lowest ebb is captive in sin like a fly in a spider's web. Humanity in sin becomes little more than a brute beast that exercises base instincts for a mixture of survival

19. Rutledge, *Not Ashamed of the Gospel*, 176.

and self-gratification. However, despite the horrible consequences that sin has for the individual, family, and friends, and even for social structures, we must not lose sight of the fact that sin is ultimately an offense against God. He is the primary party offended by our sin. Sin offends God's sovereignty, holiness, and glory. Hence Paul's words: "For although they knew God, they neither glorified him as God nor gave thanks to him, but their thinking became futile and their foolish hearts were darkened" (Rom 1:21). Sin is like a form of cosmic sedition or a repetitive mutiny against God's will as expressed in his common grace and providence over humankind.

I tend to think of sin as primarily about humanity's feeble efforts to put themselves on the throne in place of God. One of the most commonly played songs at funerals is Frank Sinatra's "I Did It My Way." In many ways, the title of the song aptly summarizes the nature of sin. Sin represents the attempt to displace God and the desire to deify the self. Humans defy their Creator, shake their puny little fists at the heavens, and say, "I will do it my way." Such an attitude means trying to usurp the prerogatives of deity, acting with impunity before the divine throne, and demanding immunity from any consequences that would warrant judgment. To insist, even in one's funeral, to having done things "my way" is to insist on the right to define right and wrong or good and evil without reference to God. Rage, rejection, and rebellion against God combined with the deification of the self: this is the essence of sin. Sin, in the end, is a form of the "Frank Sinatra Syndrome," where human beings delude themselves into thinking that their life was lived "my way" and not "God's way." If we usurp for ourselves the sovereignty of the God who is love, we will become obsessed with living a life ruled by anything other than the divine way of love. In the end sin leads to a consuming love of self with no room for the love of God and a diminishing capacity to love others.

Let me add that this leads to a bad situation for us. The English Puritan Ralph Venning wrote a small book called *The Sinfulness of Sin*. The title sounds tautological, I know. However, I think the title conveys an important point, namely, that sin is utterly consumed with its own nature of hostility toward the holiness of God. As Venning wrote: "sin is sinful, all sinful, only sinful, altogether sinful and always sinful."[20] Humanity in sin becomes all sinful. In the domain of theology this tenet is usually called the doctrine of total depravity. That is not to say that human beings are incapable of goodness or that they are as maximally evil as they can be. No, total depravity simply means that from the cradle to the grave our natural inclination is toward sin, and sin is like a virus that infects every facet of our existence

20. Ralph Venning, *The Sinfulness of Sin* (Edinburgh: Banner of Truth, 1965), 31.

including desire, intellect, imagination, and behavior. Sin leaves us stranded in a sand pit of human misery where we sink deeper and deeper into its depths. Because we are consumed in sin, the solution must be to be consumed with something else. The abounding nature of sin in the human subject can only be defeated by the superabounding grace of God expressed toward us in Jesus Christ.

### Preaching Sin to an Amoral World

How would one preach a passage as confronting as Romans 3:1–20 to, say, an urban congregation full of Millennials and Gen-Ys who were reared on a bunch of political correctness and self-help mantras from postmodern priestesses? How do you convince a class of cultural narcissists whose consuming passion is twizzlers and Twitter that they are sinners and that they need the redemption that comes by way of Christ Jesus? How do you get them to look at their behavior through a biblical worldview and not just through the instantaneous gratification of Google glasses? I submit that what one needs here is not just some good biblical hermeneutics for handling the rhetorical jujitsu of 3:1–20 but also some good cultural hermeneutics for reading the values and struggles of people immersed in the often tragic complexities of twenty-first-century urban life.

In terms of preaching on "sin," I cannot speak definitively about the USA, but I have learned from my experience in the UK and Australia that it is increasingly difficult to speak convincingly about "sin" to unbelieving audiences. It is difficult in a secular and post-Christian culture where younger generations are not only biblically illiterate, but the increasing number of "nones" (i.e., those folks with no religious connections) simply have no concept of what the words "God," "sin," "Christ," and "salvation" even mean. Let me say that I am a Gen-Xer, and growing up as a "none" everything I knew about Christianity I learned from Ned Flanders of the TV sitcom *The Simpsons*. Not exactly a perfect introduction to Christianity and the Bible. Sad to say, the situation has only got worse for Gen-Y and the Millennials, who entirely lack a Christian frame of reference and even basic knowledge of how biblical language is echoed in modern idioms. To young people like these, you cannot just tweet them Romans 6:23, "For the wages of sin is death but the gift of God is eternal life in Christ Jesus our Lord," because the word "sin" has no resonance or affront.

To most unchurched folks, the word "sin" means something like "naughty but fun." Sin is something opposed by moralizing geriatrics and happily indulged in by hip guys and gals who brazenly assert their independence against any authority that thinks can boss them around. Sin is one of those

Victorian hang-ups that we need to get over so we can get on and enjoy life to the full.

For example, near where I used to live were two businesses that both used the word "sin" in their trading name. There was an adult product shop called *Sinsational* and a tattoo parlor called *Sin the Skin*. Reflect for a moment as to how the word "sin" is used by those two businesses as a marketing tool to actually entice people into their premises. The concept of sin here is not affronting or offensive; it is rather a point of attraction. I like sinning, so I should go and buy some adult sex products or get a tattoo (I'm not prejudging what people do to spice up their marital life or whether Christians should get tattoos, just saying that these businesses were using "sin" as a positive marketing device). Alan Mann does a good job of tracking this same trend in his book *Atonement for a "Sinless" Society*, where he points out that Western culture no longer has a meaningful concept of sin and guilt. People see themselves as basically good and victims of economic, political, and social forces. People are aware, however, that their real self (who they are) and their ideal self (who they wish they were) are not identical. Thus, they are more susceptible to feelings of shame and likely to respond to a message of atonement that focuses on becoming whole and healed persons.[21]

If that is where our culture is at with "sin," then all bets are off, and we have to start from scratch. I suggest we stop using the word "sin" and find a new term to designate what is meant by the biblical words that we normally translate as sin, sinner, and sinful.[22] My own suggestion is that we start talking about "evil" instead. Whereas the word "sin" can get easily brushed off by our biblically illiterate contemporaries as just a code word for religious moralizing, the word *evil* has far more connection and capital with audiences. That is because people know about evil; they've seen evil either on the TV or in their own broken neighborhoods, and deep down they are very, very afraid of evil.

Google has as their motto, "Don't Be Evil." Whether Google has actually lived up to their own motto is an open question, and some of the deals they did about filters and freedom with the Chinese government might leave us with pause for thought. But the notion of "evil" is on peoples' moral compasses, and its very mention, like George W. Bush's "Axis of Evil," immediately arouses our attention. Evil is something we feel obligated to run from and when able, to destroy. That is because evil threatens all that we value and love: life, freedom, and the pursuit of happiness. Christianity takes evil far

21. Alan Mann, *Atonement for "Sinless" Society: Engaging with an Emerging Culture* (Milton Keynes, UK: Paternoster, 2005).

22. For a summary of the main Hebrew and Greek words for sin, see Clayton N. Jefford, "Sin," in *EDB* 1224–26.

more seriously than any other religion. In the Christian worldview, evil is not merely an outward illusion, not just the product of human desiring, not an eternal force in a symbiotic relationship with good, nor simply our name for the social and biological evolutionary forces that inhibit the propagation of our species. No, evil is an intrusive invasion into the good world that God created. Evil is not the way it is supposed to be. God's plan to put the world to rights will be achieved by vanquishing evil once and for all, and that vanquishing began with the victorious death of the Lord Jesus Christ.

## Finding Evil in the Mirror

In all of our anxiety about evil, whether we associate evil with things like barbaric atrocities in Iraq or the sadistic kidnappers like Ariel Castro, we must inevitably confront evil within ourselves. We have to ask the question: Am I evil? Usually most people's reaction to that question is, "No, of course not. There are seven billion people on this planet I haven't killed, and I help the old lady next door with her internet connection." But while we may not be evil in the same sense as a Joseph Stalin or an Osama Bin Laden, people will usually admit their moral imperfections and their capacity for evil. That's when I love to quote from Aleksandr Solzhenitsyn's *The Gulag Archipelago*: "If only there were evil people somewhere insidiously committing evil deeds, and it were necessary only to separate them from the rest of us and destroy them. But the line dividing good and evil cuts through the heart of every human being. And who is willing to destroy a piece of his own heart?"[23] Do you find the same struggle within yourself? What are you really capable of? Are you both victim and perpetrator of evil? These are the types of questions we need to be confronting people with in terms of their own capacity to see the evil within themselves.

I adore musical theater, so I loved *Les Misérables*, both the stage show and the movie, because the characters show the vastly different shades of humanity at its best and at its worst. I tell people that in my head, I like to think of myself as a modern Jean Valjean — someone who is strong yet merciful, driven and yet compassionate. However, what I think in my head is one thing, but down in my heart I know I'm more like a cross between the characters of Thénadiers and Javert, or a mixture of desperate brutality and cold self-righteousness. To use imagery from another musical, *Whistle Down the Wind,* an escaped convict tries to convince a teenage girl, who thinks he's Jesus come back, that he is not really Jesus. So he tells her, "If you look deep down inside my eyes, do you see a savior, a prophet, or a priest, or do you only see the blackness there?

23. Aleksandr Solzhenitsyn, *The Gulag Archipelago, 1918–1956: An Experiment in Literary Investigation* (New York: Harper Row, 1974), 1.168.

That's the nature of the beast." A sober and honest evaluation of ourselves might prove that we are not likely to appear at the Hague for crimes against humanity any time soon. However, an examination of the deeper recesses of our hearts, where we lock away our most insidious desires, will prove that deep down is not Valjean but Javert, not a beauty but a beast.

Such introspection can be the catalyst for coming to faith as exemplified by a story I once heard from D. A. Carson about the conversion story of a successful career woman:

> He [Mark Dever] introduced me to a woman. She was one of the editors of a Washington political weekly, she was about fifty, a PhD in journalism, a shrewd woman, divorced, two grown sons. He [Mark] said to her, "Tell Don how you got converted." Well, it turned out that she was a self-confessed postmodernist through and through and through, a complete relativist; good and evil is defined entirely by your social structure. You can't even say that Hitler was wrong because in his own lights he was right. There were a lot of people who did believe in Aryan supremacy. I don't like it and from my point of view it was wrong, but from his own perspective he thought what he was doing was right. And that was the frame of reference.
>
> Eventually she came along to a Bible study on the book of Mark that he [Mark Dever] had set up, an evangelistic Bible study, not because she was terribly interested.... She liked literature and this was studying the Bible, it was literature. Then she went off to Papua New Guinea four to five years ago during one of those political changeovers. And while she was there, just before she left, there was a priest who was arrested; he'd been there for thirty-five years or so, and just before he was due to retire and go back to America, he was arrested for paedophilia. Turned out that, as the case unpacked, he had sodomized at least 200 boys.
>
> For some reason this story grabbed her. When you start thinking of all the damage this would do to the boys and probably their marriages and because abused people often become abusers and all the people they might abuse. Where does this all end? It just really grabbed her and she came home really shaken by this and she told Mark all of this and Mark smiled and said, "Was it wicked?" And she said, "Well, probably this priest was himself abused by someone; probably he's a victim himself. There are reasons why people do these kinds of things." Mark said, "The Bible says that the sins of the fathers are visited upon the children to the third and fourth generation. All that you've told me is that sin is social. It is not merely individual. Sin has social dynamics that affect other people. I'm not asking

> whether or not there are things that help to explain why this man did certain things; the question is, the things that he did, were they wicked?"
>
> She just couldn't get away from the question. Was it wicked? Was it wicked? She was losing her sleep. She was not able to concentrate. One night some weeks later she woke up in the middle of the night, and this question was coming through her mind again and again and again. Was it wicked? Was it wicked? She stared out the window, she couldn't say "yes," but she couldn't believe "no." Finally, in a burst of intensity she said, "This was wicked. This was evil." Then it dawned on her. But that means that there is a category for wicked, maybe it means that she is wicked. Some time later she became a Christian.[24]

What I take away from that story is that once people find a category to hang their sense of moral "oughtness" on, as C.S. Lewis called it—whether that is sin, shame, evil, or wickedness—the reflexive thing for them to do is to reflect on what planet they sit in that moral universe. "Who am I?" they can ask, in a universe where there really is right and wrong and where there really is good and evil. The best strategy we can use in preaching the gospel to the unchurched is not to throw churchy language at folks about "sin" and "transgression," but to find a way to connect them to a moral universe, a moral universe in which God is judge and they are culpable to God for their shameful behavior. Then and only then will redemption, rescue, and reconciliation begin to make sense.

In preaching Romans 3:1–20 to an audience, especially one filled with Millennials and Nones, the challenge is to describe convincingly Paul's message about how humanity is both washed adrift in a sea of evil and yet also acts as seafaring marauders within it. Furthermore, we must declare with Paul that this evil, corporate and individual, must meet with the judgment of God. Evil is not something that is limited to dictators and mass murderers; rather, evil lurks within the recesses of our minds and finds a highway of delight in the veins of our own bodies. What is more, God's response to evil is his righteous rage and his holy justice. If God is to put this evil-ridden world to right, he must put us out of it. The solution to evil is not a purified ethnicity, not moral effort, nor even good education. The moral degeneration and ethical dystrophy of human existence requires something far more effective than rules and regulation; it needs redemption and renewal. But from where can such a saving justice come?

---

24. Don Carson. DC 37 Eliza Ferrie Lecture Series 2001. Sydney, Australia. "Righteousness and Justification in Paul." Tape number 4. Dated 20–08–01.

CHAPTER 6

# Romans 3:21 – 31

## LISTEN to the Story

21 But now apart from the law the righteousness of God has been
made known, to which the Law and the Prophets testify. 22 This righteousness is given through faith in Jesus Christ to all who believe. There
is no difference between Jew and Gentile, 23 for all have sinned and fall
short of the glory of God, 24 and all are justified freely by his grace through
the redemption that came by Christ Jesus. 25 God presented Christ as
a sacrifice of atonement, through the shedding of his blood — to be
received by faith. He did this to demonstrate his righteousness, because in
his forbearance he had left the sins committed beforehand unpunished —
26 he did it to demonstrate his righteousness at the present time, so as to be
just and the one who justifies those who have faith in Jesus.
27 Where, then, is boasting? It is excluded. Because of what law? The
law that requires works? No, because of the law that requires faith. 28 For
we maintain that a person is justified by faith apart from the works of the
law. 29 Or is God the God of Jews only? Is he not the God of Gentiles too?
Yes, of Gentiles too, 30 since there is only one God, who will justify the
circumcised by faith and the uncircumcised through that same faith.
31 Do we, then, nullify the law by this faith? Not at all! Rather, we uphold
the law.

*Listening to the texts in the story*: Exodus 6, 25; Leviticus 16 – 17; Isaiah 53; Psalm 98; 2 Maccabees 7:38 – 39; 4 Maccabees 6:27 – 29; 17:20 – 22.

To recap, the argument spanning Romans 1:18 – 3:20 is that God will not allow humanity to exist indefinitely in a state of rebellion against him, nor will he permit Israel to continue forever in transgression of the Torah. The ungodly and disobedient must be brought to account before the tribunal of divine judgment (2:3, 5 – 16; 3:6, 19 – 20). But judgment is not the only part of the story, and we must remember that Paul opened his letter with the good news of salvation in Jesus Messiah for Jews and Gentiles (1:3 – 4, 16 – 17).

Thus Paul has embedded an inherent tension in his letter between the good news of salvation in Jesus on the one hand, and his narration of God's intent to prosecute his contention against sinful Gentiles and disobedient Jews on the other hand. The tension even flows into Paul's gospel, which declares God's plan to judge the secret things of people's heart through Jesus Christ (2:16) and how the gospel is the power of God for the salvation of Jews and Gentiles (1:16–17).[1]

So what happens when God's impartiality as cosmic judge of the world meets with God's covenantal faithfulness to bring salvation to the world through Israel? How does God's punitive justice comport with God's saving justice? On what plane can God be both the judge of the wicked and the justifier of ungodly? That tension, of course, was not new, since God in the biblical story is always portrayed as both judge and deliverer. Paul's answer to this duality is given in Romans 3:21–4:25.[2] Here Paul begins to expound the gospel at theological depth by describing how God brings salvation to all who believe in Messiah Jesus. Sin, death, and condemnation are not the last word. God has a final word, his name is Jesus the Christ, and this word brings justification from condemnation, redemption from slavery, and reconciliation from hostility. In the end, human unrighteousness cannot indefinitely obstruct God's righteousness. God's intent to rectify, redeem, reconcile, and restore will in the end triumph over the travails of the present evil age.

Paul proceeds in this manner: (1) Romans 3:21–26 is the epicenter of his gospel with its exposition in the categories of justification, redemption, and sacrifice. (2) Thereafter, 3:27–31 is a defense of the gospel against objectors who advocate a form of ethnocentric nomism whereby God's righteousness is tied strictly to Israel, so that to be justified one must convert to Judaism. Then, 4:1–25 demonstrates the conformity of Paul's gospel to the pattern of Scripture; specifically, the story of Abraham proves that God justifies Gentiles as Gentiles on the condition of faith alone.

### Righteousness Revealed (3:21)

In rhetorical terms, Romans 3:21–26 is an *exornatio*, an elaboration of the *propositio* announced in Romans 1:16–17 concerning the revelation of God's

1. Cf. Fitzmyer (*Romans*, 307): "This Pauline message of judgment is what the Christian needs to hear first ... and in the light of that message the message of justification by grace through faith takes on new meaning. It is only in light of divine judgment according to human deeds that the justification of the sinner by grace through faith is rightly seen."

2. Wright, "Romans," 10:440.

righteousness in the gospel: "But now apart from the law the righteousness of God has been made known, to which the Law and the Prophets testify." Paul frequently uses "but now" (*nuni de*) to mark the new eschatological moment where God's saving power invades the present time (e.g., Rom 6:22; 7:6; 1 Cor 15:20; 2 Cor 6:2; Eph 2:13; Col 1:22). The events spoken about in the gospel, Jesus' death and resurrection, prove to be the eschatological turning point of world history. It conveys "all the flavor of Paul's inexhaustible excitement at what God had done in Jesus the Messiah."[3] "But now" implies a temporal contrast with what has gone before. Whereas the whole world stands in the dock waiting for divine judgment and there is no positive status to be attained before God by adherence to the works of the law (so 3:19–20), even so, condemnation need not be the end result. There is a new factor to be reckoned with "now." There is a new state of affairs that gives hope to the human predicament. There is a new event that is already imposing itself upon the morass of the present evil age. This new event is the revelation of God's righteousness in Messiah Jesus.

I have already discussed the "righteousness of God" (*dikaiosynē theou*) in the commentary on Romans 1:17. To briefly recap, such a phrase should be located in the spheres of creation and covenant. God's righteousness describes the actions whereby God rectifies creation and shows himself faithful to the covenant. God's righteousness is chiefly a way of designating his saving action as it is expressed in his feats of deliverance for his people. The righteousness of God then is the character of God embodied and enacted in his saving works. The principle benefit for humanity is that this new unveiling[4] of God's righteousness enables persons to be justified by faith in Messiah Jesus.

Note Paul's emphasis that the revelation of God's saving righteousness in the gospel is simultaneously discontinuous and continuous with the law. To begin with, when Paul says that the righteousness of God is manifested "apart from the law," he means, first, that obedience to the precepts of the law is not the basis for access to salvation. In other words, performance of the works of the law, getting your Jewish lifestyle on, will not put you in the right. Second, adherence to the law does not demarcate the community who will experience God's justifying verdict. The law is not a badge of covenant membership in the messianic age. Alternatively, "the Law and the Prophets testify to" this saving righteousness. According to Brian Rosner, Paul sees the law as possessing a

3. Ibid., 10:569. Cf. Byrne, *Romans*, 122: "'Now,' at this 'eleventh hour' on the apocalyptic time-scale when all is rushing to destruction and ruin, God has intervened to convert the situation of unrighteousness and 'wrath' into one of righteousness and hope."

4. The perfect tense of *pephanerōtai* does not signify the ongoing manifestation of God's righteousness but instead the definitive new eschatological state that is revealed in God's righteousness.

prophetic function.[5] The law (i.e., Torah) with its stories and sacrificial system all pointed ahead to the redemptive work of Israel's messianic king. Thus "the Law and the Prophets"[6] bear witness to God's promise that he would reveal his salvation in the death and resurrection of the Messiah.

This promise periodically emerges in the scenes of the biblical story like a flashing light pointing people to an emergency exit. This salvific promise is sometimes tacitly mentioned, elsewhere typified by example, and even explicitly prophesied in an array of verses, visions, victims, and victories in the biblical discourse. For instance:

The famous *protoevangelium* promises a skull-crushing victory to Eve's offspring over the serpent (Gen 3:15).
God credits righteousness to the pagan man Abram, who answers his call (Gen 12–15).
We hear that the scepter will never depart from Judah (Gen 49:10).
An explicit link is made between blood and atonement (Lev 17:11).
There is a prophecy of a future prophet-like-Moses (Deut 18:15).
David's line will rule over Israel (2 Sam 7:11–14).
Some of the prophets promise a new covenant (Jer 31; Ezek 34; Hos 2).
Isaiah writes about the ministry of the Suffering Servant (Isa 53).
Images of a future Davidic shepherd king will lead postexilic Israel (Isa 11:1–5; Jer 23:5; Mic 5:1–2; Zech 9:9–13).

All these images from the Law and the Prophets are billboards pointing ahead to God's salvation in the death and resurrection of Jesus the Messiah.

### Faith of/in Jesus Christ (3:22a)

Paul then adds, "This [God's] righteousness is given through faith in Jesus Christ to all who believe" (v. 22). Here we approach a really, really big interpretive puzzle that has vexed many exegetical minds. To begin with, the verse is elliptical as no verb is present, and no explicit mention is made as to precisely how God's righteousness "is given" (NJB, NIV) or "comes" (CEB) to believers.[7] On top of that, the phrase *pisteōs Iēsou Christou* could be rendered as either an objective genitive with "faith in Jesus Christ," or as a

5. Brian S. Rosner, *Paul and the Law: Keeping the Commandments of God* (NSBT 31; Downers Grove, IL: InterVarsity, 2013), 135–58.

6. On this expression see Matt 5:17; 7:12; 11:13; 22:40; Luke 16:16; John 1:45; Acts 24:14; 28:23; 2 Macc 15:9; 4 Macc 18:10; with discussion in Talbert, *Romans*, 108.

7. Several translations (e.g., KJV, NASB, NRSV, NET, and ESV) do not supply a verb in v. 22a, which keeps close to the Greek, though unfortunately it does render the translation rather awkward to read in English.

subjective genitive with the "faithfulness of Christ."[8] The difference is whether faith is put in Christ or whether Christ is the one who himself exercises faith or faithfulness (*pistis* can mean both). Similar verses occur elsewhere in Paul's letters (Gal 2:16, 20; 3:22; Phil 3:9; Eph 3:12), and this has led to an intense biblical and theological debate surrounding the *pistis Christou* question. In sum, the debate pertains to whether God's righteousness is revealed in the human act of faith, or whether God's righteousness is revealed in Jesus' own faithfulness to his messianic task.[9]

| **Romans 3:22 in Comparison** | |
|---|---|
| NIV | CEB |
| This righteousness is given through **faith in Jesus Christ** to all who believe. | God's righteousness comes through **the faithfulness of Jesus Christ** for all who have faith in him. |

The debate cannot be settled on the basis of semantic or syntactical factors alone, but only as informed by context.[10] Following the majority of scholars, I gravitate toward the objective genitive and render *pisteōs Iēsou Christou* as "faith in Jesus Christ." This is because the grammatical placement of *pistis* most naturally suggests that Paul was indicating that Christ was the object of faith.[11] The context of the verse also seems to zone in on the human response in appropriating God's saving work by expressing faith and loyalty in Jesus Christ, especially with the following phrase "for all who believe," making an objective genitive again more probable. In addition, the objective genitive has been overwhelmingly preferred in the history of interpretation and translation, rendering the subjective genitive interpretation, barring a few exceptions, something of a recent novelty.[12]

8. For those unfamiliar with the Greek case system, a "genitive" often describes those nouns that are possessive and that normally modify another noun, like "Bob's spanner," where "Bob's" indicates ownership of the "spanner."

9. See Michael F. Bird and Preston Sprinkle, ed., *The Faith of Jesus Christ: Exegetical, Biblical, and Theological Reflections* (Milton Keynes, UK: Paternoster, 2009).

10. Cf. Porter, *Idioms*, 95; Wallace, *Greek Grammar beyond the Basics*, 115–16.

11. Stanley E. Porter and Andrew W. Pitts, "πίστις with a Preposition and Genitive Modifier: Lexical, Semantic and Syntactic Considerations in the πίστις Χριστοῦ Discussion," in *The Faith of Jesus Christ* (ed. M. F. Bird and P. M. Sprinkle), 33–53. Cf. Byrne (*Romans*, 124–25): "To be more precise, it is 'Christ-qualified' faith in God—faith in God precisely as the One who raised Jesus from the dead."

12. Cf. R. Barry Matlock, "The Rhetoric of πίστις in Paul: Galatians 2.16, 3.22, Romans 3.22, and Philippians 3.9," *JSNT* 30 (2007): 173–203; idem, "Saving Faith: The Rhetoric and Semantics of πίστις in Paul," in *The Faith of Jesus Christ* (ed. M. F. Bird and P. M. Sprinkle), 73–89. Among Romans commentaries, see esp. Dunn, *Romans*, 1:166–67; Fitzmyer, *Romans*, 345–46; Moo, *Romans*, 224–26; Hacker, *Römer*, 87; Schreiner, *Romans*, 181–86; Esler, *Romans*, 157–59; Jewett, *Romans*, 275.

Be that as it may, there is something suspiciously right about the subjective genitive that makes it so alluring.[13] The concept of God's righteousness being revealed in the faithfulness of Jesus Christ fits squarely into Paul's christocentric view of salvation. Elsewhere the faithfulness and obedience of Jesus Christ have important functions in salvation especially in Romans 5:12–21 and Philippians 2:5–11.[14] On either side of Romans 3:21–26, Paul speaks of the faithfulness of God (3:3) and of the faith(fulness) of Abraham (4:12). We might also ask the provocative question: How can *human* faith meaningfully reveal *God's* righteousness? Would it not make better theological sense to say that God's righteousness is revealed in the faithfulness of Jesus the Messiah?[15]

My solution to this debate is to try to balance the theological, christological, and anthropological elements present in Romans 3:22. We are presented with a divine saving action, executed in Jesus Christ and appropriated by humanity through faith. The noun *pistis* is most naturally a concept associated with human believing and supports an objective genitive of "faith in Christ." But even so, God's righteousness is revealed in *Christos*, which stands for the manifestation of salvation in the faithfulness, death, and resurrection of Jesus Christ. In which case the faithfulness of Jesus Christ is implied not in *pistis* but in *Christos*. On such a reading, *pisteōs Iēsou Christou* refers to the event of the gospel itself and implies an underlying narrative about Jesus Christ as the subject of divine deliverance and object of human believing.[16] According to Francis Watson, "the christological qualification of Paul's faith terminology is intended to refer neither to 'the faithfulness of Christ' nor to 'faith in Christ' but, more open-endedly, to the faith that pertains to God's saving action in Christ—originating in it, participating in it, and orientated towards it."[17] The "faith of Jesus Christ" (KJV), much like the "love of God," is perhaps deliberately ambiguous and can elicit various connotations and connections to the notion of divine and human faith(fulness).[18] We can loosely paraphrase

13. Cf. e.g., Witherington, *Romans*, 101; Wright, "Romans," 10:467–68; Johnson, *Romans*, 59–62; Matera, *Romans*, 93–94, 97; Reasoner, *Romans through the Centuries*, 39–40; Campbell, *Deliverance of God*, 610–13.

14. Cf. Richard Longenecker, "The Foundational Conviction of New Testament Christology: The Obedience/Faithfulness/Sonship of Christ," in *Jesus of Nazareth, Lord and Christ* (ed. J. B. Green and M. Turner; Grand Rapids: Eerdmans, 1994), 473–88.

15. Douglas A. Campbell, "The Faithfulness of Jesus Christ in Romans 3:22," in *The Faith of Jesus Christ* (ed. M. F. Bird and P. M. Sprinkle), 62–66, though the notion of trusting in God's righteousness is not unknown in the Old Testament (as in Isa 51:5–8 and Dan 9:16; Dunn, *Romans*, 1:165, 167).

16. Cf. Francis Watson, "By Faith (of Christ): an Exegetical Dilemma and its Scriptural Solution," 147–64, and Preston Sprinkle "πίστις Χριστοῦ as an Eschatological Event," 165–84, both in *The Faith of Jesus Christ*.

17. Watson, *Paul, Judaism, and the Gentiles*, 255.

18. Bryan, *Preface to Romans*, 109–10.

v. 22 by saying that "God's righteousness comes to humanity through faith in his saving action revealed in Jesus' faithfulness, death, and resurrection for everyone who believes in him."

### All Have Sinned (3:22b–23)

Paul explains why the righteousness of God revealed in Jesus Christ is desperately needed: "There is no difference between Jew and Gentile, for all have sinned and fall short of the glory of God" (vv. 22b–23). The remark that "there is no difference" is a brief but crucial point.[19] The noun *diastolē* for "difference" will reappear in 10:12, where Paul says that there is no difference between Jew and Greek as both call on the same Lord. *Diastolē* is used in Romans to indicate the equality of Jews and Gentiles in judgment (1:18–3:20) and in salvation (9:1–11:36). The reason for the lack of distinction among people is that "all have sinned[20] and fall short of the glory of God." That is to say, all of humanity has either exchanged the glory of God for inglorious idolatry (1:23) or failed to seek God's glory (2:10), which is why they are liable to divine judgment (3:19–20). The result is a lack of differentiation between "all"; whether it be in the categories of ethnicity, economics, religion, or political power, all share in the shame of sin and as a result are shunned[21] from God's glory and honor.[22]

### Justification, Redemption, Sacrifice (3:24–25a)

Paul then uses three images for salvation—justification, redemption, and sacrifice—to explain how God's righteousness becomes a saving event for those who believe in Jesus Christ.

First, "all are justified freely by his grace." On *justification*, a law court metaphor,[23] I've already argued that justification is God's declaration that a person is forgiven, acquitted, and in a right relationship with God based on Jesus' death and resurrection. Justification is the act whereby God creates a

19. The NIV adds "between Jew and Gentile," which is not in the original Greek, but rightly captures the sense.

20. The verb *hēmarton* is probably a gnomic aorist and signifies an act occurring over time and is representative of something that regularly occurs (Porter, *Idioms*, 38–39). It is not an allusion to Adam's sin (contra, e.g., Dunn, *Romans*, 1:168) and should probably be translated with a present tense with "for all sin."

21. The verb *hystereō* ("fall short") has connotations of failure, inferiority, and lackingness, and in the passive voice would mean that God deliberately deprives them of his glory.

22. There may also be a connection with Adam's sin here since some Jewish literature emphasized Adam's loss of glory at the fall (*Gen. Rab.* 12.6; *3 Bar.* 4.16; *Apoc. Mos.* 21.6). Correspondingly there was an end-time hope for Adam's glory to be regained (*Apoc. Mos.* 39.2; *1 En.* 50.1; *4 Ezra* 7.122–25; 1QS 4.23; CD 3.20; 1QH 17.15; see further Dunn, *Romans*, 1:168; Fitzmyer, *Romans*, 347).

23. Morris, *Romans*, 178; Wright, "Romans," 10:398–401; idem, *Justification*, 68–70, 90–92.

new people, with a new status, in the new covenant, as part of the new age. The present participle *dikaioumenoi* does not mean that justification is a process, as if believers are in the process of becoming righteous; rather, it is an acknowledgment that God's justifying verdict covers a temporal span between Christ's death and Christ's *parousia* since justification is both a present experience (Rom 3:24, 26, 28; 4:25; 5:1, 9; 8:30) and something set for the future (Rom 2:13; 3:30; 10:9–10).

The emphasis falls squarely on the unmerited mercy by which this justifying verdict is given. It is made "freely" and "by his grace"; that is, God justifies sinners without cost to them and without external causes that prompt him to be generous to them. Believers do not warrant or win God's favor by meticulous Torah observance, cultic ritual, seeking divine patronage, or cultivating the Roman virtue of *pietas*. Instead, as James Harrison observes, "Paul's emphasis on the unilateral nature of divine grace was directed against the idea that God was compelled by acts of human piety to reciprocate beneficently."[24] Justification is a gift rooted exclusively in God's undeserved favor. No one ever earns the right to be righteous before God; indeed they cannot (Rom 3:20), which is why salvation must be all of grace (see Eph 2:8–9; Titus 3:5). In the words of Stuhlmacher: "The ground and realization of justification reside in God's grace alone, as it appeared in Jesus Christ, and only the faith awakened by God through the gospel allows a person to participate in it."[25] This image of justification means that believers have no fear of the day of judgment because the verdict has already been declared to them in advance, and that verdict is not "condemnation" but "righteousness" (see Rom 5:1; 8:1, 30).

Second, "the redemption that came by Christ Jesus." The image of salvation as *redemption* is common in both Paul (Rom 8:23; 1 Cor 1:30; 6:20; Eph 1:7, 14; 4:30; Col 1:14; 1 Tim 2:6; Titus 2:14) and in the wider New Testament (Matt 20:28; Mark 10:45; Luke 21:28; Heb 9:15; 1 Pet 1:18).[26] The mention of redemption would bring to the mind of Jewish readers the exodus, which was the great act of liberation that God wrought for the Israelites by bringing them out of Egypt (e.g., Exod 6:6; Ps 110:9), and also God's

---

24. James R. Harrison, *Paul's Language of Grace in its Graeco-Roman Context* (WUNT 2.172; Tübingen: Mohr Siebeck, 2003), 18.

25. Stuhlmacher, *Romans*, 67. Consider also Calvin (*Calvin's Commentaries: The Epistles of Paul the Apostle to the Romans and Thessalonians* [trans. R. Mackenzie; Grand Rapids: Eerdmans,1960], 74–75): "There is, perhaps, no passage in the whole of Scripture which more strikingly illustrates the efficacy of this righteousness, for it shows that the mercy of God is the efficient cause, Christ with His blood the material cause, faith conceived by the Word the formal or instrumental cause, and the glory of both the divine justice and goodness the final cause."

26. Whether redemption means the "payment of a price" or just means "deliverance," the former is more likely given the context of a "free" justification and that sacrifice involves the payment of a price in blood (see discussion in Schreiner, *Romans*, 190–91).

promise to the Babylonian exiles for a new day of redemption in a new exodus (e.g., Isa 51–52). The Torah also knew of a ransom that had to be paid when perpetrators were liable for crimes and could buy their way out of it by paying a ransom to the offended party (e.g., Exod 21:28–30).

By and large, however, redemption was associated with the release of captured prisoners of war and the manumission of slaves from service (e.g., Exod 21:8; Lev 25:25; *Ep. Arist.* 12.35; Josephus, *Ant.* 12.27).[27] Paul's notion of redemption is that it occurs "in Christ Jesus," within the realm of association with Christ, and is determined by his death and resurrection. God ransoms believers from sin by the payment of the blood of his own Son (see esp. Eph 1:7; also 1 Cor 6:20). Paul explains in Romans 3:24 the agential and locative forces that cause justification by way of reference to two prepositional phrases, i.e., justification occurs *through* redemption and *in* Christ Jesus. Grace is the efficient cause of justification, but its instrumental cause is redemption, and this redemption is of Christ.[28]

Third, "God presented Christ as a sacrifice of atonement."[29] A torrid debate surrounds the meaning of the word *hilastērion*, which the NIV and NRSV translate as "sacrifice of atonement." There is widespread agreement among commentators that the background to this word comes from the sacrificial cultus prescribed by the Torah.[30] The *hilastērion* designated the "mercy seat," the cover of the ark of the covenant over which Yahweh appeared on the Day of Atonement, and over which the blood of sacrifices was poured (see Exod 25:17–22; Lev 16:13–15; Heb 9:5). This is why the NET opts for "God publicly displayed him at his death as the mercy seat." The sacrificial context is underscored further by the reference to "the shedding of his blood"

27. Leon Morris, *The Apostolic Preaching of the Cross* (Grand Rapids: Eerdmans, 1965), 11–29; David Williams, *Paul's Metaphors: Their Context and Character* (Peabody, MA: Hendrickson, 1999), 122–24. Frank Matera (*Romans*, 103) comments: "As God had redeemed Israel from slavery and exile, so God has redeemed Israel—and with Israel the Gentiles—from slavery once more. In this act of redemption, God redeems Israel and the nations from the slavery of sin, under whose power all find themselves."

28. Constantine R. Campbell, *Paul and Union with Christ: An Exegetical and Theological Study* (Grand Rapids: Zondervan, 2012), 74, 114–15.

29. The phrase "in his blood" (*en tō autou haimati*) could modify "sacrifice of atonement" (*hilastērion*) meaning, "God presented Christ as a sacrifice of atonement, by the shedding of his blood" (e.g., NIV, NRSV, NJB, ESV). However, the word order more likely indicates that "in his blood" is the object of "faith" (*pisteōs*) resulting in "by faith in his blood" (e.g., KJV, NIV84, HCSB). Cf. Bryne, *Romans*, 133.

30. It is impossible to also rule out echoes of Jewish martyrological traditions (e.g., 2 Macc 6:13–16; 7:18, 32–33, 37–38; 4 Macc 6:27–29; 9:20; 10:8; 17:21–22). See esp. discussion in Jarvis J. Williams, *Maccabean Martyr Traditions in Paul's Theology of Atonement: Did Martyr Theology Shape Paul's Conception of Jesus' Death* (Eugene, OR: Wipf & Stock, 2010); and in Greco-Roman literature more broadly, see Martin Hengel, *The Atonement: The Origins of the Doctrine of the New Testament* (Philadelphia: Fortress, 1981), 6–18.

because it was the shedding of blood that made atonement for sins (see Lev 17:11 and esp. Matt 26:28; Eph 1:7; Heb 9:22). By using this cultic imagery, Paul was "presenting Jesus as the ultimate 'mercy seat,' the ultimate place of atonement, and, derivatively, the ultimate sacrifice."[31]

Even so, the cultic language inevitably leads to the question as to how sacrifice works or how atonement is achieved. The main options that have emerged are either *expiation* (i.e., the cleansing of sin) or *propitiation* (i.e., the placating of wrath).[32] C. H. Dodd avidly argued for expiation, where sin is cancelled and cleansed. Dodd vociferously objected to propitiation on the grounds that it was something associated with pagan religion where capricious gods needed to have their anger placated in order to make them favorable to people.[33] Propitiation is totally at odds with the God of the Old and New Testaments, who acts out of love, not anger that is assuaged.[34] However, Dodd overstated his case, and scholars like Leon Morris have successfully demonstrated the cogency of *propitiation*.[35] (1) The Old Testament frequently connects the mercy seat with the forgiveness of sins and the setting aside of God's wrath; (2) Josephus and the Maccabean literature use cognates of *hilastērion* with this same meaning of assuaging divine wrath;[36] and (3) if Jesus' sacrificial death is to be effective for salvation, it must ultimately deal with God's wrath against sin as described earlier in Romans 1:18.

According to Morris, "Paul has mounted heavy artillery in the section 1:18–3:20 to show that all are sinners and subject to the wrath of God. But unless the present term means the removal of wrath, he has left them there, still under God's wrath."[37] So while the cross undoubtedly demonstrates God's love (see 5:8), it also turns away God's righteous indignation against human

31. Carson, "Atonement in Romans 3:21–26," 129. Cf. Daniel P. Bailey, "Jesus as the Mercy Seat: The Semantics and Theology of Paul's Use of *hilastērion* in Romans 3:25," *TynB* 51 (2000): 155–58.

32. On translations, see "expiation" in RSV and NEB and "propitiation" in KJV, NASB, ESV, and HCSB. The NET has "mercy seat," the CEB opts for "place of sacrifice where mercy is found," and the NJB uses "sacrifice for reconciliation," while other translations like the NIV and NRSV go for the more general "sacrifice of atonement."

33. See the following inscription found at Cos: "The people, for the Emperor Caesar, son of God, Augustus, for salvation to the gods [offer this] propitiatory sacrifice (*hilastērion*)" cited from Witherington, *Romans*, 108.

34. C. H. Dodd, "Atonement," in *The Bible and the Greeks* (London: Hodder & Stoughton, 1935), 82–95; idem, *Romans*, 55: "The rendering propitiation is therefore misleading, for it suggests the placating of an angry God, and although this would be in accord with pagan usage, it is foreign to biblical usage." Cf. Fitzmyer, *Romans*, 349–50; Byrne, *Romans*, 126, 132–33.

35. Morris, *Apostolic Preaching of the Cross*, 144–213; idem, *Romans*, 179–83; and others, e.g., Stott, *Cross of Christ*, 168–75; Cranfield, *Romans* 1.214–18; Wright, "Romans," 10:475–76; Witherington, *Romans*, 108–9.

36. Josephus, *War* 5.385; *Ant.* 6.124; 8.112; 10.59; 2 Macc 7:37–38; 4 Macc 6:28–29.

37. Morris, *Romans*, 180–81.

wickedness. That said, we do not have to choose absolutely between *expiation* and *propitiation* since it might be more accurate to say that when sin is expiated (i.e., when ours sins are cleansed), then God is propitiated (i.e., God's wrath is turned away).[38]

There is one more profound fact we must observe, namely, that God is the one who sets forth Jesus as a sacrifice. He does not merely receive a sacrifice that is offered up to him, but God takes the initiative to shed the blood that is made for atonement. If that is the case, then God is both the subject and object of atonement.[39] God is both the offerer of a sacrifice and the one affected by it. God makes a sacrifice of his own Son, which satisfies his justice and leads to the free offer of salvation.[40]

## God's Forbearance and Justice (3:25b–26)

The stated purpose for God's setting forth Jesus as a sacrifice is described in vv. 25b–26 as the demonstration and establishment of God's righteousness: "He did this to demonstrate his righteousness, because in his forbearance he had left the sins committed beforehand unpunished—he did it to demonstrate his righteousness at the present time, so as to be just and the one who justifies those who have faith in Jesus." Paul twice repeats the phrase "demonstrate his righteousness" (*endeixin tēs dikaiosynēs autou*), which is obviously a statement about the uprightness of God's character. This righteousness is the same as that spoken about in v. 21, and it pertains to God's upright and faithful character that is expressed in his saving actions. This righteousness is exhibited in God's decision to pass over or overlook[41] the sins that men and women committed before Christ came.[42] The same thought is captured in Paul's speech to the Athenians at the Areopagus: "In the past God overlooked such ignorance, but now he commands all people everywhere to repent" (Acts 17:30). In other Pauline language this could be described as "not counting people's sins against them" (2 Cor 5:19; cf. Rom 4:8). God's overlooking of sin is not because he is fickle or forgetful, but it is part of his "forbearance," something associated with his kindness and patience in Romans 2:4.

38. Cf. similarly Dunn, *Romans* 1:171; Schreiner, *Romans*, 195; Wright, "Romans," 10:476; Talbert, *Romans*, 113; Kruse, *Romans*, 191; Andria, *Romans*, 72.

39. Stott, *Cross of Christ*, 123–28; Carson, "Atonement in Romans 3:21–26," 131, 135.

40. We might compare this verse with Apocalypse of Abraham 17.20, which contains the striking notion of a sacrifice offered by God and to God: "Accept my prayer and delight in it, and (accept) also the sacrifice which you yourself made through me as I searched for you."

41. BDAG 776, defines *paresis* as "deliberate disregard, passing over, letting go unpunished."

42. On the "sins previously committed," Carson ("Atonement in Romans 3:21–26," 137) comments: "In other words, the sins committed beforehand are not just those committed by an individual before his or her conversion, but those committed by the human race before the cross."

The reason why God can pass over sins that were committed in the *past* is because he has acted in the *present* to vindicate his justice. God has so acted in order to be "just" himself and at the same time to be the "justifier" of those who have faith in Jesus. At the cross there is a genuine satisfaction of divine justice in the sense of making reparation or amends for the offense committed.[43] While most translations here employ the language of "just" and "justifies," it is important to note that the Greek words used are cognates for "righteousness" in the adjectival (*dikaios*) and verbal (*dikaioō*) forms, meaning that there is no change of topic with what has gone previously. Paul does not explicitly say how God has established his justice, but most likely it pertains to the prosecution of God's contention against human evil in the death of Jesus. Seifrid notes that the cross is the prolepsis of the day of judgment, when God's contention with the world comes to its dramatic conclusion.[44]

Jesus' death, then, turns out to be a vicarious sacrifice and a penal substitution whereby God "condemned sin in the flesh" of Jesus as a "sin offering" (Rom 8:3) and "God made him who had no sin to be sin for us" (2 Cor 5:21). Significantly there is no justification of the sinner apart from the justification of God. In the cross, God is vindicated against the world that vilified his glory by exercising his punitive judgment against the world. In the cross, God also vindicates those who believe in the divine love and mercy displayed in Jesus' cross.

## Boasting Excluded, Gentiles Included (3:27–31)

Coming to vv. 27–31 we see that Paul draws out some immediate implications from his narration as to how God's righteousness is revealed through faith in Jesus Christ. The first implication Paul makes is not about ethics or politics; instead, he reinforces the contrast between "faith" and "works" while also eliminating the possibility that God has limited his grace to one particular people. What I find frustrating in recent studies on Romans is the bifurcation between those on the one hand who insist that Paul's primary concern lies with addressing the social problem of Jewish exclusivism, while on the other hand some scholars are adamant that Paul's main point is to deal with the anthropological problem of human sin. Yet a holistic reading of Romans reveals that Paul addresses both matters: theologies of merit and ethnic superiority.[45] To deny that a person is justified by works of the law is to deny that

43. See Cole, *God the Peacemaker*, 130–43.

44. Seifrid, *Christ, Our Righteousness*, 65–66.

45. Second Temple Jewish literature clearly evidences views that never lost sight of grace, election, and covenant (e.g., 1QH 11.11–12). However, there was a diversity of opinion of whether and to what extent God's blessings were freely given or whether they were rewards for righteousness (e.g., Philo, *Sacrifices*, 54–57). Moreover, an emphasis on works as a means to salvation can emerge when (1) one considers the basis for entrance into the age to come, heightened when it is assumed

any moral effort can earn one salvation before God. Instead, justification is by faith and given freely by grace. At the same time, the works of the law are the covenantal stipulations for the Jewish way of life. The observance of these works by Gentiles would entail following the customs of the Jewish people and even joining a Jewish community through circumcision.

What Paul rules out here is what I call "ethnocentric nomism," which is the view that you have to become a Jew in order to be a Christian, where salvation is by *performance of the law* and limited to the *people of the law*. Listen to John Chrysostom on v. 28: "For these two things were what confused the Jews; *one*, if it were possible for men, who with works were not saved, to be saved without them, and *another*, if it were just for the uncircumcised to enjoy the same blessings with the those, who had during so long a period been nurtured in the Law; which last confused them more by far than the former."[46] Chrysostom notes that the passage touches on the idea of salvation by merit and the challenge posed to Jewish privileges, and he accents the latter.

My point is that it is not possible to segregate the issues of grace and race in Paul's argument in Romans as they are intractably linked together. God's declaration that a sinner is righteous is evidence for the vertical, salvific, and relational reality in justification. At the same time, however, Paul's scriptural argument for justification out of the Abraham story as well as its application to the social situation in ethnically mixed communities means that Gentile inclusion is equally the context and content for justification. Viewed this way, justification by faith is not simply a theological preface to a plea for ethnic unity, but neither is the inclusion of the Gentiles in the church a mere happenstance as one of many possible implications of the doctrine. A thick description of justification by faith in Paul's letters must be soteriological as well as social and not expound one at the expense of the other.

Paul next includes a flurry of rhetorical questions reminiscent of Romans 3:1–9: "Where, then, is boasting? It is excluded. Because of what law? The law that requires works? No, because of the law that requires faith" (v. 27). Paul will have much more to say about the theme of boasting in Romans 4, specifically, how no one can claim to have acted in a way as to require God to reward them for their good work. In any case, in light of 2:17, 23, it is clear that the boasting mentioned here refers to Israel's boast in knowledge of God, specifically, knowledge acquired through the Torah, resulting in a status above

---

that only a remnant will be saved; (2) during intra-Jewish sectarian debates about which and whose interpretation of the law is valid; and (3) among debates within a community about the rite of entry for insiders to join the community. See Bird, "What If Martin Luther Had Read the Dead Sea Scrolls?" 118; idem, *Saving Righteousness of God*, 89–95.

46. Chrysostom, *Hom. Rom.* 7 (italics added).

and better than that of Gentiles.[47] Paul says that such a boast is "excluded," shut out as a possibility. When Paul asks, "Because of what law [is boasting excluded]?" he is rhetorically asking after the legal basis for this exclusion; that is, on what legal grounds is Israel forced to forfeit its boasting? He flat out denies that the exclusion of boasting arises from "works [of the law]" with its obligations placed on the individual. Instead, he pins the exclusion to "the law that requires faith"—literally in the Greek "through the law of faith" (*dia nomou pisteōs*). But what is this "law of faith"? There are two main options.[48]

(1) *A metaphorical principle that proves that justification by faith rules out boasting in works of the law*. Here *nomos* means something like "principle" or "rule," so that the principle of faith is the antithesis of the principle of law. Boasting is then excluded because of the principle that God has provided salvation by faith. Paul is making a play on words based on the lexical breadth of *nomos* as legal code (i.e., Mosaic law) or a general rule of prescriptive force (i.e., principle). In favor of this option is that the use of *nomos* as "principle" arguably appears later (Rom 7:21, 23–25, 8:2). Also, Paul's next move in v. 28 is to reiterate the same juxtaposition: justification is by faith and not by works of the law. Furthermore, for many commentators it is important to stress that Paul is not talking about the law in a positive relation to faith because law and faith are at odds when it comes to the grounds on which God justifies persons. Support for this view could be found in the fact that Paul often makes strong contrasts between law and faith (see Rom 9:30–33; 10:5–6; Gal 3:11–12, 23–24; Phil 3:9), and he has assumed some discontinuity between the Mosaic law and faith a few verses earlier, where God's righteousness is revealed "apart from law" (Rom 3:21–22). Thus, the "law of faith" is the principle that demands that justification is by faith and not by observance of the law, so that boasting is logically excluded.[49]

(2) *The law of Moses understood as supporting and establishing faith as the means by which God justifies persons*. Paul might be legitimating the exclusion of boasting in the law by reference to the law's prophetic function in pointing ahead to faith. When the law is understood in terms of "works," it leads to boasting, but when the law is situated in relation to "faith," such boasting is excluded. In support, we can point to how a few verses earlier Paul asserted

47. Simon J. Gathercole, *Where Is the Boasting?* 225; idem, "Justified by Faith, Justified by his Blood: The Evidence of Romans 3:21—4:25," in *Justification and Variegated Nomism: Volume 2—The Paradoxes of Paul* (ed. D. A. Carson, P. T. O'Brien, and M. A. Seifrid; Grand Rapids: Baker, 2004), 153.

48. Cf. also Rom 7:21–23, 25b; 8:2.

49. Cf. e.g., Morris, *Romans*, 144; Fitzmyer, *Romans*, 363; Moo, *Romans*, 249–50; Byrne, *Romans*, 136; Witherington, *Romans*, 100, 111; Talbert, *Romans*, 116; Arland J. Hultgren, *Paul's Letter to the Romans: A Commentary* (Grand Rapids: Eerdmans, 2001), 168; Kruse, *Romans*, 195.

that the Law and the Prophets testify to justification by faith (Rom 3:21). And, at the end of this section, Paul will conclude that faith does not abolish the law; rather, faith upholds the law (3:31). In addition, Paul often uses the law to establish the scriptural grounds for his gospel and justification by faith (e.g., Rom 4:3, 9, 17–18, 22–23; 10:5–6). Later Paul will also refer to the requirements of the law being fulfilled by those who live according to the Spirit (Rom 8:4); he will assert that Christ is the goal or climax of the law (10:4) and urge Christians to fulfill the law by living in love (13:8–10). While there is a certain law vs. faith conflict, this may be a matter of illegitimate purposes, perspectives, and practices being applied to the law rather than the law having no positive relation to faith. Thus, understanding the law in light of faith will exclude any attempt to find in works of the law any grounds for boasting. That is because the law actually supports faith in the prophetic and christological senses.[50]

In sum, while option (1) connects with Paul's law vs. faith contrast more generally, nevertheless option (2) is preferable because it better relates to the immediate context where Paul tries to lessen that contrast between law and faith by reenvisaging the law in such a way that it is supported by faith.

Paul explains in v. 28 why such boasting is an impossibility: "For we maintain that a person is justified by faith apart from the works of the law" (v. 28). The first person plural pronoun "we" indicates that Paul expects his audience to agree with him that obedience to the precepts of the law will not be the basis of vindication at the eschaton. Evidently the exclusion of national boasting applies equally to individual boasting as well. Paul's remark here shows that the Reformation catch cry of *sola fide* ("faith alone") is an authentically Pauline theme if there ever was one. Indeed, 3:27–4:25 functions as the most definitive theological argument for the sufficiency of faith as the instrument by which God communicates his salvific blessings to persons, all persons.[51] As Luther put it, "God accepts or accounts us as righteous for our faith in Christ only."[52] Even earlier Ambrosiaster said, "They are justified freely, because they have not done anything nor given anything in return, but by faith alone they have been made holy by the gift of God."[53]

The logical alternative to justification by faith is canvassed and then cancelled by Paul's logic:[54] "Or is God the God of Jews only? Is he not the God

50. Cf. e.g., Cranfield, *Romans*, 1:219–20; Dunn, *Romans*, 1:185–86; Stuhlmacher, *Romans*, 66–67; Schreiner, *Romans*, 201–2; Wright, "Romans," 10:480–81; Jewett, *Romans*, 296–97.

51. Cf. Moo, *Romans*, 243–45.

52. Martin Luther, *Commentary on Galatians* (Grand Rapids: Revell, 1988), 95.

53. Bray, *Ambrosiaster*, 29.

54. Contra Schreiner (*Romans*, 205), who thinks that if Paul intended a logical connection between v. 28 and v. 29, he would have introduced v. 29 with the coordinating conjunction *gar* ("for") whereas Paul introduces it with the coordinating conjuction *ē* ("or"), indicating a new argument.

of Gentiles too? Yes, of Gentiles too, since there is only one God, who will justify the circumcised by faith and the uncircumcised through that same faith" (vv. 29–30).[55] The conjunction "or," though left out of many translations (e.g., NIV84, NJB, NLT), is crucial because it proves that the logical alternative to justification by faith is ethnocentrism: attributing salvation to an ethnic ghettoization of grace rather than to a universal grace. If justification comes by works of the law, then obviously only those in the law can be righteous. Such a belief would mean that only the Jews can be justified since only the Jews possess the law. Paul reasons that since God is not merely the God of the Jews but the God of the Gentiles too—a point Scripture confirms from Genesis to Jonah—this one God will create for himself one people and justify them on one condition, that of faith. Byrne puts it well: "Faith recognizes that, in the Messiah Jesus, God has acted 'inclusively' with respect to the Gentiles, without compromising covenant fidelity (righteousness) towards Israel. In the face of *this* kind of divine intervention, it is impossible for Jews to maintain an 'exclusivist,' boasting attitude."[56]

Paul returns to the two catchwords of "circumcision" and "uncircumcision," which appeared in 2:25–29 and which exemplify a Jewish way of perceiving the distinctions within humanity. Yet these distinctions are no longer in force now that Christ has come. Paul has already stripped the Jewish way of categorizing people to the argumentative bone by exposing the bankruptcy of Jewish boasting in their national and moral superiority in 2:1–3:20. Then, in light of his theological convictions, an old one about monotheism and a new one about the Messiah, he describes a story whereby Israel's one God has acted in the Messiah's death and resurrection to bring justification, redemption, and atonement to Jews and Gentiles by faith. Just as there is "no difference" between Jew and Gentile in falling short of divine glory (v. 22), so now the one God "will justify the circumcised by faith and the uncircumcised through that same faith" (v. 30). Therefore, the Messiah, not Moses, by faith, not works, is the instrument for God's salvific work.

A Jewish teacher might agree with Paul that God is the God of the nations, but he would demur from Paul and suggest that Torah is the instrument for bringing Gentiles into the covenant people and into relation with the covenant God. Paul has dealt with that argument already by pointing out that adherence to the Torah cannot save anyone, even those who are properly and meticulously Jewish; therefore, it is pointless to impose it on Gentiles. And next up in Romans 4 he will argue that the story of Abraham proves that faith

55. Paul's use of two different preposition phrases in 3:30 for "by/through faith" (*ek pisteōs* and *dia pisteōs*) is stylistic rather than substantive.

56. Byrne, *Romans*, 137 (emphasis original).

is the divinely intended instrument for bringing Gentiles into a redemptive relationship with God.

As such, the Torah no longer functions as the boundary marker between those outside and inside the people of God. Paul knows instead that in the Messiah, all have equal access to God, and that is possible only if faith rather than works of the law is the entrance requirement. God is the one who will justify[57] the circumcised and uncircumcised by faith. If so, justification by faith is not a polemical doctrine that was contingently formulated to argue for the inclusion of the Gentiles in the church. No, justification by faith is rather a primitive tradition shared by Paul's Jewish Christian contemporaries (see Gal 2:15–16), and justification by faith is equally a message to be preached to Jewish audiences (see Acts 13:38–39).

Paul finishes off the section with a rhetorical question: "Do we, then, nullify the law by this faith? Not at all! Rather, we uphold the law" (v. 31). Just when commentators expect Paul to say that the law is abrogated, obsolescent, or defunct,[58] he says the opposite, namely, that his gospel and the faith that it elicits uphold and validate the Torah.[59] We must remember that while boasting in the law is excluded, the law itself is not negated; in fact, the law's validity is established by faith.[60] Paul means to stress that he is not antinomian or lawless, nor does he denigrate the law with respect to its real purpose.

While Paul can construct a concerted argument against those who would force Gentiles to obey the precept of the law to establish their identity and righteousness (see Gal 3:6–14), even so, he remains adamant that the law is "holy, righteous, and good," something that is fulfilled rather than abrogated by the life of faith (see Rom 7:7–13; 8:4; 13:8–10). Paul's gospel is the fulfillment of the prophetic voice of the law, and the love his gospel cultivates is consistent with the moral will of the law. We might even say that in Paul's gospel the law is upheld because the redemptive-historical purposes of the law are upheld.[61]

A Jewish audience might hear these arguments with confusion and consternation. A conservative Jewish Christian, who venerates Christ but is not yet quite with Paul on the Torah's redemptive-historical obsolescence, might respond with frustration. Yet our Gentile Christians in their dingy Roman

57. The future tense of the verb *dikaiōsei* is probably a logical future; however, the connotations of a real future are nearly impossible to avoid in light of 2:13. Cf. Dunn, *Romans*, 1:189; Fitzmyer, *Romans*, 365; Schreiner, *Romans*, 206.

58. Cf. Dodd, *Romans*, 63–64.

59. The verb *histēmi* here means "reinforce validity of, uphold, maintain, validate" (BDAG 482).

60. Jewett, *Romans*, 303.

61. Carson, "Atonement in Romans 3:21–26," 139.

*insula*,[62] who belong in a strange socio-religious place of being neither Jew nor Greek, who still wonder if Torah observance offers a surer path to salvation, ethics, and identity, can cry out "Booyah!" That is because God's grace in Christ reaches them by faith, not by works of the law. Hence, there is no privilege, no patronage, no status, and no salvation from God that is not theirs in Messiah Jesus and theirs by faith alone.

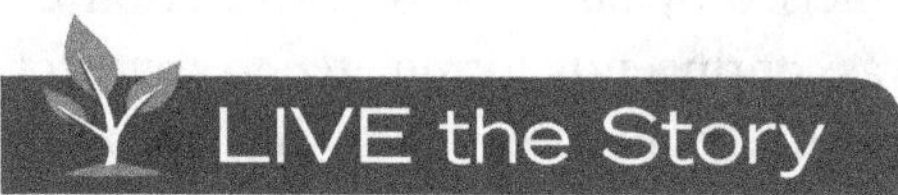


Paul's exposition of the revelation of God's righteousness in 3:21–31 brings together massive themes from the story of Scripture. There is imagery drawn from the exodus, the Day of Atonement, and Isaiah's prophetic word to the exiles. There is the picture of sin as glory lost and lacking. Paul describes the saving nature of Jesus' death with a triangulation of biblical themes of redemption, atonement, and justification. We also meet here for the first time in Romans the motif of union with Christ. Then there is the law as pointing to salvation but not itself providing it. Paul soars in between anthropological, christological, and redemptive-historical horizons. Thus, 3:21–20 is the cross section of so many biblical stories and presents Christ as the climax of God's saving purposes. As we try to live out this bountiful bonanza of biblical narrative, I would suggest that we should be led to reflect on two particular presenting ideas: grace and race.

### The Gospel of Grace: Still Amazing After Two Thousand Years

The German Reformer Martin Luther's lectures on Romans reveal a deep wrestling with the theological themes of the letter about grace, righteousness, and faith. Luther grasped the radical nature of God's grace precisely because he was grasped by it! Luther was a guy who never quite got over the fact that God saved him. He remained in awe of God's grace toward him in Christ. Luther's career was sustained by his realization that God was not a distant and merciless judge ready to squish him, but a loving and merciful Father eager to forgive him. Listen to the grace-dripping story of Luther's "tower experience" in his own words:

> I hated the expression "righteousness of God," for through the tradition and practice of all the doctors I had been taught to understand it philosophically, as the so-called "formal"—or, to use another word,

62. Juvenal commented on the shoddy nature of the insula, saying, "We live in a city supported mostly by slender props, which is how the bailiff patches cracks in old walls, telling the resident to sleep peacefully under roofs ready to fall down around them." *Sat.* 3.190–211.

> "active" — righteousness through which God is just and punishes sinners and the unjust. But I could not love the righteous God, the God who punishes. I hated him ... I pondered incessantly, day and night, until I gave heed to the context of the words, namely: "for in the Gospel is the righteousness of God revealed, as it is written: the just shall live by faith." Then I began to understand the righteousness of God as a righteousness by which a just man lives as by a gift of God, that means by faith. I realized that it was to be understood this way: the righteousness of God is revealed through the Gospel, namely the so-called "passive" righteousness we receive, through which God justifies us by faith through grace and mercy.... Here I felt that I was altogether born again and had entered paradise itself through open gates.[63]

This experience remained with Luther, and it explains why his theology was resolutely focused on the triumph of grace over human teachings about indulgences and merits. It was grace that set him free from a burdened conscience, grace that made him alive to God, and grace that showed him a God who truly loved him. In his sermons Luther wrote how Christ "is the spring and fountain from which flow sheer grace, truth and righteousness. From him we receive grace upon grace and truth upon truth." And also, "God's grace is a great, strong, mighty, and active thing. It upholds, leads, drives, draws, changes, and works all things in a person and is really felt and experienced."[64] Luther preached grace because he knew grace.

Strange as it might sound to those familiar with biblical scholarship, N. T. Wright gets his Luther on when he writes: "Paul's whole thought is characterized by the free grace of God, and any suggestion that humans, whether Jewish or Gentile, might somehow put God in their debt, might perhaps earn their good standing within God's people, would be anathema to him."[65] Yes, that is absolutely true. God's grace is not won or warranted, not earned or enticed, not manufactured or merited, and it is neither reward nor a wage. God gives out his grace like a fire hydrant bursting forth with water. God dispenses his favor like a billionaire throwing rolls of hundred dollar bills off the top of a hotel balcony. God pours forth grace like a torrent of raging waters that flows down an empty ravine.

Yet I have learned from experience that it is human nature to resist, deny, laugh at, walk away from, and even to spit on grace. One of the most dramatic moments in *Les Misérables* is when Inspector Javert is forced to accept the fact

63. Cited form George, "Martin Luther," 112 – 13.

64. Marshall D. Johnson, ed., *Day by Day We Magnify You: Daily Readings of the Entire Year: Selected from the Writings of Martin Luther* (Minneapolis: Augsburg, 2008), 26, 184.

65. Wright, "Romans," 10:479.

that he owes his life to a convict, a common criminal, Jean Valjean. Rather than show gratitude to Valjean for his act of mercy, Javert prefers suicide. He would rather die than admit that he lives in the debt of a criminal. Javert knew law, merit, and reward, but he could not live with the concept of grace. I'm sad to say that the world is full of Javerts.

Many years ago, I led a Military Christian Fellowship group at an army barracks, where service members and civilian defense staff came together to pray and to study the Bible. I remember how on one occasion we were studying the theme of grace in Paul's letters. And on this particular day, I was leading a small group in a study on Ephesians 2 and Romans 5, amazing passages about God's lavish grace. There were three of us present, the two others were fairly nominal in their faith and from mainline churches. As I began to expound and dialogue with the two of them about God's grace, especially how it is freely given and not earned, something became apparent. The idea of salvation by pure grace was foreign to both of them. The woman was amazed, awestruck, and almost moved to tears as we read through several passages. She had the excitement of a child being reunited with a long lost parent. I cannot be sure, but it may have even been a conversion experience for her, since she came to hear the gospel of grace for the first time. The guy's response, however, was totally different. He stared intently at Ephesians 2:8–10 in his Bible, perplexed by it; he looked worried, even agitated. He then spurted out: "That can't be right, it can't be that easy. I mean, I think v. 10 is okay where it talks about good works, but the whole faith alone thing sounds suspicious to me." I tried to reason with him, explain it to him, but in the end he would not give in. He would not accept that salvation was of grace alone and by faith alone. On his view, it seemed morally inexcusable for God to pardon people irrespective of whether they deserved it or not. He was still clinging to the idea that some people, himself perhaps, really did deserve eternal life.

In my movements around different places, I've been amazed at what lengths people will go to and what schemes of salvation people will dream up all in order to avoid the idea that salvation is by grace. In my short time as a follower of Jesus, I've had people tell me that in order to be saved, I need to speak in tongues, partake of some sacrament, only read the King James Bible, subscribe to a certain confession, believe in this diagram of the end times, and jump through a dozen other hoops that seem to serve the purpose of validating the rantings of some lunatic with an opinion and a desperate desire to force it on others. Fortunately for me, I was well discipled by Christian leaders and attended churches where the pastors were committed to biblical preaching, so I never got suckered into the "Jesus plus" stairway to salvation. But sadly, many do.

At the risk of generalization, I have to say that many churches have had the gospel of grace replaced by a kind of therapeutic semi-Pelagianism. I'm thinking of churches where preaching is reduced to short slots giving trite advice on how to please God by making sure that everyone around you is as happy as a dingo with a didgeridoo. Then, in some other churches, there is the constant threat of diluting grace with the poisonous waters of sectarianism and legalism—a place where pastors preach grace, but in practice they are purveyors of self-righteousness. Legalism can come in many forms and work to express itself variedly in different cultures.[66]

I hope you know that the oft-quoted phrase "God helps those who helps themselves" is not found in Scripture. Yet this nonbiblical saying, so often quoted as biblical, summarizes the sentiments that many have about salvation. God is type of self-help guru, who is urging us on to get saved by concerted self-effort. In the movie *Jerry Maguire* (1996, directed by Cameron Crowe), there is a scene where sports manager Jerry Maguire (Tom Cruise) tries to convince NFL player Rod Tidwell (Cuba Gooding Jr.) to assist him in getting a better contract for Tidwell. Maguire goes into a comical and impassioned plea that Tidwell should "help me help you." In many ways, that encapsulates what lots of people think about salvation. Salvation is God helping us help ourselves. God is not so much a savior as an enabler. Jesus is not so much a deliverer as a coach. So just try harder, compare yourself to Jesus, keep up the appearance of civil religion, avoid really awful sins like murder, and maybe in the end things will pan out for you. The tragedy is that our greatest human need is not a self-help guru; what we really need is the amazing grace of God.

One of my favorite stories of grace comes from the Gospel of Luke. In the crucifixion scene, one of the bandits being crucified alongside Jesus mocked him as a messianic fraud, joining the chorus of onlookers who heaped insults against Jesus. But the other bandit on the cross rebuked him, saying: "Don't you fear God," he said, "since you are under the same sentence? We are punished justly, for we are getting what our deeds deserve. But this man has done nothing wrong." Then he said, "Jesus, remember me when you come into your kingdom." (Luke 23:40–42). This man knew Jesus was not a fraud. He knew that Jesus was innocent whereas he himself was guilty with blood on his hands. Jesus responded to him with those memorable words: "Truly I tell you, today you will be with me in paradise" (23:43). The anonymous bandit had no good works to set before God. His life ended the way that he lived it: in gruesome violence. In the end, all he can do is cry out to Jesus for mercy—and he receives it. He does not come to faith while doing time in

66. On legalism in African culture, see Andria, *Romans*, 42–43, 121.

prison or while on death row, but during his execution. And now there is an ex-con in heaven who knows more about grace than a thousand theologians.[67]

If we are interested in the type of gospel, theology, and church life that Paul taught about, then it means we have to be deeply interested in grace. What is more, we need grace like we need air. So grace is something that we can't afford to be vague or wish-washy about. While I do not think "religion" is necessarily a bad word, especially when it denotes piety and devotion to God, still, in Western culture, "religion" means something like stuff we do to impress God. In that light, grace is *the* religion killer. Religion is about what we do, whereas grace is about what God has done. Religion is about getting a reward, whereas grace is about God's free gift. Grace is about adulterous kings being forgiven, prodigal sons returning home, cowardly apostles being restored, and crucified bandits getting offered an eternity in paradise. If we are truly justified by grace, it is the story we have to live by and no substitute will suffice. Or, as Michael Horton puts it,

> Grace is the gospel. The extent to which we are unclear about who does what in salvation is the degree to which we will obscure the gospel. At a time when moralism, self-righteousness, and self-help religion dominate much of evangelical preaching, publishing, and broadcasting, we desperately need to return to this message of grace.[68]

## Gospel of Grace: Justification by Faith and Gracism

As should be clear by now, Luther is one of my heroes. He knows that salvation is not something he earns but what God freely gives him. Luther also represents the triumph of biblical theology over a philosophically dry scholastic theology. However, as powerful and profound as Luther's reading of Romans is, at many points it becomes reducible to an allegorical interpretation of the letter composed against the background of medieval philosophy, papal corruption, monastic religion, and ecclesiastical ceremonialism.[69] I've argued elsewhere that while the Lutheran and Reformed interpretation of

---

67. Max Lucado, *The Lucado Inspirational Reader* (Nashville: Thomas Nelson, 2011), 391.

68. Michael Horton, *Putting the Amazing Back into Grace* (rev. ed.; Grand Rapids: Baker, 2011), 26.

69. Watson, *Paul, Judaism, and the Gentiles*, 25 – 26 (and esp. 27 – 56). While poor old Luther has been a bit of a whipping boy of New Perspective proponents, see the defense of Luther by Timothy George, "Martin Luther," in *Reading Romans through the Centuries: From the Early Church to Karl Barth* (ed. J. P. Greenman and T. Larsen; Grand Rapids: Brazos, 2005), 101 – 19; idem, "Modernizing Luther, Domesticating Paul: Another Perspective," in *Justification and Variegated Nomism: Volume 2— The Paradoxes of Paul* (ed. D. A. Carson, P. T. O'Brien, and M. A. Seifrid; Grand Rapids: Baker, 2004), 437 – 63. Note too Stephen Westerholm's (*Israel's Law and the Church's Faith: Paul and His Recent Interpreters* [Grand Rapids: Eerdmans, 1988], 173) comical quip, "Students who want to understand Paul, but feel that they have nothing to learn from Martin Luther, should consider a career in metallurgy. Exegesis is learned from the masters."

Paul rightly captures Paul's theological texture; it is deficient at times in grasping the concrete social realities behind Paul's letters.[70] Such a deficiency is exploited by the "New Perspective on Paul," which refers to a cohort of New Testament scholars emerging in the late 1970s who have criticized the traditional Lutheran reading of Romans as being too individualistic and narrowly focused on the salvation of sinners to the exclusion of other motifs in the letter, like the unity of Jews and Gentiles in Christ.[71]

Now is not the time to go into the pros and cons of the New Perspective on Paul. I and others have done that business elsewhere.[72] What I will say is that proponents of the New Perspective, despite their failings, are correct in at least one key aspect: Paul is deeply concerned with the unity and equality of Christ-believing Jews and Gentiles in Rome. Paul's letter to the Romans provides some theological triage to a potentially fractious cluster of house churches in Rome, which could fragment along ethnic lines due to competing claims about the ongoing validity of Torah for believers. While Romans addresses in depth the anthropological problem of human sin by Christ's death and resurrection, it is no less ecclesiological in its call for the Christians in Rome to be united in one gospel, worshiping one God, and receiving one another just as Christ received them (see 15:8–9). Romans addresses, simultaneously, the questions of "What must I do to be saved?" and "Who are God's people in Rome?" The logical corollary of a common salvation is a common worship around a common Lord.

I wish to point out that this observation is not at all new and has been around since the church fathers. The British monk Pelagius, who let it be said had a dodgy view of grace and works, says in his Romans commentary that Paul writes to intercede between two rival groups in Rome, the boasting of Jewish Christians in their Jewishness and the anti-Semitism of Gentile Christians against them. Pelagius wrote:

> Thrusting himself between those who were disputing in this way, the apostle interrupts the questions of the two parties so as to establish that neither of them deserved salvation by their own righteousness; rather, both peoples sinned knowingly and gravely, the Jews inasmuch as they dishonored God by transgression of the law, the Gentiles in that, although they ought to have worshipped as God the Creator revealed to them by creation, they changed his glory into idols fashioned by hand. With [irrefutable] logic the apostle shows, therefore, that they are equal, both having

70. Bird, "What If Martin Luther Had Read the Dead Sea Scrolls?" 107–25.

71. Cf. Kent L. Yinger, *The New Perspective on Paul: An Introduction* (Eugene, OR: Wipf & Stock, 2011).

72. Cf. esp. Bird, *Saving Righteousness of God.*

obtained in like manner, especially when in one and same law it [was] foretold that both Jews and Gentiles were destined to be called to faith in Christ. Wherefore, humbling them in turn, he exhorts them to peace and [to] concord.[73]

Ironically, Pelagius's opponent Augustine wrote something similar:

The Letter of Paul to the Romans, in so far as one can understand its literal content, poses a question like this: whether the Gospel of our Lord Jesus Christ came to Jews alone because of their merits through the works of the law, or whether the justification of faith that is in Christ Jesus came to all nations, without any preceding merits for works. In this last instance, people would believe not because they were just, but justified through belief; they would then begin to live justly. This then is what the apostle intended to teach: that the grace of the Gospel of Lord Jesus Christ came to all people. He thereby shows why one calls this "grace," for it was given freely, and not as a repayment of a debt of righteousness.[74]

Pelagius's and Augustine's short remarks contend that Romans addresses interlocking issues related to Jewish ethnicity and moral effort, and the apostle denies that either is a cause of justification but only God's grace. Let's fast forward to the British philosopher John Locke (1632–1704), who wrote a series of notes and paraphrases on Paul's letters that were published posthumously. On Romans 3:25 he commented: "[God] took Gentiles into his church, and made them his people, jointly and equally with the few believing Jews. This is plainly the sense of the apostle here, where he is discoursing of the nation of the Jews and their state, in comparison with Gentiles; not of the state of private persons. Let any one [*sic*] without prepossession attentively read the context, and he will find it be so."[75] Locke was probably reacting against the individualistic exposition of Romans by English Puritans, which passed over the historical context behind Romans. Then there was Benjamin Jowett (1817–1893), an Oxford theologian, who pointed out that a central theme of Romans is "union with Christ which breaks down all other ties of race and language, and knits men together into a new body which is His church."[76]

73. Pelagius, *Romans*, prologue.

74. Cited in Paula Fredriksen Landes, *Augustine on Romans: Propositions from the Epistle to the Romans and Unfinished Commentary on the Epistle to the Romans* 1.1 (ed. Robert L. Wilken and William R. Schoedel; Text and Translations 23, Early Christian Literature, series 6, Chico, CA: Scholars, 1982), 53.

75. John Locke, *A Paraphrase and Notes on the Epistles of St. Paul to the Galatians, First and Second Corinthians, Romans and Ephesians* (Cambridge: Brown, Shattuck, and Co., 1832 [1707]), 277.

76. Cited in William Baird, *History of New Testament Research* (3 vols.; Minneapolis: Fortress, 1992–2013), 1:356.

Evidently reading Romans as a letter concerned with the unity of Jews and Gentiles in the church, as much as declaring the gospel to them, is not out of left field.

The real avant-garde of the "new" reading of Paul's letters along sociological lines was Markus Barth, son the famous Swiss theologian Karl Barth. Barth the younger argued that justification by faith was for Paul an ecumenical doctrine that binds Jew and Gentile together in Christ. Barth acknowledged that justification brings a change in one's status before God and rules out any hint of works righteousness. However, he noted that "Paul fights for the rights of Gentiles — rights based on the justification of Jews and Gentiles through Jesus Christ — to receive blessing through the Messiah of Israel and to believe in him without becoming Jews. . . . For the two themes, justification by faith and unity of Jew and Gentile in Christ, are for him obviously not only inseparable but in the last analysis identical."[77] I think Barth is right: justification by faith not only declares that we are in the right with God, but it also declares that we are right with each other.

My point from this brief historical survey is to show that reading Romans as Paul's attempt to bring unity to Christ-believing Jews and Gentiles through the gospel is not an innovation, but is common in the history of interpretation. Such a perspective does not declaim against the central thesis of the Reformers that salvation is by grace alone, through faith alone, and in Christ alone. What it does mean, however, is that our doctrine of justification needs to be broader than the salvation of the individual and needs to encompass wider the themes of election, adoption, and church unity. A holistic and fully orbed doctrine of justification means that a theology of grace will naturally and inevitably shape our churches toward the practice of racial and ethnic unity. In other words, justification by faith is probably the best arrow in our doctrinal quiver to address the issues of race, ethnicity, and unity.

Clearly race continues to be a tough topic for civic and religious leaders in America. Matthew Emerson and Christian Smith lament that "well-intentioned people, their values, their institutions actually recreate the racial divisions and inequalities they ostensibly oppose."[78] While religion has been part of the pathway to racial equality and reconciliation, sadly, it has also been a large part of the problem by reinforcing racial divides. America is never more divided than when it is at worship. I always enjoy my visits to the USA. But whenever I go there, I am always struck by the fact that 11.00 a.m. on Sunday morning is the most

77. Markus Barth, "Jew and Gentile: The Social Character of Justification in Paul," *JES* 5 (1968): 256, 258.

78. Matthew O. Emerson and Christian Smith, *Divided by Faith: Evangelical Religion and the Problem of Race in America* (Oxford: Oxford University Press, 2000), 1.

segregated hour of the American week. Blacks, whites, and Latinos are never more segregated than when it comes to attending worship services.

In addition, I confess that I was deeply disturbed when several years ago I visited an American friend of mine in the South. He had recently been offered the senior pastorate of a white church that was located in what was quickly becoming an African-American neighborhood. He told the elders of this church that he would only accept the position if they consented to move the church to a new white-majority area. I quizzed him on how he as a Christian minister could be so racially partisan. His response was that, realistically, it would be impossible to grow a white church in a predominantly African-American neighborhood. I understood the complexities of his context, but I was still aghast with the racial prejudice that drove his approach to ministry.

I should point out that this is not exclusively an American church problem; it is a pressing matter for the entire global church. Wherever there are ethnic, racial, linguistic, or tribal divides, you will always find churches where those same divides are manifested and long-held prejudices are even promoted. White settlement in places like South Africa, Australia, and New Zealand led to the segregation of the indigenous peoples and their exclusion from places of worship dominated by white peoples. In my own Australia, the churches often acted as agents of the state in promoting segregation and facilitating the removal of children from their indigenous parents.[79] In other places like Africa, churches are often aligned with a particular tribe, and long-held rivalries against other tribes are retained, often leading to disasterous effects (as happened in Rwanda, where African Christians ended up killing other African Christians).

In China, minority ethnic groups like the Zhuang and Hui are not always able to integrate themselves into churches with Han majorities. In Fiji, the ethnic Fijian churches have sometimes supported military coups that were designed to curtail the political power and social influence of Indian Fijians. The Indian Fijians were brought to Fiji by the British in the late nineteenth century to work in the plantations and have frequently been the subject of oppression and discrimination. Evidently prejudices are pervasive and always find a place to sit comfortably on the pews. To justify any form of ethnic or racial exclusion means that one either does not understand or does not believe in justification by faith. Let me be clear. The denial of ethnic privilege and racial superiority is not merely an implication of justification by faith; rather, it is a core element of the doctrine, since Paul says so in Romans 3:27–31. Grace and racial prejudice are mutually exclusive because justification creates

---

79. See William Loader, "Australia's Day of Apology to the Stolen Generations of its Indigenous People," *ExpT* 119 (2008): 385–86.

a church, a new covenant community consisting of Jew and Gentile, slave and free, male and female, Greek and barbarian, white and black, Arab and Latino, African and Asian. Churches that practice racial segregation even for pragmatic reasons deny the biblical teaching about the doctrine of justification as it works itself out in the *koinonia* of the church.

I take no pleasure in informing my Presbyterian friends that one of their heroes of the faith, Old Princeton luminary J. Gresham Machen, was ardently prosegregationalist and fumed when black students were integrated into the Princeton Seminary dormitory.[80] Machen failed to see beyond the prejudices inherited from his own southern aristocratic tradition, and as a result he denied a fundamental tenet of justification by faith. Thankfully his senior colleague, B. B. Warfield, did have a better grasp of the biblical meaning of justification by faith, which is why he rejected the PCUSA's reunion with the Cumberland Presbyterians since the PCUSA would have been forced to accept a racially divided church. Warfield wrote on the topic of racial unity with a resolute affirmation that people of all races should worship God together.[81]

Rather than racism, what the church should be known for is what David Anderson calls "gracism." Gracism means extending favor to others irrespective of color, class, or culture.[82] Yes, I know that "gracism" sounds cornier than a cornfield in Cornville, Iowa, but it rings true. Gracism means that nobody will ever be asked to sit at the back of the church bus. Gracism means that we can never say "equal but separate." Gracism means that we deliberately desire to have multiethnic and interracial fellowships. Gracism means that we sinners who have been reconciled to God can now be agents of reconciliation with each other. Gracism issues forth in a radical deconstruction of all caste systems. Gracism means that grace is both preached and practiced toward others. Gracism means that the most ruthless and efficient way to destroy our tribal enemies is by making them our brothers and sisters in Christ.

I've seen some white-majority middle class churches do some useful things to try become deliberately multicultural, gracism-styled churches. A number of churches run English classes and consciously host foreign students with local families. Other churches deliberately partner with ethnic churches by allowing them to meet in their facilities and integrate them into fellowship groups associated with the church. Running a multicultural church brings challenges ranging from language to worship style, and just plain trying to see things from the perspective of another person's culture can be hard.

---

80. James H. Moorhead, *Princeton Seminary in American Religion and Culture* (Grand Rapids: Eerdmans, 2012), 255.

81. Ibid., 254–55.

82. David. A. Anderson, *Gracism: The Art of Inclusion* (Downers Grove, IL: InterVarsity, 2007), 21.

Thankfully the number of multiethnic churches appears to be increasing, and this is one of the most visible signs that the gospel has taken root in a believing community. The best examples I've seen and heard about in my time are Holy Trinity Brompton and the Ichthus Fellowship (both in London). These churches have provided a place where West Indian, Pakistanis, Indian, Bangledeshis, European, East African, and ordinary English people have met together for fellowship. This includes ethnic and cultural groups with a long history of colonial oppression and traditional hostility toward neighboring peoples; yet despite all their differences and their historical grievances, they join together to love and support each other in their common faith. That is gracism in action!

Richard Hays recounts a powerful story he read from a missionary letter about how the gospel brings a transformation to tribal loyalties and racial prejudices:

> The history of the church provides numerous impressive testimonies of the power of the gospel to break down the wall of separation between different races and cultures. One of the most remarkable stories of this kind from recent history emerged from the bloody conflict in Rwanda, where in 1994 members of the Hutu tribe carried out mass murders of the Tutsi tribe. At the town of Ruhanga, fifteen kilometres outside Kigali, a group of 13,5000 Christians had gathered for refuge. They were of various denominations: Anglicans, Roman Catholics, Pentecostals, Baptists, and others. According to the account of a witness to the scene, "When the militias came, they ordered the Hutus and Tutsis to separate themselves by tribe. The people refused and declared that they were all one in Christ, and for that they were all killed," gunned down en mass and dumped into mass graves. It is a disturbing story, but it is also a compelling witness to the power of the gospel to overcome ethnic division. Paul would have regarded these Rwandan martyrs as faithful witnesses to the truth of the gospel.[83]

Embracing grace means embracing more than the gift of my own salvation. Embracing grace means embracing a story that shapes and transforms an entire community. As God draws us to himself, so he also draws us closer to each other.[84] Therefore, brothers and sisters, let us glorify God and extend Christ's kingdom by preaching the glorious gospel of grace with all the passion of Martin Luther, and let us practice gracism with the courage of the Rwanda martyrs!

---

83. Richard B. Hays, "The Letter to the Galatians: Introduction, Commentary, and Reflections," in *NIB* (ed. Leander E. Keck; 12 vols.; Nashville: Abingdon, 2000), 11:248.

84. Cf. further on this theme Scot McKnight, *Embracing Grace: A Gospel for All of Us* (Brewster, MA: Paraclete, 2005).

CHAPTER 7

# Romans 4:1 – 25

## LISTEN to the Story

1What then shall we say that Abraham, our forefather according to the flesh, discovered in this matter? 2If, in fact, Abraham was justified by works, he had something to boast about—but not before God. 3What does Scripture say? "Abraham believed God, and it was credited to him as righteousness."

4Now to the one who works, wages are not credited as a gift but as an obligation. 5However, to the one who does not work but trusts God who justifies the ungodly, their faith is credited as righteousness. 6David says the same thing when he speaks of the blessedness of the one to whom God credits righteousness apart from works:

> 7"Blessed are those
> whose transgressions are forgiven,
> whose sins are covered.
> 8Blessed is the one
> whose sin the Lord will never count against them."

9Is this blessedness only for the circumcised, or also for the uncircumcised? We have been saying that Abraham's faith was credited to him as righteousness. 10Under what circumstances was it credited? Was it after he was circumcised, or before? It was not after, but before! 11And he received circumcision as a sign, a seal of the righteousness that he had by faith while he was still uncircumcised. So then, he is the father of all who believe but have not been circumcised, in order that righteousness might be credited to them. 12And he is then also the father of the circumcised who not only are circumcised but who also follow in the footsteps of the faith that our father Abraham had before he was circumcised.

13It was not through the law that Abraham and his offspring received the promise that he would be heir of the world, but through the righteousness that comes by faith. 14For if those who depend on the law are heirs, faith means nothing and the promise is worthless, 15because the law brings wrath. And where there is no law there is no transgression.

[16]Therefore, the promise comes by faith, so that it may be by grace and may be guaranteed to all Abraham's offspring—not only to those who are of the law but also to those who have the faith of Abraham. He is the father of us all. [17]As it is written: "I have made you a father of many nations." He is our father in the sight of God, in whom he believed—the God who gives life to the dead and calls into being things that were not.

[18]Against all hope, Abraham in hope believed and so became the father of many nations, just as it had been said to him, "So shall your offspring be." [19]Without weakening in his faith, he faced the fact that his body was as good as dead—since he was about a hundred years old—and that Sarah's womb was also dead. [20]Yet he did not waver through unbelief regarding the promise of God, but was strengthened in his faith and gave glory to God, [21] being fully persuaded that God had power to do what he had promised. [22]This is why "it was credited to him as righteousness." [23]The words "it was credited to him" were written not for him alone, [24]but also for us, to whom God will credit righteousness—for us who believe in him who raised Jesus our Lord from the dead. [25]He was delivered over to death for our sins and was raised to life for our justification.

*Listening to the texts in the story*: Genesis 15:5–6; 17:1–16; Psalm 32; Isaiah 53:11–12; Sirach 44:19–21; 1 Maccabees 2:51–52.

Paul continues his line of thought begun in Romans 3:21 by showing that the story of Abraham found in Genesis 15 upholds his argument that justification is by faith and not by works of the law (see table below). Importantly, Abraham, the "friend of God," was a revered figure in Jewish tradition.[1] Paul latches his gospel onto the Abraham story in Romans 4, demonstrating the prophetic nature of Abraham's faith underscoring the scriptural roots of his teaching about justification by faith.[2]

At the hub of Paul's argument is Genesis 15:6, which says, "Abraham believed God and it was credited to him as righteousness." In contrast to Jewish readings of Genesis, Paul is out to prove that Abraham is not a proto-proselyte,

1. On Abraham in Judaism, see James E. Bowley, "Abraham," in *EDEJ* (ed. J. J. Collins and D. C. Harlow; Grand Rapids: Eerdmans, 2010), 294–95 and the series of quotations conveniently listed in Jewett, *Romans*, 308–9.

2. Paul has already intimated that point by quoting a piece of traditional material about the gospel being "promised beforehand through his prophets in the Holy Scriptures" (Rom 1:3), by appealing to Habakkuk 2:4 to prove that "the righteous shall live by faith" (Rom 1:17), and by stating more broadly that "the Law and the Prophets testify" to the revelation of God's righteousness through faith in Jesus Christ (3:21–22).

| Links between Rom 3:21–31 and 4:1–25[3] | | |
|---|---|---|
| Righteousness apart from law | 3:21, 28 | 4:6 |
| Righteousness through faith | 3:22, 27 | 4:5, 11 |
| Righteousness to all who believe | 3:22, 29 | 4:11–12, 16 |
| Righteousness by grace | 3:23 | 4:4, 16 |
| The law not nullified | 3:31 | 4:14 |

the first convert to Judaism; but the proto-typical Christian, who has faith in God's life-giving power. What Paul has in mind is no mere raiding of the favorite proof text of traditionalist critics and twisting it for his own ends. Rather, Paul is concerned with the true meaning of the Torah for the revelation of God's righteousness in the gospel, a gospel that is for Jews and Gentiles. Abraham's faith, as described in Genesis 15:5–6 and when properly understood, requires a recalibration of contemporary views about God's promises, covenant, law, and salvation. That is because Abraham's faith proves that justification is by faith and not by works of the law, nor is it restricted to people of the law. In this way, Paul is able to drive a wedge between Israel's election and Israel's law, and instead redraws election around faith in Christ, with Abraham the case in point.[4]

As such, the Abraham story is invoked *sociologically* to dissolve the category of "God-fearer" as a second class of insiders within Jewish and Christian assemblies. The Abraham story is also recast *theologically* to shut down any notion of salvation as a reward. Paul's exposition of Abraham's faith illustrates the dual role of faith as the badge for membership in God's people and the instrument of salvation. As Schreiner writes: "Paul is interested in the inclusion of Gentiles and the basis of their inclusion."[5] Thus, Romans 4 stresses that all believers are Abraham's children by faith since faith is what God requires of his people.[6]

---

3. The verbal parallels indicate that Paul is dealing with the same issues throughout Romans 3:21–31 and 4:1–25, namely, the saving significance of faith (see Moo, *Romans*, 244–45; Tobin, *Paul's Rhetoric*, 126).

4. Cf. Keck, *Romans*, 118.

5. Schreiner, *Romans*, 228.

6. The relevance of Abraham for Christian faith has already come up in Paul's earlier letters. It appears that certain Jewish-Christian agitators infiltrated the churches in Galatia and urged the Gentile Christians there to be circumcised. Central to their argument was the example of Abraham. Abraham was circumcised (Gen 17:23–26; Acts 7:8), and if the Galatians wanted to be children of Abraham, they had to be circumcised too. Paul wrote to the Galatians urging them not to be circumcised and not to be fooled by such a specious argument. Paul responded in Galatians 3:6–18 by saying that: (1) Genesis 15:6 proves that faith and not circumcision is necessary for righteousness

In terms of the structure of Romans 4, Paul contends: (1) Abraham was justified by faith, meaning that salvation is by grace and not merited by works (vv. 1–5). (2) David reiterates the same point that God credits righteousness and forgives sins wholly apart from works (vv. 6–8). (3) Therefore, Abraham is the father of all who believe, circumcised or uncircumcised, because of the priority of the promise over the law (vv. 9–16). (4) Abraham's faith was steadfast and centered on God's life-giving power (vv. 17–22). (5) The story of Abraham is paradigmatic for Christians, who exercise a similar faith in God's life-giving power by believing in the God who raised Jesus Christ from the dead (vv. 22–25).

### Is Abraham Your Daddy? (4:1–3)

Paul begins with a hermeneutical technique called "midrash," where he brings together Genesis 15:6 and Psalm 32:2 in order to highlight God's gracious action in granting righteousness to believers (vv. 1–8).[7] Midrash is a broad term but basically means an "interpretive exposition." The aim of midrash is to show the relevance of one text to another in the course of constructing an exegetical argument. There were several ways to do that, and one such way was the *gezerah shewah* or "equivalent regulation," where the interpreter undertakes an exposition of two or more texts that share a common word.[8] In the immediate context, Paul links Genesis 15:6 and Psalm 32:2 by their common word "credit" or "reckon" (*logizomai*).

The point of vv. 1–2 is to declare that Abraham was no exception to the statement in 3:27–29 about the exclusion of boasting and the inclusion of Gentiles. Paul begins with a rhetorical question, as he has done often, "What then shall we say?" but thereafter we encounter some translation issues that require comment. The basic question is what does the infinitive verb *heurēskenai* ("to discover, find") modify? Does it go with the following noun

and adoption into Abraham's family. In fact, Genesis 15:6 is a prophecy of the gospel, indicating that God would justify the Gentiles by faith. (2) Those who rely on the law are under a curse, yet Christ died to save Israel from the curse of the law, so that the Abrahamic blessings would flow through to the Gentiles. (3) The Abrahamic promise came before the Mosaic law, and the law does not nullify or set aside the promises. Paul uses these arguments from Galatians 3 in a similar way in Romans 4, albeit with a few minor changes of emphasis.

7. Several commentators acknowledge that Paul's interpretive techniques here belong to the genre of midrash, yet they are reluctant to call it so apparently because midrash is such a broad category (e.g., Moo, *Romans*, 255 n. 1; Schreiner, *Romans*, 209–10).

8. Richard N. Longenecker, *Biblical Exegesis in the Apostolic Period* (Grand Rapids: Eerdmans, 1975), 32–38.

| Who "Discovers" or "Finds" in Romans 4:1? | |
|---|---|
| Abraham discovered justification by faith | "What then shall we say that **Abraham**, our forefather according to the flesh, **discovered** in this matter?" (NIV) |
| We have discovered that we are not related to Abraham by human descent but by faith | "So what are we going to say? Are **we going to find** that Abraham is our ancestor on the basis of genealogy?" (CEB) |

"Abraham," or else does it go with the subject of the preceding verb "we have found"?[9]

The traditional reading is that Abraham discovered that he was justified by faith, not by works (e.g., NIV, NRSV, ESV)—an observation that comports with the thrust of vv. 2–8 concerning the contrast between faith and works and corresponds to the definite emphasis on grace in v. 4.[10]

However, an alternative reading is proposed by Richard Hays, who contends that "we" is the subject of the verb "find" and Abraham is the object: Have *we found Abraham* to be our forefather on the basis of human descent?[11] This rendering has a number of strengths: (1) Throughout Romans the refrain, "What shall we say?" (*Ti oun eroumen;*) is normally a complete sentence and is always followed by a second rhetorical question (see Rom 3:5; 6:1; 7:7; 8:31; 9:14, 30). It is correct to see two questions being asked here rather than just one: "What shall we say? Have we found Abraham to be our forefather on the basis of genealogy?"

(2) The context of 3:27–31 and 4:9–22 deal with the question as to whether descent from Abraham and the status of "righteous" are limited to those who are circumcised. The primary point of vv. 9–22 is that Abraham is the father of all believers, whether circumcised or uncircumcised. In which case, the presenting issue is the scope of salvation with Abraham, comprising the case study for answering the question.

(3) The phrase "according to the flesh" (*kata sarka*) is inserted to address the issue of whether belonging to Abraham's family is a matter of genealogy or a matter of faith. The presence of "according to the flesh" is strange on the

9. Several manuscripts (e.g., K L P 33) notice this ambiguity and try to resolve it by placing the verb at the end of the clause to clarify that it was Abraham who did the finding.

10. Cf. Käsemann, *Romans*, 105–11; Cranfield, *Romans*, 1:224–32.

11. Richard B. Hays, "'Have We Found Abraham to Be our Forefather According to the Flesh?': A Reconsideration of Rom 4:1," *NovT* 27 (1985): 76–98; N. T. Wright, "Romans," 10:489; idem, "Paul and the Patriarch: The Role of Abraham in Romans 4," *JSNT* 34 (2013): 225–31; see earlier Theodore Zahn, *Der Brief des Paul an die Römer* (Leipzig: Deichert, 1910), 215; also Grieb, *Romans*, 46–47; Keck, *Romans*, 120. But see objections by Byrne, *Romans*, 148; Moo, *Romans*, 259 n. 13; Schreiner, *Romans*, 213; Jewett, *Romans*, 307–8.

traditional view since Paul would be claiming that Gentiles have Abraham as their ancestor according to the flesh, namely, by genealogy, when clearly they do not relate to Abraham by natural descent. Yet it makes much better sense if the issue is *whether* Abraham is our father according to the flesh (i.e., on the basis of circumcision) or *whether* Abraham is our father according to faith (i.e., on the basis of believing God's promises). What is more, later in Romans 9:7–8, Paul will state that it is not children of the "flesh" who are Abraham's seed, but the children of the "promise," i.e., believers. Viewing Romans 4 and 9 together, Paul is claiming that election is marked out by faith in the promises, not by obedience to works of the law. The stress falls on *how* believers are in the Abrahamic covenant, by flesh or by faith, and Paul says emphatically by faith.

If this is the issue, Paul is then asking, "Given our previous discussion about faith and works, grace and boasting, what should we conclude about Abraham? Is Abraham our forefather on the basis of human descent? Of course not! If that were the case, then Israel's boasting would be valid and God would be the God of the Jews only." Paul brings up "how" believers are justified in vv. 2–8 precisely because how Abraham was justified will impact both the scope of justification and the means by which Abraham becomes the father of all believers. Given the Torah's association with Jewish identity, obviously the matter of the *who* and the *how* of justification are interlocking issues. For Paul, Abrahamic sonship and justification are a matter of grace, promise, and faith, not derived from physical descent, circumcision, or works.

Accordingly Paul constructs a hypothetical proposal in vv. 2–3 about Abraham being justified by works. Whereas some thought that Abraham was a paragon of virtue, who was duly justified by his works, who could boast in his God-given privilege and steadfastness under trial, Paul asserts to the contrary that Abraham couldn't have made any such boast, especially not before God. The reason is clear: Abraham had no such works to boast in. Scripture says, rather than works warranting reward, that something different took place. Genesis 15:6 records that "Abraham believed God and it was credited to him as righteousness." The promise to Abraham did not come to Abraham on the basis of what he went on to do, but on the basis of his steadfast faith. Abraham's righteousness was not a matter of reward but of grace, for it came through faith, not by works.

### God Justifies the Ungodly (4:4–5)

To further establish this point, Paul reverts to a commercial metaphor in vv. 4–5 to categorically rule out any possibility of merit on Abraham's behalf that warranted a declaration of righteousness. Paul is adamant that Abraham's righteousness cannot be understood in contractual or commercial terms. Abraham's

| Abraham in Jewish Tradition | | |
|---|---|---|
| *Abraham as Righteous* | *Abraham as Law-Observant* | *Abraham as Faithful in Testing* |
| For Abraham was perfect in all of his actions with the Lord and was pleasing through righteousness all of the days of his life (*Jub.* 23.10). | And all of the nations of the earth will bless themselves by your seed because your father [Abraham] obeyed me and observed by restrictions and my commandments and my laws and my ordinances and my covenant (*Jub.* 24.11). | This is the tenth trial which Abraham was tried, and he was found faithful, controlled of the spirit. Because he was found faith and he was recorded as a friend of the Lord in the heavenly tablets (*Jub.* 19.8–9). |
| Therefore you, O Lord, God of the righteous, have not appointed repentance for the righteous, for Abraham and Isaac and Jacob, who did not sin against you, but you have appointed repentance for me, who am a sinner (*Pr. Man.* 8). | That is the fountain of Abraham and his generation.... For at that time the unwritten law was in force among them and the works of the commandments were accomplished at that time (*2 Bar.* 57.1–2). | Was not Abraham found faithful when tested, and it was reckoned to him as righteousness? (1 Macc 2:52) |
| Abraham was the great father of a multitude of nations, and no one has been found like him in glory (Sir 44:19). | He [Abraham] kept the law of the Most High, and entered into a covenant with him (Sir 44:20). | He [God] certified the covenant in his flesh, and when he [Abraham] was tested he proved faithful (Sir 44:20). |
| Abraham has not sinned and has no mercy of sinners (*T. Abr* 10.17). | Abraham did live by it and was considered God's friend, because he observed the commandments of God and he did not choose to follow the will of his own spirit (CD 3.2–3). | Was not our father Abraham considered righteous for what he did when he offered his son Isaac on the altar?... And the scripture was fulfilled that says, "Abraham believed God, and it was credited to him as righteousness," and he was called God's friend (Jas 2:21–23). |
| Great is circumcision, for despite all the religious duties which Abraham our father fulfilled, he was not called perfect until he was circumcised (*m. Ned* 3.11). | And we find that Abraham our father had performed the whole Law before it was given, for it is written, "Because that Abraham obeyed my voice and kept my charge, my commandments, my statutes, and my laws" [Gen 26:5] (*m. Qidd.* 4.14). | God marvelling at Abraham's faith in him repaid him with faithfulness by confirming ... the gifts which he had promised (Philo, *Abr.* 273). |

righteousness was not meted out as a payment owed but an entirely unmerited gift that was freely bestowed. By employing this imagery, Paul is refuting contemporary views that said God credited righteousness to Abraham as a reward for his character and conduct. For example, some argued that Abraham was already righteous when God called him, some speculated that Abraham must have kept the Mosaic law, and others projected Abraham's subsequent act of obedience in Genesis 22 into his justification in Genesis 15. Against all that, as Dunn comments, "Paul here attacks head-on the normal or at least widely accepted way of thinking about Abraham among his fellow Jews."[12]

In contrast to these Jewish interpretations of Abraham, Paul declares that Abraham's faith was credited as righteousness without Torah obedience; while he was uncircumcised and numbered among the "ungodly," it was given by sheer grace. This is as clear of a rejection of a work-for-reward view of salvation as one can find in the New Testament.[13] God does not justify the one working for the reward of righteousness, but God justifies the ungodly who believe in his promises.[14] Salvation is not located in human effort, but in a divine reckoning.

That God "credits" or "reckons" faith as righteousness can only mean that salvation emerges from God's act of declaring, acquitting, and creating. God does not weigh us and calculate if we are worthy; rather, he reckons us and makes us worthy to be with him. God creates a redemptive reality by declaring it to be so. This divine reckoning, based on the Greek word *logizomai*, means that we do not face an assessment as to our fittingness for a heavenly eternity on judgment day; instead, we are reckoned as righteous in the here and now. This little word *logizomai* carries big significance for in it we find our identity as God's people (Rom 2:26) and our acceptance before God's throne (4:4–6, 8–12, 24). Fleming Routledge tells the story of how a departing Episcopal priest from a congregation was given a going-away present comprised of a golden cross and chain with the word *logizomai* engraved on the back of it.[15] Salvation resides in God's great *logizomai*; we are reckoned as being in a covenant relationship with him by faith in Jesus Christ.

---

12. Dunn, *Romans*, 1:200.

13. Cf. Gathercole, *Where Is the Boasting?* 232, 242–46; Vickers, *Jesus' Blood and Righteousness*, 98–100; Watson, *Paul, Judaism, and the Gentiles*, 260–69; Jewett, *Romans*, 310, 325. Others play down the meritorious nature of the works in Romans 4:4–5, such as Hays, "Reconsideration of Rom 4:1," 93; Wright, "Romans," 10:491–92; idem, *Justification*, 220–21; idem, "Paul and the Patriarch," 209, 215–17, 232–36; Dunn, *Romans*, 1:200, 204–5, 228.

14. On the justification of the ungodly as the central theme in Pauline theology, see Otfried Hofius, " 'Rechtfertigung des Gottlosen' als Thema biblischer Theologie," *JBTh* 2 (1987): 79–105.

15. Routledge, *Not Ashamed of the Gospel*, 122.

| Abraham, Justification, and Interpretation of the Book of Genesis | |
|---|---|
| Jewish exposition: | Abraham → works → justification → boast |
| Paul's exposition: | Abraham → faith → justification → obedience |

## The Forgiven King (4:6–8)

The same point is then illustrated in vv. 6–8 by way of a citation of Psalm 32:2, where God credits righteousness apart from works. David says the "same thing," which means there is a theological agreement between Genesis 15:6 and Psalm 32:2 about the gracious nature of salvation. The one considered "blessed" is he "whose transgressions are forgiven, whose sins are covered" and "whose sin the Lord will never count against them." Significantly, David stands as one already within the covenant, already circumcised, an anointed king over Israel, who does not assert his covenantal righteousness but pleads instead for forgiveness in the face of his transgression. The appeal to the stories of Abraham and David prove that justification by faith is consistent across Israel's covenantal history.

Importantly this categorical denial of merit theology in vv. 4–8 is placed in service of a wider redemptive-historical arc that Paul draws across this chapter. For if "works" do not justify (vv. 2–8), then presumably neither does the work of circumcision (vv. 9–22), which paves the way for the uncircumcised to be justified by faith (vv. 23–25). As such, Paul insists that Abraham stood in the position of a Gentile, the quintessential example of a sinner, when he was justified. Abraham was a covenant partner with God wholly apart from the covenant symbol of circumcision. Let us note that in the Torah Abraham was a Gentile when God called him (Gen 12); Abraham's belief in God's promises (Gen 15) took place before he was circumcised (Gen 17) and before his faith was tested (Gen 22). If Abraham was justified by faith—without Torah, without circumcision, without proven obedience, by sheer grace—then the same can be true of others. Abraham is, then, truly the father of all who believe, circumcised or uncircumcised. In effect, Paul opposes a view common among Jewish authors that Abraham was the first circumcised proselyte to Judaism; instead, Paul sees Abraham typologically as the first Gentile Christian.[16]

## Blessings for the Circumcised and Uncircumcised (4:9–10)

In vv. 9–16 Paul returns to the argument that righteousness by faith applies equally to Jew and Gentile. Paul immediately unpacks the significance of Psalm 32:2 and Genesis 15:6 by asking: "Is this blessedness only for the

16. On Abraham as a proselyte, see Philo, *Cherubim* 31; *Names* 76; *Dreams* 161; *Abraham* 70; Josephus, *Ant.* 1.155; *Jub.* 12.1–21; *Apoc. Abr.* 1–8.

circumcised, or also for the uncircumcised? We have been saying that Abraham's faith was credited to him as righteousness. Under what circumstances was it credited? Was it after he was circumcised, or before? It was not after, but before!" (vv. 9–10). The question behind Paul's question is something along the lines of: If circumcision is the sign of the covenant (see Gen 17:9–14), is it not true that circumcision is indispensable for receiving covenantal grace?[17] Paul's answer is a resounding "no."

To begin with, Paul's question whether the blessedness spoken about in Psalm 32:2 pertains to both the circumcised and the uncircumcised demands an affirmative answer in light of Genesis 15:6. The blessedness, consisting of the forgiveness of sins and the noncounting of sins, comes to the uncircumcised as the example of Abraham demonstrates. The emphasis is on the "before," for it was when Abraham was not yet circumcised that he was credited righteousness. If that is the case, no one can say that circumcision is the *sine qua non* for a right standing before God because Abraham was definitely not yet circumcised.

Now is a good time to say a few things about circumcision since it features so prominently in Romans 4. Circumcision of male infants was a sign of Abraham's covenant (Gen 17:11; Acts 7.8; *Jub.* 12.26–28; *m. Ned.* 3.11) and commanded for Israelites (Lev 12:3). Circumcision was also regarded as the rite of entry for Gentiles into the covenant (Jdt 14.10; Esth 8:17; Acts 15:1; *m. Šab.* 19.3). Circumcision was thought to have a host of benefits like saving one's life (see Exod 4:24–26), avoiding destruction (*Jub.* 15.26), deliverance from wrath (*Jub.* 15.33), warding away evil spirits (CD 16.4–6), purifying the soul (Philo, *Somn* 2.25), bringing perfection (*m. Ned* 3.11), serving as a symbol for eliminating sinful desires (Philo, *Migration* 82; *Spec. Laws* 1.9–10), and even having improved hygiene and virility (Philo, *Spec. Laws* 1.2–8).

The Christianized *Odes of Solomon* say, spiritually at least, "circumcision became salvation for me" (*Odes Sol.* 1.3). Circumcision was not just a ceremonial part of the Torah because, as Mark Seifrid suggests, circumcision was understood in ethical terms, denoting faith and piety.[18] Circumcision was emblematic to Jews for covenant fidelity, while circumcising Gentiles was indicative of the triumph of Judaism over paganism (see 1 Sam 18:25–27; Gal 6:13). The ritual of circumcision denoted a whole theological galaxy of meanings related to covenant and conquest, promise and proselytes, blessings and warnings, heritage and hope, purity and prosperity, faithfulness and favor.

17. Schreiner, *Romans*, 224.

18. Mark A. Seifrid, "Blind Alleys in the Controversy over the Paul of History," *TynBul* 45 (1994): 79 (77–81).

In contrast to those who thought that circumcision was an eternal sign of an eternal covenant (*Jub.* 15.11, 23), Paul believed that what God did in Messiah Jesus, namely, "the circumcision of the Messiah" (Col 2:11), had rendered physical circumcision inoperable and insignificant in the new age (1 Cor 7:19; Gal 5:6; 6:15; Col 3:11).

### The Seal of Righteousness (4:11 – 12)

The obvious comeback to Paul is to ask: What does circumcision actually mean? Here in vv. 11 – 12 we come to the heart of the argument. Paul addresses the matter of circumcision with a straightforward chronological reading of Genesis 15 – 17 where 15:6 (faith in the promise) precedes 17:11 (circumcision as sign). Paul declares that circumcision was the sign of the promise that Abraham received by faith, not the means for attaining the promise. The result proves that Gentiles are justified in the same way as Abraham — by faith — and those who emulate the Abrahamic faith belong in the Abrahamic covenant.[19]

Paul knows full well that Abraham "received circumcision" as a "sign of the covenant." However, circumcision was not the instrument for righteousness. Rather, circumcision was a "seal of the righteousness that he had by faith" even while in his uncircumcised state (v. 11). Abraham's circumcision was a ratification that God accepted him by faith, and acceptance was not restricted only to the circumcised.[20] Paul is stating that the chronology of Genesis 15 – 17 not only shows that Abraham was righteous by faith and that circumcision was a subsequent sign of this righteousness, but more importantly, Paul is showing that the covenant promises are determined by faith, not by law, and are not restricted to the circumcised. The promise operates through the "righteousness that he [Abraham] had by faith." The Greek phrase *dikaiosynēs tēs pisteōs* (lit., the "righteousness of faith") probably means righteousness acquired by means of faith (see NIV, NRSV, ESV, CEB, NET). Such a phrase stands in contrast to a "righteousness from the law," which righteousness acquired by circumcision would imply (see *T. Dan* 6.10; *2 Bar.* 67.6).

Paul continues by adding that Abraham is the "father" of "all who believe but have not been circumcised," and Abraham is the "father" also of "the circumcised" who "follow in the footsteps of the faith that our father Abraham had before he was circumcised" (v. 12). There is no denial of Abraham's fatherhood of the Jewish people, but Paul stresses that Abraham's precircumcised

19. The discussion of Romans 4 by Peter T. O'Brien ("Was Paul Converted?" in *Justification and Variegated Nomism: Volume 2 — The Paradoxes of Paul* [ed. D. A. Carson, M. A. Seifrid, and P. T. O'Brien; Grand Rapids: Baker, 2004], 375 – 90) is particularly helpful here.

20. Dunn, *Romans*, 1:232.

state remains paradigmatic for Jews and Gentiles. Everyone, Jew and Gentile, is a son of Abraham if they believe like Abraham. Everyone, Jew and Gentile, is credited with righteousness if they follow in the steps of Abraham's faith.

### Promise Trumps Law (4:13–16)

Paul makes his point even clearer in vv. 13–16; if you get the chronology wrong, you'll get the theology wrong too. Whereas many Jewish writings subordinated promise beneath law, Paul moves to invert it and place promise over law.[21] Paul asserts that the covenantal promises made by God to "Abraham and his offspring" did not originate "through the law"; therefore, they are not dependent on the law for their continuing validity. On the contrary, Abraham and his seed enjoy "the righteousness that comes by faith" (v. 13). If only those who "depend on the law" are Abraham's "heirs," two things follow. First, "faith means nothing and the promise is worthless," and Gen 15:6 would be reduced to some kind of aberration in a saving plan otherwise focused on adhering to the Jewish way of life (v. 14). Second, since "the law brings wrath," relying on the law will mean rendering oneself susceptible to the curses of the law for transgressing its stipulations. Living under the law means living with the possible penalties for violating the law. However, the Abrahamic epoch did not have the law and therefore was without the threat of punishment for transgressing the law's demands. It was more fitting, then, for the promise to be given during the time of Abraham since "where there is no law there is no transgression" (v. 15).

Paul concludes this block of his argument by saying: "Therefore, the promise comes by faith, so that it may be by grace and may be guaranteed to all Abraham's offspring—not only to those who are of the law but also to those who have the faith of Abraham. He is the father of us all" (v. 16). I submit that Romans 4:16 is the John 3:16 of Paul's theology. It is such a good summary of Paul's reading of the Old Testament, God's fatherhood, his emphasis on grace, and the universal nature of salvation in Christ, and it marries together the individual and corporate horizons of redemptive history.

Beyond that, a few things here are noteworthy. First, the fact that the promise comes by faith means that it is based on grace, it is guaranteed, and it applies to everyone at all times. If the promise came by law, it would mean the opposite: it would be based on works, remain constantly in doubt, and be limited in scope to only a few. Rooting God's promise in Abraham rather than in Moses means that we have salvation by grace, a sense of assurance, and a universal offer of salvation.

---

21. Cf. 2 Macc 2:17–18; *Pss. Sol.* 12:6; *Sib. Or.* 3.768–69; *2 Bar.* 14.12–13. According to Byrne (*Romans*, 152): "Paul has to cut the nexus between promise and obedience [to the law]."

Second, Paul bookends v. 11 with v. 16 by again emphasizing that Abraham is the father of all who believe—whether Jews or Gentiles, under the law or outside of the law. Imagine for a moment how Christians in Rome would receive this message. The church meeting in the house of Rufus—the leader of our fictitious house church in Rome— which was comprised mostly of Gentiles, would be encouraged to be reminded that by faith in Christ, Abraham had become their father. They are not second-tier members of a religious association; they are legitimate heirs of the full promises of Abraham.

Third, salvation is described in a diverse array of images. Paul uses a number of terms for God's salvific gift: justification, forgiveness, blessing, and being made heirs. Many of the images seem to overlap with one another. The crediting of righteousness means the noncrediting of sin, and the justification of the ungodly means the forgiveness of sins.[22] There is also an abundance of familial and covenantal imagery employed. While Abraham is a model individual, the Abrahamic promise is for a worldwide family. While justification is about crediting righteousness, it is no less about covenantal relatedness. So, if we ask what salvation means in Romans 4, we would have to say that we are invited to believe with Abraham in order to belong to Abraham's forgiven family.

## Justification Ex Nihilo (4:17)

The precise object and nature of Abraham's faith is exposited in vv. 17–22. Paul begins by citing Genesis 17:5, where it is written, "I have made you a father of many nations" (v. 17a). The citation provides scriptural warrant to Paul's claim in v. 16 that Abraham is the father of all believers because God explicitly promised Abraham that he would be a father of many nations. Yet the citation also serves to introduce the content of Abraham's faith, focused as it was on God's promise and power. That is why Paul states that Abraham

22. Traditionally Romans 4:1–8 has been used as a proof text to substantiate the doctrine of Jesus' imputed righteousness. While the doctrine is theologically correct (see Bird, *Saving Righteousness of God*, 71–77; idem, *Bird's-Eye View of Paul*, 96–98; idem, "Justification,"145–52), Paul never explicitly says that Jesus' righteousness is imputed to believers. Let us observe that there is an imprecision in the language used about crediting/reckoning in Romans 4 since Paul can say that "faith is credited" (vv. 3, 5, 9 and implicitly in vv. 10, 22, 23) and also that "righteousness is credited" (vv. 6, 11, and implicitly in v. 24). Is there a double imputation of faith and righteousness? What does it mean that "faith" is imputed? I surmise that when Paul writes that "God credits righteousness apart from works" (v. 6), he is simply using the language of Genesis 15:6 to reiterate what he said in 3:28 that God "justifies apart from works," rendering the phrases coterminus. The crediting of faith means a recognition of the sufficiency of faith to please God. So Paul is not talking about the mechanism by which justification occurs with the imputation of Jesus' righteousness (see Rom 5:18–19 for something closer to that idea), but merely using biblical language to say that justification does occur by faith. See also Brian Vickers, *Jesus' Blood and Righteousness: Paul's Theology of Imputation* (Wheaton, IL: Crossway, 2006), esp. 191–232.

"believed" in God, precisely, "the God who gives life to the dead and calls into being things that were not" (v. 17b). Abraham's faith is exercised before God and is secured against the nature of God.

Two aspects of God's nature are singled out for special attention. First, God's power to bring the dead to life. That God brings down death and raises up life was a well-known notion in biblical testimony (see Deut 32:39; 1 Sam 2:6). It was God's power to create a nation from the frailty of Abraham's body and from the deadness of Sarah's womb that was the object of Abraham's hope. Indeed, Abraham's faith in God to bring life foreshadows resurrection faith. Isaac, the promised child born to Abraham and Sarah, anticipates the resurrection of Jesus. Such a faith in God's life-creating power is replicated by those who believe that God raised Jesus from the dead, which Paul will soon talk about in vv. 24–25. Thus, Christians don't just emulate Abraham's faith; they believe in the same promise, namely, that God brings life from the dead.[23]

Second, God's creates things by pure fiat or by a divine speech-act. God doesn't just announce stuff; his words literally bring things into being. Abraham believed in him who "calls into being things that were not." This could be saying no more than God's intent is to summon a nation that does not yet exist.[24] I suspect, rather, that Paul is saying more than that, namely, that Abraham had faith in God's power to create a new people, with a new status, in a new covenant, as part of a new creation. If so, justification is an event that happens *ex nihilo*, like the promise from which it comes. God's reckoning alone makes us righteous, not by a gradual moral transformation but by the launch of a new creation.[25]

### The Faith of Abraham (4:18–22)

More is said about Abraham's faith in vv. 18–22. In brief, Abraham is a model for what he did and didn't do in his faith. On the one hand, he didn't *weaken* in his faith even though he and Sarah were old and almost dead; he didn't *waver* into unbelief concerning the promise. On the other hand, Abraham *believed* that he would be the father of many nations even when it seemed hopeless; Abraham was *strengthened* in his faith and *gave glory* to God; and Abraham was *persuaded* that God could do what he promised to do.

The most important thing to note here is that Abraham does what humanity was supposed to do but did not do. Whereas humanity exchanged God's glory for idolatry (1:23), Abraham gave glory to God (4:20). Whereas

23. Seifrid, *Christ, Our Righteousness*, 69.

24. Cf., e.g., Moo, *Romans*, 282–83; Schreiner, *Romans*, 237.

25. Seifrid, *Christ, our Righteousness*, 68; Stuhlmacher, *Romans*, 74; and esp. Käsemann, *Romans*, 122–23, for whom Romans 4:17 is the quintessence of Paulinism.

the Jews lacked faith (3:3), Abraham was faithful (4:18–20).[26] This, Paul explains, is why "it [faith] was credited to him as righteousness" (v. 22). In this way, Paul uses Genesis 15:6 as an *inclusio*, beginning with it in v. 3 and ending with it v. 22 to underscore how the Abraham story is about how God creates and justifies a people for himself, according to grace, and by faith.[27]

### Written for Us (4:23–24)

In vv. 23–25, Paul turns to the direct relevance of the Abraham story for the Roman audience. When Paul writes that "the words 'it was credited to him' were written not for him alone" (v. 22), he is engaging in some theological exegesis of Scripture whereby the meaning of Genesis 15:6 is relevant to, in some cases even about, his current audience. The Torah is not just a record of revelation; it reveals and prophesies that which God intends to do for his people.

Hence Paul's statement that the words of Genesis 15:6 were written "for us, to whom God will credit righteousness—for us who believe in him who raised Jesus our Lord from the dead" (v. 24). What was true of Abraham is also true for believers. Abraham was justified by faith and so are Christ-believers justified by faith. Faith here is specified as believing in the resurrection of Jesus (see Rom 10:9–10; 1 Cor 15:3–5; 2 Cor 5:15; 1 Thess 4:14). The future tense of the promise, God "will credit righteousness" (*mellei logizesthai*), is a present reality meted out in God's declaration of justice for all believers in the here and now (3:22–24; 5:1, 9; 8:30, 33; 10:10), and yet it also awaits a future fulfillment to be enacted in the resurrection of the body (2:13; 3:30). The net point is that anyone, irrespective of ethnicity, who believes in God's life-giving power, just like Abraham did, can rest assured in the promise of Genesis 15:6; from Easter until the end of the ages, God has put them in a right relationship with himself.

### Raised for our Justification (4:25)

Paul caps off his midrashic exegesis of the Abrahamic narratives by citing what is probably a traditional formula: "He was delivered over to death for our sins and was raised to life for our justification." These are poignant words that form a fitting end to our tour through the citadel of Romans 1–4. In this verse there are strong echoes of Isaiah 53:5, 11–12, where Jesus appears as the Suffering Servant who was handed over to death, bore the sins of many, was

---

26. Cf. Edward Adams, "Abraham's Faith and Gentile Disobedience: Textual Links between Romans 1 and 4," *JSNT* 65 (1997): 47–66.

27. Or, we could say that the fall of Adam and Eve in Genesis 3 begins to be undone by the call of Abraham in Genesis 12–15.

vindicated by seeing the light of life, and resultantly makes many righteous. Importantly, the main verbs are divine passives, so that Jesus was handed over *by God* (*paredothē*) and raised up *by God* (*ēgerthē*), which indicates we are dealing with a theocentric act of God in the cross and resurrection. Furthermore, the two prepositional phrases, though both beginning with the preposition *dia*, are inexact in their parallelism. The first phrase is retrospective in that Jesus was delivered over to death *because of* our transgressions (*dia ta paraptōmata hēmōn*), while the second phrase is prospective in that Jesus was raised up to life *for the purpose of securing* our justification (*dia tēn dikaiōsin hēmōn*).[28] Taken together, Jesus' death has dealt with sins, while Jesus' resurrection establishes the justification of believers.

The link between resurrection and justification has struck some commentators as odd. While Paul often ties justification to the cross and blood of Christ (see Rom 3:24–25; 5:9), he can also put salvation in relation to Jesus' resurrection (see 1 Cor 15:17). We must remember that the resurrection constitutes Jesus' own justification since the resurrection is God's cosmic verdict that Jesus is the Messiah, Lord, and Son of God (see Acts 2:36; Rom 1:3–4; 1 Tim 3:16). So, on the cross Jesus undergoes our condemnation for sin (Rom 8:1), and in his resurrection he becomes the source of our justification (1 Cor 1:30). The death and resurrection of Jesus Christ is an apocalyptic event within which the justification of believers takes place. Thus, by a Spirit-forming faith, we have union with Christ, and what is true of him becomes true of us. In other words, we are justified because our transgressions have been forgiven at the cross and because we are incorporated into the justification of Jesus the Messiah in his resurrection.[29]

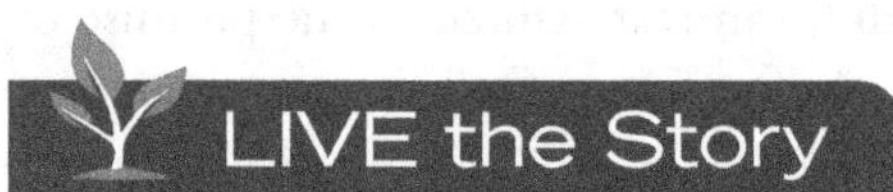


Romans 4 focuses on the theme of faith, precisely, Abraham's faith as a prototype and exemplar for Christian faith. In thinking about how we might live out this faith story, I want to explore the nature of faith, faith in the biblical story, and the link between believing and belonging.

---

28. Cf. discussion in Morna D. Hooker, "Raised for our Acquittal (Rom 4,25)," in *Resurrection in the New Testament* (ed. R. Bieringer, V. Koperski, and B. Lataire; Leuven: Leuven University Press, 2002), 323–42; Bruce A. Lowe, "Oh διά! How Is Romans 4:25 to Be Understood?" *JTS* 57 (2006): 149–57; Kirk, *Unlocking Romans*, 74–81.

29. On resurrection and justification, see Bird, *Saving Righteousness of God*, 40–59; Wright, *Resurrection of the Son of God*, 735; Howard Marshall, *Aspects of Atonement: Cross and Resurrection in the Reconciling of Humanity* (Colorado Springs, CO: Paternoster, 2007), 68–97; and Markus Barth and Verne H. Fletcher, *Acquittal by Resurrection* (New York: Holt, Rhinehart, & Winston, 1964).

## What is Faith?

Words like "faith" and "believe" get used a lot in our own culture. From the raunchy lyrics of George Michael's song "Faith," to the Monkees hit song "I'm a Believer," the words "faith" and "believe" resonate with us at some level. That is probably because it is part of our nature to believe and trust. All life is a life of faith, whether it is faith in ourselves, our friends, family, plans, people, ideologies, institutions, or even in forces beyond this earthly realm. We always look to someone or something to be an anchor that we can cling to in a world of uncertainty. We all reach out in faith somewhere, whether you are religious or not, because it is in our nature to trust. Yet we must ask, What is faith? What is faith about? Romans 4 is an exposition of "faith," but what is this "faith" to which Paul speaks?

A good place to learn about faith is the book of Hebrews, where faith is a prominent theme. Hebrews 11 provides a parade of heroes in the "Hall of Faith" as it describes men and women of ancient times who kept the faith, who believed the divine testimony, and who trusted in their God. These heroes were all commended by God for their faith even though "none of them received what had been promised, since God had planned something better for us so that only together with us would they be made perfect" (Heb 11:39–40). At one point the author gives this definition of faith: "Now faith is confidence in what we hope for and assurance about what we do not see" (Heb 11:1). Faith is a firm conviction that what we *hope* for will one day *happen*. Faith is confidence about a *future* that to many observers looks *futile*. Martin Luther put it best: "Faith is a living, unshakeable confidence in God's grace; it is so certain, that someone would die a thousand times for it. This kind of trust in and knowledge of God's grace makes a person joyful, confident, and happy with regard to God and all creatures. This is what the Holy Spirit does by faith."[30]

Returning to Romans 4, Abraham is presented as the most exemplary figure of faith in the biblical story. Abraham responded to God's call and left his house, homeland, parents, and even his ancestral gods to go to Canaan to worship the Lord and be the father of many nations. He faced hardship, division, testing, opposition, war, and even infertility. In fact, everything seemed to point in the opposite direction of what God had promised him. But Abraham did not give up; instead, he maintained his trust in God—so much so that the apostle Paul says about him:

> Against all hope, Abraham in hope believed and so became the father of many nations, just as it had been said to him, "So shall your offspring be." Without weakening in his faith, he faced the fact that his body was as good

30. "Preface to Romans," www.ccel.org/l/luther/romans/pref_romans.html.

> as dead—since he was about a hundred years old—and that Sarah's womb was also dead. Yet he did not waver through unbelief regarding the promise of God, but was strengthened in his faith and gave glory to God, being fully persuaded that God had power to do what he had promised. (Rom 4:18–21)

There are a few things we can say about Abraham's faith. First, it had to overcome fear, for all circumstances pointed to the exact opposite of the divine promises coming true. Abraham and Sarah had no children, were positively geriatric in age and appearance, and probably saw little prospect of any human life coming from their bodies. After all how could this old geezer be the father of many nations? Herdsmen might have whispered snide remarks whenever they saw Abraham, mocking his faith, or jeering at his pretentious claims that one day he'd have descendants as numerous as the stars. Despite all that, Abraham didn't give up on God. He didn't falter or think that God had failed him, but he kept his hope in God because of his confidence in God.

I do not doubt that Abraham, and a good many people around him, were scared, scared that he might die without an heir. Abraham had dragged his wife and kinsmen halfway across the Middle East based on a promise without a deposit. Abraham and the tribe around him could have remained desperately worried about the future, their ability to survive, whether the tribe would hold together. But what made Abraham unique was that he put his faith where his fear was. He trusted in God's promises and did not countenance the possibility that God would prove false. That is faith!

Second, Abraham's faith was God-centered.[31] His faith was not based on human possibility or logical probability. The faith of Abraham was oriented away from himself and directed firmly toward God. It was a faith in God's person, God's plan, God's promise, and God's power. The power of faith resides not in ourselves but in the power of the one in whom we put our trust. In contrast, faith is weak when it allows itself to be determined by or dependent on what lies within the realm of human power or human possibility or is limited to the horizon of human vision.[32] George Müller famously said: "Faith does not operate in the realm of the possible. There is no glory for God in that which is humanly possible. Faith begins where man's power ends." Faith is strong when it begins with the presupposition of God's faithfulness to us. Accordingly, our faith is strong when it properly comprehends and acknowledges the power and faithfulness of God.

In want of giving my own definition of faith, I would surmise that faith is our trusting response to God's own faithfulness. As Karl Barth put it:

31. Schreiner, *Romans*, 235.
32. Dunn, *Romans*, 1:220.

"Faith is trust in the divine faithfulness."[33] The notion that God is faithful is a bedrock of biblical teaching (see Deut 7:9; 1 Cor 1:9; Heb 3:6). We also see divine faithfulness in the faithfulness of Christ. In Revelation, John the Seer calls Jesus "the faithful witness" (Rev 1:5). Furthermore, Paul's celebration of his salvation in Philippians 3 can be rendered as: "[Hoping] I may gain Christ and be found in him, not having a righteousness of my own that comes from the law, but that which is through *the faithfulness of Christ* — the righteousness that comes from God on the basis of faith." Redemption is tied to the fact that we have union with the one who was himself faithful and obedient for us.

In light of these biblical pictures about God's faithfulness and Jesus' faithfulness, I was deeply moved by the preface to a big theological book I once read, where the author noted the last communication he received from a dying friend. His friend expressed confidence in the "Faithfulness" to whom he had entrusted himself.[34] That is a wonderful picture of faith. In light of the biblical picture of divine faithfulness, I would say that faith is entrusting ourselves to the faithfulness of God as seen in the faithfulness of Jesus Christ. Faith is our trusting response to God's faithfulness.

To give an illustration about faith, I spent several years in the Australian Army and for part of that time I served as a paratrooper. I clearly remember my parachute training in the small town of Nowra in rural New South Wales. We did two weeks of intense training before our first jump. This prepration included learning the differences between static-line and free-fall parachuting, lectures on how to put on a parachute, what to do in case of emergencies, how to activate a reserve chute, and doing all sorts of exercises that simulated what it was like to be in a parachute harness. We practiced over and over how to safely hit the ground without breaking a leg or busting a shoulder. The training was thorough, time-tested, and effective. The last parachute fatality in the Australian military I think well over fifty years ago. So I had good reason to be confident that everything would be okay when I did my first jump.

Even so, there was one thing that was lingering at the back of my mind. The parachutes we were using, called T10s, were the cheapest parachutes that the Australian Army could buy. They were the 99¢ version of parachutes. They weren't sports parachutes, where you land with a gentle pitter patter. They weren't maneuverable and permitted minimal steering. The T10s were designed to get you from the plane to the ground as fast and as safely as possible in order to minimize the time you are in the air because that is when you

33. Karl Barth, *Church Dogmatics*, II/1:460 – 61.

34. Larry Hurtado, *Lord Jesus Christ: Devotion to Jesus in Earliest Christianity* (Grand Rapids: Eerdmans, 2003), xv.

are vulnerable to being shot. Also, every parachute jump has a casualty rate of 5 percent caused by strains and sprains on landing, and that was without anyone even shooting at you. I had heard shocking stories of soldiers breaking all sorts of bones when landing in trees, powerlines, and even busy roads. I knew of one guy who broke his hip when he landed on a washing machine in someone's backyard. So I was naturally nervous about parachuting.

Eventually the time came for our first jump. When we got into the plane, it didn't take long until we were airborne and it was my stick's turn to jump. This was the moment of truth and for some a moment for a change of underwear. I didn't want to appear scared before my mates, but I kept having second thoughts as to why I was throwing myself out of a perfectly good airplane with a parachute purchased for its low-budget price. At "H hour" I saw the green light come on and I told myself that I just had to trust my training, my instructors, my equipment, and my own abilities.

As I quickly approached the bay door of the C-130, I could feel the adrenaline pulsating through my body as the jump master ever so nongently helped me step out through the door. As the cool air hit me, I instantly tumbled around for three or four seconds in a blur of blue and green until I finally stabilized and I felt myself drifting downward with my chute safely opened. I immediately began my safety drills, checking that my chords weren't tangled and I wasn't going to collide with any other paratroopers in midair. I soon landed on the ground with a heavy thud, but I rolled along the ground just as I had been taught to do. I layed on the ground for a moment, flat on my back, looking up into the blue sky, realizing that I had made it. My faith was not a blind faith, it was not an unreasoned faith, nor was it a futile faith. I believed that I would survive the jump, and thankfully I did. This faith, however, was not abstract or theoretical; it meant stepping out and laying my life on the line. I took a literal leap of faith, trusting in the integrity of my equipment and in the reliability of my training.

Now all analogies break down, and I'm sure comparing faith in God to faith in a military parachute has its limitations. Yet, in both cases there is a genuine leap into the unknown, casting oneself into the care of something else whom we do not fully see for certain. I went on to do over thirty jumps in my paratrooper career, and what it taught me was that faith means that we trust that there is someone trustworthy to keep us and preserve us in the face of danger. If we throw ourselves on God, he will always catch us.

### Faith in God's Big Story

The Bible is a book about faith. It is about God's faithfulness toward creation, toward Israel, and toward the church. It is about the faith and fidelity of Old

Testament saints from Aaron to Zechariah. It is about the faithfulness of Jesus Christ as the Son of God. It is about the belief and obedience of Christians who come to faith and are called to endure in their faith. The biblical story is a story of faith!

The reason why Paul brings up the story of Abraham is not because he wants to engage in some cheesy proof texting to prove that justification is by faith. No, far beyond that, Paul wants to show his Roman audience—perhaps Jewish Christians relegated to the fringes of a Roman synagogue community or Gentile Christians worshiping in a cramped apartment block—that they are part of the story of faith. This is their story, this is who they are! The Abraham story is for them and even, in some sense, about them. Abraham believed that God's power would create life from nothing by giving him a child. Christians believe that God's power has been supremely exercised in the resurrection of Jesus. Abraham was credited as righteous by faith without circumcision; so too are Jewish and Gentile Christians credited as righteous by faith without circumcision.

I've noticed a huge trend of young evangelicals leaving their churches either to join Roman Catholic and Greek Orthodox churches or else to embrace liturgical patterns of worship that rehearse ancient practices. This "back to the past" trend is I think being driven by the fact that many young people have become disillusioned with the never-ending church fads, cult worship of the latest and the greatest, are sick of turning pastors into celebrities, and are tired from jumping on and off ecclesiastical bandwagons. You gotta keep up on the latest doctrines, watch out for the newest heretics, and attend the coolest new conferences. I remember one church leader opining to me about all the fads that his denomination has gone through over the past decade or so. "We wanted to be seeker-sensitive churches, then welcoming churches, then healthy churches, then emergent churches, and now missional churches. I'm tired of it. I just want to be the church!" Church leadership gurus keep changing the narrative as to what is the problem and what the solution should be.

The faith that Paul speaks about is different. It is not about a fad; it is about a foundational narrative. By professing faith in Israel's Messiah, believers find themselves sharing in Israel's story of God's plan to put the world to rights through the Redeemer and a redeemed people. The example of Abraham shows that faith is the door through which we walk in order to enter a new symbolic universe pertaining to creation lost and found, humankind fallen in sin and raised in glory. The act of faith, then, is no mere personal decision that means the individual may now look forward to no more than a time of heavenly bliss in a postmortem state. Faith puts us in the story, it makes us actors in the theodrama, it recruits us into the company of the gospel so that we follow in Abraham's steps, all the way to Golgotha, to the empty tomb, to Pentecost, and then on to the new heavens and new earth. Faith means that we part of the story of God and his promises!

### Believing Means Belonging

I remember when I was in elementary school that we had a religious education teacher who would get us kids to sing a few Sunday school songs. Coming from a non-church-going family, I never went to Sunday school, so these were the only Sunday school songs that I ever learned as a child. But one song always stuck in my mind: "Father Abraham had many sons, many sons had father Abraham. I am one of them and so are you, so let's all praise the Lord." I'm sure most of you know it. I submit that this song captures the main theme of Romans 4. By faith, we are Abraham's children, and we belong in Abraham's family.

The central point of Romans 4 is about this: Who are the people of God? Paul's answer is that it is those of faith, men and women who believe; irrespective of ethnicity and independent of the Torah, they are true children of Abraham. Paul's concern is not just to legitimate a theology of justification—though he does clearly do that—but to legitimate the identity of Gentiles as members of the people of God because they have faith in Jesus who died for their sins and was raised for their justification.

This is an important point because it means that faith is not just about what I assent to; it is also about whom I belong to. Faith is about family, a Christ-shaped, Spirit-filled, and God-centered family. Faith tells me who my brothers and sisters are, and what it is that brings this family together. It would seem that faith has to do with participating in a new spiritual and social reality through acceptance of the gospel of God's righteousness made present in the death and resurrection of Jesus Christ.[35] Believing means belonging to the body of Christ through reception of the gospel about Christ!

This is why I think the images of marriage (Rom 7:1–6) and adoption (Rom 8:14–17) are so important. Those images refer to believers being bonded to God by matrimony and by patrimony and then joining the church family as a result. In light of those images, faith is more than our assent to certain ideas. Faith is the mark or badge of belonging to God's family and constitutes proof that we are his children. The joys of faith are similar to the joys of marriage and adoption. Faith means that I am not alone. I have a home and a family among those who know and name the same God that I do. Faith puts me into a relationship with God and God's other children.

---

35. Jewett, *Romans*, 329.

Sociologists regularly undertake studies as to whether believing in God requires belonging to any religious community. One interesting trend I've learned is that while rates of belief have remained fairly stable in recent years, the rates of belonging to a church or religious organization have steadily declined.[36] That might seem to contradict what I'm saying, so that believing does not really require belonging. But I would push back and ask: What kind of God do these people believe in and what kind of gospel have they received? If one has a consumerist view of religion or if one has a view of God as a kind of cosmic therapist whose sole purpose is to be there 24/7 to meet my on-call needs, understandably such a person might well choose to not involve himself or herself in a church, as it would be surplus to their religious requirements. However, if one views God as creating a worldwide family for himself, using the church as the platform for his mission into the world, then a churchless Christianity makes about as much sense as a Christless Christianity. That is because belonging to Christ's community is part and parcel of believing in Christ.

Given this nexus of believing and belonging, the challenge for pastors and leaders is to make sure that people in their churches know that faith is the only thing they need to belong and that faith is not a privatized affair but is a genuinely family event. God does not save us and then assign us a number until it is time to go to heaven one individual at a time. Rather, God saves us and puts us into his family for the purpose of sharing in the family business of worship and mission.

Lest anyone think I'm simply trying to give a plug for church membership, let me say that belonging is a vital part of believing since we need to belong to something if we are to be healthy people capable of flourishing. Any psychologist will tell you that belonging is one of the most basic human needs. We have an innate desire to form attachments and to gain acceptance from others. Our sense of identity, purpose, security, and worth is bound up with belonging. The church is the place where that identity, purpose, security, and sense of worth are formed. It is this sense of belonging that enables us to flourish as individuals and even as whole communities. Our belongingness is to be cultivated, celebrated, and even defended against those who would say that some of our family members do not really deserve to be there.

On the defensive side, Paul argued in Romans 4 that Christians belong to God's people and have all the rights, privileges, and hopes that go along with that. However, such a claim was challenged. Some Jews might have said to Jewish Christians that their belief in a crucified Messiah and fraternizing with

36. Kevin R. Ward, *Losing Our Religion? Changing Patterns of Believing and Belonging in Secular Western Socieites* (Eugene, OR: Wipf & Stock, 2013).

Gentiles disqualified them from membership (see Hebrews). Some Jewish Christians might have told Gentiles that they did not belong to the Messiah or to Abraham unless they are circumcised and followed certain elements of the Torah (see Galatians). Strangely enough, while I'm writing this section, there is an online debate going on about who is "Reformed." The label "Reformed" is obviously a prestige tag that many do not want to share with others since such an expansive definition would lower the currency of the term. So there is a melee going on in cyberspace as to whether or not Calvinistic Baptists like John Piper and Mark Dever are really part of the Reformed fold. Many voices are in fact claiming, "I'm more Reformed than thou!"

In some ways, this is the same issue as Romans 4. Who is in and who is out? Who gets to put up the fences around the farm and who gets to decide who lives on it? Sadly, as Fleming Rutledge points out, that sort of rivalry about who is worthy and who isn't has been wired into our DNA since Cain and Abel.[37] The Romans 4 story of Abraham, faith, and justification is about belonging. Yes, obviously it covers other things too, like the forgiveness of sins and justification; let's not discount them. But Paul employs the example of Abraham to demonstrate how God embraces us in his grace in Jesus Christ and establishes us as full and equal members of God's forgiven family. We bring nothing in our hands to make us worthy to be in that family, but we do not have to, for God has made us worthy by receiving his own Son in whom we apprehend holiness, righteousness, and redemption.

37. Rutledge, *Not Ashamed of the Gospel*, 114.

CHAPTER 8

# Romans 5:1–11

## LISTEN to the Story

[1]Therefore, since we have been justified through faith, we have
peace with God through our Lord Jesus Christ, [2]through whom we have
gained access by faith into this grace in which we now stand. And we
boast in the hope of the glory of God. [3]Not only so, but we also glory in
our sufferings, because we know that suffering produces perseverance;
[4]perseverance, character; and character, hope. [5]And hope does not put us
to shame, because God's love has been poured out into our hearts through
the Holy Spirit, who has been given to us.

[6]You see, at just the right time, when we were still powerless, Christ
died for the ungodly. [7]Very rarely will anyone die for a righteous person,
though for a good person someone might possibly dare to die. [8]But God
demonstrates his own love for us in this: While we were still sinners,
Christ died for us.

[9]Since we have now been justified by his blood, how much more shall
we be saved from God's wrath through him! [10]For if, while we were God's
enemies, we were reconciled to him through the death of his Son, how
much more, having been reconciled, shall we be saved through his life!
[11]Not only is this so, but we also boast in God through our Lord Jesus
Christ, through whom we have now received reconciliation.

*Listening to the texts in the story*: Psalm 22:5; Isaiah 32:17; Joel 2:28; 2 Corinthians 5:11–21.

After scaling the citadel of Romans 1–4, one can scarcely find time for a breather before having to continue the advance on the cosmic cathedral of Romans 5–8 and the olive grove of Romans 9–11 that still lie ahead. That said, 5:1–11 is a charming little section filled with so many breath-taking themes like reconciliation, peace, love, and hope. It is a short rest stop, kind of like an exegetical café that one pauses at before approaching the squalid taverns of original sin, law, and death just around the corner in 5:12–21. Respite comes because 5:1–11 is something of a bridging section.[1] Paul seems to be half recapping the wonderful story of justification by faith from 3:21–4:25 but also preparing for some meaty sections on Christian living in 6:1–8:39 that are just over the horizon.[2] In other words, 5:1–11 is a place where Paul forces us to take a deep breath, have a backward glance over the terrain we've covered, get our theological bearings, and have a quick peek at what is still to come.

In these few verses, Paul reminds his audience that they stand within God's vindication of the faithful, and this action is not only redemptive but transformative as well. Paul refers to the Spirit's operation on believers and how the Spirit begins to cultivate a host of virtues in the believer. Importantly, Paul also introduces here one of his most important themes, namely, reconciliation. By expounding reconciliation, Paul shows how the hostility between God and sinners has been removed on account of the death and life of the Lord Jesus.

For attentive listeners, this was harking back to the Old Testament promise of restoration and reconciliation. When God made a new covenant with his people, they would be forgiven, vindicated, vitalized, and renewed, and there would be peace, a "covenant of peace" in fact (see Isa 54:10; Ezek 35:25; 27:26; Mal 2:5). Now that God's epic and epochal act of deliverance has arrived in Jesus Christ, Paul is explaining what this covenant of peace looks like when it is put under a microscope. He maxes out his metaphors to describe it: justification, peace, hope, glory, atonement, virtue, and life. Our immediate response to this divine saving work, as Paul shows, is to boast in the hope of the glory of God.

The section is hard to break down because it is such a dense compilation of so many themes that appear across the letter. Generally we could divide the text into: (1) recapping justification by grace through faith (vv. 1–2); (2) rehearsing the virtues produced by faith (vv. 3–5); (3) remembering Christ's death for the ungodly (vv. 6–8); and (4) receiving a Pauline primer on reconciliation.

## Justification, Grace, and Glory (5:1–2)

Paul begins anew with: "Therefore, since we have been justified through faith, we have peace with God through our Lord Jesus Christ" (v. 1). In

1. Dunn, *Romans*, 1:242–44; Moo, *Romans*, 292; Jewett, *Romans*, 346; and further P. M. McDonald, "Romans 5.1–11 as a Rhetorical Bridge," *JSNT* 40 (1990): 81–96.

2. In rhetorical terms, then, Romans 5:1–11 is a *transitio*, a passage of text that recalls what has been said and sets forth what is to follow. On how Romans 5:1–11 summarizes Romans 1–4 and prepares for Romans 5–8, see Moo, *Romans*, 293; Keck, *Romans*, 135.

rhetorical terms, Romans 5:1 is a *conplexio*, a short statement that seeks to recapitulate the central thesis of the argument that Paul has been advancing thus far. That central point is of course that "we have been justified by faith." Believers are in the right with God, not as a reward for any accomplishment, but solely as part of a divine reckoning of faith for righteousness. On that premise Paul deduces ("therefore") that what follows from justification is the reality of "peace."[3] This peace is not a subjective experience, like a sensation of inner tranquility attained by sitting next to a quiet stream or the serenity one arrives at by engaging in meditation techniques; no, this peace is objective and entails the end of hostilities between warring parties. Because God's enemies are justified, it means that their enmity has been pacified. "Our Lord Jesus Christ" is the source of our peace, just as much as he is the source of our righteousness. Thus, God sends his Son to make peace between parties formerly at war.

Christ's benefits for believers encompass more than peace and include access to divine grace and hope for divine glory. Christ is the one "through whom we have gained access by faith into this grace in which we now stand. And we boast in the hope of the glory of God" (v. 2). There is an interesting narrative here. Faith in Christ brings us into grace and grace leads to hope, and hope basks in God's glory. Here "grace" does not appear to mean an initial saving grace, like mercy, but something more akin to the continuing favor of God on his people. It is a grace that means we always have a VIP pass into the hallways of heavenly power. Because God is our Father, the Holy Spirit fills our hearts with love for God; and since Christ died for us, believers will never experience a failure code of "access denied" when it comes to seeking God's presence. From this grace, Christians may boast in the fact that they have a hope in the glory of God. Hope and glory are often interweaved together by Paul since hope is largely for glory (see Rom 8:14–39; Eph 1:12; Col 1:27; 1 Thess 2:19; Titus 2:13). Not a hope of one day knowing God's glory, but more of a hope of sharing in it, what theologians call "glorification," to which Paul will refer in Romans 8:30.

---

3. The manuscript evidence for the "we have" in "we have peace with God" is a bit messy. Some witnesses read an indicative verb "we have" (*exomen*) while other witnesses read a subjunctive verb "let us have" (*exōmen*). There is a slight theological difference between the two options because the indicative mood would suggest that peace is a real experience while the subjective mood would imply that peace is something that we only might attain. Several commentators prefer *exomen* (i.e., "we have peace with God) as more internally consistent with Paul's theology (e.g., Moo), while others point that *exōmen* (i.e., "let us have peace with God) has slightly better external attestation in the manuscript evidence (e.g., Jewett). See further Stanley E. Porter, "The Argument of Romans 5: Can a Rhetorical Question Make a Difference?" *JBL* 110 (1991): 662–75 (655–77).

Paul's brief summation of the gospel highlights the effect of God's saving work. Believers experience a justification unto peace, a Christ-given access into divine favor, and a further hope of sharing in God's everlasting glory.

## A Factory of Virtue (5:3–5)

The boasting of Christians is not restricted to God, but even encompasses their present state of affairs: "Not only so, but we also glory in our sufferings, because we know that suffering produces perseverance; perseverance, character; and character, hope. And hope does not put us to shame, because God's love has been poured out into our hearts through the Holy Spirit, who has been given to us" (vv. 3–5). To find honor/glory/prestige in suffering seems counterintuitive. Suffering normally connotes weakness, lament, sadness, shame, and disfavor. Yet for Paul, sharing in Christ's sufferings is the criteria for one day sharing in Christ's glory (see Rom 8:17; 2 Cor 1:5; Phil 3:10).

Not only that, but suffering is formative for one's personal development, turning us to either vice or virtue, and testing the metal of our moral resolve. Christians tend to be like tea bags in that you have to put them in hot water to see how strong they really are. Successfully overcoming adversity shapes our personal traits by forcing us to endure under stress (perseverance), gain recognizable approval for our conduct under pressure (character), and look confidently toward the end of our tumult (hope). With such hope, believers can confidently rebuff any shame or derision leveled at their most deeply held convictions. Moo observes that hope is like a muscle; it degenerates if it goes unused. If hardship is met with doubt in God's goodness and promises, the result can be bitterness or despair. But if hardship is met with an attitude of confidence and rejoicing, i.e., Christian hope, the hardship can produce spiritual qualities in one's character.[4] Perhaps we could paraphrase the passage by saying that "we brag in the midst of affliction about God's glory, knowing that affliction produces a strong backbone, a strong backbone produces authenticity, authenticity produces hope, and hope does not make us shy away in shame."

The capacity to endure under duress and grow in the faith is not solely due to one's own resilience, but to the Holy Spirit's enabling. While there are certain imperatives, certain virtues that believers should strive to cultivate, the imperatives are rooted in an indicative, namely, that God's Spirit has been given to believers. The gift of the Holy Spirit is a gift of love. The Spirit is a personified form of divine love that wells up inside believers. "God's love" (lit., "love of God") could be either a love for God or a love from God. There is no

4. Moo, *Romans*, 303.

reason why it cannot be both. The Spirit is a wellspring of affection for the things of God and for God's people. Just as the Spirit is the love that unites the Father and the Son, so too is the Spirit the divine love that draws believers into communion with the everlasting God.

### Christ's Death for Powerless Sinners (5:6–8)

If the wondrous gift of the Holy Spirit filling our hearts was not proof enough of God's love, there is another, more excellent demonstration: Christ's death for sinners. Paul states: "You see, at just the right time, when we were still powerless, Christ died for the ungodly. Very rarely will anyone die for a righteous person, though for a good person someone might possibly dare to die. But God demonstrates his own love for us in this: While we were still sinners, Christ died for us" (vv. 6–8). The movement of thought pertains to how Christ died for ungodly sinners (v. 6), followed with an aside remark that someone might conceivably die for a good person (v. 7), so Christ dying for unworthy persons is a sure sign of God's extraordinary love.[5]

Paul's opening remark (v. 6) is similar to Galatians 4:4, where he wrote that God sent his Son "when the time had fully come," that is, as the climax to a redemptive-historical sequence beginning with Abraham. But here he proffers the view that Christ came at "just the right time." What made that time so "right" was that ungodly sinners were powerless to deliver themselves and were wholly reliant on God to save them from their wretched state. That Christ died for the ungodly obviously harks back to Romans 4:5 where Abraham was the model of the ungodly pagan saved by God's justifying grace. That Christ died "for" them is purposive in the sense of dying to make atonement for their sins.[6]

Paul then comments on the extraordinary nature of this act by way of an analogy as to whom we would normally consider worthy of dying for (v. 7). Only "rarely" would someone give up their own life to save the life of a good man or woman. It is conceivable, Paul admits, but such displays of self-sacrifice and altruistic behavior are rare, rarer than a cheap parking spot in Manhattan. If it is uncommon for someone to die for a good person, it is even less likely that anyone would lay down their lives to save an evil person. Giving up your life to save Nelson Mandela is one thing, but who would take a bullet to save Adolf Hitler?

And yet—and this is the shocking and affronting element to the atonement—God shows his love to sinners by sending Christ to die for them, to make atonement for their sin, for their rectification, redemption, and reconciliation

5. Wright, "Romans," 10:518.

6. Cf. Moo, *Romans*, 307 n. 65 on the connotations of the Greek word *hyper* ("for").

(v. 8). Christ does not die for the righteous, he dies to make the unrighteous righteous. This is the topsy-turvy, crazy, freaky, wildly illogical, world-denying, self-giving love that God shows sinners in Christ Jesus.

### A Reconnaissance on Reconciliation (5:9–11)

Paul proceeds to describe the manner in which God shows his love to sinners in Christ, namely, by justification and reconciliation. This divine act is thereafter the grounds for their sense of assurance. If God loved sinners enough for the Son to die to save them, then God will surely complete what was begun at such a cost.[7]

Paul states: "Since we have now been justified by his blood, how much more shall we be saved from God's wrath through him!" (v. 9). Note how Paul's argument moves from the present to the future and from the difficult to the easy.[8] The key point is that if God has in present time justified sinners by the sacrificial death of his Son (no easy thing to do), then how much more likely is it that believers will also be saved from God's coming wrath through this same Jesus (a comparatively easier thing in light of the first thing).

Paul reiterates the same point again but this time using the images of reconciliation and salvation: "For if, while we were God's enemies, we were reconciled to him through the death of his Son, how much more, having been reconciled, shall we be saved through his life" (v. 10). This is another argument that moves from present/hard to future/easy. In our prior sinful state we were "God's enemies," given the hostility of our minds and our living toward God (even "God-haters" according to Rom 1:30!). Yet it was while we were in such a state of enmity with God that God took the initiative to reconcile us to himself by the death of his Son. And if God has reconciled us by the death of his Son, then certainly he will save us by the life of his risen Son. These are some big juicy assertions and we need to unpack them.

First, note the temporal span to salvation. To be blunt, it isn't just about the cross. There is a big future that is still ahead. Now obviously the death of Jesus, the shedding of his blood, is definitive for justification and reconciliation (see Rom 3:25; 5:9–10; 8:3). Yet that is not the end of the story. Jesus did not stay dead. He was raised up for our justification (4:25), he was exalted to God's right hand (8:34), and he makes continuing intercession for believers (8:34). The death of Jesus marks the beginning of our salvation, but its consummation remains dependent on the continuing life of Christ as the one

---

7. Wright, "Romans," 10:514.

8. This was a common logical sequence in argumentation, called by the rabbis *qal wayyōmer* ("light and heavy").

who "will save" believers for a future day. Paul will speak more toward this future horizon in Romans 8.

Second, justification and reconciliation are opposite sides of the same salvific coin. In fact, we could probably add "redemption," "forgiveness of sin," "peace," and "eternal life" as the host of images for what God achieves for sinners in the death and resurrection of Christ. Salvation for Paul is so rich and so amazing that it requires a full quiver of metaphors to come even close to grasping it.

Third, New Testament scholars have long wondered what is at the center of Paul's theology. What motif or theme is the most dominating one? Several proposals have been offered, ranging from "justification by faith" to "union with Christ" and the like. However, a common proposal for a center of Paul's theology, or at least the center of his soteriology, is that of reconciliation, a proposal I agree with. The notion of reconciliation pertains to the healing of fractured relationships. New Testament examples include the restoration of relationships between persons such as a husband and a wife (1 Cor 7:11) and between fellow Israelites (Acts 7:26). Paul frequently speaks of people being reconciled to God through Christ (Rom 5:10–11; 2 Cor 5:18–21; Eph 2:14–17; Col 1:20–22).[9]

In fact, Paul considered his apostolic missionary crew to be acting as "ambassadors [of] reconciliation" (2 Cor 5:20), and he embodied the practice of reconciliation by entreating Philemon to take back the absconded slave Onesimus (Phlm 17). The key word here is *katalassō*, which basically means, "the exchange of hostility for a friendly relationship."[10] What is significant though, as Stanley Porter has shown, is that Paul was the first author to speak of God, the offended party, initiating reconciliation and using the verb *katalassō* ("I reconcile") in the active voice. For Paul, reconciliation starts with God, who reaches out to sinners through his Son. Reconciliation does not begin with the offending party pleading to God for peace and forgiveness. In this sense, reconciliation is an expression of God's grace.[11]

Finally, Paul closes the section by saying, "Not only is this so, but we also boast in God through our Lord Jesus Christ, through whom we have now received reconciliation" (v. 11). This verse forms a perfect *inclusio* with vv. 1–2, effectively bracketing vv. 1–11 with the theme of boasting in hope in God through Christ. To boast in God through Jesus Christ means a

9. See discussion on "reconciliation" in Bird, *Bird's-Eye View of Paul*, 104–6; idem, *Evangelical Theology*, 557–59.

10. BDAG 521.

11. Stanley E. Porter, *Katalassō in Ancient Greek Literature, with Reference to the Pauline Writings* (Cordoba: Ediciónes El Almendro, 1994).

rejection of boasting in all other possible avenues for the acquisition of honor like virtue, status, accomplishment, and superiority, and to look instead for the glory that is from and in Jesus.[12] John Chrysostom captures Paul's thought wonderfully: "And so the fact of his saving us, and saving us too when we're in such plight, and doing it by means of his only-begotten, and not merely by his only-begotten, but by his blood, weaves for us endless crowns to glory in."[13]

The summative nature of Paul's language easily lends itself to application in both the ancient Roman churches and in the contemporary ones, especially in relation to the real meaning of our salvation and how it proves to be transformative for our own character and conduct.

### The Access of Grace

I've worked in places where you need an access card to get into certain buildings or into special parts of certain buildings. You get to wear a special card on a piece of cord around your neck. You flash the card at security officials or else tap it on an electronic terminal to secure entry into a restricted area. If you do not have the special card, you need to either sign in or get escorted into certain places. When carrying such cards, there is always a certain feeling of privilege or exclusivity, as if one holds the key to some kind of kingdom! I can go in and out of this special secret place as often as I like but those persons over there cannot. I have special privileges! To put it another way, as Tim Keller recently tweeted (yes, I'm now quoting tweets in my commentary): "The only person who dare wake up a king at 3:00 AM for a glass of water is a child. We have that kind of access."[14]

Paul uses the word *prosagōgē* in Romans 5:2 for describing how believers now have, through Christ, "access" to God (a theme rehearsed also in Eph 2:18; 3:12). They are able to stand in God's grace because Christ is for them the means of access into God's favor. To try and approach God without Christ would mean not only access denied, but result in the social equivalent of being roughly carried out of a building by several serious-looking men wearing black suits, dark sunglasses, and pressing a finger against their ear pieces while muttering, "The weasel is being escorted from the building. I repeat, the weasel is being escorted from the building. The area is now secure, please stand down."

12. Jewett, *Romans*, 368.
13. John Chrysostom, *Hom. Rom.* 9.
14. @timkellernyc 2:05 AM - 24 Feb 2015.

Yet Christ means that the way to God's presence is forever open to us who bear his name. There is no security service, electronic door, or dead bolt that can obstruct us from entering into God's presence. We are free to enter the presence of the heavenly, royal, all-sovereign, and infinitely holy God. Not bad considering we were once godless sinners, by nature objects of wrath, at enmity with God. Yet now we can enter into the presence of God by the blood of Christ our reconciler. Such is the access of grace—a theme that is wonderfully captured in the lyrics of a modern hymn:

> Only by grace can we enter,
> Only by grace can we stand,
> Not by our human endeavor
> But by the blood of the Lamb.

### Virtues

There are different ways of conceiving of ethics. One can think in terms of consequences or duties, but these days it is common to describe ethics in terms of cultivating certain virtues.[15] Paul himself was probably no stranger to discussions of virtue by philosophers, Greco-Roman and Jewish, as Paul was able to produce his own lists of virtuous attitudes and behaviors that should typify God's people. Three virtues that Paul mentions here are endurance, character, and hope. Paul believed that Christians can even boast in affliction because affliction is the process by which such virtues are exercised as living expressions of our faith.

#### *Endurance*

Endurance was celebrated by moral philosophers of antiquity as one of the noblest of virtues. The ability to persist under adversity was a mark of strong and even royal character. We celebrate endurance in our own culture in many ways, such as the accolades offered to endurance marathoners or memorializing those who have overcome great pain and anguish in the course of their lives. There is something inherently noble about those who have kept the faith, fought the good fight, walked the line with Christ, and finished the race in the midst of external pressure, internal struggle, personal injury, constant temptation, and even self-doubt. The fact is that the Christian life is not a sprint; it's an ultra-distance marathon, or sometimes like partaking in an ultra-marathon obstacle course while being chased by tigers wearing laser guns on their heads. There are some great stations along the way that can refresh

---

15. See discussion in Scot McKnight, *The Sermon on the Mount* (SGBC; Grand Rapids: Zondervan, 2013), 4–5.

us in the often-perilous journey toward the new Jerusalem — hopefully every Sunday service, our family, and Christian friends — but that does not diminish the genuine struggle we face along the way. What gives us the impetus to keep going is seeing that the end is drawing closer. And our end is coming — either the Lord returns or we walk under the veil of death — but either way, at the end we will see the Holy City of the new Jerusalem and enjoy an everlasting intimacy with God (Rev 21 – 22).

I don't know if you've ever heard the story of the American distance swimmer Florence Chadwick, but it's a good story about endurance. In 1952 Chadwick attempted to become the first woman to swim the twenty-plus miles across the Catalina Channel from Catalina Island to Palos Verde on the American west coast. Due to the threat of surrounding sharks, cold waters, and a blanket of fog, she gave up the swim with less than a mile to go. The fog meant that she was unable to see where she was going and did not feel like she was making any progress. She could not see that she was getting nearer to her goal. So she quit the race. Afterwards she told reporters, "Look, I'm not excusing myself, but if I could have seen land, I know I could have made it." However, only two months later, Chadwick tried again, this time she made it across the channel. How true it is that we can only finish a race if we can see the end. For Christians, our endurance comes from (among other things) the fact that we can see the end, the majestic vision of God dwelling with his people, and this is the end we strive toward day by day, stepping out in faith, one foot after another, ebbing ever closer to our eternal home.[16]

### *Character*

Paul says that endurance produces "character." The word for "character" is *dokimē*, which means the quality of withstanding a test.[17] That is a way of saying that hardship shows the true nature of our personality and the natural proclivity of our desires. Character is something that is shaped by external forces, but also something that is cultivated by choice. While elements of our personality are no doubt influenced by both nature and nurture, there are traits to our person that we consciously decide to grow. If the digital age has taught us anything, it is that allowing people to say and do things anonymously is the surest sign to the true nature of their moral character. As Christians we are to have a godly, holy, and Christlike character. Some of the wisest words ever given to me when I was a still relatively new believer came

16. Karen C. Krahulik, "Chadwick, Florence May," in *Notable American Women: A Biographical Dictionary Completing the Twentieth Century* (ed. Susan Ware; Boston: Harvard University Press, 2004), 5:110 – 11; "Florence May Chadwick," www.answers.com/topic/florence-chadwick#ixzz2nz1R0c3U.

17. BDAG 256.

from the (then) young pastor of the first church I ever attended. Pastor Craig Corkill once told me:

> If you sow a thought, you reap an act.
> If you sow an act, you reap a habit.
> If you sow a habit, you reap a character.
> If you sow a character, then you reap a destiny.

Those words have stuck with me, and I hope they stick with you too. Christians should sow thoughts, acts, and habits that will produce a character worthy of an eternal inheritance. Then perhaps we will have the type of character that is genuinely approveable before God just as Paul exhorted Timothy: "Do your best to present yourself to God as one approved, a worker who does not need to be ashamed and who correctly handles the word of truth" (2 Tim 2:15).

***Hope***

Finally, Paul says that character produces hope. Hope is not some ephemeral thing like that which might be, could be, or possibly be. Hope can sometimes seem futile. Chicago Cubs fans will know all too well what I'm talking about! But hope is a big theme in Romans. Abraham's faith was really a hope in God's promises (Rom 4:18). Creation is subjected to frustration with a hope of overcoming it (8:20). Christians are saved in hope, and hope means that we have to patiently wait for what we do not yet have (8:24–25). Paul hopes that his gospel will arouse Israel to jealousy (11:14). Christians are to be "joyful in hope" even amidst affliction (12:12). The Scriptures were written so that we might have hope (15:4). Christ is the one about whom Isaiah prophesies as the hope of the nations (15:12 = Isa 11:10). Amidst the vulnerabilities and uncertainties of life, Paul urges the Romans to remain united, supporting each other, so that by their unity they will have an abundance of hope.[18]

Most Anglican prayers end by looking forward to a "world without end." Sadly though, we live today in a world without hope. The most basic of ambitions, the sweetest of dreams, and most cherished thoughts of men and women across the whole globe so often find themselves laid bare and busted by the cruel realities of the world around them. Death becomes the final destroyer of all hopes as it ends all chances of life and happiness beyond the vestiges of its dark grip. A somber thought, but hardly a new one, as such despair has been often expressed by thinkers. The ancient Roman philosopher Seneca once said, "Most men ebb and flow in wretchedness between the fear of death and the hardships of life; they are unwilling to live, and yet do not

18. Watson, *Paul, Judaism, and the Gentiles*, 272–73.

know how to die."[19] For the twentieth-century existentialist Albert Camus, "He who despairs of the human condition is a coward, but he who has a hope for it is a fool." But for us Christians, we are gladly Camusian fools because in Christ we are not sufferers of Senecian wretchedness.

The reason for that is because we have a hope that is high as heavens and as wide as the love of God in Christ Jesus. For the Scriptures point us toward a hope beyond the earthly mire and toward the sublime shores of a new heavens and a new earth. No wonder one of the most frequently repeated refrains in Psalm 119 is "I have put my hope in your word," because it is a word of promise and that promise *was* made good, *is* made good, and *will* be made good in Christ. One of my favorite books by N. T. Wright is his *Surprised by Hope*. In particular, I love his wonderful remark, "Easter was when Hope in person surprised the whole world by coming forward from the future into the present."[20] We might even say that *hope became flesh* and now the word of hope goes forth into the world. As such, the world does not end with a whimper or a slow slide into entropy. Instead, God in Christ has brought the future into the present and in doing so has given us hope that the life and love in the Lord Jesus will win in the end.

## Christ for Sinners

The other thing Romans 5:1–11 teaches most profoundly is God's enduring love for wretched and wrongful people. The first theology class I ever sat in was in northern Australia, where we had a guest lecturer from America. The lecturer's name was Jim Allman, who now teaches Bible exposition at Dallas Theological Seminary. I vividly remember the poignant testimony he gave about Romans 5:8 and how it quite literally saved him:

> When I was pastoring some years ago, I found myself in an almost impossible position. Hired to minister the Word of God to God's people, I was struggling with my own salvation. Those who have been through the experience know how desperate such a condition is. I had slipped into a persistent depression over the period of about three years. The pressure of the ministry, the responsibility to lead people spiritually, led me into a profound spiritual despair. My growing understanding of God's grace and its efficacious work in our lives compounded the despair. I felt that I must show myself worthy of the pastorate, worthy to even claim to be a Christian. I learned later that depression is anger turned inward. For me

19. Seneca, *Letters* 4.6.

20. N. T. Wright, *Surprised by Hope: Rethinking Heaven, the Resurrection, and the Mission of the Church* (San Francisco: HarperOne, 2009), 40–41.

> this was true. The anger I felt against myself led me to self-destructive thoughts. The despair grew and deepened. For most of about four years I would awaken in the depths of the night planning ways to commit suicide. I wanted my family to receive the benefits of an insurance policy on my life. Certainly I was worth more to them dead than alive. The beginning of the end of this despair came late one night when for the first time Romans 5.8 crashed into my consciousness. I became convinced that God saves man by grace. I was equally convinced that God's grace does not work by halves. His grace is sufficient. Yet I could not see any evidence that His grace was effective in my life. For the first time, that night, God made it clear to me that salvation is not for the righteous. Romans 5.8 made it plain that one key requirement for salvation is that God saves sinners. Though I could see no evidence of God's grace in my life, I could see that I was indeed a sinner. If God saves sinners, then perhaps I could be a saved man. I knew that I was trusting nothing but Christ for salvation, since I could trust nothing in my life. For the first time it became clear that for salvation, sin is absolutely necessary. That was the beginning of a six year odyssey into God's grace.[21]

I do think one can preach Romans too individualistically and lose the cosmic and christological scope of its message. However, there can be no denying the fact that the gospel confronts individuals with a message of God's love in Christ Jesus — a message they need to respond to if they are to avoid the ruin of wrath against their sin. We need to keep reevangelizing our churches, because once the gospel is simply assumed, it is soon forgotten, and what is forgotten is soon replaced with something else.[22] Too often those enmeshed in church culture, even from birth, can be lulled into trusting in their religiosity rather than trusting in Jesus for redemption. That's why we need to keep preaching the gospel in our churches, even if the choir is convinced, to make sure that our churches never become a place where the sinners can sulk in sorrow or the self-righteous will ever feel solace.

21. Personal correspondence with Jim Allman dated 02.01.14.

22. See on this, D. A. Carson, "Put the Advance of the Gospel at the Center of Your Aspiration," *Articles and Excerpts*, Acts29 Network: www.acts29network.org/article/put-the-advance-of-the-gospel-at-the-center-of-your-aspirations/. My thanks to Matt Smith for drawing attention to this article.

CHAPTER 9

# Romans 5:12–21

## LISTEN to the Story

[12]Therefore, just as sin entered the world through one man, and death through sin, and in this way death came to all people, because all sinned—

[13]To be sure, sin was in the world before the law was given, but sin is not charged against anyone's account where there is no law. [14]Nevertheless, death reigned from the time of Adam to the time of Moses, even over those who did not sin by breaking a command, as did Adam, who is a pattern of the one to come.

[15]But the gift is not like the trespass. For if the many died by the trespass of the one man, how much more did God's grace and the gift that came by the grace of the one man, Jesus Christ, overflow to the many! [16] Nor can the gift of God be compared with the result of one man's sin: The judgment followed one sin and brought condemnation, but the gift followed many trespasses and brought justification. [17]For if, by the trespass of the one man, death reigned through that one man, how much more will those who receive God's abundant provision of grace and of the gift of righteousness reign in life through the one man, Jesus Christ!

[18]Consequently, just as one trespass resulted in condemnation for all people, so also one righteous act resulted in justification and life for all people. [19]For just as through the disobedience of the one man the many were made sinners, so also through the obedience of the one man the many will be made righteous.

[20]The law was brought in so that the trespass might increase. But where sin increased, grace increased all the more, [21]so that, just as sin reigned in death, so also grace might reign through righteousness to bring eternal life through Jesus Christ our Lord.

*Listening to the texts in the story*: Genesis 3; Wisdom of Solomon 2:23–24; *4 Ezra* 3.21–22; 7.118–19; *2 Baruch* 54.15, 19.

In the cathedral of Romans 5–8, 5:12–21 is like a room of stark contrasts. It is the darkest corner of the building, yet the brightest lamp shines in it. It's a room where the blackness of human evil casts its shadow, but a luminous ray of brightness pierces through it. The mystery of evil's origins hangs in the air like a heavy fog while the candles on a messianic menorah push the darkness back. In this passage, we see both the hideousness of human evil and the hidden plan of God to redeem it.

Exegetically, Romans 5:12–21 is a rather difficult text to translate and understand. It is not just that the grammar is difficult, especially v. 12d, but Paul breaks off his argument at the end of v. 12 and does not pick it up again until v. 18. The intervening paragraph in vv. 13–17 is essentially an extended parenthetical afterthought concerning the nexus between sin, law, and death. Wright notes: "The Adam/Christ contrast of 5:12–21 is cryptic and elliptical: trying to read its Greek after the measured sentences of 5:1–11 is like turning from Rembrandt to Picasso."[1] Complexities aside, Keck calls vv. 12–21 a "theological tour de force" as it sets out the human dilemma and God's deliverance in a panoramic horizon.[2]

Paul offers here a *synkrisis*, a rhetorical comparison between two "types," two persons who are symbolic and yet determinative for human existence.[3] I would aver that the Adam/Christ typology that runs through Romans 5:12–21 is really an extended commentary on 1 Corinthians 15:22 and 15:56: "For as in Adam all die, so in Christ all will be made alive.... The sting of death is sin, and the power of sin is the law." The background story is, of course, Genesis 3 and the account of the fall of Adam and Even into sin and corruption and their subsequent expulsion from God's presence. In the course of Romans 5:12–21, Paul endeavors to demonstrate how Adam's sin brought death, but the giving of the law to the Israelites at Sinai did not fix the sin problem. The law served only to accentuate the power of sin, to activate sinful desire, and to affirm the sentence of death due to Adam's progeny on account of sin. In which case, the law did not solve the Adamic problem; rather, it made the situation much worse.

Paul locates his argument about God's saving righteousness within the arc of the biblical narrative about humanity condemned and then justified, humanity enslaved in sin and set free in Christ; thus, justification creates not only a worldwide Abrahamic family, but also a renewed humanity. Believers shift from the epoch of sin, death, and condemnation associated with Adam's

1. Wright, "Romans," 10:508.

2. Keck, *Romans*, 145.

3. Cf. Quintilian, *Inst. Or.* 3.8.23–24; Hermogenes, *Progymnasta* 2.

transgression to the epoch of righteousness, life, and justification associated with the obedience of the new Adam, Jesus the Messiah.

By taking us from the old Adam to the new Adam, Paul shows that all people everywhere stand behind one of two figures: Adam and Christ. In Adam one faces bondage to evil and the sentence of death. In Christ one faces righteousness and life.[4] The main point of the passage is that the combined power of sin, law, and death is defeated by the superabounding power of grace and righteousness in the Lord Jesus Christ.[5] The way Paul proceeds is (1) by connecting the entrance of sin and death into the world with Adam (v. 12); then breaking off from his main idea to make parenthetical remarks about (2) how sin and death were in the world before the law (vv. 13–14); (3) by contrasting the outcomes of Adam's disobedience with Christ's obedience (vv. 15–17); (4) then by returning to his main thesis about how Adam's trespass is matched by Christ's righteousness (vv. 18–19); and (5) finally by showing that it was not law but grace that triumphs over Adam's sin.

### One Man, One Sin, Lots of Death (5:12)

Paul now shifts from describing reconciliation to describing the primeval events that led to the universal human need to be reconciled to God: "Therefore, just as sin entered the world through one man, and death through sin, and in this way death came to all people, because all sinned" (v. 12). The logical connection between what precedes and what follows vv. 12–21 is not immediately obvious. In one sense, vv. 12–21 take up the themes of condemnation and justification in 1:18–4:25 and show how they can be explained by way of standing in relation to either Adam or Christ as sources of condemnation and justification respectively. In another sense, vv. 12–21 also introduce some important concepts like grace, life, sinfulness, and transformation that will be prominent in 6:1–8:17. Paul's opening words *dia touto* can mean "Therefore," but also "So it comes about that" and so grounds the hope and reconciliation of vv. 1–11 in Jesus' obedience as the new Adam in vv. 15–19.[6] In any event, in vv. 12–21 Paul places the story of God's saving

---

4. See further, Bird, *Evangelical Theology*, 677–83.

5. Jewett (*Romans*, 370) comments: "I conclude that the main theme is how Christ's life (v. 10) defines the future destiny of believers just as Adam's life defined the future of his descendants." Barth (*Romans*, 165) writes an apt summary: "There is no discovery of God in Christ, no entering into life, except men be exposed in Adam as fallen from God and under the judgment of death. But we cannot stop here: there is no falling from God in Adam, no judgement of death visible to us, except at the point where we are reconciled to God in Christ and assured of life."

6. Wright, "Romans," 10:523.

righteousness in the scope of a universal history that affects all of humanity, and he shows how the resolution to the problem of sin's entrance was not the reading of the law but the reconciliation wrought by the risen Lord.

The premise behind the "therefore" pertains to God's salvation in Christ, for which a bond of assurance now wonderfully exists (vv. 1–11). But this salvation must be understood in light of the primeval events of Adam's transgression and humanity's subsequent descent into evil, enmity, death, and decay. Somewhat frustratingly, Paul begins a comparison in v. 12 with "just as sin entered the world through one man ..." but never completes it. Later in vv. 19 and 21, Paul argues "just so ... so also" but we do not get a "so also" in v. 12, leading to some confusion.

Paul begins his train of thought by narrating the sequence of events that thrust sin and death upon the world: "just as sin entered the world through one man, and death through sin, and in this way death came to all people." Clearly Paul here is providing a synopsis of the events in Genesis 3 about Adam's transgression leading to death, a death that comes on all people.[7] Noticeably, it is not Adam's action so much that is central but sin's entrance. Sin is personified by Paul as a something that "enters" (v. 12) and "reigns" (v. 20); later we learn that it can be "obeyed" (6:20), pays "wages" (6:23), seizes "opportunity" (7:8, 11), "deceives" (7:11), "kills" (7:12), and even "dwells" in people (7:20). Sin is portrayed as the villain, death his weapon, and people his victims. Sin is the sum of evil, personal and impersonal, that found a portal into the world by the disobedience of Adam and Eve.[8] Sin immediately became a deadly pathogen, potent, lethal, instantly producing death in all with whom it came into contact. Sin brought death—spiritual death, then physical death, and then eternal death—to all people.[9] Beverly Gaventa comments: "In Romans in particular sin is Sin—not a lowercase transgression, not even a human disposition or flaw in human nature, but an uppercase Power that enslaves humankind and stands over against God."[10]

7. On Jewish views about the influence of Adam and Eve on subsequent human behavior, see Wis 2:24; Sir 14:17; 25:24; *4 Ezra* 3:7, 21–22; 4:30; 7:48; 116–18; *Jub.* 3:17–32; *Life of Adam and Eve* 3; *2 Bar.* 23:4; 54:15, 19. See discussion in Tobin, *Paul's Rhetoric*, 167–77; Kruse, *Romans*, 255–57. According to Dunn (*Romans*, 1:273–74) Paul reflects "the same broad stream of Jewish reflection on the Genesis account of Adam's fall—viz., the tension between the inescapableness of human sin operating as a compelling power from within or without ... and recognition of human responsibility in sinning."

8. On Eve's role in the primeval entrance of sin, see 2 Cor 11:3 and 2 Tim 2:14.

9. According to Morris (*Romans*, 230): "Physical death is in mind, but not physical death in itself; it is physical death as the sign and symbol of spiritual death."

10. Beverly R. Gaventa, "The Cosmic Power of Sin in Paul's Letter to the Romans: Towards a Widescreen Edition," *Int* 58 (2004): 231 (229–40).

The explanation as to why death is visited on all people is then given in a notoriously opaque clause at the end of v. 12, which the NIV translates as "because all sinned" (see also NRSV, ESV, NASB, NLT, NET). The issues here are both grammatical and theological. The context, however, indicates that the net point is that death is universal because sin is universal, and Adam was the conduit by which sin and death were unleashed in the world.[11]

First, on grammar, the clause *eph' hō pantes hēmarton* can be translated in a few different ways.[12] Augustine famously followed the Latin Vulgate *in quo* to mean "*in whom* all sinned," implying that all people sinned in Adam. That is largely the basis for the Augustinian doctrine of original sin. Others prefer to take the clause in a consecutive or purposive sense as meaning something like "with the result that all sinned."[13] Yet, this would require that death (*thanatos*) is the logical antecedent of the pronoun (*hō*) and mean that death caused sin whereas the reverse is true, that sin caused death.[14] Thus, with the vast majority of modern English versions, we prefer the translation "*because* all sinned" for the reason that the conjunction *eph' hō* is best taken causally since it has that meaning elsewhere in Paul's letters (2 Cor 5:4; Phil 3:12; 4:10). As such, death spreads to all of humanity because all of humanity engages in sin and so dies. In any event, as Dunn observes, the emphasis is not so much on "original sin," but on "original death," underscoring the consequence of death from sin and sin from Adam.[15]

Second, on theology, the location of this sinning is the interpretive problem at hand. Where and when does this sin take place? Does it somehow occur "in" Adam's sin or is it a sinning "in ourselves"? Reformed theology has a long history of identifying Adam as the representative of all people, and his disobedience is then said to be reckoned or imputed to all people. In which case, everyone is condemned because they share in and have solidarity with Adam's sin. But many will object that it is hardly fair that I be indicted for sins that someone else committed. It is surely just that I be judged only for my own failures rather than for anybody else's. This tension has been handled in different ways.

Origen believed that all humans were seminally in Adam and were exiled from Paradise with Adam. "As a result," he says, "that death which came upon him because of his transgression also passed through him into them who were held in his loins." Yet Origen was also aware that attributing condemnation and justification to identification with Adam or Christ would make it appear

11. Moo, *Romans*, 321.

12. Cf. Cranfield, *Romans*, 1:274–75; Fitzmyer, *Romans*, 413–17; Jewett, *Romans*, 375–76.

13. Fitzmyer, *Romans*, 413–17; Schreiner, *Romans*, 274–79; Talbert, *Romans*, 148.

14. Cf. Byrne, *Romans*, 183; Wright, "Romans," 10:527.

15. Cf. Dunn, *Romans*, 1:273; Byrne, *Romans*, 176; Schreiner, *Romans*, 276.

"that we ourselves do nothing for which we deserve to live or die: Adam is the cause of death, and Christ the cause of life." So he also added that human sin is not just a matter of nature, but comes from imitating one's parent. In such a case, sin emerges from Adam by both "generation" and "instruction."[16]

According to Pelagius, sin entered the world through Adam's "example" so that "through Adam sin came at a time when it did not yet exist, so in the same way through Christ righteousness was recovered at a time when it survived in almost no one."[17] Ambrosiaster emphasized human solidarity with Adam: "For it is clear that all have sinned in Adam as though in a lump. For being corrupted by sin himself, all those whom he fathered were born under sin. For that reason we are all sinners, because we are all descended from him." But he added, "We do not suffer this death as a result of Adam's sin, but his fall makes it possible for us to get it by our own sins."[18]

Chrysostom, typical of the Eastern tradition, identifies sin as a personal act and Adam's influence is limited to being the instrument through whom mortality and corruption entered and prevailed over humanity because of his disobedience.[19] Similarly, Theodoret said: "Therefore, the Holy Apostle states that because Adam had sinned and had been made subject to death because of that sin, both of these defects passed into the human race. The condition of death prevails over all humanity, then, because all have sinned. So each person stands under sentence of death, not on account of the sin of the first parent but through each one's own transgression."[20]

Augustine, in his anti-Pelagian writings, stressed that sin is not simply a matter of imitation of Adam, but propagation from Adam. Adam is the one "in whom" sin enters and extends to all. Augustine saw a transmission of guilt from Adam to people, a guilt that could only be reversed by the grace of baptism.[21] Augustine's view held sway in Reformed churches, though what was emphasized was more of the federal or representative character of Adam's transgression by which Adam's sin was imputed to the whole human race. Others have emphasized that what is propagated from Adam is primarily a corrupted nature, not an inherited guilt, so that what is passed on from Adam is a propensity to sin, and this sin results in death.[22]

16. Wilken, *Romans*, 114–25.

17. Pelagius, *Romans*, on 5:12 and 5:15.

18. Ambrosiaster, *Romans*, 40.

19. Chrysostom, *Hom. Rom.* 10. See David Weaver, "The Exegesis of Romans 5:12 among the Greek Fathers and Its Implications for the Doctrine of Original Sin: The 5th–12th Centuries," *SBTQ* 29 (1985): 122–59, 231–57.

20. Wilken, *Romans*, 119.

21. Augustine, *City of God* 13.14; 16.27; *On the Merits and Forgiveness of Sins and Infant Baptism* 1.10; *Against Julian*, 7.24; 20.63.

22. Cranfield, *Romans*, 1:278.

I should point out that a somewhat mediating view is advocated by Henri Blocher, who tries to forge a path between competing conceptions of the nexus between Adam-sin-guilt-death-humanity. He splits the horns of the dilemma as to whether we are condemned by Adam's sin or by our own sin. On Blocher's account, humans are viewed through the legal identity of Adam, and Adam's sin efficaciously secures the condemnation of all people by virtue of their representation by him as emphasized in vv. 18–19. Even so, beyond the federal headship of Adam over humanity, sin is both propagated by Adam and imitated from Adam. Blocher accordingly contends that we undergo the fact of death in solidarity with Adam like children who share in the sin of their father. Yet we do not undergo the penalty of Adam as if it were immediately ours. Rather, by sharing in the consequences of Adam's sin — in the spread of his corruption and death — our sinning certainly happens and our own guilt can be reckoned as originating with Adam. Hence his paraphrase of Rom 5:12: "Just as through one man, Adam, sin entered the world and the sin-death connection was established, and so death could be inflicted on all as the penalty of their sins."[23]

The logic of Rom 5:12 seems to support Blocher's contention, since the train of thought appears to run something like:

Sin entered the world through Adam.
Death is the consequence of the sin of Adam.
Death has spread to the whole human race.
Human beings, therefore, because they enter the world alienated from God, engage in sin.

**Sin Came before Law (5:13–14)**

The conclusion of v. 12 about Adam introducing a sin-death nexus is reinforced in vv. 13–14: "To be sure, sin was in the world before the law was given, but sin is not charged against anyone's account where there is no law. Nevertheless, death reigned from the time of Adam to the time of Moses, even over those who did not sin by breaking a command, as did Adam, who is a pattern of the one to come." The point to remember is that the association Paul makes between sin and death is open to question since Paul elsewhere draws a thick line between law and sin (see Rom 3:20; 4:15; 7:7–8; 1 Cor 15:56). So if sins depends on law, and if there was a time when there was no law, was there ever a period without sin? Obviously not! Paul preempts this

23. Henri Blocher, *Original Sin: Illuminating the Riddle* (NSBT; Downers Grove, IL: InterVarsity, 1997), 78.

objection by arguing that death follows from sin and since "death reigned from the time of Adam to the time of Moses," sin was in the world before the law. So while sin might not have been reckoned during this period as a "transgression," a deliberate violation of a known law, sin existed all the same as evidenced by the presence of death.[24] While sin existed prior to the law, it was the law that enabled sin to be fully identified and confronted. As Cranfield puts it: "It is only in the presence of the law, only in Israel and in the Church, that the full seriousness of sin is visible and the responsibility of the sinner stripped of every extenuating circumstance."[25]

## The Grace Gift Trumps the Trespass (5:15–16)

Adam is a "pattern" of the "one who is to come," namely, Christ (v. 14), and so Paul waxes eloquently in his contrast between Adam and Christ in the rest of vv. 15–19. Paul begins the contrast in vv. 15–16 by highlighting the differences between the *content* and *consequences* of Adam and Christ's actions. Paul's argument here is much like a Rembrandt painting for it is against the dark backdrop of Adam's sin that the brightness and clarity of God's grace-gift stands out so starkly.[26]

First, "But the gift is not like the trespass. For if the many died by the trespass of the one man, how much more did God's grace and the gift that came by the grace of the one man, Jesus Christ, overflow to the many!" (v. 15). Adam's transgression (*paraptōma*) is entirely unlike the grace-gift (*charisma, dōrea*). Paul switches from "sin" (vv. 12–14) to "transgression" to describe Adam's fall, and this will now become the primary term for describing Adam's disobedience in the garden (vv. 16, 17, 18, 20). While "sin" and "transgression" are synonyms (see v. 14, "those who did not *sin* by *breaking the command*"), the former has the sense of missing the mark, while the later conveys the notion of stepping over a boundary.[27]

On the positive side, the co-location of "grace" (*charis*) and "gift" (*dōrea*) in the second half of the verse emphasizes that the gift is entirely gracious; it flows from the unmerited mercy and favor of God. In the ancient Mediterranean world, gift-giving was not like our time, entirely generous and

24. Of course, this assumes that the particle *alla* at the head v. 14 is not adversative ("but" [CEB]) and instead is concessive ("Nevertheless" [KJV, NASB, NIV, HCSB]). See Cranfield, *Romans*, 1:282.

25. Cranfield, *Romans* 1:282.

26. Witherington, *Romans*, 142.

27. Cf. Hannah K. Harrington, "Sin," in *EDEJ* (ed. J. J. Collins and D. C. Harlow; Grand Rapids: Eerdmans, 2010), 1230–31.

gratuitous; rather, it was always about fittingness and reciprocation. As John Barclay notes:

> The corn-handout to citizens, the patronage of a socially-significant club, the reward of a victorious athlete, the gift of property bequeathed to an adopted heir or old friend, the political backing of a long-established family: none of these are pay, calculated duties or handed over of necessity; they are carefully calibrated gifts, given according to relation between the donor and the recipient and according to the social or moral structures governing the relationship.[28]

In contrast, what Paul says is that God gives the gift without condition to those who are unfit for it and without means of reciprocation. Such a notion would be perceived, says Barclay, as "random, bizarre, and potentially dangerous."[29] The gift itself is probably that of a righteous status leading to eternal life (see Rom 5:16, 18; 6:23). The contrast between Adam's transgression and grace-gift is about their nature: one is fatal and ghastly, the other free and gracious. For if "many"—a semitic equivalent for "all"—died by Adam's trespass, how much better is the grace-gift that flows abundantly to all, presumably through the offer of the gospel. In which case, Adam's transgression is a deed of death that is paltry when compared to God's gift and the work of grace that brings righteousness and life through Messiah Jesus.

Second, "nor can the gift of God be compared with the result of one man's sin: The judgment followed one sin and brought condemnation, but the gift followed many trespasses and brought justification" (v. 16). Paul ups the ante of the contrast by showing how much better God's gift is when compared to Adam's sin in terms of consequences. The superiority is partly mathematical. *One sin* resulted in condemnation, but this *one gift* brings liberation from the penalty of *many sins*. Adam's sin, though infectious, deadly, pervasive, and total, cannot overide the sheer immensity of the saving power contained in God's gift of justification and life. God's response to Adam's transgression is not to cancel it but to exceed it by bringing to completion the destiny of which Adam had fallen short.[30] Such grace does not counterbalance the weight of sin, it over balances it.[31]

---

28. John M. G. Barclay, "Believers and the 'Last Judgment': Grace and Recompense in Paul," in *Eschatologie–Eschatology: The Sixth Durham-Tübingen Research Symposium: Eschatology in Old Testament, Ancient Judaism and Early Christianity* (ed. H.-J. Eckstein, C. Landmesser, and H. Lichtenberger; WUNT 272; Tübingen: Mohr Siebeck, 2011), 201.

29. Barclay, "Believers and the 'Last Judgment,'" 201.

30. Dunn, *Romans*, 1:280.

31. Barrett, *Romans*, 114.

### The Reign of Righteousness over the Trespass (5:17)

Paul amplifies v. 16 by continuing the contrast between Adam and Christ in terms of the consequences of their actions, expressing the contrast by way of reference to death and life: "For if, by the trespass of the one man, death reigned through that one man, how much more will those who receive God's abundant provision of grace and of the gift of righteousness reign in life through the one man, Jesus Christ!" (v. 17). Through Adam's transgression death entered and exercised its tyranny over the entire human race, which indicates again how this "one man" is the vehicle by which humanity's mortal and immoral condition was created.

However, a better condition is created by "one man, Jesus Christ," in whom grace abounds, overflows, and erupts toward all of humanity. Or, to quote Morris, "Grace is superlative generosity. Grace is overflowing abundance."[32] There is a "gift of righteousness," the status of being in a right relationship with God on offer. It is a way of describing justification as a gift that one receives rather than as something one earns (see Rom 4:4–5). Death's reign is defeated like a sub-Saharan dictator being brought to justice and in its stead believers reign in life through Jesus Christ. There is also a tacit glimpse toward the future where the reign of death is supplanted by the reign of the saints over God's new world (see Dan 7:27; Matt 19:28; Rev 5:10; 20:4–6). While many have seen a universalism in these verses—all die in Adam, all made alive in Christ—the benefits of Jesus Christ do not flow automatically. The experience of grace, righteousness, and life is for those who "receive" it, and they receive it by believing it.

### The Victory of the Messiah (5:18–19)

Paul finally resumes the argument he began in v. 12, which he commented on parenthetically by remarking on the relationship between sin and death prior to the law (vv. 13–14) and elaborated on in vv. 15–17 by way of several sharp contrasts between Adam and Christ. He declares: "Consequently, just as one trespass resulted in condemnation for all people, so also one righteous act resulted in justification and life for all people. For just as through the disobedience of the one man the many were made sinners, so also through the obedience of the one man the many will be made righteous" (vv. 18–19). Several things merit mention.

First, Adam's "one trespass" and "disobedience" has its sequel in Christ's "one righteous act" and "obedience." This does not refer to Jesus keeping the law in the course of his life, his so-called "active obedience," but refers more

32. Morris, *Romans*, 237.

properly to his faithfulness to his redemptive vocation by suffering death on the cross as part of the Father's design for reconciliation.

Second, the respective outcomes of Adam's and Christ's actions are "condemnation" and "justification," proving beyond all reasonable doubt that justification here is clearly forensic; it denotes a righteous status before God (see Rom 8:1). Again, however, Paul marries it to the concept of "life," as he does elsewhere, showing that vindication and vivification go hand in hand (see vv. 10, 17, 18, 21).

Third, Paul essentially restates v. 18 in v. 19, but now shifts his imagery for salvation from the forensic to the transformative and amplifies the future horizon of v. 17. The verb *kathistēmi* does not mean "imputed" as it is not a synonym for *logizomai*, which Paul used throughout Romans 4. The verb conveys the idea of both appointing and making something into a certain state of affairs.[33] While the verb might be declarative, it is no less effectual for what it declares. That is to say, because of Adam, people are *constituted* as sinners and sinful; because of Christ, people are constituted as right and righteous. Schreiner agrees that both ideas are present: "One cannot separate the representative and constitutive roles of Adam and of Christ in these verses."[34]

Paul here contrasts our condemnation *and* corruption in Adam with our justification *and* transformation in Christ. Wright offers a fitting summary: "Christ's *dikaiōma* [righteous act] in the middle of history leads to God's *dikaiōsis* [justification] on the last day."[35] On top of that, the future tense of *kathistēmi* is not a logical future, but a real future; it pertains to an eschatological and cosmic transformation before God on the final day.[36] Paul prods us to look forward to the life of justification in our risen and glorified bodies. As Seifrid argues, the resurrection of the ungodly comprises the incarnation of their justification. It is the formal enactment of that verdict in their own resurrection.[37]

## Sin Is Defeated by Grace, Not Law (5:20–21)

"The law was brought in so that the trespass might increase. But where sin increased, grace increased all the more, so that, just as sin reigned in death, so also grace might reign through righteousness to bring eternal life through Jesus Christ our Lord" (vv. 20–21). An interesting feature of Romans 5:12–21 is that Paul has moved beyond the particularism of Jew vis-à-vis Gentile that

33. BDAG 492.

34. Schreiner, *Romans*, 288; cf. similarly Fitzmyer, *Romans*, 421; Witherington, *Romans*, 150.

35. Wright, "Romans," 10:529.

36. See, e.g., Käsemann, *Romans*, 157; Dunn, *Romans*, 1:285; Seifrid, *Christ, Our Righteousness*, 71; against, e.g., Cranfield, *Romans*, 1.291; Fitzmyer, *Romans*, 421; Moo, *Romans*, 345 n. 142.

37. Seifrid, *Christ, Our Righteousness*, 71.

so dominated Romans 1–4 and addressed instead the plight of humanity pitched to a universal horizon. It is not just a matter of rescuing Israel from a continuing state of exile and a few Gentile acquaintances along the way. Rather, all of humanity is understood as being in the bondage of sin and under the tyranny of death. Paul's story of salvation, then, reaches behind Isaiah 40–66, back through Deuteronomy 27–31, all the way back to Genesis 3. Evidence for the universal scope of salvation is aptly supplied by Watson: "If Adam is a 'type' of Christ, then Christ's act can hardly be narrower in its scope than Adam's."[38]

As such, vv. 20–21 must be understood as Paul sketching out the story of redemptive history with a view to showing who the true villain really is. Israel's problem is not they are like pre-fall Adam with custody of creation and yet the beasts (i.e., Gentiles) have taken over the global zoo. No, the problem is that Israel is in post-fall Adam and they need to be in the Messiah, the new Adam. What is more, the Messiah fixes the problem with humanity that Israel's covenants and law could not fix: sin and death. The solution comes not by Moses but through the Messiah in the form of grace, righteousness, and life. Barth is eloquent here: "Grace is not grace, if he that receives it is not under judgement. Righteousness is not righteousness, if it be not reckoned to the sinner. Life is not life, if it be not life from death."[39]

The substance of vv. 20–21 is that irrespective of how much sin increased and reigned, grace increased more and reigned doubly as powerful. Hence his words: "The law was brought in so that the trespass might increase. But where sin increased, grace increased all the more, so that, just as sin reigned in death, so also grace might reign through righteousness to bring eternal life through Jesus Christ our Lord" (vv. 20–21). A Jewish reader, or even our hypothetical God-fearer Rufus in a Roman house church, might be surprised by many of Paul's assertions here. The notion that "the law was brought in so that the trespass might increase" would seem odd, especially when the law was meant to decrease sin by teaching right from wrong, advocating the restraint of desire, and driving Gentiles into purity of mind, heart, and worship.[40] But, as Paul argues so frequently, the law does not fix sin; it is at best a temporary fence around it, or perhaps even bait that draws sin into the open and exposes it under the floodlights of divine justice (see Rom 3:19–20; 4:15; 7:7–9; 1 Cor 15:56; Gal 3:21; Col 2:23). The law can count sin, but cannot counter it![41] In any case, however sin increased, grace increased doubly; however sin

38. Watson, *Paul, Judaism, and the Gentiles*, 275.

39. Barth, *Romans*, 187.

40. Cf. Oakes, *Reading Romans in Pompeii*, 156.

41. Cf. Grieb, *Story of Romans*, 66.

reigned to effect death, grace reigned through righteousness to bestow eternal life. This "life" is not the immortality of the soul, but sharing in the life of the world to come, the new creation, cosmic renewal, and the consummation of God's purpose for all things.

Living out the story of Romans 5:12–21 means appropriating the narrative within the text about the entrance of sin into the world and grasping the grace that overcomes it.

### A Tale of Two Adams

One important feature of Romans 5:12–21 is that it forces us to look at the big picture. The Adam story, the Abraham story, the Israel story, and the Messiah story are all determinative for believers and shape the basic features of their worldview: identity, existence, struggle, purpose, and goal. In the scope of redemptive history, properly understood, salvation is not just about how my wretched soul gets forgiven and is granted entrance to heaven. Salvation is even bigger than bringing Jews and Gentiles together in one church. Salvation pertains to how the universal tyranny of sin and death over the human race is finally defeated by the obedience and life of the Lord Jesus Christ. Salvation is about Adam lost and Adam found, the death of death, the reversal of sin, and the reign of righteousness.

If we fail to grasp the narrative and existential connections between Adam and ourselves, we miss out on seeing a crucial feature in the biblical story. Rutledge puts it like this: "Paul says, if you don't understand what it means to be part of the race of Adam, you don't understand the situation. This roller-coaster ride ends in death. To say that we are not strapped in properly would be to put it mildly. As children of Adam, we are completely at the mercy of forces we cannot control, forces that seize our lives and dislocate them violently." She adds, it is only in light of the "enormity of the threat that hung over us" that we can understand the *how much more* of what God has done in Christ to save us.[42]

In search for some examples of the redemptive-historical horizon of Adam and Christ, we need look no further than English literature. John Milton's epic poem *Paradise Lost* (1667, second edition in 1674) rehearses in sublime language the fall of Adam and Eve from a state of innocence and their descent into reprobation. Milton begins his epic with the words:

42. Rutledge, *Not Ashamed of the Gospel*, 177–78.

Of Man's First Disobedience, and the Fruit
Of that Forbidden Tree, whose mortal taste
Brought Death into the World, and all our woe,
With loss of *Eden*, till one greater Man
Restore us, and regain the blissful Seat.

(John Milton, *Paradise Lost*, 1:1–5)

Its sequel, *Paradise Regained* (1670), was not set as you might imagine at Calvary, with Jesus bearing the sins of the world, but in the temptation of Jesus by Satan in the wilderness. Jesus' withstanding satanic assault and his obedience to his messianic task was the means by which Paradise was regained for the human race. The poem focuses heavily on the theme of reversals. Christ's obedience secures the reversal of what Adam lost and what Satan gained. Jesus proves to be the "one greater Man" to best Satan's enticements, to restore humanity, and to regain paradise. Toward the end of the fourth book, Milton writes:

True Image of the Father, whether thron'd
In the bosom of bliss, and light of light
Conceiving, or remote from Heaven, enshrin'd
In fleshly Tabernacle, and human form,
Wandring the Wilderness, whatever place,
Habit, or state, or motion, still expressing
The Son of God, with Godlike force indu'd
Against th' Attempter of thy Fathers Throne,
And Thief of Paradise; him long of old
Thou didst debel, and down from Heav'n cast
With all his Army, now thou hast aveng'd
Supplanted Adam, and by vanquishing
Temptation, hast regain'd lost Paradise,
And frustrated the conquest fraudulent:
He never more henceforth will dare set foot
In Paradise to tempt; his snares are broke:
For though that seat of earthly bliss be fail'd,
A fairer Paradise is founded now
For *Adam* and his chosen Sons, whom thou
A Saviour art come down to re-install.

(John Milton, *Paradise Regained*, 4:596–615)

Milton captures a theme that comes from the heart of Romans 5:12–21. It is by one man's disobedience that Paradise is lost and it is by another man's obedience that Paradise is regained. It is by one man's disobedience that death is unleashed and it is by another man's obedience that death is defeated. By one man's disobedience sin accedes to the throne over humanity, but by another man's obedience sin is dethroned and vanquished. By one man's disobedience corruption becomes a universal pandemic, but by another man's obedience corruption is purified. By one man's disobedience sin uses the law to multiply itself, but by another man's obedience the law is returned to its place of service against sin. By one man's disobedience Paradise becomes a jungle of horror, but by another man's obedience, as Milton puts it, "a fairer Paradise is founded now."

Milton might be a bit much for modern readers, so let me give a modern analogy of Adam's disobedience and Christ's obedience. George Lucas's *Star Wars* saga could be called "A Tale of Two Skywalkers" (Episodes 1–6). The interstellar sci-fi story in its own way reflects the Adam-Christ pattern of Romans 5, where Adam and Christ represent two states of humanity in corruption and salvation. The first Skywalker (Anakin Skywalker) faced the temptation to give in to the dark side of the Force; he gave in to it, and death, destruction, and chaos followed. In contrast, the second Skywalker (Luke Skywalker) faced the same temptation, but he was faithful and obedient to the Jedi vocation, and consequently hope, life, and the triumph of good followed. In fact, Luke was able to redeem the first Skywalker, his father Anakin, from evil through his own faithfulness to the Jedi vocation.

In fact, I've seen an interview where George Lucas said that the entire Star Wars trilogy—or at least the first trilogy—was concerned with the redemption of Anakin Skywalker. One could say that the entire story line of redemptive history is about the redemption of Adam. What humanity needs, strange as it sounds, is a new humanity. Let me explain. The human condition can only be healed by the extraction of the evil that has contaminated it and corrupted it. We need another human, also created in God's image, who can syphon away evil, suffer under its weight, and yet not succumb to its dark power. That human being, we learn from Paul, is the Lord Jesus, the one like Adam, who is the seed and son of Abraham, who fulfills Israel's vocation, and is the Lord of the entire human race. In Jesus' life, obedience, and death, the children of Adam and Eve are redeemed, restored, and renewed and may thereafter return to the Paradise that God destined them to dwell in for all of eternity.[43]

---

43. Adapted from Bird, *A Bird's-Eye View of Paul*, 43.

## Original Sin Makes Sense of Human Behavior

Romans 5:12–21 tells us quite a lot about sin. The doctrine of "original sin" or "original guilt," whichever you prefer, gets a lot of criticism from atheists, liberal theologians, and postmodern intellectuals for all sorts of reasons. It's just myth, it's all legal fiction, how can guilt be passed on to others, people are normally good, and the like. Perhaps you've heard such objections yourself.

However, as G. K. Chesteron famously said, original sin is the only Christian doctrine that is empirically verifiable. All people sin. All people imitate sin. All people have a propensity to sin. All people are habitiually addicted to sin. All people are guilty of sin. That human beings sin, transgress, break laws, violate rights, and commit immoral deeds is self-evident to everyone. I have to confess that one of the things that amazed me as a parent was that I never had to teach my children how to lie. They picked it up quite naturally. The mess that one child makes he or she will instinctively blame on another child, preferably the younger one, who cannot yet speak for himself or herself. Greed, violence, and selfishness seem like the default setting that they are born with. I sincerely believe that crying babies would throw their own mothers under a truck if it would get them what they want.

Experience has also taught me that raising toddlers is like working for Caligula and Charlie Sheen combined. A house run by teenage boys has about the same degree of law and order as lunatics running an asylum. A colony of minors stranded on an island would not resemble Peter Pan's paradisiac *Never Never Land*, but would descend immediately into violence and terror more akin to William Golding's novel *Lord of the Flies*, where the strongest ruled the weakest with merciless spite. If you ever want to see what people are like, what they are truly like, see what they do when they think no one is watching them. Whether it is under the cover of night, in a dark alley, or anonymously on the internet, that is where you see what evil desires and what lurid proclivities lurk within the hearts of men and women. I'm sure psychologists, sociologists, and anthropologists have their own models and explanation for this sort of innately inhumane behavior, but just as equally important is the theological one: human beings are born into the world with an inherent propensity to sin because they are born into the world separated from God. The whole condition of guilt, sinful behavior, and death is all traceable to the one act of disobedience in our primeval parents, Adam and Eve.

If my history is right, the Chinese built the Great Wall of China for the specific purpose of keeping out the Mongol hordes to the north. The wall was very effective; it was never breached and never successfully broken into. However, invaders did manage to get through it on at least three occasions. How you might ask? By bribing the gatekeeper! It only takes one act of betrayal and one deed of treachery to introduce horrendous consequences for a whole nation. Adam, in many ways, was the gatekeeper to the human race (I'll skip for now the debate as to whether or not Adam was literal or metaphorical).[44] It was his divinely given vocation with his female companion to tend the garden and to keep Paradise in perfection. But Eve was seduced by the serpent and Adam was duped by his companion. Our primeval parents disobeyed the primary directive they were given. And so enters evil, sin, death, disease, disorder, enmity, estrangement, terror, and violence into the human world, and humanity thereafter struggles to retain its humanness that separates it from the world of the beasts. Ever since then, the angels, all of creation, and the children of Adam and Eve cry out, "O Adam, what have you done?"

Sin has become part of our fallen human nature, messed up our moral compasses like a magnet, and become part of our constitution. Maybe you've heard the story about the scorpion and the frog. There was once a frog who was sitting on his lily pad when he noticed on the riverbank a scorpion standing around with some frustration. The scorpion called out to the frog, "Mr. Frog, will you take me to the other side of the river by letting me ride on your back." The frog was hesitant as frogs did not trust scorpions and were naturally frightened of them. So the frog replied, "Sorry Mr. Scorpion, but I cannot carry you across, for you might sting me." The scorpion retorted, "Don't be silly. If I stung you while I was on your back, you would die, but so would I, as you'd sink, and I'd drowned in the river." The frog paused and thought about it for a moment, and decided that it made sense. "Okay, then," said the Frog. "Climb on my back, Mr. Scorpion, but if you sting me we shall both surely die." So the scorpion jumped on the frog's back, and all was going well as he began to carry him across the river. Just maybe, the frog thought, his fear of scorpions was unfounded. But when they were about halfway across the river the scorpion stung the frog in the back. The frog felt a surge of pain and cried out, "Why, why did you do that, Mr. Scorpion? Now we're both gonna die." The scorpion replied, "I don't know, Mr. Frog, I don't know what came over me. I guess it's just in my nature." Tragically, sin is in our nature, a nature that results in the destruction and death of all that we care about.

The Christian worldview explains what sin is, why we sin, how sin entered the world, and what the solution to sin is. Sin's effects are pervasive as they are powerful, yet Romans 5:12–21 promises us hope from such a wretched state. Jesus, as the new Adam, comes to save us from Adam's guilt, Adam's example, and Adam's nature. We become truly and authentically human when we are

44. Cf. Matthew Barrett and Ardel Caneday, eds., *Four Views on the Historical Adam* (Grand Rapids: Zondervan, 2013).

justified by faith, when we follow Christ's example, and when we are regenerated by the Spirit into a new creation. In Christ is the model and means for humanity to be the human race that God had always intended it to be.

The story narrated in Romans 5:12–21 is that God's grace is greater than all our sin. *Whatever* Adam had done is matched by the *how much more* Christ has done for us. The death, condemnation, and corruption introduced with Adam are reversed and surpassed by the grace and gift available in the Lord Jesus. I like how the note in the Geneva Bible on v. 21 spells it out: "Grace was poured so plentifully from heaven that it did not only counterbalance sin, but beyond this it surpassed it." The gospel of grace always has the checkmate on law and sin. The German tennis player Boris Becker said that when playing his absolute best, he could theoretically beat American Pete Sampras. But he also said that if he played his best and if Sampras played his best, Sampras was always going to win, because his best was always better. If sin is Becker, then grace is Sampras. Grace is always gonna win!

## Getting a Theological Orientation

In terms of application for Romans 5:12–21, as we've seen above, we need to know the biblical story of sin and salvation from Adam to Christ. We also need to have a robust understanding of sin and to comprehend that God's grace is more powerful than our sin. In addition, the other thing that I think we need to stress when we preach a text like this is to make sure people know which Adam they are in and what it means for them. If I were to preach this text, I would want to put up a revolving sign in neon lights that said, "By faith, you are in Christ, not Adam," then "You cannot make yourself more justified than you already are," and "Whatever condemnation you think you had, it has been obliterated by grace."

People can only know who they are in Christ if they first know that they are really and truly in Christ. They need to be reminded that by putting their faith in Christ, they have, metaphorically speaking, changed their location and gone from the swamp to the oasis, from quicksand to the snowfield, from the Dead Sea to the Sea of Galilee, and exchanged a rat-infested shack for a luxurious apartment. Clearly knowing that one is in Christ has all sorts of applications as Paul will soon explain in Romans 6. It had big implications for Paul's Gentile readers when it came to their relationship to the Torah and to the Jewish communities in Rome since they no longer had to look to the Torah for the security of their salvation and identity. For contemporary readers, knowing that one is in Christ becomes the basis for appreciating the sufficiency and supremacy of grace, and it grounds the moral imperatives that flow from God's saving work in us. Let folks learn the poem:

When I was in Adam I was counted as dead,
But I'm alive in Christ, my new glorious head.
The curse of the law now carries no dread,
Because I know that Christ has died in my stead.
The ghastly garment of death has been unthread,
Since I'm clothed with the Son of the triune Godhead.
And in the resurrection of the body all our hair will be red.
(The last line is optional for those with pro-ginger theological beliefs).

CHAPTER 10

# Romans 6:1–14

## LISTEN to the Story

1What shall we say, then? Shall we go on sinning so that grace may
increase? 2By no means! We are those who have died to sin; how can we
live in it any longer? 3Or don't you know that all of us who were baptized
into Christ Jesus were baptized into his death? 4We were therefore buried
with him through baptism into death in order that, just as Christ was
raised from the dead through the glory of the Father, we too may live a
new life.

5For if we have been united with him in a death like his, we will
certainly also be united with him in a resurrection like his. 6For we know
that our old self was crucified with him so that the body ruled by sin
might be done away with, that we should no longer be slaves to sin—
7because anyone who has died has been set free from sin.

8Now if we died with Christ, we believe that we will also live with
him. 9For we know that since Christ was raised from the dead, he cannot
die again; death no longer has mastery over him. 10The death he died, he
died to sin once for all; but the life he lives, he lives to God.

11In the same way, count yourselves dead to sin but alive to God in
Christ Jesus. 12Therefore do not let sin reign in your mortal body so that
you obey its evil desires. 13Do not offer any part of yourself to sin as an
instrument of wickedness, but rather offer yourselves to God as those who
have been brought from death to life; and offer every part of yourself to
him as an instrument of righteousness. 14For sin shall no longer be your
master, because you are not under the law, but under grace.

Listening to the texts in the story: Exodus 14–15; Mark 1:9–11; 10:38–39; Acts 13:39; 1 Corinthians 10:2; Galatians 2:19–20.

Many folks assume that Romans 1–4 is about how to get saved, Romans 5 is all to do with having assurance of salvation, and Romans 6 is about how those who get saved should live. While that is not completely false—Romans 6 does have a lot to say about "ethics"—it is underselling the story. The Adamic condition runs far deeper than guilt and bad behavior. This condition means being marked, owned, and enslaved to sin. It leaves people reeking of the odious and overpowering stench of death over their spiritually dead bodies. This is a condition for which the Torah is utterly powerless to bring life.

What Paul does in the scope of 6:1–8:17 is to trace the path of freedom, not only from sin's penalty but also from its power, a path that does not use the Torah as a Winnebago to carry passengers to its destination. Paul places all of humanity between the figures of Adam and Christ. Adam stands as the head of the realm of sin, death, and condemnation, while Christ stands as the head of a new humanity by way of his obedience, life, grace, and righteousness. What Paul wants to do now, taking his cue from 5:21, is to map where believers are in relation to Adam and Christ. He wants to mark out where they sit in relation to the "reign" of sin and the "reign" of grace. Exactly whose jurisdiction are they under? To whom do they belong? And most important, what does that mean for how they are to live? Paul, like someone assisting confused visitors at an information booth in a massive shopping mall, wants us to find the part of the map that says "You are here." And by the way, "here" means "in Christ," not "in Adam."

Vital for understanding the argument of Romans 6 is what Paul means by "union with Christ." According to Constantine Campbell's recent landmark study, Paul's Christ-language in relation to believers—in Christ, with Christ, into Christ, etc.—is all about union, participation, identification, and incorporation into the Messiah.[1] Paul exposits the state of our union with Christ in terms of shifting our allegiances, reshaping our identities, altering our desires, and reconfiguring our obligations, all in light of our baptism into the Messiah's death and resurrection. As Robert Tannehill argues, union with Christ in Romans 6, at its most basic level, is about our emancipation from sin's dominion and our entrance into the new age in Christ.[2] In Romans 6, Paul treats union with Christ as bringing in a new exodus that releases believers from slavery to sin and puts them in service to God.

Paul's argument and exhortation in Romans 6:1–23 lacks any Old Testament citations. However, his entire discussion assumes that when God redeems his people, he also renews them, a point congruent with the biblical story. In essence, Paul is describing how Christians go through a new exodus and become a new people living faithfully under a new Lord. He emphasizes that baptism into Christ means being plunged and placed into the redemptive story of God's plan to consecrate a people worthy of his name. To this end, Paul

---

1. On the theme of union with Christ more generally, see Constantine R. Campbell, *Paul and Union with Christ: An Exegetical and Theological Study* (Grand Rapids: Zondervan, 2012) and Grant R. Macaskill, *Union with Christ in the New Testament* (Oxford: Oxford University Press, 2013).

2. Robert C. Tannehill, *Dying and Rising with Christ: A Study in Pauline Theology* (Eugene, OR: Wipf & Stock, 2006), esp. 30–40.

constructs this passage around a series of exhortations that are often diatribal in form, full of comparisons, replete with rhetorical questions, and make manifold injunctions. He begins his train of thought by: (1) espousing the incompatibility between sin and grace (vv. 1–2), and (2) asserting that dying and rising with Christ mean freedom from sin (vv. 3–7); (3) this necessitates believers reckoning themselves to be dead to sin (vv. 8–11), (4) because believers are not under the jurisdiction of the law, but under the reign of grace (vv. 12–14).

### Baptism and Sin (6:1–2)

Paul draws an inference from 5:12–21 by asking, "What shall we say, then? Shall we go on sinning so that grace may increase?" (v. 1). Paul used the same rhetorical question earlier when a potential objection could be raised against his main point (see 3:1; 4:1). Here Paul abruptly asks: Does the superabounding nature of grace mean that we are free to indulge in sin so that our sinning actually helps grace increase? Paul knows this accusation well since he probably encountered it periodically from Jewish and perhaps even Jewish-Christian interlocutors (see Rom 3:8; cf. Acts 20:20–21; 28:17). Gentile Christians in Rome might have been seizing on Paul's mantra of being "not under law" and misused it in relation to debates with Jewish-Christian believers to the effect that it is wrong for anyone to obey any of the law, which of course opens up the problem of precisely where believers get their ethical instruction from (see Gal 3:10–14; 4:4–5, 21; 5:18; cf. 1 Cor 9:20). What Paul asks is whether believers should "remain in sin." What Paul means by "sin" is a cross between a status, a state, and servitude. The problem with remaining in sin is the absurdity of the thought. It is kind of like asking whether one should remain stuck at the bottom of a well even while a rope has been lowered down to us. Grace is designed to get us out of that situation, not to make us feel more comfortable within it!

No wonder that Paul answers his rhetorical question with an emphatic negation: "By no means! We are those who have died to sin; how can we live in it any longer?" (v. 2). Paul's militant denial rehearses similar denials made earlier (see 3:4, 6, 31) as he is adamant that the question he just posed is a logical impossibility. For believers, sin is no longer their status, their state, or their master. Paul is claiming that believers cannot remain in sin because one of the most distinguishing features of believers is that they have died to sin. Sin and grace are utterly incommensurable.[3] You cannot reside in Sin-land when the

3. Barth, *Romans*, 191.

government posts your obituary in its local newspaper. Why would you want to remain there anyway when you recently received a letter notifying you that you had just inherited Grace-land (complete with Elvis memorabilia)?

### Baptism into the Messiah (6:3–7)

Paul expounds v. 2 in the following verses by describing the incompatibility between baptism into Christ and remaining in sin. He does that by describing the event of baptism (vv. 3–4) and by sketching its wider significance (vv. 5–7). Paul challenges his audience with the claim: "Or don't you know that all of us who were baptized into Christ Jesus were baptized into his death?" (v. 3). Baptism here refers not only to the symbolic act of immersion into water, but recalls the entire event of conversion and initiation. Baptism is the sign and seal that believers have entered into the story of Jesus' death and resurrection, and its liberating power is manifested in them. If so, the person who thinks that grace is a license to sin simply does not know the reality of what it means to die with Christ. Baptism into Messiah Jesus means baptism into his messianic death.

Jesus himself spoke of his death as a coming "baptism" where he would drink the cup of God's wrath that would be poured on him (Mark 10:38–39; Luke 12:50). For Paul, baptism is no empty symbol; it points to the reality of sharing in Christ's death and resurrection and in some way even ushers in that reality. If Jesus of Nazareth is the crucified and risen Lord, then baptism entails solidarity with him and placing our identity in him. The whole scope of our being becomes "cruciformed," shaped by his cross. Such is the presupposition of other passages in Paul, such as Galatians 2:20: "I have been crucified with Christ and I no longer live, but Christ lives in me. The life I now live in the body, I live by faith in the Son of God, who loved me and gave himself for me."

Paul goes on to explain what baptism into Jesus' death means: "We were therefore buried with him through baptism into death in order that, just as Christ was raised from the dead through the glory of the Father, we too may live a new life" (v. 4). Baptism is the instrument whereby believers are literally "co-buried" with Jesus and share his death. Burial of course means a decisive end to something—in this case, to an old way of life under an old master. It is impossible to "go on sinning" if one is dead and buried to a life of sin.[4] What is more, this burial-through-baptism into the Messiah has a purpose ("in order that" [*hina*]) and a parallel ("just as Christ" [*hōsper . . . Christos*]). The primary point is that God raised up Christ from the dead and brought

4. Jewett, *Romans*, 398.

him into resurrection life, and God does the same for believers by liberating them from sin and bringing them into new life. According to Chrysostom: "Baptism is the cross. Baptism has become for us what the cross and tomb were for Christ, although not in the same way. Christ died and was buried in the flesh, while we experience death and burial to sin."[5]

We should note here that the instrument by which Christ was raised up is stated as "the glory of Father," which is probably a circumlocution for the Holy Spirit. Later Paul will state specifically that it was the Spirit who raised up Christ, and this is the same Spirit who will raise up believers at the last day (Rom 8:11). Furthermore, what Paul has in mind in 6:4–7 is not the future horizon of being raised from the dead like Christ was at the last day, but the immediate impact that Jesus' resurrection has upon the believer's life in the present, namely, that "we might walk" in the newness of life (see Gal 5:25). Paul introduces the ethical imperative that follows on from our baptism into Christ. The new creation, which bursts on us in Christ, means that we must have a new way of life for Christ. This is the Jewish language of *halakah*, one's walk in obeying the law, but here it means walking in a new spiritual life in accordance with the cross and resurrection of Christ. As Wright puts it, "the Messiah's resurrection means that those who are 'in the Messiah' now stand, and must walk, on resurrection ground."[6]

Paul adds a parenthetical remark about death and liberation from sin. He states: "For if we have been united with him in a death like his, we will certainly also be united with him in a resurrection like his" (v. 5). Paul seems to think of baptism as a reenactment of Jesus' death and resurrection. Once we begin the first part by sharing in his death, the second part comprising resurrection necessarily follows. Baptism is the bond that places us in Christ's death and resurrection so that we experience redemption in the present and a physical resurrection in the future. If I may go freestyle: by faith we're righted, with a Messiah united, sin is defied since I'm co-crucified, I serve a new sire, dunked in the Messiah, dying and rising, no more death tyrannizing, in a glorious blaze one day I'll be raised, so all say, "Hallelujah" from Fargo to Fallujah.[7]

Paul continues by explaining the ethical implications of union with Christ: "For we know that our old self was crucified with him so that the body ruled by sin might be done away with, that we should no longer be slaves to sin" (v. 6). The reason all this make sense is that believers "know" or at least

5. Chrysostom, *Hom. Rom.* 10.

6. Wright, "Romans," 10:538.

7. See my forthcoming gospel rap album called, "The Birdman Raps the Apostles," with Sony records, produced by Katya Covrett (contract pending).

should "know" (as per v. 3) that by co-crucifixion with Christ, they have left the domain and dungeon of sin. The "old self" is literally "the old man" (*ho palaios ... anthrōpos*) and stands for the entire self as viewed as someone "in Adam." This self is co-crucified with Christ—again hear the echoes of Galatians 2:19–20—and there are two immediate consequences.

First is the abolishment of the "body of sin." The NIV has the "body ruled by sin" and the CEB has "the corpse that had been controlled by sin." But it is better to follow the rendering of the ESV and NRSV with the "body of sin," because the image is probably not of sin in the individual, but the mass of humanity in the thrall of sin that is in mind. Yes, Paul speaks later about individuals not letting sin "reign in your mortal body" (Rom 6:12), not offering "any part of yourself to sin" (6:13), and referring to the self as a "body subject to death" (7:24). However, when Paul usually speaks about the "old self" or the "old man," as in Ephesians 4:22, Colossians 2:11–13, and 3:9, it is always in the context of referring to the eclipse of the old self by the new creation, so the emphasis is cosmic, not individual.

What is more, "body of sin" may well stand as the antitype to the "body of Christ." So the body of sin is more than sin in my own body; rather, it pertains to my solidarity with the sin and death of all who share in Adam.[8] The "body of sin" is a body that is broken down in crucifixion and put back together in resurrection. T. W. Manson said about the "body of sin": "It is the mass of unredeemed humanity in bondage to the evil power. Every conversion means that the body of sin loses a member and the body of Christ gains one."[9]

A second consequence of co-crucifixion with Christ is emancipation from the bondage of sin. Believers "should no longer be slaves to sin," and it is probably wise to underline the word "should." Paul is not saying that believers will never sin, but they need not sin, since they are alive to God in a whole new way, principally, by the Spirit (more on that in Rom 8:1–17). Taking stock for a moment, Paul's remarks show that the reign of sin spoken about in 5:21 has been challenged by grace, and this grace is effective in Christ's death and resurrection. Thus, as Wright wonderfully waxes, "when grace enfolds the baptismal candidate, entwining the Jesus-story and the Jesus-reality with theirs, the communal solidarity that sin has created, generating the sense and the fact of helplessness as humans go along with all that sin suggests, is broken, and they are free to live under a different lordship."[10]

8. Cf. further Tom Holland, *Contours of Pauline Theology* (Fearn, Ross-shire: Mentor, 2004), 85–110.

9. T. W. Manson, "Romans," in *Peake's Commentary on the Bible* (ed. M. Black and H. H. Rowley; rev. ed.; London: Routledge, 2001), 945.

10. Wright, "Romans," 10:540.

Paul adds a short, albeit cryptic, explanatory gloss to clarify what he means, "because anyone who has died has been set free from sin" (v. 7). If sin is slavery, then crucifixion with Christ means liberation (more to follow on that in Rom 7:1–6). Interestingly what Paul says, literally in the Greek, is that believers have been "justified from sin" (*dedikaiōtai apo tēs hamartias*).[11] That Paul uses a perfective passive form of *dikaioō* for liberation from sin's mastery creates a lot of fretfulness for Reformed theologians. The reason is that Paul appears to be using language normally reserved for justification (the gift of a righteous status) for what is normally called sanctification or transformation (actually becoming righteous). The anxiety is that if one confuses justification and transformation, you could end up saying something like being right with God is based on right living, and then end up with some kind of scheme of legalism. So Reformed theologians have tended to insist on a theological restraining order separating justification and transformation; yet here Paul seems to allow them to fraternize freely. What is going on here? Does Paul confuse grace and works, gospel and law, justification and sanctification?

Before anyone panics, let's have a hot cup of tea, a chocolate cookie, and take a deep breath. First, what Paul says in places like Romans 4:4–5 and Ephesians 2:8–9 rules out of bounds any kind of work-for-reward scheme of salvation. Second, as a general point of order, I would maintain that justification and transformation are linked logically though not conceptually in Paul. The way that Paul structures his epistles shows that he knows the difference between what God does for us and what we do to show our thanks to God (e.g., Ephesians 1–3 and 4–6; Galatians 1–4 and 5–6). Third, what Paul says in Romans 6:7 may simply be idiomatic for "freedom from sin," given the parallel language found in Romans 6:22 and Acts 13:38–39 about release from sin.

Those reassurances aside, the fact is that Paul's linguistic register may employ semantic domains and make pragmatic applications for words that do not evince any sensitivity to the shibboleths of post-Reformation dogmatics. Paul, writing to poor and powerless Gentile Christians in the tenements of Rome, hardly has at the front of his mind the paranoid concern to partition justification and sanctification as would happen some 1,500 years later. In the case of v. 7 with "justified [set free] from sin," I suggest that Paul is announcing that co-crucifixion with Christ means that believers enter a state of righteousness because God's justifying verdict is a speech-act that begins to create the very reality it declares. Think of it this way. At a wedding ceremony, a

11. Cf. for similar phrasing, "A merchant can hardly keep from wrongdoing, nor is a tradesman *justified from* sin" (Sir 26:29), and "Behold I have told you all things, that I may be *justified from* your sin" (*T. Sim.* 6.1) [my own translations].

pastor can legally declare a marriage by saying, "I now announce you husband and wife," but he also transforms the actual relationship between the couple by his utterance and so engenders in them a new set of obligations toward each other. In the same way, God's righteousness is so comprehensive that it simultaneously declares and effects righteousness in the believer.[12]

### The Grace Reckoning (6:8–11)

What Paul said in vv. 4–7 about liberation from the body of sin and entrance into the body of Christ is given a further push in vv. 8–11, where he emphasizes the need to make a conscious appropriation of this change in our position. That is why Paul talks about believing (v. 8), knowing (v. 9), and reckoning (v. 11) the scheme of dying and rising with Christ to be something that *is* true of us and yet needs to be *made* true for us as well. Union with Christ is both indicative and imperative, a reality *in us* that requires further action *by us*.

"Now if we died with Christ, we believe that we will also live with him. For we know that since Christ was raised from the dead, he cannot die again; death no longer has mastery over him" (vv. 8–9). The assertion here rehashes vv. 4–5 about how dying with Christ logically entails rising with Christ, rising into new life and sharing in his resurrection. The believer's co-crucifixion with Christ mirrored in baptism means that believers "will live with him [Christ]" and share in a future resurrection life with the Lord Jesus in God's new creation.

The upshot is that believers escape from the lordship of death in the same way that Christ did. Resurrection is the power of emancipation from slavery in sin and from the lordship of death. Paul explains further what happened to Christ: "The death he died, he died to sin once for all; but the life he lives, he lives to God" (v. 10). Christ's death and resurrection formed a climactic and nonrepeatable action whereby he was removed from sin and given a never-ending and incorruptible life with God in his resurrection. Christ was not stuck in a cycle of sin and death that kept repeating itself or can even now impose itself on him. He was removed from it once and for all. The same is true for believers; they are free—truly, finally, definitively free—from the lure and lordship of sin.

---

12. Although I would not go this far, Talbert (*Romans*, 179–80) speaks for many when he writes: "A forensic interpretation of Paul's doctrine of justification is a reductionistic reading of the apostle's teaching. This way of interpreting the matter often sets justification as a judicial act over against regeneration or the new life in Christ. This has led people to think that salvation is a legal transaction in which they might be delivered from the penalty of sin—be declared just—whether they were ever made righteous or not. Paul's doctrine of justification is something more radical than that."

The application Paul makes about Christ's once-for-all release from sin is that believers should now consider themselves to be in a similar position. "In the same way," he writes, "count yourselves dead to sin but alive to God in Christ Jesus" (v. 11). This is the answer to the question raised in v. 1 about whether we shall go on sinning! No, of course not; we have died to sin and we live with Christ. We are part of the new reality of life and righteousness, not the old dominion of sin and death.

Before we go on, a bit of realism is required here. Obviously Christ's resurrected and postexaltation state is rather different from our own form of mortal existence and our continuing moral struggles. Let's not get too triumphalistic or overcook our union with Christ as if we are already glorified, as if we already have the whole package, as if our pews are thrones in the new Jerusalem. But, in the same way that slavery to sin and the lordship of death imposed itself on humanity to shape their identity and behavior, so now our identity and behavior are equally determined by an imposing force, namely, union with the risen and exalted Lord. That is why we "count" ourselves to be dead to sin — not that we are fully and finally dead to sin, but we need to start living as if we were. We need to live a life that shows that we don't belong in Sin-land; we need to burn our passport, renounce our citizenship, forget the language, and look instead to the risen Christ as the power that annexes portions of our minds and hearts that still feel the need to submit to the old master. Chrysostom put it like this: "Only let us go leave the strange and foreign land; for this is what sin is, drawing us far away from our Father's house; let us leave her then, that we may speedily return to the house of our Father."[13]

### The New Master (6:12–14)

Paul is drawing a picture of believers on a type of journey, leaving the land of sin and death and entering the land of life and righteousness through the waterfall of baptism into Christ. Paul drives home the point with a few more exhortations in vv. 12–14 about what they should and should not do. It comes down to one basic point: don't obey the old master, but obey the new master — a point that will provide the premise for the rest of argument in vv. 15–23.

Dying with Christ means dying to sin, and so Paul infers, "Therefore do not let sin reign in your mortal body so that you obey its evil desires" (v. 12). The background story is that "Sin" is a hostile power that uses death as its henchman and desire as its seducer to force humanity to obey its every whim. Sin reigns in death over the members of the mortal body by making them

---

13. Chrysostom, *Hom. Rom.* 10.

captive to desire. I should add that the role of "desire" in sin does not ordinarily get a lot of attention, but it should. Sin elicits desire and desire is what controls the will.[14] Ancient philosophers saw people controlled by desires for either pleasure or power, driven by hedonistic pursuit or consumed with the prestige of honor. God's judgment against sin includes handing people over to the desires of their hearts (Rom 1:24). Sin uses the law to cultivate wicked desires in persons (7:7–8). Believers, then, should give no forethought to the desires of the flesh but instead be clothed with Christ (13:14). In which case, the path toward a God-pleasing life comes by dethroning sin from our lives, so that our desires shift from obeying "Sin" to serving our Savior. Sanctification is what happens when we desire God as much as we desire oxygen and we begin to expel sin the same way our bodies expel carbon dioxide.

Not letting sin reign and disobeying evil desire is given concrete expression in the following command: "Do not offer any part of yourself to sin as an instrument of wickedness" (v. 13a). The word for "offer" (*paristēmi*) means to put at someone's disposal. Believers should not offer themselves to sin to be used and abused for whatever ends the master determines. Believers are exhorted not to allow their bodies to be used for wickedness and worldliness. In contrast, Paul says, "but rather offer yourselves to God as those who have been brought from death to life; and offer every part of yourself to him as an instrument of righteousness" (v. 13b). Paul wants believers to refrain from living in death, serving sin, and being driven by desire. Instead they should live "as those"—as *fitting for* those—who have died and risen with Christ, and offer themselves into service of God and his righteousness.

The underlying reason for all this is then laid out: "For sin shall no longer be your master" (v. 14a). Whereas one might expect Paul to say "For sin no longer *is* your master," Paul says instead "sin *shall* no longer be your master." The significance of the future tense is hard to gauge, but Paul seems to mean it as an imperative in the sense that sin ought not be the boss and bane of their lives. The reason why sin should no longer lord it over them is because "you are not under the law, but under grace" (v. 14b). These are important words and easily taken out of context. Obviously it does not mean that Paul sees no moral obligation laid on believers simply for the fact that 6:1–2 and 6:15 deny such a possibility of moral anarchism. Paul has a string of imperatives he's just laid out: don't offer yourselves to sin, offer yourselves to God. The vital thing is, however, that these imperatives do not emerge from the law, but from a different reality altogether, from the redemptive reality of Jesus' death and resurrection. What Paul is getting at is that believers do

14. Cf. Moo, *Romans*, 383.

not exist under the dominion of sin-death-law but live instead under the dominion of the life-righteousness-grace of God the Father and the Lord Jesus Christ.

The house churches in Rome to which Paul wrote would be more than familiar with the many religious connotations of "baptism." Jews knew of baptisms for ritual purification; baptism might have been part of the ritual for Gentiles converting to Judaism in some places, and pagan mystery cults had various kinds of washings for initiates. What baptism into Christ meant at its most fundamental level was a transfer of lordship, a transfer into a new realm characterized by grace, righteousness, and life. It might even imply, to some degree, a transfer from one community to another. Paul urges the Roman house churches to resource their walk not in the works of the law, but in God's grace-gift of righteousness.

In addition, to be under grace, not law, is to speak not only of one's spiritual state, but also of one's social situation. Whatever relationship the Roman churches have to the synagogues—and such an association need not be negative or adversarial—the believers are nonetheless not bound to uphold the Jewish way of life mandated by the synagogues since they have a better way of life in Messiah Jesus that is more effective in curtailing sin.

Believers are not caught between the reigns of sin and grace; rather, they belong properly under the reign of grace. Christ redeemed believers by his death, and as baptized believers they are dipped and dyed into Christ like a fabric plunged into colored water. Paul seeks to remind them of who they are in Christ and how dying with Christ means counting themselves dead to sin.

### Who Am I? I Am a New Creation!

I confess that I've always liked the chorus, "I am a new creation" by David Bilbrough. The first stanza rehearses many of the themes we find in Romans: new creation, no condemnation, standing in God's grace, heart overflowing, and love keeps growing. The new life that Paul mentions in Romans 6:4 is really the effervescent overflow of the new creation that the Spirit has wrought in our hearts. What creates the ethical imperatives for the Christian life is not a new law, but this new creation.

The substance of Christian ethics is not lists of rules with case studies on how to handle legal conundrums when laws conflict. Christian ethics and Christian living are about properly walking in the way of Christ, with the

Spirit of Christ, until the day of Christ. It is a matter of letting our behavior match our new identity. It is about working out what God has worked in. As the Greek poet Pindar said, "Be what you know you are!"[15]

Sin is entirely inappropriate for believers because sin belongs to the age of death and decay and to the world with its wickedness. We belong to Christ, his kingdom, and the world to come. So engaging in sin when engrafted into Christ is a fundamental mismatch. It is like trying to play vinyl LPs on a CD player. Or like trying to insert CDs onto an iPod. Or like trying to send tweets from a walkman. Putting our mortal body out of sin's grasp and into the grip of grace requires genuine effort, but we should not think of it as some kind of Jekyll and Hyde inner turmoil going on inside of us, as if we have a bipolar moral character. We are not half in Adam and half in Christ; no, the exodus has happened, death has occurred once and for all, we are in Christ and not in Adam, we are under grace not under law, and we are now free to serve in a whole new way of life opened up for us in Messiah Jesus.

If we have died and risen with Christ, certain attitudes and actions are simply incompatible with what God has done for us and in us. To use the language of Galatians, if we have been crucified with Christ, we've been crucified to the world (Gal 2:19; 6:14). We have changed jurisdictions, we have changed allegiances, and we have changed what we desire and what we fear. Believers are living out a story of paradise lost and regained, prodigals run away and prodigals returned, shifted from the dominion of darkness to the kingdom of light, and swapped the horror of hell for the hope of a new heavens and a new earth. What fundamentally shapes our ethics and ethos is not old law but new life. We find ourselves moved to obey the commandments of God, not by the old law with the threat of curses, but by new life and its power to conform us to Christ.

### Who Am I? I Am a Baptized Christian!

Paul says much about baptism into Christ in Romans 6:3–4 and how it represents dying to sin and living to God. In the writings of Martin Luther, baptism was a powerful reminder of the Christian's identity and a source of their moral courage to overcome sin. In his second epiphany sermon on Christ's baptism, Luther identified baptism as the place where the wretched old man is led to drown and die as well as a sign and seal of our new life from God. Luther also added the comforting words: "Now if you fall into sins, then remember to flee again to your baptism. For that is the little boat that can help us over."

---

15. Pindar, *Pythian* 2.72.

When we contemplate our baptism, we contemplate the death of our old self, what Christ has done for me, and how Christ lives in me. In the face of temptation, we may ask, "How can I sin? I am baptized into Christ! How can I offer my body into the service of this sin?" Baptism, from the symbolic to the sacramental, should soak its way into our lives and shape how we think of ourselves and how we act. Remember your baptism, remember you are baptized, remember who baptized you, and remember into whom you were baptized. Our conversion into Christ means that we are baptized into his death and resurrection in much the way that a fabric is dipped and dyed into a bath of colored water, which permanently stains it. As J. Bligh put it: "When a person is dipped in the bath of baptism, he comes out a changed man: the former color disappears, he comes out the color of Christ. Whether the person before dipping was a Jew or a Gentile, a slave or a free man, a man or a woman, no longer matters."[16] Baptism is the testimony to our new self, new master, new life, and new walk, which should never be undersold or forgotten.

Paul discourses on justification by grace alone, through faith alone; yet grace is transformative and is cultivated by genuine effort. The motive to live in righteous service to God is gratitude for grace and hunger for holiness. It is, paradoxically, by committing ourselves to slavery to Christ's lordship that we discover our freedom to be authentic human beings filled not with licentiousness or wickedness, but overflowing with holiness and righteousness. True freedom is apprehended by weaving our own story with the story of Jesus' death and resurrection as we do in baptism. We prove our baptism good by dying to sin and living to righteousness. In the daily resolution to prove our baptism, we offer head, heart, and hands in service to the pattern and power of the cross, so that our true nature, emblematized in baptism, carried by prayer, and strengthened by the Spirit, rises like Christ walking out of the tomb triumphant.

### Who Am I? Someone Who Is Dead to Sin!

"Count yourselves dead to sin," Paul says. "Do not offer any part of yourself to sin as an instrument of wickedness," he adds later (Rom 6:11, 13). The problem is that sin often feels very much alive, and we sometimes find ourselves conscripted into its service. But we have to regard ourselves as dead to sin even when we think and feel alive to it. This predicament reminds me of a curious story I heard a long time ago about ants. Celebrated American entomologist and sociobiologist E. O. Wilson did his early research with ants. Wilson and other researchers described how ants communicate with each other through a

16. J. Bligh, *Galatians* (London: St. Paul Publications, 1969), 324.

series of pheromones, chemical "words" they release to indicate certain states like "danger approaches" or "I've found food" or "I'm ready to mate" or even "I'm dying, so throw me out."

Wilson decided to do an experiment to see what would happen if he sprayed some of the "I'm dying" pheromone onto an ant that was actually alive and healthy. The result was rather amusing. The ant got sprayed with the "I'm dying" pheromone and immediately other ants from the colony picked him up and took him outside of the nest to some kind of ant graveyard. The poor little ant then walks back to the nest only to have the same routine repeated again and again. The other ants smelled the death pheromone on him and despite the fact that the ant was not really dead, they kept throwing him out of the nest.

By analogy, we need to count ourselves dead to sin, even when sin feels very alive. We need to sprinkle the waters of baptism on our sin, water that will make our sin smell of death, so we can bury it in the graveyard of our old self. For Paul, this is the act whereby we count or call or consider ourselves dead to sin and alive to God and we begin to live out our true identity as a follower of Jesus Christ. As Origen commented: "Whoever thinks or considers that he is dead will not sin. For example, if lust for a woman gets hold of me or if greed for silver, gold or riches stirs me and I say in my heart that I have died with Christ ... the lust is immediately quenched and sin disappears."[17]

### Who Am I? A Servant of Christ!

Paul goes at length to emphasize that sin is no longer our master. If we have died with Christ, then we are freed from sin, and Christ he is our new master, and we owe him our steadfast devotion. One of the things we need to emphasize in Christian living and in applied ethics is that we are called to show our loyalty to Jesus Christ by the type of choices we make and the type of actions that we undertake. There are some things that are simply inappropriate for a person who confesses Jesus Christ as Lord, like murder, adultery, and theft. Then there are some things that are absolutely mandatory for believers, like compassion, mercy, and kindness. As servants we should bring honor to our master by our life and works rather than shame or disrepute.

This reminds of a story about the ancient Greek general Alexander the Great. Alexander, one of the greatest military commanders who ever lived, was on a campaign, and on one particular night he had some trouble sleeping. So he got up out of his tent to walk around the campsite to inspect the defensive fortifications. As he was quietly walking around the campsite, he came

17. Origen, *Comm. Rom.* on 6:11 (cited in Keener, *Romans*, 82).

across a young soldier who was asleep while on guard post, a serious breach of security that could endanger the safety of the entire camp. In fact, so serious was the offense that in ancient times this usually warranted the death penalty. Alexander angrily roused the soldier from his slumber and began to berate him. The young soldier was surprised and fearful for his life when Alexander gave him a very serious talking to.

Alexander asked him, "Do you know what the penalty is for falling asleep whilst on guard duty?"

"Yes, sir," was the fearful reply.

Then Alexander questioned him some more, "What is your name, soldier?"

"Alexander, my name is Alexander," came the meek response.

Alexander was a bit annoyed by this and repeated the question "What is your name?" three times. He kept getting the same answer, "Alexander" from the soldier.

Finally, Alexander looked at him with an icy glare and said in a stern voice, "If your name is Alexander, then either change your name or change your behavior."

Romans 6 reminds us that we need to honor Christ as our master by the way we live. We need to make sure that when it comes to our Christian faith, our talk matches our walk. We must ensure a consistency between what we affirm with our mouths and what we do with our hands. We need to demonstrate that Christ is our master by refusing to let anything in the world master us.

One of the apostolic fathers and first martyrs of the church, Ignatius of Antioch, wrote: "It is better to be silent and be real than to talk and not be real," and he asked others to pray for him that "I may not merely be called a Christian but actually prove to be one."[18] Those moving words are something we can all aspire to.

If we have been crucified with Christ and if we have died to sin, we can count ourselves dead to sin, we can embrace the true meaning of our baptism, and we can offer ourselves in service to righteousness. Doing that is the proof that Jesus is our Lord and we are his servants. That is what it means to live the story of Romans 6:1 – 14.

---

18. *To the Ephesians* 15.1; *To the Romans* 3.2.

CHAPTER 11

# Romans 6:15–23

## LISTEN to the Story

[15]What then? Shall we sin because we are not under the law but under
grace? By no means! [16]Don't you know that when you offer yourselves to
someone as obedient slaves, you are slaves of the one you obey—whether
you are slaves to sin, which leads to death, or to obedience, which leads to
righteousness? [17]But thanks be to God that, though you used to be slaves
to sin, you have come to obey from your heart the pattern of teaching
that has now claimed your allegiance. [18]You have been set free from sin
and have become slaves to righteousness.

[19]I am using an example from everyday life because of your human
limitations. Just as you used to offer yourselves as slaves to impurity and
to ever-increasing wickedness, so now offer yourselves as slaves to righteousness leading to holiness. [20]When you were slaves to sin, you were
free from the control of righteousness. [21]What benefit did you reap at
that time from the things you are now ashamed of? Those things result in
death! [22]But now that you have been set free from sin and have become
slaves of God, the benefit you reap leads to holiness, and the result is
eternal life. [23]For the wages of sin is death, but the gift of God is eternal
life in Christ Jesus our Lord.

*Listening to the texts in the story*: Exodus 14–15; Mark 1:9–11; 10:38–39; Acts 13:39; 1 Corinthians 10:2; Galatians 2:19–20.

Paul has just springboarded off 5:20–21 into 6:1–14 by saying that the superabounding grace of God does not provide a license for sin. That is because believers, by dying and rising with Christ, have experienced a change of lordship from mastery under sin to freedom in a new way of life. By entering into the story of the Messiah's death and resurrection, as embodied in baptism, they have given sin its funeral rites and risen into new life themselves.

Paul finished the line of thought in Romans 6:14 not with a quaint conclusion about liberty from sin, but with a further controversial remark that would incense some readers. He said freedom from sin's reign comes from the realization that "you are not under law, but under grace." Let's remember that the baffling and bothersome conclusion of 5:20 – 21 is still in the background about escaping the triangulation of dark power in law-sin-death. Whereas 6:1 – 14 dealt with sin and grace as binary opposites, now in 6:15 – 23 Paul deals with grace and law as opposing forces, with law identified with the plight and grace cast as the solution. In brief, Paul, in 6:15 – 23 and 7:1 – 6, is really expounding 6:14 about law and grace in a way that shows that freedom from sin is not freedom to sin and freedom from the law is not freedom for lawlessness.[1]

Central to 6:15 – 23 is the theme of slavery. If sin reigns or lords over a person, such persons are slaves to sin. We might say that wherever sin is *kyrios* ("Lord"), there a person is a *doulos* ("slave"). Yet the chains of this slavery have been broken by the liberating grace of God, who has made believers his own. Believers enter into a new form of service by being slaves to righteousness (v. 18) and slaves to God (v. 22), which leads to eternal life (v. 23).

In terms of flow of thought, (1) Paul opens with a rhetorical question about the possibility of remaining in sin if one abides in grace and not law (v. 15). (2) This is answered with a further rhetorical question requiring a negative answer since servitude implies obedience. Obedience to sin leads to death, while obedience to God leads to righteousness (v. 16). (3) Furthermore, the Roman believers have been set free from slavery to sin by obeying the pattern of teaching given in the gospel and so become slaves to righteousness (vv. 17 – 18). (4) That point is underscored by contrasting slavery in sin leading to wickedness and slavery to righteousness leading to holiness (v. 19). (5) Paul follows it up with a biographical reminder about their former way of life controlled by sin, which led to shame and death, and their new life in Christ, which leads to holiness (vv. 20 – 22). (6) Finally, Paul recaps his main point that believers are free from sin and slaves to God and are thus able to receive the gift of eternal life (v. 23).

### The Problem Freshly Stated (6:15)

Paul rehearses 6:1 in 6:15 by again asking a rhetorical question that critics would be likely to bring up: "What then? Shall we sin because we are not under the law but under grace? By no means!" (v. 15). Since 5:20, Paul has argued that the superabundance of grace is premised on the negation of the law. Yet a fairly obvious question that arises is how this law-free state can

1. Talbert, *Romans*, 167.

leave sin restrained (6:1). In response, Paul remained adamant that he is not providing license for immoral behaviour or giving grounds for ethical arbitrariness, for liberation from sin is attained by union with the crucified and risen Lord in the present (6:2–14).[2] The emphatic negation, "By no means" (*mē genoito*), spells out the matter as a logical incongruity (see 3:1; 4:1; 6:2). Grace does not provide permission for one to remain in sin or permit one to sin because he or she lives beyond the jurisdiction of the law. Whereas vv. 2–14 dealt with this question in terms of the transformative effects of union with Christ, now in vv. 15–23 Paul addresses the same subject in terms of emancipation from sin and slavery to God. Schreiner summarizes it well: "One is either God's slave or sin's slave. Those who think that freedom is attained by jettisoning obedience to God opt for sin as their lord."[3]

## Obedience Implies Servitude (6:16)

Paul responds further to the hypothetical objection with a rhetorical question designed to show the ignorance and immorality of anyone who supposes that grace grants a license to sin: "Don't you know that when you offer yourselves to someone as obedient slaves, you are slaves of the one you obey—whether you are slaves to sin, which leads to death, or to obedience, which leads to righteousness?" (v. 16). The point is simple: if you offer yourself in obedience to someone, they own you as a slave. So there are only two possibilities. One can *either* enter into slavery to sin, leading to death, *or* alternatively, one can join in obedience to God, which leads to righteousness.

The comparison in the final clause is not neatly symmetrical and is therefore a little confusing. Most likely, Paul makes a juxtaposition to the effect that "*obedience* to sin" leads to "death," while "obedience *to God*" leads to "righteousness." When Paul says "obedience [to God] leads to righteousness," he is hardly advocating a works-righteousness scheme of salvation. Most likely, "obedience" is a cipher for faith, fidelity, and clinging to Christ.

## Freedom from Sin in the Gospel (6:17–18)

The two options of (a) obedience to sin leading to death, and (b) obedience to God leading to righteousness gives way to a burst of thanksgiving: "But thanks be to God that, though you used to be slaves to sin, you have come to obey from your heart the pattern of teaching that has now claimed your allegiance. You have been set free from sin and have become slaves to righteousness." Paul makes a tacit reference to his audience's own biography. They were formerly slaves to sin, but they have been set free, and now they are

2. Watson, *Paul, Judaism, and the Gentiles*, 276–77.

3. Schreiner, *Romans*, 331.

slaves to righteousness. The moment of their first obedience is probably their conversion, and following that they are called to let their allegiance to Christ be made known by their behavior.

We can note two things. First, the Romans have received the transformation of the heart spoken about by the prophets (Ezek 11:19; 18:31; 36:26; Jer 31:33), which Paul has pointed to as evidence for the presence of the new covenant blessings (Rom 2:15, 29; 5:5). The implication is clear: by confessing from the heart that Jesus is Lord (10:9–11) and by leaving behind the old heart that was foolish, full of sinful desires, and unrepentant (1:21, 24; 2:5), the Roman believers demonstrate that they are new covenant people.

Second, Paul does not say that this happened because of the "pattern of teaching" that they received (contra KJV; NLT; CEB!). Quite the reverse! He says that they've been set free by the "pattern of teaching" that the Greek literally says "you were delivered over to." The NIV translates the phrase as "claimed your allegiance," while other translations opt for something like "to which you were committed" (ESV; NASB) or "to which you were entrusted" (NRSV, NET). Better is the HCSB with "pattern of teaching you were transferred to."

What is this "teaching"? Was it something known exclusively to Paul, or was it part of a wider body of Christian instruction that the Romans had already received? Given that Paul speaks elsewhere of the Roman's own "faith" (1:8) and their competency to instruct one another (15:14), he must mean a body of teaching of which they are already knowledgeable. Most likely Paul's point is that liberation from slavery to sin comes by being arrested by the pattern of teaching that constitutes the gospel. The Romans are delivered over to the gospel and not the gospel to them. This is the gospel with the "righteousness of God," which declares unto them a new Lord, new righteousness, new life, and a new way of life.[4]

### Two Ways to Live (6:19)

Paul next calls for a reversal of conduct by urging his audience to desist from servitude in sin and instead to embark in service to righteousness. He begins with a prefatory remark: "I am using an example from everyday life because of your human limitations" (v. 19a). His precise wording is more literally translated, "I am using a human argument" (*anthrōpinon legō*), and the same expression was used back in 3:5. Paul resorts to reasoning from a human point of view, a negative but necessary manner of discourse.

Commentators disagree over whether this "limitation" or "weakness" (*astheneia*) is intellectual or moral. I think this misses the point. While Paul

4. Seifrid, *Christ, our Righteousness*, 73.

knows of weakness as a human inability (see Rom 5:6; 8:26), he also knows of weakness as a way of describing someone who has a sensitive conscience and is easily offended (see 14:1–2; 15:1). I think Paul is acknowledging that his line of reasoning might be counterintuitive, given that some of the Roman Christians are burdened with weak consciences. In other words, Paul is recognizing that he's dealing with a sensitive matter that can potentially offend. Let us remember too that the whole slavery metaphor might be an unpleasant reminder to believers who either are slaves at the present or were slaves in the recent past. Johnson suggests that Paul's slavery metaphor might not be an agreeable way of putting things; nonetheless, it remains an apt way to describe the fundamental shift that has taken place in their condition and thus their allegiance.[5]

He presses the point further by exhorting his audience: "Just as you used to offer yourselves as slaves to impurity and to ever-increasing wickedness, so now offer yourselves as slaves to righteousness leading to holiness" (v. 19b). The point is framed as "just as ... so now," to the effect that the Romans must transform their former slavery to sin into a slavery to righteousness. Although Paul keeps pressing the idea of freedom from the slavery of sin across Romans 6, he nonetheless sees this freedom as meaning entering into service to God. Humanity will serve, but it will be either sin or righteousness. The believers have, by obedience, placed themselves in service to a new Lord, who summons them to a new pattern of behavior. A shift in lords requires a change in how believers use the members of their body. Moo puts it well: "The Christian is not just called to do right in a vacuum but to do right out of a new and powerful relationship that has already been established."[6]

Furthermore, Paul's language employs a thoroughly Jewish way of talking about sin, namely, as "impurity" (*akatharsia*) and "wickedness" (*anomia*). The language might even recall Jewish criticisms that Gentile believers have encountered because they are Gentile "sinners." This is a point relevant to the wider purposes of Romans, as Dunn says: "The evocation of the Jewish critique of Gentile morality and the implicit antithesis between Jewish ideals of priestly consecration and gentile lawlessness is undoubtedly deliberate. It strengthens the implication that Paul was writing the letter with Gentiles largely or principally in view."[7]

## In Case You Forgot Your Old Self (6:20–22)

The appeal to the Romans' own experience is continued by reminding them that their former way of life was wicked, fruitless, shameful, and lethal:

5. Johnson, *Romans*, 109.
6. Moo, *Romans*, 403.
7. Dunn, *Romans*, 1:346–47.

"When you were slaves to sin, you were free from the control of righteousness. What benefit did you reap at that time from the things you are now ashamed of? Those things result in death!" (vv. 20–21). The temporal marker "when" moves the audience to consider a former time when they were captive in sin's dominion and incapable of righteousness. Paul's question about the "benefit" (more lit., "fruit" [*karpos*]) of such a lifestyle assumes a negative answer as it was a fruitless mode of life. The Romans rightly looked back on their former way of life as "shame"—no little thing in an honor/shame culture—perhaps with echoes of their shameful sexual activities (see 1:26–27). The old life lived in sin's clutches had as its end point a certain death.

Yet, as Paul is accustomed, he contrasts the bondage of the person to evil with the liberating power of the gospel. Hence his words: "But now that you have been set free from sin and have become slaves of God, the benefit you reap leads to holiness, and the result is eternal life." (v. 22). The wonderful "but now" (*nuni de*) appeared earlier in 3:21 to introduce the epochal entrance of the deliverance of God wrought in Jesus' atoning death for sinners. Here Paul rehearses the major theme of his exhortation: believers have experienced a divine liberating power to free them from slavery to sin and to put them into slavery to God. If sin is enslaving the world, then freedom from sin will mean freedom from whatever sin suppresses—in this case, God's purposes for his people. While we might think any form of slavery as odious and oppressive, peoples of the ancient world knew that they were all under the sway of some higher power, whether political or divine, and the question was what benefits and blessings accrued to them by servitude to their current master. Just as being a slave of Caesar would free someone from subjugation to a lesser master, so too slavery to God means freedom from a lesser master like sin.[8]

The end result of service to God is "holiness" and "eternal life." Let us remember that holiness and life were goals of law observance. The holiness that Paul looks for in his audience is the holiness that the law looked for in Israel (see Exod 19:6; Lev 11:44–45; 19:2; 20:26; Deut 7:6; 14:2; 26:19; 28:9), and life was the reward for obedience to the law (Deut 30:19). Paul regards his churches as positionally "holy" or "sanctified" because of their union with Christ (e.g., 1 Cor 1:2, 30), but he also exhorts believers to holiness as a virtue (e.g., 1 Thess 4:3–4, 7). Jewett puts it well: "Paul views the church as the new, holy temple of God (1 Cor 3:16–17), filled and directed by the Holy Spirit (Rom 5:5; 14:17; 15:13; 2 Cor 13:14), and called upon to exhibit holiness in its social relations (Rom 12:1; 1 Thess

8. Johnson, *Romans*, 108.

4:3)."[9] Furthermore, the notion that holiness leads to eternal life has been stated by Paul earlier (Rom 2:7) and elsewhere (Gal 6:8). Holiness for Paul is part of the experience and evidence of divine grace.[10] The holiness which God expected of his covenant people and the life at stake in Israel's covenant faithfulness is now experienced by Gentiles who have faith in Israel's Messiah and obedience to Israel's God.

### Wage vs. Gift (6:23)

Coming to 6:23 means we have traveled full circle from 5:21. Paul has explained the two ways to live: sin reigning into death versus grace reigning into eternal life. The section concludes with a description of the underlying principle behind 6:15–22: "For the wages of sin is death, but the gift of God is eternal life in Christ Jesus our Lord" (v. 23). Paul explains ("for," *gar*) the reason why the two ways to serve are characterized as they are. Sin pays "wages" like a regular payment given to a soldier for their service, and that wage is "death." In contrast, what God offers is not fitting recompense for services rendered, but an entirely undeserved reward, a "gift" in the form of "eternal life."

The language of "gift" and "wages" is reminiscent of the earlier discussion about Abraham in Romans 4:4–5 and the Adam/Christ antithesis contrasting "gift" and "trespass" in 5:15–17. A similar point holds here whereby God's offer of life is due entirely to his unmerited grace. Pelagius, of all people, gets it right: "He did not say in a similar manner: 'the wages of righteousness,' because there was no righteousness in us beforehand for him to repay: for it is not procured by our effort, but is presented as a gift of God."[11]

Peter Oakes notes that the theme of eternal life, despite being replete across Romans 1–8, is "astonishingly underplayed by scholars" who think of life after death as some kind of simplistic promise of pie-in-the-sky-when-you-die. Yet, as missionaries working with people in the majority world will tell you, the hope for eternal life for those in places of war, brutality, exploitation, injustice, and disease is among the most attractive features of Christianity. At the ground level of a Roman tenement, where poverty meant that the prospect of death was a daily reality, Paul's words about eternal life would have provided succor and hope for a life beyond the grip of the grave.[12] In addition,

---

9. Jewett, *Romans*, 421.
10. Cf. further Schreiner, *Romans*, 341.
11. De Bruyn, *Pelagius' Commentary*, 100.
12. Oakes, *Reading Romans in Pompeii*, 141, 179.

the closing formula "in Christ Jesus our Lord" implies that God is the giver of eternal life, and this is achieved through the work of Christ.[13]

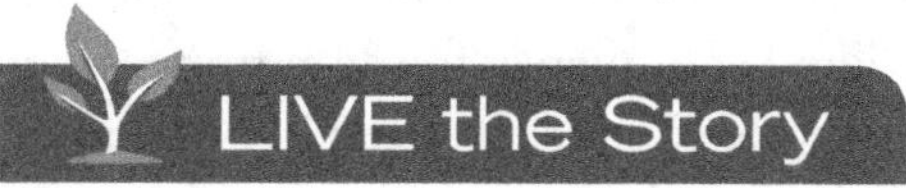


If Romans 6 has one overarching theme, it would have to be that Jesus sets us free to serve God in righteousness and holiness.

### Set Free by Grace

Romans and Galatians, despite being different letters written for different purposes, are remarkably similar in several respects. One clear connection between them is the theme of Christian freedom. Paul urged the Galatians not to be led into thinking that they needed Jesus plus Moses in order to top up their faith, so he wrote to them: "It is for freedom that Christ has set us free. Stand firm, then, and do not let yourselves be burdened again by a yoke of slavery" (Gal 5:1), and "do not use your freedom to indulge the flesh; rather, serve one another humbly in love" (5:13).

We find the same theme attested elsewhere in Paul's letters. When he wrote to the churches of Corinth, who were struggling to be a holy people in the midst of a pagan city, he reminded them: "You are not your own; you were bought at a price. Therefore honor God with your bodies" (1 Cor 6:19–20). It is a common theme: Christians are ransomed by Christ, so they must live as good and faithful servants of the master who purchased them. Returning to Romans 6:15–23 we find largely the same themes surfacing: liberation, deliverance, and freedom from sin, but such freedom is not freedom to sin. Instead believers are free to serve God with lives that burst forth with thanksgiving, holiness, love, and righteousness. The real proof that our chains have been broken is that we have freely bound ourselves to the God who loves us. According to James Dunn, "The only real freedom for a man is as a slave of God, a life lived in recognition of his creaturely dependence."[14]

To many people that will sound highly paradoxical: believers are set free from one master (i.e., sin) only to be forced into the service of another (i.e., God). However, freedom in the biblical sense is not some kind of absolute autonomy, a freedom to do and act as one pleases. Freedom is not the capacity to switch nonchalantly from virtue to vice as one pleases, but true freedom in the biblical sense is to become human by becoming like Christ. Such freedom

13. Campbell, *Paul and Union with Christ*, 75.
14. Dunn, *Romans*, 1:345.

implies a long and steady journey of being transformed by the Spirit and conformed to the pattern of the crucified Lord. This freedom, given by the Father, purchased by Christ, and expressed in the Spirit, will manifest itself in Christlike service to others just as Christ demonstrated in his own life and death. To put it simply, Christian freedom is not merely freedom from something; rather, it is freedom to follow someone. We are not freed in order to be autonomous, as if we may now happily live to please ourselves, free from any law and every master. Instead, we are to be Christonomous, living under the lordship and law of Jesus Christ.

Dietrich Bonhoeffer understood this point far better than anyone else I've come across. In one of his Berlin sermons from 1932, he called his congregation to hear again God's truth, a truth that sets us free, and enlists us in the service of love for others.

> God's truth is God's love and God's love makes us free from ourselves for others. To be free means nothing less than to be in love. And to be in love means nothing less than being in the truth of God. The man who loves because he has been made free by God is the most revolutionary man on earth. He challenges all values. He is the explosive material of human society. He is a dangerous man. For he recognizes that the human race is in the depths of falsehood. And he is always ready to let the light of truth fall upon his darkness; and he will do this because of his love. It is also true that a people cannot find truth and freedom unless it stands under the law of God's truth. A people remains in slavery until it receives and wants to receive truth and freedom from God alone; until it knows that truth and freedom will lead it into love; yes, until it knows the way of love leads to the cross. If a people would really know this, then it would become the only people who could rightly be called a free people, the only people which does not become a slave to itself, but the slave of the truth of God and therefore free.[15]

Bonhoeffer sees slavery as living in the tyranny of one's own self-centeredness, and freedom is found in God's truth about Christ. Bonhoeffer provides a portrait of what happens when God's Word comes to the world. It comes as a word of rebuke as much as a word of redemption. Out of that redemption comes a free people, a people refusing to bow down and serve the idols of self or state because they are too busy bowing down to God and doubling over to pull one another up from the ground.

---

15. Dietrich Bonhoeffer, *Dietrich Bonhoeffer's Christmas Sermons* (trans. and ed. E. Robertson; Grand Rapids: Zondervan, 2005), ePub version.

It will help considerably if we remember that the background story in Romans 6 is the exodus narrative. Israel was redeemed from slavery in Egypt so that they would be free to serve God in the Promised Land. The most repeated summary of Israel's history is that God brought them out of Egypt, out of the land of slavery; that is the presupposition for virtually everything commanded in the Old Testament (see Exod 13:3, 13; Deut 7:8; 8:14; 13:5, 10; Josh 24:17; Judg 6:8; Jer 34:13; Mic 6:4). I think it significant that the words "I am the Lord your God, who brought you out of Egypt, out of the land of slavery" preface both accounts of the Ten Commandments (Exod 20:2; Deut 5:6). God's liberating work for the people necessarily precedes God's expectations for the obedience of his people. The same pattern is carried over into the New Testament, where God's redemptive work in Christ for his people is the basis on which they are called to holiness, righteousness, and obedience. The gospel is the story of a new exodus, a new moment of redemption, where sinners are set free from the dominion of sin and are enlisted into service of their God as a holy people. I love the way Wright puts it:

> The exodus story, which stands behind so much of this chapter, remains decisive.... The story of coming out of slavery into freedom—with all the new puzzles and responsibilities that freedom brings!—is the story of the gospel, the narrative within which Jesus deliberately framed his own final moments with his followers, the story on which he himself drew to give meaning to his death. And, just as the Jewish people discovered in the exodus story the character of their rescuing God, so the covenant faithfulness of this same God has been fully unveiled in the paschal events of Golgotha and Easter. Learning about the Christian life and learning about the God revealed in Jesus Christ are two sides of the same coin.[16]

We have our own exodus in the events of Easter. We are transferred from the kingdom of darkness to the kingdom of Christ; we are redeemed and sanctified, and with this liberating work we are conscripted into the service of a new master. We serve our Lord, not by the letter of any law, but in the power of the Spirit, and where the Spirit is, Paul reminds us, there is freedom (2 Cor 3:18). By conversion to Christ and initiation into his visible body, believers have gone through a new exodus, escaped the oppressiveness of sin, so all Christians can say, "Free at last, free at last, thank God Almighty, I'm free at last."

---

16. Wright, "Romans," 10:547.

Romans is the Magna Carta of the Christian faith, spelling out as it does our emancipation from evil in the cross of Jesus Christ. The tragedy is that millions of men and women around the world live in slavery to the power of sin, mostly unbeknownst to themselves. Like mindless drones they obey its every command, completely submissive to its power. While all sin is tyrannical, we see the cruelest side of its dark reign in people who suffer from addiction. Whether it is addiction to drugs, gambling, alcohol, or pornography, sin comes to exercise such a totalizing control over the addict that gratifying the sin, even while knowing its horrid consequences, becomes the strongest impulse the addict knows. In my own country of Australia, the powerful gambling lobby, with the cooperation of political parties to the left and right, has successfully manufactured conditions to maximize their ability to entice, enslave, and exploit people through gambling. It is so sinister because it creates systematic slavery through addiction.

I know from the experience of seeing others take the journey out of addiction that it is a long and painful road. There are psychological and emotional factors that have to be faced if one is to be free. What people need to escape fully and finally from the power of sin is not only twelve-step plans, but the Savior Jesus Christ. If a person is to be free from sin, in body, mind, and soul, they need Jesus the liberator. In Paul's testimony: "Jesus Christ ... gave himself for us to redeem us from all wickedness and to purify for himself a people that are his very own, eager to do what is good" (Titus 2:13–14). Christ is the one who, in Charles Wesley's wonderful words, "breaks the power of canceled sin, he sets the prisoners free." And those whom the Son sets free, will be free indeed (John 8:36)!

## Serving God in Righteousness and Holiness

Romans 6 has several clear calls for believers to resolve to put themselves in complete service to God: do not let sin reign in your mortal body so that you obey its evil desires (v. 12); offer yourselves to God; offer every part of yourself to God as an instrument of righteousness (v. 13); and offer yourselves as slaves to righteousness (v. 19). Paul's exhortation is for believers to cultivate righteousness and holiness in their conduct because they have died and risen with Christ. It is an expectation that believers will earnestly prosecute their sanctification and improve their way of life as a believer. It is not that Christ merely *inspires* them to good deeds, nor is it that Christ merely *commands* them to try harder; rather, they are part of redemptive and transformative reality that invades the world in Jesus' death and resurrection, and that reality needs to be worked out in their own lives. The work of Christ on the cross provides the basis for the "therefore" leading to a crucicentric ethos and resurrection-driven ethic that manifests itself in real and tangible behaviors.

I have to express some degree of frustration with recent emphases among the Reformed tradition to the effect that all we should do is believe more deeply and harder in grace, and all the holiness and discipleship stuff will just take care of itself. Paul's language here is nothing like that, and he is hardly quite so blasé about it. Instead, he insists that believers must work to apply and appropriate their new identity in Christ with Christ-honoring action. While we must be ever conscious of the danger of moralism, thinking that we can earn God's favor by our own noble deeds, we must not explain away the moral imperatives that naturally flow out of union with Christ since Christ is the source our justification as well as our sanctification. A theology of the Christian life that does not lay strenuous commands on the believer is based on a cheap version of grace that is itself based on an impoverished view of Christ.

Jesus offers us what cannot be won by any moralism; that said, what God opposes is earning, not effort. As James Dunn puts it: "Moral effort is in no way antithetical to faith; it is rather the outworking and expression of faith."[17] Note what Paul says in Philippians: "continue to work out your salvation with fear and trembling," not because God is ready to smite them if they don't; rather, he explains its basis: "for it is God who works in you to will and to act in order to fulfill his good purpose" (Phil 2:12 – 13). Ultimately our pursuit of holiness and righteousness is simply the attempt to work out what God has worked into us by our union with his Son.

17. Dunn, *Romans* 1:350.

CHAPTER 12

# Romans 7:1–6

## LISTEN to the Story

[1]Do you not know, brothers and sisters—for I am speaking to those
who know the law—that the law has authority over someone only
as long as that person lives? [2]For example, by law a married woman is
bound to her husband as long as he is alive, but if her husband dies, she
is released from the law that binds her to him. [3]So then, if she has sexual
relations with another man while her husband is still alive, she is called
an adulteress. But if her husband dies, she is released from that law and is
not an adulteress if she marries another man.

[4]So, my brothers and sisters, you also died to the law through the
body of Christ, that you might belong to another, to him who was raised
from the dead, in order that we might bear fruit for God. [5]For when we
were in the realm of the flesh, the sinful passions aroused by the law were
at work in us, so that we bore fruit for death. [6]But now, by dying to what
once bound us, we have been released from the law so that we serve in the
new way of the Spirit, and not in the old way of the written code.

*Listening to the texts in the story*: Deuteronomy 24:1–4; 1 Corinthians 15:56; 2 Corinthians 3:6; Galatian 2:17–19; *4 Ezra* 9:31.

As we enter Romans 7, we are entering the most disputed and contested portion of the letter. But before we trek into the interpretive jungle of 7:7–25 with the much-debated identity of the "I," we should not simply gloss over 7:1–6. That is because, as Luke Timothy Johnson notes, 7:1–6 "seldom receives the attention it deserves."[1] This short section sums up what has gone before (Romans 6) and also sets the stage for much of what follows (Romans 7–8).[2] The provocative assertions of 5:20–21 still loom large in the background; the law unleashed sin and sin brings death, but Christ ushered in grace and grace reigns in life. Furthermore, as Paul contends in 6:1–23, the

1. Johnson, *Romans*, 114.
2. Cf. Käsemann, *Romans*, 190; Dunn, *Romans*, 1:358; Wright, "Romans," 10:558.

life of grace is not lived under the law, but it does not therefore entail lawlessness. Such is the case because dying with Christ means dying to sin and cultivating righteousness.

The implications of this are immense. Whereas many Jews saw in the Torah a hope for life, a source of group identity, and a code of conduct, Paul believes that those things — life, identity, and ethics — are apprehended in union with the Messiah. The burden of Romans 5–8 is to show that the Torah is not the source and substance of Christian hope; instead, life and righteousness are given by the Messiah and appropriated in the Spirit. The story of Paul's theology mapped into Romans 5–8 is that believers escape the Adamic triangle of law-sin-death (1 Cor 15:56 = Rom 5:20–21) by dying with Christ (Gal 2:19 = Rom 6:8; 7:4), and this brings believers into the new covenant life of the Spirit (2 Cor 3:6 = Rom 7:6; 8:1–11). If you can grasp that, then you have figured out the main plot in these central chapters of Romans.

After the controversial claim of the preceding section that believers are "not under law, but under grace" (Rom 6:14–15), Paul now moves in 7:1–6 to provide a supporting analogy from marriage. Paul does this in order to explain how freedom from the law can be conceptually linked to the new fruitful life in the Spirit. The point of the marriage illustration is to prove that death removes a person from legal obligation (vv. 1–3). Consequently, dying with Christ frees believers from the law and binds them to Christ as their new master (v. 4). His explanation essentially rehearses Romans 6, repeating the claim that believers have died with Christ to sin and so are free to serve in the new life apart from the law (vv. 5–6). In other words, 7:1–6 is a natural extension of 6:1–23,[3] but with two crucial differences.

First, what Paul says about sin in Romans 6:1–23, he attributes to the law in Rom 7:1–6:[4]

| Sin reigns | 6:14 | Law reigns | 7:1 |
|---|---|---|---|
| Died to sin | 6:2 | Died to law | 7:4 |
| Free from sin | 6:7, 18, 22 | Free from law | 7:6 |

Paul can do this because in this present evil age the law drags people into sin. The law brings knowledge of sin (Rom 3:20), increases trespass (5:20), and arouses sinful passions (7:5). Does that make the law bad? Well, no, read ahead in 7:7–25!

3. Cf. Morris, *Romans*, 260; Dunn, *Romans*, 1:358; Moo, *Romans*, 409; Tobin, *Paul's Rhetoric*, 222.

4. Cf. Dunn (*Romans*, 1:358), who sees 7:1–6 as "gathering up the main thrust of chap. 6, but now with reference to the law."

Second, the vital new element that Paul adds to his argumentative repertoire is the work of the Holy Spirit in enabling believers to produce fruit to God (7:4–6). Paul has mentioned the Holy Spirit back in 5:5 as a gift poured into our hearts, but he otherwise leaves the motif of the Spirit's work dormant until he writes 8:1–11. The absence of reference to the Spirit in Romans 6 is probably because Paul wants to emphasize that union with Christ is the conduit for life in the Spirit. Romans 7:4–6 tacitly implies that the Spirit is given in the crucified body of Christ (see 8:2), and as a logical consequence the Spirit is active in the corporate body of Christ (12:5; 14:17; 15:13, 16). This meld of Christ and Spirit explains why the Holy Spirit is called the "Spirit of Christ" (8:9) and why Paul urges the Romans pray for him "by our Lord Jesus Christ and by the love of the Spirit" (15:30).

## An Illustration from Marriage (7:1–3)

"[Or] do you not know, brothers and sisters—for I am speaking to those who know the law—that the law has authority over someone only as long as that person lives?" (v. 1). Strangely, most English translations like the NIV, NRSV, and CEB omit the coordinating conjunction "Or" (*ē*) with which Paul opens this new section (see rightly the ESV, NET, NASB). Paul implies a logical contrast whereby rejecting his previous argument in 6:1–23 would render incongruous his marital illustration in 7:1–6. Yet Paul assumes his audience's agreement with the illustration that he is about to unpack—hence his words "Do you not know," which is tantamount to "I'm sure you are with me on this one."

The reason why Paul can assume their agreement is because his audience is "those who know the law," and they know specifically "that the law has authority over someone only as long as that person lives" (v. 1). Now the "law" in question could be Roman law, which citizens are no longer obligated to obey after death. But that would be stating the blinding obvious. Moreover, in the precise legal example that Paul uses concerning the death of a husband, the surviving wife did in fact have legal obligations in Roman law to mourn her husband's death and to remain unmarried for at least twelve months after his passing. Thus it is not Roman law that the apostle has in mind here.[5]

Consequently, the "law" here has to be the Jewish law, the Torah. Specifically, Paul is probably recalling the laws in Deuteronomy 24:1–4 about marriage, divorce, and death. But if that is so, who then is Paul addressing? Is he

5. Dunn, *Romans*, 1:360.

speaking to Jews or Gentiles in the Roman congregations? While some think that Paul changes tack and speaks here directly to Jewish Christians,[6] several things count against this: (1) Paul addresses his audience as "brothers and sisters," which is the same way he addressed his Gentile audience back in his epistolary opening in Romans 1:13; (2) Paul never refers to Jews as those who "know the law" but those who are "in the law" or "under the law" (see 2:12; 3:19; 1 Cor 9:20–21; Gal 4:4, 21; 5:18); and (3) God-fearers and proselytes would certainly "know the law" from their experience of Jewish socio-religious life.[7] Thus, Paul expects the following legal example to reinforce his Gentile audience's agreement with his line of argument about Christ, grace, and freedom from the law.

The actual "example" that Paul gives in vv. 2–3 states that the death of a husband ends a wife's legal responsibilities to him. Sexual relations with another man while the husband is alive would be adultery, and the wife would be duly condemned as an "adulteress." But if the husband dies, "she is released from the law that binds her to him" (v. 2), and "she is released from that law and is not an adulteress if she marries another man" (v. 3). While the example might seem prosaic, the driving point is that death *releases* and *frees* a person from the obligation of the law.

### Explanation of the Marital Illustration (7:4)

Paul explains the meaning of the illustration about marriage to his audience with the words: "So, my brothers and sisters, you also died to the law through the body of Christ, that you might belong to another, to him who was raised from the dead, in order that we might bear fruit for God" (v. 4). The point, of course, is that, just like marriage, death removes one from the jurisdiction of the law. The verse harks back to 6:6–8, where dying with Christ means that one has died to sin; so it goes here, by dying to sin one has died to the law. We might observe too that 6:6–8 and 7:4 are themselves much like Galatians 2:19: "For through the law I died to the law so that I might live for God." The key difference is that whereas in Galatians Paul says that "through the law" he died to the law, here in Romans he states that believers have died to the law "through the body of Christ." Here the "body of Christ" is the crucified body of Christ that believers identify with in their baptism.[8]

The problem many find with Paul's illustration in vv. 2–3 and its application in v. 4 is that it does not appear to be fully consistent. *If* in vv. 2–3 the "first husband" signifies the law, the "second husband" signifies Christ, and

---

6. Cf. e.g., Rosner, *Paul and the Law*, 55; Watson, *Paul, Judaism, and the Gentiles*, 276–78.
7. Cf. Dunn, *Romans*, 1:369.
8. Cf. e.g., Käsemann, *Romans*, 189; Tobin, *Paul's Rhetoric*, 222; Jewett, *Romans*, 433–34.

the "wife" signifies the Christian, *then* how can Paul say that in v. 4 "you died to the law" when it was the first husband and not the wife who died in v. 3? However, before we fault Paul's logic, we should carefully follow his train of thought. Paul's point in v. 1 is that death severs one's relationship to the law, which is illustrated by a marital example in vv. 2–3; and the premise of v. 1 is then applied in terms of dying to the law in v. 4. Or, as Moo paraphrases it, "Recognizing the validity of the principle that 'death severs one's bondage to the law,' you believers can understand that, like this woman, you have through a death been severed from your bondage to the law and been enabled to be joined to another."[9]

Two purpose clauses round off the verse and describe what dying to the law achieves. First, "that you might belong to another, to him who was raised from the dead," indicates that the illustration of vv. 2–3 is applied to the believer with a view to their union with the risen Messiah. Second, "in order that we might bear fruit for God" goes to show that Paul envisages this union as ethically transformative and produces an abundance of spiritual fruit in the life of the believer. Behind it all is—yet again—5:20–21, where God's epochal act of deliverance rips believers from the tyrannical grip of the triumvirate of sin–death–law and places them in the reign and realm of the Lord Jesus Christ.

### Bad Fruit and New Covenant (7:5–6)

The assertions in 7:5–6 are significant because they are a summary of all that is about to follow in 7:7–8:17. This helps solve an issue with the narrative. Paul describes in v. 5 all human experience as a life lived in the clutches of sin and lived under law, with the law utterly powerless to help. This state is then contrasted with v. 6 with freedom from the law and the work of the Holy Spirit. Understood this way, v. 5 previews 7:7–25 and v. 6 previews 8:1–17.[10]

Paul makes a marked contrast by saying: "For when we were in the realm of the flesh, the sinful passions aroused by the law were at work in us, so that we bore fruit for death" (v. 5). Whereas dying with Christ brings forth a bounty of good fruit in the life of the believer (v. 4), the old life in sin and even life under the law produced a crop of poisonous fruit (v. 5). Paul refers to the former way of life of his readers when they were in the "realm of the flesh" (lit. "in the flesh"). While "flesh" (*sarx*) can simply mean one's bodily existence or the weakness of human constitution (e.g., Gal 2:20, "the life I now live in the body [*sarx*]"), for Paul, "flesh" can also signify the carnal, sinful, and immoral nature of human existence (e.g., Rom 13:14, "do not

9. Moo, *Romans*, 414.
10. Dunn, *Romans*, 1:358.

think about how to gratify the desires of the flesh"). To be "in" the flesh is to be controlled and dominated by the flesh. It means to be in the condition that characterized those who are in Adam (5:12–21) and trapped under Sin's power (6:16–21).

Significantly, Paul says that "sinful passions" were "aroused by the law," so the law makes sin worse, not better — something implicit already in 5:20 and 6:14–15, but spelled out fully here. This is highly a provocative remark. Most Jews would have said that the law was God's instrument for restraining sinful desires and putting a lid on sin. For instance, consider this passage from *4 Ezra*: "For I sow my law in you, and it shall bring forth fruit in you, and you shall be glorified through it forever" (*4 Ezra* 9.31). But Paul says the exact opposite, that the law was an enabler of sin. That is an admittedly outrageous claim, and he will return to it in 7:7–25. Paul's immediate point is that the law enables sin to permeate the entire person and produces a pattern of behavior for which death is the most fitting end.

This brings us to the solution: "But now, by dying to what once bound us, we have been released from the law so that we serve in the new way of the Spirit, and not in the old way of the written code" (v. 6). What Paul says here just repeats what he's said in so many other places like 2 Corinthians 3, Galatians 5–6, Colossians 2, and earlier in Romans 2:25–29, and he expounds it in Romans 8:1–17. That contention is that believers are free from the law, but not thereby lawless. That is because dying with Christ, living in the Spirit, and entering into the new creation kills their old self and quickens their new self to live for holiness and righteousness.

The "but now," as in 3:21 and 6:22, marks the new redemptive moment where God's saving power invades the present time. By dying with Christ, believers have died to the law and therefore are freed from the law. But, as per Romans 6, this is not a freedom to return to the old life; instead, it means "we serve in the new way of the Spirit, and not in the old way of the written code." That is reminiscent of 2 Corinthians 3:6 ("He has made us competent as ministers of a new covenant — not of the letter but of the Spirit; for the letter kills, but the Spirit gives life"), with the new covenant reality impinging on them, proving that God always intended to redeem his people by the Messiah and to renew them by the Spirit. In fact, Augustine believed that Romans was basically an extended commentary on 2 Corinthians 3:6.[11]

Think again on our gang of ex-God-fearers, ex-proselytes, and ex-pagans meeting in a Roman *insula*. How might they hear this? Obviously doing their best to keep the law, at least key parts of it, was not setting them onto a path of

11. Augustine, *Letter and Spirit*, 6, 8, 20, 24–25.

salvation, because the law could not kill the pagan in them; it only made them realize how pagan they were and even enticed them to paganize further. Does that mean that the law promotes sin, that the law had its origins in the devil, or that the law is opposed to God's goodness? To such matters Paul now turns!

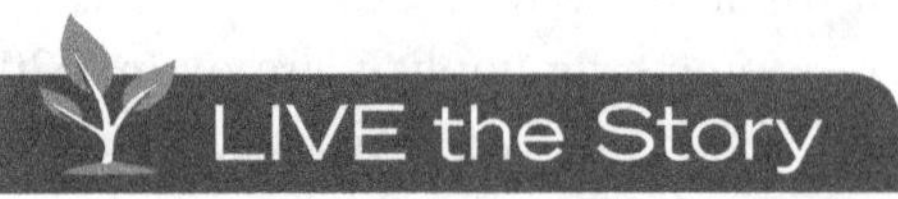


Paul draws on a whole host of images related to marriage, dying to the law, and bearing fruit to God. At their core is the redemption and transformation wrought by Christ and the Spirit. And such things are well worth pondering anew.

**Nuptials and New Covenant Fruit**

The marital imagery in vv. 2–4 implies dying to the law and a new marriage to the living Messiah. Whereas Romans 6:4 says that believers are crucified and buried with Christ, here in Romans 7:4 we see that believers are now nuptially united with the risen Jesus. Paul's exact words in v. 4 are "you also died to the law through the body of Christ, that you might belong to another, to him who was raised from the dead, in order that we might bear fruit for God." The point is that our death to the law has as its sequel our matrimonial union to the one whom God raised from the dead (see 1:4; 4:24–25; 6:4, 9).[12] We are effectively freed from the old husband and are now literally wedded to the Messiah. No wonder that Martin Luther used marriage as one of his favorite images for justification by faith. In marriage, the riches of the Bridegroom are given to the bride to adorn her with love, grace, and righteousness. This means that ecclesiology follows hot on the heels of Christology. For by dying with the crucified body of Christ (7:4), we become part of the corporate body of Christ on earth (12:5; 1 Cor 12:27), who is also the bride of Christ destined for the new heavens and the new earth (Eph 5:23–24; Rev 19:7; 21:2, 9; 22:17).

At least two implications emerge from this. (1) All believers have the same relationship with Christ, all are part of his body, and all are the bride of Christ. Paul will explore this topic later in chapters 12–15, but for now we can say that the oneness of the body of Christ is crucial for the unity and mission of the church. The mission of Christ's body is inhibited where Christ's body is not inhabited by a spirit of mutual love and shared commitment. Where there are bitter divisions, petty squabbles, and even violent factionalizing, the

12. Jewett (*Romans*, 435) states: "As always in Pauline theology, the resurrection of Christ lies at the foundation of faith."

church looks less like a bride adorned for her wedding and more like a bridal party that has engaged in mixed martial arts cage fighting.

(2) Some complain that Paul mixes metaphors by shifting from the marital to the agricultural. But it's nit-picking and to no good end. The metaphors of marriage and fruitfulness can easily be correlated. Children are the fruit of marriage and the union of the believer with Christ should produce a quiver of spiritual progeny. Matthew Black inferred that "the believer is free to contract a new union with his Risen Lord, and obtain new progeny through this fresh 'marriage.'"[13] The fruit of such marriage may not simply be a series of new God-honoring habits and the avoidance of vices; perhaps Paul also envisages the fruit of this marriage including the birth of new believers. In the same way that Paul wanted the Romans to support his mission to Spain as part of their spiritual fruitfulness, so too when we support the mission to spread the message of the gospel, we are birthing, nurturing, and raising up new believers, producing a fruitful abundance of babes of Christ.

### Making Bad People Good

How do you get idolatrous, immoral, pork-eating, emperor-worshiping, ignorant pagans to live and act like the people of God? Well, the Jewish view, quite understandable from a certain perspective, was to urge Gentiles to come under the wings of the Torah. Moses can make Roman Rufus and Corinthian Chloe better people. Yet Paul's controversial argument in Romans 1–5 is that it does not work. What people need is not rules or religion, but a new nature, and from that new nature will flow transformed behaviors.

Now obviously there are a lot of moral imperatives in the Christian faith. True as that is, however, these imperatives are never divorced from the prior acts of what God has done for us in Christ nor divorced from the Holy Spirit's work to continually renew us. The pattern of prescribed behavior for believers is never given in isolation from our relationship with God through Jesus Christ. Christian ethics flows from the event of the gospel. Our good works stem from God's grace; our good works are not the cause of grace.

To put it differently, there are certain rules and expectations that shape my relationship with my wife; even so, those rules do not characterize it as purely a legal relationship determined by rewards and punishments. What primarily shapes our behavior to each other is our relationship as man and wife and the fact that we have created something together that neither of us could do individually, namely, a marriage and a family. It is this mixture of relationship and marriage that provides the matrix in which our obligations to each other

13. Cited in Jewett, *Romans*, 435.

exist. We are not two strangers just living together, with a list of rules written down to be rigorously followed, and just happen to engage in intermittent coitus for procreation. The union is determined by a love commitment resulting in the existence of a new entity, a marriage, into which we both submerge our own identities. Within that marriage relationship we have expectations to each other that make the relationship enjoyable and fulfilling. We do not always meet those expectations to each other; we often fail, which is why our relationship needs to be repairable and open to constant reconciliation. My point is that a marriage is not two persons living by a rule book. It entails a loving relationship culminating in a new entity of a union of man and woman and that provides the context for the obligations and expectations.

If you attempt to foist rules and regulations on someone apart from a relationship, you can end up with a person who is either despondent or disobedient because they do not have the capacity to obey all the rules all the time. Here's an analogy I once heard, which, according to oral tradition, is traceable to Max Lucado. Once upon a time there was a woman with a very controlling and manipulative de facto partner. Every day before he went to work he would write a long list of all the chores that he expected her to do before he returnd home—chores like vacuum the floor, wash the dishes, iron his clothes, walk the dog, fix dinner, and so forth. If she did not do those jobs every day to his satisfaction, her partner would verbally abuse her, call her "lazy" and "useless," and sometimes prohibit her from leaving the house. So every day the poor woman worked tirelessly and fearfully to please her partner, hoping that she did everything on the list and did it to his satisfaction. Sadly, she rarely did, and daily she was scolded for some failure.

Eventually she left her partner and was soon married to a lovely and caring man. He worked in insurance in the city while she kept the house and managed their internet business. Her husband never wrote a horrid list of all the things he expected her to do while he was at work. He never complained about what she had or had not done, but they worked out their differences together with give and take. Many years later, the woman found one of the lists that her ex-partner had written for her, complete with the dozens of chores on it. She could not help but cry as she noticed that she was still doing all those things, still doing the same routines, still working hard to keep a nice home. However, she was no longer motivated by a fear of abuse, but spurned on by devotion to her husband to make their lives together happy.

Yes, I know the analogy is stereotypical with a stay-at-home wife and all, but please take on board the main point. Rules do not necessarily motivate people to do good things. What motivates people to act for the good is rarely fear but more properly love. Israel's Torah was never meant as an end for itself;

it pointed ahead to a greater redemptive reality, the coming of the Messiah. The Messiah was born under the Torah, to redeem those under the Torah, to make a people who had a new heart with a new law written on it. The Torah was intended to prepare God's people for the Savior, not to provide salvation for either Israel or the nations.

What the Torah could not do, God has done in the Messiah, to bring redemption and transformation to the peoples of the world. To overturn the sentence of death on Adam's children with the sentence of righteousness issued in the raising up of God's Son. God has sent his Spirit to draw us into the love of the triune Godhead so that we might love him and love others with a love that comes from the heart of God. We will never live in a world without rules—the anarchists and libertarians are wrong on that score. However, it is from God's deliverance wrought in Jesus, out of this redemptive relationship where God first loved us even while we were sinners, that we come to serve God. This is an obedience that comes not from the writ of the letter, but from the love of Christ and the power of the Spirit: the obedience of faith.

CHAPTER 13

# Romans 7:7 – 25

## LISTEN to the Story

[7]What shall we say, then? Is the law sinful? Certainly not! Nevertheless, I would not have known what sin was had it not been for the
law. For I would not have known what coveting really was if the law
had not said, "You shall not covet." [8]But sin, seizing the opportunity
afforded by the commandment, produced in me every kind of coveting.
For apart from the law, sin was dead. [9]Once I was alive apart from the
law; but when the commandment came, sin sprang to life and I died.
[10]I found that the very commandment that was intended to bring life
actually brought death. [11]For sin, seizing the opportunity afforded by the
commandment, deceived me, and through the commandment put me to
death. [12]So then, the law is holy, and the commandment is holy, righteous
and good.

[13]Did that which is good, then, become death to me? By no means!
Nevertheless, in order that sin might be recognized as sin, it used what
is good to bring about my death, so that through the commandment sin
might become utterly sinful.

[14]We know that the law is spiritual; but I am unspiritual, sold as a slave
to sin. [15]I do not understand what I do. For what I want to do I do not
do, but what I hate I do. [16]And if I do what I do not want to do, I agree
that the law is good. [17]As it is, it is no longer I myself who do it, but it is
sin living in me. [18]For I know that good itself does not dwell in me, that is,
in my sinful nature. For I have the desire to do what is good, but I cannot
carry it out. [19]For I do not do the good I want to do, but the evil I do not
want to do—this I keep on doing. [20]Now if I do what I do not want to
do, it is no longer I who do it, but it is sin living in me that does it.

[21]So I find this law at work: Although I want to do good, evil is right
there with me. [22]For in my inner being I delight in God's law; [23]but I
see another law at work in me, waging war against the law of my mind
and making me a prisoner of the law of sin at work within me. [24]What a
wretched man I am! Who will rescue me from this body that is subject to

death? [25]Thanks be to God, who delivers me through Jesus Christ our Lord!

So then, I myself in my mind am a slave to God's law, but in my sinful nature a slave to the law of sin.

*Listening to the texts in the story:* Genesis 1–3; Exodus 20:17; Leviticus 18:5; Isaiah 49–50; 4 Maccabees 2:5–6; *4 Ezra* 3:6–8; *2 Baruch* 15.5–6.

## The "I" of the Storm[1]

Reading Romans 7:7–25 is like that moment in an airline flight where your plane goes through a bit of turbulence and the pilot tells you to fasten your seat belts. So, yeah, it's time to fasten your exegetical seat belts, because this is where it gets bumpy! The text of 7:7–25 is among the most contested passages in all of Romans.[2] Commentators have wild disagreements over whether the moral struggle of the "I" reflects the normal experience of a Christian or refers to someone in their morass of guilt under the law before coming to faith. A cursory glance at any recent commentary will show that 7:7–25 is one of the most vexing parts of Holy Scripture.[3] So please indulge a slightly longer preface before we get into the "explain" and "live" sections.

Discussion of this passage has a long historical pedigree.[4] For example, Augustine, in his early works, regarded the "I" as a reference to humanity without Christ. However, in light of his dispute with Pelagius—perhaps because he wanted to deprive Pelagius of the opportunity to use 7:22 about the unregenerate delighting in God's law—he changed his mind and argued that 7:7–25 instead referred to Paul the Christian in his struggle with sin.[5]

---

1. The title is inspired by M. P. Middendorf, *The "I" in the Storm* (Saint Louis: Concordia Academic Press, 1997).

2. According to Philipp Melanchthon: "This part of the Pauline epistle must be pondered in a particularly careful manner, because the ancients also sweated greatly in explaining these things, and few of them treated them skillfully and correctly" (cited in Witherington, *Romans*, 181).

3. Cf. Terry L. Wilder (ed.), *Perspectives on Our Struggle: Three Views of Romans 7* (Grand Rapids: Baker, 2011), and see the balanced weighing of options in Schreiner, *Romans*, 379–92. A good survey can also be found in Stephen Voorwinde, "Who Is the 'Wretched Man in Romans 7:24?" *Vox Reformata* 54 (1990): 12–18.

4. Cf. Mark Reasoner, *Romans in Full Circle: A History of Interpretation* (Louisville: Westminster John Knox, 2005), 67–84; Mark W. Elliott, "Romans 7 in the Reformation Century," in *Reformation Readings of Romans* (ed. K. Ehrensperger and R. W. Holder; London: T&T Clark, 2008), 171–88.

5. In Augustine's own words: "At one time, I thought that in this passage the Apostle was describing a person who was under the law (rather than in grace), but afterwards these words forced themselves on me: **Now it is not I that do it.** What he says next is also related to this: *There is now*

This view has come to dominate the medieval and Reformed theological traditions.[6] But then again does the "I" have to be Paul's own moral autobiography, or does Paul even have to be addressing the moral state of Christians at all? There are other options to consider. Could the "I" be Adam, Israel, Jews, Jewish Christians, or even God-fearers narrating their moral struggle under the law? Several interpretations are possible, and as such there are several factors that we must consider as we work through 7:7–25.[7]

First, Romans 7:7–25 should principally be understood as Paul's *apologia* for the Torah.[8] Paul here is expounding 7:5 and trying to show that the sinful desires aroused by the law do not thereby mean that the law is identifiable with sin or with sin's chief effect, death.[9] Paul mentions the law sixteen times in 7:7–25. In vv. 7–12 he deals with the question "Is the law sin?" and then in vv. 13–25 he deals with the question "Did the law become death for me?" Remember that in places like Galatians, Paul makes a rather robust contrast between the Torah and Christ to the effect that Christ and not the Torah is the sole means of salvation and the sole mode for identifying God's people (see esp. Gal 2:15–3:29). Romans continues the same train of thought by constantly referring to the law's salvific inability, its redemptive-historical redundancy, its ethnic relativity, and the law's entrenchment with sin and death.

Think about what Paul says about the law in Romans and how it might sound to an audience who, at one time or another, observed the law. The law

---

*no condemnation for those who are in Christ Jesus* (Rom 8:1). Nor do I see how this statement could be true about a person under the law: **I delight in the law of God, in my inmost self.** This very delight in good, by which he does not consent to evil out of a love of justice rather than from fear of punishment—this is what it means to delight—must be attributed to the grace of God alone" (cited in Burns, *Romans*, 180 [bold original]).

6. Cf. Reasoner, *Romans in Full Circle*, 70–73; R. Ward Holder, "Calvin's Hermeneutic and Tradition: An Augustinian Reception of Romans 7," in *Reformation Readings of Romans* (eds. K. Ehrensperger and R. W. Holder; London: T&T Clark, 2008), 98–119.

7. Personally, I think that if a pastor wants to preach from a disputed text like this, they should double or even triple the amount of preparation time normally spent on a sermon. In regards to classic pieces that one should read, I'd recommend Ambrosiaster; Augustine; Chrysostom; Luther; Calvin; Lloyd-Jones, plus more recent works by Rudolf Bultmann, "Romans 7 and the Anthropology of Paul," in *Existence and Faith: Shorter Writings of Rudolf Bultmann* (ed. and trans. S. M. Ogden; London: Collins, 1964), 173–85; J. I. Packer, "The 'Wretched Man' in Romans 7," *SE* 2 (1964): 621–27; Jan Lambrecht, "Man before and without Christ: Rom 7 and Pauline Anthropology," *LS* 5 (1974–75): 18–33; Douglas J. Moo, "Israel and Paul in Romans 7.7–12," *NTS* (1986): 122–35; Mark A. Seifrid, "The Subject of Rom 7:14–25," *NovT* 34 (1992): 313–33; Robert H. Gundry, "The Moral Frustration of Paul before His Conversion: Sexual Lusts in Romans 7:7–25," in *The Old Is Better: New Testament Essays in Support of Tradition Interpretations* (WUNT 178; Tübingen: Mohr Siebeck, 2005), 252–71; Karl Deenick, "Who Is the 'I' of Romans 7:14–15?" *RTR* 69 (2010): 119–30.

8. Cf. Dunn, *Romans*, 1:376–77, 385–86, 403; Fitzmyer, *Romans*, 463; Byrne, *Romans*, 220, 229; Witherington, *Romans*,190; Wright, "Romans," 10:551; Schreiner, *Romans*, 359; Tobin, *Paul's Rhetoric*, 219–20.

9. So Jewett, *Romans*, 440, against Dunn, *Romans*, 1:406, who thinks 7:6 is being teased out.

discloses sin without remedying it (3:9, 20), performance of the law is not the basis of eschatological salvation (3:21–30), the law no longer defines the people of God (4:14–16), the law brings wrath (4:15), the law is unnecessary for the practice of righteousness (6:14–23), the law increases sin (5:20), and the law arouses sinful passions (7:5). If all of that is true, one might legitimately ask: What was the point of the giving the law in the first place? Is the law opposed to the gospel? Is the law sinful? In light of such questions and concerns arising from Paul's Christ/law contrast, Paul proceeds to explain how the law fits into God's plan in redemptive history and how the law's purpose, properly understood, is positive.

Second, in terms of genre, Romans 7:7–25 is best understood as a *prosopopiia* or "speech-in-character."[10] In ancient rhetoric a speech-in-character was a rhetorical device where a writer or speaker would give a discourse in which he takes on the character of somebody else, either real or fictional, and speaks on their behalf. Ancient commentators as far back of Origen recognized that Paul was employing some kind of literary device like impersonation in the text.[11] What that means is that the "I" is not necessarily Paul's own autobiographical cameo; it may reflect the experience of a person or class of persons whom Paul is impersonating here as a way of making a point about the struggles of trying to keep the law and the law's inability to restrain sinful desires.

Third, on the identity of the "I," let me suggest that it reflects *generally* the moral struggle of any person confronted by the law and becoming aware of their own inability to keep it; but it probably refers *specifically* to Gentile God-fearers who, at some time, tried to keep elements of the law, but found that they were unable to do so. Several lines of argumentation support this hypothesis.[12]

(1) The "I" is not a Christian and cannot be a Christian.[13] While many might take great comfort in a Christian reading of Romans 7:7–25, furnishing proof that even the apostle Paul struggled with sin in his Christian life, providing hope and succor for the rest of us in our struggle against the flesh—and it's a position supported by scholars no less than Augustine, Aquinas, Luther, Calvin, Dunn, and Cranfield—yet the basis for such a reading is flimsy. Paul is not talking about Christians in this section since the statement

10. David E. Aune, *The New Testament in Its Literary Environment* (Cambridge: James Clark & Co., 1987), 168; Stanley K. Stowers, "Romans 7.7–25 as a Speech-in-Character (προσωποποιία)," in *Paul in His Hellenistic Context* (ed. T. Engberg-Pedersen; Minneapolis: Fortress, 1995), 180–202.

11. Stowers, *A Rereading of Romans*, 268–69; on Origen, see Burns, *Romans*, 170, where Origen sees Paul "speaking as a teacher of the Church" and "assumed the voice of the weak."

12. What follows is an extended version of Bird, *Bird's-Eye View of Paul*, 140–43.

13. As established by the well-known and celebrated study of Werner G. Kümmel, *Römer 7 und die Bekehrung des Paulus* (Leipzig: Hinrichs, 1929).

"I am unspiritual, sold as a slave to sin" (7:14) conflicts with what he says about Christians in Romans 6, where he declared that they have been freed from sin (6:6–7, 17–18, 22). The speaker struggles to obey the law (7:22, 25), whereas Christians are free from the law (6:14–15; 7:6).

If this is a Christian being spoken about, then goodness me, where is the Holy Spirit? Surely the transforming work of the Holy Spirit should get a word in somewhere here, but it doesn't! We have to wait until Romans 8:1–17 to hear about the Holy Spirit, and there we are informed that the Spirit "has set you free from the law of sin and death" (8:2), the requirements of the law are fulfilled by those who "live ... according to the Spirit" (8:4), "by the Spirit you put to death the misdeeds of the body" (8:13), and "the Spirit you received does not make you slaves" (8:15). In other words, reading 6:1–7:6 and 8:1–17, which bracket 7:7–25, shows that those who are in Christ Jesus and who share in the Spirit have been saved from the horrible things spoken about in 7:7–25. So the "I" of 7:7–25 *cannot* be a Christian if Christ has delivered us from slavery to sin, if believers are under grace not law, and if the Holy Spirit enables believers to fulfill the just requirements of the law. Yes, there is an ongoing struggle with the flesh for Christians (see 8:9–11; 13:14; 1 Cor 3:1; Gal 5:13, 16–18); however, that is not the point here. Instead Romans 7:7–25 is a redemptive-historical argument about the law's goodness and its inability to put the power of sin in check.

(2) The "I" is not necessarily a normal pre-Christian experience of wailing in guilt and longing for a deliverer. The problem is, as Krister Stendahl has pointed out, that Western theology has read Paul through the lens of the introspective consciences of thinkers like Augustine and Luther, who had an unusual fixation on their moral failings prior to coming to faith. Yet the preconversion anxieties of Augustine and Luther should not be regarded as paradigmatic for the moral struggle of every soul prior to coming to faith.[14] In fact, as far as we know, Saul of Tarsus did not have a guilt-ridden conscience and was not longing for a merciful God to save his soul from the fires of everlasting damnation. In an autobiographical passage, Paul claims that as a Pharisee he thought he was "blameless" in regards to the law (Phil 3:8), and his zeal for the law meant that he genuinely believed that God was pleased with his religious efforts (Gal 1:14; Phil 3:6).

The language of "blamessless" is not necessarily forensic and is a relative term expressing moral intentionality, not complete sinlessness. Certainly

14. Krister Stendahl, *Paul among Jews and Gentiles* (Philadelphia: Fortress, 1976), 78–96. But see in counterpoint Talbert (*Romans*, 197–203) who thinks that Paul must have had some introspective thoughts about his own guilt!

Paul, like other Jews,[15] was probably aware of his sinful habits and looked to expunge them through the sacrificial rites of the cultus. But in any case, before his conversion on the Damascus Road, Paul thought he was doing alright, and he was certainly not fixated on his moral inadequacies. He was probably more like the hypothetical Jewish teacher in Romans 2:1–11, 17–24, who is confident in his election, convinced of the goodness of his own moral effort, and believes he has earned a right to be comparatively boastful over others. In which case, the moral struggle of the "I" narrated in 7:7–25 is probably retrospective and reflects an inner anxiety about keeping the law that is only perceptible from the vantage point of faith. It spells out what Douglas Campbell calls "the horrifying view backward."[16] The person speaking is saying, "Ah, yes, in coming to Christ now I can see the struggle I formerly had, a struggle to obey the law, a struggle I could not win, because the law could not help me overcome the flesh."[17] Paul, from a Christian perspective, can now view his mix of pricked conscience and presumption of righteousness as part of the deception and death that he experienced under the law.

(3) The "I" is probably a composite character. There are echoes of Adam, Israel, perhaps Paul himself, and especially God-fearers or proselytes who tried to live under the law but now see in hindsight that they had always failed to keep it.[18]

---

15. Cf. 1QS 11.9–10: "I belong to evil humankind to the assembly of wicked flesh; my failings, my transgressions, my sins ... with the depravities of my heart, belong to ... those who walk in darkness. For to man does not belong his path, nor to a human being the steadying of his steps" (cited from Talbert, *Romans*, 193).

16. Douglas A. Campbell, "Christ and the Church in Paul: A 'Post-New Perspective' Account," in *Four Views on the Apostle Paul* (ed. M. F. Bird; Grand Rapids: Zondervan, 2012), 133.

17. That is not to say that Jews and Gentiles were unaware of their moral failures and ethical calamities. Jews knew that they often failed to live up to the standards of the covenant (e.g., Ps. 51) and Gentiles had genuine struggles of conscience (e.g., Rom 2:14–15). But the depiction of Jews or Gentiles as incessantly bemoaning their moral wretchedness and powerlessness in sin seems foreign to the experience of most ancients.

18. Cf. Brian Dodd, *Paul's Paradigmatic "I": Personal Examples as Literary Strategy* (JSNTSup 117; Sheffield: Sheffield Academic Press, 1999); Stephen J. Chester, "The Retrospective View of Romans 7: Paul's Past in Present Perspective," *Perspectives on Our Struggle with Sin: Three Views of Romans 7* (ed. T. L. Wilder; Nashville: Broadman & Holman, 2011) 57–103 (esp. 73). Moo (*Romans*, 425–31) sees "Paul in solidarity with Israel," Wright (*Climax of the Covenant*, 197) observes that "Israel recapitulated the sin of Adam," and Grieb (*Story of Romans*, 74) detects Paul describing "humanity in general and especially Israel living the Adamic existence under Sin's power." Jewett (*Romans*, 442–44) rejects the composite theory as "bizarre in its complexity" and argues instead that the "I" is Paul describing his preconversion religious zealotry that opposed God's Messiah. However, Jewett also thinks that the speech is "formulated in such generic terms that persons outside of Paul's circle of experience can apply the argument to themselves," and "Paul's analysis of the human plight generalized from his Jewish experience" (*Romans*, 444, 466). The latter observations mute his critique of the composite view.

To begin with, there are some striking parallels between Genesis 2–3 and Romans 7:7–25. For instance this statement, "Once I was alive apart from the law ... [then] the commandment came" (Rom 7:9), reflects the pattern where God "took the man and put him in the garden" and then afterward gave him a "command" about the Tree of Life, which could potentially yield death (Gen 2:15–17). Also, "sin ... deceived me and through it killed me" (Rom 7:11) corresponds with "the serpent deceived me, and I ate" (Gen 3:13). More generally, the sequence of sin leading to death (Rom 7:9–11) reflects the introduction of death with the "fall" of Adam (Gen 3:19). These parallels show that the experience of the "I," who is deceived into sin leading to death, recapitulates the experience of Adam in the Garden of Eden. At a bare minimum we could confidently affirm that the subject of the speech has discovered within himself the dark vestiges of the Adamic self.[19]

In addition, the "I" language of 7:7–25 might represent Israel under the law. The anxiety of the speaker is reminiscent of several psalms where the psalmist oscillates between the "I" and "Israel" as the subject of the psalm (e.g., Pss 17; 69; 119; esp. 130; 131).[20] The commandment "you shall not covet" in v. 8 is a clear citation of the Decalogue, Israel's covenant charter (Exod 20:17; Deut 5:18). In fact, the whole narrative in Romans 7:8–10 evokes the image of Israel's reception of the law at Sinai and its failure to obey it. Furthermore, if one grants the echoes of Isaiah 49–50 in vv. 14–25, one could discern echoes of Israel's exile within the story of the text.[21] So Romans 7:7–25 may well have as its subject the position of Israel under the law, even under the exilic curse for disobedience, and becoming suddenly aware their inability to obey the law.[22]

Finally, given Paul's Gentile audience, who were drawn mainly from the ranks of God-fearers and proselytes, perhaps Paul is trying to get the Roman

---

19. Keck, *Romans*, 180. On the echoes of Adam, see esp. Käsemann, *Romans*, 195–96, 200 ("*egō* means mankind under the shadow of Adam") as well as Cranfield, *Romans*, 1:350–51; Dunn, *Romans*, 1:378, 399–400; Witherington, *Romans*, 184–92; Watson, *Paul, Judaism, and the Gentiles*, 279–87; Grieb, *Story of Romans*, 72. Even so, making Adam the actual speaker fails because (1) commentators are forced to treat Sin/Serpent as the same character (e.g., Dunn, *Romans*, 1:385; Witherington, *Romans*, 191); and (2) while some of the later rabbis thought that Adam had a version of the Torah in Eden (e.g., *Tg. Neof.* Gen 2:15), it is unlikely that Paul thought so, since it would evacuate his argument in Romans 4:13–15, 5:13, and Galatians 3:17 about the introduction of the law after the time of Adam and Abraham.

20. On the significance of the Psalms for the "I" see Dunn, *Romans*, 1:378, 382 and more fully Beverly R. Gaventa, "The Shape of the 'I': the Psalter, the Gospel, and the Speaker in Romans 7," in *Apocalyptic Paul: Cosmos and Anthropos in Romans 5–8* (ed. B. R. Gaventa; Waco, TX: Baylor University Press, 2013), 79–91.

21. John K. Goodrich, "Sold under Sin: Echoes of Exile in Romans 7.14–25," *NTS* 59 (2013): 476–95.

22. Cf. e.g., Moo, *Romans*, 430–31; Byrne, *Romans*, 216; Bryan, *Preface to Romans*, 141; Kruse, *Romans*, 321; Goodrich, "Sold under Sin," 489–90.

Christians to reflect on how in hindsight they can see that their prior life under the law was a continuous moral struggle where they were never able to arrive at a sense of assurance that they were right with God or that they really belonged to God's people.[23] The law was able to remind them of their sin but unable to redeem them from it.[24] A Gentile God-fearer seems a likely candidate for the "I," considering that the speaker refers to a time when he did not "know" the law (vv. 7–8), a time when he was "alive apart from the law" (v. 9), and only later did the commandments come and make him cognizant of his sinful desires (vv. 9–10). This sounds much like the experience of a Gentile God-fearer and his encounter with the law.

Furthermore, Greco-Roman philosophers were aware of the danger of falling into a state of moral duplicity where one acted against one's better moral judgment, a state called *akrasia*. This state was characterized by a lack of self-control, where the soul was deceived into doing wrong by giving into passion over reason.[25] If feelings of *akrasia* were aroused by an encounter with the Torah, this partly explains the angst of the Gentile speaker, who is opining: "I want to live an overall plan of life like the Jewish law teaches,

---

23. A Gentile audience for Romans 7:7–25 is likely because (1) earlier in Romans 6:21 ("What benefit did you reap at that time from the things you are now ashamed of? Those things result in death") seems to have a Gentile audience in mind; and (2) Romans 7:1 ("I am speaking to those who know the law") is not necessarily referring to Jews, but to Gentiles who know about and have experienced some form of life under the law.

24. Even those Gentiles who had little exposure to the Jewish law, would still know about the perils of "desire" (vv. 7–8) from Greco-Roman moral philosophers, particularly the Stoics, who urged their followers to extricate themselves from the power of desire. Gentile Christians converted from paganism might be inclined to see themselves in 2:15, 7:7–25 as the "I" who is unable to keep a "natural law" on account of their illicit desires. See Troels Engberg-Pedersen, *Paul and the Stoics* (Louisville: Westminster John Knox, 2000, 38–39; Markus Bockmuehl, "The Conversion of Desire in St. Paul's Hermeneutics," in *The Word Leaps the Gap: Essays on Scripture and Theology in Honor of Richard B. Hays* (ed. J. R. Wagner, C. K. Rowe, and A. K. Grieb; Grand Rapids: Eerdmans, 2008), 498–513; Oakes, *Reading Romans*, 157–58.

25. There are some interesting Greco-Roman parallels to note: Plato (*Republic*, Bk 9): "Then will you say that such a soul is enslaved or free? 'Enslaved, I should suppose.' Again, does not the enslaved and tyrannized city least of all do what it really wishes? 'Decidedly so.' Then the tyrannized soul — to speak of the soul as a whole — also will least of all do what it wishes, but being always perforce driven and drawn by the gadfly of desire it will be full of confusion and repentance. 'Of course.' And must the tyrannized city be rich or poor? 'Poor.' Then the tyrant soul also must of necessity always be needy and suffer from unfulfilled desires.... And do you not think you will find more lamentations and groans and wailing and anguish in any other city?" Ovid (*Metam.*, 7.19–20): "Desire persuades me one way, reason another. I see the better and approve it, but I follow the worse"; Epictetus (*Diatr.* 2.26.4): "What I wish, I do not do, what I do not wish, I do." Seneca (*Hippolytus*, 177): "I know what you say is true but passion forces me to take the worser path." The parallels do, of course, have their limitations, see Ronald V. Huggins, "Alleged Classical Parallels to Paul's 'What I Want to Do I Do Not Do, but What I Hate, That I Do' (Rom 7:15)," *WTJ* 54 (1992): 158–61. More positively, see Emma Wasserman, "The Death of the Soul in Romans 7: Revisiting Paul's Anthropology in Light of Hellenistic Moral Psychology," *JBL* 127 (2007): 793–816.

but my overpowering but transitory desires consistently frustrate that larger goal."[26]

In regards to the identity of the speaker then, as Tobin avers, it is most naturally identified as one of the Roman Gentile Christians who came to know the law through their association with local synagogues, and Paul verbalizes how he imagines their prior experience of the law now looks to them. "The speaker is describing the situation of someone in whom Paul thinks the Gentile Roman Christians will see themselves and their own experience of trying to observe the commandments of the law," and "Paul uses the speech-in-character to illustrate something he hopes the Roman Christians will see reflected in their own experience so that, through seeing this reflection they come to understand how the law can be both good yet limited and something by which believers in Christ are no longer bound."[27]

The structure of Romans 7:7–25 breaks down into two distinct sections: (1) answering the question whether the law is sinful (vv. 7–12); and (2) answering the question whether the law is death (vv. 13–25).[28]

## EXPLAIN the Story

### Is the Law Sin? (7:7–8)

Paul launches into the provocative question: "What shall we say, then? Is the law sinful?" (v. 7). In light of the whole sweep of Romans 2:1–7:6 about the law's inability to provide salvation and its role in snowballing rather than solving sin, Paul asks a question that his audience might be quietly thinking: Is the law itself sinful? Paul responds with his emphatic negation, "Certainly not" (*mē genoito*), to make it crystal clear that the law not identifiable with sin nor is it inherently sinful.[29]

In what follows Paul exonerates the law from such a charge by describing how Sin conspires to lead people into sin through the law. He states: "Nevertheless, I would not have known what sin was had it not been for the law. For I would not have known what coveting really was if the law had not said, 'You shall not covet.' " (v. 7). Ambrosiaster notes: "Here Paul shows that the law is not sin but the yardstick of sin."[30] To say it differently, the law is a channel

26. Stowers, *Rereading of Romans*, 280.

27. Tobin, *Rhetoric of Righteousness*, 237–38. See also Rafael Rodriguez, *If You Call Yourself a Jew: Reappraising Paul's Letter to the Romans* (Eugene, OR: Cascade, 2014), 136–45.

28. According to Talbert (*Romans*, 196), these are likely Jewish objections Paul had encountered in his missionary work.

29. The Greek text says literally, "Is the law sin?" (*ho nomos hamartia;*) as per the NRSV, ESV, CEB.

30. Cited in Bray, *Ambrosiaster*, 55.

for sin but not its cause; the cause of sin lies in desire as activated by sin. The law facilitates knowledge of sin by setting forth the divine commandments that prohibit sin (see 3:20). For case in point, knowledge of coveting is first given by the tenth commandment of the Decalogue, which forbids coveting a neighbor's people or possessions (Exod 20:17; Deut 5:21). The law, by prohibiting coveting, introduced the idea of coveting, and so opened up the possibility of coveting.

The process whereby one moves from knowledge of the law to actually violating its commands is spelled out: "But sin, seizing the opportunity afforded by the commandment, produced in me every kind of coveting. For apart from the law, sin was dead" (v. 8). The notion of "Sin" here is that of a personal power awakened by the law. Without the law "sin was dead" and unable to affect anyone. However, with the law, sin rises up and seizes the opportunity afforded by the law to sow its seeds and to cultivate sinful desires. Importantly, Sin is characterized as a devious personal agent who conspires to produce all kinds of desire "in me."[31]

### Why I Sin (7:9–11)

While Paul has spoken in the first person in vv. 7–8 about the one in whom Sin produces sinful desires through the law, here in vv. 9–11, he embarks on the first movement of his speech about the "I" who is trapped between law and sin. It is here that we first get the impression that Paul is not talking strictly about himself, but about a particular person or about a particular class of persons who can identify with the situation concerning which he speaks.

"Once I was alive apart from the law; but when the commandment came, sin sprang to life and I died" (v. 9). This verse summarizes the assertion behind vv. 7–8 about how sin used the law to bring in sinfulness and death. The new element is that Paul now situates that miniature epic in relation to the story of the "I's" own journey from life to death. The "I" was "alive apart from the law," which implied that the person was not born under the law like the Jews and so it naturally connotes a Gentile. Yet when the commandment comes—and "commandment" is probably a synecdoche for the whole law—sin springs to life, and with its life comes the advent of death upon the "I." The "I," by coming under the jurisdiction of the law, becomes trapped in the triangle of law-sin-death.

Paul next explains exactly how the "I" goes from life to death. He is careful to note that while the law produced death, even so it was inadvertent rather than intentional: "I found that the very commandment that was intended to

31. The middle voice of *kateirgasato* ("it produced") suggests that sin effectively reproduces itself in the action of activating desires, in other words, sin produces sinfulness.

bring life actually brought death. For sin, seizing the opportunity afforded by the commandment, deceived me, and through the commandment put me to death" (vv. 10–11). The idea that the law with its commandments was intended to bring life rather than death is formulated at several places in the Torah, such as, "Keep my decrees and laws, for the person who obeys them will live by them" (Lev 18:5), and "If you fully obey the LORD your God and carefully follow all his commands I give you today ... you will be blessed in the city and blessed in the country" (Deut 28:1–3). It is by violating the commandments that one receives the penalties of the law, which results in death for both the individual and the nation (see Deut 28:15–68). Sin operates in this two-way theme of obedience unto life or disobedience unto death.

The manner of sin's deception is not altogether clear. It obviously calls to mind the deception of Adam and Eve in the garden of Eden (Gen 3:13; 2 Cor 11:3; 1 Tim 2:14). Some think that it refers to Israel being deceived into thinking that the promise of life held out by the law could be achieved by trying to keep the law.[32] This latter option is tempting, especially in light of Romans 9:30–10:4 and Galatians 3:6–13, which highlight Israel's failure to keep the law. However, it probably requires a bit more nuance. I surmise that the deception in question probably refers to anyone, Jew or Gentile, who thinks that keeping the law provides a sure path to life, with "life" defined as belonging to the people whom God will deliver in an eschatological future. In other words, the deception pertains to the belief that the law provides security in election and a surety for final vindication. Paul is saying that taking up the law means coming under a death sentence, and joining ethnic Israel means joining a community experiencing national death. This is precisely why Gentiles should not do it.

### The Law Vindicated (7:12)

Paul recaps his defense of the law with the words: "So then, the law is holy, and the commandment is holy, righteous and good" (v. 12). This is the full answer to the question issued in v. 7, "Is the law sinful?" It is more than a mere negative answer as the law is positively described as "holy, righteous, and good." The law might be a channel for sin, arousing it and enabling it, with death close behind, but the law does not deliberately cause sinning. Paul affirms that the law is God-given and expresses divine holiness and divine goodness, and it reveals God's faithfulness. Such words put up a permanent embuggerance against those who would try to drive a Marcionite bulldozer over Paul's theology to make the law wicked, profane, and unjust.

32. Cf. e.g., Moo, *Romans*, 440.

### Is the Law Death? (7:13)

The sequence in vv. 13–25 follows a similar pattern to vv. 7–12.[33] Paul again begins with a provocative question, which meets with an emphatic denial (v. 13), follows it up with a first-person speech (vv. 14–23), and finishes with a closing remark (vv. 24–25). Paul has concluded in v. 12 that the law is not sinful, but that is not the end of the charges against the law, for he asks: "Did that which is good, then, become death to me? By no means!" (v. 13). Since the law is caught up in the triangle of law-sin-death (see Rom 5:20–21; 8:2; 1 Cor 15:56) it naturally leads to the question of whether the law is death. Again, the answer is an emphatic "By no means!" (*mē genoito*). The law is not identifiable with death, nor is the law inherently fatal. Paul explains where the law fits into the nexus of sin and death: "Nevertheless, in order that sin might be recognized as sin, it used what is good to bring about my death, so that through the commandment sin might become utterly sinful" (v. 13). The law puts a spotlight on sin with dual effects. On the one hand, the law provides sin with a platform to ply its trade as a merchant of death. But on the other hand, the law exposes sin for what it truly is and highlights the full measure of its brutality. To give an analogy, the law lures an assassin into the open, where he kills his intended victim, but the identity of the assassin is then revealed. The law, though good, brought death, so that sin might be revealed as the killer it is. Even while sin uses the law to produce death, God's main purpose for the law still remains in effect; sin is unmasked and given visible recognition.

### Why Do I Die? (7:14–23)

Paul proceeds to explain his vindication of the law against charges of promoting sin by again reverting to a biographical speech in the first person: "We know that the law is spiritual; but I am unspiritual, sold as a slave to sin" (v. 14).[34] What Paul means by "spiritual" (*pneumatikos*) here is things pertaining to the Spirit or filled by the Spirit.[35] In other words, the law is God-given and expresses God's own will. In contrast, Paul says that the "I" is the

---

33. In Romans 7:7–12 this pattern took the form: Q&A (vv. 7–8), biographical speech (vv. 9–11), and conclusion (v. 12).

34. Some commentators (e.g., Bruce, *Romans*, 143–45 and Murray, *Romans*, 1:155–59) see a transition with vv. 7–13 talking about a pre-Christian and then vv. 14–25 talking about a Christian. This view flounders on the fact that vv. 14–25 rehearses many themes about the state of the non-Christian world in 1:18–3:20 and 5:12–21 (Käsemann, *Romans*, 199). What is more, the shift from the aorist tense in vv. 7–13 to the present tense in vv. 14–15 does not imply that Paul is talking about his present experience. Greek verbs are aspectival with the temporal sense given by context. The present tense is aspectivally imperfective and meant to underscore an insider perspective on an action (see Constantine R. Campbell, *Basics of Verbal Aspect* [Grand Rapids: Zondervan, 2008], 40–43).

35. BDAG 837.

exact opposite—"unspiritual" as the NIV puts it, but more literal is "of the flesh" (see ESV, NRSV). The meaning of the word *sarkinos* most likely refers to humanity in a sinful, self-centered, self-seeking, and worldly state before God (see 1 Cor 3:1, "I could not address you as people who are spiritual but as people who are still *fleshly*" [pers. Trans.]). Käsemann describes the flesh as "the workshop of sin," and a person in the flesh abounds in "cosmic fallenness to the world."[36]

This "fleshly" state is further described as being "sold as a slave to sin." According to John Goodrich, "It is difficult to overstate the rhetorical and theological importance of the phrase 'sold under sin' in Rom 7.14."[37] Käsemann even says that "Paul's theology as a whole stands or falls with this statement" since it assumes that humanity is "engulfed in the power of sin" and needs justification by faith.[38] The plight of the "I" is not just internal angst about sin, but externally imposed slavery under sin, which is decisive for thinking that a Christian is not in view here.[39] While these words could allude to several Old Testament texts about people selling themselves to do evil (1 Kgs 21:20, 25; 2 Kgs 17:17), a good case can be made for an allusion to Isaiah 50:1 about Israel being sold into the punishment of exile on account of their sin.[40] Paul may be doing something similar to what he did in Galatians 3:6–14 by arguing that anyone who comes under the law comes under the curses of the law for disobedience. Thus, the "I" finds himself enslaved in sin even while he tries to obey the God-given law.

The succeeding description of the plight of the "I" in vv. 15–20 is difficult to follow in English and even more so in Greek. In summary, the "I" finds himself confused by his conflicting desire and wicked behavior (v. 15a), totally unable to do good and drawn to doing wrong (v. 15b). He proves by his disobedience that the law is good and that sin is residing within him (vv. 16–17); he realizes that no good is within him, and he is controlled by his sinful nature (v. 18), so much so that he is unable even to begin to do good and instead persists in doing evil (v. 19). His sinful behavior, doing what ought not be done, reiterates the helpless state he is in as one totally under the sway of sin (v. 20). The "I" is a tragic figure, powerless, pathetic, and pitiful, as he knows what he *ought* to do but is entirely *unable* to do it.

The travails of the "I" described in vv.15–20 are then put in explicit relation to the Torah in vv. 21–23. First, in reflection, the speaker says, "So I find

36. Käsemann, *Romans*, 199, 205.
37. Goodrich, "Sold under Sin," 477.
38. Käsemann, *Romans*, 200.
39. Cf. e.g., Käsemann, *Romans*, 200; Stuhlmacher, *Romans*, 115; Moo, *Romans*, 454.
40. Cf. Goodrich, "Sold under Sin."

this law at work: Although I want to do good, evil is right there with me" (v. 21). The word "law" here seems to be a principle rather than a reference to the Mosaic law.[41] The principle is that even with the best of intentions, evil remains upon him, like a parasite clinging to its host.

Second, the "I" is caught between his desire to obey the law on the one hand and his sinful desires on the other hand that prevent him from obeying the law. The conflict is described in terms of a struggle between warring factions: "For in my inner being I delight in God's law; but I see another law at work in me, waging war against the law of my mind and making me a prisoner of the law of sin at work within me" (v. 22–23). Paul switches from referring to "law" as a principle in v. 21 to the notion of "law" as something like a power in vv. 22–23. The "I" delights in God's law, the Torah, because it is holy, righteous, good, and spiritual (vv. 12–14). He is like the many voices found in the Psalter about people who take delight in God's law as a holy guide and a wellspring of goodness (see Pss 1:2; 19:7; 40:8; 119:70, 72, 97, 113).

Yet there is "another law" in the equation, an irresistible power of sorts, which wages war against the "I" by pitting his delight in God's law against the desires of his flesh. This "law" commences open hostilities against the "law of the mind." This foreign "law" comes into open conflict with his noble intention to delight in and to obey the law. Tragically, however, this other "law" is revealed to be none other than the "law of sin." This "law of sin" is like a virus that enters and infects the "I's" mind. It works so effectively that it imprisons the "I" under sin, turning his delight in the law to disobedience of the law, and then leaving him in the spiral of confusion and carnality spoken about in vv. 15–20.

### The Wretched Man Rescued by the Wonderful Savior (7:24–25)

The "I" has finally and fully answered his question about whether the law is sin and whether the law brings death in vv. 7, 13. The answer on both counts is "no." That is because God's law is good and holy, the "I" delights in the law, but this delight is overpowered by the "law of sin," which enslaves him within the vestiges of its vile grip. The end result is that the "I" is trapped in a totally helpless state. He finds himself under the curse of the law, captive to its power and worthy of its penalties.

It is from within this plight that Paul presents the "I" as crying out in despair, "What a wretched man I am! Who will rescue me from this body that is subject to death?" (v. 24). The answer to the question uttered by the

41. Cf. e.g., Cranfield, *Romans* 1:361–62; Käsemann, *Romans*, 205; Fitzmyer, *Romans*, 475–76; Byrne, *Romans*, 228, 232.

miserable speaker as to who can rescue him is posed in such a way as to imply, "Nobody can!"[42] The "I" is alone and helpless in sin, but at least he now knows it. The "I" is pathetic and powerless, which is why he recognizes his utterly "wretched" condition. The "I" is like the penitent person in the psalms who begs the Lord not to hold their sins against them and pleads for mercy in the face of judgment (e.g., Pss 6; 38; 51; 102; 130; 143).[43] The "I" is on the precipice of a place that we can only call "conversion."[44]

Paul, however, cannot jump to his conclusion in v. 25b about slavery in sin without first giving a burst of thanksgiving to Jesus Christ. Paul, the apostle of grace, has to give a spoiler as he knows that the wretched man meets the wonderful rescuer. So he interjects a note of thanksgiving and praise: "Thanks be to God, who delivers me through Jesus Christ our Lord!" (v. 25a). Jesus is the agent through whom God's redemptive activity is manifested. Also, while the "I" is a composite character of Adam/Israel/God-fearers narrated in a speech-in-character, even so, the "me" of the thanksgiving probably includes Paul himself, meaning that Paul does identify with the character in the speech at least to some degree.[45]

Finally, Paul resumes his line of thought by recapitulating the main theme of the speech, "So then, I myself in my mind am a slave to God's law, but in my sinful nature a slave to the law of sin" (v. 25b). Deep down the "I" desperately wants to be obedient to God's law, but his desire is thwarted by a sinful nature that renders him subservient instead to the "law of sin," a law that is tantamount to the "power of sin." The "I," then, knows the law's goodness, but remains powerless in sin, to the point that he is corrupted by sin and condemned for sinning. The "I" cannot save himself; he is a living corpse, a body of death, whose only hope is to be rescued.[46] However, Paul has argued in 3:21–5:11 that the rescue has already begun, sin's penalty has been paid, sin's poison has been cured, and sin's power can be overcome by Jesus' death and resurrection, union with Christ, and the pouring out of the Holy Spirit.

Imagine a gaggle of Gentile Christians, crammed together in a squalid apartment somewhere in the Trastevere, listening to Phoebe or one of her companions read these words to them. They might have had perplexing

42. Morris, *Romans*, 297.

43. In contrast to some scholars (e.g., Dunn, *Romans*, 1:377, 389, 394, 398–99, 407), the "I" is not eschatologically divided between the old age and the new age. Rather, the cry for help in vv. 24–25 shows that he is in desperate need for any deliverance!

44. Contra, e.g., Dunn (*Romans*, 1:397), who thinks that the deliverance here is not about an initial "conversion" but about "final deliverance" at the end of the age. More correct is Jewett, *Romans*, 471–72.

45. Cf. Dunn (*Romans*, 1:382): "What is true of everyman is true also of him."

46. Keck, *Romans*, 194.

questions about Paul's characterization of God's righteousness as coming "apart from law" but "attested by the law" (3:21), how the law caused sin to multiply (5:21), and how they are not "under law but under grace" (6:14–15). The speech-in-character in 7:7–25 brings some of these threads together by showing that the law is good and godly, but the law becomes a weapon of sin when the law meets human wickedness. According to Paul, the law has not restrained the sinful nature as his kinsmen believe; on the contrary, the law has proved how much Adam and Israel have in common.

In light of that, Gentile Christians too could see themselves as the "I" at one time trapped in sin when they became aware of the Torah. In hindsight they might view their one-time affiliation with Jewish communities and the Torah as not giving them assurance of belonging to God's people and to God's future, but instead reinforcing how far away they were from deliverance. Furthermore, since Jesus Christ has rescued them from the triangle of law-sin-death, they have made the right decision to believe in Messiah Jesus, to receive the gospel about him, to join a Christ-centered community, and to rely on Christ rather than Roman religion or the Torah for deliverance.

## LIVE the Story

In thinking about how to "live," Romans 7:7–25 can be a bit tricky. Augustine's interpretation that the "I" was a Christian has ruled the day through Luther and Calvin, but I'm not convinced it is either correct or helpful. We are confronted with a real challenge as to how we are to preach, teach, and apply this passage when so many of the popular explanations of the text are not feasible. So, for instance, if Paul is not talking about humanity facing up to its own inauthentic existence under the law, then what do we say? If we refuse to go the route of overly psychologizing the text, pitting the "super-ego" against the "id," can some relevant remarks be salvaged? If Paul is not talking about carnal Christians still stuck in the flesh and still longing for extrication from sin's power, then how do we explain the story? Stephen Chester hits the nail on the head when he says: "The history of Protestant interpretation of Romans 7 thus sets before our generation of interpreters a challenge: how do we forge interpretations of Romans 7 that are exegetically and theologically credible and yet still have something definite enough to say to be usable in the praxis of Christian conversion?"[47] Well, I do have a few ideas about how Romans 7 can connect with both lost people and with devout Christians!

47. Stephen J. Chester, "Romans 7 and Conversion in the Protestant Tradition," *Ex Auditu* 25 (2009): 135–71 (here at 71).

**Reading Romans 7 with "I's" Wide Open**

Part of the problem is assuming that we can manufacture the type of moral frustration and existential crisis experienced by the "I" in Romans 7 through our own homiletical devices. The fact of the matter is that in our day and age, any such attempt to guilt people into conversion will prove mostly fruitless. This flies in the face of a lot of theology that has conventionally seen the preaching of the law as the necessary prerequisite to the preaching of the gospel. In Reformed theology—broadly defined—there is a long tradition of treating the law as a big stick to drive people to the gospel of Jesus Christ, which is the carrot. Just think of John Bunyan's allegorical narrative *Pilgrim's Progress*. At one point poor old Christian is walking up a hill when out of nowhere some maniac comes running down the incline with a big stick and beats the living daylights out of him. Poor Christian tumbles back down the hill, wondering what on earth just happened, and he learns the identity of his assailant was none of other than Moses, the Law-giver. Such was a common theme among English Puritans: the law is there to beat the snot out of you, to remind you what a perverse little creature you are before God, and to drive you to repentance and faith in Jesus Christ your Savior.

John Wesley was not an English Puritan, but in many ways he was much like the Puritans in believing that the law prepares for the gospel. John Wesley was once asked how he goes about preaching the gospel, and in a letter he replied:

> I think the right method of preaching is this. At our first beginning to preach at any place, after a general declaration of the love of God to sinners and His willingness that they should be saved, to preach the law in the strongest, the closest the most searching manner possible; only intermixing the gospel here and there, and showing it, as it were, afar off. After more and more persons are convinced of sin, we may mix more and more of the gospel, in order to beget faith, to raise into spiritual life those whom the law hath slain; but this is not to be done too hastily neither. Therefore it is not expedient wholly to omit the law; not only because we may well suppose that many of our hearers are still unconvinced, but because otherwise there is danger that many who are convinced will heal their own wounds slightly: therefore it is only in private converse with a thoroughly convinced sinner that we should preach nothing but the gospel.[48]

The notion that the purpose of law is to reveal sin as sin is biblical; in fact, we've encountered that precise view in Romans 3 and 7. So there is some

48. John Wesley, "Letter to Ebenezer Blackwell," 1751. http://wesley.nnu.edu/john-wesley/the-letters-of-john-wesley/wesleys-letters-1751/4.

legitimacy to the idea of the law playing the "bad cop" to the gospel's "good cop." However, that kind of approach will only work in a cultural environment where Judeo-Christian ethics are the recognized norm, recognized by people who do not even practice such values themselves. Such people, whether nominally Christian or culturally Christian, are more likely to be persuaded by such an approach as they know that they do not live up to the moral ideals of their own culture.

Even so, for a person not reared in an environment where Judeo-Christian ethics are the norm, using the law as a pre-evangelistic tool might not be an optimal opening move. Whether that is a Scythian blacksmith in ancient Rome or a secular, educated accountant in Portland, the Ten Commandments and levitical laws about purity will probably not drive them to their knees in repentance. The reason is simply that the biblical commands belong to a different moral universe than the one they inhabit. In a post-Christian age of self-esteem coaches and moral relativism, we cannot assume that all people are conscious of failing to live up to a standard of righteousness commanded by a deity and long to have their burden of guilt taken away by an offering of blood sacrifice.

Do not get me wrong. I'm not saying that it is impossible to draw people into the biblical story of creation lost and creation regained. God's Word is efficacious, and the Holy Spirit will draw people to Christ any way he wishes. But if my reading of Western culture is right—and I have some experience here—we are entering a cultural space where Moses is not likely to drive sinners to Jesus any more than throwing a dictionary at an illiterate person is going to force them to take an adult reading class. People who do not know or respect the Ten Commandments are not going to cower in fear of violating them. As such, we need a far more savvy strategy for engaging "nones," millennials, and people from cultures where Christianity is not the historical heritage. For many people, their biggest problem is not a sense of guilt, but hopelessness.

Thankfully, a point of contact between the gospel and our secular world does exist. God has hardwired a moral compass into the fabric of humanity in the form of "conscience" (see Rom 2:15–16). People are configured to sense their moral weaknesses, and even the darkness within their own souls. As C. S. Lewis noted, God has created humanity with a sense of moral "oughtness." Certain things ought to be and others things ought not to be. Even the most secular of folks resonate with notions of moral evil, slavery, powerlessness, and genuine crises of conscience even if they do not verbalize them in the language of Christian theology.

The notion of moral struggle is readily found in the magazines, movies, and music that people absorb around them. For example, Bob Dylan's song "Gotta Serve Somebody" leaves listeners with a choice between serving the devil or serving the Lord. Dylan, still in his Christian phase, recognized that service is inevitable, and the choice is restricted to two options. So wherever we can find sayings and stories in our culture that follow the biblical script about humanity trapped in wickedness and in need of redemption, we might have to use them as an entrée into the subject of sin and self. In other words, if we are to persuade men and women of their sinfulness, our first port of call might have to be through Marie Claire or Marvel Comics rather than through Moses.

Most people are usually aware that they do not live up to the standards of their own values, and they cope with that failure in various ways ranging from self-denial to self-flagellation. In the long run, without some kind of mechanism to cope with moral failure, people will end up in a cycle of decadence, dejection, and denial. In the end, people either train their consciences to be desensitized to their own behavior or else internally barter their way out by latching onto some kind of belief system that might make them better. Along this line, Henry David Thoreau famously said that "the mass of men lead lives of quiet desperation." By this he meant that people have misplaced values and have a misplaced sense of security.

What is more, every attempt to end that desperation leads them to immerse themselves deeper in the very things that hold sway over them. Their sense of anxiety and powerlessness leads them to seek comfort in the things that enslave them: sex, money, pleasure, and power. When a person truly grasps that they are in such a state of desperation, they are a step closer to realizing that every code, creed, ritual, resolution, and philosophy that they've tried has epically failed to make them a complete human being. Neither a Buddhist therapist nor a Hindu guru, neither Hollywood religion nor holiday religion, neither rules nor religion, neither karma nor the Dalai Lama—none of these has made a difference in their behavior, nothing has fixed the evil impulse inside them, and no one has led them to a point of actual transformation.

Once people have seen themselves within a cycle of sin and slavery that even the most charismatic TV shrink has failed to solve, then hopefully a text like Romans 7:7–75 might really speak to them. Bringing people to a point where they realize that: I'm a slave of my lusts. I'm a slave of my fears. I'm a slave of porn. I'm a slave of my career. I'm a slave of my possessions. I'm a slave of my insecurities. I'm a slave of greed. I'm a slave of money. Challenging people to identify themselves as the "I" who does the things he doesn't want to do and doesn't do the things that she knows she ought to do. People all too often see that they hurt the ones who love them and love the things that hurt them. Letting people realize the things that they thought made them better serves only to point out the heights of their hypocrisy. One aim in our evangelistic preaching should be to bring people to a point where, like Jean Valjean in *Les Misérables*, they look back on their life and groan with pained regret, "I know the meaning of those nineteen years, a slave of the law."

Now there will always be those people who are allergic to any form of moral introspection—people whose consciences are seared to the point that they no longer really know or care about right from wrong. Folks who are so deep down in sin they don't even know which way is up anymore. People who know only their own perverse impulses and don't even understand their irresistible urge to satisfy them at any cost. In fact, there are even some people out there who don't want to sing the famous hymn "Amazing Grace" because they don't want to see themselves as one of the "wretches."[49] But in contrast, there will also be those who think that the "I" of Romans 7:7–25 is the story of their lives. For some, hearing the text for the first time can be horribly confronting, as if someone has found and opened their secret moral diary detailing their lifelong struggles to live rightly. People have an epiphany and learn that a struggle between good and evil has constantly been waged in their inner being, and it feels as if good has always been the loser. In fact, a pastor-friend of mine came to faith precisely through reading Romans 7:7–25. Rev. Dr. Craig Lloyd, a Reformed Baptist pastor in Brisbane, Australia, came from a non-Christian family; while at university he encountered some Christians and was eventually led to read the Bible. He recounts his story here:

> Romans 7 has a place of prominence in my heart for the role it played in my coming to a conviction of sin. I was in the fifth year of my Medical degree and living a life totally oblivious to the gospel and the affront my sin was before the Lord. Yet in His grace He chose to place two Christians in my life at that time. They faithfully shared with me and challenged me for months. They explained the gospel to me in very clear terms and yet I still found their words to be foolishness and unworthy of serious thought. (They later told me that they had basically given up on me. It seemed that God had not chosen to show me the truth of His grace.) It was at this time that I found myself alone one night. It was during the university vacation and no one was still around. Basically, I was bored. To this day I do not know what caused me to do what I did—but I pulled down the Bible my friends had given me from my shelf. It had sat there unopened since the day they gave it to me.

49. Gaventa, "The Shape of the 'I,'" 80.

I opened it at random. It opened to Romans 1 and I began to read. I found myself fascinated with the argument Paul was making but I was not personally affected — until I reached Romans 7 — in particular verses 21–25:

*So I find this law at work: Although I want to do good, evil is right there with me. For in my inner being I delight in God's law; but I see another law at work in me, waging war against the law of my mind and making me a prisoner of the law of sin at work within me. What a wretched man I am! Who will rescue me from this body that is subject to death? Thanks be to God, who delivers me through Jesus Christ our Lord!*

*So then, I myself in my mind am a slave to God's law, but in my sinful nature a slave to the law of sin.*

In reading this I lived the immortal words of Charles Wesley:

Thine eye diffused a quickening ray;
I woke, the dungeon flamed with light;
My chains fell off, my heart was free,
I rose, went forth, and followed thee.

The Spirit of God convicted me deeply. I was pierced to my soul. I understood sin. I knew I was a sinner. I knew I was lost before a Holy God. I knew I was a wretched man — needing to be delivered and only Jesus Christ could do it. I understood Romans 7 better that day than I have since and I thank God for His grace in opening my heart to its truths.[50]

I'm sure Pastor Craig's story is not an isolated incident, and many others have found Romans 7:7–25 to be a passage through which the Holy Spirit has brought even the most resilient of unbelievers to a point of conviction about sin.

I want to suggest that 7:7–25 is such a powerful text because it can speak to people from a variety of contexts. I do not have time to give a lesson on hermeneutics; however, at this point it might be beneficial to utilize Umberto Eco's distinction between "closed" and "open" texts. Closed texts are those that evoke a predetermined meaning encoded by an author in a text, which is then decoded by a reader (e.g., "Paul, apostle of Christ Jesus" means Paul is an apostle sent by Jesus the Messiah). Open texts, in contrast, are those where the author does not necessarily encode a single meaning within a text; rather, the language that the author uses is plastic enough that it creates a web of possibilities that can be activated based on the resonances of the text with a

50. Email from Rev. Dr. Craig Lloyd (06.07.14). See more about Craig's ministry at http://gracebible.org.au/.

reader's own experiences.[51] Texts, then, can be either open or closed based on the nature of their discourse.[52]

Since Paul does not explicitly nominate the identity of the speaker in the speech, the identity of the "I" remains open, perhaps deliberately. The open-endedness of the speaker's identity explains precisely why so many divergent interpretations have arisen over the centuries. If postmodern literary theorists have taught us anything, it is that meaning is a matter of context. One's own context will then inevitably shape how we identify the "I" in the text.

Contemporary readers of Romans 7:7 – 25, therefore, could quite naturally and reasonably detect a whole host of resonances and allusions in the first person speech. A Muslim reading this passage might think of themselves as powerless to obey the Qur'an and thankfully see Jesus Christ as the only one who rescues them from condemnation. An atheist may be forced to see themselves as one controlled by their own primal and perverted impulses and completely unable to escape from them even through the best humanist philosophy. A Jewish reader might be led to remember how after their *bar mitzvah* or *bat mitzvah* they soon felt the lure of sexual temptation and struggled to contain it. A Buddhist could understand the passage as teaching the slavery of the self to desire and their inability to follow the noble eightfold path and that Jesus is better than the Buddha in delivering them from this predicament.

That is not to say that the text is just a mirror and reflects whatever we project on it. Romans 7:7 – 25 does give us a few clues about the speaker's identity, especially with the reference to the tenth commandment, being alive without the law, delighting in the law, and so on. Everyone, irrespective of their background, is led to see sin as enslaving them, the law as promoting sin, and Jesus Christ as the only hope of rescue. But — and this is my point — the open nature of the "I" means that 7:7 – 25 is capable of meaningfully connecting with people from all sorts of cultures and backgrounds.

### Finding Yourself on the "I" Chart

What about the "I" and the Christian? If Romans 7:7 – 25 is about a preconversion past, how does this passage speak to those currently engaged in the Christian life? Part of the problem with traditional readings of the "I"

51. For example, reading the Gospels as one who has lived in Middle Eastern village life brings the text to light in whole new ways, as Kenneth Bailey has done in his book *Jesus through Middle Eastern Eyes* (Downers Grove, IL: InterVarsity, 2008).

52. We have to remember that "meaning" is not located just in authorial intent, not just in the text, not just in the mind of readers. Interpretation is the science of decoding the authorial intent embedded with a text, identifying the internal coherence of a text, and then mapping authorial intention and textual coherence in relation to the reader's own experiences. Thus, "meaning" is the sum of the associations and resonances that occur in the fusion of author, text, and reader.

as representing a Christian, be they Catholic or Protestant, is that they can lead to what I call "worm theology." You know, "I'm just a pathetic and lowly worm before God, still unfit to gaze upon his glory, still trapped in this sewer of sin, and still as wretched as the day I first believed." The underlying idea here is that even the most saintly of Christians are still worthless and unworthy before God.

The problem on this account is an underrealized view of salvation. Christians are not worthless; they bear the image of God and the image of Christ, and God will never suffer any accuser to tell his children that they are worth less than worms. Yes, Christians were once unworthy in their unregenerate state, but the gospel is the good news that God has declared you to be worthy and his Holy Spirit is working in your life to make you worthy!

The biggest problem with worm theology, apart from mistaking self-degradation for spiritual maturity, is that it fails to grasp the extravagant and epochal eschatological deed that God has wrought in the death and resurrection of Jesus Christ. What God has done is take us from Adam to Christ, justify the ungodly, reconcile his enemies, make the spiritually dead become spiritually alive, and adopt rebels into his family. In what can only be called the greatest social reversal since Cinderella, God has taken unworthy sinful orphans and declared them worthy to be his righteous children. God has issued his verdict, and the verdict is not, "I declare you a lowly worm"; rather, it is "I declare you my righteous child because you are one with my righteous Son. I declare you to be holy because you bear my Holy Spirit."

So we are not like the sorrowful characters in the Shannon Noll song "What about Me?" where he laments that "nobody's been changed, nobody's been saved." We cannot talk about our lives as if nothing good has happened to us and as if God's transforming work has come to naught. We are saved, we are changed, and we are changing still. I know, for all my failings, I am not the man I was before. I *was* the "I" of Romans 7, but by the grace of God I'm *now* the "I" who has been "crucified with Christ" (Gal 2:19–20), and I am part of the "we" who has "been buried with him through baptism into death in order that, just as Christ was raised from the dead through the glory of the Father, we too may live a new life" (Rom 6:4). We need to put faith in God's transforming work and to have the courage to work out what God has worked in! We need to whack the worm theology that undersells the gospel and work hard to give the Spirit more room to work within our own lives.

Let me add an important caveat here lest I be misunderstood as promoting a hypervictorious and overrealized view of sanctification. I'm not suggesting that believers attain, ever, moral perfection. I'm not alleging that a struggle with sin no longer afflicts the believer.[53] No, that's not the wicket I'm batting on! The burden of my song is to suggest that if we identify the "I" and "wretched" man as a Christian, we are invariably drawn into lessening or even denying the effectiveness of God's transforming work in the life of believers. Yet the gospel that I read in the New Testament, the gospel I see taking root of the lives of friends and family around me, is more like Romans 6:1 – 23 and 8:1 – 11 than like 7:7 – 25. We are best described not as weary wretches saved by grace; we are more like saints who sometimes sin.[54]

So when we, as Christians, read Romans 7:7 – 25, it should not be as if we are holding up a mirror to ourselves. It is more like a former drug addict looking back at the moment when he or she finally began the journey out of addiction. It is more akin to the story of someone reading entries from their journal from a time when they began wrestling with questions of God, sin, faith, and gospel. It is analogous to how it might feel to watch a home movie of oneself at a wild party from years past and realizing how irresponsibly one acted and how guilty one felt afterward. Such retrospection then gives way to jubilation as we also remember that Jesus Christ has set us free from this body of death!

---

53. Some have tried to connect the moral frustration of Romans 7:7 – 25 with the struggle against sin in Romans 8:10 – 13 and Galatians 5:16 – 17 with a view to proving that the "I" of Romans 7:7 – 25 (esp. vv. 14 – 25) is definitely a Christian. However, a chief difference is that while the Christian in Romans 8 and Galatians 5 may struggle with sin, the "I" in Romans 7 is characteristically dominated by it. See further Bruce, *Romans*, 143 – 44; Gundry, "Moral Frustration," 269 – 70.

54. I recommend readers take a few minutes to read the excellent piece by Robert Saucy, " 'Sinners' Who are Forgiven or 'Saints' Who Sometimes Sin" as he gives a good challenge to what he calls "miserable-sinner-Christianity" (even though I strongly disagree with his view of Romans 7:14 – 25!) www.reclaimingthemind.org/blog/2012/01/sinners-who-are-forgiven-or-saints-who-sin-robert-saucy/.

CHAPTER 14

# Romans 8:1 – 17

## LISTEN to the Story

[1]Therefore, there is now no condemnation for those who are in Christ Jesus, [2]because through Christ Jesus the law of the Spirit who gives life has set you free from the law of sin and death. [3]For what the law was powerless to do because it was weakened by the flesh, God did by sending his own Son in the likeness of sinful flesh to be a sin offering. And so he condemned sin in the flesh, [4]in order that the righteous requirement of the law might be fully met in us, who do not live according to the flesh but according to the Spirit.

[5]Those who live according to the flesh have their minds set on what the flesh desires; but those who live in accordance with the Spirit have their minds set on what the Spirit desires. [6]The mind governed by the flesh is death, but the mind governed by the Spirit is life and peace. [7]The mind governed by the flesh is hostile to God; it does not submit to God's law, nor can it do so. [8]Those who are in the realm of the flesh cannot please God.

[9]You, however, are not in the realm of the flesh but are in the realm of the Spirit, if indeed the Spirit of God lives in you. And if anyone does not have the Spirit of Christ, they do not belong to Christ. [10]But if Christ is in you, then even though your body is subject to death because of sin, the Spirit gives life because of righteousness. [11]And if the Spirit of him who raised Jesus from the dead is living in you, he who raised Christ from the dead will also give life to your mortal bodies because of his Spirit who lives in you.

[12]Therefore, brothers and sisters, we have an obligation—but it is not to the flesh, to live according to it. [13]For if you live according to the flesh, you will die; but if by the Spirit you put to death the misdeeds of the body, you will live.

[14]For those who are led by the Spirit of God are the children of God. [15]The Spirit you received does not make you slaves, so that you live in fear again; rather, the Spirit you received brought about your adoption to

sonship. And by him we cry, "*Abba,* Father." [16]The Spirit himself testifies with our spirit that we are God's children. [17]Now if we are children, then we are heirs—heirs of God and co-heirs with Christ, if indeed we share in his sufferings in order that we may also share in his glory.

*Listening to the texts in the story*: Exodus 4:22; Leviticus 5:6–8; Deuteronomy 14:1; Isaiah 44:1–4; Ezekiel 36–39; Mark 14:36; Galatians 4:1–7.

To recap Romans 5–7, Paul spelled out the consolation of believers in terms of a justification and reconciliation that will lead most assuredly to final salvation (5:1–11). Thereafter, he takes us back to the wide screen shot by describing the condemnation that entered the world by the disobedience of Adam with the result that sin and death extended to all humanity. The disobedience of the first Adam, however, has been undone by the obedience of the new Adam, Jesus Christ. It is Jesus who brings us into righteousness and life.

The Torah, it must be said, did not fix Adam, but merely gave opportunity for the contagious transmission of sin and the horrid proliferation of death. Despite the tyrannical triumvirate of law-sin-death, grace reigned through Christ to bring eternal life (Rom 5:12–21). This grace is not a license for sin; rather, the arresting grace of Christ unites believers with him so that, by the bonds of baptism, they die to sin and live to righteousness. Being bound to Christ means that the slavery of sin is broken. Believers are genuinely in a position now where they need not offer themselves in service to sin and reap its wages of death (6:1–23).

Furthermore, dying with Christ means dying to sin and to the law. So entering into Jesus' death means being removed from the law's jurisdiction (Rom 7:1–6). That does not mean that the law is identifiable with sin or with death. To the contrary, the law is good, holy, and just. What happens is that "Sin" hijacks the law to bring about death. Any person striving to live under the law will find—as even Roman God-fearers themselves discovered in retrospect—that the law condemns them, but it cannot acquit them, nor can it change them. And that is why we need a deliverer to save us from this wretched state. Praise be to God that we have a Savior in the Lord Jesus Christ (Rom 7:7–25).

The next episode in Paul's train of thought is Romans 8, which, much like the final movement of a symphony, brings resolution to the contrasting motifs that have thus far been building. Looking back at 5:20–21—for the umpteenth time I know—remember the tension. There "sin reigned in death," and the law was conscripted to serve that reign by increasing transgression. But we also heard good news that "grace [will] reign through righteousness to bring eternal life through Jesus Christ." The same sharp contrast was played out in 7:5–6. In 7:5 we observed that for those in the flesh, their sinful passions aroused by the law lead to death, while in 7:6 dying to sin means release from the law and freedom to live in the Spirit. The central claim of 7:5 was about humanity in slavery to sin, a state personified by the "I" of 7:7–25. The central claim of 7:6 about dying to sin and law and the liberation of the Spirit finds its sequel in 8:1–17.

The cluster of dichotomies that Paul constructs between sin and righteousness, law and grace, and death and life cannot go on forever in some kind of infinite theological tango. Paul's opening words, "Therefore, there is now no more condemnation for those who are in Christ Jesus" (Rom 8:1), are designed to put a definitive end to the juxtaposition of justification and condemnation. From here on, the dominating point of view is what it looks like from the vantage point of Christ's death and the giving of the Spirit.

The discourse of Romans 8, as Fitzmyer observes, is "a certain peak in Paul's whole discussion" because it seeks to bring out the reality of the new age and of the new life that believers can now share in union with Christ and through his Spirit.[1] Romans 8:1–17 in particular involves rehashing some earlier themes from 5:1–11 and 6:1–23 about our righteous standing before God, the beginnings of moral transformation, and our spiritual vivification. For the most part, however, Paul's argument here is breaking new ground in Romans as it centers on how to live a life pleasing to God, a life that is lived in accordance with the Spirit rather than in accordance with the flesh.

There are many precedents for these thoughts from Paul's other letters, not the least of which is Galatians 5, about Christian freedom and life in the Spirit, plus Paul's terse remark to the Corinthians that "where the Spirit of the Lord is, there is freedom" (2 Cor 3:17). What is new here is the overwhelming dominance of the Holy Spirit in cultivating holiness and empowering moral transformation. The Holy Spirit leads believers away from the flesh and guides them into their inheritance as adopted children of God.

All this would not be surprising to anyone who knew the teachings of the prophets about the future. Ezekiel looked forward to a time when God would give Israel a new heart and put a new spirit in them (Ezek 11:19; 18:31; 36:26). Several of the prophets had a vision of a time when God would pour out his Spirit like a gushing waterfall of life (Isa 44:1–4; 59:21; Ezek 39:29; Joel 2:28–29). The Spirit leads people to know the Lord and remember their

1. Fitzmyer, *Romans*, 481.

sins; he compels them to obey and leads them in thanksgiving (Jer 31:34; Ezek 16:60–63; 20:42–44; 36:24–38). It is reception of the Spirit that proves beyond doubt that Jews and Gentiles are the vanguard for the renewed Israel of the new exodus that God has been promising (see esp. Isa 44:1–4; Ezek 39:25–29).

The overall construction of Romans 8 develops the theme of the Christian life empowered by the Spirit (vv. 1–17), Christian life, and the unshakeable hope (vv. 18–30), and then Christian life and the victory of God (vv. 31–39). Zooming in on 8:1–17, the main flow of thought pertains to: (1) the liberating work of the Holy Spirit (vv. 1–4); (2) the mutual hostility between flesh and Spirit (vv. 5–8); (3) the indwelling of the Spirit in the believers (vv. 9–11); (4) the obligation to live in the Spirit and to deny the flesh (vv. 12–13), and (5) the Spirit's adoption of believers into God's family (vv. 14–17).

## EXPLAIN the Story

### Condemnation No More (8:1–4)

Paul's sentence in Romans 8:1–4 forms a perfect summary as any as to what the whole of Romans 5–8, or even the entire sway of Paul's theology, has been getting at: the Spirit gives the life that the law promised but could not deliver.[2] Note that after the speech-in-character section in 7:7–25 about the wretched man who is a "slave to the law of sin," Paul now turns to the subject of deliverance from this plight through Christ's sin-bearing death and the liberating work of the Holy Spirit. Given the previous context about the "I's" state of slavery, what Paul says in 8:1–4 about freedom from the law of sin and death bursts upon us like a bright light falling on captives who have been locked inside a darkened cave.

Paul's opening words, "Therefore, there is now no condemnation for those who are in Christ Jesus" (v. 1), are startling and shocking, and just like a prisoner having sunlight beam on him for the first time in years, we can hardly be forgiven for blinking several times before looking at it directly. The first blink is obviously the question as to how the tragic analysis of 7:7–25 can lead to such a wondrous conclusion. The answer is that Messiah and Spirit have wrought a redemptive work to emancipate believers from the realm that sin and death once occupied. God's saving work, so lavishly described in 3:21–26; 5:1–11, 15–21; 6:4–7; 7:6, is distilled and described here with a series of succinct phrases like "no condemnation" (v. 1), "set free" (v. 2), "sins

2. Wright, "Romans," 10:574; Campbell, "Christ and the Church in Paul," 117.

dealt with" (v. 3), and "law fulfilled" (v. 4). The "reign of grace" (5:21) and the "new life of the Spirit" (7:6), which sounded like wishful thoughts drowned out by the dark depths of human depravity in Romans 5–7, now burst forth with incandescent light in 8:1–4 with its description of the Messiah's vicarious death and the Spirit's liberating work. Thus, Sin's power has not prevailed and its darkness recedes in the light of God's Son and Spirit.

Coming to v. 1—and blinking more and more as we go on—"There is therefore now" (*ara nyn*) constitutes an abrupt yet emphatic opening. The accent falls on the "now" as describing the invasive action of God launched in the present time to inaugurate salvation by means of Christ's death and resurrection (see Rom 3:21; 5:9; 6:19; 7:6). What now "is" is that there is "no condemnation" (*ouden ... katakrima*). The verdict of condemnation that has fallen on everyone in the aftermath of Adam's sin does not reach those who are in Christ (see 5:16, 18). The state of "condemnation" stands for the general "lostness" that all of humanity experiences in their estrangement from God.[3] Yet those who are "in Christ Jesus" are removed from that state as Christ is the vessel by which believers shift from condemnation to justification and from death to life.[4] What guarantees escape from the final judgment is not law, but location, being "in Christ Jesus."

The language here is clearly judicial[5] as "no condemnation" is simply the flip side to "justification" (see 2 Cor 3:9, which contrasts the ministry of *katakrisis* and the ministry of *dikaiosynē*, and Rom 8:33–34, which juxtaposes the one justifying with the one condemning). In other words, 8:1 is exactly like 5:1 and constitutes a rhetorical *conplexio*, a short recap of the central thesis about God's saving righteousness stated in 1:17 and expounded in 3:21–26. In addition, the eschatological horizon should not be far from our minds as the verdict of the last day has been declared in the present. Fabulously, the verdict is one of acquittal, and so the judgment day should now not be feared—a thought that is, according to Wright, "quite simply, the solid foundation for Christian joy."[6]

The basis for "no condemnation" in v. 1 is explained in v. 2: "because through Christ Jesus the law of the Spirit who gives life has set you free from the law of sin and death." The reason[7] why there is no condemnation

3. Moo, *Romans*, 473.

4. Campbell, *Union with Christ*, 120.

5. BDAG 518: "judicial pronouncement upon a guilty person." According to Keck (*Romans*, 196) a "courtroom idiom" and for Morris (*Romans*, 300) a "forensic term which here includes both the sentence and the execution of the sentence."

6. Wright, "Romans," 10:575.

7. The Greek word *gar* is usually translated as "for" (e.g., KJV, NRSV, ESV, NASB) though "because" conveys the causal sense more clearly (e.g., NIV, NJB).

is because the Holy Spirit has brought about a liberation of the believer in Christ from the domain of sin and death. One immediate problem we are confronted with is that Paul uses the word *nomos* to characterize both sides of the situation: the *law* of the Spirit and the *law* of sin and death. By "law" does Paul mean either "Torah" or something like "principle/power/authority"?[8] To begin with, the "law of sin and death" clearly means the Torah as it leads to sin and death, as that has been the burden of much of Paul's song in Romans 3:1–20; 5:12–21; and 7:1–25 (see 1 Cor 15:56). But what on earth does the "law of the Spirit" mean? There are two options.

(1) Torah in the sphere of the Spirit, where Torah is experienced in its fuller and truer sense as embodying God's verdicts and declaring God's promises—a view enhanced by the observation that the Torah testifies to God's righteousness (3:21), upholds faith (3:27), intends to bring life (7:10), and is spiritual (7:14). What is more, 8:4 states clearly that walking in the Spirit fulfills the "righteous requirements of the law." Indeed, the remaining references to *nomos* in the rest of Romans are undoubtedly references to the Torah (see 8:7; 9:4, 31; 10:4–5; 13:8, 10). So "law of the Spirit" could designate something like "Torah in the sphere of Spirit shows us God's intention to set us free in Christ Jesus."

(2) The "law of the Spirit" as a principle or power to describe the Spirit's work of liberation. Paul may be making an intended pun. It is likely that *nomos* as principle or power was used a few verses earlier in 7:21, 23. Even more persuasive is the fact that to make the Torah the liberating agent in 8:2 would flat out contradict 8:3, where God sends his Son precisely because of the Torah's inability to save! Such a view reflects generally well within both Romans and Paul's letters as a whole: no one is justified by "works of the law" (3:20, 28), the righteousness of God is revealed "apart from law" (3:21), one enters the Abrahamic covenant by faith not by law (4:12–15), the believer is under grace "not law" (6:14), and believers are "released from the law" (7:6). In light of this—and without even venturing into Galatians—we can observe that Paul consistently places *nomos* as Torah on the opposite side of the ledger to Spirit, righteousness, and faith. As such, Paul appears to be saying that the *power* of the Spirit, as the outflow of Christ's redemptive work, has rescued believers from the Torah as the agent of sin and death. That is not to say that the Torah is inherently bad (Paul dealt with that red herring in 7:7–25), but his chief point is that the Torah was not and is not the instrument for divine deliverance.

---

8. See Romans 3:27 and 7:21–23, 25 for the same dilemma about the "law" as Torah or principle. See Moo (*Romans*, 473–76) and Johnson (*Romans*, 127–28) in contrast to Wright ("Romans," 10:576–77) and Dunn (*Romans*, 1:416–17) for sharply diverging perspectives here.

This controversial point is then defended: "For what the law was powerless to do because it was weakened by the flesh, God did by sending his own Son in the likeness of sinful flesh to be a sin offering. And so he condemned sin in the flesh" (v. 3). The explanation as to why the Spirit operating in Christ rescues believers from condemnation is that the Torah was unable to do it on account of the weakness of human "flesh." Here "flesh" (*sarx*) refers to the moral weakness of the human condition. The problem with the Torah is that when it meets human wickedness, it inevitably produces sinning (see 3:19, 28; 5:13, 20; 7:7–8). Torah can flay the flesh but cannot fix it! The Torah's salvific impotence is why God sent his own Son in the same human nature as any sinner to be a sacrifice for sin and to condemn sin in its fleshly abode. Several things call out for comment here.

First, the "sending" of the Son is implicit to Jesus' preexistence and incarnation. Jesus comes from the Father to earth by taking on "flesh," which naturally suggests that the Son moves from one state (i.e., preexistence) to another state that he did not previously possess (i.e., "flesh").[9] In any case, the purpose of that sending is chiefly redemptive as the Son comes to redeem and restore the covenant people and to include the Gentiles in the patriarchal promises (see Rom 8:32; 15:8; Gal 3:14; 4:4–5).

Second, the "likeness of sinful flesh" should not be taken in a docetic sense as if Jesus' humanity was merely an external layer over his divinity. Paul clearly affirms Jesus' full humanity (see Gal 4:4 with "born of woman"), yet he is aware that humanity is not natural to him (see Phil 2:7–8 with "made in human likeness" and "found in appearance as a man"). The issue here is that Paul does not want to say that God sent Jesus in sinful flesh, since that would imply that the enfleshing of the Son took on the sinful condition, which itself needs deliverance. What Paul wants to say is that Jesus' humanity was the same as ours and yet not totally like ours to the point that he was tainted with sin.[10] Jesus was *just like* us in possessing human flesh, and yet *totally unlike us* by not participating in a sinful nature. It may be more appropriate, therefore, to translate the phrase along the lines of God sending Jesus in the "same body as humans, who are controlled by sin" (CEB; cf. NJB).

Third, sacrificial allusion abounds in the words "sin offering" and "condemned sin in the flesh." The prepositional phrase "sin offering" (*peri hamartias*) is the same expression used in the LXX to refer to Old Testament sacrifices that atone for guilt (see Lev 5:6–8, 11; 6:25; Num 6:16; Ezek

9. Simon J. Gathercole, *The Pre-Existent Son: Recovering the Christologies of Matthew, Mark, and Luke* (Grand Rapids: Eerdmans, 2006), 28–29; contra, e.g., Dunn, *Romans*, 1:420–21. See interesting background references in Jewett, *Romans*, 483 n. 76.

10. BDAG 707; Keck, *Romans*, 198.

42:13). Paul undoubtedly sees Jesus' death as a sacrifice that deals with sin in the sense of removing its stain, burden, and penalty (see Rom 3:25; 1 Cor 5:7). Jesus' sacrificial death means that God has "condemned sin in the flesh," specifically, in the flesh of Jesus. God does not condemn Jesus; more precisely God condemns sin, but Jesus sucks the poison of sin from us and draws its vile venom into his own flesh, where it is denounced and defeated.

Here, and in other places like Galatians 3:13 and 2 Corinthians 5:21, we have one of the clearest presentations of penal substitution, where Jesus dies our death in our stead, bearing our penalty in his body.[11] As Wright says, "in Jesus' death the condemnation that sin deserved was meted out fully and finally, so that sinners over whose heads that condemnation had hung might be liberated for this threat once and for all."[12] Several scholars are theologically allergic to substitutionary atonement and, like David Brondos, venture to suggest implausible alternatives: "The idea is rather than sin is condemned in the flesh of human beings or believers in some general sense."[13] If that were the case, we would struggle to explain why God sent Jesus, why Jesus had to die at all, and how the condemnation of sin is actually taken away from us. Far more likely, as the old hymn "Man of Sorrows" says, "In my place condemned he stood, sealed my pardon with his blood: Hallelujah, what a Savior!"

The goal of God's saving work in Christ and the Spirit is then described with reference to the spiritual life of believers who fulfill the law by their conduct: "in order that the righteous requirement of the law might be fully met in us, who do not live according to the flesh but according to the Spirit" (v. 4). The opening purpose clause ("in order that") relates not only to v. 3 about Jesus' sacrificial death, but to the whole sway of vv. 2–3 about God's liberating work.

The end for which the Spirit frees believers and the goal as to why God sent his Son is to fulfill the righteous obligations of the law by those who are no longer controlled by the flesh but controlled by the Spirit. This might seem like an intrusive moralizing thought that interrupts some good old gospel preaching, but it is really paramount. Paul's gospel is not about saving souls for heaven, but redeeming and renewing a whole people. Remember, Paul says the purpose of his apostolate is to bring Gentiles to the "obedience of faith" (Rom 1:5; 16:26). Paul hinted that there are some (Christian) Gentiles who are effectively circumcised because they keep the law's commandments (Rom 2:25–29). In the ethical section stretching from 6:1–7:6, Paul labors the point that freedom from the law is not freedom to sin.

---

11. On substitutionary atonement, see Bird, *Evangelical Theology*, 402–10.

12. Wright, "Romans," 10:575.

13. David A. Brondos, *Paul and the Cross: Reconstructing the Apostle's Story of Redemption* (Minneapolis: Fortress, 2006), 123.

Paul has said the same thing elsewhere. In Galatians, Paul broadcasted a powerful message of freedom from the law coupled with an obligation to walk in the Spirit and to fulfill the law of Christ (Gal 5:16; 6:2). To the Corinthians, he says that he can rock on with or without the law, but he remains bound to the law of Christ (1 Cor 9:21). The law is fulfilled, Paul says, when Christians love one another (Rom 13:8, 10; Gal 5:14).[14] Take careful note, Paul does not say that Christians "do" or "obey" or "keep" the law in the power of the Spirit. His point is rather, as Gordon Fee notes, that the "Spirit himself fulfills Torah by replacing it and he does so by enabling God's people to 'fulfill' the 'whole of Torah.'"[15] Therefore, the "righteous requirement of the law" (*dikaiōma tou nomou*)[16] is fulfilled when believers "walk," not according to the control and values of the flesh, but according to the control and values of the Spirit.

### Mind the Flesh (8:5–8)

Paul next wants to juxtapose even more sharply the difference between the spheres of flesh and Spirit. The two succeeding pair of verses asserts the incompatibility between spiritual and fleshly ways of living and thinking (vv. 5–8). The two spheres, "flesh" and "Spirit," are characterized by a certain mode of thinking and a certain type of lifestyle (v. 5). Paul's line of thought continues when he contends that the mind-set controlled by the flesh ultimately leads to "death," while the mind-set controlled by the Spirit yields up "life and peace" (v. 6). This is because "the mind governed by the flesh is hostile to God; it does not submit to God's law, nor can it do so," and "those who are in the realm of the flesh cannot please God" (vv. 7–8). "The mind governed by the flesh" (*phronēma tēs sarkos*; lit., "mind-set of the flesh") is a state defined by hostility and rebellion toward God and incapable of obtaining divine approval. This is more or less explains why the "weakening of the flesh" (v. 3) renders the law ineffective. The answer is that the flesh stands in opposition to God's purposes in both thought and deed.

Paul's purpose in vv. 5–8 is not to warn Christians about the perils of walking, living, and thinking in the realm of the flesh. He will do that soon enough in v. 13, but here he presents more of a contrast between those who belong to the flesh and those who belong to the Spirit. In other words, Paul is not making an exhortation to believers at this point but is juxtaposing two

14. Rosner (*Paul and the Law*, 124) comments, "If in Romans 8 Christ fulfils the law *for* us, in Romans 13 and Galatians 5 Christ fulfils the law *through* us."

15. Gordon D. Fee, *God's Empowering Presence: The Holy Spirit in the Letters of Paul* (Peabody, MA: Hendrickson, 1994), 536.

16. While *dikaiōma* can mean "righteous verdict" (Rom 1:32), "righteousness," or "justification" (Rom 5:16), the translation of "righteous requirement" in terms of the demands of the Torah is probably intended here (see BDAG 249; Cranfield, *Romans*, 1:383–84).

groups of people, the converted and the unconverted. It is a kind of argument to the effect "think of what you were when you were called" to underscore their sinful state prior to coming to Christ, set in direct contrast to the spiritual life that they now possess (see 1 Cor 1:26; 6.11; Eph 2:1–3). According to Moo: "Paul's main purpose is to highlight the radical differences between the flesh and the Spirit as a means of showing why only those who 'walk/think/are' after the Spirit can have eschatological life."[17]

### You Are in the Spirit (8:9–11)

Paul immediately contrasts those who belong to the flesh in vv. 5–8 with those who belong to the Spirit in vv. 9–11. The key differences are that those who belong to the Spirit experience the indwelling of the Spirit and Christ, possess life, and await the hope of resurrection. None of this is true for those in the flesh. Paul is here outlining the spiritual make-up of the new covenant people, something he intimated in 2:25–29, but now he expounds it more fully.

"You, however, are not in the realm of the flesh but are in the realm of the Spirit, if indeed the Spirit of God lives in you. And if anyone does not have the Spirit of Christ, they do not belong to Christ" (v. 9). Paul switches to the second person and declares to his audience that they do not belong to the flesh side of things but to the Spirit side of things. The conditional clause beginning "if indeed" (NIV, NASB) or "if in fact" (ESV, CEB) is not meant to imply a cause for doubt, but stresses that which is precisely true about them. The audience belongs to the realm of the Spirit because the Spirit of God dwells in them.

Furthermore, possession of the "Spirit of Christ" is itself the condition for belonging to Christ. This is one of only three places in Scripture that mention the "Spirit of Christ" (see Phil 1:19; 1 Pet 1:11). The association of the Spirit and Christ is natural since the Spirit raised Christ from the dead (Rom 1:4; 8:11), Christ is the giver of the Spirit (John 14:26; 15:26; Acts 2:38), Christ and Spirit cooperate in the work of salvation (1 Cor 6:11), and both stand within the trinitarian nature of God as Father, Son, and Holy Spirit (2 Cor 13:14). The net point is that if one possesses the Spirit of Christ, Christ in turn possesses them!

The first implication of belonging to Christ is: "But if Christ is in you, then even though your body is subject to death because of sin, the Spirit gives life because of righteousness" (v. 10). Paul shifts from speaking of being "in Christ" (v. 1) to speaking of "Christ in you," which signifies the indwelling of believers with the divine power that will transform them in the future (see Gal

17. Moo, *Romans*, 486.

2:20; 4:19; Eph 3:17; Col 1:27). The upshot is that, on the one hand, their physical bodies remain subject to death because of sin. The corruption and mortality introduced by Adam's sin have not as yet been fully eradicated. The eschatological tension of the "not yet" remains as the tragic cycle of birth, life, and death continues for the time being. On the other hand, the Spirit gives life in the present time, and this life consists of a new relationship with God in Christ (Rom 6:4) and a life marked by peace (see 5:1; 8:6).

Paul adds a further explanation as to why life has arrived: "because of righteousness." Here "righteousness" (*dikaiosynē*) could be a circumlocution for "Christ," could refer to the righteous act of Christ in contrast to Adam's disobedience (see Rom 5:18), or else could signify God's righteousness understood as his saving activity. It is hard to pick a winner here, but the vibe of the verse inclines me towards "God's saving righteousness."[18]

The second implication is based on the first and moves readers toward the glorious future horizon: "And if the Spirit of him who raised Jesus from the dead is living in you, he who raised Christ from the dead will also give life to your mortal bodies because of his Spirit who lives in you" (v. 11). Paul has shown earlier that the goal of grace is eternal life (2:7; 5:21; 6:22–23). The spiritual life enjoyed in the present is only a deposit of the life to come and not an end in itself (see 2 Cor 1:22–23; 4:16–5:5; Eph 1:13–14). Johnson's description is perfect: "The transforming Spirit that God has given to humans is the pledge and portent of future life in the resurrection."[19] There is a future life that is yet to arrive in the form of the resurrection of the coming age. If the Spirit who raised Jesus from the dead dwells in believers, this same Spirit who imparted glorious immortal life to Jesus will impart the same life to them. The nature of that resurrection life is explored elsewhere by Paul (see 1 Cor 15:35–58; Phil 3:21; 1 Thess 4:17). What should be emphasized is that for Paul, this God-given "life," both now and in the future, is the concrete incarnation of his righteous verdict. Righteousness reigns in life through resurrection life (see 5:17; 8:34). Thus, God's righteousness is a verdict that vivifies.

### Two Ways to Live (8:12–13)

The logical conclusion to be drawn from the Spirit's indwelling and the prospect of the Spirit's gloriously transforming the body of believers is that believers are not indebted to the flesh but to the Spirit. "Therefore, brothers and

18. Cf. Dunn (*Romans*, 1:432), who takes *dikaiosynē* to denote "the gracious outreach of God in accordance with his role as creator and redeemer ... it could be used almost interchangeably with *pneuma* and *zōē*."

19. Johnson, *Romans*, 131.

sisters, we have an obligation—but it is not to the flesh, to live according to it" (v. 12). Paul, somewhat confusingly, begins a train of thought only to break it off. The "obligation" he intends to speak about is that believers are indebted to the Spirit as the source of their life. Yet Paul changes tack and accents what the obligation is *not*, namely, to live in and according to the flesh. The logic is that if Christ lives in them and if the Spirit enlivens them, it is unimaginable for anyone to live in the realm of the flesh.

"For if you live according to the flesh, you will die; but if by the Spirit you put to death the misdeeds of the body, you will live" (v. 13). Paul next spells out the deadly consequences of living according to the flesh, namely, death! At this point it is uncertain if Paul thinks that this is a genuine possibility for Christians, that believers might return to the flesh and jeopardize their future salvation. The echo of the two ways to live of Deuteronomy 30:15, 19 might imply the possibility of falling away. More likely though, in light of the flame of assurance that shines from 8:1 through to 8:39, Paul is perhaps questioning whether there are some in their circle who do not have the Spirit and continue to live in the flesh. For those without the Spirit and who persist in living in the flesh—those described in vv. 5–8—the prospect of death in its full eschatological sense as eternal separation from God is real.

In any case, irrespective of exactly who the warning is aimed at, the subsequent exhortation is for those in the Spirit to put the misdeeds of the body out of their fleshly misery by killing them. The idea here, just like Colossians 3:5–11, is that sin is so deadly that it is no good to merely contain it or restrain it; the prospect of its escape looms too dangerous, so it must be destroyed. Importantly, this is not something done on one's own steam. It is by the agency of the Spirit that the believer mortifies the deeds of the body and attempts to erect a barricade against fleshly intrusion.

### Heirs of Heaven (8:14–17)

By v. 13 Paul has finished his demarcation of the two opposing forces of redemptive history, Spirit and flesh, where he placed believers on the side of the Spirit. Christians, therefore, are those who are indwelt by the Spirit of Christ, who have been set free from sin and death, and who are empowered to resist the flesh. What we find in vv. 14–17 is a transitional passage that uses the theme of adoption to move between the Spirit/flesh contrast of vv. 1–13 to the following section on the future dimension of Christian hope in vv. 18–39. The substance of vv. 14–17 is that those led by the Spirit are adopted as children of God. Such adoption brings a new status, it provides an intimate relationship with God, and it secures a glorious future as co-heirs with Christ in glory.

"For those who are led by the Spirit of God are the children of God" (v. 14). The "for" (*gar*) links to the preceding verses by providing an explanation as to why Christians are indebted to the Spirit. The debt is not merely gratitude; it is filial, as those who are led by the Spirit are made/declared/constituted[20] as "children of God." As per Galatians 4:1–7, the God who sent the Son now sends the Spirit in order to adopt all those in whom the Spirit dwells.[21] Notably "led by the Spirit" is a compressed summary of everything that Paul said about the Spirit in vv. 4–9, and it describes someone whose whole direction of life is determined by the Spirit.[22] The experience of being led by the Spirit is a "distinguishable sign" of being a child of God.[23] Thus, the behavior of Christians is motivated in no small part because they belong to God's family. The bond of belonging is the Holy Spirit.

The imagery of adoption and sonship requires some comment. First, on translation, while it is perfectly feasible for translators to render *huioi theou* inclusively as "children of God" (e.g., NIV, NLT, NRSV, CEB), the Greek more literally reads "sons of God" (e.g., KJV, RSV, NASB, ESV, NET, HCSB). Opting for "children of God" correctly captures the intention to include men and women in purview of adoption since Paul speaks inclusively about "those who [*hosoi*] are led by the Spirit" in v. 14, and he switches from *huios* ("son") to *teknon* ("child") in v. 16. However, translating *huios* as "child" loses a particular nuance associated with adoptive sonship in the ancient world. In the patriarchal world of the first century, an adopted son was associated with a certain status, honor, and inheritance that even biological children of the family might not share.[24]

Second, the language is allusive of the exodus story, which was the quintessential act of divine adoption in Scripture. When Paul talks of believers being "led," being adopted as "sons," and escaping "slavery" in vv. 14–17, it is difficult not to be reminded of a cohort of texts about the exodus tradition.[25] Remember that the exodus was the event where Israel was brought out of the land of slavery and made a "son of God" (Exod 4:22; Isa 1:2; Hos 1:10; 11:1). Paul might imply here that Christians have gone through their own exodus in the waters of baptism, by coming out of the slavery of sin, and are led by the Spirit just like Israel was led by the pillar of cloud and fire in the wilderness.

---

20. Romans 8:14 is elliptical and no verb is supplied as to how believers become children. Given adoption practices in the ancient world, some kind of declarative function is implied.

21. Wright, "Romans," 10:593.

22. Murray, *Romans*, 295; Moo, *Romans*, 498; Schreiner, *Romans*, 422.

23. Morris, *Romans*, 313.

24. Cf. Johnson, *Romans*, 132–33.

25. Cf. Sylvia C. Keesmaat, "Exodus and the Intertextual Transformation of Tradition in Romans 8.14–30," *JSNT* 54 (1994): 37–49.

It also means that by bearing the Holy Spirit, these Gentile Christians share in the adopted sonship of Israel (see Rom 9:4), and they are the eschatological people of God (see Ezek 36–37).[26]

"The Spirit you received does not make you slaves, so that you live in fear again; rather, the Spirit you received brought about your adoption to sonship" (v. 15a). Paul moves to explain the link between the Spirit and sonship. Initially he says that it is not slavery. However, the metaphor of slavery runs differently across Romans. Christians were once enslaved by sin and put under law (Rom 6:6, 16–17, 20; 7:14, 25), they have been freed by Christ and the Spirit (6:7, 18, 22; 7:6; 8:15), yet they are now slaves of righteousness (6:18–19) and slaves of God (6:22). If so, they have become like Paul, a "slave of Christ" (1:1). Many of the Roman Christians, who were either slaves or former slaves, knew all too well that slavery was a state of living death. Slavery meant being treated like a piece of furniture with a soul, yielding up one's body to whatever task or torment that a master demanded. Although the fortunes of slaves were mixed depending on the household and the particular purpose of the slave, generally speaking, slavery was defined by servility and suffering.

More positively, since believers are "in Christ" and "led by the Spirit," they are slaves no more. They have instead "adoption to sonship" (*huiothesia*). The word *huiothesia* means etymologically "to have the place of a son," or "to be adopted as a son." Its legal sense is well attested in several inscriptions, though it is used in the New Testament only by Paul (Rom 8:15, 23; 9:4; Gal 4:5; Eph 1:5). Accordingly, believers are released from fealty and fear because they have been adopted as sons into a new household, with a new *paterfamilias*, and are made co-heirs with the Lord Jesus Christ.[27] As Keck notes, the adoptive metaphor is a perfect fit for Paul's theology because adoption bestows a status on the "son" to which he has no right but which he receives solely because of the father's decision. Theologically, then, "adoption is an act of grace."[28]

"And by him we cry, '*Abba*, Father.' The Spirit himself testifies with our spirit that we are God's children" (vv. 15b–16). The ultimate proof that believers are adopted into God's family is through the way they are led by the Spirit to address God. They address him not only as "Lord," but by the intimate Aramaic name "*Abba*." The language here is a "familial, familiar, and

26. Byrne, *Romans*, 249.

27. Cf. Trevor Burke, "Pauline Adoption: A Sociological Approach," *EQ* 73 (2001): 119–34 on the background. He writes: "For these early Christians, and the Pauline communities in particular, their adoption/conversion was perceived as belonging to the divine family where a new loyalty had replaced all others, one in which 'God acts as a proper, well-to-do *paterfamilias*'" (125).

28. Keck, *Romans*, 206.

affectionate term suggesting great intimacy and trust."[29] This way of addressing God in prayer seems to have been a characteristic aspect of Jesus' own prayer life (Mark 14:36), and it was taken up by Christians who address God with similar sense of intimacy (Rom 8:15; Gal 4:6). Linguists debate whether *Abba* means "Daddy" and whether it was unique to the early Christians.[30] What matters to Paul is that the Spirit of Christ has been sent into the hearts of Christians, so they may address God in prayer like a child speaking to a loving father, and so that they would know as well that they are no longer slaves but sons, with all the rights and privileges of sons (see esp. Gal 4:6–7).

Paul then looks to the future horizon by marrying sonship to glory: "Now if we are children, then we are heirs—heirs of God and co-heirs with Christ, if indeed we share in his sufferings in order that we may also share in his glory" (v. 17). The logic is that *if* sons, *then* heirs of God, *if* heirs, *then* co-heirs with Christ. A child is a normal recipient of a father's estate. However, it was the "firstborn"—an appointed status, not necessarily a birth order—who would inherit the lion's share of it. Christ is the firstborn and therefore the true "heir" of the Father (see Rom 8:29). Yet believers are made co-heirs with Christ and share in his inheritance in terms of immortality, exaltation, and glory. The implication is that our adoption is rooted in Christ's own sonship. What Paul has in mind is the ultimate reversal: going from the destitution of slavery to being the little brother of the crown prince of the universe.

The reason for this adoption is stated in the last two clauses of v. 17. Believers have a "share in his suffering" with a view to one day possessing a "share in his glory." Christians participate in Christ's sufferings in two ways. First, in baptism they have entered into the story of the cross and made it their own story (see Rom 6:4–6). Second, suffering for the sake of Christ is the inevitable result of uniting oneself with the crucified Lord, where shame, scorn, abuse, and even persecution may follow (see Phil 1:29; 3:10; 2 Cor 1:5). Witherington sums things up eloquently: "One must follow the path Christ followed to glory, the path of self-sacrifice, or suffering with him and for him in the cause for which he suffered."[31] In sum, sonship sets Christians on the path to glory; yet such a path takes us under the shadow of the cross, into the waters of baptism, and through many trials of despair as we track toward our final destination (see Acts 14:22; Rom 8:30; 2 Cor 4:17). The reference to suffering is the perfect springboard into vv. 18–30 about Christian comfort in the face of adversity.

29. Johnson, *Romans*, 134.

30. Cf. the balanced treatment by Dunn, *Romans*, 1:453–54.

31. Witherington, *Romans*, 219.

A text as rich as Romans 8:1 – 17 has so many dimensions we could explore and think about in terms of application. It confronts us like a deep-sea diver emerging from the water and punching his fist in the air in victory after fending off a reef shark. It feels much like a defendant hearing that, on appeal, the case against her has been thrown out and her character vindicated. We almost want to cheer like a crowd of onlookers watching a firefighter pull a small child out of a burning building. All sorts of emotions are evoked by the text, such as relief, joy, praise, and thanksgiving. Probably the three main themes that stand out for my mind are assurance, living in the Spirit, and contemplating our adoption in Christ.

**Anxiety and Assurance**

Paul's climactic assertion is that for those in Christ there is "no condemnation." The verdict of the final day has been declared and the verdict is "righteous" for those belonging to Christ. The verdict cannot be changed, and thus we face the judgment day with complete assurance that what lies ahead of us is not a life-or-death assessment of our deeds but the divine disclosure of our acquittal.[32]

The concept of assurance is close to the heart of the Protestant faith. Indeed, for the Reformers, a major part of their protest against medieval Catholicism was their claim that it was possible for persons to have a complete sense of assurance that the Father loved them, the Spirit was in them, and Christ truly died for them. They could really, truly, deep down, and fully know without any hesitation that they were saved. God's love in Christ, stretching from eternity to eternity, had seized hold of them and would never let them go. Such assurance was the joy and comfort of those who believed in Jesus Christ. The ground of assurance is not in ourselves or even in our experiences, but in the gospel, in the grace offered us in Christ, and in the mercy of God. We can rest rather than be restless about our eternal state. We can have assurance rather than carry anxiety about the future. We can be at peace rather than worry ourselves to pieces about how it will turn out for us before our Judge and Maker. We can take our final breath knowing that all will be well.

It was this apparently outrageous and assumptive claim to complete assurance that Roman Catholic theologians found highly objectionable. Cardinal Robert Bellarmine (1542 – 1621) was a key Catholic figure during the European Reformation. He was Pope Clement VIII's personal theological advisor

32. Cf. Morris, *Romans*, 308; Moo, *Romans*, 490.

and one of the most capable leaders in the Counter-Reformation movement within sixteenth-century Roman Catholicism. According to Bellarmine, "the greatest of all Protestant heresies is assurance." His fear was that such a doctrine would give license to sin and promote antinomianism.[33] Later the Council of Trent (1545–63) recognized the rich nature of God's mercy and the efficacy of Christ's blood, but it still claimed in one of its sessions that "no one can know with the certainty of faith, which cannot be subject to error, that he has obtained the grace of God."[34]

The retort of the Reformers, incipiently channeling the message of children's cartoon character Bob the Builder, was "Yes, we can!" We can know for sure that we have obtained the grace of God. The Reformed and evangelical churches — with several variations on the theme among Wesleyans, Baptists, Lutherans, and Presbyterians — have normally maintained that Christian believers can have full and confident assurance of their standing in God's mercy and grace. Such is the "blessed assurance" that Christ is mine and I am his for all eternity.[35]

But what if I or someone I know struggles with assurance? It is true that there are some people out there with a sham faith who probably should struggle with assurance. In those instances a little bit of self-examination and asking themselves if they are truly living in the faith is a genuinely good idea (see 2 Cor 13:5). Such persons need to stop sitting on the fence and take faith and its consequences seriously. Nevertheless,, there are plenty of people who really should feel the comfort of their heavenly Father's joy in them because they have entrusted themselves to the one who died and rose for them.

In those instances where people with genuine faith wrestle with spiritual insecurity about their standing before God, I usually take the following approach. First, I ask them, "Do you have any love for God? However imperfect or incomplete, is there any love for God in you?" Normally they answer "yes, some love I guess." Next, I tell them that loving God is something that God himself enables us to do. It does not come from depraved humanity, but derives from the love that God dispenses and decants into our heart from heaven. This is precisely what Paul says: "God's love has been poured out into our hearts through the Holy Spirit, who has been given to us" (Rom 5:5). Similar is 1 John 4:7: "Dear friends, let us love one another, for love comes from God. Everyone who loves has been born of God and knows God." So my

33. Sinclair B. Ferguson, "The Greatest of All Protestant Heresies?" *Ligonier Ministries*. www.ligonier.org/learn/articles/greatest-all-protestant-heresies/.

34. J. H. Leith, *Creeds of the Churches* (Richmond, Virginia, 1973), 413–14 cited in Anthony S. Lane, "Calvin's Doctrine of Assurance," *Vox Evangelica* 11 (1979): 47.

35. For a treatment of assurance and perseverance, see Bird, *Evangelical Theology*, 595–605.

love for God is proof that God loves me! Obviously there are other issues we could broach, like our obligation to love others, how doubt and repentance fit into the normal Christian life, and so forth. Suffice to say for now, we should remember that our affection for God is the affective work of the Holy Spirit, who draws us to love God and to love others in the name of Jesus Christ.

Bill Hybels gives a good illustration about assurance. He noticed that when you're at an airport, you can always tell the difference between those with confirmed tickets and those on standby. "The ones with confirmed tickets read newspapers, chat with their friends, or sleep. The ones on standby hang around the ticket counter, pace and smoke, smoke and pace."[36] The good news is that we are not anxiously fretting about whether we will get a ticket and make it on the plane. There is no need for consternation over our reservation since it is done. The gospel is good news that our tickets have been issued by the Father, purchased by Christ, and ratified by the Holy Spirit. And it's not just a ticket to heaven! It's more like a joining a rescue boat that we have been recruited on, and we go forth to pick up refugees and survivors from the storms of evil until the day when the admiral returns to take charge of fleet. While on that boat, we can be assured of our deliverance, knowing that no storm of sin, no wave of wickedness, and no typhoon of tragedy can remove us from the love of the one who called us and set us on his vessel named the *Ecclesia Dei*.

## Spirit vs. Flesh

Another thing we should reflect on is the sharp contrast between Spirit and flesh that dominates Romans 8:5–13. Let me get one thing clear. Paul says that believers are not in the flesh but are in the Spirit (see 7:5; 8:9). He's talking about a state, not an ideal to aim for! As a result, the tension between Spirit and flesh is not some kind of internal war waged within us with our fleshly nature battling against our spiritual nature. The hostility between Spirit and flesh is not the hostility between two conflicting components of one's self, but two external powers vying for control over the self.[37]

The struggle against sin, old habits, and temptation—and don't get me wrong, they are real—should not be construed as the ongoing conflict within me. Rather, the struggle denotes the force of my old self trying to come back and regain control over me! It's not that our heart is in a perpetual state of civil war with itself; instead, it's more like our heart is a fortress that is constantly besieged by a wicked tyrant who once resided there, was defeated and exiled, yet desperately wants to get back in by launching a mixture of frontal

36. Bill Hybels, *Too Busy Not to Pray* (Downers Grove, IL: InterVarsity, 1998), 113.

37. Keck, *Romans*, 201.

and covert assaults. The Sultan of Sin, leading the armies of "World" and the "Devil," wants to force his way into a territory that was never rightfully his and will never be his again. While he might seize the odd outpost, shake the walls with artillery, wound the morale of the men guarding the towers, even smuggle the odd enemy soldier over the wall, yet his power to annex our hearts is hampered by the fact the Spirit of Christ is there, and he has never surrendered any city to the tyrant.

The pursuit of holiness and the cultivation of obedience require moral courage. As Paul says later on: "Rather, clothe yourselves with the Lord Jesus Christ, and do not think about how to gratify the desires of the flesh" (Rom 13:14). To resist the flesh requires discipline on what we think, do, say, run from, and run to. It requires vigilance and keeping our hearts on guard at all times against intrusion. In the same way that you don't give your credit card details to a suspicious website ... don't give into the flesh. In the same way that you don't hand over your children to a babysitter who is drunk ... don't give into the flesh. In the same way that you don't allow a doctor to operate on you if he has a degree from the "University of Kelloggs" hanging on his wall ... don't give into the flesh. Don't think about, entertain, dream, or imagine what surrender to a dangerous, unwholesome, or sordid thing would be like. Don't let it in and don't give in to the flesh.

Paul tells us that we are not indebted to the flesh (8:12). So, metaphorically speaking, if a so-called debt collector from "Flesh Financial Services" comes to your house and demands payment or threatens to repossess your house, tell him in no uncertain terms, "I don't owe you anything." You do not owe the flesh even the slightest courtesy, but you are obligated to give the Spirit your utmost devotion. Don't haggle or negotiate with the flesh. Instead, put the false fleshly debt collector to death like you would to a cobra you found in a child's bedroom.

### An Adoption Court

In the big picture, the story of Romans 8 is the story of God finding a people who are not his people and adopting them as his children. It's like a cosmic version of the musical *Annie*. You know, the story of orphan Annie set during the Great Depression, and how she was eventually adopted by American billionaire Oliver Warbucks. Okay, admittedly it's not a perfect analogy since God is not an industrial war profiteer who has his heart softened by a little girl, but keep to the main point. We have gone from spiritual destitution to being co-enthroned with the risen and exalted Lord of the universe. This is far better than a rags-to-riches story. We have gone from worldly wretchedness to royal status. We are princes and princesses of our heavenly Father, with Christ our brother and the Holy Spirit our advocate. We can enter the presence of the heavenly tabernacle with confidence and boldness that we truly belong there as sons belong in a father's house.

Ultimately God's courtroom, where he declares us to be one of his covenant people, is an adoption court. It is where God declares that we, irrespective of our natural parents and without due regard for our sinful past, belong to him as children belong to a parent. The Father loves us like a parent and we may call to him with the words "*Abba*, Father." Christ takes our sin and we take his name as Christians. No wonder that this image of salvation as adoption has inspired some of the most moving hymns and choruses. In a world where people sing songs like "Cat's in the Cradle" to grieve a fatherless childhood, we can sing songs in worship like "Father God I Wonder," "Abba, Father," "See What Manner of Love," and Fanny Crosby's famous hymn "Adopted," which includes the memorable words:

I am adopted, O wonderful love,
Heir to a heritage purchased above;
Tell it, my soul, and joyfully sing,
I am a child and an heir of a King.

CHAPTER 15

# Romans 8:18–30

## LISTEN to the Story

[18]I consider that our present sufferings are not worth comparing with
the glory that will be revealed in us. [19]For the creation waits in eager
expectation for the children of God to be revealed. [20]For the creation
was subjected to frustration, not by its own choice, but by the will of the
one who subjected it, in hope [21]that the creation itself will be liberated
from its bondage to decay and brought into the freedom and glory of the
children of God.

[22]We know that the whole creation has been groaning as in the pains
of childbirth right up to the present time. [23]Not only so, but we ourselves,
who have the firstfruits of the Spirit, groan inwardly as we wait eagerly for
our adoption to sonship, the redemption of our bodies. [24]For in this hope
we were saved. But hope that is seen is no hope at all. Who hopes for
what they already have? [25]But if we hope for what we do not yet have, we
wait for it patiently.

[26]In the same way, the Spirit helps us in our weakness. We do not
know what we ought to pray for, but the Spirit himself intercedes for
us through wordless groans. [27]And he who searches our hearts knows
the mind of the Spirit, because the Spirit intercedes for God's people in
accordance with the will of God.

[28]And we know that in all things God works for the good of those
who love him, who have been called according to his purpose. [29]For
those God foreknew he also predestined to be conformed to the image
of his Son, that he might be the firstborn among many brothers and
sisters. [30]And those he predestined, he also called; those he called, he also
justified; those he justified, he also glorified.

*Listening to the texts in the story*: Isaiah 24–27; 65–66; Psalm 44:21; Zechariah 12:10; 2 Corinthians 4:17; 5:2–4.

The focus in Romans 8:1–17 was about how the Spirit gives life and grants sonship to believers. It began with a triumphal note of "no condemnation" (v. 1) and ended with a spectacular vision of believers being co-glorified with Christ (v. 17). The unstated question, though, is that if believers have been freed from the "law of sin and death," why does death still engulf them? If believers have a share in the glory of Christ, where is this glory now?

Paul anticipates this question and reminds his audience of the "not yet" of Christian hope and turns their gaze on the future horizon of divine glory. In the midst of the sufferings of the present time, there remains a longing for a future glory that will be revealed in us, which will redeem our bodies, heal the wounded creation, and seal our adoption. The gist of vv. 18–30 is that believers must walk in the footsteps of the Lord and travel the path of suffering before entering into glory (see 2 Cor 4:17). Moo is right that Paul "assumes the fact of suffering as the dark backdrop against which the glorious future promised to the Christian shines with bright intensity."[1]

Paul intimated this theme of enduring-suffering-into-future-salvation earlier at the beginning of Romans 5–8. Suffering is a cause of celebration because it produces a panoply of virtues like patience, character, and hope (see 5:3–5). The new element here in 8:18–30 is that Paul introduces the notion of glory. The purpose of persevering through pain is that at the end of it, believers "may also be glorified with him" (v. 17) and "be conformed to the likeness of his Son" (v. 29).

In other words, the final goal is what we might call *Christification* or even *Christosis*.[2] The meaning is that humanity will recover the glory lost in Adam by sharing in the glory arrayed in Christ. The divine purpose for humanity to reign over creation on God's behalf is recovered by the Messiah and shared with his people. For believers the redemption of their bodies and the revelation of their sonship will be a cosmic event that will spill over and lead to the renovation of the cosmos. In the meantime, however, Christians must exhibit a hope characterized by "patient fortitude"[3] and rely on the Spirit's intercession to get them through it. They do so knowing that the golden chain of salvation, from God's eternal decision to our eschatological deliverance, is immutable, and it will bring believers into the glorified family of the Son of God.

This passage is a good reminder that the biblical story is about creation fallen into corruption and restored into glory. We look ahead to a day when

1. Moo, *Romans*, 509.

2. See Ben Blackwell, *Christosis: Pauline Soteriology in Light of Deification in Irenaeus and Cyril of Alexandria* (WUNT 2.134; Tübingen: Mohr Siebeck, 2011), 152–73; Graham Cole, *God the Peacemaker: How Atonement Brings Shalom* (NSBT 25; Downers Grove, IL: InterVarsity, 2009), 223.

3. Moo, *Romans*, 510.

"the mountains and hills will burst into song before you, and all the trees of the field will clap their hands" (Isa 55:12), and "let all creation rejoice before the Lord, for he comes, he comes to judge the earth. He will judge the world in righteousness and the peoples in his faithfulness" (Ps 96:13). The redemption of Israel and the rescue of the nations will lead to the renovation of the world—a world where "God's dwelling place is now among the people, and he will dwell with them. They will be his people, and God himself will be with them and be their God" (Rev 21:3). The groaning of creation and creatures in the meantime is part of our anticipation as we wait for the "not yet" to give way to the "hope of glory."

In terms of structure, (1) Paul opens with mention of present sufferings in the context of the groaning of creation (vv. 18–22); (2) then he refers to the groaning of Christians who wait in hope for their final salvation (vv. 23–25); (3) Paul next comments about the groaning of the Spirit who intercedes for the saints in the interim period (vv. 26–27); and (4) he describes how God's goodness prevails for those who love him (vv. 28–30).

### Creation Groaning for the Children's Glory (8:18–22)

Paul proceeds to explain how it is possible to cope with sharing in Christ's sufferings without yet sharing in Christ's glory. He emphasizes that the glory that is to come is so wondrous that it is not worthy of comparison with the travails that we endure now. In the meantime, even creation groans in pain, waiting for its release from bondage at the freedom of the glory of the children of God.

"I consider that our present sufferings are not worth comparing with the glory that will be revealed in us" (v. 18). Several translations (e.g., NIV, NRSV, CEB) omit the particle *gar* ("for") in their rendering and so lose the connection between v. 17b and v. 18, which is about explaining the tension of sharing in Christ's sufferings without yet sharing in his glory (but see ESV, NASB, and NET: "For I consider ..."). When Paul says "I consider" (*logizomai*), he means to calculate or reckon from the vantage point of faith in Christ.[4] From such a vantage point, he says, "our present sufferings" (lit., "the sufferings belonging to this age," i.e., "the now time" [*tou nyn kairou*]) do not warrant comparison with the coming glory. The present travails are not "worth" or even "worthy" (*axia*) of the glory that will be "revealed in us."

At the end, God's glory is not like a vision that will be shown "to us" (NRSV, NASB, CEB), or a spectacular display put on "for us" (NJB), but

4. Moo, *Romans*, 511 n. 14.

will properly be revealed "in us" (NIV). What it means to have God's glory revealed "in us" is probably best left to being a mystery of faith rather than an exegetical question. When it comes to future glory outweighing current hardship, Paul expressed a similar thought in 2 Corinthians 4:17: "For our light and momentary troubles are achieving for us an eternal glory that far outweighs them all." Even more elegant is Theresa of Ávila: "In light of heaven, the worst suffering on earth will be seen to be no more serious than one night in an inconvenient hotel."

This tension between suffering-in-the-now and waiting-for-glory is then placed in a cosmic context in vv. 19–22. Paul personifies the created order as itself groaning for release from its anguish at the future revelation of the children of God. I suggest that vv. 19–22 make better sense logically if we read them in reverse order: (1) Creation is groaning up to the present time like a woman in labor (v. 22); (2) the reason for the groaning is that creation has been subject to frustration, bondage, and decay as it waits in hope for the glorious freedom of God's children to be revealed (vv. 20–21); and (3) thus, creation is waiting with eager anticipation for the children of God to be revealed (v. 19).

"For the creation waits in eager expectation for the children of God to be revealed" (v. 19). Paul leads with his conclusion that creation,[5] personified with the emotion of eagerness and the hope of expectation, is waiting for something to happen. Just as biblical writers could portray creation as shouting and singing for joy (Ps 65:13) or mourning (Isa 24:4; Jer 4:28; 12:4), Paul envisages creation as withering and writhing in pain while waiting for liberation from its afflicted estate. What creation anxiously awaits is the "revelation" (*apokalypsis*) of the "children of God," or more precisely the "sons" (*huioi*) of God. There will come a time at the end of history when God lifts a veil to reveal the contested identity of those who are truly his children, and the name of that family is the church of God. In other words, as Wright says, "The reason why present suffering cannot compare with the coming glory is because the whole creation is on tiptoe with excitement, waiting for God's children to be revealed as who they truly are."[6]

The premise behind that conclusion is this: "For the creation was subjected to frustration, not by its own choice, but by the will of the one who subjected it, in hope that the creation itself will be liberated from its bondage

5. Here *ktisis* means "non-human creation" as in Wis 2:6; 16:24; 19:6.

6. Wright, "Romans," 10:596. Cf. Moo (*Romans*, 515): "The 'revelation' of which Paul speaks is not *only* a disclosure of what we have always been but also a dynamic process by which the status we now have in preliminary form and in hiddenness will be brought to its final stage and made publicly evident" (emphasis original).

to decay and brought into the freedom and glory of the children of God" (vv. 20–21). The reason why creation is anxiously awaiting the revelation of God's sons to be revealed is because it knows that once they are revealed in the resurrection, creation itself is next in line to receive release from the mire of corruption. Creation has been subject to "frustration" or "futility" (*mataiotēs*),[7] experiencing a "slavery of corruption" (*douleias tēs phthoras*), which, as a genitive of apposition, means a slavery consisting of corruption. This slavery is not by choice, but by imposition.

Who imposed this corrupted state of servitude on creation? Was it God? Or was it imposed by Adam or by Satan? The answer is probably God, who allowed creation to be drawn into the decaying effects of Adam and Eve's sin. The NLT puts it well by referring to how "creation was subject to God's curse." Paul drops us into the back story of Genesis 1–3, where human rebellion against God disrupted the relationships between God, humanity, and creation. The exile of humanity from God's presence led to the gradual decay of the natural order and the introduction of death.

However, the divine intention for the world is not corruption but new creation, as passages like Isaiah 24–27; 65–66 make clear, and Paul probably has them in mind. Paul taps into a popular Jewish view that just as the fall brought the curse of creation, so too deliverance will mean the restoration of the natural order.[8] In which case—and this is the load-bearing wall of a Christian view of ecology—the destinies of humanity and creation are intertwined.[9] Creation, just like humanity, must now wait "in hope" for what is promised but not yet fully delivered. The subject of that hope is that creation will obtain, be brought into, or join in[10] "the freedom and glory of the children of God."[11] I know of no other verse in all of Scripture that better describes the majestic vision of Christian hope. The shackles of slavery replaced with freedom. The darkness of destitution driven away by rays of divine glory. That is good news for God-fearers in the tenements of Rome, good news for the poor in the slums of Rio, and good news for the working poor in Reno, Nevada.

7. Cranfield (*Romans*, 1:413) is right to think that the frustration refers to creation's inability to "attain its goal," and Paul means that "the sub-human creation has been subjected to the frustration of not being able properly to fulfil the purpose of its existence."

8. Cf. Isa 65:17; 66:22; *1 En.* 45:4–5; 51:4–5; 72:1; *4 Ezra* 7.30–31, 75; 2 Pet 3:13; Rev 21:1.

9. Cf. Jonathan A. Moo and Robert S. White, *Let Creation Rejoice: Biblical Hope and Ecological Crisis* (Downers Grove, IL: InterVarsity, 2014), 101–14.

10. The action of creation to "obtain," "be brought," "share," or "join" is implied by the preposition *eis*, which assumes that creation will go from corruption and decay *into* the glorious freedom of God's children on a future day.

11. It is probably better to take *eleutherian tēs doxēs* as a genitive of quality and render it "glorious freedom" (see KJV; CEB; NLT).

The premise behind vv. 20–21 is succinctly summarized: "We know that the whole creation has been groaning as in the pains of childbirth right up to the present time" (v. 22). Creation is experiencing a time of "groaning," which indicates an involuntary action of sighing or lamenting in the face of undesirable circumstances.[12] In fact, "groaning" is something that creation (v. 21) and humanity (v. 23) have in common, showing that creature and creation share in the anguished "agh" of the not-yet. Let us remember that at the end of the Roman road is not a swagger of saved souls, but a glorious new heaven and a new earth. When God's purposes come to pass, God rectifies sinners, he renews Israel's covenant, and he renovates the universe. The inheritance of the saints—as God promised Abraham (Rom 4:13)—is for a redeemed people inhabiting a new creation. In the interim, the agony and anticipation of creation in its travails are likened to a woman in labor waiting for the suffering to be over and for new life to come forth. According to Moo and White:

> The fact that Paul uses an analogy of the pains of childbirth draws attention again to the long-term perspective of the hope for the future of new birth, of the new beginning that will come with the new creation. Labor pains are certainly agonizing and all-consuming at the time. Yet they are quickly forgotten and relegated to the past in the joy of birth and the arrival of new life.[13]

### Christian Groaning for Redemption and Adoption (8:23–25)

Paul changes the focus in vv. 23–25 from the cosmic to the anthropic. He places humans in this state of groaning as they wait for the substance of their hope to come to pass.

"Not only so, but we ourselves, who have the firstfruits of the Spirit, groan inwardly as we wait eagerly for our adoption to sonship, the redemption of our bodies" (v. 23). It is "not only" creation that groans since the groaning is shared by those who possess the "firstfruits of the Spirit." The idea of "firstfruits" is that the present experience of the Spirit is but the first stage (see 2 Cor 1:22: 5:5; Eph 1:14) of the Spirit's final impartation of life into the body (see Rom 8:11).[14] Paul has sounded out the same idea elsewhere where believers are said to "groan, longing to be clothed instead with our heavenly dwelling ... we groan and are burdened, because we do not wish to be

12. BDAG 942.

13. Moo and White, *Let Creation Rejoice*, 108–9.

14. Cf. Moo (*Romans*, 519): "The word ['firstfruits'] alludes to both the *beginning* of a process and the unbreakable *connection* between its beginning and the end. As applied to the Spirit, then, the word connotes that God's eschatological redemptive work has begun and that this redemptive work will surely be brought to its intended culmination" (emphasis original).

unclothed but to be clothed instead with our heavenly dwelling, so that what is mortal may be swallowed up by life" (2 Cor 5:2, 4).

The groaning for glory aches after two things: "adoption to sonship" and "redemption of our bodies." Paul has already referred to adoption and redemption as present experiences of believers (see 3:24; 8:15). However, the whole gamut of Paul's theology is pervaded by the now and the not-yet, and so it is with adoption and redemption. While Christians have already received adoption and been redeemed, these facets of salvation still await a final consummation. In the case of adoption, what awaits is the final revelation of sonship in glory. In the case of redemption, it is not just redemption from the penalty of sin, but the redemption of the body from the presence of sin that remains outstanding. The resurrection of the body will be the event that will consummate both adoption and redemption.

"For in this hope we were saved. But hope that is seen is no hope at all. Who hopes for what they already have? But if we hope for what we do not yet have, we wait for it patiently" (vv. 23–25). Paul's gospel is not simply doctrinal; it is also a promise.[15] Paul characterizes the intervening period as a time not only for groaning, but also of hope. Believers are "saved" with a "hope" for their adoption and redemption to be finalized. Hope, however, assumes that one does not possess what one currently awaits. Precisely because it is a hope in "what we do not yet have," one must "wait for it patiently." Christian hope looks forward, not vainly, but with confidence in God's promise, that they will inherit the world (see Rom 4:13).

### Holy Spirit Groaning in our Prayers (8:26–27)

Paul is quick to point out that Christians are not left with nothing but hope to sustain them for the future. An important partner in their lives is the Holy Spirit, who helps them, intercedes for them, and even groans for them in the midst of a groaning world.

"In the same way, the Spirit helps us in our weakness. We do not know what we ought to pray for, but the Spirit himself intercedes for us through wordless groans" (v. 26). The adverb *hōsautōs* is better rendered "in this manner" than "in the same way." Paul wants to show the manner in which the Holy Spirit assists believers while they are groaning and hoping. The Spirit's work is described as *synantilambanomai*, which means "to help by joining in an activity or effort—'to join in helping.'"[16] The imagery pertains to the Spirit's ministering to those weak in strength, courage, and endurance.

15. Käsemann, *Romans*, 238.
16. LN 35:5.

As an example (*gar*, "for"), the Spirit helps believers when they do not even know what they "ought to pray for." Christians are committed to the task of intercession, but when they are at a loss as to what to pray about, perhaps in the midst of tragedy, the Spirit is said to "intercede for us through wordless groans." The Spirit is portrayed as interposing himself to help believers present their pleas to God the Father. Paul's description of this assistance as taking place through "wordless groans" (NIV) is a perplexing description (see ESV and NASB "groanings too deep for words"; CEB "unexpressed groans"; RSV "sighs too deep for words"; HCSB "unspoken groanings"). Some commentators think that this refers to *glossolalia* or speaking in tongues,[17] while others suggest that what is in mind is more generally a Spirit-inspired prayer. I have no bones to pick with speaking in tongues, but I'm inclined toward the latter view since it coheres with the Spirit-led prayer "*Abba*, Father" in Romans 8:15 and resonates with a possible echo of "the spirit of grace and supplication" from Zechariah 12:10, about God's enabling the people of Jerusalem to pray in the midst of a sociopolitical catastrophe.[18] This phenomenon of "wordless groans" describes the Spirit's imperceptible murmurings into our imperfect hearts to animate them in God-glorifying prayer.

A further work of the Spirit is then stated: "And he who searches our hearts knows the mind of the Spirit, because the Spirit intercedes for God's people in accordance with the will of God" (v. 27). God is the one who searches and knows the human heart (see, e.g., 1 Chr 28:9; Pss 44:21; 139:23; Jer 17:10; Acts 15:8; Rom 2:16; 1 Cor 14:25), and it is God who knows the Spirit because he is the Spirit of God (not to mention that "the Lord is the Spirit," see 2 Cor 3:17–18). Because of the unity between God and the Spirit in one mind and will, the Spirit is effective when he intercedes for the saints. Wright has a good take on this: "This hints at something deeper than merely prayer in the way that God wants or approves; God's own life, love and energy are involved in the process. The Christian, precisely at the point of weakness and uncertainty, of inability and struggle, becomes the place at which the triune God is revealed in person."[19]

### The Golden Chain of Salvation for a Christ-Shaped Family (vv. 28–30)

The undergirding premise behind the certainty of hope and the effectiveness of the Spirit's intercession is one of the most encouraging verses of all of Scripture: "And we know that in all things God works for the good of those who love him, who have been called according to his purpose" (v. 28). For those

17. Cf. e.g., Käsemann, *Romans*, 241.
18. Wright, "Romans," 10:598.
19. Ibid., 10:600.

who love God, God — the implied subject of the verb *synergeō*[20] — works together everything for their benefit. An important pastoral note is that it does not always look or feel that way. It is often hard to discern God's goodness in the midst of a throbbing pain of grief or in the uncertainty of an oncology ward. However, at the end of history, in light of a glorious eternity, the goodness of God's purposes will be fully understood. What Paul tells the Romans is not that we live in the best possible world, but we are being prepared for the best possible world in the best possible way. As Augustine memorably wrote: "God is so good as to permit no evil to exist, except that God is so powerful as to be able to draw something good from any evil."[21]

The God lovers are further defined as "those who been called according to his purpose." God's purpose is seen initially in the call to conversion that comes with the gospel message. God's "purpose" (*prothesis*) pertains to that which God has resolved in advance to do (see Rom 9:11; Eph 1:11; 3:11).[22] The call is not for those who already love him, but it is a call that will elicit love for him and confidence in his good purposes.

Paul explains in greater depth the meaning of God's purpose by way of a sequence in vv. 29–30 that William Perkins labeled as the golden chain of salvation: "For those God foreknew he also predestined to be conformed to the image of his Son, that he might be the firstborn among many brothers and sisters. And those he predestined, he also called; those he called, he also justified; those he justified, he also glorified" (vv. 29–30). The "for" is explicative as Paul expounds the meaning of the divine purpose as expressed in the call.

At this point we must refrain from reading into the text debates about divine sovereignty, the basis of election, and human free will. While the text no doubt raises the question for readers, even so, answering it is not Paul's main concern.[23] Suffice it to say, God's foreknowledge here is not a prescience of whether persons may or may not answer his call, but is simply an intimate foreknowing of the persons themselves (see Acts 26:5; 2 Pet 3:17). Paul later says about Israel, "God did not reject his people, whom he foreknew," with no reference to how or why he foreknew them (Rom 11:2). Similarly, God's predestination here is not an absolute decree to elect some and not others, but highlights that God's redemptive work takes place at his initiative and isn't merely a response to a human decision (see esp. Rom 9:11; 1 Cor 2:7; Eph 1:5, 11).

20. Cf. esp. Hultgren, *Romans*, 326–27.

21. Augustine, *Enchiridion*, 3.11.

22. BDAG 869.

23. On the theological issues, see Bird, *Evangelical Theology*, 513–47. For different views on the predestination in 8:29–30, compare Witherington, *Romans*, 227–30, and Schreiner, *Romans*, 450–55.

Careful note should also be taken concerning the goal behind the divine foreknowing and predetermining, namely, that there will be a people "conformed to the image of his Son" in order that Christ "might be the firstborn among many brothers and sisters." In other words, God's before-the-ages plan was to create a Christ-shaped family, a renewed humanity modeled on the Son.[24] Christ, as the "firstborn," has preeminence and supremacy over all things, specifically, over the glorified saints, to whom he is like an older brother (see Col 1:15, 18; Heb 1:6; 12:23; Rev 1:5). Here Christology and ecclesiology converge[25] as believers will one day become miniature Jesuses who reflect his image, just as Jesus reflects the image of God (see 1 Cor 15:49; 2 Cor 4:4; Phil 3:21; Col 1:15; Heb 1:3). In that day, they achieve *Christosis* or *Christification*, sharing in the life and likeness of the Lord Jesus Christ.[26]

Paul further enumerates the chain of saving events, referring again to those "called." The call here is probably not a general call in the sense of a universal offer of the gospel, but refers to a more effectual call that results in conversion (see Acts 16:14; 1 Thess 1:4–5; 2 Thess 2:13–14). Those called are "justified." Justification is a forensic metaphor for salvation that gives a right standing before God (see Rom 2:13; 3:20, 24, 26, 28, 30; 4:2, 4; 5:1, 9; 8:32, cf. 8:1). Here justification stands as an inclusive term for the whole sway of images that Paul uses for salvation, like redemption, forgiveness, peace, and reconciliation. Justification, in its broadest sense, is such a head term because it denotes our entire standing before God.[27]

Then Paul adds that the foreknown, elected, called, and justified persons are also "glorified." Commentators have wondered how glory can be described as a past or present experience when believers are said elsewhere to await "the hope of glory" (Rom 5:2; Col 1:27) and one day share in Christ's glory when it is finally revealed in them (Rom 8:17–18, 21). First, even glorification is something that is now and not-yet. On the present side, Paul wrote to the Corinthians that believers even now "are being transformed into his [Christ's] image with ever-increasing glory" (2 Cor 3:18), and Peter wrote to the churches of Asia Minor, "The Spirit of glory and of God rests on you" (1 Pet 4:14). On the future side, glory is not fully possessed since Paul looks forward to a day when God "will transform our lowly bodies so that they will be like his glorious body" (Phil 3:21). In other words, one can view

24. Wright, "Romans," 10:601.

25. Cf. Hultgren, *Romans*, 329.

26. Cf. Blackwell (*Christosis*, 167): "Being glorified, or experiencing the resurrection life of Christ through the agency of the Spirit, is the pinnacle of being conformed to Christ's image."

27. R. Michael Allen, *Justification and the Gospel: Understanding the Contexts and Controversies* (Grand Rapids: Baker, 2013), 62.

glorification as simultaneously present and future, but probably with an asterisk on the future side.

Second, also to be remembered is that aorist verbs do not signify a completed past event as is commonly (mis)thought, since Greek verbs are not strictly temporal but principally aspectival. The aorist conveys perfective aspect in that it views an action as a simple whole with connotations of remoteness. If so, the verb *edoxasen* perhaps functions as a proleptic aorist, to indicate that those whom God has justified he *will* also glorify. The aorist would be fitting because God has already decreed that glorification will take place.[28]

All in all, the anchor holding steady the big five verbs in vv. 28–29—foreknown, foreordained, called, justified, and glorified—is that God has always intended to create a new covenant family, a redeemed and renewed people, bearing the Spirit and imaging Christ. Believers form a forgiven family of Jews and Gentiles, groaning for glory, sustained by Spirit-inspired prayer, with creation anxiously waiting for the unveiling of the glorious freedom of these children in the age to come.

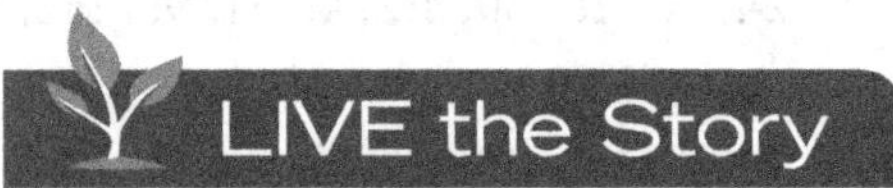

## LIVE the Story

Entering the world of Romans 8:18–30 forces us to understand Christian life as a pilgrimage that takes us from groaning to glory. We are all spiritual sojourners making our way in a fallen world and looking ahead to the celestial city as the hope that lies before us. We follow Christ, who paved the way ahead of us, a way of suffering, the way of the cross; yet it is also the way to life and glory. Those who bear Christ's name are not excused from this journey; on the contrary, it is precisely because they are in Christ that they too must share in Christ's sufferings so that they might also share in his glory. As Käsemann said: "The Spirit who makes Christ present on earth is the very one who imposes on them a pilgrim theology.... Only he who participates on earth in the passion of the Kyrios will participate in his glory."[29] Thus we go on in our pilgrimage, in the throes of heartache, while lifting our eyes on the joy set before us. Happily we are sustained in each step by God our Father, Christ our brother, and the Spirit our helper. In light of that, it is worth briefly reflecting on the two crucial elements of our pilgrimage, groaning and glory.

---

28. Porter, *Idioms of the Greek New Testament*, 37. Campbell (*Basics of Verbal Aspect*, 147) thinks that the aorist verbs in Romans 8:30 are "gnomic" or "timeless."

29. Käsemann, *Romans*, 229.

**Groaning Pains**

As humans we groan; we groan about all sorts of things—political upheaval, social unrest, economic hardship, workday stress, emotional problems, relationship breakdown, and physical ailments. The Christian life is one filled with groaning. I groan when I read the news headlines. I groan when some of my students fail to put much effort into their term papers. I groan when I hear about the persecution of the church around the world. I groan when I hear about the petty squabbles in adjacent churches. I groan when I see my former students mistreated by others. I groan when I hear of a relative who has been diagnosed with a serious illness. Life can often feel like one soul-crushing and heart-wrenching blow after another that leads us into incessant groaning. Or as Wesley said in the movie *The Princess Bride* (1987): "Life is pain, highness. Anyone who says differently is selling something."

In fact, as I write this, I am literally groaning in acute discomfort with a stomach complaint, having just had a gastroscopy this morning, which has led (thankfully and finally!) to a diagnosis of severe acid reflux. Today I am the groaning exegete. Not the worst pain in the world I know, but still enough to slow me down, to make me grasp my midsection every few minutes, and to make me groan as only a middle-aged man who likes spicy food can. Of course, I should not be surprised as Christians are not immune from this-worldly groanings. We not only groan about the usual everyday stuff of life that all people have to put up with. We also groan about church divisions, theological error, poor conduct by ministers, gossip, and other disappointments. We groan in this way because we live in a world that is cursed with sin. Even while grace and glory are incipient experiences for those in Christ and possessed by the Spirit, they are not the full receipt of our inheritance, and so we grimace in the struggles of this life, looking forward to a day when groans are no more.

I am of the opinion that one thing we should perhaps consider having in our churches are lament and groaning services. Perhaps our groaning should be formally liturgicalized. We have services for harvests, thanksgiving, veterans, mothers and fathers, Easter, and Christmas, so why not a lament service? We need a time when we can offer up our grief and groanings, our pain and strain, and our laments and complaints to God.

Such a time is biblical. Think of the lament psalms, the prayers of Jeremiah, the entire book of Lamentations, and the grievance of Job. Read the language; it is highly charged, deeply emotional, almost irreverent in its approach to God. God is asked questions, like what is he doing, where is he right now, where is he taking his people, does he even know what he's doing, has he forgotten his covenant, and does he even care? There is a place in our own prayers and even in our worship for us to groan before God — not like a whining child who cannot have his or her own way, but offering up petitions and prayers like the pain of a child who asks a parent why this or that trauma has come on them and will it be okay in the end. Churches need to groan together more, joining with creation, and listening to the wordless groans of the Spirit who leads us in intercession for those in need of prayer.

A number of churches actually do this sort of thing. I've known churches that hold lament services at times of local and national tragedy. They invite the wider community into their building to share in the grief and despair of the moment and hold out the hope of the gospel that God's love will still triumph in the end. Some churches have a regular "Blue Christmas" service during the advent season a few days before Christmas Day. It is traditionally a day set aside for mourning the loss of loved ones who will, perhaps for the first time, not be with us on the coming Christmas celebration. A Blue Christmas can be a time of reading from the book of Lamentations, parts of Romans and Revelation, reflecting on poetry, offering thanksgiving for those we have loved and lost, and solemnly singing Horatio Spafford's famous hymn, "It Is Well with My Soul" (itself written after the death of his children in a ship collision in the Atlantic Ocean).

Services like this are important because they show that grief, lament, and loss are not unchristian; they are normal, since we all go through seasons of groaning. We are not to brush them under the carpet and pretend that every day abounds from glory to glory. The fact is that some days we do feel defeated and in despair, and that is okay, because we worship a God who can heal our brokenness and raise us up out the slough of despond. It is the depths of sadness that makes the glories of the future so much more resplendent and joyous.

### The Hope of Glory

Psychologists ponder which, out of all of our needs — beyond the immediate necessities like air, water, food, and shelter — we need the most to feel happy, safe, secure, and to promote human flourishing. Some might say it is "love," others opt for "purpose," and others still suggest something like "significance." In any case, somewhere along the way, "hope" would have to feature prominently as one of our most important needs, both existentially and even for survival. We know the importance of hope because we know what it does to people without it.

The Scriptures describe all too well the despair of hopelessness. Job lamented in his pain: "My days are swifter than a weaver's shuttle, and they come to an end without hope" (Job 7:6). King David said in his final address to the Israelites before he passed away that even the covenant people feel like "our days on earth are like a shadow, without hope" (1 Chr 29:15). The apostle Paul wrote that Gentile Christians were once a people "without hope and without God in the world" (Eph 2:12). There is perhaps no place more despairing than one in which a person does not know hope for the future.

German philosopher Friedrich Nietzsche once sneered that "in reality, hope is the worst of all evils, because it prolongs man's torments." Hope is often vilified as a thief to logic and a fool to reason. But like the crazy homeless man under the bridge, it just won't shut up! Hope often fortifies itself in the most pathetic and pitiful of places and takes root in the most desperate and despondent of people. Hope has a habit of keeping the faith when others have long since retired from the race.

I once read a study about soldiers from various wars who survived extensive periods of captivity as prisoners of war. The common factor that sustained them was that they never lost hope. They never gave up the prospect of their release and one day being reunited with their families. People suffering from debilitating depression are at the most susceptible to suicide when they lose hope in their circumstances. While the varieties, causes, and treatments for depression are varied, recovery from depression often begins when those in the midst of its thick fog begin to rediscover hope. When all seems lost, hope can find a way.

In order to be happy and whole we need hope. Jürgen Moltmann captures perfectly the necessity of hope for human existence: "Living without hope is no longer living. Hell is hopelessness and it is not for nothing that at the entrance of Dante's hell there stands the words: 'Abandon hope, all you who enter.' "[30] In contrast, one could say that at the gates of heaven is a sign that says, "Lay down your hopes, all who grieve, for what your hearts longed for you now receive."

The evangelical faith is one that is indelibly connected to hope in God. That is why Paul spoke about a "hope stored up for you in heaven and about which you have already heard in the true message of the gospel" (Col 1:5), and the "hope held out in the gospel" (1:23). Because our hope is stored up in heaven does not mean we have to go to heaven in order to access it. That would be like me saying that I've got a beer cooling in the fridge for you and you thinking that you had to crawl into the fridge in order to drink it.[31] Hope has come to us in the incarnation of Christ, the promise of the gospel, the gift of the Spirit, and the anticipation of life everlasting. The gospel of hope gives us assurance that what God has begun in the present he will complete in the future.

30. Jürgen Moltmann, *Theology of Hope* (New York: Harper & Row, 1967), 32.
31. N. T. Wright, *Surprised by Hope*, 164.

Hope is not optimism; rather, hope is the audacity of faith under adversity. Hope is the cheering in triumph for what others deem a lost cause. Hope expiates the misery of life. Hope is currency in the land of melancholy. Hope is the dancing when the music has long ceased. Hope is bread for the soul that is starved. Hope is the voice that whispers to us that "all things are possible." Hope is the grace to face our fears, knowing that there is someone greater than the sum of all fears. Hope holds out a light rather than curses the dark. Hope is the physician of a terrified soul. Hope is the hero of the weak. Hope is defiance in the face of the tyrant.

The gospel is the story of the invasion of hope into a world that knows only despair and doubt. The gospel tells us about men and women doomed for a hopeless end discovering in Christ Jesus an endless hope. Hope is that shameless confidence that Jesus Christ is who he said he is and that his promises to us are totally trustworthy. If so, as Käsemann puts it: "True theology ... has to remain a pilgrim theology under the message of the gospel as a promise for the whole world—a theology of hope."[32]

At the end of hope is the glory that is to come. Let it be noted and underlined that God's glory has an important place in the contours of Paul's theology, as Romans aptly illustrates. God had always intended to make the riches of his glory known to Jews and Gentiles (Rom 9:23). Glory is what humanity was meant to seek after and to receive from God (2:7, 10), yet humanity foolishly exchanged the glory of God for an inglorious idolatry (1:23), with the result that all humans have fallen short of God's glory (3:21). Abraham was an exception as someone who gave glory to God (4:20), while the Israelites were the custodians of the divine glory in their worship (9:4). It was God's glory that raised Jesus from the dead (6:4). Christ is glorified because the Gentiles have been made holy to God (15:17). In Jesus Christ the "hope of glory" is recovered (5:2), and it enables people to even "glory in our sufferings" (5:3). Christians suffer with Christ and will one day be glorified with Christ (8:17). God's glory will be revealed in the very fabric of their being (8:18). Creation anxiously awaits the glorious freedom of the children of God (8:21). It is for this reason that Paul can burst into praise and acclaim, "To him be the glory forever! Amen" (11:36), and "to the only wise God be glory forever through Jesus Christ" (16:27).

I like to think of glory as the incandescent splendor of God's beauty and majesty. The new heavens and the new earth will be the dimension of future existence, which will be illuminated by the glory of God (see Rev 21:11, 23). Thus, the hope of glory refers to the end of the often painful pilgrimage of

32. Käsemann, *Romans*, 242.

the self toward God and the reanimation of the body in the glory that God has always intended it to be (see 1 Cor 15:43; 2 Cor 4:17; Titus 2:10). Glory is the place where groanings are no more, where groanings are only a faint memory of what came before, a wrinkle in time amidst an eternity of peace, praise, and joy with God.

An engineer friend of mine once visited an African town that had been ravaged by civil war. Most families had fled the violence and had little thought of going back because there was nothing to go back to. Virtually all of the houses were ruined or damaged, all the shops had been looted, the schools and hospital had been demolished, and what little infrastructure there was had been destroyed. He said that while everything seemed hopeless, when a new well was dug by a foreign engineering team, the mood of the town changed virtually overnight. People got excited, they began repairing buildings, shops recommenced their business, they reopened schools and a medical center, and some families began to return to their homes. The creation of a new well meant that the town had clean water, a source of life, and they could have a go at getting life back to normal. Hope overcomes the inertia of despair and energizes people with a vision that the future might be better than what it is like in the present. Our Christian hope is what enables us to cope with the groanings in our lives, to move beyond the paralysis of pain, because we know that something better is on the horizon.

CHAPTER 16

# Romans 8:31–39

## LISTEN to the Story

[31]What, then, shall we say in response to these things? If God is for us,
who can be against us? [32]He who did not spare his own Son, but gave him
up for us all—how will he not also, along with him, graciously give us all
things? [33]Who will bring any charge against those whom God has chosen?
It is God who justifies. [34]Who then is the one who condemns? No one.
Christ Jesus who died—more than that, who was raised to life—is at
the right hand of God and is also interceding for us. [35]Who shall separate
us from the love of Christ? Shall trouble or hardship or persecution or
famine or nakedness or danger or sword? [36]As it is written:

> "For your sake we face death all day long;
> we are considered as sheep to be slaughtered."

[37]No, in all these things we are more than conquerors through him who
loved us. [38]For I am convinced that neither death nor life, neither angels
nor demons, neither the present nor the future, nor any powers, [39]neither
height nor depth, nor anything else in all creation, will be able to separate
us from the love of God that is in Christ Jesus our Lord.

*Listening to the texts in the story*: Genesis 22:12–16; Psalm 44:22; 110:1; Isaiah 50:4–9; 53:12.

The heart of the argument set forth in Romans 8 is for assurance in the unshakable and sovereign love of God. To this end Paul constructs a rhetorical peroration in 8:31–39 to recap the key tenets of his argument about assurance and to make an emotional appeal to his audience for their consent to the pathos of his speech. The main premise, harking back to 5:1–11, is that God's love is a love that comes to us in Christ and triumphs over all adversity. Paul's words constitute a dramatic crescendo to the discourse as he weaves together the well-worn motifs of cross, resurrection, grace, justification, the priesthood of Christ, the exaltation of Christ, suffering, triumph, and divine love. Paul puts his rhetorical pedal to the homiletical metal as he waxes eloquently about the majestic span of God's love for us in Christ Jesus. Paul is almost hymnlike in his account of how God's love in Christ Jesus secures a victory for humanity over all things that might conceivably oppose them.

Paul's song of divine love is really playing the cover of an old and familiar melody from the biblical story. God's love did not begin with Romans 5 and 8, but had always been with God's people from the beginning. God's love is the prologue to Israel's covenants: "Know therefore that the LORD your God is God; he is the faithful God, keeping his covenant of love to a thousand generations of those who love him and keep his commandments" (Deut 7:9). Despite all the judgments that came on Israel for their unfaithfulness, one of the most repeated refrains in Scripture is that "the LORD is compassionate and gracious, slow to anger, abounding in love" (see Exod 34:6; Num 1:18; Neh 9:17; Pss 86:15; 103:8; 145:8; Joel 2:13; Jon 4:2; Nah 1:3).

You only have to read the book of Hosea to see that God's love is infinitely stronger than anyone's unfaithfulness. The God of the Old Testament is the same God of the New Tesatment, who demonstrates his love for us by sending his Son to die on the cross for sinners (Rom 5:8), is known as the "God of love" (2 Cor 13:11), and is even the God who "is" love (1 John 4:8). The divine love that is poured into our hearts and manifested in Jesus Christ is the unbreakable bond between God and his people across the whole sweep of redemptive history. This is the love that Paul exalts in Romans 8:31–39.

| **Questions and Answers on Divine Love**[1] | | |
|---|---|---|
| *Romans 8:31–39* | *Question* | *Answer* |
| Verses 31–32 | 1. If God is for us, who can be against us? | Nobody! Why? Because God, having not spared his own Son, will give us all things. |
| Verse 33 | 2. Who shall bring any charge against those whom God has chosen? | Nobody! Why? Because God justifies the elect. |
| Verse 34 | 3. Who is the one who will bring charges against the elect? | Not Christ, for he died, rose, and intercedes for us. |
| Verses 35–37 | 4. Who shall separate us from the love of Christ? Any of the usual suspects? | Nobody! Why? Because God's love makes us super-conquerors. |

1. Based largely on Wright, "Romans," 10:610.

The passage is largely a diatribe and is structured around a series of rhetorical questions, where each question is followed by a statement to the effect that the answer must be "nobody" (vv. 31, 33, 34, 35). Yet as the questions unfold, it becomes clear that God has already rendered his judgment in favor of believers and no one can call his verdict into question. The only one capable of condemning them is the risen and exalted Christ, who is interceding on their behalf. This means that nothing can come between them and his love—not any of the trials and tribulations they have suffered or any of the dark spiritual powers arrayed against them—none can remove them from the circle of God's unchanging love for them.

(1) Paul begins with a general question about what 8:1–30 means for his audience (v. 31a). (2) He states that God is for us, and the chief evidence is that he did not spare his own Son, ensuring the continuance of divine favor (vv. 31b–32). (3) God and Christ are on their side, as proven by God's verdict for them and Christ's intercession for them (vv. 33–34). (4) This leads to the logical impossibility of separation from God's love in Christ Jesus, even as many of them face death, because God's love conquers all (vv. 35–37); and (5) the victory of God extends over all realms and planes so that believers may rest with splendid assurance that nothing can steal them from the grip of divine love (vv. 38–39).

**Love That Spares No Expense (8:31–32)**

Paul rounds off his argument in 8:1–30 by asking, "What, then, shall we say in response to these things? If God is for us, who can be against us?" (v. 31). Paul uses the interrogatory formula "What, then, shall we say ..." in several places in the letter to make provocative questions that introduce new phases in his argument (see 4:1; 6:1; 7:7; 9:14, 30). It spells out the inference as to where his case does or does not lead. In this instance, the rhetorical question reinforces the notion of God's unswerving favor for the believer. Also, when Paul says "these things," he means not only his immediately prior remarks in 8:28–29, but includes the sweep of the entire argument in 8:1–30, and with most commentators, it probably also concludes 5:1–8:30 since 8:31–39 forms an *inclusio* with 5:1–11.[2] In any case, the arc of Paul's argument brings

2. Cf. e.g., Käsemann, *Romans*, 246; Moo, *Romans*, 538; Wright, "Romans," 10:609; Jewett, *Romans*, 535; Hultgren, *Romans*, 336; Byrne, *Romans*, 279; Schreiner, *Romans*, 458; Grieb, *Story of Romans*, 80–81. Jewett (*Romans*, 535) notes the following links between Romans 5:1–11 and 8:31–39:

| | | |
|---|---|---|
| Set right: | 5:1, 9 | 8:33 |
| Suffering: | 5:3 | 8:35–37 |

him now to call for reflection on what it all means for his audience. As Paul will clarify, it means the unwavering security of resting in divine love.

The conditional clause in v. 31b is a summary of the entire theme of the chapter about God's saving righteousness revealed in Jesus Christ: "God is for us."[3] The meaning of this phrase is far more than the platitude that God is on our side. The underlying idea is that God has demonstrated his righteousness toward his people in such a way as to leave no doubt that their relationship to him is graced and privileged. On that premise, Paul asks, "Who can be against us?" or we might say, "Who would dare be against us?" If God is for us, any opposition of any order is irrelevant as it is futile, a point Paul will emphasize again in vv. 38–39.

Keep in mind that these are not the words of an armchair theologian for an audience safely elevated up in their ivory towers from the ordeals of life. Paul had experienced great opposition in his ministry from fellow Jews, Jewish Christians, Roman authorities, and even his own churches, and he expects a lot more when he gets to Jerusalem (see Rom 15:31). Likewise, the Christians in Rome may well have had their own share of hardships over Torah observance and of living out the economic and social costs of holding to the Messiah's gospel over against Caesar's gospel. But Paul, being the good monotheist and messianist that he is, believes that all that opposition will prove to be futile in the end as God's love in Christ triumphs over everything.

The evidence that God is "for us" is that God handed over Christ to die for believers: "He who did not spare his own Son, but gave him up for us all—how will he not also, along with him, graciously give us all things?" (v. 32). This verse is a rich blend of intertextual links with the Old Testament and intratextual resonances with the whole of Romans. The statement that God "did not spare his own Son" is highly allusive of the *Aqedah* tradition, where Abraham was willing to sacrifice his own beloved son Isaac (Gen 22:12, 16). That God "gave him up for us all" is also a likely allusion to Isaiah 53:12, where the Suffering Servant "poured out his life unto death," which itself

---

| | | |
|---|---|---|
| God's love: | 5:5, 8 | 8:35, 39 |
| Christ's death: | 5:6, 10 | 8:34 |
| Saved from wrath: | 5:9 | 8:31–34 |
| Christ's resurrection: | 5:10 | 8:34 |
| Rejoicing in God: | 5:11 | 8:31–39 |

Several commentators see 8:31–39 as the conclusion to an argument begun as far back as 1:16–17 or 18. See Cranfield, *Romans*, 1:434–35; Fitzmyer, *Romans*, 529; Witherington, *Romans*, 220; Dunn, *Romans*, 1:499.

3. Cf. Dunn (*Romans*, 1:500): "The more the phrase 'God for us' is understood as a summary of Paul's gospel, the more important the Jewish character and continuity implicit in it." Barth (*Romans*, 326): "In the words *If God be with us* is summed up all that can be said concerning fulfilment, perfection and redemption."

stands behind Romans 4:25 and 5:8–9. The "for us" is shorthand for "for our sins," meaning to expiate or remove our sins from us (see Rom 4:25; 1 Cor 15:3; Gal 1:4).

Importantly, the atonement is the guarantee for divine blessing. Just like Romans 5:8–10, Paul employs a from-harder-to-easier style of argument. We should probably assume too a conditional clause in the framing of the verse to the effect: "*If* God has, indeed, given his Son for us, *then* how can anyone doubt that he will not also freely give us all things along with him?"[4] To put it differently, if God is willing to hand over his beloved Son for us (a hard thing), he must surely be willing to give us all things (an easy thing). Paul does not explicitly state the scope of the "all things" that are graciously bestowed on believers. However, the "with him [i.e., Christ]" clues us into thinking that he has in mind the inheritance and glory that believers share with Christ (see Rom 8:17).

### God the Justifier, Christ the Intercessor (8:33–34)

Paul's rhetorical questions shift from general opposition to legal opposition. Paul asks: "Who will bring any charge against those whom God has chosen? It is God who justifies" (v. 33). The presumed setting is a type of heavenly courtroom where the fate of Christians supposedly hangs in the balance (see Job 1–2; Zech 3, with possible echoes of Isa 50:8, "He who vindicates me is near. Who then will bring charges against me? Let us face each other! Who is my accuser? Let him confront me!"). Paul opens up the possibility of a legal challenge to the status of Christians, though by whom is not stated, and supposing it is Satan is not remotely suggested. In light of Paul's earlier argument about justification by faith (Rom 3:24, 26, 28, 30; 4:1–8, 25; 5:9, 18; 8:10, 30) and given his short recaps (5:1 and 8:1), any punitive charge (*egkaleō*) or condemnation (*katakrinō*) is simply impossible. So Paul predictably states, "It is God who justifies," meaning that God has justified the elect, executing his verdict against evil while showing his faithfulness to his people.[5]

The second legal question, "Who then is the one who condemns? No one. Christ Jesus who died—more than that, who was raised to life—is at the right hand of God and is also interceding for us" (v. 34) is grammatically disputed. When it comes to the question of who is the "one who condemns," no precise answer is supplied in the text. Then there is the matter of what relationship "Christ Jesus" has to the question. The NIV and NLT supply

4. Moo, *Romans*, 540–41.

5. The present tense of the substantive participle *ho dikaiōn* (lit., "the one justifying") does not mean that God is continually justifying believers (contra, e.g., Dunn, *Romans*, 1:502), but is more likely gnomic (Moo, *Romans*, 584; Schreiner, *Romans*, 462).

the answer "no one," and the NLT also adds the explanatory particle "for," to indicate that Christ' death, resurrection, and exaltation is the reason why believers cannot be condemned. Logically, these additions make sense of the passage, but the problem is that the words "no one" and "for" are not actually given in the Greek text.[6]

More likely, a question is made about whether Christ Jesus is the one who will condemn believers, i.e., "Is it Christ Jesus?" (KJV, RSV, CEB) or to put it more paraphrastically, "Are we not sure that it is Christ Jesus, who died—yes and more, who was raised from the dead and is at God's right hand—and who is adding his plea for us?" (NJB). That makes sense theologically because Paul already said in Romans that God will judge the secrets of all people through Jesus Christ (Rom 2:16),[7] which corresponds with other biblical images for Jesus as the appointed judge (see Matt 25:31–46; John 5:22, 27; Acts 17:31; 2 Cor 5:10; 2 Tim 4:1). But Christ cannot condemn believers because he died for ungodly sinners (Rom 4:25a; 5:6–8), he bore the condemnation of their sin in his flesh (8:3), he was raised for their justification (4:25b), he was exalted to glory so that they would be glorified with him (8:17, 30), and he intercedes for his people just as the Spirit intercedes for them (8:27). In other words, Paul says that the only one capable of condemning believers is Christ Jesus, and he has died, risen, and ascended for them and is now interceding on their behalf.[8] If Jesus acts as an advocate on behalf of believers, then he will not turn around in the next minute and condemn them![9] So the verdict of 8:1 stands firm: "no condemnation."

### No Separation Anxiety (8:35–37)

The train of thought switches from the lawcourt metaphor to the message of Christ's love: "Who shall separate us from the love of Christ? Shall trouble or hardship or persecution or famine or nakedness or danger or sword?" (v. 35). Given God's judicial verdict issued in the handing over and raising up of Jesus, there is nothing at all that can remove believers from the love of Christ. This love is the love that Christ has for his people (see Gal 2:20; 2 Cor 5:14; Eph 5:2) and is a telescoped way of referring to "the love of God in Christ" (see

6. Cf. Wright, "Romans," 10:612–13.

7. Yes, Romans 14:10 refers to "God's judgment seat," but then again 2 Corinthians 5:10 refers to "Christ's judgment seat."

8. On the intercessory work of Christ see also Hebrews 7:25; 9:24; 1 John 2:1 (with echoes of Isaiah 53:11).

9. Johnson, *Romans*, 145; cf. Talbert, *Romans*, 229. According to Aquinas, "Will Christ Jesus accuse or even condemn the elect of God? And he indicates that the answer is 'NO' because Christ Jesus confers great benefits on the saints through his humanity as well as through his divinity" (Ian Christopher Levy, Philip D.W. Krey, and Thomas Ryan, trans. and eds., *The Bible in the Medieval Tradition: The Letter to the Romans* [Grand Rapids: Eerdmans, 2013], 213).

Rom 8:39; Eph 3:18). The list of afflictions is similar to Paul's accounts of the hardships he faced in his apostolic labors (see 2 Cor 4:7–15; 11:23–29; 12:10; Col 1:24). It is a sobering reminder that the Christian life can be filled with the most brutal of adversaries, deriving from both human wickedness and from natural evils.

Paul injects a citation of Psalm 44:22 to underscore the true emotional depth of the plight experienced by God's people: "As it is written: 'For your sake we face death all day long; we are considered as sheep to be slaughtered' " (v. 36). This was probably a verse that Paul recalled on many a day when things were, well, not going swimmingly for him, like when he was chased by mobs, stoned, flogged, imprisoned, or shipwrecked. Psalm 44 begins with a celebration of the Lord's victories for Israel in the exodus and conquest of the land, but then quickly turns to a lament because Israel's loyalty to the Lord has led them to suffer a mix of mockery and massacres at the hands of the surrounding nations. The psalmist pleads with God to get his act together and to show his covenant love to Israel.

To tell the truth, I write these words with a heavy heart, having heard in the background that Sunni jihadists in Iraq have turned Mosul into a virtual slaughterhouse for Christians. Sadly, for many, like those who suffered in Rome under Nero's persecution of Christians in the mid-60s or like those Christians in Iraq-Syria experiencing inhumane treatment in the present, Psalm 44:9–25 is the nightmare that they find themselves caught in. Paul does not think of the Christian walk as "Your best life now!" but as being granted to share in the sufferings of Christ (see Rom 8:17; 2 Cor 1:5; Phil 1:29; 3:10; 2 Tim 2:3).

Paul finally returns in v. 37 to answer the question he gave in v. 35 as to whether anything can separate believers from the love of Christ: "No, in all these things we are more than conquerors through him who loved us" (v. 37). Most translations supply the word "No" (NIV, NRSV, ESV, NET, NJB, NLT) whereas what the Greek actually has is the strong adversative "but" (NASB). Probably something like "but despite all this" is what is intended. In the face of "all these things" that stand against believers, they are nonetheless "more than conquerors."

The word *hypernikaō* is literally to "hyper-conquer" or "super-conquer" and denotes their superlative triumph over all adversity (see NET, "we have complete victory"; NASB, "overwhelmingly conquer"; NJB, "triumphantly victorious"). Paul is not engaging is some kind of cognitive dissonance, reconfiguring his beliefs to manufacture a metaphorical triumph in the ashes of misery. Far from it! He believes instead in the Easter message that God, on the cross of Christ, has dealt a decisive blow to the world, the flesh, and the devil (see 1 Cor 15:57; Col 2:14–15), and one day the old foes will be made no more (see Rom 16:20; 1 Cor 15:55–56). Such victory takes place not in the evolution of human society into a Marxist utopia nor even under the aegis of divine providence, but through "him who loved us," and such love is shown in his cross (2 Cor 5:14; Gal 2:20; Eph 5:2).

### The Geometry of Divine Love (8:38–39)

Paul finally brings this section to a close, not with another rhetorical question, but with his own reflection: "For I am convinced that neither death nor life, neither angels nor demons, neither the present nor the future, nor any powers, neither height nor depth, nor anything else in all creation, will be able to separate us from the love of God that is in Christ Jesus our Lord." The word *peithō* for "convinced" or "persuaded" signifies Paul's definitive view of the matter (see Rom 14:14; 15:14; Gal 5:10; Phil 1:6, 25; 2:24; 2 Thess 3:4; 2 Tim 1:5; Phlm 21), namely, the impossibility of separation from God's love.

The note of triumph is anchored in Paul's unshakable confidence that the bond of love between God and believers cannot be thwarted or broken by anything. In terms of what might oppose God's people, Paul moves beyond the description of this-worldly hardships in v. 35 and mentions a near-universal list of adversaries who might assail them in v. 38. These include the natural processes of life and death, spiritual beings whether good or bad, the temporal nodes of past and present, elemental forces, the entire created order, and even spatial dimensions. He lists them all in order to make the point that nothing, not even the most malevolent of metaphysical powers, can unfasten them from the divine love that is known and experienced in the Lord Jesus Christ (see Eph 3:17–18, "I pray that you may ... grasp how wide and long and high and deep is the love of Christ"). This point is not only a summary of the chapter but is close to the sum of Paul's theology.[10] Paul's thought is elegantly captured by Wright: "Those who follow their Messiah into the valley of the shadow of death will find that they need fear no evil. Though they sometimes seem sheep for the slaughter, yet they may trust the Shepherd, whose love will follow them all the days of their life."[11]

In sum, Romans 8 would be comforting words for the house churches in Rome as their congregants can rest assured in God's love for them. Remember that these Christian Gentiles consisted mostly of slaves and ex-slaves, living on or beneath the poverty line, often with no surviving relatives, facing opposition on every corner, usually with no prospect for any inheritance, no priesthood or temple to visit, and no visible symbol of divine presence. Yet Paul

10. Käsemann, *Romans*, 252.
11. Wright, "Romans," 10:615.

shares with them a joyous message about the end of their suffering, the vindication of their hope, a glorious inheritance, an honor without comparison, a bond of love with unbreakable cords, and the victory of God on their behalf.

And so ends our tour of the cosmic cathedral of Romans 5–8, quite rightly in the spiral of the highest power, looking toward the heavens, choir singing below us, bells ringing around us, reminding us to rest in God's love for us.

## LIVE the Story

Where to begin trying to live the story of Romans 8:31–39 is like trying to figure out which pizza restaurants in New York one must visit on a two-day trip or which Indian restaurants one should stop at on the way through Birmingham. There are just too many options to choose from. Nonetheless, I find myself gravitating toward the themes of singing about God's love, remembering the constancy of God's love, knowing the victory of God's love, and relying on the priestly work of Christ.

### Singing of God's Love

Paul asks in v. 30 what our response is to "these things," namely, the story of God's saving righteousness summed up in 8:1–30 and more broadly perhaps the whole sweep of 5:1–8:30. However, he never tells us what our response should actually be. Presumably, he has in mind the host of actions and attitudes given in the exhortations contained in 12:1–15:13. Of course, I would suggest that an instinctive response of ours to this lavish description of God's love in Christ has to be joyous worship. As Keck comments: "If Paul assumed that this letter would be read through—as is likely—then in composing this peroration he set his argument to music."[12] In my mind, what 8:31–39 drives us to do is sing in praise to the God who is love, the Messiah who first loved us, and the Holy Spirit who is the love poured into our hearts. The whole time I've been writing up the exegesis for this section I've had the Vineyard Music version of "I Am Convinced" playing in my head. It should be in your head too!

Given what God has done for us, Christians should never tire of singing the sweet melodies and the beautiful lyrics of songs that remind us of God's love for us. It is a love that is eternal, arresting, captivating, and even a little crazy if you think about it. It is hard for hymns and choruses about God's love ever to be dull. Yes, I know you can get some shallow and cheesey choruses, songs that commit high crimes against church music with banal phrases like

12. Keck, *Romans*, 223.

"Jesus you're terrific, for you I'd swim the Pacific, yeah, baby, yeah, baby, yeah, yeah, yeah." I'm sure you know the hideous kind of songs I'm thinking about, usually with three notes, two chords, about seven words, and tragically sung twelve times over.

But in the broad range of Christian hymnody, both ancient and modern, there are many abounding classic songs about God's love. There's the famous "Hymn of Love" from the Greek Orthodox Church, which is basically 1 Corinthians 13 set to music; get the Kleenex ready, because it's a tear jerker. If you haven't ever experienced the Scottish *Sing Psalms*, a metrical version of the Psalms sung acapella, with lyrics like "But in the morning I will praise your strength and loving care, Because you are my strong defence, my refuge from despair" (Ps 59:16), and "O satisfy us with your love always, That we may sing, rejoicing all our days" (Ps 90:14), then I'm sorry, but there's a depth of worship you haven't yet experienced. In addition, who could forget Charles Wesley's classic works like "Love Divine All Loves Excelling" and "Love's Redeeming Work Is Done." My wife, Naomi, and I had the relatively new chorus "Amazing Love" by Bebo Norman sung at our wedding. Then there's my personal favorite all time hymn, "O the Deep, Deep Love of Jesus" by Samuel Trevor Francis, which features the memorable words in the final stanza:

> O the deep, deep love of Jesus, love of every love the best!
> 'Tis an ocean vast of blessing, 'tis a haven sweet of rest!
> O the deep, deep love of Jesus, 'tis a heaven of heavens to me;
> And it lifts me up to glory, for it lifts me up to Thee!

Romans is a love story about God's love for creation, for Israel, for his Son, and for the church. That might sound sappy, but I think 8:35–39 proves the point beyond all reasonable doubt. Paul wants the Roman Christians to rest assured in God's love for them, but also he wants their love for God to unite them in a common worship. If so, our worship ought to reflect this story of God's long-promised, never-giving-up, freely-given-without-price, overcoming-all-adversity, crazy-kinda love. The key biblical passages about God's love (e.g., Deut 30:16; Ps 36:7; Rom 5:5; 8:35–39; Gal 2:20; Eph 5:2; 1 John 3:1) should be safely lodged in our heads, while psalms, hymns, and spiritual songs about God's love should reverberate in our hearts. So then, in Scripture and in song, we should always have close to us the big story about God the Father's love, the Son of his love, and the Spirit, the love of God sent upon us.

### Remembering a Love Supreme

Remember how Paul says, "And we know that in all things God works for the good of those who love him" (Rom 8:28)? It sounds good in theory, but it will not always feel like that. Mark Reasoner writes, "A retired professor has repeatedly told me, within the safe walls of the faculty lounge, that he does not believe that 'all things work together for good.' Tragic events in his own life have disproved his individualistic understanding of this verse."[13] Seeing the verse pertaining to the state of affairs in our lives can quickly leave us discouraged since things do not always work out for good in a way that we can visibly see. It is in light of the end, the eschaton, the glory of eternity, that God works all things for good. Be sure to remember that!

Accordingly, there will be times in our lives when we might doubt God's love for us. There can be times when we know that God is there, but wonder if he really cares. Days when we ask, like the psalmist, " 'Why have you forgotten me? Why must I go about mourning, oppressed by the enemy?' My bones suffer mortal agony as my foes taunt me, saying to me all day long, 'Where is your God?' " (Ps 42:9–10). Or else be like the disciples in the boat with Jesus during the storm, who pleaded in desperation, "Teacher, do you not care that we are perishing?" (Mark 4:38 ESV). Does God see, know, and care about my pain? There will be days when God's love will seem distant or even dormant. What do we do then?

Several years ago I heard Prof. Karen Jobes give a sermon where she recounted the final days of her late mother. Karen's mother, lying on her death bed, asked, "What if it is not true?" by which she meant the promise of eternal life. Karen had to quickly flick through her mental theological filing system to find something comforting to say in reply. In the end, she turned to her mother and said, "Jesus loves you and he wouldn't lie." It's a simple yet profound point. The love of Jesus and the surety of his promises are what we cling to in this life even in the face of death. The love of Jesus sustains us during the dark night of the soul because we know the one who loved us and gave himself for us. If you ever doubt God loves you, remember the love that Jesus showed by giving himself for us on the cross (Gal 2:20). If you ever doubt God loves you, remember that God did not spare his own Son, but gave him up for you (Rom 8:32). If you ever doubt God's love, remember the love of God that has been poured on you in God's Spirit (5:5).

What is more, there is nothing that can separate us from this love. To quote the Kiwi Christian rock band *The Lads*, "Your love is like a beetroot stain, that never ever goes away from me." So there are no jaws-of-life, no pliers, no chainsaw, no firewall that can keep us from the love of God in Christ Jesus. God's love sticks to us like a post-it note made with heavenly glue, like divine bubble gum that was predestined to be mashed into our hair, like a

13. Reasoner, *Romans in Full Circle*, 86.

tattoo of Jesus with Holy Spirit ink that cannot be removed, or like a teenage girl holding onto tickets for a One Direction concert. God's love is like God himself: constant, unchanging, immoveable, and faithful.

**Knowing the Victory of God's Love**

The reason we sing about God's love and remember God's love is because God's love has overcome all things.

A couple of years ago, there was a famous postgame interview with Ray Lewis after the Ravens beat the 49ers (in some strange sport that Americans incorrectly call "football"). When interviewed, Lewis quoted Isaiah 54:17 that "no weapon forged against you will prevail." It was dramatic, exciting, and entertaining, though truth be told, I'm not so sure that NFL or the Baltimore Ravens were what Isaiah had in mind when he prophesied those words (if anything, rugby and the Queensland Reds would be a more fitting option since rugby is the sport of heaven). The quotation was a bit frivolous and is certainly not a template for how I would explain the victory of God's purposes in all things. However, it is certainly true to say that no weapon will finally prevail against God's love in Christ. God's love is a tower of refuge and champion for those who love him. It is indefatigable, inexhaustible, and insuperable.

It is worth remembering that the saying "Love conquers all" is famous and makes a lot of cameos across cultures. The Latin phrase, *omnia vincit amor*, goes back to Virgil who said, "Love conquers all; let us, too, yield to Love!"[14] If memory serves me right, the Italian artist Caravaggio has a painting of Cupid trampling over the trinkets of human existence called *Amor Victorious*. Pop songs called "Love Conquers All" have been written and performed by bands like Deep Purple, Yes, and ABC. *Love Conquers All* was also the name of a 2006 Malaysian film by Tan Chui Mui. Evidently the notion that love wins is something that people want to see and hear in art, song, and drama.

So in a world that looks and longs for the triumph of love, we have the opportunity to tell the story about the victory of love in the gospel of Jesus Christ. We could readily say that in Jesus love became flesh and dwelt among us, was crucified, and rose triumphantly. The gospel is the good news about the depth and power of God's love for us. This love is not a fleeting romance in song or a torrid love story on DVD. It is a love that brought a world into being, a love that called a nation out of slavery, a love that forgave a people for breaking their marriage covenant, a love that was expressed in the sacrifice of a beloved son, a love that springs eternal in the resurrection of the dead. This

---

14. Virgil, *Eclogues* 10.69.

love is experienced like a blanket of joy in the Holy Spirit, and one day this love will fill the universe like a torrential flood that consumes all in its path. God's love triumphs over tyrants and defeats even death. God's love is like a light shone into the darkness, which the darkness cannot overcome. The day when "God is all in all" is the day when God's love conquers all (see 1 Cor 15:28). When people in the world cry out with the lyrics to the Foreigner ballad, "I Want to Know What Love Is," we can tell them that real love is from God, seen in the self-giving actions of Jesus, and experienced in the fruit of the Holy Spirit. This is the love that conquers everything!

### Our Lover, the Great High Priest

Another feature we should highlight is its picture of the priestly work of Christ. The reason why nothing can separate us from God's love is because Christ himself intercedes for believers (Rom 8:34). Be aware that this is not Jesus persuading an unloving Father to reluctantly love us, but more like Jesus' presence in the courtroom of heaven providing warrant for God to continue to pour his love on believers. What is more, it is good to know that whatever we sing or pray to God, it is filtered through the priestly work of Jesus our great high priest. When our prayers are like a rudderless ship or inchoate mutterings, Jesus provides a kind of auto-tune to our prayers to make them poignant before God the Father.

Scottish theologian Alan Torrance tells about how important the priestly work of Christ was at a particularly low point of his life:

> In January 2008, my wife, Jane, died of cancer. She was the most wonderful Christian woman, wife, and mother. Watching her die in pain as the cancer spread through out her body was hard, and seeing our children witness her gradual disintegration not only physically but mentally as the cancer spread through her brain was extremely hard. There were times when, in my grief, I really struggled to find the wherewithal to pray and, indeed, to know how to pray and what to pray for. In sum, I did not know how to pray as I ought. In the depth of that valley the continuing priesthood of Christ became more relevant than I can begin to articulate—the fact that as I held Jane in my arms, the risen, ascended Priest of our confession was present by the Spirit interceding on our behalf meant that we could repose in his presence and know that communion that is the beginning and *telos* of everything.[15]

15. Alan Torrance, "Reclaiming the Continuing Priesthood of Christ," in *Christology Ancient and Modern* (eds. O. Crisp and F. Sanders; Grand Rapids: Zondervan, 2013), 190.

Jesus is more than a heavenly defense attorney. His co-enthronement with the Father means that those for whom he died and rose are forever known as "chosen" and "loved" by God (Col 3:12; 1 Thess 1:4). He is seated there as a constant reminder that there is no condemnation against us and no greater love for us.

CHAPTER 17

# Romans 9:1–5

## LISTEN to the Story

[1]I speak the truth in Christ—I am not lying, my conscience confirms
it through the Holy Spirit—[2]I have great sorrow and unceasing anguish
in my heart. [3]For I could wish that I myself were cursed and cut off from
Christ for the sake of my people, those of my own race, [4]the people
of Israel. Theirs is the adoption to sonship; theirs the divine glory, the
covenants, the receiving of the law, the temple worship and the promises.
[5]Theirs are the patriarchs, and from them is traced the human ancestry of
the Messiah, who is God over all, forever praised! Amen.

*Listening to the texts in the story*: Exodus 4:22; 16:10; 32:31–32; Deuteronomy 14:1 Hosea 11:1.

### Summary of Romans 9–11

According to Dunn, "At this point [in the letter] we may well envisage Paul stopping in his dictation and sending Tertius home to return the next day."[1] If Paul were British, he'd probably pause after Romans 8:39, have a cup of tea, whine to Tertius about the latest defeat of the English cricket team to Australia, have another cup of tea, bite his stiff upper lip, and then jump right into 9:1–5. In any case, Paul would certainly have had to pause for repose and take a deep breath before leaping into the huge rhetorical, theological, and scriptural argument that he intends to mount in Romans 9–11. What we find here, as Wagner summarizes, is: "In Romans 9–11, scriptural testimonies entwine with Paul's own interpretive comments to create a majestic tapestry displaying the righteousness of the God of Israel."[2] Or, as I like to think of it, these three chapters form an olive grove chapel, bidding Christians to pray to

1. Dunn, *Beginning from Jerusalem*, 907.
2. Wagner, *Heralds of the Good News*.

God through the Messiah because of Israel and for Israel. It is a complex and contested section that requires an extended introduction.

The argument can be summarized as teaching that God's saving righteousness is for everyone, not despite Israel, but precisely because of Israel. The underlying problem is that the gospel has brought a rupture within Israel that is now divided between "Israel according to the promise" (Christ-believers) and "Israel according to the flesh" (non-Christ-believing Jews). The rupture is not permanent, but will have an eschatological resolution since ethnic Israel's failure will be overpowered by God's faithfulness. The swarm of Gentiles who come to faith in the Messiah will provoke Israel to jealousy so that she will finally cling to her own Messiah. The present time of Israel's obduracy is tragic yet providential since it provides the occasion for the inclusion of Gentiles in God's saving purposes. In the meantime, Gentile Christians should not look down on these unsaved Jews since they themselves only get in on the coattails of Israel's promises. Instead they should heed the warning of Israel's example and look ahead to the day when all Israel will be saved.[3]

## Paul and Israel

That all sounds well and good, but is it really necessary? Isn't this whole argument a bit strange, as if Paul is just rambling on about his favorite hobby horse? Is Paul just repackaging an old sermon from his bottom drawer to try to beef up his word count? Romans would entirely make sense to us if Paul went from " … the love of God in Christ Jesus our Lord" in 8:39 to "Therefore, I urge you, brothers and sisters, in view of God's mercy to offer your bodies as a living sacrifice … " in 12:1. It would mean that Romans 1 – 8 is about "salvation" and Romans 12 – 15 approximates to what we would call "ethics." In fact, several scholars have cheekily suggested that is precisely how Paul ought to have framed the letter.

However, to its original recipients, skipping over the "Israel question" would be like ignoring the elephant in the room. If Phoebe, or perhaps one of her literate companions, read the letter aloud to the Romans and decided to skip over chapters 9 – 11, sooner or later someone would have to butt in and ask, "Ahem, excuse me for interrupting, Phoebe, but, well, what about Israel? I mean, you know, if God's righteousness is *so* righteous, and if God's

---

3. Among the many things to read on Romans 9 – 11, I recommend: Johannes Munck, *Christ and Israel: An Interpretation of Romans 9 – 11* (trans. I. Nixon; Philadelphia: Fortress, 1967); Stephen Voorwinde, "How Jewish Is *Israel* in the New Testament?" *RTR* 67 (2008): 61 – 90; J. R. Wagner, F. Schleritt, and F. Wilk, eds., *Between Gospel and Election: Explorations in the Interpretation of Romans 9 – 11* (WUNT 257; Tubingen: Mohr Siebeck, 2010); Mark D. Nanos, "Romans 11 and Christian-Jewish Relations: Exegetical Options for Revisiting the Translation and Interpretation of This Central Text," *CTR* 9 (2012): 3 – 21.

faithfulness is *so* faithful, then why has Israel missed the boat? Why are most of the Jews we know in Rome antagonistic toward *your* message about *their* Messiah? When Jewish followers of Jesus first came to Rome, we Gentiles heard the message with gladness, we thought it was great! Jesus gives us eternal life and an inheritance among the people of Israel, all by faith. But it did lead to quite a kerfuffle in the Roman synagogues, bitter divisions, and public brawling, and it resulted in the imperial expulsion of several Jewish Christian leaders from the city. Even worse, some of us have been told never to return to the synagogues because we are now *minim* or apostates! So when it comes to Israel's cold shoulder to Messiah Jesus, well, what's up with that? And how does that square with God's righteousness and faithfulness to his chosen people?"[4]

You have to admit that it is a good question! What is more, it is not a new one either. In other letters Paul deals at length with the relationship of Israel to Christian assemblies. Just read passages like 1 Corinthians 10, 2 Corinthians 3, and Ephesians 2:11–3:12. When setting out the big picture, Paul shows with a back-and-forth argument with Scripture how Israel's story culminates in Jesus the Messiah, with the result that all believers, Jews and Gentiles, have a lot in the inheritance of Israel. That is not because God offered Israel the first bite of the pie, they rejected it, so now the offer has gone out to the Gentiles. It's not as if Israel has been voted off the island and Gentile newbies have been added to the cast to make up for the loss. No, the new exodus and the covenant renewal to which the prophets looked ahead has taken place in Jesus' death and resurrection, and the sequel to that show was always Gentiles flocking to Israel's God. A redeemed Israel would lead to the redemption of the nations.

So ultimately, as Richard Hays argues, Paul is tethered to Israel because his gospel is tethered to Scripture, and Scripture is the tether that tells the story of God's choosing of Israel.[5] Yet tragically, what has happened is that Israel has not had the eyes of faith to see it, they've stumbled over the rock of salvation, and they've been blinded by the god of this age. Thankfully there is a remnant of Jewish Christians like Paul, Barnabas, Priscilla, and Aquila who have embraced the gospel of Jesus the Messiah, but they are a minority. As a result, it is the Gentiles who are proving to be fertile soil for this Jewish message about the Messiah to take root. Eventually, Paul hopes, his kinsfolk will notice that these God-worshiping, Messiah-shaped, Spirit-filled Gentiles

4. Cf. Keck (*Romans*, 224): "One cannot insist too strongly that while Rom 9–11 is elicited by the need to account for the Jews' No to the gospel, the real problem is the faithfulness of God, for only a faithful God is righteous."

5. Hays, *Echoes of Scripture*, 47.

are the vanguard for the promises that properly belong to them (see Rom 2:25–29; 11:14). Thus, we are back full circle to the argument initially given in 3:1–9: because God is impartial, he is inclusive of Gentiles; because God is faithful, Israel's failure will not be final.

The place of Romans 9–11 in the letter is naturally contested. On the one hand, many scholars of an older generation said that it was pretty much a detour in Paul's train of thought. Silly Paul gets sidetracked with a bellicose rant about Israel when he should have gone straight to the subject of ethics like any good liberal Protestant should.[6] On the other hand, more recent scholars have suggested that Romans 9–11 was in fact the "climax" of the letter, where Paul finally gets around to dealing with the elephant in the room, namely, the position of the gospel vis-à-vis unbelieving Israel.[7] In contrast to both perspectives, I would suggest that Romans 9–11 is not a needless digression, but neither is it the climax. It is would be more proper to say that these three chapters are "integral" to the argument and constitute a minor peak in the arduous journey toward the summit in Romans 15:8–9.[8] Romans 9–11 crystallizes several of the early themes about God's righteousness and faithfulness in Romans 1–8, as well as preparing for the exhortation to ethnic unity in Romans 12–15. As a result, Romans 9–11 cannot be an excursus on Israel, but comprises an integrative block of the letter.[9]

It was necessary for such an argument to be made since Paul's own circumstances, the situation in Rome, and even the structure of the letter make addressing the matter of Israel's unbelief mandatory.

First, Paul must provide an apology that his views are not anti-Torah and anti-Israel (see 3:8; 6:1; 7:7; 9:1–5). The Roman Christians had undoubtedly heard of Paul's Torah-free gospel and the controversy it caused among Diaspora synagogues. Paul's views of Messiah and Torah were indeed highly objectionable to Diaspora Jewish communities and even to many Jewish Christians because they were taken to imply that the way to salvation could take a detour around conversion to Judaism. His insistence on justification apart from works of the law meant that belonging to the people of God was no longer the exclusive property of ethnic Jews. The fundamental problem

6. Cf. Dodd, *Romans*, 148–49; Sanday and Headlam, *Romans*, 225; Bultmann, *Theology of the New Testament*, 2:132.

7. Cf. Fitzmyer, *Romans*, 541; Dunn, *Romans*, 1:lxii; 2:518–21; Byrne, *Romans*, 282; Wright, "Romans," 10:620–26; idem, *Climax*, 234; Grieb, *Story of Romans*, 87; Tobin, *Paul's Rhetoric*, 102; Johnson, *Romans*, 149–50.

8. Moo, *Romans*, 551; Talbert, *Romans*, 241; Dumbrell, *Romans*, 21; Bird, *Saving Righteousness*, 148–49.

9. Christoph Stenschke, "Römer 9–11 als Teil des Römerbrief," in *Between Gospel and Election: Explorations in the Interpretation of Romans 9–11* (ed. F. Wilk and J. Wagner; WUNT 257; Tübingen: Mohr Siebeck, 2010), 224.

was not that Paul took the gospel to *Gentiles*, but it was *the gospel* he took to Gentiles, one that dissolved the differences between Jews and Gentiles and allegedly denied the advantages of Israel's inherited privileges (see Rom 3:22; 10:12; 1 Cor 7:19; Gal 3:28–29; 5:6; 6:15; Col 3:11–12).[10] To some hearers of the letter, Paul had lowered the currency of Israel's election and denied the efficacy of the Torah for defining and saving a community. Even some Gentile Christians might have raised their eyebrows at Paul's teaching because it looked as if he was doing away with the elements of the Jewish faith that they had found so attractive in the first place.[11] Then again, other Gentile Christians might have seized on Paul's apparently Torah-less faith and insisted that the Torah was effectively unwritten and that ethnic Israel could be written off.

In response to these accusations, Paul's remarks in Romans 7:7–25 prove that he is not anti-Torah, since he affirms the Torah's divine origins and views Torah as preparatory for the gospel by revealing sin as sin (3:20; 7:7, 12). In addition, he sees the Torah as having a prophetic role in pointing to the gospel and the renewed people of God (1:3–4; 3:21, 31; 4:1–25), retaining some normative function for defining love even among Gentile communities (13:8–10), with liberty afforded for those who wished to retain some Torah observances (14:1–23). On the Israel question, Paul believes that Gentile Christians are "inward Jews" (2:29), true heirs of Abraham (4:11–17), sharers of divine glory (5:2; 8:18–30), adopted children of God (8:14–17), and "elect" (8:33), but it does not require that Israel is now *persona non grata* before God, or as if they had missed the ark completely.

Paul emphasizes his own membership in Israel (9:3; 11:1), he makes an impassioned prayer wish for Israel's salvation (9:1–5), he states that God has not rejected Israel (11:1–2), he reminds his audience that God's call and gifts are irrevocable (11:29), and he expresses his hope for Israel's eventual deliverance (11:26), which should put rest to rumors that he talks as if God has broken faith with Israel. Tobin states: "Paul consciously and insistently portrays himself as someone whose belief in Christ is in continuity with the Jewish scriptures and whose mission to the Gentiles has not lessened his concern for his fellow Jews or his conviction about their ultimate salvation."[12]

Second, the social situation of the Roman Christians themselves cannot have been far from Paul's mind. For them, "Israel" was not an abstract question about a religious state far away in the east, but was a people embodied in local communities comprised of synagogues and prayer houses.[13] In fact, the

10. Keck, *Romans*, 224.
11. Cf. Tobin, *Paul's Rhetoric*, 73–78.
12. Ibid., 318.
13. Watson, *Paul, Judaism, and the Gentiles*, 303.

Christians of Rome, be they Gentile or Jewish, may still be enmeshed in the social networks of Roman Jewish life to some degree. The problem of Israel's unbelief was compounded by two further factors. On the one hand, there might have been those Gentile or Jewish Christians who wanted to keep at least one foot in "Israel" with some token gesture of Torah-observance as a security for their status as "chosen." On the other hand, another real danger was that Gentile Christians might be tempted to imitate the anti-Semitism of imperial elites,[14] or else think that Israel's "No" to the gospel was in fact God's "No" to Israel, leading to a full blown supersessionism.[15] To that end, Paul addresses the question where Israel fits into redemptive history, partly to explain Israel's failure to embrace God's righteousness, but with the hope that God's righteousness will yet embrace them on the eve of the eschaton.

Third, the preceding arguments in Romans 1:18–8:39 have laid the groundwork for Paul to canvass the topic of Israel's unbelief in relation to the gospel.[16] Up to this point, Paul has constructed a series of arguments comprised of kerygmatic proclamation, laced with rhetorical verve, saturated with quotations and allusions to Scripture, and injecting traditional material about Jesus' death, all in order to persuade Gentile Christians to strive toward forming a community whose identity and status are determined by Christ, not by Torah. Thereafter, they can live together in a common life, in a common worship, serving a common Lord.

The gospel that creates such a community, however, stands firmly on the shoulders of Israel to the point that Jewish and Gentile Christians have interconnecting identities and interlocking destinies. Paul argued that it is *in* the Messiah and *by* the Spirit that Jews and Gentiles attain salvation and transformation. The Torah's role in redemptive history is seen to be prefatory rather than permanent. It is through the gospel that God brings Gentiles into the redemption, adoption, sonship, and inheritance of Israel. But therein lies the rub. Is the logical conclusion to Paul's Torah-free gospel that Israel has stumbled (9:30–33) and disbelieved (10:18–21) to the point that they have become enemies of the gospel (11:28) and been rejected by God (11:1–2) without any hope of recovery (11:11)? Can the Pauline *euangelion* ("good news") for Gentiles be anything but *dysangelion* ("bad news") for Israel? Thus Paul remains to show how the theology of his gospel relates to Israel in light of what might be negatively implied about Israel. For if Paul's gospel nullifies Israel's election, then God's prior dealings with his people were false,

---

14. Cf. J. C. Waters, *Ethnic Issues in Paul's Letter to the Romans* (Valley Forge, PA: Trinity, 1993), 28–55.

15. Keck, *Romans*, 225.

16. Cf. Cranfield, *Romans*, 2:445–47; Fitzmyer, *Romans*, 539.

and God is reneging on the promises he made. What is at stake is the entire character of God.[17]

Fourth, from a literary point of view, Romans 8 is a natural segue into Romans 9–11. For a start, by emphasizing the quality of assurance in salvation in 5:1–11/8:18–39, Paul naturally beckons the question about Israel's unbelief. That is because Israel's unbelief is the most likely avenue for undermining Paul's confidence in the inviolability of God's electing purposes and the constancy of God's faithfulness. Israel's failure might be taken to imply that God's Word has failed. And if God's Word to Israel has failed, could not the word of the gospel to Gentiles equally fail to achieve its purposes?[18] This single question threatens to bring down the citadel and the cathedral Paul has erected in Romans 1–8. Paul's answer is a definite "no," and he reminds his audience that God's purpose for Israel will yet come to fruition at a future time.

In addition, Paul seems to have deliberately left open the possibility for Israel to embrace the fulfillment of her own scriptural promises in Jesus. Certainly Paul is clear that the church partakes of the promises given to Israel. Israel was promised the Spirit so that they could keep the law (Ezek 36:26–27), and this has come to fruition in the church through the gift of the Spirit (Rom 8:4). Israel had the hope of resurrection (Ezek 37:1–28; Dan 12:1–2), and Paul refers to the resurrection of believers (Rom 8:10–11). Israel was the son of God (Exod 4:22), precisely what Paul attributes to Christians (Rom 8:14–17). The inheritance promised to Israel (Isa 60) is also pledged to the church (Rom 8:17). Israel was called "elect" (1 Chr 16:13; Ps 89:3; Isa 42:1) and "foreknown" by God (Amos 3:2); so are Christians (Rom 8:28–30).[19]

While some see a supersessionist theology here, others detect an emphasis on a broadened inclusion that embraces the Gentiles in Israel's hopes. Optimism for the inclusion of Israel is also spurred on by the fact that the "all" who benefit from Christ's death in 8:32 is matched by the "all Israel will be saved" in 11:26 (see Rom 5:18; 2 Cor 5:14–15).[20] If so, Romans 8 is assertive in its position that Gentiles partake of Israel's blessings, while Romans 9–11 is affirmative of the goodness of those blessings for their original recipients too.

---

17. Richard B. Hays, *Echoes of Scripture in the Letters of Paul* (New Haven: Yale University Press, 1989), 47.

18. Cf. *LAB* 12.9, which depicts Moses asking God to forgive Israel after the golden calf incident, where Moses insists: "Therefore, if you do not have mercy on your vine, all things, Lord, have been done in vain, and you will have no one to glorify you. For even if you plant another vine, it will not trust you, because you destroyed the former one."

19. Schreiner, *Romans*, 466–67.

20. Cf. Dunn, *Romans*, 1:501; Schreiner, *Romans*, 459; Tobin, *Paul's Rhetoric*, 298, 307.

In sum, by the end of Romans 8, Paul has developed the theological architecture, the literary connections, and the pastoral context in which he can intentionally deal with the subject of the gospel in relation to unbelieving Israel. The way he proceeds in Romans 9–11 is as follows: (1) 9:1–5 describes Paul's affirmation of Israel's inherited privileges and his impassioned hope for Israel's deliverance; (2) 9:6–29 describes Israel in the past with particular reference to God's electing purposes; (3) 9:30–10:21 outlines the plight of Israel in the present and the necessity of a continuity mission to Israel; (4) 11:1–32 discusses Israel in the future with a warning to Gentile Christians not to treat Israel and Jewish Christians with contempt, coupled with an affirmation of Israel's eventual deliverance; and (5) 11:33–36 is a doxology for the God who is wise as he is merciful.[21]

## EXPLAIN the Story

**Paul's Anguish over Israel (9:1–4a).**

Paul launches into an impassioned speech about the depth of his concern for his fellow Jews as they languish in their state of unbelief: "I speak the truth in Christ—I am not lying, my conscience confirms it through the Holy Spirit—I have great sorrow and unceasing anguish in my heart" (vv. 1–2). The strange thing is that Paul never explicitly says what the cause of his anguish is. Yet we know from what follows that his grief is evoked by Israel not obtaining righteousness (9:31), stumbling over the message (9:32–33), still needing salvation (10:1), and facing the question whether their "fall" is permanent (11:1, 11).

Paul prefaces his concern with a triple emphasis: "I speak the truth ... I am not lying, my conscience confirms it." The first verse is bookended with "Christ" as the guarantor to his truth-telling and the "Holy Spirit" as the co-witness to his conscience. Paul provides the testimony of a man in Christ who possesses a conscience renewed and illumined by the Holy Spirit.[22] This is all said to confirm the deep sense of grief and constant frustration he carries in his heart over Israel's recalcitrance toward their messianic Redeemer. Paul arguably raises these points in such emotive language precisely because he thinks the Romans have heard the accusation that he holds no concern for Israel. What is more, Paul might also have an eye on the possibility that his little *apologia* for his apostolate might be accessed directly or indirectly by

21. Following largely Tobin, *Paul's Rhetoric*, 321.
22. Cranfield, *Romans*, 2:453.

Roman Jewish Christians and perhaps even by non-Christ-believing Jews in Rome too.

"For I could wish that I myself were cursed and cut off from Christ for the sake of my people, those of my own race, the people of Israel" (vv. 3–4a). The depth of Paul's distress is seen in his wish to be anathematized if it would benefit his fellow Jews. Paul prayerfully wishes to forfeit final salvation from Christ (the meaning of *anathema* in this context) if it would spare his kinsfolk from permanent exclusion. Paul here looks like Moses, who stood before God at Sinai and asked God that he might himself be blotted from God's book if it would save the people from condemnation for their idolatry (Exod 32:30–34). Paul is willing to sacrifice his own salvation if it would provide salvation for Israel. Eugene Peterson's paraphrase is poignant: "If there were any way I could be cursed by the Messiah so they could be blessed by him, I'd do it in a minute" (MSG).

While the NIV describes Paul's kinsfolks as "my people" and "my race," the Greek has "brothers" (*adelphoi*) and "kinsmen" (*syngeneis*) who are related to Paul "according the flesh," signifying shared ethnicity. "Flesh" is an important description for ethnic Israel, which will resurface later in 9:8 and 11:14. Paul also defines this group, furthermore, as "the people of Israel" (*Israēlitai*). It is notable that for Paul "Israelite" is always a positive and even prestigious term for God's people. Paul is asserting that his fellow *Jews* are *Israelites*, that is, members of the chosen people of God (see Acts 13:16; Rom 11:1; 2 Cor 11:2).

### Israel's Inherited Privileges (9:4b–5).

Paul then expounds eight privileges of the Israelites: "Theirs is the adoption to sonship; theirs the divine glory, the covenants, the receiving of the law, the temple worship and the promises. Theirs are the patriarchs, and from them is traced the human ancestry of the Messiah, who is God over all, forever praised! Amen" (vv. 4–5). The list is reminiscent of 3:1–2, where Paul affirmed Jewish "advantages"; here he expounds the idea further by listing Israel's privileges:

*Adoption*: This highlights the well-known scriptural image for Israel as God's "son," which marks out the Israelites as having a special relation with the Creator (see Exod 4:22; Deut 14:1–2; Isa 63:16; 64:8; Jer 31:9; Hos 11:1; Mal 1:6; 2:10).

*Glory*: The most likely background for this is either the idea of God's glory as something revealed to the Israelites (Exod 33:18–23; Isa 35:2; 40:5; 66:18), or else signifies God's presence with his people (Exod 16:7, 10; 24:16; 40:34–35; Lev 9:6, 23; Ezek 1:28).

*Covenants*: The plural here is important and fosters debate as to which covenants are intended. The most natural inference is that it includes the covenants mentioned in the Old Testament involving Abraham, Noah, the Israelites, David, and the new covenant (on "covenants" see Eph 2:12; Sir 44:12, 18; 2 Macc 8:15; Wis 18:22).

*Receiving the law*: The emphasis here falls on the God-given nature of the law, not its negative effects as usual, especially the privileges of receiving it (Deut 31:10–11; Ezra 7:6, 10; Neh 8:1; Ps 78:5; Sir 45:5, 17). It is probably identical to the idea expressed in 3:2 that the Jewish people were "entrusted with the very oracles of God."

*Worship*: The worship in question most probably refers to the sacrificial system that was a form of reverence toward the God of the covenant and a means of maintaining the relationship (1 Sam 1:3; 1 Kgs 17:35–36; Isa 19:21; John 16:2; Heb 9:1, 6).

*Promises*: The "promises" undoubtedly refers to the promise of blessings given to Abraham and the other patriarchs, which figure prominently in Galatians and Romans (Gen 12:1–2; 15:1–5; 17:1–27; Rom 15:8; Gal 3:16, 21; Wis 12:21).

*Patriarchs*: The relative pronoun opening v. 5 is naturally translated "theirs" to signify that the Israelites have the privilege of being descended from the very persons to whom the covenants and promises were given.

*Messianic lineage*: The final privilege is that it is from Israel that "the Messiah" comes. The titular use of *ho Christos* makes it clear that Paul means "Messiah" as a formal title rather than as a proper name.[23] The element of shared ethnicity or singular family is emphasized by the phrase "human ancestry" (more lit., "according to the flesh" [*kata sarka*]). Just as Paul shares a genealogical relationship with the Israelites (v. 3), so does the Messiah (v. 5).

An acute interpretive conundrum surrounds v. 5 concerning its Greek grammar and English punctuation. It is far from a pedestrian debate over the specificity of Paul's syntax because the result determines Paul's conception of the Messiah as a divine person. It comes down to whether the final clause "God be blessed" (*theos eulogētos*) modifies "Messiah" or constitutes an independent eulogy of praise to God. Several translations, like the NIV, take the former option and ascribe deity to Jesus, while other translations, like the NRSV, take the latter option and assume an independent ascription of praise to God.

There are several good reasons for seeing Paul as identifying the Messiah as "God" in this passage. (1) The clause "the one who is over all" most naturally

23. Cf. further Bird, *Jesus Is the Christ*, 15–22.

| Comparisons of Romans 9:5 | |
|---|---|
| *Messiah as "God"* | *Messiah not "God"* |
| "... from them is traced the human ancestry of the Messiah, who is God over all, forever praised! Amen." (NIV) | "... Christ came, who is over all, God blessed for ever. Amen" (KJV) |
| "... the Messiah descended from those ancestors. He is the one who rules over all things, who is God, and who is blessed forever. Amen" (CEB) | "... comes the Messiah, who is over all, God blessed forever. Amen." (NRSV) |
| "... came the Christ, who is God over all, blessed forever! Amen" (NET) | "... from whom is the Christ according to the flesh, who is over all, God blessed forever. Amen" (NASB) |

relates back to "Messiah" as the nearest subject, while the alternative view of regarding the clause as modifying "God be blessed" would be to assume a rather abrupt change of topic. (2) The doxology "God be blessed" cannot be independent of the preceding words since that would imply a awkward asyndetic construction and the participle *ōn* ("being") would be rendered superfluous (in other words, a subsequent and independent doxology needs a better joining word like "and" to delineate a new subject for the clause, and it would be simpler without the participle *ōn* with the definite article *ho* functioning as a relative pronoun for "he"). (3) Paul's doxologies are always tied to the preceding context and not independent (e.g., Rom 1:25; 11:36; 2 Cor 11:31). If it was an independent clause, one would expect the word *eulogētos* to appear first in order (e.g., 2 Cor 1:3; Eph 1:3; 1 Pet 1:3). (4) The identification of the Messiah as God is not so radical when one remembers that Paul elsewhere refers to "the glory of our great God and Savior, Jesus Christ" (Titus 2:13). (5) Paul habitually ascribes divine functions to Jesus and even uses Old Testament passages about the "Lord" to describe him (see Jesus as "Lord" in Rom 10:13).[24]

Paul's aim in 9:1–5 is to point to his genuine pathos for Israel and to the cohort of Israelite privileges that the gospel affirms rather than denounces. He is trying to build a secure bridge between the faith of Israel and the gospel

---

24. See Bruce Metzger, *A Textual Commentary on the Greek New Testament* (2nd ed.; London: United Bible Societies, 1994), 459–62; Murray J. Harris, *Jesus as God: The New Testament Use of Theos in Reference to Jesus* (Grand Rapids: Baker, 1992), 144–72; Brian J. Wright, "Jesus as THEOS: A Textual Examination," in *Revisiting the Corruption of the New Testament: Manuscript, Patristic, and Apocryphal Evidence* (ed. D. B. Wallace; Grand Rapids: Kregel, 2011), 232–33; Hans-Christian Kammler, "Die Prädikation of Jesu Christi als »Gott« and die paunlinische Christologie: Erwägungen zur Exegese von Röm 9,5b," *ZNW* 92 (2003): 164–80; George Carraway, *Christ Is God over All: Romans 9:5 in the Context of Romans 9–11* (LNTS 489; London: Bloombsbury T&T Clark, 2013).

of the Messiah before he launches into what will be a radical reorientation of election and eschatology in light of messianic faith. Andrew Lincoln puts it well:

> Paul is at pains to stress that he is the *Jewish* apostle to the *Gentiles* and that one does not need to renounce one's Jewish heritage in order to hold to his particular string of convictions about Scripture, Messiah, and gospel. He wants to demonstrate that the distinctive elements of his gospel are not only compatible with Judaism, but also provides the best possible way of reshaping the Jewish tradition; a necessary reshaping in light of what God has done in Christ.[25]

## LIVE the Story

These verses form a short and sharp entrée into Romans 9–11. Above all, they provide a perfect moment for repose and reflection on the Jewishness of Paul and of the Christian faith itself. Contemplating the Jewish roots of Christianity is all the more important given the long and dark history of Christian anti-Semitism that culminated in the Holocaust. This passage challenges us to evaluate how we think, talk, and act toward Jewish people and the state of Israel.

### Paul the Jew

Paul's remarks in 9:1–5 show how unabashedly clear he was about his Jewish ancestry (see Rom 11:1; 2 Cor 11:22; Phil 3:3–9). Yet Paul seems to have been regularly accused of being something of a troublemaker, traitor, or turncoat toward to his familial religion. While the Jews on the whole were more focused on orthopraxy than orthodoxy, they were well aware of heretics and defectors from their ranks who had left mainstream Judaism either for a deviant form or to become pagans. The responses that Paul got from Jewish communities suggest that Paul was thought of as some kind of sectarian agitator or even as a dangerous apostate (see Acts 14:19; 17:4–5, 13; 20:3; 21:21, 27–28; 23:12; 24:5–9; 2 Cor 11:23). While many Jewish scholars have tried to reclaim Jesus, there hasn't been an equal enthusiasm for a Jewish reclamation of Paul (although my dear friend Mark Nanos is certainly having a courageous attempt at it!).[26] Sadly, there is little wonder why, since the

25. Lincoln, "From Wrath to Justification," 134.

26. Cf. Michael F. Bird and Preston Sprinkle, "Jewish Interpretation of Paul in the Last Thirty Years," *CBR* 6 (2008): 355–76, and Mark D. Nanos, "Paul: A Jewish View," in *Four Views on the Apostle Paul* (ed. M. F. Bird; Grand Rapids: Zondervan, 2012), 169–93.

history of persecution aimed at Jewish communities was inspired partly by a (mis)reading of Paul, and it has left a lasting impression on modern Jewish memory (see Acts 18:6; Phil 3:1; 1 Thess 2:14–16!).

Yet Paul has a degree of concern for Israel that is as palpable as it is undeniable. Although he was the apostle to the Gentiles, he never gave up his mission to the Jewish people, which is why he said that the gospel is "first" for the Jew, and why he was willing to live like a Jew when ministering to other Jews, so that he "might save some" (Rom 1:16; 1 Cor 9:20, 22). In fact, I tend to think that Paul himself was probably Torah-observant with some flexibility—partly from habit, not for meritorious gain, not according to the letter of the Pharisaic oral code, but as a matter of personal default. The Jewish texture of Paul's discourse should be unsurprising because Paul's letters betray a constant intertextual dialogue with the Old Testament, and they focus frequently on Jewish questions like how to live faithfully in a pagan environment. Paul believed that by telling the story of the gospel, he was telling a thoroughly Jewish story. He never gave the remotest hint that by placing his faith in Messiah Jesus he was thereby repudiating his Jewishness; rather, he was upholding it by affirming its fulfillment in Jesus the Messiah and his people (see Acts 13:32–33; 1 Cor 10:11; 2 Cor 1:20). Thus Paul was not the Benedict Arnold of Judaism; he was more like a theological Albert Einstein trying to usher new paradigms and new discoveries for the benefit of the whole world.

Paul reminds me of the character of Anton in the musical *Chess*. Toward the end of the second act, Anton wins the world chess championship, but then defects from the USSR to the USA. Soon after, a mob of reporters asks Anton why he has deserted his own country, to which he answers with the stirring ballad "Anthem" that his land's only borders lay around his heart. I want to suggest that Romans 9:1–5 is Paul's "Anthem" as he is confronted with an accusation of betrayal to his people, and he responds with an impassioned plea for his affection for his kinsfolk, not despite his faith in Messiah Jesus, but as the highest expression of it! The chorus to Paul's song is that the Messiah who took on the "likeness of sinful flesh" took on Jewish flesh (Rom 8:3; 9:5). The "love of Christ" comes to "all" including Israel and in many ways because of Israel (8:32, 35).

The image we should have of Paul should not be modernized as if he was a cosmopolitan church planter or Caucasian-looking hipster theology professor. Remember Paul the Jewish-Christian apostle to the Gentiles! Remember Paul standing in the synagogues teaching about Jesus from the law and the prophets (e.g., Acts 14:1; 17:1–2, 10; 18:19; 19:8). Remember Paul telling Gentile Christians to respect the scruples of Jewish Christians when it came to food sacrificed to idols (Rom 14:1–23). Remember Paul calling for Gentile believers to uphold the back half of the Decalogue (13:9). Remember Paul purifying himself before he entered the temple (Acts 21:26) and in the temple praying and receiving a vision to go to the Gentiles (22:17–21). Note too how Paul planned his trips around Jewish festivals like Pentecost (Acts 20:16; 1 Cor 16:8).

For all Paul's rancor and rhetoric about the Torah being imposed on Gentiles (see Rom 3:21–4:25; Gal 2:11–3:39), he retained a Jewish conception of monotheism, election, and eschatology. Paul urged Gentile Christians to live at peace with those who were Jewish by birth or by practice (Rom 14:19; 1 Cor 10:32; 2 Cor 11:13). Paul, who considered Gentile Christians like us his "brothers and sisters," could also address his fellows Jews as "brothers and sisters." If people are bothered by you referring to "Paul the Jew," keep saying it until they are uncomfortable with you not saying it.

### Getting along with the Family of Jesus and Paul's Brothers

How do Christian Gentiles relate to the Jewish people, be they secular, orthodox, progressive, or reformed? I would suggest that we pursue friendship without forfeiture. We can cultivate cordial relationships with Jewish communities without denying some of the theological differences between us. We can promote peace and harmony without asking anyone to deny the wisdom of their own tradition.

We need to offer friendship. Let us never forget that there has been a long and sad history to Christian anti-Semitism. Yes, it had its beginnings in a sectarian context when Christians were a minority and experiencing spasmodic persecution from Jews and pagans. However, Christian polemic against religious competitors quickly became more than name-calling and took an ugly turn in the post-Constantine era, Middle Ages, post-Enlightenment period, and even in Modern European history. Reading the paschal homily of Melito of Sardis in the second century, John Chrysostom's "Eight Homilies against the Jews" in the fourth century, and Martin Luther's tract "The Jews and Their Lies" in the sixteenth century should leave contemporary Christian readers confused and alarmed that anyone claiming to be a follower Jesus the Jew could say such things about Jesus' own people. It was "theology" of this order that was a contributing factor in the Holocaust, and we need to reflect on how such could happen in the middle of Christianized Europe.

I've always wondered whether if Jesus's crucifixion had been portrayed in art as he was truly was on the cross—stark naked, not with a loincloth conveniently covering his genitals, but with his circumcision visible to all—would the history of Jewish and Christian relations have been any different? One can only wonder! In any case, since Paul writes Holy Scripture, we can hardly have a view of the Jewish people different from the one he himself had. We need to be careful how we think about, talk about, and refer to "the Jew." It should not be in stereotypical, caricatured, or even strangely idealized categories. These are a people with whom we share a religious history, and they are the ones from whom the Messiah himself came—a fact that should be acknowledged and appreciated by all Christians irrespective of how they understand the precise relationship between Israel and the church.[27]

The other thing we must be conscious of is not forfeiting our testimony to Jesus the Messiah. A big trend in Pauline studies and in interreligious dialogue between Jews and Christians is to insist that Israel is still saved in their own covenantal arrangement under the Torah and without Christ. I'll have more to say on this later, but for now I want to note that this is deeply problematic position if one accepts, as I do, Paul's testimony to the finality of God's revelation in Lord Jesus the Messiah. Paul was not a postmodern theologian saying all religions are basically the same or that Judaism and Christianity are two parallel tracks to God. Paul is adamant that if salvation can come through the Torah, "Christ died for nothing" (Gal 2:21), and he believes that Christ is the end/goal/climax of the Torah "so that there may be righteousness for everyone who believes" (Rom 10:4). One cannot push aside Paul's strong claims about the exclusivisity of salvation in Christ for both Jews and Gentiles unless one denies the sense of ultimacy that Paul himself attributes to Christ's saving work. For case in point, take heed of the following story by Helmut Koester:

> Almost 30 years ago, a conference about Judaism and Christianity was held at Harvard University, with very high-powered participation from theologians and scholars from the USA and from abroad. But one of the key addresses was a complete disaster and caused great embarrassment. It was a lecture by the well-known German theologian Wolfhart Pannenberg, who insisted that the Hebrew Bible (which he called the Old Testament) can be understood properly by both Jews and Christians only if it is acknowledged that its ultimate meaning is seen as a prophecy for the fulfillment in Jesus the Christ. I still remember that my hands froze when I wanted to join in the polite applause at the end of the lecture.[28]

Whereas I genuinely sympathize with the interreligious and theological reasons for rejecting anything that reeks of hardcore supersessionism, I'm not prepared to forfeit the claims to finality and fulfillment that Christians have traditionally attributed to Jesus. Jettisoning such claims might prove to be

27. On which, see Bird, *Evangelical Theology*, 719–27.

28. Helmut Koester, "Strugnell and Supersessionism: Historic Mistakes That Haunt the Relationship between Christianity and Judaism," *BAR* 21.2 (1995): 26–27.

conducive to promoting concord between different faith communities, but it comes at the high price of ditching the biblical view of Jesus Christ as the goal of Israel's redemptive history. If I had been at the Harvard conference mentioned above, I probably would have given Wolfhart Pannenberg a big old high-five!

It should come as no surprise that many Jewish theologians have no qualms about trying to be good global citizens while also affirming the distinctiveness and integrity of their own particular tradition in contrast to other religious beliefs like Christianity. According to Tsvi Bisk and Moshe Dror:

> The future of Jewish-Christian relations must be based upon a reaffirmation of Jewish cultural particularity and the end of Jewish apologetics. We Jews are the minority and are obliged to be unambiguous regarding our differences with Christianity. Ecumenism does not mean the blurring of differences for fear of offending those with a different view of life, or shading our view of the world in order to be socially acceptable and immune to physical and political intimidation.... It is a Jewish responsibility to make Judaism stronger and more attractive by clarifying its basic principles. We must be proactive in publicizing differences between Christianity and Judaism. In a constitutional democracy that protects the citizen against religious coercion the success of missionary activity is dependent on Jewish ignorance. We are now paying the price for years of shallow and kitschy Fiddler-on-the-Roof Judaism, and the cultivation of colorful ethnicity. This must be replaced by uncompromising clarity.[29]

I strongly suggest that those in the Christian tradition interested in interreligious dialogue heed similar advice for their own tradition. We are obligated to have good manners toward those of other religions, especially the Jewish people, but it doesn't mean that we have to deny central tenets of our precious faith if we are to promote tolerance and social cohesion.

I agree with a talk I heard by Miroslav Volf that interreligious dialogue between religious pluralists is utterly boring and almost entirely useless. That is because all the cast of participants do is sit around apologizing for their own kind who aren't pluralists, engage in a never-ending series of compliments to each other, and use the most vague and meaningless language to affirm each other's position. It's more boring that watching NASCAR reruns! If you want to do something interesting, exciting, confronting, and even a little risky, get religious exclusivists to talk to each other. The best thing evangelical Christians can do in interreligious dialogue with Jewish folks, whether in an

29. Tsvi Bisk and Moshe Dror, "Future Rules of Jewish-Christian Relations," *On Jewish Matters: A Contemporary Jewish and Israeli Magazine*. www.onjewishmatters.com/judaism-and-christianity/.

academic colloquium or on an airplane to Tel Aviv, is not to sell out our historical orthodox faith in Jesus to appear tolerant or inclusive. The best thing we can do is remain faithful to Jesus the Jew and his Jewish-Christian apostles Peter and Paul by affirming Jesus as the Savior of Jews and Gentiles. Then in a spirit of humanity and humility, make a concomitant commitment to live in peace and harmony with the Jewish people.

Taken together, these themes of friendship without forfeiture are neatly summarized by N. T. Wright:

> On the one hand, any church that took Romans 9:1–5 seriously would find it impossible to engage in any of the anti-Jewish, still less the anti-Semitic, rhetoric that has disfigured would-be Christian discourse for many centuries. On the other hand, Paul's position is clearly incompatible with the Enlightenment position that treats all "religions" as equally valid paths to God, or to "the divine," or the local variation on this that sees Judaism and Christianity as parallel though separate "covenants." The whole point of vv. 4–5 is that what has happened in Jesus the Messiah is indeed the paradoxical fulfillment of God's Israel-shaped promises and purposes. Only if we follow Paul's own argument through the section will we understand his own unique proposal for a way forward from this impasse.[30]

The single most important application I think we can take from this is that we Christians shouldn't just talk about Jews, we should talk to them. By developing relations with Jewish friends, we begin a process of mutual listening to each other and learning from each other. Meeting your local rabbi, visiting a nearby synagogue, sharing a cup of chicken soup with your Jewish friend, and asking them what it was like to grow up Jewish in a Christian country can leave lasting impressions. Hopefully they will want to hear your story as well, and it will develop into a time of mutual listening and reciprocal sharing. We do that hoping that Israel according to the flesh and Israel according to the promise will one day be one and the same people!

30. Wright, "Romans," 10:632.

CHAPTER 18

# Romans 9:6–29

## LISTEN to the Story

6 It is not as though God's word had failed. For not all who are
descended from Israel are Israel. 7 Nor because they are his descendants
are they all Abraham's children. On the contrary, "It is through Isaac that
your offspring will be reckoned." 8 In other words, it is not the children
by physical descent who are God's children, but it is the children of the
promise who are regarded as Abraham's offspring. 9 For this was how the
promise was stated: "At the appointed time I will return, and Sarah will
have a son."

10 Not only that, but Rebekah's children were conceived at the same
time by our father Isaac. 11 Yet, before the twins were born or had done
anything good or bad—in order that God's purpose in election might
stand: 12 not by works but by him who calls—she was told: "The older
will serve the younger." 13 Just as it is written: "Jacob I loved, but Esau I
hated."

14 What then shall we say? Is God unjust? Not at all! 15 For he says to
Moses:

> "I will have mercy on whom I have mercy,
> and I will have compassion on whom I have compassion."

16 It does not, therefore, depend on human desire or effort, but on God's
mercy. 17 For Scripture says to Pharaoh: "I raised you up for this very
purpose, that I might display my power in you and that my name might
be proclaimed in all the earth." 18 Therefore God has mercy on whom he
wants to have mercy, and he hardens whom he wants to harden.

19 One of you will say to me: "Then why does God still blame us? For
who is able to resist his will?" 20 But who are you, a human being, to talk
back to God? "Shall what is formed say to the one who formed it, 'Why
did you make me like this?'" 21 Does not the potter have the right to make
out of the same lump of clay some pottery for special purposes and some
for common use?

[22]What if God, although choosing to show his wrath and make
his power known, bore with great patience the objects of his wrath—
prepared for destruction? [23]What if he did this to make the riches of his
glory known to the objects of his mercy, whom he prepared in advance
for glory—[24]even us, whom he also called, not only from the Jews but
also from the Gentiles? [25]As he says in Hosea:

"I will call them 'my people' who are not my people;
and I will call her 'my loved one' who is not my loved one,"

[26]and,

"In the very place where it was said to them,
'You are not my people,'
there they will be called 'children of the living God.' "

[27]Isaiah cries out concerning Israel:

"Though the number of the Israelites be like the sand by the sea,
only the remnant will be saved.
[28]For the Lord will carry out
his sentence on earth with speed and finality."

[29]It is just as Isaiah said previously:

"Unless the Lord Almighty
had left us descendants,
we would have become like Sodom,
we would have been like Gomorrah."

*Listening to the texts in the story*: Genesis 18:10–14; 21:12; 25:21–23; Exodus 4:21; 7:3; 9:12; 14:4, 17; 9:16; 33:19; Deuteronomy 32:4; Isaiah 1:9; 10:23; 29:16; 45:9; Jeremiah 18:1–6; 50:25; Hosea 1:10; 2:23; Malachi 1:2–3; Wisdom of Solomon 12:12; 15:7.

Given the totality of ethnic Israel's privileges listed in Romans 9:1–5, how did they come to the point where they failed to believe in the long-promised messianic Redeemer, and what will happen to them now? Paul's answer to that implied question consumes the bulk of 9:6–11:32. The passage is a literary unity that deals with Israel in the past, Israel in the present, and Israel in the future. The ultimate point is that Israel's failure is not final, for God's electing purposes run through Israel, reaching even the Gentiles, to the point that Israel will be prompted to jealousy, so that in the end there is hope that "all

Israel will be saved." The irony of Romans 9–11 is that Paul will argue that God has rejected part of ethnic Israel, but still intends to inject them back into his saving purposes.

The first stage in that argument is 9:6–29, which explains how God's electing purposes run within Israel but do not necessarily encompass all of ethnic Israel (at least not initially, more anon in 11:25–32!). The discourse is an expanded commentary on the initial statement made in 9:6a, "It is not as though God's word had failed." The failure of *some* within ethnic Israel to believe and the inclusion of *some* Gentiles to belong do not cast aspersions on God's faithfulness. Rather, it proves the point of a recurrent pattern in redemptive history, where God's choice and mercy always precede human decision. Salvation was never about ethnicity or effort, but about God's gracious gift, which is why God can include the Gentiles in the purview of his saving work. The end result is that Israel can be divided between those of the "flesh" and those of the "promise." The latter includes believing Jews and Gentiles (4:1–16; 9:8, 24–29), called elsewhere the "circumcision" (Phil 3:3), "like Isaac, children of the promise" (Gal 4:28), and perhaps identifiable with those whom Paul calls "the Israel of God" (Gal 6:16).

Romans 9:6–29 has long been regarded as providing teaching about "election" or "predestination." Patristic and Reformed commentators have ordinarily focused on how Paul's remarks here contribute to a theology of divine predestination, whereby God chooses some people for salvation but not others and on what basis God does so.[1] I have a twofold response to that topic. (1) Paul's argument is operating primarily on the horizons of "peoples," not "predestination." He is explaining how God's choice of Israel is consistent with a mixture of belief and unbelief within ethnic Israel and also consistent with the inclusion of Gentiles in the divine promises. As such, the focus is corporate, not individual. (2) What Paul says here undoubtedly contributes to a theology of divine predestination. For a start, he talks about the choosing of individuals for salvation as examples of corporate election (9:7, 11–13). On top of that, there is a strong emphasis that God's choosing is based on pure mercy, never merited, not attributable to foreknowledge of any person's actions (9:11–12, 16).[2]

---

1. Cf. Reasoner, *Romans in Full Circle*, 95–112.

2. Cf. Thomas R. Schreiner, "Does Romans 9 Teach Individual Election unto Salvation?" in *Still Sovereign: Contemporary Perspectives on Election, Foreknowledge, and Grace* (ed. T. R. Schreiner and B. A. Ware; Grand Rapids: Baker, 2000), 89–106; Brian J. Abasciano, "Corporate Election in Romans 9: A Reply to Thomas Schreiner," *JETS* 49 (2006): 351–71; Thomas R. Schreiner, "Corporate and Individual Election in Romans 9: A Response to Brian Abasciano," *JETS* 49 (2006): 373–86. Contrast also Morris, *Romans*, 352; and Kruse, *Romans*, 391–92, both in the Pillar series.

Central to the argument is Paul's use of the Old Testament in 9:6–29.[3] The whole passage is incredibly dense and saturated with citations of the Torah and the Prophets. By these citations Paul telescopes the story of the patriarchs, exodus, exile, and restoration with a view to demonstrating how God's electing purposes run through Israel to the Messiah and embrace the Gentiles. The reason for this thick intertextual arrangement is easy to appreciate. Jewish rejection of the gospel is a big problem, and Gentile acceptance of the gospel makes it even worse![4] How does this square with the story of Scripture? Paul embarks on a bold task to show not only the conformity of his gospel to the story of Scripture, but to explain how the current situation of Israel's unbelief and Gentile belief is actually scripted by Scripture.

Paul's argument musters a mixture of emotive diatribe and dense citation of Old Testament texts to make the point that God's Word has not failed Israel because God's election was meant for a remnant within Israel and for a residual number of Gentiles. The progression of thought runs as follows: (1) God's promises apply to the elect within Israel, not to the entire *ethnē* of Israel (vv. 6–9); (2) this point is proven by Esau and Jacob (vv. 10–13); (3) Paul dismisses a first objection that this makes God unjust by referencing the exodus story (vv. 14–18); (4) Paul dismisses a second objection that this makes God arbitrary by appealing to divine sovereignty (vv. 19–21); (5) Paul expounds the principle undergirding God's electing choices, namely, that God's dealings with Israel were marked by patience, so when he shows mercy to Jews and Gentiles, it is proof of his mercy and glory (vv. 22–23); and (6) Paul concludes that God's promises include both a cohort of Gentiles and a remnant of Jews (vv. 24–29).

## Will the Real Israel Please Stand Up (9:6–9)

Without any perceptible marker to indicate a transition, Paul simply launches into his discussion: "It is not as though God's word had failed" (v. 6a).[5] Presumably some were thinking that Paul's gospel casts aspersions on God's moral uprightness. After all, if God has chosen Israel, then why has Israel rejected the message? Why are Gentiles accepting it instead? And does this not look as

---

3. Cf. Brian J. Abasciano, *Paul's Use of the Old Testament in Romans 9.1–9: An Intertextual and Theological Exegesis* (LNTS 301; London: T&T Clark, 2005); idem, *Paul's Use of the Old Testament in Romans 9.10–18* (LNTS 317; London: T&T Clark, 2011); Wagner, *Heralds of the Good News*, 43–117; Seifrid, "Romans," *CONTUOT*, 638–50.

4. Moo, *Romans*, 549.

5. On the effectiveness of God's word, see Isa 40:8; 55:11.

if the whole sway of covenantal promises and prophetic hopes for the future, i.e., "God's word," has come to naught? That is the presenting issue that Paul deals with now.

It is worthwhile to remember that Paul has already intimated this issue in Romans 3:1–9, where he said that God's faithfulness to Israel does not preclude his judgment of Israel. Now in 9:6–9 he wants to add that God's choosing of Israel does not require his choosing everyone within Israel. God's electing purposes do not flow through lineage but through the call that God places on persons attached to the promises. So, to the Israel of the promise, God's word remains faithful and effective.

Paul reasons in vv. 6b–7 that God's word has not failed, but it has certainly been misunderstood. Paul asserts that God's election does not guarantee the immediate salvation of all Israelites—rather, only selected persons within Israel—and it is to this narrower band of Israel-within-Israel for whom God's word remains effective. Hence his explanatory statement: "For not all who are descended from Israel are Israel" (v. 6b). In other words, tucked away within ethnic Israel is a "true" Israel.[6] Paul doesn't use the precise term "true Israel," but his reference to a subset of persons inside ethnic Israel being identified as "God's children," "children of the promise," and "Abraham's offspring" (9:8) certainly works to the same effect.[7] Although some in the early church used the term "true Israel" to designate the church,[8] I prefer the nomenclature "promissory Israel" to match the language Paul uses.

Side note: There was in Paul's day a wide range of perspectives on how God's election of Israel related to the individual persons who comprised Israel. To be sure, some Jewish authors equated God's election with the entire Jewish nation, concurrent with a strong emphasis on its inviolability.[9] Yet we must remember that for others, amidst the sectarian rivalries of ancient Judaism, "Israel" was a contested entity that some authors did not think automatically applied to all Jews. The result often led to some rancorous polemics to the effect that "I'm-more-Israel-than-thou" or "thou-art-about-as-Jewish-as-a-pork-sausage."[10] For example, Philo's conception of "Israel who sees God" appears to designate an elitist group of philosophically minded and ethically

6. Moo (*Romans*, 568–59) prefers "God's true spiritual people."

7. Notice how several translations use the adverb "truly" in Romans 9:6 with "truly belong to Israel" (NRSV), "truly members of God's people" (NLT), and "truly Israel" (NETS).

8. Justin Martyr, *Dial. Trypho*. 135; Bray, *Ambrosiaster*, 80.

9. Cf. Sir 17:17; 24:6–8; *Jub.* 15.29–34; Wis 4:15; 19:22; Matt 3:9//Luke 3:8; Justin, *Dial* 140; *m. Sanh.* 10.1.

10. Cf. Johnson (*Romans*, 151–52): "To a large extent, being a Jew in the first century meant to take part in a debate over the meaning of Torah, with each sect and group finding in the tradition the basis of its own claims to uniquely represent the people to the exclusion of the claims of others."

upright persons,[11] while the Qumranites identified their own sect as the "congregation of Israel," designating themselves over against the rest of Israel.[12]

In other writings like *1 Enoch*, *Jubilees*, and *Psalms of Solomon*, authors equate "Israel" or the "elect" with the righteous who obey the Torah properly.[13] Many authors in the Second Temple period were aware of Israel's unfaithfulness and apostasy, with the result that judgment had fallen or would yet fall on all Israel, leaving only a remnant.[14] In much of the literature, then, salvation was hardly ever the lot of all Jews, but open, indeterminate, and prospective. Those who continued in sin would face judgment, while those who repented and obeyed the Torah would obtain mercy. Election in Israel was often configured backward from a sectarian view of obedience and belonging.[15]

Now back to the text: Paul's understanding of ethnic Israel embedded with a promissory Israel is then reiterated with a further negation. Paul adds: "Nor because they are his descendants [i.e., 'seed'] are they all Abraham's children" (v. 7a). The point is that (1) not everyone belonging to ethnic Israel ("Abraham's children") is part of promissory Israel ("his seed"); which entails that (2) hereditary connection to Abraham is not the basis for belonging to Abraham's chosen "seed" (see Rom 2:25–29; 4:13, 16; 9:29; 11:1; Gal 3:29).[16] The assertion is then justified with Genesis 21:12: "On the contrary, 'It is through Isaac that your offspring will be reckoned'" (v. 7b). This text recalls God's word to Abraham in response to his reluctance to banish the slave woman Hagar and her son, Ishmael, by reminding him of the distinction between his two sons. Although Ishmael would be blessed (Gen 17:20; 21:20), God's covenant people would come through Isaac (17:21).

Anyone familiar with the patriarchal narratives would hardly bat an eyelid at what Paul is saying thus far: God chose Isaac, not Ishmael. Yet the conclusion that Paul draws from v. 7b (God chose Isaac) and that bolsters his

11. Philo, *Migration*, 46, 113–14, 201; *Posterity*, 13–21; *Rewards* 44.

12. 1QS 5.22; 1QSa 1.2; 2.12.

13. Cf., e.g., *1 En.* 1.1–3; 3.7–8; 93.10; *Jub.* 2.19–28; *Pss. Sol.* 12.6.

14. Cf., e.g., 1QS 5.22; *Pss. Sol.* 10.6; 1 Macc 1:53; 7:9.

15. Cf. further Graham Harvey, *The True Israel: Uses of the Names Jew, Hebrew and Israel in Ancient Jewish Literature and Early Christian Literature* (AGAJU 35; Leiden: Brill, 1996), 148–261, 271–73; Timo Eskola, *Theodicy and Predestination in Pauline Soteriology* (WUNT 2.100; Tübingen: Mohr Siebeck, 1998); M. A. Elliott, *The Survivors of Israel: A Reconsideration of the Theology of Pre-Christian Judaism* (Grand Rapids: Eerdmans, 2000), 245–49, 307; Sigurd Grindheim, *Crux of Election: Paul's Critique of the Jewish Confidence in the Election of Israel* (WUNT 2.202; Tübingen: Mohr Siebeck, 2005), 35–76 (esp. 67–69).

16. I am assuming that in v. 7 the "seed" (*sperma*) refers to promissory Israel and "all Abraham's children" (*Abraam pantes tekna*) refers to ethnic Israel, esp. in light of v. 8 and Galatians 3:29, which refer to the "seed" as the promised line of Abraham (but see 2 Cor 11:22 where "seed" means "Abraham's descendants" as ethnic Israel). See also Dunn, *Romans*, 2:540; Moo, *Romans*, 575; Wright, "Romans," 10:636.

assertion in v. 6b (there is an Israel within Israel, i.e., "promissory Israel") would court controversy because he alleges that ethnic descent is basically irrelevant. Paul continues: "In other words, it is not the children by physical descent who are God's children, but it is the children of the promise who are regarded as Abraham's offspring [i.e., "seed"]" (v. 8). Paul divides Abraham's children into the two camps, "flesh" and "promise," with the privilege of belonging to Abraham's "seed" limited to the children of the promise.

Paul next explains the meaning of the "promise" as it relates to Isaac and those like him. The way that "the promise" of Genesis 21:12 was first stated was that: "At the appointed time I [God] will return, and Sarah will have a son" (v. 9). The original promise was that Abraham and Sarah, despite their old age, notwithstanding his good-as-dead body and her barren womb, would still have a child (see Gen 18:10, 14). The text supports the stated point because it is Sarah's son, Isaac, rather than Hagar's son, Ishmael, who is the heir of the promises. Furthermore, God—the "I" in Gen 18:10—is the one who "returns" or "comes" to fulfill his promise to the patriarchal couple by miraculously enabling them to conceive a child. The promise is yielded by divine action, not by Abraham's vigor or by Sarah's fertility. Isaac is truly the child of a divine promise.

To back up for a moment: God's word has not failed, because God promised Abraham a son (Gen 18); when the time came for a choice, God confirmed his earlier word concerning Isaac (Gen 21), with the result that ethnicity has basically nothing to do with belonging to the children of the promise.[17]

### Consider Jacob and Esau (9:10–13)

If "flesh" or "physical descent" is not the means for obtaining the divine promises, then what is? Paul discusses this in vv. 10–13 concerning Jacob and Esau, where his point is that belonging to promissory Israel is not about mere ethnicity or moral effort, but simply originates in God's gracious and sovereign call.

Paul switches to the next generation of Isaac and Rebekah with their children, Esau and Jacob, to continue his argument about the lineage of the promise. "Not only that, but Rebekah's children were conceived at the same time by our father Isaac" (v. 10). The phrase "not only that" means that the contrast between the children of the flesh and the children of the promise is not restricted to Isaac and Ishmael, but is also perceived in the story of Jacob and Esau (Gen 25–28). In fact, the contrast between these twins is more

17. Cf. Wright, "Romans," 10:636.

acute! Whereas Isaac and Ishmael had different mothers, Jacob and Esau have one mother in Rebekah and were even "conceived at the same time by our father Isaac." Nevertheless, despite their shared parents, the twin boys would have very different destinies.

At this point we might expect Paul to drop in the citation from Genesis 25:23 to underscore that Jacob would be blessed and be greater than Esau. But before he does that, Paul adds further commentary in vv. 11–12 to make it crystal clear that Jacob's destiny rests on the gracious nature of God's call and not on Jacob's moral qualities. "Yet, before the twins were born or had done anything good or bad—in order that God's purpose in election might stand: not by works but by him who calls—she was told: 'The older will serve the younger'" (vv. 11–12). Paul explains that the election of Jacob took place before either son was born and before either did good or evil. God's choice of Jacob was not merited for his behavior. In fact, Jacob turned out to be a liar and a cheat who would be far from likely to deserve the reward of an impartial deity. The basis for the choice of Jacob lay not in Jacob's moral fiber, but is given in the subsequent purpose clause: "in order that God's purpose in election might stand: not by works but by him who calls." The statement is radical in that it grates against the idea that God is a divine arbiter who finds traces of fitness in persons as the basis for his mercy.

When we think of God's purposes, we are not to think of an abstract order of decrees, but God's intention to bring salvation to the world through Abraham's seed, through Israel, and in the Messiah. God's electing purpose "stands," "remains," or we could say "carries forth" (*menō*) on the basis of his effectual call, and not as a just reward for "works."[18] Obviously the "works" in question are the precepts of the Torah. Paul has stated the same point about the inadequacy of Torah works earlier (3:20, 27–28; 4:4–6) and will repeat it again soon (9:32–33; 11:6). The debate as to whether these works are moralistic deeds of self-righteousness or Jewish boundary markers of identity is moot.[19] The emphasis is that striving in the Jewish way of life codified in the Torah will never merit salvation on account of the inescapable effects of sin on Jews and Gentiles (see 3:20; 5:12–21; 7:7; 8:3). If so, Paul is eliminating

18. Schreiner writes, "It is important to note as well that Paul does not contrast 'faith and works' but 'God's call and works'" (*Romans*, 500).

19. See discussion about "works" in Bird, *Saving Righteousness*, 89–94. Helpful also is Abasciano (*Romans 9.10–18*, 226): "The traditional perspective that Paul's 'works' language can refer to any meritorious human effort or deed receives some support from our exegesis of Rom 9.12. But the New Perspective also receives support as correctly identifying Paul's specific emphasis, particularly as we observed that the concepts of total Law-keeping and Jewish identity are inextricably linked and that Paul construed the divine purpose in these matters to be set on the blessing of the world facilitated by opening up salvation to the Gentiles."

the prospect that a potential remnant of Jews and their Gentile clientele might somehow follow the Torah with sufficient precision and intensity to establish their own "righteousness" (9:31–33; 10:3) and avoid a verdict of "disobedience" that had come upon all other Jews (11:32). Only the unmerited favor of grace will create, redeem, and renew a people worthy of God.

Paul then quotes from Genesis 25:23, " 'The older will serve the younger' "; this was the divine word spoken to Rebekah concerning her yet unborn twins, reversing the natural assumptions of birthrights going to the firstborn and proving that God's favor goes to unexpected recipients.[20] This is supported with an additional quotation from Malachi 1:2–3 with "Jacob I loved, but Esau I hated." The language of "love" and "hate" is probably a Semitic idiom for chosen status than an emotional expression.[21] More to the point, the context of Malachi is that the kingdom of Edom (i.e., Esau's descendants) has suffered devastation, and their efforts to rebuild will be thwarted. In contrast, the kingdom of Israel (i.e., Jacob's descendants) has failed to show gratitude to God, evidenced by their substandard sacrifices, but will still experience the blessings of restoration. In other words, God certainly loves "Jacob" over "Esau" even though "Jacob" is far from deserving of it.[22]

In sum, Paul has been telling the story of Abraham, Isaac, and Jacob with a view to establishing an important premise: God always intended that only some of Abraham's progeny would carry his saving purposes forward. That is the view of election that "stands" or "remains." It had nothing to do with merits, but only with the divine purpose. On the one hand, anyone familiar with the Torah would find that unobjectionable; after all, God chose Isaac not Ishmael, God chose Jacob not Esau. There was a holy line reaching from Abraham to Israel. On the other hand, it is the application that Paul draws from this principle that would have aroused indignation.[23] Paul was not merely suggesting that the promises bypass some of Abraham's descendants, but that physical descent does not seem to matter at all.

Even worse, the precepts of the Torah, even if followed with the utmost scruples, do not merit salvation for anyone. The identity of Israel was never determined by lineage or law, but exclusively decided by God's effectual call

20. Some Jewish (e.g., Philo, *Alleg. Interp.* 3.88; *Jub.* 35.13) and Christian (e.g., John Chrysostom, *Hom. Rom.* 16; Bray, *Ambrosiaster*, 75) commentators often attributed God's choice in Genesis 25:2 or Romans 9:10–13 to God's foreknowledge. Dunn (*Romans*, 2:543), following K. Schelkle, says: "The early Greek and Latin commentators who argued that election is based on God's foreknowledge of good works completely turn Paul's argument on its head."

21. Cf. e.g., Dunn, *Romans*, 2:544–45; Fitzmyer, *Romans*, 563; Keck, *Romans*, 232.

22. Ironically, this is the opposite of what is said about Jacob and Esau in Pseudo-Philo, where the author states, "And God loved Jacob but he hated Esau because of his deeds" (Ps-Philo, *Biblical Antiquities*, 32.6).

23. Wright, "Romans," 10:635.

and mercy. Barclay observes the shocking nature of Paul's claim: "Paul has directly or indirectly ruled out numerous possible qualifying criteria for divine selection: birth (natural rights of descent), status (comparative 'greatness'), and action ('works'), all forms of superiority humanly ascribed or achieved.... Thus the only principle that Paul will identify as operative in Israel's history is the principle of call/election, which operates by mercy alone."[24] The upshot is that when it comes to the divine promises, as N. T. Wright puts it, "what counts is grace, not race."[25]

### God's Choice is not Unrighteous (9:14–18)

With the words "What then shall we say? Is God unjust?" (v. 14), Paul anticipates a counterargument from an imaginary interlocutor as to whether his preceding remarks mean that God is unrighteous. The presumption of the opponent seems to be that if God does not save all of Israel, then God is not righteous. The objection harks back to 3:3–5 and the insinuation that God's impartiality nullifies God's faithfulness and righteousness. Paul emphatically denies such a possibility: "Not at all!" (again, *mē genoito*, just like 3:4). For the record, he believes that God has been faithful to Israel in the handing over of the Messiah to death and raising him back up to life in order to bring forth justification, reconciliation, and eternal life as argued in 3:21–5:11. Paul backs up the denial of God's unrighteousness with a quotation from Exodus 33:19: "For he says to Moses: 'I will have mercy on whom I have mercy, and I will have compassion on whom I have compassion' " (v. 15). This quotation comes from the scene where Moses asked the Lord to show him his glory and the Lord responded by passing by Moses as he was tucked away in the cleft of a rock face. The point of the quotation is God's freedom to bestow his mercy on whomever he so chooses, and this is the only determinative cause of God's people continuing to carry his promises forward.

However, context is important! Prosaic as it might sound, the important thing about Exodus 33 is that it follows right after Exodus 32! Recall that Exodus 32 narrated the golden calf incident, and it was after that incident in Exodus 33 that God revealed himself to Moses as the God who shows mercy. So do not imagine that Paul is talking about all of humanity who are all equally deserving of God's mercy, yet God willy-nilly only wishes to give it to a few. Rather, on closer inspection, Paul is addressing an Israel known for its covenant rebellion and pagan-like idolatry. Whereas God could have been

---

24. John M. G. Barclay, "Unnerving Grace: Approaching Romans 9–11 from The Wisdom of Solomon," in *Between Gospel and Election: Explorations in the Interpretation of Romans 9–11* (ed. F. Wilk and J. Wagner; WUNT 257; Tübingen: Mohr Siebeck, 2010), 106–7.

25. Wright, *Climax of the Covenant*, 238.

just and judged them all, he has opted to be merciful instead. The currency that Paul gets from this is to imply that Israel, when left to its own devices, becomes unfaithful and apostate, just as they were in the golden calf incident in Exodus 32, needing Moses to ask for himself to be blotted out of God's book so Israel would be spared.[26] It is but for the mercy of God that any person in Israel is able to endure.

Hence Paul's explanation: "It does not, therefore, depend on human desire or effort, but on God's mercy" (v. 16).[27] This shows that Israel's covenant relationship with God has nothing to do with whether Israel intends to do what God wants or whether Israel intends to run on the right track. God opted to stay with Israel even after the golden calf incident. In the end, as far as Israel is concerned, divine justice is primarily a matter of mercy.[28]

A further quotation from Exodus 9:16 reiterates the same idea, albeit in a negative sense, with God's hardening of Pharaoh's heart: "For Scripture says to Pharaoh: 'I raised you up for this very purpose, that I might display my power in you and that my name might be proclaimed in all the earth'" (v. 17). The flip side of election is rejection, and Paul uses Scripture to shed light on the dark side of the moon in God's electing purposes.[29] Drawing on an earlier part of the exodus narrative, we learn that God could have wiped out Pharaoh in the same way that he could have wiped out Israel in the wilderness. Instead God raised him up and appointed him to infamy by letting his defiance bellow out, so that he would be made the means by which God's name is announced to all the earth. Lest the "hardening" of Pharaoh's heart be misunderstood, it is vital to remember that Pharaoh was not a neutral figure forcibly cast in the role of a villain.[30] Pharaoh was an arrogant tyrant who chose to be deliberately cruel to God's people by abusing the Hebrews under harsh slavery (Exod 1:8–22).

As to precisely "how" Pharaoh was hardened is not clear, but it is probably analogous to the "handing over" of Gentiles to their wickedness in Romans 1:18–32. God surrenders the wicked to their own depravity so that their rebellion increases. The net effect is that such persons "store up wrath for themselves" (2:5). Importantly, the reason for God's hardening of Pharaoh was not just so God could magnify his power, but that his fame might spread

26. Wagner, *Heralds of the Good News*, 52–53.

27. Contrasted with *Pss. Sol.* 9.4–5; Sir 15.15; *4 Ezra* 8.56–61; *m. 'Abot* 3.7, which focus on the sufficiency of the human will to obey the Torah.

28. Jewett, *Romans*, 581.

29. Dunn, *Romans*, 2:561.

30. On the "hardening" of Pharaoh's heart, see Cranfield, *Romans*, 2:488–89; Morris, *Romans*, 361–62; Moo, *Romans*, 596–600.

to other nations apart from the Israelites.[31] As Stowers puts it: "Paul probably suggests here that without the miracle of the Exodus and the establishment of the land of Israel, the other nations of the earth would not have heard the good news."[32] In the end, those who think they are taking a stand against God or against God's people are in fact unwittingly conscripted to be objects that display his might to the world.

From this Paul draws the conclusion: "Therefore God has mercy on whom he wants to have mercy, and he hardens whom he wants to harden" (v. 18). Paul denies that God is capricious or that he has the right to treat human subjects like a bauble to be used and then thrown away. If we place this passage in the wider context of 9:6–10:21, we see that the take-home point is that God's plan for Israel is deliverance, despite all that they faced, despite pagan kings, and even despite their own rebellion. God's purposes hold fast. Emphasized as well is that the single force that determines the future of Israel is not the whim of emperors, nor even the strength of Israel's own faith, but the mercy of God.

### God's Choice Is Based on Sovereignty (9:19–21)

The counterobjection is that Paul makes God look utterly random in his mercy with no rhyme or reason to whom he gives it. The imaginary interlocutor digs his heals in by complaining that if God decided whom he will be merciful to and whom he will harden without recourse to foreknowledge of deservedness, then it is nonsense for God to make humans culpable for their choices.[33] Anticipating this, Paul has his imaginary interlocutor respond: "One of you will say to me: 'Then why does God still blame us? For who is able to resist his will?' " (v. 19).

Paul answers with a highly charged retort drawing from Isaiah 29:16 and probably Isaiah 45:9 (see Jer 18:6–10; Wis 15:1–7): "But who are you, a human being, to talk back to God? 'Shall what is formed say to the one who formed it, "Why did you make me like this?"' Does not the potter have the right to make out of the same lump of clay some pottery for special purposes and some for common use?" (vv. 20–21). Through these citations Paul stresses divine freedom and the incongruity of humans trying to impugn God's wisdom. In the case of Isaiah 29, it describes God's right to judge Jerusalem for its wickedness, mocking the idea that David's city can reverse the covenant relationship and make God beholden to their will, which would be like clay making demands of the potter. In Isaiah 45, the language takes place

31. B. J. Oropeza, "Paul's Theodicy: Intertextual Thoughts on God's Justice and Faithfulness to Israel in Romans 9–11," *NTS* 53 (2007): 64–65.

32. Stowers, *Rereading Romans*, 300.

33. Schreiner, *Romans*, 515.

in the context of God's selection of Cyrus to be his agent for the restoration of the exiles, and Israel has no right to complain against their maker for raising up a Gentile to achieve his purposes.[34]

In the end, God has decided to create from one "lump of clay," that is, from "Israel," one group for special purposes like a wine decanter (i.e., a remnant of Christ-believing Jews) and another group selected for lesser ends like a chamber pot (i.e., the remainder of ethnic Jews). The choice is rooted in divine purposes and in the freedom of the divine prerogative. Therefore, the clay has no right of reply to the potter for the potter's purposes are paramount. Eugene Peterson's paraphrase is apt: "If God needs one style of pottery especially designed to show his angry displeasure and another style carefully crafted to show his glorious goodness, isn't that all right?" (MSG).

The imagery of God as potter and humans as clay has annoyed quite a few commentators who think that Paul has fallen off his rocking horse in making such a comparison.[35] To that I say, obviously analogies are just that, analogies, anecdotal images that serve to explain one particular point, but not everything. It would be irresponsible to use this analogy of the potter and the clay to account for the totality of a divine view of humanity. To haggle over that is to entirely miss the point of Paul's allusions to the potter and clay imagery from Isaiah. That point is to declare that Israel, who sits in the dock, has no right to tell God that he is not permitted to judge them, nor to dictate to God whom he will or will not include in his saving righteousness.

### Vessels of Wrath and Mercy (9:22–23)

Paul next attempts to blunt any lingering concern that God arbitrarily consigns some to salvation and others to perdition. While God's choice remains mysterious, his dealings with Israel have always been marked by patience. He adds: "What if God, although choosing to show his wrath and make his power known, bore with great patience the objects of his wrath — prepared for destruction?" (v. 22). To begin with, a problem with the text is that Paul's syntax is incomplete as he begins an "if" clause (protasis) but does not follow it up with a "then" clause (apodosis); this forces readers to complete his train

34. Cf. Oropeza ("Theodicy," 69): "The questioning of the clay to the potter is associated with Israel's questioning Yahweh's plan to use a Gentile as Israel's liberator. The idea that a Gentile would be included in Israel's anticipated redemption and that God would be acknowledged among Israel's enemies may have been interpreted as a blow to Israel's pride."

35. Cf. Dodd (*Romans*, 159) on the potter/clay imagery: "It is a well-worn illustration. But the trouble is that a man is not a pot.... It is the weakest point in the whole epistle." J. C. O'Neill (*Paul's Letter to the Romans* [Harmondsworth: Penguin, 1975], 158) labels this part of Paul's argument "a thoroughly immoral doctrine." Johnson (*Romans*, 163–64) is a bit better as he is thankful that "Paul does not follow through on the merciless determinism of his primary analogue."

of thought for themselves. Specifically, we are forced to reckon with the fact that the scope of salvation might be broader or narrower than we think. In addition, commentators also differ on whether the participle *thelōn* (choosing/wishing/willing/desiring) is causal (i.e., "because God chose"), meaning that God chose some for destruction *because* he wanted to demonstrate his wrath and power, but he bore them with patience anyway (KJV, RSV, NRSV, ESV). Or perhaps the participle *thelōn* is concessive (i.e., "although God chose"), meaning that despite the fact that God intended to show his wrath and power, he nonetheless decided to bear them with patience (see NJB, NASB, NIV). Like others, I favor the concessive sense, envisaging God as willing to hold Israel to account, to judge all the earth, even with a powerful wrath; yet his patience provided a stay of proceedings for his mercy to win over all rebels in the meantime.[36]

Paul asserts in the form of a further question that even God's purposes in judgment serve to benefit a particular class of people: "What if he did this to make the riches of his glory known to the objects of his mercy, whom he prepared in advance for glory?" (v. 23). The verse actually starts with a purpose clause "in order that" (*hina*), which clarifies the purpose of his patient forbearance, namely, to make known the riches of his glory to the objects of his grace. Some have, by their own impenitence or by a divine handing-over, been prepared for destruction, yet God withholds his final judgment against them, leaving them with time for contrition (v. 22); and it is in this manner that the riches of his glory are made known for those objects prepared for mercy (v. 23). In context, the point is that God's choosing or hardening ultimately has the end result of showing mercy; in its initial stage this mercy is particular (9:23), but in its ultimate stage it is potentially universal (11:32).

So God's dealings with Israel, bound up with all the promises of curses and blessings, have led to a divide within Israel among those heading to destruction (in line with Ishmael, Esau, Pharaoh) and those headed for mercy (in line with Isaac, Jacob, Moses). None of this should be new, since Paul has already said that Israel stands condemned by the Torah (see Rom 3:20; cf. 11:28), but that is not the end of story as God has sent the Messiah to rescue Israel and the whole world (see 3:21–4:25). Paul will bring us back from the precipice of the cliff that God has utterly washed his hands of Israel by what he says about ethnic Israel's reconciliation later (Romans 11). In which case, the theodicy problem is solved, not by God refusing to punish Israel with judgment, but by God telescoping Israel's judgment into the flesh of his Son (8:3), and in

36. A view that goes back as far as Origen (Burns, *Romans*, 236).

the aftermath creating an "object of mercy" who partakes of his glory (9:23), so that "all Israel" will be saved (11:26).

### A New People: Jews and Gentiles (9:24–29)

The switch from v. 23 to v. 24 is seamless, and yet there is a discernible change in direction as Paul mounts an intertextual argument to demonstrate the identity of the "objects of mercy," the "us," as consisting of Christ-believing Gentiles and Jews (v. 24). God's choice of Israel and the preservation of a remnant to be objects of his mercy and patience always had in mind a wider purpose to show mercy to Jews and Gentiles alike. God is not replacing Israel with the church. Instead, God is preserving a remnant within Israel and then expanding it to include Gentiles as well.

Before we continue, let's remember that Paul is not writing this to people who have John Calvin's *Institutes* in one hand and a copy of Jacob Arminius's *Works* in the other hand and are a bit confused as to which author Paul's theology supports when it comes to individual predestination. Instead, imagine some Gentiles, familiar in varying degrees with the prophets, listening to Paul talking about unbelieving Israel in terms reminiscent of preexilic Israel, Israel who possessed a plethora of covenantal privileges, yet despite experiencing the exodus, were persistent in idolatry, persecuted the prophets, trusted in pagan powers to deliver them, and tragically reached the point of divine judgment, culminating in exile, with God promising to save only a remnant. Paul taps into that story but makes the provocative point that God's remnant includes Christ-believing Jews and Gentiles! The shock is with a mere pronoun: "us." The "us" of 9:24 designates the united body of Jewish and Gentile believers in Jesus as the "objects of mercy" (9:23), "children of the promise," and "Abraham's offspring" (9:8), who are identical to the "us" taken into God's unfailing and unbreakable love in the Messiah (8:31–39).

The citations from Hosea 2:23 and 1:10 in vv. 25–26 refer to restoration following judgment. In Hosea, God said he would cast off Israel for her unfaithfulness, but then takes her back to the wilderness for a new betrothal in a new covenant for a new people. Paul's reasoning is that Gentiles, as covenant outsiders, are the best example one can get of "not my people," and they become "my people" by answering the call of the gospel to believe in God and the Messiah.[37] That is not a forced interpretation since the Scriptures are remarkably consistent that Israel's postexilic restoration would involve the Gentiles streaming to Zion with the returning remnant to worship God (see

37. Paul might be thinking that the future tense of *kalesō* ("I will call") is prophetic for the call of the Gentiles in the last days.

Isa 2:2–4; Amos 9:11–12; Mic 4:1–4; Zech 8:21–23).[38] God's saving righteousness expressed in Messiah Jesus brings covenant renewal, not only for Israel, but also for the Gentiles. These are the ones who are properly God's "children" (see Rom 8:16–17, 19; 9:7–8).

Two further quotations from Isaiah 10:22–23 and 1:9 come in vv. 27–29, returning the focus to Israel. The common focus in the quotations is that Israel faces judgment for her sins and will go into exile, but a remnant will survive the day. According to Isaiah 10:22–23, even the Abrahamic promise of descendants as numerous as the sand (Gen 13:16; 28:14; 32:12) becomes limited to the remnant who are delivered from the Assyrian onslaught (vv. 27–28). And in Isaiah 1:9 we are reminded that if God had not spared this remnant, Israel would have been left desolate like Sodom and Gomorrah, suffering a fate no worse than theirs (v. 29). This "remnant" will be revisited by Paul later when he refers to Israel's future (see 11:1–5). What to take away for now is that the remnant is an important element as it shows that judgment has not overtaken Israel and there is an embryonic hope for the future of the rest of Israel.[39]

As should be clear by now, Paul surveys Israel in the past to clarify how God's electing purposes were always fastened to an Israel-within-Israel (i.e., promissory Israel), who are manifested in the present as a remnant of Jewish Christians together with their Gentile Christian companions, who together comprise the chosen children of the promises. God has not chosen the rest of ethnic Israel for this, because his promises are neither merited nor coterminous with all of Abraham's physical descendants. Along the way, Paul draws in various citations and allusions to Israel's Scriptures, including the stories of the patriarchs, the exodus, and the exile, to show that God's long-awaited deliverance would lead to a renewed Israel and the inclusion of Gentiles centered on God's cross-bearing and death-defeating Messiah.

## LIVE the Story

I do not want to complain, but Romans 9:6–29 has got to be the hardest part of Romans for a humble commentator to try think up pastoral illustrations and practical applications that can be linked to the big story line of the Bible. After Texas-style barbequing my brain, I consulted several application commentaries and was grievously disappointed to find only terse remarks

38. A topic near and dear to my heart as I wrote my Ph.D thesis on it, see Bird, *Jesus and the Origins of the Gentile Mission*, 26–38.

39. Cf. Mark W. Elliott, "Remnant," in *NDBT* (ed. B. Rosner and T. D. Alexander; Downers Grove, IL: InterVarsity, 2000), 723–26.

about the doctrine of divine predestination. Even Karl Barth's theological interpretation of Romans 9 yields only a labored and occasionally tortured (re-)interpretation of the text as pitting God against religious man with Israel, cruelly cast as a cryptic analogue for the religious man.[40]

I read over the sermons of several celebrated preachers and, to be honest, there wasn't a lot out there that I found particularly helpful. What word of exhortation will any good preacher have for his or her congregation after reflecting on God's election of promissory Israel over against ethnic Israel? Can anything sensible and stirring be offered up to feed the flock without (1) lurching into predictable debates over Calvinism and Arminianism; and without (2) uttering things about Israel that are distasteful and insensitive in a post-Holocaust context? What's a responsible preacher to do with this text? I'm going to go out on a limb and suggest that this text invites us to a new view of God, God's purposes, and God's people.

## A New View of God

One of my favorite childhood movies is the British sci-fi flick *Flash Gordon* (1980). The villain of the film is the cartoonishly evil "Ming the Merciless," the emperor of the planet Mongo, who acts true to his name. Ming is a true despot who kills and tortures without regard for life and rules by instilling fear into his subjects. For some readers of Romans 9, God might seem a little too much like Ming the Merciless. God's rejection of Ishmael, his hating of Esau, the hardening of Pharaoh's heart, the description of some people as mere pots of clay meant for common use, and peoples regarded as objects of wrath prepared for destruction might make some folks think that God treats humanity like worthless ants. It is texts like these that are usually seized on by atheists to suggest that the God of the New Testament is just as monstrous as the God of the Old Testament. Yet on closer inspection nothing could be further from the truth. Romans 9:6–29 is about the God who elects in mercy![41]

The premise is not that humans are basically good with a blank slate and then, for no apparent reason, God just randomly happens to choose to save some and consign others to perdition. In Romans, Paul has been telling the story of a world in open rebellion against him (1:18–32), a rebellion that Israel shares in (3:19; 5:20; 7:7–25), evidenced by the golden calf incident (9:15–18), disobeying God's word (10:16–21), with Israel even becoming enemies of the gospel (11:28). Yet this failure by Israel in the end proves to be part of the wisdom and will of God as God determines to work through Israel's failures to call a people to himself.

40. Barth, *Romans*, 340–61.

41. Cf. Cranfield, *Romans*, 2:448 on "mercy."

We should locate Paul's arguments against the backdrop of the story of Israel, a story about a tragic catastrophe, with Israel pruned further and further down to a remnant. Yet God allowed Israel to endure for the same reason that he allowed Pharaoh to stand, in order that his mercy would spread into the whole world. This is the story about how the Creator has worked through his chosen people's failure to bring the purposes of the covenant to their appointed goal: the Messiah revealed, the Spirit given, resulting in a multiethnic forgiven family of Abraham's children (see 9:5; 10:4).[42]

The God of Romans is immeasurably sovereign and unquestionably righteous. We observe in Romans 9 that his word does not fail and his electing purposes never falter. He cannot be undone by either the arrogance of pagan kings or by the wiliness of nomadic tribesmen. God does not hesitate to show his wrath, to flex his power, or to withhold the riches of his glory. But—and this is crucial—to that picture we must add that he is also inscrutably merciful. God's "kindness, forbearance and patience" are meant to lead people to repentance (Rom 2:4), he "justifies the ungodly" (4:4), while people were "sinners" and "enemies" Christ died to reconcile them (5:8–10), God offers the gift of eternal life in Messiah Jesus (6:23), he rescues the most wretched of persons from the body of death (7:25), and God did not spare his own Son but set him forth as a sin offering (8:3, 32). If we focus on Romans 9–11, God showed mercy to the covenant people after the golden calf incident (9:15), and he has prepared "objects of wrath" who may yet become "objects of mercy" because of his forbearance (9:22–23; 11:30–31). In fact, Paul says in the climax of this section that "God has bound everyone over to disobedience so that he may have mercy on them all" (11:32). If that is true, then "mercy" should be held up as the lens through which we view God's eternal purposes as they are worked out in redemptive history. John Barclay puts it well:

> The purposes of God are reducible to his will, a will that initially appears equally set to harden or to save, but turns out on closer inspection, and in the end, to harden only in order to save, to hate only in order to love, and to consign all to disobedience only in order to have mercy on all. What has twisted Paul's theology into this strange shape is his understanding of a "gift" that has redefined the meanings of *charis* [grace] and *eleos* [mercy] and defies explanation or rationale. That gift is the Christ-event which reconciled the world "while we were enemies" (Rom 5:6–10) and "justified the ungodly" (4:4–6).[43]

42. Cf. Wright, "Romans," 10:640, 642.

43. John Barclay, "Unnerving Grace: Approaching Romans 9–11 from The Wisdom of Solomon," in *Between Gospel and Election: Explorations in the Interpretation of Romans 9–11* (ed. F. Wilk and J. Wagner; WUNT 257; Tübingen: Mohr Siebeck, 2010), 109.

No wonder, then, that Paul can summarize God's saving work in Romans 1–11 as "mercies" (Rom 12:1) and look for the day when the Gentiles will praise God because of his mercy (15:9). If we understand God's eternal election in light of his particular mercy, we are confronted with a God who wills and works to be merciful because of his very nature. God is not moved or manipulated into being merciful; he acts mercifully because he truly is a merciful God. What is more, God wants his mercy declared to all the earth (9:17) because God has determined to manifest his mercy to those who have faith in Messiah Jesus (11:32).

I submit that this has to change the way we think about God. He is absolutely sovereign but is also unimaginably merciful. Martin Luther struggled in his preconversion days to find a merciful God. In the pages of Romans he found him, or we could say, was found by him! Romans presents us with a God of mercy, which is why salvation can be summed up as the "mercies of God" in 12:1.

My favorite story of mercy is the one about Jean Valjean and the bishop in *Les Misérables*. The homeless and angry Valjean seeks lodgings with a bishop, who kindly feeds him and houses him for a night. Yet in the morning, Valjean rises early, steals the valuable silver, and flees. When Valjean is caught by the police, they take him to the bishop to return the silver and to hear the bishop's testimony against him. However, the bishop corroborates Valjean's story that the bishop gave the silver to him, and the bishop hands over even more silver to him saying that he forgot to take the best with him. Valjean is released and able to go free, though he is forever changed by the encounter.

What is so striking about the story is that it is the opposite of what most of us would do to a criminal. If someone robbed my house, I would probably want to punish him or her severely, even physically, to make the person pay for their crime against me. When it comes to crime, our natural inclination is toward punishment and retribution. However, mercy is what happens when someone dishes out exactly the opposite of what someone duly deserves. Mercy is never earned; it is simply given at the good pleasure of the giver. The God revealed in Jesus Christ is a God of mercy.

### A New View of God's Purposes

That might all sound well and good, but others will retort that the language about God's choosing and rejecting is like trying to swallow a pillow. The whole predestination thing just sounds so mechanical and deterministic and is just a major turn-off for many folks. When it comes to those who are resistant to what I would consider a biblical doctrine of election, part of me would like to turn to them and quote Acts 13:48 and Ephesians 1:3–14, and then say,

"There you are, plain and simple, God choses people to salvation." I do not want to offer an apology for a doctrine of election, but I do want to explain the proper way to configure the doctrine and how best to appreciate it.

The primary thing to remember about election and predestination is that its overarching relevance is pastoral. Election gives believers a sense of assurance that God's grace has found them and will never leave them. Election means that if God has saved someone, this is what he always purposed to do, and that purpose will never fail. Election means that our salvation is anchored safely in divine initiative and will come to fruition because of divine security. If God has determined to save, salvation will happen, and neither hell nor high-water is going to prevent it.[44]

The doctrine of election should not be developed protologically (i.e., by speculating about God's decrees before the fall), but eschatologically (i.e., by examining God's purposes worked out in the eternal future). It is only in light of the consummation of all things that God's electing purposes in all their fullness can be properly understood. As a consequence, whatever we say about election will always be provisional. Even wrestling with things like free will and persevering faith, complicated as they are, can only be grasped by looking forward to what God intends to do beyond history. How we understand the tripartite tension between God's predestination of the elect, God's universal call to all humanity, and the realities of judgment for those persisting in unbelief will only be resolved in light of eternity.

What we can say with more certainty from looking at the gospel is that God's determination to judge is matched by God's determination to deliver, with Christ as the singular factor shifting people from "objects of wrath" to "objects of mercy." Apparently Billy Graham explains election as saying that at the entrance to the gates of heaven is a sign saying, "Come, whosoever will believe," but then as you walk through the gates on the inside is a sign saying, "Chosen before the foundation of the world." A little quaint, I know; it doesn't solve all major debates as to why some come and others do not, but its simplicity is the key to its poignancy. In light of eternity we will know who the elect are, their salvation will only ever be attributable to God's mercy and grace, and we might be surprised as to exactly whom his electing purposes intended.

This big picture of a God who is sovereign in salvation can completely reshape one's view of theology, life, and ministry. John Piper, while he was a seminary professor, embarked on a lengthy study of Romans 9, and it left a lasting impression on him. Piper writes:

44. Cf. Talbert, *Romans*, 234, and Dunn, *Romans*, 2:545–46.

> I was on sabbatical from teaching at Bethel College. My one aim on this leave was to study Romans 9 and write a book on it that would settle, in my own mind, the meaning of these verses. After six years of teaching and finding many students in every class ready to discount my interpretation of this chapter for one reason or another, I decided I had to give eight months to it. The upshot of that sabbatical was the book, *The Justification of God.* I tried to answer every important exegetical objection to God's absolute sovereignty in Romans 9. But the result of that sabbatical was utterly unexpected — at least by me. My aim was to analyze God's words so closely and construe them so carefully that I could write a book that would be compelling and stand the test of time. What I did not expect was that six months into this analysis of Romans 9 God himself would speak to me so powerfully that I resigned my job at Bethel and made myself available to the Minnesota Baptist Conference if there were a church who would have me as a pastor. In essence it happened like this: I was 34 years old. I had two children and a third on the way. As I studied Romans 9 day after day, I began to see a God so majestic and so free and so absolutely sovereign that my analysis merged into worship and the Lord said, in effect, "I will not simply be analyzed, I will be adored. I will not simply be pondered, I will be proclaimed. My sovereignty is not simply to be scrutinized, it is to be heralded. It is not grist for the mill of controversy, it is gospel for sinners who know that their only hope is the sovereign triumph of God's grace over their rebellious will." This is when Bethlehem contacted me near the end of 1979. And I do not hesitate to say that because of Romans 9 I left teaching and became a pastor. The God of Romans 9 has been the Rock-solid foundation of all I have said and all I have done in the last 22 years.[45]

If you lose yourself in the text of Romans 9, you might find yourself driven to doing amazing and even risky things for the sake of the glory of the "only wise God [to whom] be glory forever through Jesus Christ!" (16:27).

Bear in mind that Romans is a theocentric letter about God's renewal of his creation and his faithfulness to the covenant in the gospel of Jesus Christ. Romans forces one to look at the big story, develop a big theology, so that we can grasp just how big God is. If you want to have a big ministry, if you want to live big for God, you have to have a big picture of God. That bigness begins by getting your head around the depth and breadth of God's person as Paul

45. John Piper, "The Absolute Sovereignty of God: What Is Romans Nine About?" Preached 03 Nov 2002. *Desiring God*: www.desiringgod.org/sermons/the-absolute-sovereignty-of-god-what-is-romans-nine-about.

tells us about him in Romans. If you wrestle with a big God, you will begin to develop big faith muscles. That is the kind of faith training that our churches need. Nobody needs nugget-size bits of advice from a puny God who wouldn't scare a fly, or lifestyle tips from a God who looks like a cheap ripoff from a TV therapist. What we should give people, the best thing we can give people, is a big God who leaves them in awe of his character and his grace.

Preaching through Romans should be like helping people look at a distant planet for the first time through a powerful telescope. Just as a telescope makes something millions of miles away visible, so too preaching through Romans should make God's power, majesty, might, and mercy become visibly captivating to the audience. Our congregations and fellowships need to have their cheesey assumptions about God blown away and their domesticated images for God transformed by a fresh encounter with the God revealed in Paul's letter to the Romans. So we need to introduce people to God's wrath, God's impartiality, God's faithfulness, God's justice, God's wisdom, God's love, God's own Son, and God's Spirit in ways that leave them astounded by grace and abounding in joy.

The things about God that Paul teaches in Romans—his nature, character, and work—need to connect with people and open their eyes to a whole new dimension of the God-centred reality in which we live. People should have that sense of amazement like a deaf man or woman hearing their own voice for the first time. Do not let your congregation or Bible study fellowship listen to you talk about Romans and reply, "Wow, isn't Paul an amazing apostle!" or "Man, you really are a good preacher, you got good theology, and you know your Greek." Those things aren't bad, but they are missing the point. You need to make sure that people go away from hearing Romans believing that they have met the God who is totally unlike anything they have seen or heard before. They have met a God who is truly worthy of their worship, thanksgiving, faith, and devotion.

### A New View of God's People

My wife likes watching a TV show called *Who Do You Think You Are?* In this program viewers get to watch a celebrity attempt to trace their family ancestry as far back as they can, noting the heroes and villains who inhabit their lineage, and learn about themselves in the process. It can be highly entertaining, shocking, and even quite moving. I want to suggest that Romans 9 is much like *Who Do You Think You Are?* for Christians. In reading over the text, Christians are forced to look at the lineage of the family of faith from whom they came. It is of paramount importance that the history of Israel is treated as the history of church (see also 1 Cor 10:1–12). The story of the Old Testament is about a gradual narrowing down of "Israel" until it reaches the postexilic remnant, while the story of the New Testament is about the broadening of "Israel" to include Jews, Samaritans, Greeks, Romans, Scythians, and barbarians.

The Christian community is by nature a racially and ethnically inclusive community (see Rom 1:16; 3:29; 4:11–16; 9:24–29; 10:11–13). While God's electing purposes were cocooned around Israel, they were so only until the Messiah came, and in the chosen Son is a chosen people, drawn from every tribe, tongue, and nation, who are made partakers of God's glorious grace. The reason why on any given Sunday you can walk into a church with people as diverse as African Americans, native Americans, Asians, Latinos, Europeans, and even Australians is because of what Paul talks about in 9:24–29. God has called a people who were not his people. God has saved a remnant, even though all deserved judgment. The result is that the "children of the living God" includes both Jews and Gentiles. Who should the church think they are? Well, a scan over Romans 8–9 shows that they are Abraham's multiethnic offspring, united in the Messiah, bonded by the Spirit, bestowed with the rights of children and heirs, and brought together to work for the kingdom and to worship the Lord in peace and joy. The task for us, wherever it is possible, is to deliberately plant and cultivate the sorts of multiethnic churches that look like the new creation people of Paul's letter to the Romans.

CHAPTER 19

# Romans 9:30 – 10:21

## LISTEN to the Story

[30]What then shall we say? That the Gentiles, who did not pursue
righteousness, have obtained it, a righteousness that is by faith; [31]but the
people of Israel, who pursued the law as the way of righteousness, have
not attained their goal. [32]Why not? Because they pursued it not by faith
but as if it were by works. They stumbled over the stumbling stone. [33]As it
is written:

"See, I lay in Zion a stone that causes people to stumble
and a rock that makes them fall,
and the one who believes in him will never be put to shame."

[1]Brothers and sisters, my heart's desire and prayer to God for the
Israelites is that they may be saved. [2]For I can testify about them that they
are zealous for God, but their zeal is not based on knowledge. [3]Since they
did not know the righteousness of God and sought to establish their own,
they did not submit to God's righteousness. [4]Christ is the culmination of
the law so that there may be righteousness for everyone who believes.

[5]Moses writes this about the righteousness that is by the law: "The
person who does these things will live by them." [6]But the righteousness
that is by faith says: "Do not say in your heart, 'Who will ascend into
heaven?' " (that is, to bring Christ down) [7]"or 'Who will descend into
the deep?' " (that is, to bring Christ up from the dead). [8]But what does it
say? "The word is near you; it is in your mouth and in your heart," that
is, the message concerning faith that we proclaim: [9]If you declare with
your mouth, "Jesus is Lord," and believe in your heart that God raised
him from the dead, you will be saved. [10]For it is with your heart that you
believe and are justified, and it is with your mouth that you profess your
faith and are saved. [11]As Scripture says, "Anyone who believes in him
will never be put to shame." [12]For there is no difference between Jew and
Gentile—the same Lord is Lord of all and richly blesses all who call on
him, [13]for, "Everyone who calls on the name of the Lord will be saved."

[14]How, then, can they call on the one they have not believed in? And how can they believe in the one of whom they have not heard? And how can they hear without someone preaching to them? [15]And how can anyone preach unless they are sent? As it is written: "How beautiful are the feet of those who bring good news!"

[16]But not all the Israelites accepted the good news. For Isaiah says, "Lord, who has believed our message?" [17]Consequently, faith comes from hearing the message, and the message is heard through the word about Christ. [18]But I ask: Did they not hear? Of course they did:

"Their voice has gone out into all the earth,
their words to the ends of the world."

[19]Again I ask: Did Israel not understand? First, Moses says,

"I will make you envious by those who are not a nation;
I will make you angry by a nation that has no understanding."

[20]And Isaiah boldly says,

"I was found by those who did not seek me;
I revealed myself to those who did not ask for me."

[21]But concerning Israel he says,

"All day long I have held out my hands
to a disobedient and obstinate people."

*Listening to the texts in the story*: Leviticus 18:5; Deuteronomy 9:4; 30:12–14; 32:21; Psalm 19:4; Isaiah 8:14; 28:16; 52:7; 53:1; 65:1–2; Joel 2:32; Nahum 1:5.

The argument in Romans 9:6–29 explained Israel's current rejection of the gospel in two ways: (1) by showing that their present state of obstinacy merely rehearses Israel's prior failures, and (2) by showing that God's elect people have always been a subset of ethnic Israel, a promissory Israel embedded within empirical Israel, but the two are not coterminus. Paul's discussion of Israel in the past has been necessary to frame his forthcoming arguments about the precise reason for Israel's failure in 9:30–10:21. The point, of course, is that Israel did not submit to the righteousness of God, but the Gentiles have. Consequently, as Johnson notes, Paul engages in what was probably the "most painful part of his argument," trying to show that God has both contracted and expanded Israel on the basis of Jesus the Messiah.[1] Accordingly, the section

1. Johnson, *Romans*, 166.

is far from excursive as it fortifies Paul's theses about Israel, Torah, Gentiles, and justification by faith through highlighting the Messiah as the "goal" of redemptive history.[2] More than that, even while emphasizing the depth of Israel's intransigence through the jealousy motif in 10:19, Paul lights a candle of hope for Israel that will flicker across 11:1–32.

The point of contention in this passage is that Israel pursued a law of righteousness rather than the righteousness that is by faith. This explains why Israel has not "attained" righteousness (9:30); they did not "know" or "submit" to God's righteousness (10:3), to the point that they "stumbled" over their own Savior (9:32–33). They heard the message but did not "accept" it or "understand" it (10:16–19), and before God they now appear as "a disobedient and obstinate people" (10:21). In contrast, precisely because "righteousness" is by faith, it is available to all without "distinction" (10:12), which is why believing Gentiles have obtained salvation (9:30; 10:18–19). In the end, it is this mixed family of faith, living under Jesus' lordship, who constitutes the climax of Israel's covenantal hopes and the goal of redemptive history (10:4, 12).

Those who call on the name of the Lord will suffer no shame, they can expect a fount of blessings, and they will experience the fullness of God's salvation in the future (10:12–13). The array of Pauline themes that we find in 9:30–10:21 pertaining to gospel (10:15–16)—salvation (10:1, 9, 10, 13), the inclusive "all" (10:4, 11, 12, 13), no difference between Jew and Greek (10:12), righteousness (9:30, 21; 10:3, 4, 5, 6, 10), faith (9:32, 33; 10:4, 6, 8, 9–11, 14, 17), and Old Testament fulfillment (10:4, 5–8, 15)—means that we are dealing with a microcosm of Paul's entire theology in Romans.[3]

The argument Paul constructs is once again densely intertextual with eleven citations of the Old Testament in only twenty-five verses. Isaiah 28:16 is quoted in Romans 9:33 and 10:11 about God's rock of offense, with an emphasis that those who believe on it will not be put to shame. In what we might call the justification juxtaposition, the Isaianic rock is the reason for both Israel's stumbling and for the inclusion of Gentiles (see 9:30; 10:11–13). Furthermore, the premise of Leviticus 18:5 about life through law is set in contrast to the promise of Deuteronomy 30:12–14 concerning God's saving word drawing near through the early church's word of faith. On closer inspection, the word of the gospel is the prophetic gospel of Isaiah 52:7 (10:15)—a word that has gone out into all the earth *à la* Psalm 19:4 to include the Gentiles (10:18). This word will provoke ignorant Israel to jealousy in accord

2. Contra Moo, *Romans*, 618, and with Wright, "Romans," 10:645, though Munck (*Christ and Israel*, 90) calls it an "independent section."

3. Dunn, *Romans* 2:577; Moo, *Romans*, 618.

with Deuteronomy 32:21 (10:19). Then from Isaiah 65:1–2 Paul avers that Israel's God was embraced by Gentiles even while Israel herself has resisted the Messiah (10:20–21). All this is to say that Paul believes there are precedents in the biblical story for showing that God keeps faith with those who have faith in him.

The unfolding stage of the argument runs as follows: (1) the Gentiles have attained righteousness by faith, while Israel has not obtained it by seeking righteousness through the law (9:30–33); (2) Israel, despite her zeal, remains ignorant of the fact that her covenantal history attained its climax in the Messiah (10:1–4); (3) the condition of Leviticus 18:5 pertaining to life through law is redundant since the promise for covenantal renewal in Deuteronomy 30:12–14 comes not by law obedience but by the Messiah (10:5–8); (4) the result is that confession of Jesus as Lord is the means of righteousness for Jew and Gentile (10:9–13); and (5) the Christian mission has gone out into all the world, where it has met with a mixed response (10:14–21).

## The Justification Juxtaposition (9:30–33)

After the assertions of Romans 9:6–29, Paul poses his now stock-standard rhetorical question to introduce a controversial point (see 3:5; 4:1; 6:1; 7:7; 8:31; 9:14), "What then shall we say?" (v. 30). By asking such a question he invites his audience to adopt his own perspective on the matters raised, namely, "that the Gentiles, who did not pursue righteousness, have obtained it, a righteousness that is by faith; but the people of Israel, who pursued the law as the way of righteousness, have not attained their goal" (vv. 30–31). Paul is describing how the Gentiles, despite not "pursuing" (NIV) or not "striving" (CEB) for a right standing before God, presumably by Torah-observance, have in fact obtained it by way of faith. This description merely rehearses what Paul has emphasized at length throughout the letter, that justification is by faith and not by works of the law (see 1:16–17, 3:22; 4:1–25; 5:1).

The spikey barb in the statement is the contrast this response has with Israel, who pursued "the law as a way of righteousness." Part of the Greek is notoriously awkward here, with *nomon dikaiosynēs eis nomon* (lit., "law of righteousness unto law"). A paraphrase might be helpful here: "But Israel, pursuing a law supposedly promising them righteousness,[4] did not succeed in attaining such a law nor the righteousness they were looking for." On the one

4. The Greek *nomon dikaiosynēs* is probably a genitive of purpose along the lines of a "law leading to righteousness." See Moo, *Romans*, 625.

hand, the Torah prescribes regulations for right conduct and for a right covenant standing before God. But on the other hand, this could be accentuated to the point that covenant righteousness becomes the presumption of those who think they are adhering to the Torah rightly, whether by sacred violence (Zealots), by promoting priestly purity (Pharisees), by revisioning calendrical regulations and cultic purity (Essenes), or by continual sacrifice and temple purity (Sadducees). All of these efforts attempted to press their own claim for righteousness and look to God to vindicate it.[5]

Furthermore, Jewish authors sometimes made an explicit identification of the law as a source of "righteousness," like *Testament of Dan* 6:10, where the patriarch tells his children to "depart from all unrighteousness, and cling to the righteousness of the law of God, and your race will be saved forever." According in *2 Baruch* 67:6, the author worries that if Gentiles conquer Jerusalem, "the incense of the righteousness of the law" will be extinguished.

According to Paul, however, Israel's problem was that they tried to apprehend a righteous standing that avails before God based on their own Torah-keeping, whereas what they really need is the righteous status that God freely bestows by faith in Jesus. Hence Paul explains their failure to attain righteousness that way: "Why not? Because they pursued it not by faith but as if it were by works. They stumbled over the stumbling stone" (v. 32). At the mention "stumbling stone" Paul adds a blended quotation of Isaiah 28:16 and 8:14: "As it is written: 'See, I lay in Zion a stone that causes people to stumble and a rock that makes them fall, and the one who believes in him will never be put to shame' " (v. 33). Both of these Isaiah passages refer to salvation in the aftermath of judgment, with Israel experiencing renewal after retribution, a renewal centered on God's new work. Paul identifies Jesus with the stone that God has placed in Zion, the foundation for the future of the new people of God. The root of Israel's failure is christological; their failure to believe in their own Messiah has caused their current misstep. As such Israel's tragedy is that they have stumbled over the very source of their salvation and have taken offense at what could save them from shame.

Moo is right that 9:30–33 carries an importance out of proportion to its length.[6] That is because the juxtaposition between a justification by faith and a justification by works is sharp and deliberate. While it undoubtedly entails no less than a rejection of any kind of work-for-reward scheme of salvation (see 3:21–26; 4:4–8), it is certainly more than that too (see 3:27–31; 4:9–17). If "righteousness" is by faith, then it is not by Israel's *ethos* or *ethnos*; neither

5. On sectarian and ethnic context of trying to establish one's own righteousness, see Jewett, *Romans*, 618.

6. Moo, *Romans*, 620.

Jewish effort nor Jewish ethnicity puts someone in the right. Gentiles need to know that righteousness is not acquired by excelling in achievement in Jewish rites of religion or by sharing in Jewish social life. God saves Gentiles *as* Gentiles!

### Christ Is the Climax of the Covenant (10:1–4)

Paul's tale of two righteousnesses in 9:30–33, of faith and law, now meets with his redemptive-historical explanation in 10:1–4 as to why righteousness comes by faith. Paul begins by rehearsing his earlier heartfelt plea for his Jewish kinsfolk in 9:1–5 with the words: "Brothers and sisters, my heart's desire and prayer to God for the Israelites is that they may be saved" (v. 1). Paul reiterates his acute interest in the welfare of his fellow Israelites partly to ward off his Gentile readers from taking delight in Israel's failure, but also to offset the controversy that his subsequent remarks about Israel, law, and righteousness might well initiate. The "salvation" Paul desires for Israel is that they would be gathered into the new people that God is forming on the basis of faith in the Messiah with the abounding promise of eternal life.[7]

Paul then witnesses on behalf of Israel with the claim: "For I can testify about them that they are zealous for God, but their zeal is not based on knowledge" (10:2). Israel is "zealous" for God principally through a zeal for God's law, its correct interpretation, its instruction, its preservation under pagan domination, and even its promulgation to the entire world. Paul's former zeal for the law in his pre-Christian state was manifested in his willingness to inflict violence on those suspected of endangering the purity of the covenant people (see Acts 22:3; Gal 1:4; Phil 3:6; in the tradition of Num 24:11–13; 2 Sam 21:2; 1 Macc 2:24–27, 50, 54, 58; 2 Macc 4:2; 14:38; Sir 45:23–24; Josephus, *Ant.* 12.271). Paul spotlights Israel's zeal to showcase their devotion to God much in the same way the Jewish seer who wrote 2 Esdras complained that Israel's zeal should excuse them from judgment: "But we your people, whom you have called your firstborn, only begotten, zealous for you, and most dear, have been given into their hands" (2 Esd 6:58). Nevertheless, despite their zeal, Israel lacks "knowledge," knowledge in the sense of both awareness and assent to the divine saving action in Jesus the Messiah.

Paul explains why Israel is lacking in knowledge: "Since they did not know the righteousness of God and sought to establish their own, they did not submit to God's righteousness" (Rom 10:3). Paul's description of Israel's problem is curter than what the NIV ("did not know") and CEB ("did not understand") let on, saying more precisely that Israel is "ignoring" the righteousness

7. Johnson, *Romans*, 168.

of God (see NRSV, ESV, and NET). The charge that Israel has acted in ignorance about Jesus appears in apostolic preaching (Acts 3:17), and Paul claimed that ignorance was the reason for his own persecution of the church (1 Tim 1:13). Israel's ignorance has led to further problematic behavior.

First, Israel sought to establish their own righteousness[8] in the sense of trying to establish a claim for a righteousness that avails before God from their zeal for God. Israel has pursued righteousness in the wrong way, seeking righteousness by acts of Torah obedience and a righteousness that is exclusively their "own" by fact of election (see Rom 2:17; 9:32; 10:5).[9] Yet, by pursuing this line of action, Israel has demonstrated her ignorance of God's deliverance wrought in the Messiah. It shows a lack of awareness about the Torah's intrinsic limitations and an accompanying denial of Israel's own disobedience to the Torah. In addition, some in Israel denied God's impartiality toward all people and have not accepted the arc of prophetic promises that embrace the nations. In other words, they are ignorant of the entire sweep of argumentation set forth in Romans 1:16–9:33.

Second, Israel did not submit to God's righteousness. Here God's righteousness is not something imputed or even a gift. One receives a gift; one does not submit to it.[10] Here God's righteousness signifies his saving action and connotes something of God's own authority. God's righteousness, then, is the saving power of God, and it is identifiable with his own authority and might. The great misfortune is that Israel, despite her inherited privileges and notwithstanding her zeal for God, has become like the nations who "do not know God" because she did not submit to the righteousness of God in the Messiah (see Gal 4:8–9; 1 Thess 4:5; 2 Thess 1:8).

The reason why Israel is wrong to try to establish their own righteousness and wrong for not submitting to God's righteousness is then explained: "Christ is the culmination of the law so that there may be righteousness for everyone who believes" (v. 4). If you read the initial words of v. 4 in a Greek manuscript like codex Sinaiticus, the line runs:

Greek: ΤΕΛΟΣΓΑΡΝΟΜΟΥΧΣ
Transliteration: TELOS GAR NOMOU CH[RISTO]S

8. Some manuscripts include "righteousness" (*dikaiosynē*) here to supply the implied noun.

9. I see no reason to split the individual and corporate connotations of "their own" in v. 3, as both can be simultaneously true, i.e., individual Jews who perform the law with a view to maintaining or acquiring righteousness or the Jewish nation as a whole who received the law and is therefore the sole race capable of being righteous before God. Cf. Seifrid ("Romans," *CONTUOT*, 653): "Israel's own righteousness would be a particular righteousness, of course, which set it apart from the nations. Yet neither ethnic particularity nor the self-righteousness bound up with it is Paul's concern at this moment, even though both fall within the scope of his following argument."

10. Cf. Bird, *Saving Righteousness*, 16; Wright, "Romans," 10:654.

Interlinear: End for law [is] Christ
NIV: Christ is the culmination of the law

Those three little nouns—*telos, nomos, Christos*—create such a big headache for interpreters as they try to understand what Paul means when he said that "*Christ* is the *telos* of the *law.*" I call this the TNX dilemma (i.e., *telos, nomos, Christos*). Most of the debate centers on whether the word *telos* means "end" (KJV, NRSV, ESV), "goal" (CEB, NTE), "culmination" (NIV), "climax" (VOICE), or "fulfillment" (WEB).[11] Then there is the matter of how that applies to the whole discussion about the continuing role of the law in the dispensation of the new covenant. In a nutshell, the options are generally thought to be that Christ brings the law to a temporal termination whereby its authority comes to an end, or alternatively, that Christ is the one to whom the law was pointing and promising. I'm not sure these are mutually exclusive alternatives; both could be true in their own way, for something about the law ends because the law is fulfilled in Messiah.[12]

In my solution to the TNX dilemma, I suggest that the main idea is that the Messiah has brought the law to its intended goal, namely, covenant renewal (see below Rom 10:6–8 based on Deut 30:12–14). By doing so, he terminates the law as the mechanism for relating to God, so that righteousness is now available to all on the basis of faith and not on the basis of performing works of the law. In other words, Paul's remarks about the law here pertain to its eschatological redundancy in a new epoch of redemptive history.

Thus, to pursue righteousness through Torah observance is wrong because it is futile; it is like trying to spend your K-Mart gift card at a K-Mart store that has been sold and converted into a Macy's store. Note as well that Paul does not refer to human inability to do the law on account of sin as he said earlier (see 2:21–25; 3:9, 20; 4:15; 7:7–8), nor does he allude to the law's impotence to save (see 5:20; 8:3), nor does he expound on the law's innate redemptive-historical limitation, given as it was after Abraham without nullifying the Abrahamic promises (see 4:13–14). Instead, Paul proposes that the law has its climax in the revelation of the Messiah, with the result that the Messiah is the means of righteousness for everyone.

Let me add that I do not think Paul means that Christ "ends" the law in the sense that it is a bad thing that has been done away with. While Paul can

11. Cf. the more paraphrastic translations: "But Christ makes the Law no longer necessary for those who become acceptable to God by faith" (CEV); "For Christ has already accomplished the purpose for which the law was given. As a result, all who believe in him are made right with God" (NLT).

12. Cf. e.g., Barrett, *Romans*, 184; Bruce, *Romans*, 105–6; Moo, *Romans*, 641; contrasted with Fitzmyer, *Romans*, 584.

accent the discontinuities between the Torah and Christ (see 3:21; 6:14–15; 7:1–6), even so, these discontinuities are usually situated in a wider span of redemptive history that includes promise and fulfillment. More positively, the Torah is a prophetic pointer to the gospel (3:21); faith upholds the Torah (3:31), while life in the Spirit fulfills the Torah (8:4; 13:8, 10). Viewed this way, Christ is the end of the law in the sense that Christ is the climax of the Mosaic covenant by being the agent of the covenantal renewal to which the law itself pointed. The Messiah is the new "stone" for a renewed people of God, made up of believing Jews and Gentiles, who show their covenantal identity by their obedience of faith and by praising God for his mercies.

### The Law-Word of Leviticus and the Faith-Word of Deuteronomy (10:5–8)

Paul adduces further support for his claim that the law finds its "climax" in Christ by devising an intricate scriptural proof about the law's fulfillment in Christ. Paul lodges a contrast between Leviticus 18:5 and a blend of Deuteronomy 9:4/30:12–14 in order to reiterate his denial of righteousness by works (9:31–32; 10:3) combined with an affirmation of righteousness by faith (9:30; 10:4).

> Moses writes this about the righteousness that is by the law: "The person who does these things will live by them" [Lev 18:5]. But the righteousness that is by faith says: "Do not say in your heart, [Deut 9:4] 'Who will ascend into heaven?'" (that is, to bring Christ down) "or 'Who will descend into the deep?'" (that is, to bring Christ up from the dead). But what does it say? "The word is near you; it is in your mouth and in your heart," [Deut 30:12–14] that is, the message concerning faith that we proclaim (Rom 10:5–8).

To us this is an odd-looking argument, as if Paul is preying on Moses for having some kind of split personality about whether the law is legalistic or prophetic.[13] Paul's citation of Deuteronomy 30 in particular has been understood in various ways among researchers. For example: (1) Paul uses Deuteronomy 30 to make an antithetical response to pursuing a righteousness by the law since it tries to do for oneself what Christ does for us (F. Watson).[14] (2) Paul takes Deuteronomy 30 as pointing ahead to

13. Dodd (*Romans*, 166) labels Paul's interpretation of the text "purely fanciful." According to Byrne (*Romans*, 318), Paul's "exegetical procedure is forced." Johnson (*Romans*, 170) calls it a "daring maneuver." Jewett (*Romans*, 626) labels it a "historically apt depiction of the goals of some of the Jewish parties in Paul's time."

14. Watson, *Paul and the Hermeneutics of Faith*, 329–41; idem, *Paul, Judaism, and the Gentiles*, 329–30.

eschatological restoration in Jesus Christ (G. Waters).[15] (3) Paul engages in a christological rewriting of Deuteronomy 30 to indicate that God has fulfilled the conditions for restoration in Christ (D. Lincicum).[16] (4) Deuteronomy 30 is a prophetic prefiguration of God's dealings with Israel through the gospel (R. Hays).[17] (5) Paul detects in Deuteronomy 30 a redefinition of obedience by the postexilic gift of God's word about Jesus (N. T. Wright).[18] (6) Paul constructs a speech of Christ projected into the promises of Deuteronomy (M. Bates).[19] If you are confused, relax, you're not alone, but keep the coffee pot close by, put your thinking cap on, have your Bible software open; we have a lot of work to do!

First, Paul begins with "Moses writes this about the righteousness that is by the law" (v. 5a) to indicate that he is about to address the perspective of those who think that righteousness is by Torah observance (see 3:20, 28; 4:14, 16; 9:12, 31–32; 10:3). Thus Paul confronts those who would dispute 10:4 that Christ is the culmination of the law so that there is righteousness for everyone.[20]

Second, what Moses actually says is found in Leviticus 18:5, "The person who does these things will live by them" (v. 5b). In its original context, Leviticus 18:1–5 is about not living like the Egyptians and Canaanites with special reference to proscribing certain sexual relations in Lev 18:6–30. The Israelites were to obey the law, and by obeying the law they preserved life under the covenant. While evangelicals might be aghast as the prospect of God commanding obedience as a condition for life, no such distaste was shared by Jewish authors who earnestly believed that the law was actually quite doable (see Sir 15:15; *Pss. Sol.* 9.4–7; 14.2; *m. 'Abot* 3.7), and even the pre-Christian Paul himself thought so (see Phil 3:6–7). For Ben Sirach, Torah was a "law of life" in that keeping Torah was both a way of life and a way to life (see Sir 17:11; 45:5). The promise in Leviticus 18:5 about "doing these things" and receiving "life" was thought to set out the conditions for preserving temporal life under the covenant and for receiving eschatological life in the future. For

15. Guy Waters, *The End of Deuteronomy in the Epistles of Paul* (WUNT 2.226; Tübingen: Mohr Siebeck, 2006), 162–85.

16. David Lincicum, *Paul and the Early Jewish Encounter with Deuteronomy* (WUNT 2.284; Tübingen: Mohr Siebeck, 2010), 153–58, 166–67.

17. Hays, *Echoes of Scripture*, 77–82, 163–64.

18. Wright, "Romans," 10:658–64.

19. Matthew W. Bates, *The Hermeneutics of the Apostolic Proclamation: The Center of Paul's Method of Scriptural Interpretation* (Waco, TX: Baylor University Press, 2012), 225–40, 334.

20. Waters (*End of Deuteronomy*, 180) rightly identifies two mutually exclusive clusters in 9:30–10:3, which Paul builds on here: (a) righteousness associated with law, works, striving on one's own; and (b) righteousness associated with faith, not works, not striving, of God. See also Schreiner, *Romans*, 551–56.

Paul and for many Jews, Leviticus 18:5 was a summary of the entire law; it was the John 3:16 of Second Temple Judaism![21]

Third, remember also that Paul pitted Leviticus 18:5 against Habakkuk 2:4 in Galatians 3:11–12 to underscore that justification is by faith and not by works of the law.[22] In Galatians, Paul asserted that Torah observance leads one under the curse of the law, from which Christ has redeemed believers, which is why it is foolish for Gentiles to submit to the law. That said, I do not think that Paul's "problem" with Lev 18:5 is that the law requires perfect obedience; no one can obey the law perfectly, so righteousness and life do not come from the law. It is more accurate to say that Paul invokes Lev 18:5 to say that whatever it is that the law requires of people, people are unable to fulfill it. That is not because Leviticus teaches merit theology, but because of the "conditional logic of the covenant" where the conditions are unfulfilled by human effort.[23] The law, as Paul understands it through Lev 18:5, sets forth the conditions for life, but it does not provide it. So Paul's juxtaposition of Lev 18:5 and Deut 9:4/30:12–14 is probably revisiting the same point albeit in a new context and perhaps for a different end.

Fourth, there are several elements of the Deut 9:4/30:12–14 citation that should be noted.

(1) Paul identifies the speaker as "the righteousness that is by faith," thereby personifying "righteousness" as a character in the discussion (see Isa 41:2–4 similarly). I suspect that Paul regards this "righteousness by faith" (*ek pisteōs dikaiosynē*) as the voice of new covenant faith in Christ reading Deuteronomy in retrospect (much like Gal 3:23 with "before faith came," where "faith" is a metonym for Christ!).

(2) Paul splices the words of Deuteronomy 9:4 (cf. Deut 8:17), "Do not say in your heart" onto the beginning of his citation of 30:12–14 in order to underscore the gracious provision of God's saving righteousness. Deuteronomy 8–9 emphasizes that God's deliverance of the Hebrews from Egypt and their conquest over the Canaanites is not attributable to their own righteousness, but to God's faithfulness to his covenant with the patriarchs (8:18; 9:5). Paul places Deuteronomy 9:4 at the head of his subsequent citation to

---

21. Cf. esp. the study by Preston M. Sprinkle, *Law and Life: The Interpretation of Leviticus 18:5 in Early Judaism and in Paul* (WUNT 2.241; Tübingen: Mohr Siebeck, 2008); idem, *Paul and Judaism Revisited: A Study of Divine and Human Agency in Salvation* (Downers Grove, IL: InterVarsity, 2013), 153.

22. On the similarities and differences between Galatians 3:12 and Romans 10:6–8 see Waters, *End of Deuteronomy*, 181–83.

23. Lincicum, *Encounter with Deuteronomy*, 155.

censure self-praise and self-reliance as the keyhole through which we should look at Deuteronomy 30:12 – 14.[24]

(3) Deuteronomy 30 is written from the perspective of Israel's exile as a fait accompli; in other words, it is going to happen (see Deut 30:1)! Only when Israel has returned to the Lord and obeyed him with all their heart and soul will the exile come to an end (30:2 – 5). When God does that, it will be evidenced by a regathering of the dispersed peoples, abundant prosperity, agricultural fecundity, circumcised hearts, and curses for their enemies (30:6 – 9). The condition on which this renewal takes place is obeying the Lord and keeping his commands (30:10). The commands are not too onerous for the people (30:11), akin to ascending to the heights of heaven to retrieve them or else journeying across the sea to obtain them (30:12 – 13). Instead, the word of the law is in close proximity to the people and is obeyable (30:14).

The central blessing of the law is the life that God has set before the Israelites (30:15). This life is obtained by obeying the commandments and lost by disobeying them (30:16 – 18). The Israelites must then choose life and love the Lord if they are to receive blessings and avoid the curses (30:19 – 20). It is no wonder that Jewish interpreters understood Deuteronomy 30:12 – 14 to teach that the law is accessible and doable (Bar 3:29 – 30; Philo, *Posterity* 84 – 85). Paul's exposition of Deuteronomy 30:12 – 14 is akin to other Second-Temple interpretive approaches in that Paul does not engage in a straight-out interpretation of the text along the lines of paraphrasing its contents or simply summarizing its assertions. Paul seems to offer something more like a creative retelling of the text shaped by factors external to the text — in this case, the perspective of messianic faith (i.e., the "righteousness that is by faith"). The extrinsic nature of Paul's interpretation is implied by the observation that he has "righteousness" speaking "in the manner of" (*houtōs*) Deuteronomy 30:12 – 14, which is to say that "righteousness" can use 30:12 – 14 to explain what messianic faith is about, without claiming that 30:12 – 14 is itself talking explicitly about messianic faith.

For the same reason, Paul's drapes the text with glosses that "this is Christ" (*tout' estin Christon*), implying the artificial introduction of an idea not explicit in the text, but which the text helps to explain nonetheless. Before one disparages Paul's creative interpretation of Deuteronomy 30:12 – 14, it is worth remembering that Paul's construal of the text receives legitimacy from the theological claims of Deuteronomy itself. In the horizon of Deuteronomy, we find a close identification of God with the word of the law (see Deut

24. Cf. Lincicum, *Encounter with Deuteronomy*, 155; Wagner, *Heralds of the Good News*, 161 – 62.

4:7–8), so that Paul's extension of the "near word" of Deuteronomy to the "word of faith" is simply extending a trajectory already begun in Deuteronomy.[25] This is not a hermeneutical sleight of hand, but rests of the conviction that Scripture finds its *telos* in Christ, and the law genuinely witnesses to Christ (see Rom 1:2; 3:21). In other words, Paul's reading is explicitly "Christian."[26] Thus, I surmise that Paul utilizes Deuteronomy this way because he believes that its theological framework of grace *prefigures* the gospel and the text can be *reconfigured* to show how the law points to the gospel.

(4) Careful attention should be given to how Paul handles Deuteronomy 30:12–14 in terms of what he omits and what he adds to his citation, as a side-by-side comparison of Deuteronomy 30:12–14 (LXX) and Romans 10:6–8 demonstrates.

| Deuteronomy 30:12–14 (LXX) | Romans 10:6–8 |
|---|---|
| It is not in the sky saying, "**Who will go up to the sky** and get it for us? And when we hear it, we shall do it." Neither is it beyond the sea, saying, "**Who will cross to the other side of the sea** for us and get it for us? And when we hear it, we shall also do it." **The word is very near to you, in your mouth and in your heart** and in your hands, to do it. (NETS) | But the righteousness that is by faith says: "Do not say in your heart, '**Who will ascend into heaven?**'" (that is, to bring Christ down) "or '**Who will descend into the deep?**'" (that is, to bring Christ up from the dead). But what does it say? "**The word is near you; it is in your mouth and in your heart,**" that is, the message concerning faith that we proclaim. (NIV) |

To begin with, Paul omits all references to "doing" in 30:12–14 (i.e., the shaded sections in the left column), and he intersperses parentheses to suggest that "this is" really about the word of Christ's death and resurrection (i.e., the underlined sections in the right hand column). What's up with that?

On the one hand, it is tantalizingly tempting to say that Paul switches from Leviticus 18:5 to Deuteronomy 9:4/30:12–14 and makes these cosmetic changes in order to redefine "doing the law" as "believing the gospel," whereby the word that was near Israel in the law is identical to the word that

25. Lincicum, *Encounter with Deuteronomy*, 157; Jewett, *Romans*, 626.

26. Cf. Watson, *Hermeneutics of Faith*, 340; Bates, *Apostolic Proclamation*, 239. Cf. esp. Kirk (*Unlocking Romans*, 167): "By reading Deut 30:12 as a reference to Christ's birth and Deut 30:13 as a reference to Christ's resurrection from the dead, Paul has made Deuteronomy a witness to both prongs of the gospel proclamation he has articulated in [Rom] 1:3–4."

is near Israel in Christian proclamation.[27] But I must sadly demur against this reading since it scales down the contrast that Paul mounts between Leviticus 18:5 and Deuteronomy 30:12 – 14 concerning righteousness by law and righteousness by faith. Such a reading assumes that Christ as the end of the law entails redefining "righteousness of the law" as the "righteousness of faith," which seems a stretch.

It is perhaps more fitting to see Paul as arguing that the conditional promises of Leviticus 18:5 are not only unfulfilled but redundant, because the Messiah himself has fulfilled the conditions for Israel's postexilic restoration by his death and resurrection.[28] The *telos* of the law is God's salvation for his people in the Messiah rather than Israel's obedience to the law for their own deliverance.[29] Therefore, Israel should not try to obtain by obeying the law what the Messiah himself has obtained for them: end of exile and covenant renewal (i.e., "Do not say in your heart, 'The Lord has brought me here to take possession of this land because of my righteousness' "). Paul is delving into the story of Deuteronomy 30 and declaring that Israel's exile described in Deuteronomy 30:1 – 10 has ended, and the appropriate response is not law observance but messianic faith. That is because the obedience necessary for the end of exile in Deut 30:10 – 11 has taken place in the Messiah's fulfilling his vocation as the *telos* of the law.

The "doing" of Lev 18:5 and the "obedience" of Deut 30:10 – 14 has been absorbed under the mantle of the Messiah's own faithfulness and obedience (see Rom 5:19; Phil 2:8).[30] For the Messiah is truly the climax of the covenant in taking the curse of the law on himself (see Deut 30:1 – 5; Rom 8:3; Gal 3:13), ushering in covenant renewal (Deut 30:6 – 11, 15 – 16; Rom 2:25 – 29; 8:1 – 17; 12:1 – 2; 13:8 – 10) and confirming the promises of the patriarchs by forming a united people of Jewish and Gentile believers (Deut 30:4 – 5, 20; Rom 3:22; 4:16; 9:24 – 26; 10:12, 18 – 20; 15:8 – 12). We have here not so much a contrast of believing vs. doing as in Galatians 3:1 – 14, but a claim that the Messiah has done what was necessary to bring Israel into the renewal of the covenant. The gift of Torah has been replaced by the gift of Christ.[31] So what is required now is not obedience to the law, but faith in the Messiah.

---

27. Cf. Hays, *Echoes of Scripture*, 81 – 82; Wright, "Romans," 10:660; Wagner, *Heralds of the Good News*, 159 – 65.

28. Cf. Munck, *Christ and Israel*, 86 – 88; Cranfield, *Romans*, 2:521 – 25; Johnson, *Romans*, 171; Schreiner, *Romans*, 557 – 58; Keck, *Romans*, 252 – 54.

29. Kirk, *Unlocking Romans*, 170.

30. But see Dunn, *Romans*, 2:601, and Jewett, *Romans*, 624 – 25 for the view that Christ is not the one doing the law in these verses — a view that, in my mind, represents a failure to see Paul's argument here as thoroughly christological.

31. Seifird, "Romans," *CONTUOT*, 657.

This means that rather than looking to the law, Israel should look to the Messiah for deliverance and covenant renewal. As Sprinkle comments: "To continue to live as if the conditional offer is still in effect, is to embark on an arduous quest that practically nullifies the work of God in Christ."[32]

Given this line of argument we might paraphrase Romans 10:6–8 as follows:[33] Moses certainly provided the premise for Israel's pursuit of righteousness by observing the law: "The person who does these things will live by them." That sounds kosher I know, but it is not the whole story. The righteousness of faith (i.e., the view from our vantage point) replies by pointing out that Israel's exile was caused by Israel's disobedience to the law and that exile ends, not by Israel striving in law observance, but in a different way, through the Messiah. If you deny this, then either: (a) you will end up trying to manufacture the conditions for covenantal renewal on your own steam, but before you try that option does anyone remember what the words "Do not say in your heart" introduce? Or (b) you will simply be denying what God has done for us in the Messiah and end up complaining that God hasn't brought his saving word to us yet. You'll be all melodramatic like: "Who will ascend into heaven?" as if to bemoan that no one can launch himself into the sky to bring us some salvation from above (that would be to deny that the Messiah came down from heaven to redeem his people) or complain, "Who will descend into the deep?" as if to bemoan that no one can go on an underworldly journey to bring us back some salvation from below (that would be to deny that the Messiah died and rose for us). But what does Moses say? "The word is near you; it is in your mouth and in your heart." My point is that the striving in the law or waiting for someone to traverse heaven or hell to bring salvation is over because the word that brings covenantal renewal is here in the message of faith that we proclaim in the gospel of Jesus the Messiah.

### Faith as Confession of Jesus as Lord (10:9–13)

Paul goes on to explain in vv. 9–13 that the "word of faith" in v. 8 is the announcement that Jesus is the risen Lord and by that word one is saved: "If you declare with your mouth, 'Jesus is Lord,' and believe in your heart that God raised him from the dead, you will be saved" (v. 9). At the center of Christian faith is the confession of the lordship of Jesus and the belief that God raised him up from the dead. The organs of "mouth" and "heart" are vital here. For it is by confession with the mouth that one publicly declares one's allegiance, and it is in the heart that one finds the most cherished reserve of one's convictions. Lying underneath this, of course, is the liturgical-like

32. Sprinkle, *Law and Life*, 183.

33. Cf. also the paraphrase of Wright, "Romans," 10:662, and Hays, *Echoes of Scripture*, 76–77.

formulas we saw earlier in Romans 1:3–4 and 4:25 about God handing over Jesus to death and raising him up to new life. It is because God acted in and through Jesus that believers call on him as Lord and Savior (see Acts 22:16; 1 Cor 12:3; 2 Cor 4:5; Phil 2:11).

This verse is perhaps the best explanation of what it means to be a Christian. A Christian is someone who professes to live under submission of King Jesus and believes that God has acted in Jesus to usher in the age to come. Not only that, what is provocative is that Paul writes these words to a cluster of house churches in the heart of the Roman empire, living right under the emperor's nose and boldly declaring the lordship of a Jewish man executed by the Romans as a common criminal. It's provocative because the Roman emperor was the one hailed as *Kyrios* by supplicants and clients across the empire. At the time that Paul was writing, one can find inscriptions, papyri, and ostraca all attesting that "Nero is Lord," even the grandiose claim that "Nero, the Lord of the entire world."[34] Whether Paul intends the statement "Jesus is Lord" to be heard as a deliberate sociopolitical protest against the propaganda of the imperial cult is debatable. But at least we should acknowledge that the claim was potentially incendiary and could be perceived as politically disloyal. To claim that "Jesus is Lord" on Lord Nero's own turf was not going to endear the Christians to imperial authorities.

"For it is with your heart that you believe and are justified, and it is with your mouth that you profess your faith and are saved" (v. 10). Paul makes clear that the faith that proceeds from heart and mouth becomes determinative for one's standing before God and one's state in the coming age. Here "justification"[35] and "salvation" are basically synonymous and refer to God's deliverance of the believer, not just freedom from the penalty of sin, but freedom for sin, death, and evil altogether.

Paul backs that up with a scriptural citation from Isaiah 28:16: "As Scripture says, 'Anyone who believes in him will never be put to shame'" (v. 11). Paul adds the word "anyone" at the head of the citation in order to emphasize its universal relevance to as many as would believe.[36] The citation of Isaiah 28:16 in Romans 9:33 and 10:11 forms an *inclusio*, allowing us to see Romans 10:1–11 as an intertextual commentary drawn predominantly from Isaiah about Israel's particular stumbling and God's upholding the honor of believers. The reason Paul is not ashamed of the gospel (see 1:16) is because the

---

34. On the title "Lord" applied to Nero, see Joseph D. Fantin, *The Lord of the Entire World: Lord Jesus, a Challenge to Caesar* (NTM 31; Sheffield: Sheffield Phoenix, 2011), 132–33, 196–202.

35. The Greek is more properly "righteousness" (*dikaiosynē*) as per the CEB: "Trusting with the heart leads to righteousness, and confessing with the mouth leads to salvation."

36. Cf. Tobin, *Rhetoric of Righteousness*, 347.

gospel declares that God has reversed the verdict of anyone who might try to shame his people. Whereas some detractors might have alleged that Christian faith is shameful in what it implied about God, Israel, and Torah, Greek religion, and Roman empire, Paul says that those who confess such a faith in fact abound in honor before God.

Paul unpacks the universal dimension pregnant in the "everyone" and "anyone" in Rom 10:4, 11 with respect to righteousness by faith: "For there is no difference between Jew and Gentile — the same Lord is Lord of all and richly blesses all who call on him, or, 'Everyone who calls on the name of the Lord will be saved' " (vv. 12–13). When God's impartiality is worked out in practice, it means that there is no distinction among Jew and Gentile. This of course was the principle underlying 1:18–3:20, which stated that Jews and Gentiles are both condemned in sin; therefore, Jews and Gentiles both need justification by faith as made clear in 3:22, 29–30. Clearly, sharing in the same plight entails sharing in the same solution.

But the picture here is far more than Jews and Gentiles simply being stuck with each other in the same lifeboat. Jesus is the same Lord of both Jews and Gentiles[37] because God intends to put all of his people under the headship of one person, Messiah Jesus. God's plan, first annunciated to the patriarchs, was always to form a worldwide family of faith to live under the reign of the Messiah. So Paul's reference to Jesus' lordship is no mere abstract affirmation of his deity. It means in the first instance that our relationship with God is mediated *through* Jesus as the one appointed as Messiah and Lord. On top of that, Jesus' lordship necessitates a radical configuration of how believers relate to each other, including followers of Jesus belonging to different ethnicities. There is no "them" and "us," but only "us" under the lordship of Jesus. Those who believe in the same Lord belong in the same community — a point with significant ramifications later in the letter (see 14:1–11).

All believers, irrespective of race, have received in Christ a grace that abounds in rich blessings. The image of "wealth" signifies the unlimited resources of God bestowed on his people through his Son (see 1 Cor 1:5; 2 Cor 8:9; Phil 4:19; Eph 1:7; 2:7; 3:8; Col 1:27).[38] Paul then rounds off this section by way of a citation of Joel 2:32 that "everyone who calls on the name of the Lord will be saved." Once more the inclusive term "everyone" is crucial as it implies that any person who calls on the name of the Lord will share in salvation (see Acts 22:16; 1 Cor 1:2). Notable too is the fact that the "Lord" whom Israel called upon was YHWH, whereas Paul here identifies the Lord as Jesus; this

37. A more exact translation is "Greek" (*Hellēnos*).

38. Moo, *Romans*, 660.

is clear evidence that Jesus was regarded within the early church as part of the divine identity.[39]

## Christian Mission — Part 1: The Beginning (10:14–17)

We should not underestimate the missional theme that runs through Romans 9–11. After all, the gospel is for the Jew first and then the Gentile (1:16), and Romans 9–11 is about the gospel in relation to the story of Israel in past, present, and future. In the divine plan Jews and Gentiles have interlocking destinies since Gentiles get in on the coattails of Israel's covenantal promises (9:1–5; 11:18–25), Gentile inclusion will eventually prompt Israel to jealousy (10:19; 11:11, 14–15, 30–31), and in this way ethnic Israel and promissory Israel will both be saved (11:25–26). Paul's prayer for Israel's salvation (10:1) will one day come to fruition when God's call and love overpowers Israel's "stumbling," "hardening," and "disobedience" and leads them into his mercy (11:28–32).

Understandably then, Paul, as the Jewish Christian apostle to the Gentiles (see 1:1, 5, 13–16; 11:13; 15:18), takes a moment in 10:14–21 to place the Christian mission to both Jews and Gentiles on the map of prophetic promises. First, he places the mission in the coordinates of Isaiah 52–53 and proceeds to describe the mission's urgency and the necessity of preaching the gospel for people to come to faith (Rom 10:14–17).[40] Second, Paul pulls in parts of the Psalms, Deuteronomy, and Isaiah to lament Israel's failure to acknowledge that God had always intended to bring the Gentiles into salvation (10:18–21). This paves the way for Paul to argue in 11:1–32 that God is far from done with Israel since Israel's salvation is still on the cards as God will use the nations to provoke Israel to jealousy. Viewed this way, the primary issue is not Israel's failure, but God's mission to Jews and Gentiles and its surprising effects.[41]

Paul's citation of Joel 2:32 in v. 13 that everyone who calls on the name of the Lord will be saved leads Paul to a series of questions posed by way of a rhetorical device called *klimax* or *gradatio*, where the final word of each question generates in turn the next question: "How, then, can they call on the

39. Cf. David Capes, *Old Testament Yahweh Texts in Paul's Christology* (WUNT 2.47; Tübingen: Mohr Siebeck, 1992), 116–23; C. Kavin Rowe, "Romans 10:13: What Is the Name of the Lord?" *HBT* 22 (2000): 135–73.

40. Wagner (*Heralds of the Good News*, 180) says, "Paul's claim that Isaiah's 'message' concerns the 'word of Christ' raises the intriguing possibility that he understands the Servant Song of Isaiah 52:13–53:12 to refer to Christ and, in some sense, to be Isaiah's preaching of the same 'gospel' that Paul, now Isaiah's 'co-worker,' also preaches."

41. Contra Munck, *Christ and Israel*, 91; Cranfield, *Romans*, 2:533; Fitzmyer, *Romans*, 595; Stuhlmacher, *Romans*, 158; and more properly with Dunn, *Romans*, 2:620; Watson, *Paul, Judaism, and the Gentiles*, 332.

one they have not believed in? And how can they believe in the one of whom they have not heard? And how can they hear without someone preaching to them? And how can anyone preach unless they are sent? As it is written: 'How beautiful are the feet of those who bring good news!' " (vv. 14–15). Paul's point is that the only way that people can call on the name of the Lord and share in this fantastic renewal of the covenant is by having faith. However, no one can have faith unless they've heard the gospel about the Messiah's death and resurrection. For this to happen someone needs to preach the word to them, and the preachers needed to be sent out! On the back of that Paul adds a quotation from Isaiah 52:7, "How beautiful are the feet of those who bring good news!" Paul is saying that he and those like him are announcing that God has restored the covenant in the Messiah and God calls both Jews and Gentiles into a renewed community.[42]

Paul then adds a slightly darker note that this mission to the world has not met with universal success: "But everyone hasn't obeyed the good news" (CEB). The NIV translates *pantes* ("all") as "all the Israelites," but that is not what the text says, and it wrongfully reads Israel's failure in vv. 19–21 back into v. 16. Also, some translations tone down the demand expected of people and render *hypakouō* as "welcomed" (NLT), "accepted" (NIV), or "responded" (NJB) rather than as the more fitting "obeyed" (see RSV, ESV, NRSV, CEB, NET, HCSB). The gospel is not only to be believed, but also to be obeyed (see 2 Thess 1:7–8 and 1 Pet 4:17) because the gospel brings us to the "obedience of faith" (Rom 1:5; 16:26). The gospel is not just religious data we expect people to agree with; the gospel is a royal summons to receive Jesus as Savior and to submit to him as Lord. Paul's own experience in the synagogues and agoras was that the gospel was not always well received and was often rejected with mockery and hostility (see 1 Cor 4:9–13; 2 Cor 11:23–28). So he adds a citation from Isaiah 53:1, "Lord, who has believed our message?" Evidently Paul knew what it was like to reap a harvest of new believers, but other days it probably felt like sowing seed on concrete or trying to fish in a dry lake. Some days it feels like Isaiah 52:7, other days it feels like 53:1.

The experience of failure, far from discouraging Paul, simply reaffirms what he knows from his evangelical mission: "Consequently, faith comes from hearing the message, and the message is heard through the word about Christ" (v. 17). Irrespective of whether the audience is receptive or hostile, faith comes by hearing the news and the news is the word of the Messiah! The power of salvation is the power of the word of the gospel that bruises the hardest of hearts and breaks down resistance to God's grace (see Acts 16:14; Jas 1:21).

42. Wright, "Romans," 10:667.

### Christian Mission—Part 2: The Result (10:18–21)

Paul transitions from the general rejection of the gospel across the world (v. 18) to spelling out Israel's particular rejection of God's plan to include the Gentiles in the scope of salvation (vv. 19–21).

The worldwide "hearing" of the gospel is supported with the claim of Psalm 19:4 about the effusion of the message to all of creation: "But I ask: Did they not hear? Of course they did: 'Their voice has gone out into all the earth, their words to the ends of the world'" (v. 18). The statement is certainly peculiar if taken literally (after all, the indigenous populations of the Americas and Australia did not hear the gospel until the seventeenth and eighteenth centuries). Paul is obviously making a rhetorical claim about the spread of the gospel across the Mediterranean basin and parts of the Middle East (see Col 1:23; 1 Tim 3:16).[43] Paul himself knows that there are still other regions like Spain that must yet hear the message (Rom 15:24, 28, 30). In general, though, the inhabited world has heard the gospel, though not all have believed it.

Paul then claims in vv. 19–21 that Israel should "understand" or "know" that God had always intended to bring the nations into salvation. He shows this, first, from a citation of Deuteronomy 32:21, "Moses says, 'I will make you envious by those who are not a nation; I will make you angry by a nation that has no understanding'" (v. 19). The text is drawn from the Song of Moses in Deuteronomy 32, which is a poetic panoply of praise to God combined with a vehement indictment of Israel. The list of judgments against Israel given in Deut 32:19–25 is that if Israel lurches into idolatry, God will make them jealous by (adopting?) a senseless people (see Rom 1:21, 31) who are not his people. Paul takes this as a prophecy that the Gentiles will one day enjoy Israel's privileges, driving Israel to a fit of jealousy.[44] The motif of jealousy will prove to be the hinge on which Israel's future turns because Israel will be roused to envy by Gentile acceptance of their Messiah and by Gentiles experiencing their covenant renewal (see Rom 11:11, 14).

Paul backs that up with a further citation, this time from Isaiah 65:1: "And Isaiah boldly says, 'I was found by those who did not seek me; I revealed myself to those who did not ask for me'" (v. 20). This text is for Paul a prophecy of the same point: Israel is rejecting the blessings on offer, so God finds a foreign people, who were not seeking him, and he makes them part of his covenant people. In essence, the citations of Deuteronomy 32:21 and Isaiah 65:1 are conscripted to say exactly the same thing that Paul drew from Hosea

---

43. Cf. Cranfield, *Romans*, 2:537; Moo, *Romans*, 667.

44. Cf. e.g., Wright, "Romans," 10:669; Moo, *Romans*, 668.

1:10 and 2:23 back in Romans 9:25–26, namely, that God has called a people who were not his people to be his people. That should hardly be surprising, because when the patriarchal promises were fulfilled (Gen 12:1–3; 15:1–6) and Israel's covenant was renewed (Deut 30–32), the Gentile outsiders would become covenant insiders (Hos 1:10; 2:23; Isa 65:1). That is what Israel should "know" and "understand," but they haven't seen it that way! This is why God's word has not failed (Rom 9:6).

Whereas Paul thinks that Isaiah 65:1 refers to Gentile inclusion, he understands Isaiah 65:2 as putting Israel back in the spotlight, or we might say "shame light": "But concerning Israel he says, 'All day long I have held out my hands to a disobedient and obstinate people'" (v. 21). Israel is in that position because, as Paul said back in 9:30–33, they are pursuing righteousness by Torah with the result that they have not attained their goal. They have stumbled over the messianic stone and tried to establish their own righteousness. Instead of being the renewed people of God who herald the message of God's mercy to the nations, Israel has become stubborn and recalcitrant to what God is doing for the nations through the Messiah.

To recap, in Romans 10:1–21 Paul has taken us from Abraham, to the exodus, to the exile, to covenant renewal, to the inclusion of the Gentiles. The Messiah has come and acted to end the exile and to bring in the renewal of the covenant so that Jews and Gentiles could be justified by confession of Jesus as Lord. A message has spread to the inhabited world, meeting with mixed responses, but the upshot is that Gentiles are entering into the heritage of Israel even while Israel herself does not have the eyes to see it. Paul prays that his fellow Israelites will see it, but for the time being they haven't just missed the boat; they are throwing rocks at it. N. T. Wright provides a good distillation of the kind of story that Paul is telling:

> It is the story of how people who had no airs and graces of their own, no thought of being sought by Israel's God, the creator, nevertheless found themselves grasped by the divine call and love as an act of sheer grace. And it is also the story ... of the shock received by the people who thought the God-and-world story could only be told, and would always be told, with them coming out on top. The climax of their own history was Messiah who, from their point of view, was as it were an anti-Messiah. The king came, and instead of setting his people free he died their death and invited them to follow him. Only if they do so will they find the fulfillment of their own story: he is indeed, the true king, and the world's true Lord, and will give salvation to all who call on his name.[45]

45. Wright, "Romans," 10:670.

The Gentile Christians in Rome, who probably did not get the complete significance of all of Paul's Old Testament citations, would nonetheless probably have had an "aha" moment after hearing Romans 9 – 10. Careful reflection on these words would provide them with a better grasp of why most Jews have rejected the message and how this relates to God's purposes to bring Gentiles into the inheritance of Israel. But they might ask, does that mean that God has now rejected Israel (11:1), that Gentile believers can consider themselves to be superior to Israel (11:18), or that Israel can be regarded as the dead wood pruned off a tree to make room for them (11:19)? Paul will give an emphatic "no" to all these questions. But, to be fair, after reading Romans 9 – 10, it certainly looks as if Paul is giving Israel a hard time for their failure to believe, and he even leaves their position before God up in the air.

Yet Paul only emphasizes Israel's failure at such length so that Israel's salvation will appear all the more striking. Israel's reconciliation will serve to magnify the depths of God's mercy and the constancy of God's faithfulness toward Israel (see 11:33 – 36). Keep in mind that there is still another chapter of the story to be told. After telling his version of Israel in the past, after narrating the tragedy of Israel in the present, Paul will now go on to tell a story of hope for Israel in the future.

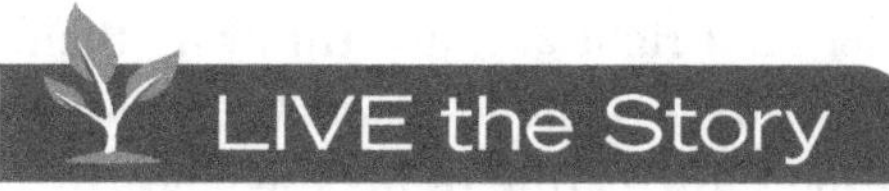

## LIVE the Story

Our appropriation of the story of Romans 9:30 – 10:21 needs to wrestle long and hard with several things that Paul raises. First of all, because it is just too plain to avoid, we need to reflect on Paul's christological reading of the Old Testament. While his interpretation of texts like Isaiah 52 and 53 or Deuteronomy 30 and 32 might seem strange to us, Paul's interpretation flows from his belief that the totality of the Torah witnesses to Christ. Such a hermeneutical conviction must be absorbed by responsible interpreters who want to read the Old and New Testaments as Christians. We need to understand how the story of Romans is unlocked by the story of the Old Testament.

Second, we are presented with a remarkably high view of preaching in 10:17, where the proclaimed word is the instrument that creates faith. This really should instill into us the high calling of being a preacher and the great responsibility that we carry in leading men and women into faith through preaching the word to them.

Then, third, there is no ignoring the missional theme that runs through 10:14 – 21, where we are confronted with the need for people to be sent as heralds of the good news. Paul confronts the issue of Israel's recalcitrance to the gospel; yet such recalcitrance only takes place in the context of mission. Even despite the cool and hostile response that Paul's gospel received from his fellow Jewish compatriots, there is no abandoning the mission either to Israel or to the nations. Paul doesn't explain why he has given up in the face of rejection; rather, he explains why the mission must keep going.

### Reading Your Bible with a Jesus Lens

If you are new to the whole plethora of issues about how the New Testament authors interpret the Old Testament, then Romans 9–11 can be quite a shock to the system.[46] Obviously Romans 9–11 is dense with manifold citations, allusions, and echoes of the Old Testament. Depending on how you calculate them, Romans as a whole has about sixty-five or so direct citations of Old Testament texts, of which about half appear in Romans 9–11. So after the dearth of Old Testament citations in Romans 5–8, intertextually speaking, coming into Romans 9–11 can feel like walking out of a desert and into a snowstorm. While some might think that Paul' s use of the Old Testament is strange or arbitrary, we have to let him engage in whatever interpretive oddities he likes because, you know, he is an apostle!

Instead I want to suggest that Paul's reading of the Old Testament has a lot more reason and intentionality behind it than meets the eye. Paul isn't blindly pulling out passages from the left and right and just throwing them at his audience with the hope that they won't actually look any of them up. For Paul, the Old Testament provided the substructure of his theology; that is, Paul believed that his gospel was prepromised and even authorized by the narrative of Israel's Scriptures. The way Paul utilizes passages like Habakkuk 2:4; Genesis 15:5–6; and Isaiah 28:16 illustrate his belief that the gospel is conformed to the pattern of Scripture.[47]

As a seminary professor, I have to tell you that I am routinely frustrated by how little incoming students know about the way that the Old Testament points to Jesus. Only yesterday I was leading a seminar for a parachurch organization on "What Is the Gospel?" During the seminar, I spoke at length

---

46. For a primer, I recommend Kenneth Berding and Jonathan Lunde, ed., *Three Views on the New Testament Use of the Old Testament* (Grand Rapids: Zondervan, 2008); the select studies in Steve Moyise, *Evoking Scripture: Seeing the Old Testament in the New* (London: T&T Clark, 2008); on methodology see Stanley E. Porter, "Further Comments on the Use of the Old Testament in the New Testament," in *The Intertextuality of the Epistles: Explorations of Theory and Practice* (ed. Thomas L. Brodie, Dennis R. MacDonald, and Stanley E. Porter; NTM 16; Sheffield: Sheffield Phoenix, 2007), 98–110; on Jewish interpretative techniques in antiquity see Matthias Henze, ed., *A Companion to Biblical Interpretation in Early Judaism* (Grand Rapids: Eerdmans, 2012); and for an encyclopedia treatment of the subject, see G. K. Beale and D. A. Carson, eds., *Commentary on the New Testament Use of the Old Testament* (Grand Rapids: Baker, 2007).

47. Calvin, *Romans*, 384.

about the content of the gospel, and then quickly moved on to how the gospel lines up with the Old Testament promises. When I asked the students, who were drawn from the ranks of Bible-believing churches, which exact Scriptures accord with the gospel, they looked back at me with embarrassed and blank faces. So I asked them, "When Peter and Paul embarked on their missionary travels and went into synagogues and tried reasoning from Scriptures that Jesus is the Messiah, what texts did they begin with?" The result: stunned silence, some eyes looking away, others flicking through their Bibles.

Then I hear "Psalm 23" yelled out by one brave young girl. A sensible choice since Psalm 23 is a bit of a personal favorite for many people. Sadly though, I had to tell the young lady that Psalm 23 is never once quoted in the New Testament. After more painful silence, I slowly took them through Psalms 2, 110, and 118 to show what texts were prevalent in apostolic evangelism and teaching. I should confess also that this was not a unique experience for me. Many Christians out there simply do not know how their Bible fits together, how the Old and New Testaments provide a singular testimony to God, the kingdom, Israel, Jesus, the cross, and the church.

What our churches desperately need, not just in pulpit preaching but as part of any discipleship training, is a basic introduction to biblical theology[48]—in short, getting a grip on the basic story line of Scripture.

It is sad and yet a little encouraging that many Christian parents are for the first time learning about biblical theology by reading Sally Lloyd-Jones's volume *The Jesus Storybook Bible* to their children.[49] I don't know what impact the book is having on toddlers and preschoolers, but I know from anecdotal evidence that a whole generation of parents are having big "aha" moments since they are finally getting a grasp of the story line of Scripture by reading it to their children. Many parents are getting into the biblical story by reading a condensed and child-friendly version of the biblical story to their small children. One of the strengths of the Australian theological scene, provincial as it may be to Americans, is that we've always had a strong tradition of biblical theology. Leaders like Graeme Goldsworthy and Brian Rosner have had a strong hand in highlighting the importance of biblical theology

48. For those getting started, I recommend Tim Chester, *From Creation to New Creation: Understanding the Bible Story* (Carlisle, UK: Paternoster, 2003); Vaughan Roberts, *God's Big Picture: Tracing the Storyline of the Bible* (Downers Grove, IL: InterVarsity, 2002); and Michael D. Williams, *As Far as the Curse Is Found: The Covenant Story of Redemption* (Phillipsburg, NJ: Presbyterian & Reformed, 2005).

49. Sally Lloyd-Jones, *The Jesus Storybook Bible: Every Story Whispers His Name* (Grand Rapids: Zondervan, 2007).

for preaching and teaching.[50] I would point out that the *Story of God Bible Commentary* series is premised on the idea of showing how a biblical book is situated within the wider story of Scripture itself.[51] We want the whole story, the whole counsel of God to shape how we read and apply Scripture today.

We do not have time for a crash course in biblical theology. But if you want to glean one basic insight, one thought to file away in your mind, it has to be this: all of God's promises to Israel receive their fulfillment in Jesus Christ. Goldsworthy drilled into his students two particular texts that reflect this. First, 2 Corinthians 1:20, which says: "For no matter how many promises God has made, they are 'Yes' in Christ." Second is Acts 13:32–33, which says, "We tell you the good news: What God promised our ancestors he has fulfilled for us, their children, by raising up Jesus." According to Goldsworthy, "The promises of a new covenant, a new restored people of God, a new dwelling place of God amongst men, are all fulfilled in Christ. Furthermore, they are fulfilled in the gospel event."[52] Young gospelizers should heed those words well because when it comes to biblical hermeneutics, they are sheer gold(sworthy)!

In practice that means we read Scripture as if Jesus really, genuinely, truly, and assuredly is the climax of the covenant (Rom 10:4). Paul read his Bible this way. That is why Paul sees Jesus as Isaiah's "stone" of stumbling (9:33), the "near word" of Deuteronomy (10:8), the prophet Joel's "Lord" (10:13), and the one proclaimed by Isaiah-inspired heralds (10:15). The Old Testament is filled with signs and shadows that point to the person and work of Jesus the Messiah. Or as Calvin put it: "Whatever the law teaches, whatever it commands, whatever it promises, [it] has always a reference to Christ as its main object."[53]

Scholars often debate whether we should read the Old Testament as the apostles did. Some look at Paul's allegory in Galatians 4:21–31 and his exposition of Deuteronomy 30:12–14 in Romans 10:5–8 and say, "Good grief. No! Do as Paul says, but not as he does!" In my mind, such objectors have bought into a narrow, literalistic way of reading Scripture that owes more to Thomas Hobbes than it does to Jesus and the apostolic church. This is a

50. Cf. Graeme Goldsworthy, *Preaching the Whole Bible as Christian Scripture: The Application of Biblical Theology to Preaching* (Grand Rapids: Eerdmans, 2000); idem, *The Goldsworthy Trilogy (Gospel and Kingdom, Gospel and Wisdom, Gospel and Revelation)* (Carlise, UK: Paternoster, 2001); idem, *According to Plan: The Unfolding Revelation of the Bible* (Downers Grove, IL: InterVarsity, 2002); idem, *Gospel-Centered Hermeneutics: Foundations and Principles of Evangelical Biblical Interpretation* (Downers Grove, IL: InterVarsity, 2010); and the reference work by Brian Rosner and T. D. Alexander, eds., *New Dictionary of Biblical Theology* (Downers Grove, IL: InterVarsity, 2000).

51. See the website http://storyofgodseries.com/.

52. Goldsworthy, *Trilogy*, 173.

53. John Calvin, *Commentary on the Epistle of Paul the Apostle to the Romans* (Bellingham, WA: Logos Bible Software, 2010), 384.

failure of hermeneutical nerve that refuses to take seriously the truth of Jesus as the centerpiece of Scripture. If the apostles cannot be trusted to serve as exemplars of Christ-centered or christotelic exegesis, who can?

What we should take away from Romans 9:30 – 10:21 is the importance of knowing the Old Testament and knowing it through the story of Jesus. In other words, we read the Bible through a Jesus lens! On this "Jesus lens" approach, Michael Williams says:

> Reading the Bible through the Jesus lens is reading it the way it was intended. It keeps our reading, understanding, teaching, and preaching properly focused on God's grand redemptive program that centers on his own Son. Seeing how each biblical book makes its own contribution to that redemptive focus enables us to use these diverse materials with much more confidence and accuracy. The Jesus lens ensures that our exegetical bowling balls stay within the lane and don't go crashing over into areas where they can cause a lot of damage to the faith of believers and to our ability to use the Bible fruitfully in our service to God.[54]

One of the best things we can do is learn to read the Bible that Jesus and the apostles read and learn to read it in the sense that it is about Jesus. If we apply this, it means that in places like adult Sunday school, in home groups, or in Bible study fellowships, Christian leaders need to make a concerted effort at teaching people how to read Scripture in a Jesus-centered fashion. The danger is that this can end up becoming a mushy spiritualizing of the text or else descend into an exercise in allegory or eisegesis. So it takes patience and hard work to get people's heads into the position whereby they can see a witness to Christ in God's word in the Old Testament. Yet the hard work is worth it as the people in our churches will often find themselves reading the Old Testament and understanding the New Testament with a depth and precision that they had never had before.

### Preaching the Word

What is striking about Romans 10:17 is the high value placed on the preached word and the high virtue of being a preacher. Paul says that "faith comes from hearing the message, and the message is heard through the word about Christ." This "Pentecostal fire," as Karl Barth called it, has nothing to do with our manipulated extravagances or human enthusiasm but is exclusively about bringing the word of Christ near to the people.[55] It is this Christ-word, the

54. Michael Williams, *How To Read the Bible through the Jesus Lens* (Grand Rapids: Zondervan, 2012), 9.

55. Barth, *Romans*, 378.

*verbum Christi*, that creates faith. It is the Christ-word that brings a spiritual oasis to those in a spiritual desert. It is the Christ-word that brings effervescent life to those in the throes of death. It is the Christ-word that is the good news of judgment, love, redemption, and hope. The role of the preacher is to bring the Christ-word to bear against the resistant wills and despondent hearts of men and women. For it is through the Christ-word alone that we find salvation offered and actualized. Robert Jewett says that "the compelling power of the gospel resides not in its preachers but in Christ himself, who becomes present in the preached gospel for those who believe."[56] What Jewett says aligns exactly with the Second Helvetic Confession:

> THE PREACHING OF THE WORD OF GOD IS THE WORD OF GOD. Wherefore when this Word of God is now preached in the church by preachers lawfully called, we believe that the very Word of God is proclaimed, and received by the faithful; and that neither any other Word of God is to be invented nor is to be expected from heaven: and that now the Word itself which is preached is to be regarded, not the minister that preaches; for even if he be evil and a sinner, nevertheless the Word of God remains still true and good.[57]

When the preacher brings the "word" to a congregation, it is not mere opinions, empty sentiments, or religious musings that are set before the flock. It is genuinely the word of God *insofar* as it is expresses the truth of God's incarnate Word and reflects his inscripturated word. The preached word brings the power, substance, conviction, and authority of the divine word to bear on the hardened, the broken, the proud, the wise, the foolish, the miserable, the haughty, and the contrite. In the mouth of the preacher, the word becomes a sword with authority to judge the self-righteous and to justify the ungodly. God's word never fails, precisely because it is a God-word; so it is infallible as it is indefatigable (see Isa 55:11; Rom 9:6).

This theology of the preached word from Romans 10:17 is a great encouragement for pastors, preachers, and teachers since it shows that God can use the most unlikely and unqualified of people to be vessels of his word of grace. Let us not forget that across redemptive history, God has consistently used ineffective speakers like Moses (Exod 4:10), Isaiah (Isa 6:5–8), and Paul (1 Cor 2:5) to give his word to the people. This is a heartening thought for anyone engaged in the high office of preacher or teacher. It means that irrespective of the character or talent of the preacher, the word is effective because the Spirit gives their words unction and Christ is the subject received in faith

56. Jewett, *Romans*, 642.

57. Second Helvetic Confession, chapter 1.

by the hearers. In this word, God's word, trembling on the lips of men and women, dogged by feelings of inadequacy and unworthiness, stuttering and stressed, that we see God's word become power in weakness. Here we experience the word not as a contest in public speaking, not as entertainment or rhetoric, but as God's raw redemptive power to transform the utterances of human people and to enable their speech to teach, rebuke, correct, and instruct in righteousness. The efficacy of the word resides in the ministry of the Spirit, not in the spirit of the ministers.

Do not think that this view of the preached word as animated by the Spirit and quickened by Christ excuses the preacher from the arduous work of preparation and practice. Yes, God can speak through creatures as pitiful as Balaam's ass (Num 22), but pity the fool who is content to be God's ass when they could be a royal herald (Isa 52:7). The Spirit will always use us despite ourselves, but by honest exegesis, hermeneutical design, and homiletical practice, we give the Spirit more to work with in the delivery of our sermons. When it comes to preaching, remember, the only place where "success" comes before "work" is the dictionary. So we must labor hard in the vineyard of God's word so that our audiences will be doubly blessed by our own efforts and by God's work through us.

Preachers carry the responsibility and pleasure of presenting Christ to those who hunger for him. If so, then regardless of the good of our programs, the virtue of our ancillary ministries, the benefits of our community events, nothing compares with the value of Christian proclamation. If what people want most of all is to know that Christ loves them and died for them, anything else we can give them will be comparatively less. That means, dear pastor, that your main vocation is not to be a community activist, a social worker, a counselor, a political pundit, a little league coach, a fund raiser, or anything else. Good, noble, and important as those things are, they are not the primary task with which you are to be concerned. If God has called you to be a preacher, preach with all the passion and desperation of someone holding out an antiserum to a people dying from a venomous poison. If God has called you to be a preacher, don't settle for being something less like a president or king. But remember that the best thing you can offer your people is Christ! I cannot put it better than John Updike's novel *Rabbit Run* (1960), which includes the thunderous denouncement of pastoral ministry by the Lutheran Pastor Fritz Kruppenbach, who says to a junior colleague:

> Do you think this is your job, to meddle in these people's lives? I know what they teach you at seminary now: this psychology and that. But I don't agree with it. You think now your job is to be an unpaid doctor, to

> run around and plug up holes and make everything smooth. I don't think that. I don't think that's your job.... I say you don't know what your role is or you'd be home locked in prayer.... In running back and forth you run away from the duty given you by God, to make your faith powerful.... When on Sunday morning, then, when you go out before their faces, we must walk up not worn out with misery but full of Christ, *hot* with Christ, on *fire*: burn them with the force of our belief. This is why they come; why else would they pay us? Anything else we can do and say anyone can do and say. They have doctors and lawyers for that.... Make no mistake. Now I'm serious. Make no mistake. There is nothing but Christ for us. All the rest, all this decency and busyness, is nothing. It is Devil's work.[58]

Don't get me wrong. I'm not telling leaders to lock themselves in their study six days a week and to avoid their parishioners because they are busy with sermon preparation. I'm trying to emphasize that the high point of our ministry is that moment, whether in the pulpit or beside a hospital bed, when we bring the Christ-word to them, the word of love divine and hope eternal. If we owe people our best, our best is the good news of Christ himself.

Finally, I used to love the Brother Biddle comic strips about the trials of a balding Presbyterian minister (who looks uncannily like Tony Campolo). In one particular episode, when Brother Biddle was despondent with what he should be doing with himself as a minister, all of a sudden a mysterious black crow flies into his study and—in the tradition of Edgar Allen Poe's *The Raven*—begins taunting him; but it taunts him to "preach the truth forevermore." As Brother Biddle soon realizes, the crow is speaking the truth to him. Preaching the word, that is his business, that is his bread and butter, that is his calling, that is his task; everything else should distract him nevermore.

### How Will They Hear Unless Someone Is Sent?

Anyone claiming the designation *evangelical* for themselves ought to have their hearts both warmed and burdened by reading the words, "How, then, can they call on the one they have not believed in? And how can they believe in the one of whom they have not heard? And how can they hear without someone preaching to them? And how can anyone preach unless they are sent? As it is written: 'How beautiful are the feet of those who bring good news!'" (Rom 10:14–15). It remains true that "We've a Story to Tell to the Nations," as the old hymn goes. We must tell all people from Azerbaijan to Zimbabwe that "God was reconciling the world to himself in Christ" (2 Cor 5:19), that

58. I have to thank Peter Orr and Ben Myers for alerting me to the relevance of John Updike for preaching.

"now is the time of God's favor, now is the day of salvation" (2 Cor 6:2), and that God "wants all people to be saved and to come to a knowledge of the truth" (1 Tim 2:4). Paul was a crosscultural apostolic missionary who believed that the church's mission participated in God's own mission to repossess the world for himself. That is why Paul and his coworkers traveled around Syria, Asia Minor, and Greece and engaged people in their cultural and linguistic diversity irrespective of whether they were Jewish, Greek, or Roman. They did it because they believed that they were ambassadors of reconciliation, taking the word of faith to the nations.

It is true to say, then, and merits repeating, that the church today has the same mission and the same urgency that it had two thousand years ago: to know Christ and to make him known, to advance the gospel, to work for the kingdom, and to magnify the majesty of God across the world. To use the language of the Lausanne Covenant's "Cape Town Commitment," evangelical mission requires "the whole Church taking the whole gospel to the whole world." That is a task we undertake as God's people, at God's command, in God's own mission, for the redemption of God's creation, and for the ultimate glory of God himself. We still have a story to tell the nations, a story that goes from creation to the cross to the consummation.

In doing that we have to remember that in many parts of the world, like Papua New Guinea, what is needed is not so much evangelism by foreign missionaries but partnership in theological education and mentoring leaders to help develop the existing churches. In other cases, however, there is a real need for tentmaker missionaries to establish churches in places where the gospel has trouble penetrating. I think of countries like Yemen, which has only three thouand Christians in a country of twenty-four million people. My own heart swells for the number of Arabic-speaking Christians coming to Australia from Egypt, Sudan, and Syria who need churches to worship in and need help rebuilding their lives.

Just the other day my friend Sean Winter (Pilgrim Theological College) posted on Facebook the startling fact that the Anhui province in China has 1.8 million Protestant Christians, meeting in around 5,000 churches, served by 102 ordained ministers, 208 elders, and 180 evangelists, which leads to a ratio of one minister per 18,000 members. Talk about sheep without a shepherd! I know we say it a lot in evangelical churches, and citing this verse at missions conferences has become almost cliché, but Jesus' words are true that in every generation, "The harvest is plentiful, but the workers are few. Ask the Lord of the harvest, therefore, to send out workers into his harvest field" (Luke 10:2). We must remind ourselves and our congregations time and time again that we have a corporate mission to the nations.

I am more than aware that not everyone is called to crosscultural and overseas missionary work. It takes a certain set of skills, particular personal attributes, and a lot of family, church, and agency support. To use Acts 1:8 as a template, some are called to work in their own local "Jerusalem," some in their nearby "Judea," and some in the adjacent "Samaria." I'm not trying to guilt people into going into missions, but others are indeed called to go to the "ends of the earth." God places his call on people to go to distant and difficult places to establish a church as a beacon of light in the midst of darkness. A call that resonates with the experience of Isaiah, who felt the burden of God's call, and responded, "Here am I. Send me!" (Isa 6:8); or others, who hear the plight of peoples in faraway lands as if someone is from that territory is earnestly beseeching them, "Come over to Macedonia, *or Mongolia, or Mozambique, or Macau, or Montenegro* and help us" (Acts 16:9 [my own annotations]).

In reflecting on Romans 10:14–15 we should be asking ourselves and each other whether this passage is describing the missional vocation that any of us are called to. Do our hearts tug for some particular people group? Does some country or province keep lodging itself in our minds? Do we keep coming across things that remind us of a particular ministry need that we feel drawn to? If so, maybe God is calling you to missions! N. T. Wright says about these verses, "All Christians, reading them, should at least ask themselves, and more important ask God in prayer, whether they are among those who will be 'sent' as heralds, enabling men, women, and children in every country and race to hear the good news, so that some at least may come to believe."[59]

My former colleague Peter Law told several cohorts of students that when it comes to mission, "Buddhists give their firstborn, Mormons give two years, and Christians give excuses." Perhaps overstated, but with a sad grain of truth in it. Thankfully, many have taken their feet to the mission field. Steve Mosher tells one such story about missionary feet: "I knew an older Filipino circuit pastor whose churches were in the remote mountains. There were no roads, and he had no car anyway. In fact, he usually didn't wear shoes. His feet were wrinkled, rough, and rugged. After hearing about his mission in the mountains, I thought his feet looked beautiful."[60] That's a moving story about someone who took his preaching feet to a far off place where they were needed the most!

What we need to do then, metaphorically speaking, is to check whether God has given us feet that have been especially blessed to go and tell it on the

59. Wright, "Romans," 10:672.

60. Steve Mosher, *God's Power, Jesus' Faith, and World Mission: A Study in Romans* (Scottdale, PA: Herald, 1996), 209.

mountain, in the river, in the valley, in the slums, in the country, and in the city, that Jesus Christ is Lord. We need to check if we have "feet fitted with the readiness that comes from the gospel of peace" (Eph 6:15). To live the story of Romans 10 might mean for you taking those blessed feet for a walk that's a long way from home!

CHAPTER 20

# Romans 11:1–32

## LISTEN to the Story

[1]I ask then: Did God reject his people? By no means! I am an Israelite myself, a descendant of Abraham, from the tribe of Benjamin. [2]God did not reject his people, whom he foreknew. Don't you know what Scripture says in the passage about Elijah—how he appealed to God against Israel: [3]"Lord, they have killed your prophets and torn down your altars; I am the only one left, and they are trying to kill me"? [4]And what was God's answer to him? "I have reserved for myself seven thousand who have not bowed the knee to Baal." [5]So too, at the present time there is a remnant chosen by grace. [6]And if by grace, then it cannot be based on works; if it were, grace would no longer be grace.

[7]What then? What the people of Israel sought so earnestly they did not obtain. The elect among them did, but the others were hardened, [8]as it is written:

> "God gave them a spirit of stupor,
> eyes that could not see
> and ears that could not hear,
> to this very day."

[9]And David says:

> "May their table become a snare and a trap,
> a stumbling block and a retribution for them.
> [10]May their eyes be darkened so they cannot see,
> and their backs be bent forever."

[11]Again I ask: Did they stumble so as to fall beyond recovery? Not at all! Rather, because of their transgression, salvation has come to the Gentiles to make Israel envious. [12]But if their transgression means riches for the world, and their loss means riches for the Gentiles, how much greater riches will their full inclusion bring!

[13]I am talking to you Gentiles. Inasmuch as I am the apostle to the Gentiles, I take pride in my ministry [14]in the hope that I may somehow

arouse my own people to envy and save some of them. 15For if their
rejection brought reconciliation to the world, what will their acceptance
be but life from the dead? 16If the part of the dough offered as firstfruits is
holy, then the whole batch is holy; if the root is holy, so are the branches.

17If some of the branches have been broken off, and you, though a
wild olive shoot, have been grafted in among the others and now share
in the nourishing sap from the olive root, 18do not consider yourself to
be superior to those other branches. If you do, consider this: You do
not support the root, but the root supports you. 19You will say then,
"Branches were broken off so that I could be grafted in." 20Granted. But
they were broken off because of unbelief, and you stand by faith. Do not
be arrogant, but tremble. 21For if God did not spare the natural branches,
he will not spare you either.

22Consider therefore the kindness and sternness of God: sternness to
those who fell, but kindness to you, provided that you continue in his
kindness. Otherwise, you also will be cut off. 23And if they do not persist
in unbelief, they will be grafted in, for God is able to graft them in again.
24After all, if you were cut out of an olive tree that is wild by nature, and
contrary to nature were grafted into a cultivated olive tree, how much more
readily will these, the natural branches, be grafted into their own olive tree!

25I do not want you to be ignorant of this mystery, brothers and
sisters, so that you may not be conceited: Israel has experienced a
hardening in part until the full number of the Gentiles has come in, 26and
in this way all Israel will be saved. As it is written:

> "The deliverer will come from Zion;
> he will turn godlessness away from Jacob.
> 27 And this is my covenant with them
> when I take away their sins."

28As far as the gospel is concerned, they are enemies for your sake; but
as far as election is concerned, they are loved on account of the patriarchs,
29for God's gifts and his call are irrevocable. 30Just as you who were at
one time disobedient to God have now received mercy as a result of their
disobedience, 31so they too have now become disobedient in order that
they too may now receive mercy as a result of God's mercy to you. 32For
God has bound everyone over to disobedience so that he may have mercy
on them all.

*Listening to the texts in the story*: Numbers 15:17–21; Deuteronomy 29:4; 1 Kings 19:10, 14, 18; Psalm 69:22–23; Isaiah 27:9; 29:10; 59:20–21; Jereremiah 11:16–19; 31:33–34.

Paul concluded his argument in Romans 9:30–10:21 by drawing the picture of God holding out his hands to a disobedient and stubborn Israel, who constantly refused him (10:21). While he has certainly developed this theme of Israel's obstinacy, he will now emphasize that God is still holding out his hands to Israel. Paul will insist, much as he did in 3:3, that Israel's infidelity will be overcome by God's own faithfulness.[1] We are brought, then, to the next phase in Paul's argument about how Israel relates to the gospel through his discourse on Israel and the future, a future that includes Israel's salvation. We find Paul in 11:1–32 describing the hope for his kinsfolk of the flesh to one day find salvation by faith in Israel's Messiah.

The argument that Paul has set forth in Romans 9–10 might seem on first glance to lead to the inescapable conclusion that God has rejected Israel because of their rejection of the Messiah. After all, he has asserted that ethnic Israel and promissory Israel are separate entities (9:9); unbelieving Israel can be likened to Ishmael, Esau, and Pharaoh (9:9–18); Israel might be like a clay pot made for ignoble purposes (9:21), or even "vessels of wrath" (9:22). In terms of the reason why, Israel did not submit to God's righteousness because they pursued righteousness the wrong way and stumbled over the messianic stone of salvation (9:30–33), they missed the climax of the covenant by seeking to establish their own righteousness (10:3–4), and they did not understand because they were disobedient and obstinate (10:16, 19, 21).

Some might say that the weight of Paul's own cruel logic is that Israel has been cast off so that Gentiles could be brought in. Israel had their chance, but now it's too late for them (see 11:18–20). Because of Israel's "ignorance" (10:3, 19), "disobedience" (10:16, 19; 11:31), and spiritual "stupor" (11:8), Israel has become "enemies of the gospel" (11:28). But before anyone from an Ivy League Divinity School appoints Paul to "The Marcion of Sinope Chair in Supersessionist Theology," I would point out that such "logic" is precisely what Paul resists and refutes in Romans 11. Paul escapes the logic of Israel's permanent rejection with a Houdini-like exegetical and theological move in making God's wrath against Israel vanish and making their corporate election reappear. Yet what Paul does is not magic; rather, it's a majestic vision of God's mercy, Christ's *parousia*, all set against the backdrop of the redemptive-historical drama and the interlocking destiny of Jews and Gentiles.

Remember that throughout the course of the argument, Paul has dropped clues for a huge plot twist that would even leave Agatha Christie or Stephen King stunned. That twist is that in the end Israel actually gets saved. Hence Paul's words: "For God has bound everyone over to disobedience so that he

1. Wagner, *Heralds of the Good News*, 219.

may have mercy on them all" (11:32). God's covenantal purposes turn out to be somewhat analogous to the machinations of Severus Snape in the Harry Potter series. What looks like failure or betrayal turns out in the end to be the mystery by which good triumphs, and in hindsight one can see that love, faithfulness, and self-sacrifice were the driving forces all along.

This should be unsurprising, since in Romans 1–8 we saw that the gospel is for the Jew "first" (1:16). God is the God of Jews and Gentiles (3:29); this one God will justify the circumcised and the uncircumcised by faith (3:30). Abraham is the father of the "circumcised" who "walk in the footsteps of faith" (4:12). Jesus brings righteousness and life "for all people" (5:18), and God gave up his Son for "us all" (8:32). So, Paul's gospel remains tethered to the story of Israel, and salvation remains open to the Jewish people. Even within Romans 9–10, we still find a few subtle hints that ethnic Israel might yet make it onto the messianic ark. Israel belongs to the covenants that the Messiah consummates (9:4–5; 10:4). Promissory Israel begins within ethnic Israel (9:6), including Abraham's physical descendants like Isaac and Jacob (9:9–13). God's unmerited mercy is always the decisive factor for Israel, and it just might be so again in the future (9:15–18).

Paul builds on Romans 9–10 in order to show in 11:1–32 that Israel is savable precisely because of God's promises (see the accompanying table). This is not a frantic change of mind, but rests on Paul's theology of Israel's story, including *God's promise* of a new covenant to forgive Israel's sins (11:26–27), *God's election* of Israel, which is "irrevocable" (11:28–29), and *God's plan* to use Israel's disobedience to usher in Gentile inclusion and to use Gentile inclusion to bring Israel to jealousy and thus to salvation (11:14, 30–32). If the biblical story teaches us anything, it is that if God is God and if Israel is his people, then rejection and condemnation cannot be God's last word for them. Paul rehearses what we read in the Law, the Prophets, and the Writings, that there must be a better ending for Israel if God is to be faithful to his covenant.

On structure, while 11:1–32 is undoubtedly a literary unity, it seems that vv. 1–10 and vv. 11–32 constitute an obvious subdivision within the section. Both subsections open with a rhetorical question presuming a negative answer and then proceed to unpack the correct point of view on the topic by a mixture of Old Testament citations and theological reflections.[2] To put it simply, vv. 1–10 deal with "Can any Jews be saved?" while vv. 11–32 deal with "Can any more Jews be saved?"[3] To break it down further, (1) Paul establishes the possibility of Israel's salvation by appealing to the idea of remnant (vv. 1–6); (2) he briefly recaps Israel's failure in trying to obtain righteousness by works

2. Cf. e.g., Cranfield, *Romans*, 2:542; Moo, *Romans*, 671.
3. Wright, "Romans," 10:673.

| Israel's Salvation across Romans 9–11 | |
|---|---|
| *Romans 9–10* | *Romans 11* |
| God's word has not failed (9:6) | God has not rejected his people (11:1) |
| In judgment Israel is reduced to a remnant (9:27–29) | God has thankfully preserved a remnant (11:5) |
| Salvation not by works but by grace (9:12, 32) | A remnant chosen by grace (11:5–6) |
| Israel stumbled (9:32–33) | Israel did not stumble beyond recovery (11:12–13) |
| God will prompt Israel to jealousy (10:19) | Gentile salvation makes Israel jealous to salvation (11:11, 14) |
| God hardens Israel (9:18; cf. 11:7–8) | Israel was hardened temporarily (11:25) |
| Paul prays for Israel's salvation (10:1) | All Israel is saved (11:26) |
| God's purposes in election stand against achievement (9:11) | God's election means Israel is loved (11:28) |
| Israel's disobedience (10:16, 21) | Gentile disobedience and Israel's disobedience (11:30–31) |
| God has mercy on whom he has mercy (9:15, 16, 18) | Israel receives mercy (11:31–32) |

(vv. 7–10); (3) Paul asserts that Israel's failure is not final, but leads to the Gentiles coming into salvation, which in turn may arouse Israel to jealousy (vv. 11–15); (4) the relationship between Gentiles and Israel can be likened to an olive tree with foreign branches grafted in and natural branches, once broken off, regrafted back in (vv. 16–24); and (5) God's new covenant promises ensure that there is still hope for Israel to receive mercy either before or at the Messiah's second coming (vv. 25–32).

## EXPLAIN the Story

### A Soft Remnant within Hardened Israel (11:1–5)

Paul launches into the next section of his argument with a rhetorical question, "I ask then: Did God reject his people? By no means!" (v. 1). Just like 9:1 and 10:18–19, Paul uses "I ask" (*legō*) to indicate a transition to the next phase of his argument. The question about whether God has rejected his people is demanded by Paul's discussion across 9:30–10:21 as to whether Israel's obstinacy means that Israel has reached a point of no return. Paul responds with an emphatic denial, "By no means!" (*mē genoito*) to underscore its impossibility (see 3:4, 5–6; 9:14; 11:11). The immediate reason why God cannot reject his people is because there are some among his people, like Paul, who have embraced the Messiah. As he did earlier (see 9:3), Paul stresses his genealogical relationship to Israel: "I am an Israelite myself, a descendant of Abraham, from the tribe of Benjamin" (v. 1). Paul is genuinely conflicted between his identity as a Jew and his conviction regarding salvation residing exclusively in the gospel. The resolution is that Paul knows that his Jewish heritage does not guarantee any status of "righteousness" (see 2 Cor 11:22; Phil 3:5–9); nonetheless, Paul still holds onto his inherited privileges as an Israelite since they are the conduit for the revelation of God's righteousness. In the end, the existence of Jewish Christians like Paul is telling evidence that God has not rejected his people.[4]

Paul asserts in affirmative terms what he denied in v. 1a, that "God did not reject his people, whom he foreknew" (v. 2a). The precise wording derives from Psalm 94:14 and 1 Samuel 12:22, though Paul adds the description of Israel as those "whom he foreknew." The appeal to divine foreknowledge is meant to locate Israel within God's pretemporal plans and to stress how Israel's position before God rests on God's choice of them to be his people. The irrevocable nature of Israel's election is based on the immutability of God's knowledge; God cannot unknow the people whom he knows are his (see Rom 8:29).

In addition to believing Israelites like Paul (v. 1b) and divine foreknowledge (v. 2a), Paul adds a third reason as to why God cannot reject Israel, that is, scriptural testimony to a remnant: "Don't you know what Scripture says in the passage about Elijah—how he appealed to God against Israel: 'Lord, they have killed your prophets and torn down your altars; I am the only one left, and they are trying to kill me'?" (v. 3). Paul brings up the story of King Ahab's persecution of the prophets faithful to the Lord from 1 Kings 19. After Ahab massacred the prophets and after Jezebel sent Elijah death threats, Elijah fled to Mount Horeb. Paul cites Elijah's lament in 19:10, 14 that Israel is in willful violation of the covenant and he is the last prophet left. The words probably resonated with Paul given the often fierce response that his message incited from his fellow Jews (see Rom 15:31; 1 Cor 4:12; 2 Cor 4:9; 11:24–26; Gal 5:11; 1 Thess 2:15). Repeated expulsions from Jewish communities may have left him and his coworkers feeling as if they were the last of the messianic Mohicans (see Acts 13:50–51; 14:2; 17:5–9; 18:6–8; 19:8).

4. Käsemann, *Romans*, 299; Moo, *Romans*, 673.

However, the stories of Elijah and Paul carry a ray of hope as well. There, in the wilderness, the Lord assured Elijah that Ahab had not destroyed all the prophets, for the Lord had preserved seven thousand men. So Paul asks: "And what was God's answer to him? 'I have reserved for myself seven thousand who have not bowed the knee to Baal' " (v. 4). The citation of 1 Kings 19:18 is congenial to Paul's purpose here, which is to show that God's faithfulness to his people outweighs the depths of Israel's rebellion. Just as God preserved a remnant in the days of Ahab, so too has God preserved a remnant in the days of Israel's disobedience to the gospel.

Here we see the flip side of a remnant theology. A remnant can be viewed negatively in judgment, in that *only* a remnant will be saved (Rom 9:27); or else positively, *at least* a remnant will be saved (9:29; 11:4). In any case, building on what he said before (see 9:24), Paul holds that this remnant includes believing Jews. God's preservation of a Jewish remnant not only proves God's faithfulness to Israel, but it is the seed with which God sows and grows the renewed people of God.

The application of 1 Kings 19 to Paul's own context is then made explicit: "So too, at the present time there is a remnant chosen by grace. And if by grace, then it cannot be based on works; if it were, grace would no longer be grace" (vv. 5–6). The "present time" is the eschatological moment of salvation (see 3:21; 8:18), where grace invades the world to set free those enslaved to sin and death (5:20–21). These two verses arguably summarize the whole of Romans 9–10 thus far by emphasizing that the remnant comes into existence only through God's choosing (9:6–29), to the exclusion of any effort to lay a claim for deliverance based on works (9:11–12; 9:30–10:4). The grace vs. works contrast underscores that Israel has no nationalistic privileges or achievement in Torah obedience that she can cling to as the basis for salvation (see 2:1–29; 3:20; 4:2–8; 9:10–13). As Paul has done earlier, he has stressed that grace is the efficacious cause of salvation (see 4:16; 5:2, 15, 17, 20–21). Grace is God's unmerited favor, but it ceases to be grace when someone claims to have merited it.

### A Recap of Israel's Failure (11:7–10)

In light of vv. 5–6, Paul goes on to explain why only a remnant has been chosen: "What then? What the people of Israel sought so earnestly they did not obtain. The elect among them did, but the others were hardened" (v. 7). The rhetorical question announces Paul's wish to show the implications of what a remnant of Jewish Christians means for Israel as a whole. Paul, largely abbreviating 9:30–32, states that "Israel" as an entire people "did not obtain" a righteous standing before God by Torah obedience. However, the "elect among them did," we may presume because they had faith in the Messiah (see 10:6, 8–11, 17; 11:20). But if God has chosen a Jewish remnant to receive his blessings, then the obvious implication is that the rest of Israel is not elected to be part of the remnant. Instead, the rest of Israel has been "hardened." In 9:17–18 Paul invoked the language of "hardening" in relation to Pharaoh and applied it implicitly to unbelieving Israel to describe their spiritual antagonism to God's purposes. He deploys once more the language of "hardening" to account for Israel's exclusion from the blessings of the remnant.

To clear the deck, I do not think this hardening relates to a notion of eternal reprobation unto damnation for the nonelect. Let us remember a few things. First, the language of v. 7 balances both divine sovereignty and human responsibility, since it conveys equally notions of God's "elect" and a deliberate "hardening" in addition to notions of human "striving" and efforts to "obtain."[5] Second, Paul does not say that Israel was hardened so that they were made to fail; rather, if we read it in sequence, Israel has been hardened because they failed. According to Morris, "we must remember that those who failed God did not do so because they had been hardened, but they were hardened because they had failed him."[6] Paul is probably tapping into a standard apocalyptic theme that those who do not use the delay in God's judgment to repent and turn back to God will themselves be hardened by God to increase their culpability at the final judgment.[7] Third, Paul cannot be talking about an eternal decree of hardening akin to an "eternal reprobation" because when we get to 11:25, we discover that Israel's hardening is only temporary.

The citations from Deuteronomy 29:4, Isaiah 29:10, and Psalm 69:22–23 in vv. 8–10 underscore that Paul sees Israel as suffering a type of spiritual blindness and an incapacity to perceive God's work in their midst. As Moses warned, Israel is inherently stupefied and unable to appreciate God's act of deliverance for them. As Isaiah lamented, Israel has reached a point of spiritual stupor where revelation proves ineffectual. As David sang, Israel has become like enemies standing in futile opposition against God's anointed king. Tragically, ethnic Israel will be blinded and remain hardened so long as they refuse to see the crucified one as their Messiah and Lord.

## God's Call, Israel's Fall, and the Mission of the Apostle Paul (11:11–15)

The dilemma of Israel's failure is now placed into a redemptive-historical and even cosmic framework that reveals, in the end, the potential riches that

5. Moo, *Romans*, 679 n. 45.

6. Morris, *Romans*, 403.

7. Wright, "Romans," 10:677.

could flow from Israel's "full inclusion" and "acceptance." Paul clearly turns a corner here and begins to outline how it might be that rebellious Israel finds reconciliation with their God.

"Again I ask: Did they stumble so as to fall beyond recovery? Not at all!" (v. 11a). Just as in v. 1, Paul opens v. 11 with a rhetorical question. The question pertains to whether Israel's stumbling means that they have fallen into a permanent and irretrievable state of loss (*pesōsin*; see "fallen permanently" [CEB]; "lead to their downfall" [NJB]; "fallen off the deep end" [VOICE]; "Are they down for the count?" [MSG]). To which Paul gives his final emphatic negation, "Not at all!" (*mē genoito*). Israel has not stumbled *in order to* irreversibly fall away.[8] Israel's failure does not put them beyond the pale of redemption.

Paul sets the question in sharp contrast to his own view, which espouses the interlocking destiny of Jews and Gentiles: "Rather, because of their transgression, salvation has come to the Gentiles to make Israel envious" (v. 11b). Israel's "transgression" for not believing in the Messiah has given occasion for the Gentiles to receive "salvation." And "salvation" here must involve the whole scope of Romans 3–8 in terms of belonging to God's forgiven-justified-reconciled-adopted-renewed family united in the Messiah and sharing in the Spirit. This "salvation" may also provoke Israel to jealousy just as Paul intimated in Romans 10:19 with his citation of Deuteronomy 32:21. The difference is that whereas jealousy was originally intended in Deuteronomy 32 as a curse, jealousy becomes now a means of drawing Israel back to God.

The picture is that of Israel, seeing the Gentiles enjoying *their* messianic blessings and *their* covenant renewal, in turn become desirous for it and want it for themselves, and resultantly come to faith so that they might possess the riches of God in Christ. In other words, Israel will get jealous when she sees Gentiles playing her part in the redemptive drama![9] This salvation boomerangs in that it comes from Israel, goes to the Gentiles, and then returns to Israel. The premise behind all this is that Israel is not only savable, but God really wants to save Israel. If so, then it was not a matter of courtesy that Paul said the gospel brings salvation "first to the Jew" (1:16). It was not out of feigned concern that Paul prayed for Israel's salvation (10:1). Paul's claim that the offer of salvation applies to anyone who calls on the name of the Lord Jesus was not an empty offer (10:9–11). The point of all this is simply that ethnic Israel may yet be saved!

---

8. Porter, *Idioms*, 236.

9. Richard H. Bell, *Provoked to Jealousy: The Origin and Purpose of the Jealousy Motif in Romans 9–11* (WUNT 2.63; Tübingen: Mohr Siebeck, 1994), 199; cf. similarly Wagner, *Heralds of the Good News*, 357.

Paul continues his line of argument by emphasizing how Israel's full inclusion brings even greater blessings for the Gentiles: "But if their transgression means riches for the world, and their loss means riches for the Gentiles, how much greater riches will their full inclusion bring" (v. 15). Israel's failure meant an opulent abundance of divine riches like kindness (2:4) and glory (9:23) extending to the whole world and the Gentile peoples who inhabit it.[10] On the premise that Israel's destitute state yielded a blessed state for Gentiles, Paul infers that Israel's "full inclusion" will produce an even more bountiful array of riches for the world.[11] If Israel's loss is the Gentiles' gain, Israel's gain will be the Gentiles' mega-super-duper-über gain! Paul makes clear that the Gentiles stand not to be impoverished, but to be enriched by Israel's full inclusion in the Messiah's family.

Paul turns from his line of argument to an aside remark about his role as an apostle to bring Israel to jealousy: "I am talking to you Gentiles. Inasmuch as I am the apostle to the Gentiles, I take pride in my ministry in the hope that I may somehow arouse my own people to envy and save some of them" (vv. 13–14). Paul addresses his Gentile audience to correct any erroneous assumption on their part that the reason that he himself ministers to Gentiles is because he has given up on the Jews. Quite the contrary. Paul labors in Gentile territory as part of his apostolic call (see Gal 1:13–14), yet he does so knowing that his work serves a wider purpose to rouse Israel to jealousy. By his labors, Paul wants to "save some" of his "own people" ("my flesh," *mou tēn sarka*) by either preaching to them (1 Cor 9:20–22) or by provoking them to envy through the spiritual riches of the Gentiles (Rom 11:13).

Paul returns to his initial assertion about the interlocking destinies of Gentiles and Jews in v. 12 by adding a conditional expectation for Israel in v. 15: "For if their rejection brought reconciliation to the world, what will their acceptance be but life from the dead?" (v. 15). Israel's "rejection" is equivalent to their hardening for disbelieving the message of Jesus. Yet this casting off of Israel led to the Gentiles experiencing "reconciliation" through the message of the cross (see Rom 5:10–11; 2 Cor 5:18–21; Col 1:22). If so, Israel's eventual "acceptance" by God[12] will not only be beneficial to Gentiles, could it even be, he asks, "life from the dead?"

---

10. Although "world" and "Gentiles" might be synonymous, I think it better to see the latter as a subset of the former.

11. Commentators differ as to whether "full inclusion" (*plērōma*) has a qualitative meaning of "fullness" or a quantitative sense of "full number." It might be a bit of both as Paul envisages the fullness attained through a numerical process (see Moo, *Romans*, 690). Or, as General Norman Schwarzkopf once said about the numerical size of the Iraqi Army, "there is a certain quality to quantity."

12. On acceptance by God, see Rom 14:2 and 15:7.

In keeping with the apocalyptic orientation of Paul's theology, he might be suggesting that Israel's acceptance of the Messiah will usher in the day of resurrection (see John 11:24; 1 Cor 15:22–24; Phil 3:10–11; 1 Thess 4:14; Rev 20:4–6).[13] Perhaps, but more likely Paul is saying that Israel's coming to faith will be so amazing and so miraculous that the only metaphor apt describe it is resurrection. This image is an appropriate metaphor for Israel's political restoration and their return from exile (see Ezek 37; Hos 13:14). If so, Paul is saying that Israel has finally experienced the story of salvation as narrated in Romans 5:10 by going from hostility to reconciliation to acceptance to life.[14] Paul holds out the prospect that Israel may yet find in Christ the fullness of covenantal and eschatological life.

### Redemptive History and Divine Horticulture (11:16–24)

Paul continues his exhortation to his Gentile readers about the savableness of Israel through a horticultural metaphor of an olive tree. The olive tree represents the people of God, the root is the patriarchal promises, ethnic Israel is the "natural branches," and Christian Gentiles are the "wild olive shoot." What Paul sets out to do here is try to adjust the attitude of his Gentile audience toward Israel — hence the repeated use of the personal pronoun "you" throughout. He wants to make sure that they do not bask in Israel's failure or think that Israel is excluded from a future place in God's people. The proper perspective they should have is to see Israel and Gentile Christians as potential exemplars of each other. Just as Gentiles were grafted into the tree, so too can Israel be regrafted into the tree. Just as Israel was cut off from the tree, so too can Gentiles be cut off from the tree. Gentile boasting is excluded because the cutting off of branches and the grafting in of shoots cuts both ways for both ethnic groups. So rather than boast over Israel, Gentiles should look at unbelieving Israel and say, "There but for the grace of God go I," or else the Gentiles should testify to unbelieving Israel in saying, "We benefit from the spiritual nourishment that was first yours and can still be yours."

Paul begins with metaphorical language about bread offering and botany to prove that what is true of the part of something is also true for the whole of something: "If the part of the dough offered as firstfruits is holy, then the whole batch is holy; if the root is holy, so are the branches" (v. 16). The thought is clearly transitional as Paul tries to tie together his claim about the interlocking destiny of Jews and Gentiles in vv. 10–15 with his forthcoming

13. Cf. e.g., Käsemann, *Romans*, 307; Fitzmyer, *Romans*, 613; Dunn, *Romans*, 2:658, 670; Moo, *Romans*, 694–96; Schreiner, *Romans*, 599; Jewett, *Romans*, 681.

14. Cf. e.g., Ambrosiaster, 90; Morris, *Romans*, 411; Wright, *Climax of the Covenant*, 248; idem, "Romans," 10:682; Kirk, *Unlocking Romans*, 184–93.

olive tree metaphor in vv. 17–24. In general, the imagery of dough and a tree stresses that the qualities associated with an item's germinal state extends to its germane parts. More specifically, in the case of a bread offering (see Num 15:19–21), once the firstfruits of the dough have been offered to God, the whole batch is considered holy and consecrated for use. In the case of an olive tree, if the root is holy, then so are its extended branches (see Jer 11:16–17; Hos 14:6).

It is generally agreed that the "whole batch" and "branches" are symbols for ethnic Israel in its state of unbelief, but what precisely is symbolized by the "firstfruits" and the "root"? Given the surrounding context, I am inclined to see the "firstfruits" as the remnant of Jewish Christians who have been chosen by grace, including Paul himself. Paul often uses "firstfruits" to refer to "first converts" (Rom 16:5; 1 Cor 16:15; 2 Thess 2:13).[15] These Jewish believers are the firstfruits of believing Israel, who are sanctified by their faith. A corollary is that the whole of Israel, from whom the remnant was drawn, must be regarded as holy too — somewhat analogous to how an unbelieving person is sanctified by their believing spouse in 1 Corinthians 7:13–14. The identity of the "root" is open to conjecture, and numerous suggestions have been made in the history of interpretation — e.g., that it refers to the Jewish Christian remnant, the Messiah, or God. The most likely option is the patriarchs[16] since Paul sees the patriarchs as one of Israel's greatest privileges (9:5), the patriarchs are the basis for God's love for Israel (11:28), and the Messiah served the Jews to confirm the promises made to the patriarchs (15:8). Unpacking the symbolism of the root and branches, Paul means that the holiness and belongingness of Israel's patriarchal origins extends even to Israel's current position.[17]

The imagery of the tree root and tree branches is then transformed into a metaphor for which his readers are meant to identify themselves: "If some of the branches have been broken off, and you, though a wild olive shoot, have been grafted in among the others and now share in the nourishing sap from the olive root, do not consider yourself to be superior to those other branches. If you do, consider this: You do not support the root, but the root supports

---

15. Dunn, *Romans*, 2:659.

16. On the patriarchs as the "root" of Israel, see *1 En.* 93.5; Philo, *Heir* 279; *Jub.* 21.24.

17. Thus I side with several commentators (e.g., Nicholas of Lyra; Cranfield, *Romans*, 2:564–65; Fitzmyer, *Romans*, 614; Bell, *Provoked to Jealousy*, 123; Keck, *Romans*, 273) in identifying the firstfruits with the Jewish remnant and the root with the patriarchs because it sums up the discussion of both the "remnant" and the "rest" of Israel in 11:1–15. Others see a consistent reference to the patriarchs in both images (see e.g., Chrysostom, *Hom. Rom.* 19; Moo, *Romans*, 700–701; Byrne, *Romans*, 340; Schreiner, *Romans*, 600; Talbert, *Romans*, 261–62). Wright ("Romans," 10:683–84) takes the firstfruits as the Jewish remnant and the root as the Messiah.

you" (vv. 17–18).[18] The basic plot is that some of the "branches" (i.e., ethnic Israel) may have been broken off (i.e., stumbled, hardened, rejected, stupefied), while you/wild olive shoot (i.e., Gentile Christians) have been grafted onto the tree and share in its nutrients (i.e., salvation in Israel's Messiah). Yet the point that Paul initially draws from the metaphor is to reprimand his Gentile readers for a disparagement of ethnic Israel. Paul does not want Gentiles to think that their elect status somehow licenses them to gloat over unbelieving Israel. Paul will not allow them to rewrite redemptive history as if Israel was merely the cocoon and Gentile Christians were the butterfly and to brag over Israel as now dispensable and discarded. To do that would be to engage in the very kind of boasting that Paul censures his hypothetical Jewish interlocutor for performing (see 2:17, 23).

The principle of the gospel is that all boasting is excluded (see 3:27; 4:2) save boasting in the glory of God (see 5:2, 11). At ground level in the city of Rome this means that Gentile Christians cannot indulge themselves in the ethnic prejudice and cultural bigotry that Roman satirists and political elites often exercised toward Rome's Jewish minority.[19] The basis for that injunction is Paul's claim: "You do not support the root, but the root supports you." Christian Gentiles stand on the patriarchal promises for Israel, not vice-versa. The Gentiles must remember that they get in only on the coattails of the patriarchal promises given to Israel.

Immediately following, Paul broaches and rebuts a potential objection: "You will say then, 'Branches were broken off so that I could be grafted in.' Granted. But they were broken off because of unbelief, and you stand by faith. Do not be arrogant, but tremble" (vv. 19–20). Paul presents his imaginary Gentile Christian interlocutor taking a supersessionist view whereby Gentile Christians have replaced Israel *in toto*. Out with the menorahs and in with the

18. In ancient arboricultural practice it was normal to graft in a cultivated olive shoot into a wild olive tree rather than the other way around as Paul has it. Mark Nanos ("'Broken Branches': A Pauline Metaphor Gone Awry?," in *Between Gospel and Election: Explorations in the Interpretation of Romans 9–11* (ed. F. Wilk and J. Wagner; WUNT 257; Tübingen: Mohr Siebeck, 2010], 356) writes: "According to modern genetic research, the cultivated olive (*olea europaea*) and the wild olive (*olea oleaster*) of the Mediterranean basin have the same chromosome number and are interfertile; however, the wild differ in that they have smaller fruit, a thinner mesocarp, poorer oil content, and a long juvenile stage accompanied by the appearance of spinescent shoots. In terms of productivity, one does not graft wild olive cuttings onto cultivated trees, because the wild branches do not produce good fruit." Whether Paul was a city slicker who knew nothing about ancient farming techniques is beside the point. Metaphors bend reality. It might be the case that Paul is deliberately reversing normal practice to emphasize that the Gentiles are like a wild olive tree, which was usually unfruitful, and have been grafted in "contrary to nature" (v. 24) to highlight God's grace to the Gentiles.

19. For example, Tacitus (*Histories* 5.1) said that the "customs of the Jews are base and abominable, and owe their persistence to their depravity." See further John Gager, *The Origins of Anti-Semitism* (Oxford: Oxford University Prress, 1983), 35–112.

foreskins! Paul actually accepts the premise (*kalōs*, "Granted" [NIV]; "Fine" [CEB]; "Quite so" [Dunn]), but only to the extent that a part of Israel has been broken off and the Gentiles have been included within Israel's inheritance (hence the "*some* [*tines*] of the branches have been broken off" and "you have been grafted in *among them* [*en autois*]" in v. 17).

Yet it is the implications Paul draws that set his position apart from the interlocutor's view. Paul does not see this breaking off and engrafting as the grounds for some kind of replacement theology, with the Gentile church supposedly replacing Israel once and for all. Gentile inclusion *within* Israel does not entail the replacement *of* Israel. Once more the determinative factor is faith, since unbelief led to Israel being "broken off" and belief is what enables Gentiles to be "grafted in." If so, Gentiles have no right to hubris or haughtiness, since they may well find themselves in the same position as Israel if they do not "stand by faith."

The warning against smug self-superiority and willful arrogance becomes even more explicit in the following explanation: "For if God did not spare the natural branches, he will not spare you either. Consider therefore the kindness and sternness of God: sternness to those who fell, but kindness to you, provided that you continue in his kindness. Otherwise, you also will be cut off" (vv. 21–22). The reason why Gentile Christians need a healthy fear of the Lord is because God did not spare Israel from the consequences of their unbelief even though they naturally belonged to the patriarchs. Therefore, God is even less likely to spare Gentiles who are outside the covenants made with the patriarchs. While Christian Gentiles currently enjoy the "kindness" of God, they would do well to remember that God's "sternness" can equally fall on those who fall away from faith. Thus, the place of Gentile Christians is conditional in that it depends on keeping side with God's kindness by staying in the faith.

How this rather serious warning about falling away relates to the promises of assurance in 8:18–39 is a genuinely good question. I. Howard Marshall simply embraces the tension by concluding that "side by side with the stress on divine initiative in election and salvation there is a warning to show awe in the sight of God lest anyone should be cut off for failing to continue in His kindness."[20] In the very least we must surmise that Paul is saying that the only saving faith is a persevering faith (see Rom 8:13; Col 1:23; Heb 3:6, 14).[21]

The fact that faith is what matters not only gives Gentile believers cause for trepidation, but might also count in Israel's favor as Paul continues: "And

20. I. Howard Marshall, *Kept By the Power of God: A Study of Perseverance and Falling Away* (Minneapolis: Bethany, 1969), 105. Dunn (*Romans*, 2:664) adds, "A doctrine of 'perseverance of the saints' which does not include the lessons of salvation-history has lost its biblical perspective."

21. On issues of security and perseverance, see Bird, *Evangelical Theology*, 595–605.

if they do not persist in unbelief, they will be grafted in, for God is able to graft them in again" (v. 23). Here we find the point that Paul has been getting at. Israel can still be saved if they come to the position of faith. Already we have heard that God is willing to save ethnic Israel (see 9:22–23; 10:1, 21); now we learn that God is able to do so as well.

The point is then defended by framing the matter in a rhetorical form that moves from the harder to the easier. Paul adds: "After all, if you were cut out of an olive tree that is wild by nature, and contrary to nature were grafted into a cultivated olive tree, how much more readily will these, the natural branches, be grafted into their own olive tree!" (v. 24). If God can bring pork-eating, idol-worshiping, bisexual pagans into his new covenant people (a hard thing to do), how much more can he incorporate the people who already possess an adoption to sonship, divine glory, the covenants, receiving of the law, temple worship, the promises of the patriarchs, and a shared ancestry with the Messiah into his renewed covenant people (a comparatively easier thing to do). While the Gentiles get in, they do so as unnatural outsiders to the olive tree, whereas Israel, by faith, can come back to their own olive tree.

### Plot Twist Revealed: All Israel will be Saved (11:25–32)

We enter the climax that Paul has been building toward since 11:11. Paul enters the end game of his theological gambit in trying to persuade Gentile Christians in Rome to hold—or continue to hold—his view about the prospect of Israel's eventual deliverance. In brief, Paul thinks Gentiles can avoid conceitedness toward Israel by realizing that God's plan was to harden Israel temporarily until the full measure of the Gentiles was saved, and then God would save "Israel" at the return of Christ (vv. 25–27). Thereafter, Paul provides a summation of his argument that God's purposes are driven chiefly by his desire to have mercy on disobedient Jews and Gentiles (vv. 28–32).

Paul sums up the significance of his olive tree metaphor with these words: "I do not want you to be ignorant of this mystery, brothers and sisters, so that you may not be conceited: Israel has experienced a hardening in part until the full number of the Gentiles has come in" (v. 25). The plea to avoid ignorance frequently accompanies teaching that Paul regards as crucial (see 1:13; 1 Cor 10:1; 12:1; 2 Cor 1:8; 1 Thess 4:13). Specifically, Paul wants them to avoid ignorance of "the mystery," not a secret teaching divulged only to initiates in elaborate ceremonies, but God's long-hidden plan that is now unveiled in the gospel of Jesus the Messiah. This plan is to make Jews and Gentiles co-heirs of God's kingdom (see Rom 16:25; 1 Cor 2:1, 7; Eph 1:9; 3:3–9; 6:19; Col 1:26–27; 2:2; 4:3).

The substance of the mystery is the sequence of events in which it unfolds: Israel's disobedience and hardening, until the fullness of Gentiles come in, and then all Israel will be saved. Knowing this "mystery" will keep them from being arrogant about their own place in redemptive history as they'll realize that Gentile believers form a mutual, symbiotic, soteriological relationship with Israel.[22] Paul affirms that Israel has experienced a hardening, but it pertains only to "part of Israel" (NJB, CEB) rather than a "partial hardening" (ESV, NRSV, NASB, HCSB, NET).[23] In step with Romans 9:6 and 11:7, Paul envisages the rest of ethnic Israel as the part that is hardened and a promissory Israel who is not hardened. Not only that, but the hardening is temporary and lasts "until" (*achri*) the full cohort of Gentiles comes to join God's people. Paul does not envisage all Gentiles everywhere getting saved, but looks to the full number of Gentiles appointed to salvation entering the family of the Messiah (see Acts 13:48). It would seem that the final judgment is stayed and Israel's hardening continues until such time as the Gentile mission is completed.

Paul turns to the final item in the chain of events, which is the actual circumstance of Israel's salvation: "And in this way all Israel will be saved" (v. 26a). Let me say that whole schemes of theology, complete with charts, modern prophecy, novels, and theo-political lobby groups for the US policy in the Middle East, hinge on these few words. Three different sets of questions present themselves for us to answer:

| 1. Who is all Israel? | 2. When does Israel get saved? | 3. How does Israel get saved? |
|---|---|---|
| (a) A combined cohort of elect Jews and Gentiles; (b) the elect within ethnic Israel; (c) the whole of ethnic Israel to the very last individual. | (a) Across the history of the church's missionary outreach to Israel; (b) immediately before the second coming; or (c) during the second coming. | (a) Through faith in the Messiah; (b) through a miraculous act at the second coming; (c) through the Mosaic covenant remaining effectual for them. |

The first question is, "Who is all Israel?"[24] It is tempting to say that "Israel" is the elect group of believing Jews and Gentiles. That view has merit in light of 9:9b that not everyone from *ethnic* Israel belongs to *elect* Israel, and

22. Cf. e.g., Moo, *Romans*, 716; Witherington, *Romans*, 272.

23. Most likely *apo merous* ("from a part") modifies *Israēl gegonen* ("come upon Israel") rather than *pōrōsis* ("hardening") since the prepositional phrase is normally adverbial, as in Rom 15:15, 24.

24. Cf. survey in Mark A Nanos, *The Mystery of Romans: The Jewish Context of Paul's Letter* (Minneapolis: Fortress, 1996), 256–58.

9:24–29, where God's "people" are comprised of believing Jews and Gentiles (cf. other passages in Paul's writings like Gal 6:16 and Phil 3:3, which use Jewish language for the church).[25] However, the overwhelming weight of usage in Romans 9–11 is that "Israel" consistently means "ethnic Israel' (9:6a, 27, 31; 10:19, 21; 11:2, 7, 11). In addition, the "all" in "all Israel" is probably rhetorical, given that Paul knows that some of his kinsfolk can fall into divine judgment (see 2:1–16). So while Paul does not think that every individual Jew will necessarily be saved, he remains hopeful that much of Israel will be saved at a future time when the "remnant" (11:5) is joined with the elect from the "rest" of Israel (11:7).[26] So my position on the chart is 1 (b).

On "When does Israel get saved?" that too is a complex matter. To begin with, Paul clearly knows that Jews like himself as well as Peter, Barnabas, Priscilla and Aquila, John Mark, and many others have come to faith. Indeed, he seems to assume the necessity of a continued preaching mission to Israel in 10:14–21. So we can think that the salvation of Jews will happen over the course of the church's missionary activity present and future. So yes to option 2(a). Yet Paul does *not* seem to know of a mass conversion of Jews to Christian faith as some kind of catalyst for the second coming as maintained in some dispensational readings of Revelation (so no to option 2 [b]). Even so, there is definitely a future horizon to his thought.

The adverb *houtōs* in context could be either modal for "in this way" or temporal "and thereafter." I think the temporal meaning is supported by three things.[27] First, Paul has already given a temporal sequence in v. 25 by asserting that Israel's hardening will last "until" the full number of Gentiles are saved. So the natural sequel is that he looks ahead in v. 26 to a future moment after the fullness of Gentiles are saved and when Israel's hardening ends. Second, the future tense of *sōthēsetai* ("will be saved") in v. 26 is a real future as opposed to a logical future and underscores the temporal sequence all the more. Third, the compressed citation of Isaiah 27:9; 59:20; and Jeremiah 31:33 in vv. 26–27 looks like a description of what will happen at Jesus'

25. Cf. Barth, *Romans*, 416; Wright, *Climax of the Covenant*, 249–50; idem, "Romans," 10: 688–90; Fitzmyer, *Romans*, 622–23.

26. Cf. Tobin, *Rhetoric of Righteousness*, 373; see also Christopher Zoccali, "'And So All Israel Will Be Saved': Competing Interpretations of Romans 11.26 in Pauline Scholarship," *JSNT* 30 (2008): 303–4.

27. Cf. Munck, *Christ and Israel*, 136; Barrett, *Romans*, 223; Käsemann, *Romans*, 313; Witherington, *Romans*, 274; Talbert, *Romans*, 264; Jewett, *Romans*, 701. See esp. P. W. van der Horst, "Only Then Will All Israel Be Saved: A Short Note on the Meaning of *kai houtōs* in Romans 11.26," *JBL* 119 (2000): 521–25, who lists several extrabiblical examples where *houtōs* has a temporal sense of "thereafter" or "then" (contra Wright, "Romans," 10:691; Moo, *Romans*, 719–20; Fitzmyer, *Romans*, 622–23; Schreiner, *Romans*, 620).

return when Israel comes to repentance and experiences the new covenant blessing of forgiveness. So a yes also goes to option 2 (c).

As to "How does Israel get saved?" a strange coalition of ultradispensationalists and liberal scholars has suggested that Israel is saved without faith in Jesus since their own covenantal arrangement remains effectual. I'll have more to say on that below in "Live the Story," but such a view can be easily set aside. Paul began his letter with a thesis set out in 1:16–17 that salvation is by faith for Jew and Gentile as backed up by Habakkuk 2:4. If that were not enough, 4:1–25 discourses on the necessity of faith for Jew and Gentile to belong to the renewed family of Abraham. Throughout Romans 9–11, Paul has emphasized that salvation comes by faith (9:30, 33; 10:4, 6–8, 9–11, 14, 17), and Israel's problem has been unbelief (9:32; 11:20, 23). Faith in Messiah Jesus is the essential and nonnegotiable condition for fellowship in God's people and a right standing before God. So it has to be option 3 (a).

Paul uses a blended citation of Isaiah and Jeremiah to describe the circumstances when "all Israel is saved": "As it is written: 'The deliverer will come from Zion; he will turn godlessness away from Jacob [Isa 59:20]. And this is my covenant with them [Jer 31:33] when I take away their sins [Isa 27:9]'" (vv. 26b–27). An immediate conundrum with the Isaiah 59:20 quote is that the MT says that the Deliverer will come "to Zion," the LXX says that the Deliverer will come "for the sake of Zion," while Paul says that the Deliverer will come "from Zion." We can probably solve the problem once we realize that Zion is probably a designation for heaven (see Pss 9:11; 50:2; Joel 3:17; Gal 4:26; Heb 12:22; Rev 3:12; 21:2). The image is analogous to statements affirming Jesus' return "from heaven" (Phil 3:20; 4:16; 1 Thess 1:10; 2 Thess 1:7). Paul is drawing on prophetic language to say that the Messiah's return will mean that Israel finally enters the new covenant with its promises of forgiveness and national restoration (i.e., renewed covenant, new exodus, rebuilt temple, God's return to dwell with his people, etc.).

Paul rounds up the discussion of Gentile Christians vis-à-vis unbelieving Israel with the statement: "As far as the gospel is concerned, they are enemies for your sake; but as far as election is concerned, they are loved on account of the patriarchs, for God's gifts and his call are irrevocable" (vv. 28–29). What will enable these Gentiles to stand firm in the faith without arrogance toward Israel is getting a gospel perspective on the subject. In light of the gospel, Israel are "enemies" insofar as they refuse to believe the gospel message, they disobey the summons, and they even oppose what the message is saying about Gentile inclusion in Israel's heritage. And yet, on account of "election," with respect to God's purpose and plan, Israel is "loved" by God because of what God promised the patriarchs. The result is that God's gift of salvation and his call to salvation are "irrevocable."[28] God still has hands open to ethnic Israel no matter how obstinate they remain. If it were otherwise, God's word to Israel would have rested on a false promise.

This means that Paul's desire for Israel's salvation (10:1) is the same as God's desire (10:19) — a desire that, on closer inspection, is for Gentiles and Israel to enter into God's mercies. "Just as you who were at one time disobedient to God have now received mercy as a result of their disobedience, so they too have now become disobedient in order that they too may now receive mercy as a result of God's mercy to you" (vv. 30–31). Paul's remarks are a compressed summary of 11:11–15 concerning how Israel's disobedience led to Gentile inclusion and Gentile inclusion will lead to Israel's acceptance. By using the pronouns "you" and "they," Paul forces the Gentiles to see themselves as actors in the drama that will lead to Israel's salvation. The assertion is framed in such a way that what is true of the Gentiles in receiving mercy will also become true for Israel to receive mercy (*hōsper* ["Just as"] v. 30 ... *houtōs* ["so too"] v. 31). The Gentiles were once disobedient to God (see 1:18–31; 6:20–21) but have received mercy on account of Israel's disobedience to this offer of mercy (10:16, 19, 21; 11:20–23). Israel's casting away for unbelief has yielded a cache of Gentile believers. The flip side of the coin is that Israel's disobedience will be temporary since the Gentile reception of mercy will be the catalyst for Israel to apprehend this mercy for themselves. Gentile reception of mercy will yield up an Israel who finds mercy.

This gives way to Paul's concluding remark, "For God has bound everyone over to disobedience so that he may have mercy on them all" (v. 32). The notion is highly reminiscent of Galatians 3:22, "Scripture has locked up everything under the control of sin, so that what was promised, being given through faith in Jesus Christ, might be given to those who believe." The backstory is important. All of humanity, Gentile and Jew, are condemned in Adam. Israel was meant to be the bearer of the promises of deliverance from this condition, yet they found that the Torah convicted them along with Gentiles rather qualifying them for their role as rescuer. It was the Messiah, the new Adam, the true Israelite, who reversed the curse of sin and overturned the sentence of death. Yet Israel lapsed into further disobedience to the message of the Messiah with the result that the Gentiles would be freed from their disobedience. Still, Israel will one day be rescued from their disobedience as they come to see the Gentile rescued with the mercy that is properly theirs.

28. The word *ametamelētos* means literally "without regret." See BDAG 53.

So how might Romans 11 resonate with a group of Gentile Christians meeting in a shop or by the river? How would Paul's words challenge them? Peter Oakes takes a good estimate:

> This all made [a fictitious Gentile person named] Holoconius reconceptualize the world around him in Transtiberium. He had thought of his gentile house church as a bright light (hidden from view by the workshop shutters) in a dark, largely irredeemable society, Jew and gentile, from which a few people escaped into the light. Paul called him, instead, to see the Jews around him as still part of God's redemptive future, and to see every single person as, in some sense, an intended object of God's mercy.[29]

## LIVE the Story

Duke University Professor Susan Eastman recounts an experience that forced her to think through the question of Israel and the church in a pastoral context.

> Several years ago I led a weekday worship service in a home for elderly people who could no longer care for themselves, many of whom had some form of dementia. One particular day, a lovely woman in a wheelchair sat staring into space and saying quietly, over and over, "I love you and you love me. I love you and you love me. I love you and you love me." She repeated this throughout the service, creating a rather beautiful refrain—a love song—underneath the words of the liturgy. But suddenly another resident stood up and rudely interrupted both the liturgy and the song, saying quite angrily, "I have a lot of questions!" I responded, "I have a lot of questions too. What are your questions?" And she answered, "What about the Jews?" In subsequent private conversation, she clarified her question: "Well, what about the Jews? I mean, God made all those promises. What happened?"[30]

I doubt whether you'll ever be so abruptly confronted with a question about Israel as happened to Dr. Eastman. More likely, and as routinely happens to me, students and parishioners often ask me questions about Israel in relation to politics and biblical prophecy, for which I have fairly stock answers prepared. However, it is clear that Romans 11 drives us to address the matter of the church's relationship to the Jewish people and to the global Jewish

29. Oakes, *Reading Romans*, 160–61.

30. Susan Eastman, "Israel and Divine Mercy in Galatians and Romans," in *Between Gospel and Election: Explorations in the Interpretation of Romans 9–11* (ed. F. Wilk and J. Wagner; WUNT 257; Tübingen: Mohr Siebeck, 2010), 147.

diaspora. We need to develop a biblically informed and theologically coherent account of our continuing responsibility to the other branch of the olive tree. We do that not in a position of neutrality, but in light of two thousand years of poor church and synagogue relations, under the dark shadow of the Holocaust, amidst various Middle Eastern crises, and in an age that is increasingly pluralistic and religiously secular. Given that background, I want to ask what can we say *about* Israel, *for* Israel, and *to* Israel?[31]

### What Can We Say about Israel? Celebrating Our Shared Olive Tree!

I think a proper reading of the New Testament shows that the church does not replace Israel (contra some Reformed theologies), nor is the church a parenthesis in God's plan entirely separate from Israel (contra some dispensational theologies). Quite clearly the story of Israel is fulfilled in Jesus and continued in the story of the church — so much so that Israel's history is the history of the Christian church. It is not that Israel has been put on hold, but Israel has been expanded to include Gentiles who believe in Jesus the Messiah. Paul looks ahead to a time when the Jewish people, either in whole or in large numbers, will come to believe in Messiah Jesus. If we are informed by Scripture, we cannot conceive of any salvation without Israel or an Israel without Christ.

Here Paul's analogy of the olive tree in Romans 11:17–24 is a poignant and powerful image for the interlocking destiny of Jews and Gentiles together. While one branch is temporarily broken off and a wild shoot has been artificially grafted in, both branches belong in the one tree and receive mutual benefit from each other. The Gentiles owe their salvation to Israel's heritage, and Israel's future will only come to its appointed climax by the messianic witness of the Gentile-dominated church. The olive tree is a beautiful metaphor about the shared roots of Jews and Christians, their bonds in the Messiah, and their fecundity when joined together. In reflecting on the metaphor, Douglas Moo is on the money when he comments:

> His olive tree metaphor makes an important contribution to our understanding of the people of God. It is notoriously easy to squeeze more theology out of such a metaphor than it is intended to convey. But basic to the whole metaphor is the unity of God's people, a unity that crosses both historical and ethnic boundaries. The basic point of the metaphor is that there is only one olive tree, whose roots are firmly planted in OT soil, and whose branches include both Jews and Gentiles.[32]

31. I highly recommend Talbert for anyone reflecting on Romans 9–11 theologically, missionally, and pastorally (*Romans*, 269–74).

32. Moo, *Romans*, 708–9.

To switch metaphors, there is a place for Jews and Gentiles in the bosom of Abraham.

In practice this means that it is is worth remembering and teaching just how much Jews and Christians share in common with belief in one God, creation, humanity as bearing the image of God, the covenants, God's action in Israel's redemptive history, a shared body of Scriptures in the Hebrew Bible/ Old Testament, a shared tradition of Judeo-Christian ethics, and similar eschatological hopes for the resurrection of the dead. Even baptism and the Lord's Supper have antecedents in Jewish tradition. Ultimately, the church draws theological content and spiritual nourishment from its Jewish roots.[33] James Dunn goes so far as to say: "A church which is not drawing upon the sustenance of its Jewish inheritance (including the OT, but not only the OT) would be a contradiction in terms for Paul."[34]

When churches speak about Israel, it should not be with a condescending confidence of their own theology, but as if we are speaking about our separated brothers and sisters who are yet to see how the light of Christ shines on them. However we speak about Israel and to Jewish audiences, it should always be with deep affection and bonds of familial embrace.

### What We Can Say for Israel? Speaking Up Against Anti-Semitism!

I spent several years working in military intelligence back in the 1990s. One thing I learned from my time in that unwholesome business — I say "unwholesome" because intelligence is the second oldest profession with less morals than the first oldest profession — is that there are some evil folks in the world who would like to do great harm to the Jewish people. Some want to drive all the Israelis into the Mediterranean, and some would like to reactivate the concentration camps of continental Europe. Others would like to blow up every synagogue in the known world. Whether that is Neo-Nazis of Europe, Islamic extremists, or even secular anti-Semites, many would do great harm to the Jewish people for no other reason than they are Jewish.

In this last year in Europe we've witnessed senseless and bloody attacks on Jewish communities in Paris, Brussels, and Denmark. In fact, I just found on my Twitter feed a reference to an Op-ed piece in the *New York Times* by Debra Lipstadt that harrowingly describes recent surges in anti-Israel, anti-Jewish activities throughout Europe, including an assault on an elderly Israeli in Berlin, the firebombing of a Jewish community center in Toulouse, Jewish men in Denmark instructed not to wear their yarmulkes in public, the vandalization

---

33. Cf. Marvin R. Wilson, *Our Father Abraham: Jewish Roots of the Christian Faith* (Grand Rapids: Eerdmans, 1989).

34. Dunn, *Romans*, 2:662.

of the kosher aisles of grocery stores in London, and the anti-Semitic shooting at a Jewish museum in Brussels.[35] What can contemporary churches do about this sort of thing?

If Christians should speak up for all persecuted peoples of the world, how much more should we speak up for our Jewish friends with whom we share the same olive tree! But it is gonna take a little bit more effort than just purchasing your own copy of *Fiddler on the Roof* or *Schindler's List* to demonstrate your support for the Jewish people against anti-Semitism. It takes a mixture of resolve and activism to make sure that our cities and countries never again succumb to the unholy and unchristian scourge of anti-Semitism. I would urge every church, every seminary, and every Christian school to take their folks on a tour of a local Holocaust museum, found in most major cities, to get a grip on the brutal persecution that a supposedly Christian nation inflicted on its Jewish minority. You cannot oppose anti-Semitism until you've learned something of its insidious nature. Once you've felt the sorrow and shame on that day trip, the next step is to cultivate a resolve that says, "Never again! Not on my watch!" No nation, ethnic group, tribe, or religious minority should ever have to experience the horrors of genocide. To quote the British statesman Edmund Burke, "the only thing necessary for the triumph of evil is that good men do nothing."

Big side note! In the interest of being sensitive and balanced I need to add a few parenthetical remarks. I do not think that the founding of the modern state of Israel in 1948 is the fulfillment of biblical prophecy. Modern Israel is a secular state, not a theocracy that operates through priests, prophets, and kings. We do better to see the modern state of Israel as part of God's providence and blessing for the Jewish people, not as a step toward Armageddon.[36]

Also, I am not advocating unqualified support for the modern state of Israel and all of its policies. For a start, Israel's policies habitually change with circumstances and with the transition of its political leaders. I must confess also that I've met several Palestinian Christians and supporters who have made me see dimensions of the situation in Israel that I was otherwise blinded to, and their story of oppression and dispossession needs to be heard. One need not sympathize with Hamas or Hezbollah in order to sympathize with the plight of Palestinians, including the Christians in their ranks, who suffer as a result of the ongoing conflicts. Israel's right to defend itself must be balanced

35. Debra E. Lipstadt, "Why Jews Are Worried," *NYT* (20 Aug 2014). www.nytimes.com/2014/08/21/opinion/deborah-e-lipstadt-on-the-rising-anti-semitism-in-europe.html?_r=0.

36. See the wise advice from dispensational theologian Darrell Bock, "Some Christians See a 'Road Map' to End Times," *LA Times* (18 June 2003). http://articles.latimes.com/2003/jun/18/opinion/oe-bock18.

with the proportionality of its response to the threat it faces. Israeli politicians must be held accountable by the international community for how they treat the Palestinians, and they should not get a *carte blanche* of support irrespective of how they act. It is not about being pro-Israel or pro-Palestinian but about being pro-peace for the Israelis and the Arabs living in Israel and the Occupied Territories. Israel needs to be held to the standards of its own religious tradition in the Old Testament about how it treats refugees living in its lands (see Exod 22:21; 23:9; Deut 10:18; 24:14–21).[37]

The title "Righteous among the Nations" is an honorific designation given by the Israeli state to describe the brave actions of Gentiles who risked their lives to save Jews during the Holocaust. Recipients have their name added to the Wall of Honor in the Garden of the Righteous at the Yad Vashem Holocaust Memorial in Jerusalem. The accounts of these righteous Gentiles, what they did and what happened to them, are absolutely amazing, quite moving, with tales of both triumph and tragedy. Women such as Maria Agnese Tribboli, the head of an order of nuns in Italy, hid Jewish families in her convent, and Lois Gunden, an American Mennonite, saved Jewish children in France. André Trocmé, a French Protestant pastor, led his family and church to shelter hundreds of Jews either permanently or led them across the mountains into Switzerland. Another French clergyman, Pastor Jean Séverin Lemaire, a pastor and Bible lecturer, helped shelter Jews and assist in their escape abroad. Most who assisted the Jews in escaping the Nazis were killed. The European churches' response to the Holocaust was mixed; it included complicit support, willful ignorance, and spasmodic resistance. That heritage will remain with us, and we cannot forget it. What I would like to see is Christians treat the Jews in such a way that the churches themselves would be known to Israel as "Righteous among the Nations."

### What Can We Say to Israel? We Have Found Your Messiah?

On several occasions I've been on a plane and found myself sitting next to a Jewish gentleman and even beside a few obviously orthodox Jewish guys. We usually enjoy the normal exchange of pleasantries about the flight, food, and entertainment system. Frequently the conversation goes deeper, and I can find myself explaining my vocation to a passenger whom I know is not really interested and probably a little bit worried that they are going to spend the next thirteen hours on a flight with a religious fanatic. I don't know whether it helps the evangelical cause, but I have developed a system for trying to get a conversation on Jesus going. After I tell the person that I'm a Christian

37. Cf. Gary M. Burge, *Whose Land? Whose Promise? What Christians Are Not Being Told about Israel and the Palestinians* (Cleveland: Pilgrim, 2003).

biblical scholar, they normally reply, "Really, um ... how about that. Well, I'm Jewish so ..." and before they can say another word I deliberately interject, "You're Jewish! What an amazing coincidence." To which they often retort rather curiously, "What, are you Jewish?" I smile broadly and respond, "No, but I believe in your Messiah! Would you like to know why?" To be honest, I haven't netted any converts this way, but I have had several honest and illuminating two-way exchanges with Jewish guys about God, religion, Jesus, and the church. In the very least it has been an eye-opening experience for me and hopefully for them too.

Sadly the church quickly abandoned its evangelical mission to the Jews mostly on account of sectarian rivalries and replaced it with a horrible penchant for anti-Semitic tendencies in theology all the way from Melito of Sardis to Adolf von Harnack. However, that is not the whole story as there has been a long history of Jewish believers in Jesus since the infancy of the church as well as two centuries of modern missions to the Jewish people in Israel and elsewhere.[38] There are now vibrant messianic Jewish communities scattered over the whole world, even in the state of Israel.

I was delighted to hear from Darrell Bock that a messianic congregation had been established in Berlin, a city from which the Jews were evicted and almost completely exterminated during the Second World War and which has a thriving Jewish community around it. We need to tell our Jewish friends that to become a Christian does not mean that they have to cease being Jewish culturally, socially, or historically. Jews do not have to Gentilize to be followers of Jesus; rather, they need only accept him as Lord and Messiah and accept those who worship him as well. Just as Africans can express Christian faith as Africans and Arabs express Christian faith as Arabs, so too can Jews express the richness of the heritage and traditions as followers of Jesus.

Paul, for a guy who was the apostle to the Gentiles (see Rom 11:13; Gal 1:15–16; 2:8; 1 Tim 2:7), spent a lot of time debating and dialoguing with Jews about Jesus (see Rom 15:19; 1 Cor 9:20–23; Acts 26:20).[39] Since Paul ministered *among* the nations (Rom 1:4), he was drawn to preaching to the Jews who were living *among* the nations too. That is why Paul says that the

---

38. See esp. the magisterial Oskar Skarsaune and Reider Hvalvik, eds., *Jewish Believers in Jesus: The Early Centuries* (Peabody, MA: Hendrickson, 2007); as well as Abraham Kovács, *The History of the Free Church of Scotland's Mission to the Jews in Budapest and Its Impact on the Reformed Church of Hungary 1814–1914* (New York: Peter Lang, 2006); Yaron Perry, *British Mission to the Jews in Nineteenth Century Palestine* (Portland, OR: Frank Crass, 2003); Yaakov S. Ariel, *Evangelizing the Chosen People: Mission to the Jews in America, 1880–2000* (Chapel Hill, NC: University of North Carolina Press, 2000).

39. Cf. Michael F. Bird, "Paul: Apostle to the Gentiles *and Jews*?" in *Paul: An Anomalous Jew* (Grand Rapids: Eerdmans, forthcoming).

gospel is "first for the Jew" (1:16), and he implies that a continuing mission to Israel should continue in the future (10:15–21). However, many folks for different reasons have argued that it is religiously insensitive and theologically inappropriate to try to convert Jews to Christianity.

E. P. Sanders is frank about his willingness to demur from Paul on whether the Jews need Jesus:

> I do not know what Paul would have thought if he had lived for 2,000 years, or if he had foreseen the length of time between his own ministry and the eschaton. I think I know what he thought in the particular circumstances in which he wrote. He thought that the only way to be saved was through Christ Jesus. If it were to be proposed that Christians today should think the same thing, and accordingly that the Jews who have not converted should be considered cut off from God, and if such a proposal came before a body in which I had a vote, I would vote against it.[40]

As such, a number of scholars, some liberal and some dispensationalist, have accordingly argued that Paul teaches a two-covenant or two-track way of salvation whereby the Jews get saved under their own covenant, whereas the Messiah is the Savior of Gentiles in the new covenant. Israel's *Sonderweg* ("Special Way") allows them to maintain their position before God without coming to faith in Messiah Jesus. Israel's "misstep" was not failing to believe in the Messiah, but failing to recognize Jesus as the Messiah, who facilitates the inclusion of Gentiles in God's people.[41]

The gravity of this view hit me when I heard a Catholic theologian tell a colloquium of scholars that preaching Jesus to Jews was a fundamental violation of their human rights! To which I retorted that I have some Jewish friends who are very keen on Jesus and are very grateful that their human rights were violated because it gained them eternal life. Even more troublesome is that not only have some evangelicals adopted this two-covenant position, but even a leading messianic Jewish leader has been pushing for a similar view.[42]

---

40. E. P. Sanders, "Paul's Attitude toward the Jewish People," *USQR* 33 (1978): 185.

41. Cf. Lloyd Gaston, *Paul and the Torah* (Vancouver: University of British Columbia Press, 1987), 33, 143–50; Krister Stendahl, *Final Account: Paul's Letter to the Romans* (Minneapolis: Fortress, 1995), 39–40; John Gager, *Reinventing Paul* (Oxford: Oxford University Press, 2000), 135. Importantly, Mark Nanos should not be identified with this school (see Nanos, *Mystery of Romans*, 7 n. 13). While Nanos concurs that Jews do not need Jesus as Savior, nonetheless he views Jesus as "the Jewish Messiah who had come *first* to restore the Jewish people, and *also* to bring salvation to non-Jewish people as the Savior of the world" (Nanos, *Mystery of Romans*, 4 [italics original]). According to Nanos, Jewish believers in Jesus are not an anomaly but an anticipation of what Paul hopes for Israel as a whole in the future.

42. Mark S. Kinzer, *Postmissionary Messianic Judaism: Redefining Christian Engagement with the Jewish People* (Grand Rapids: Brazos, 2005), and the response by Craig L. Blomberg, "Freedom

The anxiety I have is that the two-covenant view leads to a denigration of messianic Jews/Jewish Christians and will diminish the church's enthusiasm to preach Jesus to the Jewish people. Fortunately the two-covenant position is not without its critics in its reading of Paul in general and Romans 11 in particular.[43]

Perhaps the strangest thing on the two-covenant scheme is that Jewish Christianity is viewed as a necessary mistake to bring about a Gentile church. Yet one can hardly imagine such a view emerging from any of the Jewish Christians who contributed to the New Testament. The wretched man of Romans 7:7–25 is not miffed by his need to come to faith in Jesus, but rejoices in it! In its more illiberal forms the two-covenants perspective yields some disparaging remarks about Jews who come to faith in Jesus.[44] Yet "messianic Judaism" is not an interreligious oddity but has a rich history and a vibrant number of congregations/synagogues around the world.[45] The supposed tolerance of the two-covenant position dissipates when one finds advocates responding to the entire notion of religious propagation with mocking contempt or venomous rhetoric. I have heard a leading professor of religious studies in the UK utter the derisive comment about "missions" that the only thing one should ever try to convert is a loft into a bedroom. What two-covenants advocates tend to embody is a desire to censure all forms of missionary activity.

That strikes me as an attack on religious freedom itself since religious freedom must include the freedom to practice and promote one's religious beliefs. All of this confirms what many of us suspect, namely, that the two-covenants approach is merely a back door for religious pluralism.[46] I'm even prepared to go one further and allege that two-covenant advocates are the ones advocating a robust anti-Judaism. N. T. Wright states that "to imagine that Jews can no

---

from the Law Only for Gentiles? A Non-Supersessionist Alternative to Mark Kinzer's 'Postmissionary Messianic Judaism,'" in *New Testament Theology in Light of the Church's Mission: Essays in Honor of I. Howard Marshall* (Eugene, OR: Cascade, 2011), 41–56.

43. Reidar Hvalvik, "A 'Sonderweg' for Israel: A Critical Examination of a Current Interpretation of Romans 11.25–27," *JSNT* 38 (1990): 87–107; Terence L. Donaldson, "Jewish Christianity, Israel's Stumbling and the *Sonderweg* Reading of Paul," *JSNT* 29 (2006): 27–54; Michael F. Bird, "Salvation in Paul's Judaism," in *Paul and Judaism: Crosscurrents in Pauline Exegesis and the Study of Jewish-Christian Relations* (eds. Reimund Bieringer and Didier Pollefeyt; LNTS 463; London: T&T Clark, 2012), 15–40.

44. As implied by the illiberal remarks of postliberal theologian Douglas Harink, *Paul among the Postliberals: Pauline Theology beyond Christendom and Modernity* (Grand Rapids: Brazos, 2003), 181–82.

45. See esp. David Rudolph and Joel Willitts, eds., *Introduction to Messianic Judaism: Its Ecclesial Context and Biblical Foundations* (Grand Rapids: Zondervan, 2013).

46. Wright, *Climax of the Covenant*, 254.

longer be welcomed into the family of the Messiah" for Paul "would be the very height of anti-Judaism."[47]

Romans is a missionary letter written by a Jewish missionary, asking a network of Gentile Christians in Rome for support in his witness to Jesus in Jerusalem and his future missionary endeavors in Spain (see Rom 15:15–33). It reflects the situation of a continuing mission to both Jews and Gentiles. If so, the application of Romans to the contemporary missional church will not entail the abandonment of a Jewish mission for a Gentile mission, nor replacing mission with interreligious dialogue or evangelical preaching with comparative religious studies. What Romans means is preaching Jesus to Jews and to Gentiles until the "full number of Gentiles has come in," in the hope that "all Israel would be saved" (11:25–26). This is an important point, as Richard Bell says: "Paul's theology *demands* a mission to the Jewish people. Provoking Israel to jealousy is no replacement for mission. It is just one possible precursor for mission. The gospel must be preached for it is only the gospel, God's reconciling word, which can make someone a Christian (Rom. 10.17)."[48]

A continuing mission to the Jewish people—whether to secular, progressive, liberal, or orthodox Jews—remains necessary since Christ is the *telos* of Israel's covenants and the only means for apprehending a right standing with God (Rom 10:4; Gal 2:21). So if we want to live the story of Romans 11, we need to partner with the existing churches within Israel to promote the gospel. We must examine demographic data on the heavily populated Jewish suburbs of New York, Berlin, Melbourne, and Buenos Aires and plant some churches that are capable of reaching them. We must earnestly pray that, whether by evangelistic efforts or by cordial friendship, the Jewish people will be magnetically drawn to their Messiah.

If we take seriously the command to try and make the Jews jealous for Jesus, it behooves the churches to live and act toward Jews in a way that will make them jealous. To practice a public faith that makes Jews of all walks of life look at followers of Jesus and say in the tradition of *When Harry Met Sally* (1989), "I'll have what she's having!" Or even get them uttering the chorus of the Thomas Rhett song, "Get me some of that." To which we may respond, "Of course, it was meant to be yours anyway."

47. Wright, "Romans," 10:697. Note too what Jewett (*Romans* 702) writes: "The missional horizon of Romans must be kept in view, despite all of the difficulties with subsequent interpretation and historical developments. . . . To whittle back the details of Paul's vision to more 'reasonable' levels, reflecting the fact of their nonfulfillment in the twenty centuries past, undercuts the magnificent scope of the 'mystery' that Paul believed he had been given."

48. Bell, *Provoked to Jealousy*, 354–55 (italics original).

I have been blessed to have met a number of Jewish men and women who have come to faith in Jesus and did not thereby think that by doing so that they were abandoning their Jewish heritage; on the contrary, they were enriching it! One such chap is my friend Bob Mendelsohn, the national director of *Jews for Jesus* in Australia. Here is what Bob has to say on the topic:

> Jesus and Paul both taught that our first priority should be to witness to the Jewish people. Unfortunately for both the church and the Jewish people, the church has often settled for a diminished witness among the ancient people of God. In that evangelical lull, not only are the Jewish people shortchanged by a lack of witness to them, but I believe the church is shortchanged as well. Unless the Jewish people are given a chance to hear the gospel and come to faith, then the church will remain indefinitely awaiting her Saviour, and the fullness will never eventuate.
>
> Thankfully since the late 18th and early 19th Centuries, God has been wooing His own Jewish people to Himself in visible and dramatic fashion. According to the French historian, during the 19th century, more than 200,000 Jewish people joined the churches worldwide. Since the 1960s again that number has been reached, and from Israel, England, the US, and even here in Australia we continue to see this evangelical reality and are delighted in God's activity among His own people.
>
> In the Australian chapter of *Jews for Jesus*, we have made Israeli tourists a major focus of many missions in the South Pacific since young Israelis travel here at the conclusion of their tour of duty in the Israeli Defense Force (required of all 18 year olds in Israel). Several outreaches and intentional ministries have been established to host these travelers who are open to the Gospel like never before.
>
> Gil (not his real name) is an example of these young people. He toured New Zealand staying in homes of Christians who were part of this network of hosts. At each, he heard a bit more of the Gospel. When he came to Sydney to finish up his travels, he listened to our missionaries and professed personal faith in Yeshua [i.e., Jesus] and was born again. He was baptized and joined in a community of faith. He continues in that faith now that he is back in Israel and married.
>
> Paul (not his real name) is a dentist and a centrist in the Jewish community in Sydney. He attends synagogue regularly, but when he met one of our missionaries, he didn't even believe in a personal God. Over the course of three years of discussions and irenic arguments Paul's objections

> were answered and he too professed faith in Yeshua as Messiah and was baptized this year. He now is buying books to give away to Jewish colleagues and friends to help them discover the joy and peace he has found in Yeshua.[49]

That is a wonderful account of a great ministry and we can hope and pray that many more like it abound with great fruitfulness in the future.

---

49. Taken from correspondence dated 26 Sept 2014.

CHAPTER 21

# Romans 11:33–36

## LISTEN to the Story

[33]Oh, the depth of the riches of the wisdom and knowledge of God!
How unsearchable his judgments,
and his paths beyond tracing out!
[34]"Who has known the mind of the Lord?
Or who has been his counselor?"
[35]"Who has ever given to God,
that God should repay them?"
[36]For from him and through him and for him are all things.
To him be the glory forever! Amen.

*Listening to the texts in the story*: Job 41:11; Isaiah 40:13.

We see here, according to Wagner, that "the drama of redemption is for Paul the grand cosmic display of the mercy of God, lavished on Jew and Gentile alike."[1] These mercies lead Paul into a theocentric hymn of praise celebrating the wisdom of God in working his way of salvation for all people. It is the longest of the Pauline doxologies (see Rom 16:27; Gal 1:5; Eph 3:21; Phil 4:20; 1 Tim 1:17; 2 Tim 4:18) and is distinguished by its connection to Jewish wisdom traditions about the ineffable mystery of the divine will (see, e.g., "But who, O Lord, my Lord, will comprehend your judgment? Or who will search out the profoundness of your way? Or who will think out the weight of Thy path?" [*2 Bar* 14.8–9]), and to Stoic traditions pertaining to God's immanence within the universe (see e.g., "from you are all things, in you are all things, for you are all things" [Marcus Aurelius, *Meditations*, 4.23]).

The emphasis is not so much on divine hiddenness but on the way in which the hidden wisdom of God has been partially revealed.[2] As such, the connection of the hymn to the preceding context in Romans 9–11 concerning the relationship between the gospel of God and God's faithfulness to Israel

1. Wagner, *Heralds of the Good News*, 300.
2. Moo, *Romans*, 740.

should not be forgotten. God's hidden wisdom is manifested in the word of the gospel. According to Wright, the placement of the doxology at this point in the letter entails: "What is revealed in the gospel of Jesus is not something other than the wisdom that ancient Jewish sages sought and celebrated, but the same thing made known for the salvation of the world."[3]

To live out this story, it will help to remember that when contemporary audiences read and ponder the doxology, we are joining with patriarchs like Job and prophets like Isaiah in marveling at the mysterious and manifold wisdom of God. The biblical story is filled with people who never lost their sense of awe at God, and this doxology reminds us to be like those people. In outline the doxology runs: (1) a celebration of God's inscrutable wisdom (v. 33); (2) two biblical citations (one from Isaiah and the other from Job) about the absolute otherness of divine wisdom compared to human advice (vv. 34–35); and (3) a celebration of God's role as Creator and sustainer of all things.

### Deep Riches and Impenetrable Wisdom (11:33)

"God is vindicated! Paul becomes a poet," says Hultgren.[4] That's a good preface to reading Paul's opening words in his hymn of praise: "Oh, the depth of the riches of the wisdom and knowledge of God! How unsearchable his judgments, and his paths beyond tracing out!" (v. 33). The interjection "Oh" instantly shows us that Paul is embarking on an expressive acclamation of divine qualities. Paul's initial words describe the riches of God's wisdom and knowledge like a Hobbit describing the vault of a castle filled with gold and gemstones.[5]

No wonder, since across the letter Paul has drawn the intersection between God's wrath and mercy, his faithfulness and truthfulness, his impartiality and justice, and sternness and kindness. These attributes of God are revealed in the mystery of the gospel, where God makes Jews and Gentiles co-heirs with the Messiah. It is more than God's ways are higher than our ways (see Isa 55:9). Paul is saying that God's purposes are unequaled in their extravagance (riches), are unsurpassed in effectiveness (wisdom), and are unmatched in their overarching coherence (knowledge). God's judgments in all these matters cannot be adequately comprehended by the human mind.

---

3. Wright, "Romans," 10:695; cf. Barth, *Romans*, 422.
4. Hultgren, *Romans*, 430.
5. It is possible that "riches" (*ploutos*) defines the nature of God's "wisdom" and "knowledge" (e.g., "depth of the riches *of the* wisdom and knowledge of God" [NIV]). Alternatively, the genitive in v. 33 could be coordinate (e.g., "the riches *and* wisdom *and* knowledge of God" [NET; Porter, *Idioms*, 85]).

### God Needs No Advisors (11:34–35)

Paul pulls in Scripture to explain what he means by the riches of God's wisdom and knowledge, namely, that God is so beyond human reasoning that no human can presume to counsel him on any matter: "Who has known the mind of the Lord? Or who has been his counselor?" The words from Isaiah 40:13 appear near the beginning of a lengthy series of songs about God's power to rescue Israel from exile and to usher in his saving reign all over the world. Just like Romans 10:14–17, Paul again sees himself like the Isaianic herald declaring the good news of God's reign, God's power, and God's wisdom.

The second citation, "Who has ever given to God, that God should repay them?" comes from Job 41:11, where God asks Job over sixty questions that emphasize God's sovereignty over the created order and the impossibility of mortal minds querying the operation of God's power or the wisdom of God's workings. The citations both pose a question and the implied answer is "no one," because God has no advisors and no creditors. He acts in his own wisdom and is obligated to no person. God is entirely "other."

### God as Creator and Provider (11:36)

Paul closes his doxology with a climactic praise to God as the beginning and end point of all that exists: "For from him and through him and for him are all things. To him be the glory forever! Amen" (v. 36). Paul elsewhere uses similar language in direct relation to God the Father and the Lord Jesus (see 1 Cor 8:6; 15:28; Col 1:15–20). God is the source of all things as Creator ("from him"), God is the agent by which all things are created and sustained ("through him"), and God is himself the ultimate end for which he made all things, namely, to bring glory to himself ("for him"). This God, who created heaven and earth, was meant to be prized and glorified by humanity, but humanity failed and instead glorified lesser creatures (1:18) to the point that they fell short of God's own glory (3:23). The reversal started with Abraham, who gave glory to God (4:20); Christ was raised through the glory of God, so that those for whom he died and rose might share in God's glory (Rom 5:2; 8:17, 30).

Doug Moo asks: "What should be our response to our contemplation of God's supremacy in all the universe? Like Paul's doxology."[6] Taking my cue from Moo, Romans 11:33–36 reminds us about the vital importance of wor-

6. Moo, *Romans*, 744.

ship as part of our response to God for his glorious salvation. What is more, if 11:33–36 is a kind of abbreviated template for worship, worship of this order should be God-centered and trinitarian, and it should celebrate the manifold wisdom of God. To praise the God whom Paul celebrates here is to acclaim the God who is rich without limit, wise without peer, entirely self-sufficient, and altogether glorious[7]—a God who is truly worthy of our worship.

Worship like this is not a show but an event where the Spirit quickens our hearts and where Jesus leads us into the praise of heaven to God the Father. The most synchronized and sublime of liturgies can be lackluster and lethargic if divorced from a sense of joyous acclaim. Liturgy without a deep affection for God risks becoming an empty ritual and as spiritually dry as the Gobi desert. On the flip side, I am all for contemporary music styles and multimedia; technology is a tool to be used. Even so, the risk is that contemporary worship can be filled with so many distractions that it becomes more focused on the pyrotechnics than on cultivating genuine piety. I remember once hearing a pastor from a big church lament that he wished the people in his church loved God as much as they love to worship God. What he meant was that some of his parishioners were more exhilarated by the experience of worship than with marveling at the God who is there to be worshiped. The problem was that they enjoyed the medium more than the message, and they were more entranced with worship entertainment than with authentic and heartfelt worship.

We need to remember that, to echo Matt Redman's chorus, "When the music fades" all we have left is God. Worship leaders come and go. Data projectors break down. Hymns and choruses go in and out of fashion. But God is the one thing that matters in our life and should matter in our worship. He is our rock and our fortress. It's not about the presentation as much as it is the direction of our worship. To worship is to capture a God-centered vision of the world, to offer up a Godward prayer, and to make God-glorifying thanksgiving. Worship is not for the sensory elation or emotional release it gives us; rather, it is to prize and enjoy the God who loves us. I'm not saying worship should be dull; far from it, it should be austere and awesome all at once. Yet worship must be Godward and God-soaked; otherwise, it's just religious noise for consumers.

Viewing worship this way will mean that we no longer ask what this service or that hymn did for me or how it made me feel. If it is a buzz you want, then lick your finger, and insert it into an electric socket. If it is emotional highs and lows that you relish, rent a DVD of *Downton Abbey* or read a

7. Cf. the in-depth study by Andrew D. Naselli, *From Typology to Doxology: Paul's Use of Isaiah and Job in Romans 11:34–35* (Eugene, OR: Pickwick, 2012).

Jane Austen novel. Worship inspired by Romans 11:33–36 will lead you to magnify God. We should pursue the type of worship that would make the angels of heaven green with envy that they are not in our choir. You are not to try to make a tiny God look big, but to enable a puny you to appreciate the immense majesty and indescribable beauty of God the Father, God the Son, and God the Holy Spirit. The task of worship, taken along this trajectory, is simply to know and enjoy the trinitarian God of the gospel.

CHAPTER 22

# Romans 12:1–2

## LISTEN to the Story

[1]Therefore, I urge you, brothers and sisters, in view of God's mercy, to offer your bodies as a living sacrifice, holy and pleasing to God—this is your true and proper worship. [2]Do not conform to the pattern of this world, but be transformed by the renewing of your mind. Then you will be able to test and approve what God's will is—his good, pleasing and perfect will.

*Listening to the texts in the story*: Leviticus 1:1–2:16; Psalm 27:6; 50:14, 23; 96:8; 107:22; 116:17; 2 Corinthians 4:16; *Testament of Levi* 3.6.

Romans 12:1–15:13 can be likened to "Christ College" where Paul attempts to engender certain attitudes and behaviors appropriate for those for whom Romans 1–11 is true. In essence, Paul begins to expound the "imperative" that follows from the "indicative" of the gospel. Or, because of what God has done for us in Christ, this is how we ought to live before God. Paul wants those who are declared righteous and united to the Messiah to exhibit a set of distinctive behaviors that show that they live under Jesus' lordship and are led by the Spirit. Call it ethics, applied theology, or Christian living, label it whatever you like, but remember that Paul's goal is to bring Gentiles to the obedience of faith (1:5; 15:18; 16:26), and he shows us now what this obedience looks like in real life. Paul is outlining how the gospel is lived out in faithful obedience among the tenements, markets, and hustle and bustle of ancient Rome.[1]

This is simply the outworking of the covenantal renewal that Paul has kept referring to with his assorted citations of Hosea, Isaiah, Jeremiah, and Deuteronomy, which is realized in the sacrificial bodies and consecrated community of

1. Highly instructive is Oakes on what Romans 12 would look like in a Roman house church (*Reading Romans*, 98–126).

the Roman believers.[2] In the biblical story, God's people always stand out from the crowd because they stand on God's word and look ahead to God's promises.

We are not to think of Paul's exhortation here merely as an appendix listing a number of do's and don'ts, nor as a general compendium of his ethical instruction. It is more like a synthesis of his theological, christological, eschatological, and ecclesiological convictions given in the letter that are then integrated and worked into the Romans' own context. In many ways this is the goal of Paul's letter: that those who bear Christ's name will learn to walk in Christ's way (hence the many echoes of the Jesus tradition throughout).[3] This is an important preface to Paul's call for mutual acceptance within the Roman churches. Paul urges the Roman Christians, whether Jew or Gentile, to not only obey the pattern of teaching they were entrusted with (6:17), but to accept one another as Christ has accepted them (15:7). The Roman Christians, diverse as they are, must join in a common life together, in work and witness, in fellowship and hardship, and intentionally embody the values of righteousness, peace, joy, and above all love. The Roman community's ethos will then be defined by mutuality rather than by mistrust and represent a unified front to a hostile environment.

In sum, Paul spells out in 12:1–15:13 how the Roman Christians are to be God's people in a pagan world. Romans 12–13 lays a general foundation for the specific exhortations to reciprocation and mutuality in 14:1–15:13. Coming to Romans 12 in detail, (1) Paul embarks on an introduction to his exhortation with its accompanying call for transformation (vv. 1–2). (2) He next urges the Romans to use their spiritual gifts for each other's benefits (vv. 3–8). (3) This is followed up with a series of ethical aphorisms that will produce Christlike behavior in believers (vv. 9–21).

### From Mercy to Living Sacrifices (12:1)

Paul opens his new section in vv. 1–2 with a much-quoted call for Christians to appropriate God's mercy by offering their bodies as sacrifices to God and not to imitate the world around them. Paul highlights the importance

---

2. Thus I demur from Wright ("Romans," 10:702) that Romans 12–15 has no "underlying biblical references, allusions, and echoes" of a "larger scriptural narrative." The citation of Deut 32:43 in Rom 15:10 leads me to think that Deuteronomy 32 has been in the background the whole time, as argued cogently by Sarah Whittle, *Covenant Renewal and the Consecration of the Gentiles in Romans* (Cambridge: Cambridge University Press, 2014), 13–16.

3. Cf. Michael Thompson, *Clothed with Christ: The Example and Teaching of Jesus in Romans 12.1–15.13* (JSNTSup 59; Sheffield: JSOT Press, 1991); Seyoon Kim, "Jesus, Sayings of," in *DPL* 477–81.

of dedication to God in both body (v. 1) and mind (v. 2). This exhortation brings together several earlier threads of Romans, including the reversal of having a depraved mind (1:28). It reiterates the command for Christians to "offer yourselves" to God as "those who have been brought from death to life" (6:13, 19), and assumes the transforming work of the Spirit in those who "live according to the Spirit" (8:4–5, 13).

"Therefore, I urge you, brothers and sisters, in view of God's mercy, to offer your bodies as a living sacrifice, holy and pleasing to God—this is your true and proper worship" (v. 1). The "therefore" shows that the exhortations constructed in Romans 12–15 are built on the theological foundations of Romans 1–11. Paul alerts his readers to the gravity of his call with the expression, "I urge you"; the underlying Greek word *parakaleō* carries the sense of "I appeal" (ESV, NRSV), "I plead" (NLT), or "I exhort" (NET) and signifies an urgent matter posed as a request. The basis of the exhortation is "God's mercy"; mercy in Romans is the cause of God's gracious action (9:15–16), the purpose of election (9:18; 11:31–32), the grounds for unity between Jews and Gentiles (11:31–32), and a fitting summary for the experience of salvation (15:9).

It is "in view of" (lit., "through" [*dia*]) God's mercy that believers must "offer your bodies as a living sacrifice, holy and pleasing to God." That is not a unique idea since Greco-Roman and Jewish authors could use sacrifice as a metaphor for religious devotion.[4] However, generally speaking, Christianity looked strange to Greeks and Romans because it was hard to conceive of "religion" apart from temple, priesthood, and sacrifice.[5] What we find in Romans 12:1 is part of a wider phenomenon in the New Testament where the language of temple, priesthood, and sacrifice is used without the actual physical apparatuses associated with them. New Testament authors often take up Old Testament cultic imagery in order to apply the themes of temple, priesthood, and sacrifice to the Messiah and his people. For instance, "sacrifice" (*thysia*) is metaphorically applied to Christian service in 1 Peter 2:5 with "offering spiritual sacrifices," in Hebrews 13:15 with "sacrifice of praise," and in Philippians 2:17 Paul refers to his imprisonment as comparable to "being poured out like a drink offering on the sacrifice and service coming from your faith."

4. Cf. Isocrates (*Nicocles*, 20 cited by Jewett, *Romans*, 727–28): "In the worship of the gods, follow the example of your ancestors, but consider that the noblest sacrifice and greatest service is to show yourself the best and most righteous person, for such persons have greater hope of enjoying a blessing from the gods than those who slaughter many victims"; Psalm 51:17: "My sacrifice, O God, is a broken spirit; a broken and contrite heart you, God, will not despise"; Sirach 35:1–5: "The one who keeps the law makes many offerings; one who heeds the commandments makes an offering of well-being. The one who returns a kindness offers choice flour, and one who gives alms sacrifices a thank offering. To keep from wickedness is pleasing to the Lord, and to forsake unrighteousness is an atonement."

5. Cf. Dunn, *Romans*, 2:710.

In a similar vein Paul calls on believers to offer their "bodies" as "sacrifices" to God. The language of "offering" recalls Romans 6, where believers are to offer their members to God "as those who have been brought from death to life" and "an instrument of righteousness" and "as slaves to righteousness leading to holiness" (6:13, 19). The difference is that Paul now utilizes language of "offering" in its more technical sense of making a sacrifice, flesh surrendered to God for death.[6] Paul's reference to "bodies" designates physical and material existence rather than just some spiritual plane, where their consecration to God is embodied in location and exercised in action. Sacrifices are offered on behalf of others, so Paul means more than a mode of corporate worship, but probably refers to self-giving deeds for the well-being of others. In the hardship of Roman street life, this was essential for survival.

This sacrifice is described by three adjectives that should not be separated: "living," "holy," and "pleasing."[7] First, a "living sacrifice" is one that does not die by bloodletting, it is not burned up or consumed like regular sacrificial offerings, but its life continues to endure.[8] So believers are living sacrifices *in the specific sense* that they have been crucified with Christ (6:6) and live as slaves of righteousness leading to holiness (6:19).

Second, "holy" denotes something set apart and dedicated to God as opposed to something common or profane. The Roman believers are "called holy" (1:7) because of the Holy Spirit "given" to them (5:5), who has "sanctified" them (15:16), and who empowers them for righteousness, joy, hope, peace (14:17; 15:13).

Third, "pleasing to God" expresses the result of sacrifices that are "living" and "holy," in that they receive divine favor (see Phil 4:18). A good commentary on this language occurs in Romans 15:16, where Paul describes the goal of his apostolic ministry as to make the Gentiles "become an offering acceptable to God, sanctified by the Holy Spirit." Put in that light, Sarah Whittle is correct that "this is more than a contextualising of Greco-Roman sacrifice or a 'replacement' for Israel's cult. Rather, this is fulfilment language, and these cultic motifs from Israel's Scripture help Paul to develop the role and status of the Gentiles in Israel's salvation history."[9]

What is difficult to determine is the precise meaning of the subsequent description of the sacrificial body as "your true and proper worship." The problem is that the word *logikos* is notoriously difficult to specify and it is usually translated as something like "rational," "logical," or "reasonable" (see

6. Cf. Cranfield, *Romans*, 2:598.
7. Cranfield, *Romans*, 2:600.
8. Moo, *Romans*, 751.
9. Whittle, *Covenant Renewal*, 78.

2 Pet 2:2).[10] Hence is the variety of translations: "your reasonable service" (KJV), "spiritual worship" (RSV, NRSV, ESV), "spiritual service of worship" (NASB), "appropriate priestly service" (CEB), and "the kind of worship for you, as sensible people" (NJB). Wider usage of the word in Greek philosophy and Hellenistic Judaism seems to support a designation of *logikos* along the lines of rationally true, authentic, and fitting.[11] If so, the NIV's "true and proper worship" is an apt description. It means that the "worship" that is "true and proper" is that which is a living-holy-pleasing sacrifice of the body.

This "true and proper worship" does not take place through the veneration of finite images found in Greco-Roman idolatry (1:24), nor in the quest for virtue by the philosopher or rabbi (2:1–16), nor by the service of the Jerusalem temple (9:4). Such is replaced by the sacrificial death of Christ (3:24–25) and the bodily service of a community in their living-holy-pleasing way of life.[12] Nijay Gupta sums up well: "What Paul is calling for in Romans 12.1, then, is an invitation to live out the freedom of Christ (especially freedom from unrestrained passions) by surrendering oneself wholly, especially bodily, to God in worship."[13]

### Transformed and Renewed (12:2)

Paul adds two further commands: "Do not conform to the pattern of this world, but be transformed by the renewing of your mind" (v. 2a). The imperative verbs dominate the verse with "do not conform" and "be transformed." The verb *syschēmatizesthe* could be passive ("do not *be* conformed") or middle ("do not conform *yourselves*"). In either case the result is the same; do not allow yourselves to become like your surroundings.

Paul urges his audience not to imitate "this age," a term that often describes the present yet transitory state of human wickedness in its opposition to God, (see 1 Cor 1:20; 2:6–8; 3:18; 2 Cor 4:4; Titus 2:12; cf. Gal 1:40). What Paul calls "this age" is analogous to "life according to the flesh" (see Rom 8:4–5, 12–13). On the ground in Rome, "this age" would mean the Greco-Roman way of a life, a way of wickedness described in 1:18–32. Despite the historical grandeur, cultural wealth, and promotion of virtues like justice in the Roman Empire, truth be told, the Romans were often little more than Latin-speaking savages dressed in a toga. The Roman Empire was cruel,

10. Cf. BDAG 598; LSJ 1056.

11. Cf. Epictetus, *Discourses*, 1.16.20–21; 2.9.2; Philo, *Sacrifices*, 88; *Moses* 2.108; *Special Laws*, 1.201, 272, 277, 287, 290; and esp. *T. Levi* 3.6, which refers to angelic worship in heaven where angels make an "offering to the Lord a sweet-smelling aroma, a reasonable and a bloodless offering."

12. Barrett, *Romans*, 232; Dunn, *Romans*, 2:711; Jewett, *Romans*, 730–31.

13. Nijay K. Gupta, *Worship That Makes Sense to Paul: A New Approach to the Theology and Ethics of Paul's Cultic Metaphors* (BZNW 175; New York: de Gruyter, 2010), 123.

repressive, and merciless, especially to non-elites and those on its margins. The Calendonian chieftain Calgacus, who fought the Romans in Britain, said about them, "They ransack the world, and afterwards, when all the land has been laid waste by their pillaging, they scour the sea.... They plunder, they murder, they rape, in the name of their so-called empire. And where they have made a desert, they call it peace."[14]

In this context, Paul says Christians are consciously to resist and to reject the attempt to bring them into concord with their surrounding culture. On the contrary, they are to be "transformed." As far as I am aware, no moral philosopher in the ancient world ever touted the virtues of a moral reconstruction of the self. You can find teachers advocating conformity to nature, advocating the necessity of self-mastery, or disengaging from the desires of the world. But the idea of "transformation" as a moral do-over was not a category anyone seems to have been seriously entertaining.[15] Yet Paul is urging a fundamental renovation of a person at the deepest level of his or her desires, intellect, and will.

Paul calls for transformation conceived as a "renewing of the mind." The word "renewal" (*anakainōsis*) appears only in Christian literature and buttresses the view that Paul is making a distinctive claim. This renewal comprises a "mind" that has shifted away from the "debased mind" of pagans (1:28), from the "mind of the flesh" typifying sinful humanity (8:7), and becomes instead a mind governed by the new way of the Spirit (7:6; 8:27) and that is conformed to the image of the Son (Rom 8:29; 1 Cor 2:12, 16; 2 Cor 3:17–18; Phil 4:2).

The purpose of a transformed self and a renewed mind is then spelled out: "Then you will be able to test and approve what God's will is—his good, pleasing and perfect will" (v. 2b). A renewed mind is able to recognize and appreciate that which belongs to God proper. The word *dokimazō* means to approve of something or to uncover its true quality.[16] The mind renewed by the Spirit is able to discern the good, the pleasing, and the perfect purposes of God with a view to aligning their own attitudes and values with it.

## LIVE the Story

In its barest elements Romans 12:1–2 is about worship, worship with the body and worship with the mind—worship that is sacredly somatic and noetically sanctified. Paul urges us to dedicate our bodies to God and to conform

14. Tacitus, *Agricola*, 30.

15. The closest one finds is Seneca, *Epistles* 6.1; 94.48 (cited in Jewett, *Romans*, 732), but even then the transformation is limited mainly to new insight.

16. BDAG 255.

our minds to the will of God. Worship of this order is fundamentally about offering ourselves to God and transforming ourselves into the image of the Son of God. This is what Charles Talbert calls "a liturgy of life."[17]

### Bodies Fit for Sacrifice

The other day I learned a very disturbing fact. During the 1980s, the song that spent the most number of weeks at #1 on the Billboard Hot 100 American music charts was Australian singer Olivia Newton-John with her hit number "Physical," which was number one for ten consecutive weeks. The chorus line is, "I wanna get physical ... let me hear your body talk." Do not watch the clip on YouTube unless you really like 1980s fitness fashion apparel. But if you think about it, striving to "get physical" might be a catchy way of summarizing what Paul is talking about when he says to "offer your bodies as sacrifices" to God. Worship that is living, holy, and pleasing to God does not take place on some spiritual plane, but occurs through what we do with our physical bodies.

This completely rules out any kind of crass dualism between body and spirit that was prevalent in the Hellenistic world and as so often passes nowadays for spirituality. On the contrary, Paul says the "life I now live *in the body*, I live by faith in the Son of God" (Gal 2:20), so as to make it absolutely clear that his embodied and fleshly existence is the locus where his faith is exercised. Similarly, when some of the Corinthians were trying to use a body/spirit dualism in order to justify sexual immorality, Paul responds that one cannot treat the body with indifference, because "Do you not now that your bodies are temples of the Holy Spirit, who is in you, whom you have received from God? You are not your own; you were bought at a price. Therefore honor God with your bodies" (1 Cor 6:19–20). What we do with our bodies shows what we value with our soul.

The logic of worship as Paul describes it is that it is entirely fitting for believers to train their bodies with the discipline needed to please God. Given that Western culture is highly consumer oriented and driven by the constant need for instant gratification, I seriously wonder if ingraining a bit of asceticism into our lives might not be a bad idea. Yes, I know that asceticism can be harsh and legalistic (see Col 2:23), but there is good evidence that the spiritual practices of Jesus included elements of self-denial and self-discipline that can properly be called asceticism.[18] I'm not saying that everyone should take a vow of silence, embark on a two-week fast, and even married folks should go

17. Talbert, *Romans*, 284.

18. Cf. Dale C. Allison, *Jesus of Nazareth: Millenarian Prophet* (Minneapolis: Fortress, 1998), 172–216.

on a celibacy binge. One of the things we can simply do is to trim our lives of excesses, whether that is in food, drink, entertainment, or anything that is self-indulgent. We should live in such a way as to make clear that our bodies belong to God and not to Starbucks, Netflix, Forever21, or Apple.

The other thing we can do is to live sacrificially for others. Sacrifice presupposes the idea of one life given for another. Applied metaphorically sacrifice means bearing the cost of other people's burdens (Gal 6:2). It entails showing generosity at your own expense (Heb 13:16). Sacrifice is acting selflessly when you see the needs of others (Jas 2:15–16). Such a perspective will manifest itself in the various attitudes and behaviors that Paul goes on to speak about at length in Romans 12:9–21. A person who makes their body a living sacrifice is one who tries to share the pain of another person's loss, grief, rejection, and need as if it were their own.

In sum, if our worship is to "get physical," then we must consciously treat our bodies as a vessel of holiness rather than as temples of self-indulgence. In addition, sacrifice is always for others, expressing itself in doing good itself even at our own personal expense. To this end Chrysostom asked, "How should the body be a sacrifice?" to which he answered:

> Prevent your eye from looking at something evil; it has become a sacrifice. Do not let the tongue say something shameful; it has become an offering. Do not let the hand perform a lawless action; it has become a whole burnt offering. Yet these things are not enough; we must also perform good works: let the hands give alms, let the mouth bless those who abuse, let the hearing devote itself continuously to listening to divine speech. For sacrifice has nothing impure about it; sacrifice is the firstfruits of all other actions. Let us then make a sacrifice to God of the firstfruits of our hands, feet, mouth, and all the other members of our body.[19]

### From Conformity to Transformity

In addition to "getting physical" with our worship, we also have to pursue worship that is noetically renewed by the Spirit and cognitively attuned to God's will. To put it simply, we have to get our minds aligned with God's purposes and plans. To pursue such a pattern entails refusing to conform to the intellectual fashions of our day and pursuing transformation through the renewal of our minds.

Wherever we go, we are bombarded with messages in advertisements and in the media to adopt a certain perspective on things, whether that is fashion, cars, politics, or entertainment. We are given information not simply to

---

19. Cited in Burns, *Romans*, 292.

inform us about something, but to cajole us into thinking about something in a certain way. Marketing experts want us to change the way we think about ourselves or a certain product in order to lure us into purchasing that product. Media outlets and movies often aim to engender sympathy for a certain person or to provoke prejudice against a certain argument. It is all rhetoric, the art of persuasion, vying for attention, mining for recognition, and courting influence over the hearts and minds of the masses. Christians are part of the contested territory that ideologues, journalists, actors, academics, writers, comedians, and politicians are striving to sway. Our TV, newspapers, and internet are awash with a constant battle of ideas with people competing for our adherence to their ideas.

Understandably, there is no shortage of political pundits and postmodern pontiffs trying to shape what we believe about God, family, faith, sexuality, sports, truth, church and state, and the life to come. I've noticed that what really, really annoys some folks is that Christians seem unwilling to budge. Some time ago British Prime Minister David Cameron said that the church needs to "get with the programme" when it comes to supporting women bishops.[20] Former Church of England Bishop, N. T. Wright, who is strongly in favor of women bishops, took issue with Cameron's reprimand of the church for refusing to conform to the myth of cultural progress. Wright responded in *The Times* with a piece saying:

> It won't do to say, then, as David Cameron did, that the Church of England should "get with the programme" over women bishops. And Parliament must not try to force the Church's hand, on this or anything else. That threat of political interference, of naked Erastianism in which the State rules supreme in Church matters, would be angrily resisted if it attempted to block reform; it is shameful for "liberals" in the Church to invite it in their own cause. The Church that forgets to say "we must obey God rather than human authorities" has forgotten what it means to be the Church. The spirit of the age is in any case notoriously fickle. You might as well, walking in the mist, take a compass bearing on a mountain goat. What is more, the Church's foundation documents (to say nothing of its Founder himself) were notoriously on the wrong side of history. The Gospel was foolishness to the Greeks, said St Paul, and a scandal to Jews. The early Christians got a reputation for believing in all sorts of ridiculous things such as humility, chastity and resurrection, standing up

20. Jerome Taylor and Nigel Morris, "'Get with the Programme': David Cameron Condemns Church of England Decision to Block Women Bishops," www.independent.co.uk/ news/uk/politics/ get-with-the-programme-david-cameron-condemns-church-of-england-decision-to-block-women-bishops–8340352.html. 21 Nov 2012. *Independent.*

> for the poor and giving slaves equal status with the free. And for valuing women more highly than anyone else had ever done. People thought them crazy, but they stuck to their counter-cultural Gospel. If the Church had allowed prime ministers to tell them what the "programme" was, it would have sunk without trace in fifty years. If Jesus had allowed Caiaphas or Pontius Pilate to dictate their "programme" to him there wouldn't have been a Church in the first place.[21]

The David Cameron vs. N. T. Wright melee is specific to the British context. Yet what I detect happening in more secularized countries like Australia and parts of northern Europe is a rank antagonism against Christians for maintaining Christian beliefs. That is because such beliefs are perceived as the final obstacles preventing society from becoming more inclusive and tolerant. Lest this seems foreign, I ask my American friends not to think they are immune from this trend since the expulsion of InterVarsity college fellowships from Georgetown University and California State University on the pathetic grounds of "equal opportunity access" should be proof enough that the illiberal tendencies of secular liberalism are coming to a town near you soon.

And therein lies the problem! The church is not called to get with any program, whether it is to exit stage left, to sponsor a certain political party, or to endorse a particular social vision. We measure our faithfulness fundamentally by a refusal to conform to the pattern of this world. Yes, we contextualize our message and the expressions of our faith, but we do not mix and match beliefs to fit with anyone's program. So if you are going to stand up for your faith, be prepared to stand alone. Do not be surprised when a contemporary Caiaphas says your views on the uniqueness of Christ are blasphemous to a pluralist society and he tears his Armani tunic in disgust. Get ready for postmodern Pilates to mockingly ask you, "What is truth?" Be prepared to have the secular Sanhedrin forbid you from speaking about Jesus. All this comes from a refusal to be conformed to the world.

It is sobering to consider how much of our values and habits already are conformed to worldly culture rather than to a kingdom culture and we just don't know it. We can happily resist the political left and the political right, depending on our own political disposition. But what if we're wrong and we're blind and we can't see it? What if the "conservatism" that we so prize is really a cultural construct and our faith has been manipulated to provide religious capital to neoconservatives, big corporations, and libertarian tendencies just because we like them? What if the "progressivism" we champion is because we

21. N. T. Wright, "Women Bishops: It's about the Bible, Not Progress," *Virtue Online*. 23 Nov 2012. www.virtueonline.org/women-bishops-its-about-bible-not-progress-tom-wright-updated-retort.

want to avoid the shame of secular elites, who want to dismantle the enduring structures of society like family so that they can create a vacuum in which their own social ideology may flourish? What if Jesus really does want us to give free health care to poor people? What if God really is angered by the killing of the unborn?

We have to wonder if many of our cosy middle class values like "security" and "mobility" really matter all that much to God or whether they have been imposed on us by our culture and we've not only accepted them, but we've baptized them. Whether you are conservative or progressive, you have to keep asking whether your faith and practice are really conformed to a kingdom culture or whether you are being played for a pawn in someone else's game of ideological chess. Be wary of the ideologues to the left or right who have complete confidence that God is on their side all the time.

Instead of being conformed to our surrounding culture, we are to be transformed by the renewing of our minds; that is to say, we must cultivate a habit of thinking that reflects the biblical vision and the catholic core of the Christian faith. Fill your head with Scripture, hymns, novels, art, and songs which will strengthen your cerebral capacities to understand and articulate your faith. Christian faith cannot bide intellectual laziness.

No, I'm not saying go get a PhD in theology, but put some effort into growing in your knowledge of all things pertaining to God. If you would engage in professional development to enhance your career, why not engage in some spiritual development to enhance your faith? Then you'll be better able to discern between the things of this world and those that belong to God. You'll be equipped to test all things and hold onto that which is good (see 1 Thess 5:21). As D. A. Carson writes: "Here the assumption is that the transformation of character and conduct brought about by the renewal of the Christian's mind is precisely what equips such a Christian to test and approve God's will—that is, to discover personally and experientially that his ways are best."[22]

22. D. A. Carson, *A Call to Spiritual Reformation: Priorities from Paul and His Prayers* (Grand Rapids: Baker, 1992), 102.

CHAPTER 23

# Romans 12:3–8

## LISTEN to the Story

[3]For by the grace given me I say to every one of you: Do not think of yourself more highly than you ought, but rather think of yourself with sober judgment, in accordance with the faith God has distributed to each of you. [4]For just as each of us has one body with many members, and these members do not all have the same function, [5]so in Christ we, though many, form one body, and each member belongs to all the others. [6]We have different gifts, according to the grace given to each of us. If your gift is prophesying, then prophesy in accordance with your faith; [7]if it is serving, then serve; if it is teaching, then teach; [8]if it is to encourage, then give encouragement; if it is giving, then give generously; if it is to lead, do it diligently; if it is to show mercy, do it cheerfully.

*Listening to the texts in the story:* 1 Corinthians 12:1–31; Philippians 2:3.

After laying the foundation for his exhortation (Rom 12:1–2), Paul urges the Roman Christians to avoid arrogant attitudes (12:3) and to embrace the diversity of their own spiritual giftedness (12:4–8). These commands are given because humility and unity are among the first steps toward becoming "living sacrifices" and experiencing the "renewal of your mind." Gospel transformation requires a modest view of self and a generous view of others.

We find numerous examples in the biblical story where God promises to raise up the humble and to bring down the arrogant (see Prov 3:34; Jas 4:6; 1 Pet 5:5). Figures like King Saul are a tragic example of how those raised to great heights can so easily fall from grace on account of their arrogance. God has also taken unassuming persons and equipped them to be his messengers. Neither Moses nor Paul were men of great eloquence (see Exod 4:10; 1 Cor 2:1; 2 Cor 10:10), yet God used them to lead and guide his people into his grace. Whenever God raises up persons to greatness by his special *charisma,* they are always called to humility and service, lest they too stumble over their own accomplishments. The same is true in the church; with great giftedness there should be great humility.

## EXPLAIN the Story

### Don't Get Full of Yourself (12:3)

"For by the grace given me I say to every one of you: Do not think of yourself more highly than you ought, but rather think of yourself with sober judgment, in accordance with the faith God has distributed to each of you." The conjunctive "for" (*gar*) suggests that Paul is unpacking his exhortation in vv. 1–2 by spelling out the means by which the Romans can express fitting worship and be renewed in their minds when they have sober thoughts about themselves. Paul speaks in his authority as an apostle who has been given "grace," specifically, the grace of apostleship to bring about their obedience (1:5). The words "I say to every one of you" indicates that the command is corporate and inclusive of all persons in the Roman congregations. The main thrust is to censure inflated self-estimation, "Do not think of yourself more highly than you ought, but rather think of yourself with sober judgment."

This sentence is dominated by four infinitive verbs based on "to think." To put it clumsily but accurately: Do not over-think (*hyperphronein*) what you ought to think of yourself (*phronein*), but think of yourself (*phronein*) in a sober-thinking way (*sōphronein*). Or as the NLT puts it: "Don't think you are better than you really are, devote your minds to sound judgment." For Paul, Christianity embodies the very best of the Stoic ideal of sober-mindedness.[1]

The significance of this seemingly benign command to humility should not be underestimated for its countercultural ethos. Humility was not an ancient virtue. Humility was for inferiors—for slaves, plebs, and retainers. You won't find Plato or Epictetus extoling the virtue of *tapeinophrosynē* or *humilitas* as it would amount to self-debasement. Remember that social life in ancient Rome was fiercely competitive and consumed with the pursuit of honor and status; raising yourself above others was the aim of the game. Yet Paul expects believers to do the opposite: to think of themselves with self-modesty instead of self-promotion.

Paul wants believers to cultivate humility as a way of pursuing unity. The origins of this teaching is that humility was a characteristic of Israel under God (e.g., Deut 8:2; Ps 18:27; Dan 10:12); it was a virtue taught by Jesus (Matt 20:25–28; 23:12), exemplified by Jesus (Phil 2:8), and instructed by the apostles (2 Cor 10:1; Phil 2:3; Col 3:12; Jas 3:13; 4:6, 10; 1 Pet 3:8; 5:5–6). This is significant because, as John Dickson has successfully argued,

1. Cf. Jewett, *Romans*, 739–41; but see Kruse on the relationship between Paul and Stoicism (*Romans*, 486–89).

humility emerged as a distinctive feature of Christian ethics and came to shape the nature of ethical teaching in Western civilization.[2]

The believer's self-estimation should be "in accordance with" the "faith" that God has "distributed to each of you." The barometer for self-estimation is the divinely given "measure of faith," as most English translations put it (*metron pisteōs*). What does this mean? Here are the options: (1) Perhaps the "measure of faith" refers to the degree or intensity of one's faith.[3] Yet the notion that faith has degrees of gradation is foreign to Paul's thought and he focuses on the object of faith and not on the intensity of one's faith. The language of those "weak" and "strong" in faith in Romans 14–15 is about faith impinging itself on conscience, not about varied degrees of believing. It is also difficult to imagine God assigning quantities of faith to certain persons and not to others in the community since a common "faith" is what binds believers together.

(2) Others contend that the "measure of faith" refers to a shared faith by which Christians are to regard themselves. Here *the* faith is the standard by which persons are to make their self-evaluation.[4] That sounds right, but it does not make sense of the "measuring" or "proportion" of faith that God assigns as God does quantify the "faith" to some degree.

(3) Others think that the "measure of faith" refers to different spiritual capacities that God apportions to each person and constitutes the equivalent of spiritual gifts. In light of the following context in vv. 5–8 about spiritual gifts that does make sense. However, the problem has always been that it seems a stretch to treat "faith" (*pistis*) as a synonym for spiritual gifts (*charisma*). Yet this objection can be blunted if we follow the argument of Jack Poirier, who translates the phrase as the "measure of stewardship" so as to understand Paul to be referring to the callings to which people have been entrusted.[5]

In support of this last option, we should note that *pistis* has a lexical range including a position of trust or trusteeship (see Rom 3:2, where the Jews have been "entrusted" with the oracles of God).[6] Not only that, but in 12:6 Paul uses similar language when he says that prophecy should be performed in accordance with the "proportion of stewardship" (*analogian tēs pisteōs*).

2. Cf. John Dickson, *Humilitas: A Lost Key to Life, Love, and Leadership* (Grand Rapids: Zondervan, 2011). See also Johnson, who makes a similar point (*Romans*, 195).

3. Cf. e.g., Dunn, *Romans*, 2:721–22.

4. Cf. e.g., Moo, *Romans*, 761; Wright, "Romans," 10:709; and esp. Kuo-Wei Peng, *Hate the Evil, Hold Fast to the Good: Structuring Romans 12.1–15.13* (LNTS 300; London: T&T Clark, 2006), 212–14.

5. John C. Poirier, "The Measure of Stewardship: *Pistis* in Romans 12:3," *TynBul* 59 (2008): 145–52.

6. LSJ 1408.

Paul is referring to behavior that befits prophecy in the sense of prophesying in a manner appropriate to what has been granted to them. Whereas in 1 Corinthians 12 Paul calls believers to be content with their assigned function within the church, here in Romans 12 he brings definitional focus to the callings and makes them the basis for humility.[7] Thus, Paul is saying in 12:3 that believers should think of themselves in light of the stewardship or calling that God has placed on their lives whether that is in "prophecy ... service ... teaching ... encouragement ... giving ... leading ... showing mercy."

### One Body, Many Gifts (12:4–8)

Paul moves on to expound the unity-in-diversity of the church by way of a body metaphor (see 1 Cor 12:12–31; Eph 2:16; 3:6; 4:4, 25; 5:29; Col 3:15): "For just as each of us has one body with many members, and these members do not all have the same function, so in Christ we, though many, form one body, and each member belongs to all the others" (vv. 4–5). Paul probably borrows from a well-known Greco-Roman metaphor about the "body politic" to stress that all believers are "members" of the "one body," and while the members are diverse in their function, they remain inalienably dependent on each other. The fact that no member is self-sufficient or expendable provides further reason for avoiding any boasting over others.

The precise expression of their diversity is seen in the diversity of spiritual gifts present among them: "We have different gifts, according to the grace given to each of us" (v. 6a). The gifts are graciously given by God to persons who are to exercise their gifts for a common good. The gifts are then enumerated in a series different from 1 Corinthians 12:7–10, 28 and Ephesians 4:11, though it is hardly meant to be an exhaustive list. It is more of a summary for the types of gifts that churches possess.

Paul calls for the gifts to be exercised with excellence: "If your gift is prophesying, then prophesy in accordance with your faith; if it is serving, then serve; if it is teaching, then teach; if it is to encourage, then give encouragement; if it is giving, then give generously; if it is to lead, do it diligently; if it is to show mercy, do it cheerfully" (vv. 6b–8). The sentence is verbless and consists of nouns and substantive participles, so one has to mentally insert a permissive command like "let us use then ..." (RSV) and imagine each ministry put into action e.g., prophecy to prophesying, service to serving, and so on. Paul calls on the Romans to release the grace given to them through the exercise of their spiritual gifts.

---

7. Poirer, "Measure of Stewardship," 151.

In general, the gifts include two main varieties, the didactic (prophecy, teaching, leading) and the holistic (service, encouragement, generosity, mercy), precisely what is needed for a congregation to become living sacrifices and to have their minds renewed. The chief idea behind Paul's list is, as Wright notes, that "God gives the church grace for its multiple and mutually supportive tasks, and whatever they are they must be exercised to the full extent of one's powers."[8]

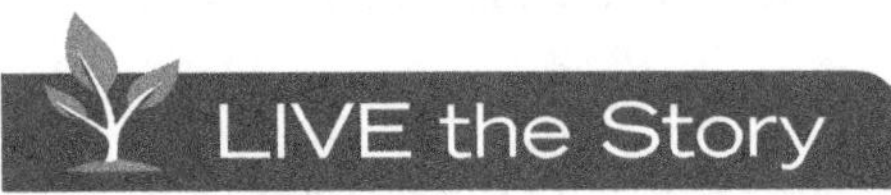


A genuine humility before God and before others is one of the best ways of cultivating a healthy spirituality and a wholesome view of Christian ministry. In applying Romans 12:3–8 to our own context and congregations, we are to exemplify a humble faith that makes much of others rather than ourselves. We should engage in regular humility self-checks to keep our priorities in order, and make a concerted effort to value the giftedness of others and their contribution to the church's corporate life.

There are two verses I cite to myself every day: Romans 12:4 ("Do not think of yourself more highly than you ought, but rather think of yourself with sober judgment") and 2 Corinthians 4:5 ("For what we preach is not ourselves, but Jesus Christ as Lord, and ourselves as your servants for Jesus' sake"). There is a reason for that. I have an ego the size of Nebraska and have a horrible tendency to engage in feats of self-promotion that would even make a Kardashian feel ashamed. This is why I love American grad students. They hero-worship their professors, and their barrage of compliments is like helium to my already swollen pride (as opposed to Aussie grad students, who treat professors with what I can only call jovial contempt). To paraphrase Marlon Brando, an academic can be a lot like an actor: if you ain't talking about him, he's probably not listening. So I think Mac Davis was right, "Oh Lord, it's hard to be humble." All this is to say that for me to lecture on humility is like asking Hannibal Lecter to lecture on vegetarianism.

In my defense, I haven't gone around trying to degrade others for the sole purpose of elevating myself. I should also point out that there are certain features of my biography and psychology that molded me into becoming an overachieving blowhard. When your primary source of self-esteem is achievement and its recognition, you can easily be driven into becoming a workaholic show pony, constantly craving attention and acclaim. Self-congratulatory

8. Wright, "Roman," 10:710.

overachievers may exude excessive confidence and make elevated descriptions of their own significance, but deep down they are often insecure people.

Thankfully, I have reached a point of maturity in my spiritual walk where I've learned that "it's not about me," and I can find my sense of self-worth in Christ rather than in my CV. I no longer feel the need to impress others, but I find greatness in a service that will lead to others receiving recognition and praise for their own work. I enjoy finding ways to highlight the wonderful work of my colleagues and students and seeing them get due recognition for the hard work that they have done in academia and ministry. A turning point for me came after a sermon I once gave where I used probably too many personal illustrations. My pastor came to me afterward and gave a polite rebuke, "I've heard of Christo-centric preaching, but not Mike-o-centric preaching." Those words initially hurt, I felt they were unfair and exaggerated, but eventually I had to accept that they were true. I must decrease, Christ must increase.

For those who are spiritually gifted, it is vital that they nurture humility in themselves. Otherwise their giftedness is not an offering to God or a tool for growing the church; instead, it becomes an idol to the cult of self. The most gifted of preachers, teachers, musicians, deacons, or janitors are like an annoying alarm clock if their giftedness is not matched with humility. We need fewer primadonnas in the pulpit and more pastors who use their gifts as servants.

An easy way to tell if you have a servant heart is how you act when you're treated like a servant. Do you see some services as beneath your calling, are you willing to go wherever you're needed, or would you do any job that needs to be done even if crowds won't throng to thank you and even if your achievements go hardly noticed? Whenever I get asked for advice from churches on what kind of man or woman they should get to fill a particular ministry role, whether a preacher or a youth worker, I always tell the same thing. Get someone gifted and godly—both, not one or the other. The great evangelical Anglican priest Charles Simeon wrote a letter to his friend Abnew Brown in which he said, "The three lessons which a minister has to learn are; 1) Humility, 2) Humility, 3) Humility."[9]

Humility is also important if we are to appreciate the giftedness of other people in our churches. The famous conductor and composer Leonard Bernstein was once asked what the hardest instrument to play is. "Second fiddle," he replied. For people who like to lead, who like to be up front, who like to take the reins, consciously deciding to take backstage position to enable others to exercise their gifts can be difficult. But it reminds me of a story. There was

9. A. W. Brown, *Recollections of the Conversation Parties of the Rev. Charles Simeon* (London: Hamilton, Adams, and Co., 1863), 17.

once a first-time gardener who was sick and tired of going out to his raspberry bushes, gazing down on them and not seeing any raspberries growing. He was just about to uproot the bush when his neighbor told him to get down low and look for raspberries under the lower leaves. So he did. The gardener got down on his belly, looked up into the bush, and beheld several clusters of luscious and ripe raspberries. The moral of the story is that you will only appreciate the fruitfulness of some people if you get down low and look up to them, rather than look down on them in stern judgment.

CHAPTER 24

# Romans 12:9–21

## LISTEN to the Story

[9]Love must be sincere. Hate what is evil; cling to what is good. [10]Be
devoted to one another in love. Honor one another above yourselves.
[11]Never be lacking in zeal, but keep your spiritual fervor, serving the Lord.
[12]Be joyful in hope, patient in affliction, faithful in prayer. [13]Share with
the Lord's people who are in need. Practice hospitality.

[14]Bless those who persecute you; bless and do not curse. [15]Rejoice with
those who rejoice; mourn with those who mourn. [16]Live in harmony with
one another. Do not be proud, but be willing to associate with people of
low position. Do not be conceited.

[17]Do not repay anyone evil for evil. Be careful to do what is right in
the eyes of everyone. [18]If it is possible, as far as it depends on you, live at
peace with everyone. [19]Do not take revenge, my dear friends, but leave
room for God's wrath, for it is written: "It is mine to avenge; I will repay,"
says the Lord. [20]On the contrary:

> "If your enemy is hungry, feed him;
> if he is thirsty, give him something to drink.
> In doing this, you will heap burning coals on his head."

[21]Do not be overcome by evil, but overcome evil with good.

*Listening to the texts in the story:* Deuteronomy 32:35; Psalms 18:8, 12; 120:4; 140:10; Proverbs 25:21–22; Amos 5:15; Matthew 5:9, 38–39, 44; Mark 9:50.

Beyond Paul's call for worship in both body and mind (Rom 12:1–2), his plea for humility (12:3), and his entreaty to cultivate unity by the exercise of spiritual gifts, he now embarks on some generalized ethical exhortations (12:9–21). The collection of ethical maxims appears eclectic and even ad hoc; yet this is the closest Paul comes to the *paraenesis* of Greco-Roman moral exhortation.[1] Johnson rightly understands 12:9–21 as "a Christian virtue list that responds to the vice list that Paul used as the climax of his attack on idolatry in 1:28–31."[2] His series of short, sharp, tweet-length statements provides ethical instructions designed to engender a particular ethos into his audience.

Paul has already talked about a believer's moral compass, deriving from union with Christ and life in the Spirit, so now he endeavors to provide instructions to cultivate a specific moral culture within the church community. This moral culture is to be an *agape* culture since the love command in v. 9a provides a thematic key that informs the various commands and prohibitions that follow. In love, one must hate evil and hold fast to whatever is good, as v. 9 and v. 21 stress. As such, Paul makes a series of ethical instructions about how Christians are to behave lovingly toward others with a specific view to building up the church as a whole.[3] This, of course, was simply living out the teachings of Judaism and Jesus about love of God and love for neighbor (see Lev 18:19; Deut 6:4–5; Mark 12:28–33). Paul wants the churches in Rome to love God by loving others and thereby set up their own unique community in a city not known for its loving ambiance.

In terms of sources, Paul's teaching here exhibits a mixture of Old Testament ethical teachings, Jewish wisdom traditions, echoes of Jesus' teachings, and some strands of Greco-Roman moral philosophy. If a structure is discernible, it is thematically based on love (v. 9a) and built around: (1) holding fast to the good within the Christian community (vv. 9c, 10–13, 15–16a) and outside of the Christian community (v. 14); and (2) hating what is evil within the Christian community (vv. 9b, 16b-c) and outside of the Christian community (vv. 17–21).[4]

### Paul Tweets Christian Love Ethics (12:9–16)

"Love must be sincere. Hate what is evil; cling to what is good" (v. 9). The first ethical exhortation pertains to the priority of love and is meant to inform

1. Abraham J. Malherbe, *Moral Exhortations: A Greco-Roman Sourcebook* (Philadelphia: Westminster, 1986), 124–29.

2. Johnson, *Romans*, 194.

3. Several commentators (e.g., Wright, "Romans," 10:712; Dunn, *Romans*, 2:738; Peng, *Hate the Evil*, 97–98, 99–114, 197) see vv. 14–21 as part of 12:14–13:7 about Christian responsibility toward outsiders. While that is possible, vv. 9–21 seem like a discernible unit bracketed by the cling to good/hate evil theme in v. 9 and v. 21, the exhortations in vv. 15–16 look as if they are oriented toward relations within the church rather than outside of it, and 13:1–7 is a change of topic to some degree going from relationships with individuals to governing authorities.

4. Cf. Peng, *Hate the Evil*, 63–65, 197. Though Stuhlmacher's proposal (*Romans*, 194–96) is simpler with the two poles of love of one's neighbor within the church (vv. 9–13) and love of one's enemies outside of the church (vv. 14–21).

all the subsequent commands and injunctions. Love must be "sincere" in the sense of devoid of hypocrisy and full of authenticity. The importance of love as the highest of Christian virtues and the singularly greatest command is indebted directly to Jesus and manifests itself across early Christian literature.[5] Paul will return to the theme of love later (13:8–10), but here he defines love with a succeeding description as hating evil and cleaving to all that is good. Such emotive language of "hate" and "cling" is clearly indebted to Jewish tradition.[6] Paul means that authentic love repels malice but magnetically clings to all things good. According to Origen, "A person who does not hate the vices cannot love and preserve the virtues."[7]

"Be devoted to one another in love. Honor one another above yourselves" (v. 10). This pair of commands emphasize mutual relations by use of the reciprocal pronoun "one another" (*allēlōn*). The first command is bracketed with two nouns, which both share the *philo-* stem for "love": *philadelphia* ("brotherly love") and *philostorgos* ("loving dearly"). The notion of brotherly love is found elsewhere in the New Testament (see 1 Thess 4:9; Heb 13:1; 1 Pet 1:22; 2 Pet 1:7), while the notion of devoted love was a more Hellenistic concept.[8] Both words for love can have familial connotations, hence the merit of the CEB translation: "Love each other like the members of your family." If love defines the Christian life, then, as Tertullian said, "See how they love one another" is what pagans should be saying when they observe an authentic Christian family.[9]

The second command about honoring others could be taken as "outdo one another in showing honor" (RSV, NRSV, ESV), although it is preferable to take the participle *proēgoumenoi* as "considering better," akin to Philippians 2:3 with "value others above yourselves," resulting in the NIV's "honor one another above yourselves." The statement is profound in an honor/shame context as Paul is telling Christians not to pursue honor for themselves, but for others. In practice this would imply a situation with "slave-owners giving honour to their slaves. In first century terms this is outrageous."[10]

"Never be lacking in zeal, but keep your spiritual fervor, serving the Lord" (v. 11). The first part of the command is that Christians should not become

---

5. Cf. 1 Cor 13:1–10, 13; Gal 5:13–14; 1 Thess 4:9; Jas 2:8–9; 1 Pet 1:22; 1 John 2:7–11; 3:10–18; 4:7–12, 18–21; and e.g., *1 Clem.* 21.7; 33.1, 47.5; 48.1; 49.4–6; 50.1–3; 53.5; 54.1; 62.2; *Did.* 1.3; 2.7.

6. Cf. Amos 5:15: "Hate evil, love good"; 1QS 1.4–5: "to love all that he has chosen and hate all that he has despised; to depart from all evil and cling to all good works"; and *T. Benj.* 8.1: "Do away with evil, envy, and hatred of brothers, and cling to goodness and love."

7. Burns, *Romans*, 301.

8. *NDIEC* 2:100–3; 3:41–42; Jewett, *Romans*, 761 n. 46.

9. Tertullian, *Apol.* 39.7.

10. Oakes, *Reading Romans*, 110.

complacent in their divine service. They should not allow their diligence to dwindle. In contrast, they should serve the Lord with a fiery fervency. Several translations miss out on the metaphor of fire that stands behind the word *zeō* as it means to be emotionally stirred up, to boil over, and be on fire.[11] Once more the CEB is preferable with "be on fire in the Spirit as you serve the Lord!" Instead of letting the flame of love fade, believers need to keep the spiritual fire in their bellies freshly kindled! Oakes puts it well: "Having lifted them all up to seats at a convivial gathering, Paul pushes them all firmly down into the world of hard work and service. All are of high status in God's eyes. All need to serve."[12]

"Be joyful in hope, patient in affliction, faithful in prayer" (v. 12). These three virtues of hope, endurance, and prayerfulness are natural partners since they describe how Christians are to keep their faith in the not-yet of their salvation.[13] In many ways, the trio summarizes the exhortations in 5:2–3 and 8:24–27, with hope fostering endurance, and endurance in turn requires constant prayer.

"Share with the Lord's people who are in need. Practice hospitality" (v. 13). Paul expects the churches to put love into practice by sharing material resources with those in need among their circle. This is the true meaning of "fellowshiping," not merely friendship within a religious club of equals, but an unhesitant desire to give to those in need without thought of return. By stressing the pursuit of "hospitality" Paul does not mean having your middle class friends over for a BBQ, but taking in those travelers who have no place to stay, especially itinerant Christian missionaries (see 1 Tim 5:10; Heb 13:2; 1 Pet 4:9; 3 John 8). If a cohort of Jewish Christians had recently returned to Rome or if Paul's own delegation led by Phoebe was looking for lodgings, the importance of hospitality would be all the more imperative.

"Bless those who persecute you; bless and do not curse" (v. 14). The exhortation here has a lot of familiarity with Jesus' own teaching about loving your enemies and praying for those who persecute you (see Matt 5:44/Luke 6:27–28). Christians often appealed to the same formula about blessing those who curse you as a way of expressing their nonretaliatory ethos (see 2 Cor 4:12; 1 Pet 3:9; *Did.* 1.3; *Ep. Diog.* 5.15). As to what kind of persecution the Roman Christians may have been experiencing at this point, before the Neronian persecution, it is hard to say. It could have included a mixture of social ostracism, slander, boycott of business, and legal action. If the epistle to the Hebrews has a Roman provenance, the believers may have experienced the

11. BDAG 426.
12. Oakes, *Reading Romans*, 112.
13. Moo, *Romans*, 779.

various hardships described therein, including public insult, imprisonment, and confiscation of property (see Heb 10:32–34). Such things may have happened to them when they came to faith and during the expulsion occasioned by the Edict of Claudius.

"Rejoice with those who rejoice; mourn with those who mourn" (v. 15). Given the preceding context with v. 14 about blessing persecutors, it is possible to see the command as a call to show sincere love to non-Christians as well as to Christians. However, in light of the parallel idea in 1 Corinthians 12:26 with, "If one part suffers, every part suffers with it; if one part is honored, every part rejoices with it," Paul most likely has the church in mind, not outsiders. As such, a further feature of fellowship is that members of the church are to share in the highs and lows of each other's journeys.[14] This was a unique notion in the Greco-Roman context, for philosophers normally associated virtue with *apatheia*, apathy, a deliberate lack of involvement with the care of others.[15]

"Live in harmony with one another. Do not be proud, but be willing to associate with people of low position. Do not be conceited" (v. 16). In keeping with the call in his other letters for single-minded unity (see 2 Cor 13:11; Phil 2:2; 4:2 and again in Rom 15:5), Paul exhorts his audience to "live in harmony with one another," or more literally, "Be of the same mind toward one another" (NASB). The focus is not on uniformity in thought, but on a single- minded pursuit of harmonious relations. They are to be thoughtful for how they treat each other. Paul will provide further specification on that point in 14:1–15:13 when it comes to some nitty-gritty details.

The barriers to such harmony are, of course, any kind of arrogance, pride, or high-mindedness (see Prov 3:7, "Do not be wise in your own eyes"). In addition, building up mutual consideration of each other rules out any kind of caste system. The Roman social order was intensely hierarchical. In the Roman world, senators did not associate with plebs, equestrians did not consider themselves equal to peasants, and masters did not dine with slaves. Everything, from seating arrangements at a trade association dinner to occupying positions during a ceremony in a temple, was ordered according to social hierarchy. Yet, just as he did in Corinth (see 1 Cor 11:17–34), Paul censures any attempt to impose such hierarchies within the churches. Persons should not think that they are socially better or philosophically smarter than anyone else and use it as an excuse to avoid associating with those who have neglible status.

14. Ibid., 782.

15. Johnson, *Romans*, 195.

While the natural social instinct for any upright Roman was to avoid fraternizing with inferiors, Paul demands that all be willing to share in fellowship with those of lesser social stations. For Paul, such socioeconomic distinctions are meaningless and broken down in Christ (see Gal 3:28–29). Oakes says, "The basis of honour in the house churches has no connection with human status. In Christ, the honour distinctions of ethnicity, servitude and gender are defunct."[16] Paul is not interested in homogenous church planting in Rome, with one church for patricians, one for equestrians, one from freedmen, one for citizens, one for foreigners, and one for slaves. Instead, they are all members of the "one body" of Christ (see Rom 12:5).

### God Is the Only Avenger (12:17–21)

On the treatment of outsiders, Paul builds on v. 14, where he called for believers to bless their persecutors rather than curse them. In vv. 17–21 he prohibits believers from seeking retaliation against foes. This is something he taught earlier to the Thessalonians: "Make sure that nobody pays back wrong for wrong, but always strive to do what is good for each other and for everyone else" (1 Thess 5:15; cf. 1 Pet 3:9).[17] It is impossible to tell if there is some situation in Rome that Paul might be addressing with these remarks. The closest we can guess is that maybe some of the believers were members of street gangs in the impoverished parts of Rome. The purpose of belonging to a gang was not the pursuit of crime but personal security. In the absence of a police force, the only deterrent for would-be assailants came by belonging to a gang who threatened to harm anyone who attacked one of its members.[18] Alternatively, Paul may simply be echoing Jewish traditions against revenge in contrast to Greek philosophers like Aristotle, who urged revenge as a virtuous enterprise: "To take vengeance on one's enemies is nobler than to come to terms with them; for to retaliate is just, and that which is just is noble; and further, a courageous man ought not to allow himself to be beaten."[19]

"Do not repay anyone evil for evil. Be careful to do what is right in the eyes of everyone" (v. 17). The Old Testament laws of legal retaliation with "eye for an eye" are based on the idea of inflicting a proportionate punishment

16. Oakes, *Reading Romans*, 111.

17. Cf. *T. Jos.* 18.2: "And if anyone wishes to do you harm, you should pray for him, along with doing good, and you will be rescued by the Lord from every evil"; and *Jos. Asen.* 23.9: "And we are men who worship God, and it does not befit us to repay evil for evil."

18. Cf. Oakes, *Reading Romans*, 123–26.

19. Aristotle, *On Rhetoric*, 1.9.24. Although a Pythagorean maxim said, "It is much more pious to suffer injustice than to kill a person; for judgment is ordained in Hades" (*Life of Pythagoras* 155, 179, cited in Talbert, *Romans*, 292).

on a criminal for their deed (see Exod 21:24; Lev 24:20; Deut 19:21). Yet Scripture provides a clear injunction against seeking revenge (see Lev 19:18; Prov 20:22; 24:29; Sir 28:10), and Jesus taught that retaliation was not how his followers should treat others (see Matt 5:38–39). The spiral of pain and loss would only be amplified if everyone attempted to exact revenge on their adversaries. Similarly, Paul urges believers not to retaliate when wronged, not to perpetuate a cycle of violence and victimization.

Instead of pursuing repayment for wrong, Paul urges his audience to show regard for what everyone believes is "good" (*kalos*). Christians then are to commend themselves by doing good things that even outsiders acknowledge and approve. The notion of doing good before others is then extended further: "If it is possible, as far as it depends on you, live at peace with everyone" (v. 18). Believers are urged to work as far as they are humanly able to cultivate peaceful relations toward outsiders. Jesus himself blessed the "peacemakers" (Matt 5:9) and taught his followers to "be at peace with each other" (Mark 9:50). In context, Paul calls on the Roman churches not to pursue an antagonistic relationship with their surroundings but to promote peace with others in the sense of not giving cause to conflict.

Paul returns to the revenge theme begun in v. 17a by way of two scriptural citations—Deuteronomy 32:35 and Proverbs 25:21–22: "Do not take revenge, my dear friends, but leave room for God's wrath, for it is written: 'It is mine to avenge; I will repay,' says the Lord. On the contrary: 'If your enemy is hungry, feed him; if he is thirsty, give him something to drink. In doing this, you will heap burning coals on his head' " (vv. 19–20). The message is clear: do not seek revenge because that is God's prerogative. The VOICE puts it well: "*Again*, my loved ones, do not seek revenge; instead, allow God's wrath *to make sure justice is served. Turn it over to Him*" (italics original). The renunciation of retaliation is not so the perpetrator can get away free. Paul knows that rulers and authorities bear the sword of justice (13:4), but God is the one who will ultimately avenge all wrongdoing. God's "wrath" is the distributive justice of heaven against all wickedness.

Paul reinforces his exhortation to defer to God's retributive will with a quotation of Deuteronomy 32:35: "It is mine to avenge, I will repay."[20] The point is singularly important, as Miroslav Volf comments, "The certainty of God's judgment at the end of history is the presupposition for the renunciation of violence. The divine system of judgment is not the flip side of the

---

20. Cf. Sir 28:1: "The vengeful will face the Lord's vengeance, for he keeps a strict account of their sins"; 1QS 10.17: "I will pay no man the reward of evil, I will pursue him with goodness. For judgment of all things is with God and it is he who will render to man his reward."

human reign of terror, but a necessary correlate of human nonviolence."[21] This decision to leave retribution up to God yields a different practice. One can provide an enemy with food and drink and in this way live out the command of v. 14 to bless those who persecute us and do the good that is approved by all people. The purpose of providing sustenance to an enemy as Proverbs 25:21–22 narrates is not to deliberately increase his or her liability to divine wrath. By showing kindness to our adversaries, we are giving them the opportunity to change. As Abraham Lincoln said, "The best way to destroy an enemy is to make him a friend."

By showing unexpected and undeserved kindness we can make our opponents become friends and break down hatred, prejudice, and ignorance. However, for those who do not change, who wish to continue their hatred for hatred's sake, such kindness does have a negative impact. A brutish response to kindness demonstrates their fitness for divine recompense and is tantamount to piling coals of fire on their head, symbols for God's coming in judgment (see Pss 18:8, 12; 120:4; 140:10).

Paul returns to the theme of "evil" and "good" with which he began in 12:9 and uses it to sum up his short exhortation: "Do not be overcome by evil, but overcome evil with good" (v. 21). Christians do not conquer the evil done to them by returning evil in equal measure; rather, they triumph over evil by performing good to a disproportionate degree than deserved. Refusing to retaliate is how we worship with our bodies, and it is by refusing to adopt the revenge culture of our world that we show forth the renewal of our minds.

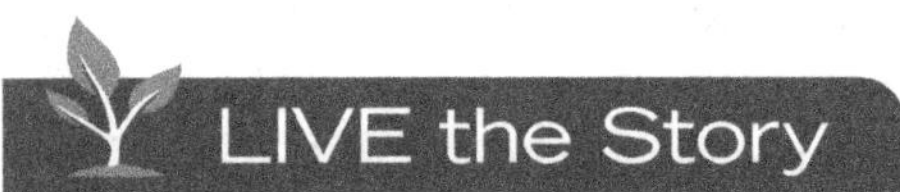


There are a whole host of themes, ideas, and motifs that could be explored in this densely packed exhortation. Without doubt, love is a dominating theme here, and all that is said about hope, joy, endurance, honor, and prayer flows from it. What also stands out in my mind here is vv. 17–21 with its teachings about revenge.

### Love Must Be Sincere

The key characteristics of love in Romans 12:9–10 are that it must be authentic and outward looking. An authentic love is one without pretense and hypocrisy. There is no pretending to love someone and no harboring hate underneath a thinly veiled smile of friendship. Those who love must empty

21. Miroslav Volf, *Exclusion and Embrace: A Theological Exploration of Identity, Otherness and Reconciliation* (Nashville: Abingdon, 1996), 302.

out what is hypocritical and hateful in their hearts and cling to everything that is noble and kind. The Danish philosopher Søren Kierkegaard put it the best: "The best defense against hypocrisy is love; indeed, it is not only a defense but a chasmic abyss; in all eternity it has nothing to do with hypocrisy. This is also a fruit by which love is known—it secures the loving one against falling into the snare of the hypocrite."[22]

To work this out in practice, Christians must live lives of sacred love. If Christians hold to Jesus' creed about loving God and loving others, and if we apply this creed as Paul does here, then several praxes will become discernible in our church community. According to Scot McKnight, the Jesus creed of sacred love transforms our lives in several ways. First, it will transform our speech so that we talk with charity and reserve. It is okay to speak one's mind as long as one speaks with the mind of Christ. Second, sacred love converts our actions so that what we do to others is determined principally by what we can do for them. It comes down to a simple golden rule of treating others how you would want to be treated. Third, sacred love inspires our worship as it forces us to realize that we are sinners and God is merciful. When we comprehend how God's love reaches those who were loveless toward him, we are ready to kneel before him in humility and to sing to him in praise.[23]

When it comes to loving sincerely and loving outwardly, it all comes down to creating an *agape* culture in our churches where people are consumed with love and our churches are known by their love. We need to cultivate a theology and practice that lead to an inward love for each other and an external love for others because we love God. To quote Kierkegaard again: "The last, most blessed, the unconditionally convincing mark of love remains—love itself, the love that becomes known and recognized by the love in another. Like is known by like; only someone who abides in love can know love, and in the same way his love is to be known."[24]

## Reversing the Revenge Culture

I do not know how if you've noticed this, but *revenge* is possibly the singularly dominant theme underlying much of our favorite novels, movies, and TV shows. The most epic revenge story I can think of is the *Count of Monte Cristo* by Alexandre Dumas (1844) about the ruin, rage, and revenge of Edmond Dantès. When it comes to movies, you could almost list indefinitely the

22. Søren Kierkegaard, *Kierkegaard's Writings, XVI: Works of Love* (eds. H. V. Hong and E. H. Hong; Princeton, NJ: Princeton University Press, 2013), 15.

23. Scot McKnight, *The Jesus Creed: Loving God, Loving Others* (Brewster, MA: Paraclete, 2004), 46–50.

24. Kierkegaard, *Kierkegaard's Writings*, 16.

number of blockbusters based on revenge. In the last few years you've got: *Django Unchained*, *Inglorious Bastards*, *Munich*, *Man on Fire*, *Gladiator*, and that's just off the top of my head. Oh, and look what just came up on my Twitter feed, *The Equalizer* with Denzel Washington, another revenge flick. Even classic movies like my all-time favorite movie *The Princess Bride* has a major revenge plot summed up in that famous line, "My name is Inigo Montoya, you killed my father; prepare to die." Then there is the recent hit TV series *Revenge*, which is a positively soap operatic story with more twists and turns than a Parisian backstreet.

It seems that revenge stories sell well. Big box office sales and big ratings for the networks! Why is that? Probably because deep down inside, all of us have thought about what it would be like to get some payback on our enemies. Whether those enemies are political, national, cultural, tribal, professional, criminal, or personal, we want to see the wicked brought to justice. We even want to go outside the law and extract some cold, hard justice of our own making without the restraints of civility or legal process. We fantasize about indulging the more violent tendencies of our imagination where we stand over evil persons and give them what we think they deserve. We would like to take the gloves off and make the wicked pay with blood for their crimes. We imagine a situation where we disempower our enemies, deprive them of their freedom, activate their deepest fears, and inflict on them recompense without remorse. If you think hard enough, you can probably visualize a number of people you'd like to see get theirs and then imagine it as a movie with either Denzel Washington or Liam Neeson cast as the vengeful hero who unleashes all hell on the perpetrators. Revenge entertains and excites, but that is not the way of Jesus Christ.

The day I came to revise this section was the same day that a Libyan faction of ISIS callously beheaded twenty-one Egyptian Copts for no other reason that being Christian. My initial response to this act of evil was to hope that some government, any government, would get revenge for the victims, that the perpetrators would be blown into a zillion pieces. We envision violence and suffering raining down on the animals who did such unspeakable things. But then I remembered that that would be repaying evil for evil. It is the way of the world but not the way of Jesus Christ. What we should do as Christians is grieve for the victims' families, pray for those who suffer and even for our enemies, hope for justice to be done, work for peace where we can, and look forward to the judgment of God.

Christians are not to seek revenge because that means usurping for ourselves what is a divine prerogative. God and God alone has the right to avenge. That is what Paul says here. That is not to say that we cannot hope and work for evildoers to be brought to justice and experience the full penalty for their crimes; we clearly should want that (see Amos 5:15; Rom 13:4). But revenge is simply not an option for those whose way of life is determined by the teaching of Jesus and his apostles. When hurt by someone, we must fight the temptation to act out the revenge fantasies of our culture. Such things are inappropriate for a follower of Jesus. As Moo says: "Evil can overcome us when we allow the pressure put on us by a hostile world to force us into attitudes and actions that are out of keeping with the transformed character of the new realm. Paul urges us to resist such a temptation."[25]

In practice, the prohibition on revenge means that we cannot pursue a private vendetta against anyone no matter how injured or wronged we might feel. Let me add that there are also good reasons to refrain from fantasizing about or pursuing revenge. Revenge is not healthy. For a start, it can be dangerous. The Chinese war strategist Sun-Tzu famously said, "Before you embark on a journey of revenge, you should first dig two graves." By seeking revenge you can end up putting yourself in further harm, emotionally and physically, magnifying your hurt rather than curing it. Second, evil triumphs when we feel compelled to do evil to destroy evil. Evil taunts us, teases us, torments us, and tempts us into thinking that we must emulate evil in order to defeat evil.

I'm not a big admirer of Friedrich Nietzsche, but he got one thing right in this saying: "Beware that, when fighting monsters, you yourself do not become a monster.... For when you gaze long into the abyss, the abyss gazes also into you." In pursuing revenge we risk becoming worse than the evil we think we are struggling against. Evil begets evil, and we end up giving further momentum to the never-ending cycle of pain and repayment. If we are to *resist* evil, we cannot *repay* evil by *replicating* evil. If everyone pays back an eye for an eye, the whole world will be full of one-eyed people. There has to be another way! Craig Keener tells the story of praying for Christians under siege from Muslims in Nigeria with a Nigerian student named "Sunday":

> Sunday was one of my students at Eastern Seminary four years ago, when we learned of a riot in his home state of Kaduna. Thousands of radical Muslim youth had marched for several days in the state capital to demand *sharia*, so Christians decided to stage a peaceful countermarch, pleading that *sharia* not be imposed. Muslims controlled the politics of the state, but Kaduna had a large Christian population that finally decided to speak up. As we heard the story, some Muslim youths began hurling stones at the Christian marchers, most of whom had traveled from the southern

25. Moo, *Romans*, 789.

part of the state for the march. When some Christian youth hurled stones back, extremist Muslims suddenly attacked with automatic weapons and machetes, slaughtering hundreds, most of them women. Children were slaughtered on their way home from school; others returned to find their parents dead. I prayed with Sunday; his cousin had been killed, and he did not know whether his brothers, now missing, were dead or alive. "Rise up, O God," I cried passionately. "Avenge the blood of your servants!" When I finished, Sunday prayed. "Please forgive the Muslims and spare them," he pleaded, "because they do not have hope." I bowed my head in shame. Sunday's compassion was right. And for the safety of millions of our brothers and sisters like Sunday, as well as for those Muslims, we need to keep praying for peace—and speaking for truth.[26]

26. Craig Keener, "The Truth about the Religious Violence in Jos, Nigeria," *Christianity Today* (21 Jan 2010). www.christianitytoday.com/ct/2010/januaryweb-only/13-42.0.html.

CHAPTER 25

# Romans 13:1–7

## LISTEN to the Story

[1]Let everyone be subject to the governing authorities, for there is no authority except that which God has established. The authorities that exist have been established by God. [2]Consequently, whoever rebels against the authority is rebelling against what God has instituted, and those who do so will bring judgment on themselves. [3]For rulers hold no terror for those who do right, but for those who do wrong. Do you want to be free from fear of the one in authority? Then do what is right and you will be commended. [4]For the one in authority is God's servant for your good. But if you do wrong, be afraid, for rulers do not bear the sword for no reason. They are God's servants, agents of wrath to bring punishment on the wrongdoer. [5]Therefore, it is necessary to submit to the authorities, not only because of possible punishment but also as a matter of conscience.

[6]This is also why you pay taxes, for the authorities are God's servants, who give their full time to governing. [7]Give to everyone what you owe them: If you owe taxes, pay taxes; if revenue, then revenue; if respect, then respect; if honor, then honor.

*Listening to the texts in the story:* Jeremiah 29:1–23; Daniel 4:17; 5:21; Wisdom of Solomon 6:1–11; Sirach 10:4–5; *2 Baruch* 82:9.

It is impossible to plot a path for God's people through pagan culture without saying something about pagan political authorities. Based on the pragmatics of Jewish diaspora life, the theocentric perspective of the Jewish wisdom tradition on kings and rulers, and the particular context of Christians in Greco-Roman cities, Paul addresses the topic of Christians living under imperial rule. On the Roman context, it is likely that in the aftermath of the Edict of Claudius that things began to change for the perception of Christ-believers. They would no longer be regarded as a subbranch within the *religio* of Judaism, but were gradually perceived as a foreign *superstitio* with no legal status and largely on the margins of Roman society.[1]

So, given this situation, how were Christ-believers to relate to Roman authorities? Remember that the Romans were among the "rulers of this age" who "crucified the Lord of glory" (1 Cor 2:8), who imprisoned believers (Rom 16:7; 2 Cor 11:23), and who exiled some of their number from Rome (Acts 18:2). One might expect Paul to stir up fervor for Rome's overthrow, or at least to wait anxiously for God to rain down fire and brimstone on them and their minions. But there is none of that; instead he calls for submission! As Keck observes, the problem with 13:1–7 is not its opaqueness but its clarity, its plain and unqualified call for submission.[2] Origen, who knew Roman brutality all too well, said: "I am disturbed by Paul's saying that the authority of this age and the judgment of the world are ministers of God."[3]

No single occasion for Paul's remarks has won widespread approval. Käsemann popularized the position that Paul was calling certain "enthusiasts" back to an earthly order and resisting the view that heavenly citizenship meant treating political authorities with indifference. To forego obedience to authorities would lead to anarchy, which would destroy love and peace in the community and discredit Christianity in the eyes of the world.[4] Thus, Paul refutes the idea that those reigning with Christ need pay no attention to ruling authorities of this defunct age.[5]

It might also be the case that some of the Christians in Rome were sympathizing with the increasing anti-Roman zeal that was beginning to ferment in Judea in the 40s and 50s.[6] Jews in Palestine had earlier revolted over paying taxes to Rome since it meant recognizing Caesar as king and Israel was supposed to have no king but God.[7] By the time Paul wrote to the Romans, the seed for revolution had been sown in Judea. Paul doesn't want Christians to become a messianic variation of the "Fourth Philosophy" with its zealous sedition against Rome.[8]

So Paul's call for submission seeks to avoid these two extremes of over-realized eschatology (kingdom is here, so ignore Caesar), and under-realized eschatology (kingdom is not here, so pick up your sword against Caesar and

1. Giorgio Jossa, *Jews or Christians? The Followers of Jesus in Search of Their Own Identity* (WUNT 202; Tübingen: Mohr Siebeck, 2006), 125–31.

2. Keck, *Romans*, 311.

3. Cited in Burns, *Romans*, 315.

4. Käsemann, *Romans*, 350–59.

5. Moo, *Romans*, 791.

6. Cf. Marcus J. Borg, "A New Context for Romans XIII," *NTS* 19 (1972–73): 205–18.

7. Josephus, *War* 2.118; *Ant.* 18.23.

8. Josephus, *Ant.* 18.9, 23.

let's make the kingdom come). Paul might be saying something like, "Jesus is the Lord, the new age has dawned, but be that as it may, we cannot get ahead of ourselves and live as if authorities are not there. They are here, and for good reasons; God has appointed them to provide justice for their peoples. What is more, some hot-heads in Judea might be sharpening their swords for holy war, looking for opportunities to revolt, but that will not solve the problem; instead, it will replace imperial rule with lawless anarchy. God can bring Rome to its knees, and he does not need your sword to do it."

Paul's remarks in 13:1–7 are sage advice if you think about it because, as Christians have learned from the Arab Spring, the rule of the dictator is often preferable to the brutal sectarian violence of anarchy. This is why Christians were largely in favor of government (see Titus 3:1; 1 Pet 2:13–14; *Mart. Pol.* 10.2). Given Rome's role in promoting some order amidst the injustices of Mediterranean life, even Paul (Acts 25:11) and Philo (*Flaccus*; *Embassy*) could appeal for intervention. Paul probably wants to emphasize that when he comes to Rome, it is as a missionary apostle, not a political agitator.[9] As we read the biblical story, we learn that God often uses pagan authorities like Nebuchadnezzar (Dan 3:28–30) and Cyrus (Isa 45:1) for his purposes, and God's people have to seek the welfare of even a pagan city during times of exile (Jer 38:4).

Romans 13:1–7 breaks down into four sub-sections: (1) the call for submission to governing authorities (v. 1); (2) the need for submission to governing authorities (vv. 2–3a); (3) practical reasons for submitting to governing authorities (vv. 3b–5); and (4) the proper way to submit to governing authorities (vv. 6–7).[10]

## EXPLAIN the Story

### Submit to Governing Authorities (13:1)

"Let everyone be subject to the governing authorities, for there is no authority except that which God has established. The authorities that exist have been established by God" (v. 1). The injunction against seeking revenge in 12:17–21 receives further support from 13:1–7, since governing authorities are the agents of divine revenge (13:4–5), who are part of the ongoing revelation of divine wrath (see 1:18). By affirming submission to governing rulers (13:1–5), Christians are also clinging to what others regard as commonly

9. Byrne, *Romans*, 386–87; Johnson, *Romans*, 199.
10. Largely following Jewett, *Romans*, 784–85.

"good" (12:9, 17, 21).[11] Paul's immediate point, then, is that "everyone" (lit., "every soul" [*pasa pseuchē*]) is to submit to the governing authorities. In Rome, the governing authorities were the emperor, senate, consuls, and magistrates with their administrative apparatus and military forces.

To us this looks a servile position that uncritically accepts the status quo without objection.[12] We tend to fear too much government. We are wary of government becoming too big, too bureaucratic, too corrupt, and too intrusive in our lives. However, in the ancient world, too much government wasn't the problem; it was too little government. Most cities and regions were never far from anarchy. Government was the only means of ensuring some kind of public order, justice system, and collective defense. Plutarch sums up what many thought: "Rulers serve God for the care and preservation of men."[13] Government, then, is a gift like marriage and family, given to preserve and better humankind.

The reason for submission is clear: all authorities exist exclusively by divine appointment, and since God has appointed them, they must be obeyed. The underlying idea is a scriptural one, namely, that kings and kingdoms, rulers and republics, only exist by the decree of God. Pagan kings like Nebuchadnezzar and Cyrus only attained their place of power by divine appointment (see Isa 45:1; Jer 27:4–7; Dan 2:21, 37–38; 4:17, 31–37; 5:18–21). In Proverbs, God says: "By me kings reign and rulers issue decrees that are just; by me princes govern, and nobles—all who rule on earth" (Prov 8:15–16). Ben Sirach declared: "The government of the earth is in the hand of the Lord, and over it he will raise up the right leader for the time" (Sir 10:4). Josephus wrote that "no ruler attains his office save by the will of God" (*War* 2.140).

Government is a form of common grace instituted by God where God uses human rulers to provide justice, order, and civility for the peoples governed. As Moo comments: "Government is more than a nuisance to be put up with; it is an institution established by God to accomplish some of his purposes on earth."[14] Thus, Paul acquiesces to political submission for the sake of respecting God's appointed servants who genuinely benefit its citizens with the exercise of their authority.

### Theological Reasons for Submitting (13:2–3a)

"Consequently, whoever rebels against the authority is rebelling against what God has instituted, and those who do so will bring judgment on themselves"

11. Numerous topical links also exist between Rom 2:7–11 and 13:3–4; see Dunn, *Romans*, 2:758.
12. On the difference between "submit" and "obey," see Moo, *Romans*, 797, 807–10.
13. *To an Uneducated Ruler* 3.
14. Moo, *Romans*, 809.

(v. 2). Paul next explains the reason for submission. Assuming that governing authorities are appointed by God, to resist or disobey these authorities is to rebel against God himself. Persons who rebel against God, as any Jew could tell you, are bringing "judgment on themselves." God brooks no rivals to either his reign or that of his appointed servants. To that Paul adds further support: "For rulers hold no terror for those who do right, but for those who do wrong" (v. 3a). This is obviously a broad generalization, but as a general principle it rings true. Whatever abuses an authority perpetuates, it rarely attempts to inflict punishment on upright citizenry. Paul's point is that only those who do wrong have anything to fear from governing authorities.

### Personal Reasons for Submitting (13:3b–4)

Paul shifts from general exhortation to a specific address to his audience with the second person, "you." "Do you want to be free from fear of the one in authority? Then do what is right and you will be commended" (v. 3b). The way of escaping fear of the authorities is not by overthrowing them, but by obeying them. There is no fear of penalty for those who do what is good; in fact, they can expect to receive praise from their political masters for noble conduct. Inscriptions testify to rulers heaping praise on those who contributed to the common good by their service. Here one thinks of "Erastus," who in Corinth was "the city's director of public works" (Rom 16:23).[15]

Paul again clarifies his thought: "For the one in authority is God's servant for your good. But if you do wrong, be afraid, for rulers do not bear the sword for no reason. They are God's servants, agents of wrath to bring punishment on the wrongdoer" (v. 4). The governing authorities are divine servants who, ideally, administer the city for the benefit of their citizens. So to do evil would be to incur culpability for the due penalties that leaders are authorized to inflict. Rulers, Paul says, "do not bear the sword for no reason," which is to say that the threat of capital punishment is real. Paul might be thinking here of the Roman *ius gladii*, the authority possessed by provincial governors to execute Roman citizens, or else, the state's right to inflict capital punishment. Although Seneca could boast that Nero had effectively sheathed the sword of government, the reality was that criminals were still routinely executed, often in the amphitheater for sport.[16] In addition, "sword-bearers" is also attested in papyri as a name for local police.[17] Governing authorities are divine servants who, by their use of punishment, execute God's wrath against evildoers. As

---

15. Cf. Bruce Winter, "The Public Honoring of Christian Benefactors: Romans 13.3–4 and 1 Peter 2.14–15," *JSNT* 34 (1988): 91–92.

16. Seneca, *On Clemency*, 1.4.

17. Jewett, *Romans*, 795.

Schreiner comments: "The judgment of the state against evildoers in history anticipates the eschatological judgment of God at the end of history."[18]

### Practical Ways for Submitting (13:5–7)

Paul concludes his short section on Christians and governing authorities with a recap of his main point and some practical suggestions on what submission actually looks like. "Therefore, it is necessary to submit to the authorities, not only because of possible punishment but also as a matter of conscience" (v. 5). Christians should submit to divine authorities because they are appointed by God (vv. 1–2), they have the divine authority to punish evildoers (vv. 3–4), and he adds another reason, "conscience" (v. 5). This "conscience" (*syneidēsis*) refers to an inner moral compass that points people to a manner of life recognized as right by both God and people (see Acts 23:1, 16; Rom 2:15; 9:1; 1 Cor 8:7, 10, 12).

To keep a good conscience requires doing certain things: "This is also why you pay taxes, for the authorities are God's servants, who give their full time to governing" (v. 6). Taxes are appropriate and should not be despised as they provide the financial resources for governing authorities to carry out their governance. Nero's taxation policies were highly unpopular, and Paul is saying that Christians should not get embroiled in the backlash against them.[19]

What Paul teaches is aptly summed up with a maxim: "Give to everyone what you owe them: If you owe taxes, pay taxes; if revenue, then revenue; if respect, then respect; if honor, then honor" (v. 7). One is obligated by law and by conscience to give rulers what they are owed, whether that is taxes, duties, respect, or honor. Although this might seem like a servile approach, it is sober advice for a group regarded with suspicion. Paul also recognizes that respect for rulers is a sensible way of staying under the radar of imperial authorities when you belong to a marginal group.[20]

Paul would be aware that these divinely appointed authorities do not always govern justly or treat people rightly. Authorities can be hostile to God and God's people, but at the end of the day, survival is the best form of defiance. In that light, Wright contends that 13:1–7 is about establishing a community right under Caesar's nose in Rome that witnesses to the work of the one true God, but avoids the view that loyalty to Jesus would mean civil

18. Schreiner, *Romans*, 684.

19. Tacitus, *Annals* 13.50; Suetonius, *Nero* 44.1. Cf. Thomas M. Coleman, "Binding Obligations in Romans 13:1–7: A Semantic Field and Social Context," *TynBul* 48 (1997): 325–27.

20. Cf. Dunn (*Romans*, 2:770): "Little gatherings of Christians, living in the capital city, without political power, dependent on the good will of the authorities, who could be very arbitrary and unpredictable in their rulings regarding minority ethnic or religious groups, were only acting prudently if they sought to avoid giving any cause for offense."

disobedience in a way that would just reshuffle the cards of political order. Rome could cope with ordinary revolutions, but a community committed to the crucified and risen Lord, living out his story and teachings—now that was dangerous![21]

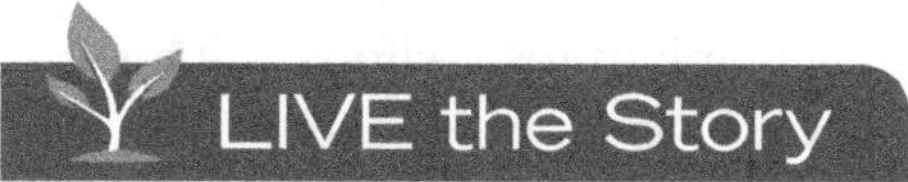


Paul's assertions here are controversial and always have been. No surprises, then, that 13:1–7 has prompted several different views as it relates to Christians and the state in general[22] and Paul and empire in particular.[23]

### Gospel and Empire

In the last twenty years, Paul has been mapped against a background of socio-political resistance to Roman imperial power.[24] For instance, N. T. Wright argues that for Paul, "the power and pretensions of Rome are downgraded, outflanked, subverted and rendered impotent by the power of love: the love of the one God revealed in the crucified and risen Jesus, Israel's Messiah and Caesar's lord."[25] However, others have insisted that the anti-imperial Paul is either overstated or else a scholarly fad. Paul was not a political activist, much less a revolutionary.[26] At first glance, 13:1–7 seems like solid support for the view that Paul harbored no anti-imperial ambitions and merely wanted to behave as a good subservient citizen of the empire. Paul calls for submission to government, not violent insurrection against it.

---

21. Wright, "Romans," 10:716–23.

22. Cf. L. Pohle, *Die Christen und der Staat nach Römer 13: Eine typologische Untersuchung der neueren deutschsprächigen Schriftauslegung* (Mainz; Mattias-Grünewald, 1984); S. Krauter, *Studien zu Röm 13,1–7. Paulus und der politische Diskurs der neronischen Zeit* (WUNT 243; Tübingen: Mohr Siebeck, 2009), 4–38.

23. Cf. Bird, *An Anomalous Jew*, chap. 7 (forthcoming).

24. Cf. Warren Carter, "Paul and the Roman Empire: Recent Perspectives," in *Paul Unbound: Other Perspectives on the Apostle* (ed. M. D. Given; Peabody, MA: Hendrickson, 2010), 7–26; idem, *The Roman Empire and the New Testament: An Essential Guide* (Nashville: Abingdon, 2006); Scot McKnight and Joseph B. Modica, eds., *Jesus Is Lord, Caesar Is Not: Evaluating Empire in New Testament Studies* (Downers Grove, IL: InterVarsity, 2013); John Anthony Dunne and Dan Batovici, eds., *Reactions to Empire: Sacred Texts in their Socio-Political Contexts* (WUNT 2.240; Tübingen: Mohr Siebeck, 2014).

25. Wright, *Paul and the Faithfulness of God*, 1319.

26. Cf. Christopher Bryan, *Render to Caesar: Jesus, the Early Church, and the Roman Superpower* (New York: Oxford University Press, 2005), 9–10, 91–93; Denny Burk, "Is Paul's Gospel Counterimperial? Evaluating the Prospects of the 'Fresh Perspective' for Evangelical Theology," *JETS* 51 (2008): 309–37; Seyoon Kim, *The Gospel and the Roman Empire in the Writings of Paul and Luke* (Grand Rapids: Eerdmans, 2008); Joel White, "Anti-Imperial Subtexts in Paul: An Attempt at Building a Firmer Foundation," *Bib* 90 (2009): 305–33.

I have argued elsewhere, with due caveats and qualifications, that there is certainly a sociopolitical texture to Paul's theology, one that stands in clear opposition to the religious and totalizing claims made by imperial authorities, a texture identifiable in Romans.[27] What bolsters the point is Paul's citation of Isaiah 11:10 in Romans 15:12: "Isaiah says, 'The Root of Jesse will spring up, one who will arise to rule over the nations; in him the Gentiles will hope.'" Paul clearly believes that at some point Jesus' kingdom is going to take over and supplant Roman power and its client states. That was a deeply subversive claim, and the Romans knew it.

Roman elites were aware of Jewish messianic prophecies and did not think highly of them. Tacitus referred to a prediction from Israel's sacred traditions about how "at this very time the East was to grow powerful, and rulers, coming from Judea, were to acquire a universal empire."[28] Suetonius writes, "There had spread over all the Orient an old and established belief, that it was fated at that time for men coming from Judaea to rule the world."[29] The Romans did not persecute Christians because they said, "Jesus is Lord of my heart," but because they insisted that "Jesus is Lord" and his kingdom will eclipse that of Caesar.

Roman persecutions against Christians were largely localized and spasmodic in succeeding centuries. The Decian (ca. AD 250) and Diocletian (AD 303) persecutions were the most deliberate empire-wide attempts to weed out Christians by using violent means. However, they failed, and Christianity did not just continue, it took over the empire. When Constantine put the symbol of the cross on the shields of his troops at the Battle of Milvian Bridge (AD 312), it meant the triumph of Christianity over the Roman imperium. As historian Will Durant famously said: "Christ met Caesar in the arena—Christ had won!"[30]

Funny enough, my aunt and uncle used to have three beautiful Labradors, one of whom was named "Nero." I had always thought that "Nero" was an odd name for a dog, especially when names like "Lucky" or "Lucy" were more common. But there was once in the UK a tradition of naming dogs after first-century Roman emperors. There is something fiercely ironic in that. Paul the apostle was put to death by Nero. Nero had sentenced many men and women to death. Nero probably thought nothing of ordering another Jew, another religious fanatic from the east, to his death. Yet, as T. R. Glover noted, little

27. Michael F. Bird, "'One Who Will Arise to Rule over the Nations': Paul's Letter to the Romans and the Roman Empire," in *Jesus is Lord, Caesar is Not* (ed. S. McKnight and J. Modica; Downers Grove, IL: InterVarsity, 2013), 146–65.

28. Tacitus, *Histories* 5.13.

29. Suetonius, *Vespasian* 4.5.

30. Will Durant, *The Story of Civilization: Part III* (New York: Simon & Schuster, 1944), 652.

did Nero know that a day was to come when men would call their sons "Paul" and their dogs "Nero."[31]

Wherever a menacing empire casts its shadow—whether from the east or from the west—Christians have a responsibility to order their lives around the story and symbols of Jesus. We are to live our lives as exemplary citizens, and we must yet let it be known that our loyalty is owed first and foremost to the true Lord of the world. Christians are to make a nuisance of themselves by setting up a benevolent alternative society to the tyrannical one that surrounds them.

## When We Should Not Be Submissive

I remember once watching a documentary about the English Reformation and its impact on church/state relationships. I recall one segment where the narrator described how under Edward VI a particular church had its ornate medieval artwork on one of its walls washed off and replaced with a quotation of Romans 13:1–7. Rather than allowing the congregation to enjoy some fine Christian art, they were given a permanent warning about disobeying the monarch! Governments have always been quick to use 13:1–7 to urge Christians to tow the line and to submit under their authority.

It is worth remembering, though, that 13:1–7 does not give governments a license to do whatever they want to whomever they want and the citizens just have to take it. Stanley Porter believes that 13:1–7 should not be seen as teaching unqualified obedience to the state. Paul thinks authorities can be called to account because they are exercising divinely given powers and disobedience is warranted when this power is misused. When Paul refers to "governing authorities" (*exousiais hyperechousais*), he does not mean any authority; the verb *hyperechō* can have a qualitative sense of superiority in quality (e.g., Dan 5:11; Sir 33:7; Phil 2:3; 3:8; 4:7). According to Porter, Paul only expects Christians to obey authorities who are qualitatively superior, that is, authorities who know and practice justice.[32]

In addition, it would be naïve to take 13:1–7 as the last word on church/state relations (excluding the fact that our idea of a "state" is conditioned by post-Enlightenment views of government, nationalism, identity, and democracy). Paul's remarks were written during a setting of relatively benevolent and well-behaved authorities, as Nero arguably was in the early years of his reign. However, a resistant approach might be required when dealing with a crazed

31. Cited from F. F. Bruce, *Paul: Apostle of the Free Spirit* (rev. ed.; Carlisle, UK: Paternoster, 1980), 5.

32. Stanley E. Porter, "Paul Confronts Caesar with the Good News," in *Empire in the New Testament* (ed. S. E. Porter and C. L. Westfall; Eugene, OR: Cascade, 2011), 184–89.

Nero, while living under Nazis in Nuremberg, when dealing with a Hindu nationalist government in Nagpur, or when terrorists take over an Iraqi town like Najaf.

Resistance can take many forms, such as economic boycott, disseminating the truth about a regime, engaging in peaceful protest, and even in armed revolution. Normally I would say that violence and revolution should be left off the table. And yet, while I do not have absolute clarity in my own mind on the matter, personally I think Dietrich Bonhoeffer's involvement in the plot to assassinate Adolf Hiter was probably the right thing to do. Though I would want to stress that such an action would clearly be exceptional and can be justified only by achieving a greater good than could otherwise be achieved by resisting entirely through passive means. It is a dangerous thing to ponder. Violence and warfare can be all too easily justified in some minds, but sometime war is the morally responsible thing to do when grave peril approaches not only the church but an entire civilization.

Furthermore, Samuel Rutherford's seventeenth-century political tract, *Lex Rex*, contested the idea that Christians have to swear absolute fealty to oppressive governments. Rutherford gave a theo-political reading of Romans 13:1 – 7 that showed that resistance, even violent resistance, to tyrannical rule could be warranted.[33] So there are occasions when resistance to government is not only required but even demanded by discipleship. Just as we have to submit to governing authorities on the basis of conscience, sometimes we have to rebel against governments because of the same conscience. In my own country, Christians have been at the forefront at protesting at the unethical treatment of asylum seekers by the Australian government by engaging in peaceful protests at the offices of political leaders. In the face of government misuse of power, you just have to say, "We must obey God rather than human beings" (Acts 5:29), and refuse to "be afraid of the king's edict" (Heb 11:23). I like how John Stott summed it up: "Whenever laws are enacted which contradict God's Law, civil disobedience becomes a Christian duty."[34]

33. Cf. Ryan McAnnally-Linz, "Resistance and Romans 13 in Samuel Rutherford's *Lex, Rex*," *SJT* 66 (2013): 140 – 58.

34. Stott, *Romans*, 342.

CHAPTER 26

# Romans 13:8–14

## LISTEN to the Story

[8]Let no debt remain outstanding, except the continuing debt to love one another, for whoever loves others has fulfilled the law. [9]The commandments, "You shall not commit adultery," "You shall not murder," "You shall not steal," "You shall not covet," and whatever other command there may be, are summed up in this one command: "Love your neighbor as yourself." [10]Love does no harm to a neighbor. Therefore love is the fulfillment of the law.

[11]And do this, understanding the present time: The hour has already come for you to wake up from your slumber, because our salvation is nearer now than when we first believed. [12]The night is nearly over; the day is almost here. So let us put aside the deeds of darkness and put on the armor of light. [13]Let us behave decently, as in the daytime, not in carousing and drunkenness, not in sexual immorality and debauchery, not in dissension and jealousy. [14]Rather, clothe yourselves with the Lord Jesus Christ, and do not think about how to gratify the desires of the flesh.

*Listening to the texts in the story:* Exodus 20:13–15, 17; Leviticus 19:18; Deuteronomy 5:17–19, 21.

In Romans 13:8–14 we find a crucial exhortation that combines ethics and eschatology, daily living in light of the end of days. In this way, Paul ends the section begun at 12:1–2 by stressing that their moral imperative to love others is to be understood in light of their impending salvation.[1] Paul promotes a love ethic for the Roman believers, but it is not an ordinary love. This is a love that is expressed within a particular apocalyptic story, where God's love has already found them (5:5, 8) and they yearn to be taken into the bosom of divine love once and for all (8:39). This harks back to a common theme in the biblical story, namely, that godliness is the best way to prepare for the coming of God. That was the burden of the song from Moses to John the Baptist. It

1. Keck, *Romans*, 329.

is all the more important when Christians find themselves living in the dark interval just before the dawn, where the love that they have for one another is a lamp that keeps them ready and alert in the meantime.

The section obviously breaks down into two discernable parts: (1) the love command (vv. 8–10); and (2) the call to live uprightly as believers wait for the consummation of their salvation (vv. 11–14). While many commentators separate the love command of vv. 8–10 from the future hope of vv. 11–14, Paul clearly connects the two together. Paul begins v. 11 with "And *do* this," with "this" relating back to the prior love command.[2] Love of neighbor is to be undertaken in the context of waiting for "salvation" (v. 11). Believers should avoid the immoral excesses of pagan living (v. 13) and instead clothe themselves with Christ as they prepare for the return of Christ (v. 14).

## EXPLAIN the Story

### A Debt of Love (13:8–10)

"Let no debt remain outstanding, except the continuing debt to love one another" (v. 8a). Paul uses the idea of Christian obligation to pay taxes in v. 7 to spring into a metaphor about Christian indebtedness to love one another in v. 8. Paul has used the verb "I am indebted" (*opheilō*) earlier as a metaphor to describe his obligation to bring the gospel to the whole world (1:14) and to indicate how Christians are obligated to live by the Spirit and not to gratify the flesh (8:12). This suggests that Paul sees Christians as caught up in a three-way obligation toward mission, Spirit, and love. Believers are bonded together in a mission to proclaim Christ, to keep in step with the Spirit, and to live out love for each other.

Paul then provides the rationale for love as mutual obligation, "for whoever loves others has fulfilled the law" (v. 8b). Paul is filling out what he urged earlier when he said that "love must be sincere" (12:9) and the Roman believers should be "devoted to each other in love" (12:10). Later he will say that if they do not respect each other's convictions on disputable matters like food, they are "no longer acting in love" (14:15). Love is at the epicenter of Pauline ethics because of its foundations in the Torah and because of Jesus' teaching about love. Paul from the outset of his ministry urged new believers to practice love toward one another as to family members (see 1 Thess 4:9–10; 5:13). Paul's moving *encomium* about love to the Corinthians praises love as the highest of Christian virtues (1 Cor 13:1–13). Paul also strenuously argued that the Galatians should regard love as the fulfillment of the Torah

2. Cf. Fitzmyer, *Romans*, 682.

(Gal 5:14). When Christians act in love, they "fulfill the righteous requirements of the law" as enabled by the Spirit (Rom 8:4).

Paul explains that the way the Roman believers are to discharge their debt of love is by doing the back half of the Decalogue: "The commandments, 'You shall not commit adultery,' 'You shall not murder,' 'You shall not steal,' 'You shall not covet,' and whatever other command there may be, are summed up in this one command: 'Love your neighbor as yourself' " (v. 9). Here Paul follows the Septuagint's list of the Ten Commandments from Deuteronomy 5:17–21 (rather than Exod 20:13–17). This list provides concrete examples of what love for others should look like in practice. Keck puts it well: "Mutual love is *not* the alternative to obligatory law-fulfillment but its mode; mutual love is the way that requisite obedience to the law is actualized."[3]

In the law and gospel debate, Romans 13:10 causes a bit of a headache. Hasn't Paul already said that believers are "not under law, but under grace" (Rom 6:14), and wasn't the whole point of Galatians that believers do not—and perhaps should not—try to keep the Torah? So how can Paul expect Christians to keep the Ten Commandments, or at least four of them?

In response to this one could say: (1) Paul is just inconsistent. He likes to impose the Torah on Gentiles when it suits him. To that I retort, well, yes, any individual figure can have argumentative inconsistencies—my students frequently point out mine to me—but I find it hard to buy into any view that Paul would so brazenly contradict himself on a major theological theme on what is a major point of this letter. (2) One could break up the law into civil, ceremonial, and moral components and say that the civil and ceremonial aspects of the law were fulfilled by Christ, but we still have to keep the moral law as summarized by the Decalogue. An attractive option, popular in some circles, but it suffers from a few fatal problems. For a start, Jewish authors did not divide up the law into these three components. For them Torah was Torah and comprised an indivisible unity. Then there is the problem that the Decalogue includes a ceremonial commandment with keeping the Sabbath (e.g., Exod 20:9–10; Deut 5:15), and there is moral law found outside of the Decalogue that we also have to keep (e.g., Lev 19:18).

The solution I think, largely following Brian Rosner, is that the Torah no longer functions as a definitive moral code for Christians since it has been replaced by the example of Christ, the teaching of Christ, and life in the Spirit. Instead, the Torah operates now as prophecy (see Rom 3:21) and as wisdom for Christian living like counseling us against seeking revenge (see 12:19). The Torah remains hermeneutically valid as a gauge for discerning God's will and provides

3. Keck, *Romans*, 326 (emphasis original).

a helpful starting point for ethical practice. Without actual commands, love is merely empty sentimentality without content or conviction.[4] So the Torah is part and parcel of Paul's ethics, not as a binding obligation to which believers are woodenly committed, but more as an advisor rather than an authority. The key premise is that the Torah commands love and love fulfills the purposes of the Torah. As Rosner says, "If in Romans 8 Christ fulfils the law *for us*, in Romans 13 and Galatians 5 Christ fulfils the law *through us*."[5]

Paul rounds off his thought by repeating v. 8b that love is the fulfillment of the Torah: "Love does no harm to a neighbor. Therefore love is the fulfillment of the law" (v. 10). Paul alludes to Leviticus 19:18 when he refers to love doing no wrong to a neighbor (see Gal 5:14; Jas 2:18), and perhaps he has in mind Jesus' particular teaching about love of neighbor as a summary of the Torah (see Matt 5:43; 19:19; 22:39). Neither Jesus nor Paul was the first to say such a thing, but it certainly became a distinctive Christian belief.

### Wake Me Up before You Go to Heaven (13:11–12a)

Paul makes a short, almost excursive, comment in vv. 11–12a on the radiant eschatological hope that casts its light on believers as they strive to love each other before he returns to more ethical admonition in vv. 12b–14. Paul adds: "And do this, understanding the present time: The hour has already come for you to wake up from your slumber, because our salvation is nearer now than when we first believed. The night is nearly over; the day is almost here" (vv. 11–12b). Paul elsewhere entertained the possibility that he might pass away prior to Christ's *parousia* (see 2 Cor 5:1–10; Phil 1:20–24), so his belief about the proximity of Christ's return was not imminent, but more like an intense notion of nearness.

The metaphor of watchfulness through the night was common in Jesus' teachings (Matt 24:42–44; Mark 13:33–37; 26:45; Luke 12:35–36; 21:36) and in Paul's own exhortations (Eph 5:8–16; 1 Thess 5:1–11). The opening phrase "And do this" is elliptical with no actual verb for "do" present, but it is strongly implied (see NIV, NASB, CEB, NET), rather than merely an additional point like "Besides this," as other translations suggest (see NRSV, RSV, ESV, NJB). Paul wants the Roman believers to "do" loving things for each other, "knowing" the reality about the shortness of the "present time." If it is true that the new age had dawned, that new life was bursting through the frost of a world in winter, then, he insists, it's time to wake up.

The reason for our arousal from slumber is that "our salvation is nearer than when we first believed." This salvation, of course, refers to the events that

4. Schreiner, *Romans*, 694.

5. Rosner, *Paul and the Law*, 124 (italics original).

Paul narrates in his eschatological teachings about the end in 1 Corinthians 15:20–58; Philippians 3:20–21; 1 Thessalonians 1:10; 4:1–5:10. Salvation will transpire on this "day," which is the "day of the Lord," the moment when Christ returns (see 1 Cor 1:8; 5:5; 2 Cor 1:14; Phil 1:6, 10; 2:16; 1 Thess 5:2; 2 Thess 2:2; etc.). The end of the story includes a final judgment, a glorious resurrection, and heaven married to earth. For us, the "night" of the old age is nearly over and the "day" of the new creation comes closer and closer.[6]

### Soldiers of the Light (13:12b–14)

Paul then draws the inference: "So let us put aside the deeds of darkness and put on the armor of light" (v. 12b). The imagery here is reminiscent of 1 Thessalonians 5:4–6 about not living like those in darkness; the weapons metaphor is drawn from 2 Corinthians 6:7, 10:3–4, and Ephesians 6:11–17. Paul calls on believers to discard anything that is inappropriate for them and to dress themselves with the apparel of a soldier waiting to be inspected by a returning king. Wright says that Paul "seems to be drawing attention to the sovereignty of Jesus, not simply over the believer (who is bound to obey the one whose servant he or she is), but perhaps more particularly over the forces of evil that are ranged against the gospel and those who embrace it."[7]

The imagery of shedding something and dressing in readiness is then put in relation to negative and positive behaviors. First, on the negative side: "Let us behave decently, as in the daytime, not in carousing and drunkenness, not in sexual immorality and debauchery, not in dissension and jealousy" (v. 13).[8] You only have to read accounts of Greco-Roman *symposia* (i.e., drinking parties) or various religious festivals (e.g., Dionysius) to know what Paul was getting at. Greco-Roman revelry could make a frat house toga party look like a convent in comparison.[9] Paul is censuring a type of rapacious party culture that featured wild excess, drinking bouts, sexual immoralities of every kind, and violent quarreling; or as I like to call it, Las Vegas during spring break with Caligula as MC. Since they still belong to the old unredeemed age, in both their natural appetites and social context, they must remain on guard lest they find themselves enticed to embrace the darkness.[10]

---

6. Cf. on Paul's expectation of the end, Murray, *Romans*, 167–68; Cranfield, *Romans*, 2:682–84; Schreiner, *Romans*, 698.

7. Wright, "Romans," 10:729.

8. These words had a profound effect on Augustine, who heard a child singing, "Take up and read," when he stumbled on a copy of Romans. He opened to Romans 13:13–14 and had his melancholic state healed and wrote in his *Confessions* (8.29): "No further would I read, nor did I need; for instantly, as the sentence ended—by a light, as it were, of security infused into my heart—all the gloom of doubt vanished away."

9. See Petronius, *Satyricon* 15.26.6–15.78.8 and Philo, *Planting*, 160.

10. Dunn, *Romans*, 2:792.

Second, and more positively, Paul says: "Rather, clothe yourselves with the Lord Jesus Christ, and do not think about how to gratify the desires of the flesh" (v. 14). Paul is rehearsing the basic commands in Romans 6:12–13 and 8:12–13 about putting to death the desires of the flesh. Here he uses the image of clothing oneself with Jesus as if he were a garment (see Col 3:12). Those who put on Christ in baptism (Gal 3:27) have robed themselves with the full array of the armor of light, which is none other than Christ himself (Rom 13:12). Ultimately, to put on Christ is also to be empowered by Christ.

The metaphor clearly represents putting on the full cohort of values, virtues, and vision of God's people summed up in Jesus Christ. Moo comments that this means that "we are consciously to embrace Christ in such a way that his character is manifested in all that we do and say."[11] Furthermore, Paul wants fleshly desires to be interdicted at the cognitive root. Do not give them forethought or the prospect for provision lest one darkly reasons one's way toward them. As a wise pastor once told me, it is always easier to sin the second time, so don't think about how to do it the first time!

For the Roman believers, Romans 12:1–13:14 prescribed a set of behaviors based around themes of love and doing good. In the dog-eat-dog world of Rome, where the believers lived in perpetual fear of the *princeps* as much as poverty, practicing family love was their best hope of enduring through it together. Where survival was a struggle, they were not to be self-concerned, but self-sacrificial. In other words, Paul's gospel in its full theological vision and ethical sweep will enable these Gentile believers to be consecrated to God in holiness, peace, and love even in the darkness of a pagan city.

## LIVE the Story

Paul's blend of ethics and eschatology forces us to think of innovative ways in which we can live out our sense of mutual obligation to each other in light of the impending return of Jesus to consummate God's purposes on earth. The three main practical consequences that emerge are our debt of love, fleeing to God, and putting on the armor of light.

### Messiah Card

Although the command to love others was not unique to Jesus, it was certainly distinctive of his teaching. Whereas the Pharisees taught love of Torah, Jesus

11. Moo, *Romans*, 825–26.

taught a Torah of love (see Mark 12:28–34; John 13:31–35).[12] Jesus' teaching on love is summed up famously in the "new command" recorded in John's gospel: "A new command I give you: Love one another. As I have loved you, so you must love one another. By this everyone will know that you are my disciples, if you love one another" (John 13:34–35). What is shocking and sobering here is that Jesus says "By this," by acting in love, everyone will know that we are disciples of Jesus. The world not only knows *that* we are disciples by our love, but *whether* we are disciples by our love.

Think about that for a moment. Francis Schaeffer comments on this verse that Jesus "gives the world the right to judge whether you and I are born-again Christians on the basis of our observable love towards all Christians." He adds, "That is pretty frightening."[13] Loving behavior toward others determines if we have the right to call ourselves followers of Jesus. The love command of Jesus that Paul rehearses is easily the greatest commandment because it sorts out the sheep from the goats, the followers from the fans, and the contenders from the pretenders.

Romans 13:8–10 raises a stack of issues about law and ethics. Irrespective of how we parse the continuing role of the law in the Christian life, we should all be agreed that love is the norm by which our behavior is measured. A consistent feature of the New Testament witness is that love is a responsive obligation; it is received and given on to others. Jesus said, "As I have loved you, so you must love one another" (John 13:34). Or in Peter's words, "Now that you have purified yourselves by obeying the truth so that you have sincere love for each other, love one another deeply, from the heart" (1 Pet 1:22). It's like you've been given a ticket to every seat at a major league baseball game and you cannot help but share it with everyone you come into contact with. Discipleship means receiving God's love and reflecting it to others.

When Romans 13:8–10 is taken seriously, it challenges our assumptions about love.[14] We are forced away from culturally dominant notions of sentiment and infatuation into the realm of mutuality, commitment, and community. In Romans, we see that love is a virtue (5:5; 12:9), a duty (12:10), and a debt (13:10). The idea of love as a debt is certainly open for deep reflection. For me personally, I hate getting into debt. I just realized the other day that if I had less children, I could pay my mortgage off quicker! Don't get me wrong, I love my kids, children are a gift from God ... and tax deductible. But even kids can't help me that much because in recent years I've got a tax debt rather

12. Scot McKnight, *Kingdom Conspiracy: Returning to the Radical Mission of the Local Church* (Grand Rapids: Baker, 2014), 51, 159–78.

13. Francis Schaeffer, *The Mark of the Christian* (Downers Grove, IL: InterVarsity, 2006), 22.

14. Keck, *Romans*, 328.

than a tax return on my annual submission to the Australian Taxation Office. Also, I love Christmas in December, but I hate the credit card bill in January. As a responsible husband and father I try to manage our finances with propriety and avoid unneeded debt.

However, when it comes to love, Paul tells us to let the debt remain outstanding. In other words, imagine that love is a credit card with no borrowing limit, and your job is to try to max it out. Make yourself indebted and obligated to love others. Make your love higher than the interest rates on an American Express card. The best way to avoid moral bankruptcy is to rack up love-based debts. Think of yourself as possessing Jesus' own credit card, *Messiah Card*, an interest free credit card of love. Imagine some mottos or advertising slogans for a card like this (guess which cards I'm parodying!):

Messiah card. Don't leave church without it!
There are some things money can't buy. For everything else there is Messiah card.
Messiah card. The missionary's passport.
Messiah card. Life takes love!
Messiah card, because love is priceless.

As Origen memorably said: "The debt of charity, however, should be with us always and never cease. We must pay this daily and always owe it."[15]

### Messiahship Down

As a child, one of my favorite stories was *Watership Down*. It is about a warren of rabbits in England and their struggle for survival. A young runt rabbit named Fiver is a prophet who receives a vision about the imminent destruction of the warren. Sadly the only other rabbits who believe Fiver are his brother Hazel and a small group of friends. Sensing the danger, the group flees and makes their way through various struggles to Watership Down to establish a new warren.

Paul's words to "wake up" remind me of Fiver's warning to the warren. When everyone is "sleeping," unaware of what is approaching, Paul tells us his audience to wake up. Paul writes with the urgency of someone waking people in a burning building, telling them that its time to flee down a ladder that is about to be put up against their window. In a world of moral darkness, Paul tells his audience to wake up, get up, and run to safety. Like Fiver, we hear the sounds of what is coming, salvation for some and judgment for others, and we get ourselves ready for it (see 1 Thess 5:8; Phil 1:28).

---

15. Cited in Burns, *Romans*, 324.

We need to tell ourselves and our congregations to wake up, get up, and get ready to flee to Messiahship Down. In my experience you can tell a lot about a person by learning not just what they are willing to fight for, but what they are eager to flee from! I tell my seminary students, especially my male students, that the undoing of many a minister is gold, glory, and girls. Or else everyone has to be wary of the addictiveness of feelings of power and influence over others and how it can contort our character. One should not just avoid these things like avoiding dog poo on the sidewalk; you should flee from them like a great white shark chasing after you in your swimming pool.

There is nothing wrong with running from something that has the power to destroy you, destroy your relationship with God, destroy your relationship with your spouse and children, and destroy your ministry. If we are to fight the good fight of the faith, that will involve doing some tactical retreats when necessary. If we are to be clothed with Christ, we have to run for our lives from stuff like pornography and gossip. That is why Paul talks about "fleeing" so often: flee from sexual immorality (1 Cor 6:18), flee from idolatry (1 Cor 6:10), flee from love of money (1 Tim 6:10–11), and flee from the desires of youth (2 Tim 2:22). This is why Paul told Timothy: "But you, man of God, flee from all this, and pursue righteousness, godliness, faith, love, endurance and gentleness" (1 Tim 6:11).

### Jesus' Clothing Brand Is Made of Steel

In addition to our indebtedness in showing loving behavior and fleeing from godlessness, believers are to be clothed with Christ, which means we put on the armor of light. This armor is tantamount to the list of virtues that the New Testament authors give us in several places. For instance, Paul told the Colossians to "clothe yourselves with compassion, kindness, humility, gentleness and patience" (Col 3:12). There is a reason for morally arming ourselves with these attitudes and actions; that is because Christian virtues, just like armor, serve to protect us from harm. I confess that I have never worn ancient Israelite armor such as a leather jacket with copper plates sown on, or the fully metal body armor of a Middle Ages knight, but I have worn modern combat armor with a kevlar vest and kevlar helmet. Let me tell you something, they are heavy and hot, and they can be hard to move. However, without that sort of protection, you are vulnerable to shrapnel and being shot, or a soft target. Kevlar body armor, for all its clunkiness and girth, is absolutely necessary; otherwise a soldier is vulnerable to being wounded or killed.

Similarly, without clothing yourself with the armor of light, you are a soft target for temptation, the devil, and the world to prey on you. Yes, I know that even the best of saints has a chink in his or her armor; we are all human after all. However, if we are fully armored up with Christian virtue, it will be much harder for us to be taken down by anything that would seek to separate us from Christ. Such armor not only shields us but also those around us.

CHAPTER 27

# Romans 14:1 – 15:13

## LISTEN to the Story

1Accept the one whose faith is weak, without quarreling over
disputable matters. 2One person's faith allows them to eat anything, but
another, whose faith is weak, eats only vegetables. 3The one who eats
everything must not treat with contempt the one who does not, and the
one who does not eat everything must not judge the one who does, for
God has accepted them. 4Who are you to judge someone else's servant? To
their own master, servants stand or fall. And they will stand, for the Lord
is able to make them stand.

5One person considers one day more sacred than another; another
considers every day alike. Each of them should be fully convinced in
their own mind. 6Whoever regards one day as special does so to the Lord.
Whoever eats meat does so to the Lord, for they give thanks to God;
and whoever abstains does so to the Lord and gives thanks to God. 7For
none of us lives for ourselves alone, and none of us dies for ourselves
alone. 8If we live, we live for the Lord; and if we die, we die for the Lord.
So, whether we live or die, we belong to the Lord. 9For this very reason,
Christ died and returned to life so that he might be the Lord of both the
dead and the living.

10You, then, why do you judge your brother or sister? Or why do you
treat them with contempt? For we will all stand before God's judgment
seat. 11It is written:

> " 'As surely as I live,' says the Lord,
> 'every knee will bow before me;
> every tongue will acknowledge God.' "

12So then, each of us will give an account of ourselves to God.

13Therefore let us stop passing judgment on one another. Instead,
make up your mind not to put any stumbling block or obstacle in the
way of a brother or sister. 14I am convinced, being fully persuaded in
the Lord Jesus, that nothing is unclean in itself. But if anyone regards
something as unclean, then for that person it is unclean. 15If your brother

or sister is distressed because of what you eat, you are no longer acting in love. Do not by your eating destroy someone for whom Christ died. [16]Therefore do not let what you know is good be spoken of as evil. [17]For the kingdom of God is not a matter of eating and drinking, but of righteousness, peace and joy in the Holy Spirit, [18]because anyone who serves Christ in this way is pleasing to God and receives human approval.

[19]Let us therefore make every effort to do what leads to peace and to mutual edification. [20]Do not destroy the work of God for the sake of food. All food is clean, but it is wrong for a person to eat anything that causes someone else to stumble. [21]It is better not to eat meat or drink wine or to do anything else that will cause your brother or sister to fall.

[22]So whatever you believe about these things keep between yourself and God. Blessed is the one who does not condemn himself by what he approves. [23]But whoever has doubts is condemned if they eat, because their eating is not from faith; and everything that does not come from faith is sin.

[15:1]We who are strong ought to bear with the failings of the weak and not to please ourselves. [2]Each of us should please our neighbors for their good, to build them up. [3]For even Christ did not please himself but, as it is written: "The insults of those who insult you have fallen on me." [4]For everything that was written in the past was written to teach us, so that through the endurance taught in the Scriptures and the encouragement they provide we might have hope.

[5]May the God who gives endurance and encouragement give you the same attitude of mind toward each other that Christ Jesus had, [6]so that with one mind and one voice you may glorify the God and Father of our Lord Jesus Christ.

[7]Accept one another, then, just as Christ accepted you, in order to bring praise to God. [8]For I tell you that Christ has become a servant of the Jews on behalf of God's truth, so that the promises made to the patriarchs might be confirmed [9]and, moreover, that the Gentiles might glorify God for his mercy. As it is written:

> "Therefore I will praise you among the Gentiles;
> I will sing the praises of your name."

[10]Again, it says,

> "Rejoice, you Gentiles, with his people."

[11]And again,

> "Praise the Lord, all you Gentiles;
> let all the peoples extol him."

[12]And again, Isaiah says,

> "The Root of Jesse will spring up,
> one who will arise to rule over the nations;
> in him the Gentiles will hope."

[13]May the God of hope fill you with all joy and peace as you trust in him, so that you may overflow with hope by the power of the Holy Spirit.

*Listening to the texts in the story:* Deuteronomy 32:43; 2 Samuel 22:50; Psalm 18:49; 69:9; 117:1; Isaiah 11:10; 45:23.

**Summary to Here**

Time to recap. Paul writes to the Gentile believers in Rome to gospelize them, to conform them to his theological vision of the righteousness of God revealed in the gospel. This is the gospel that will bring the Gentiles to a holy obedience and make them a consecrated people. So Paul sets out the theological scope of his gospel, showing how Christ's death and resurrection cancels the debt of sin and defeats death. Justification by faith without Torah observance establishes the righteousness of Jews and Gentiles who are united in Messiah Jesus. True righteousness is about dying with Christ and following the Spirit, not obeying the letter of the Torah. The Gentiles experience the covenant renewal that Israel longs for and has erstwhile rejected; but Gentile acceptance may yet provoke Israel to jealousy and then to salvation. The ethical paradigm for Gentiles is based on the predominance of love expressing itself in mutual obligations to each other. If this vision becomes embedded in Rome, Paul can return to Jerusalem with the Roman Gentiles behind him and he can count on their support for his future mission trip to Spain.

**Problems of Disunity**

But there is just one last little thing that could hinder Paul's quest. The Roman churches had some problems, problems of disunity it seems. The problems may be potential or actual, it's hard to tell, and Paul's own information is undoubtedly secondhand from one or more of the folks listed in Romans 16:3–16. The situation appears to be that there were probably competing views on Torah observance in Rome. Whether it was socially, ethnically, or theologically motivated, there were differences of opinion among the Roman congregations about what role the Torah should have in the life of the believers. The expulsion (AD 49) and return (AD 54) of the Jewish Christians probably exacerbated some of these tensions especially over who has authority to arbitrate on these disputes. Paul's center of gravity is that he does not want the Roman churches to fragment along ethnic lines or to have violent divisions over how to fuse Torah and Messiah. He's been there, done that, bought the t-shirt, and it has a lot of polemical blood spilt on it after acrimonious divisions in Antioch and Galatia. So Paul engages in some preventive pastoral care to get the Roman churches united around the Lord Jesus and the mission of God through apostles like himself.

Paul's solution was simple. He tells the Romans that you have one Lord, who is Lord over all believers, so welcome one another just as the Messiah welcomed you! He sets before them his "charter of Christian liberty and mutual tolerance" rooted in the Messiah and expressed in love.[1] Paul can say that because in his mind the climax of the biblical story is the Messiah restoring Israel and leading the Gentiles to praise God, as the dense collection of Old Testament citations in Romans 15:7–12 indicates. Paul sees Jesus as the Lord who presides over the united people of God.

Paul draws heavily on his previous exhortations to his churches (esp. 1 Corinthians 8–10); in many ways he is dealing with a universal problem that happens in any faith community where there is a mixture of the scrupulous and the accommodating or the conservatives and the progressives.[2] It would be wrong, however, to infer that Romans 14:1–15:13 is just a generalized summary of his ethical teaching from his earlier letters about how to handle differences of opinion.[3] Whereas the disputes in Corinth were about whether believers could eat idol meat (1 Cor 8:1–10; 10:24–33) and attend banquets in pagan temples (1 Cor 10:1–23), in Romans 14 the presenting matters are vegetarianism (14:2, 20–21), observing sacred days (14:5–6), and wine (14:17, 21). Whereas the weak in Corinth were converted pagans who were trying to break with their pagan past, in Romans the weak are probably Jewish Christians and maybe judaizing Gentiles who were varyingly entrenched in the Jewish way of life.[4]

As we will see, these matters of vegetarianism, sacred days, and wine had various connotations in the Roman context.[5] These matters were not just a fastidious fad or a mark of over-ardent piety, but encompassed the life or

1. Dunn, *Romans*, 2:815.

2. Fitzmyer, *Romans*, 686.

3. Contra R. J. Karris, "Romans 14:1–15:13 and the Occasion of Romans," in *The Romans Debate* (ed. K. P. Donfried; Peabody, MA: Hendrickson, 2001), 81–84, and Johnson, *Romans*, 209–12. Ambrosiaster (Bray, *Romans*, 103–4) regarded the disputes as resulting from the Jewish origins of Christianity in Rome.

4. Talbert, *Romans*, 312.

5. Cf. Augustine: "At that time, meat which had been offered in sacrifice was sold in the market; the Gentiles poured out libations of the first fruits of the wine for their idols, and some of them even made the offerings right in the pressing rooms" (cited in Burns, *Romans*, 336).

death issue of covenant loyalty for Jews living in a pagan world. It is crucial to grasp that if we are to understand what the disputes were about and how to apply Paul's exhortations to our own context.

Paul proceeds by: (1) urging the Romans to embrace diversity under the lordship of Jesus (14:1 – 12); (2) offering practical advice on cultivating unity in the churches (14:13 – 23); (3) petitioning them to imitate Christ in these matters and thereby glorify God (15:1 – 6); and (4) exhorting them to welcome each other just as Christ welcomed them (15:7 – 13).

## EXPLAIN the Story

### Jesus Is Lord of the Weak and the Strong (14:1 – 12)

Paul continues the theme of the debt of love and shows how it should work itself out in a community where there are disputable matters. His immediate point in vv. 1 – 12 is to urge the Roman Christians to accept each other, though he accents the need for the "strong" to accept "weak" probably because the majority of his audience are among the "strong." Everyone stands under the Lord and everyone will stand before the Lord, so it is not their place to judge one another.

"Accept the one whose faith is weak, without quarreling over disputable matters" (v. 1). The imperative verb "accept" (*proslambanomai*) dominates the opening sentence, and its appearance again in 15:7 with "accept one another" forms an *inclusio*. This bracketing of 14:1 – 15:13 by the theme of "acceptance" helpfully identifies the main point of the exhortation as urging the Roman believers to "accept" each other (though "welcome" is probably a better translation as per the ESV, CEB, NJB, etc.).[6] The root for the command is not pragmatic; it is christological, "just as Christ accepted you" (15:7). Instead of being contentious over "disputable matters," they should imitate Christ. These disputable matters we will see pertain to meat, sacred days, and wine.

Paul counsels, implicitly the "strong," to welcome those who's "faith is weak." But who are the "weak" (14:1 – 2; 15:1) and who are the "strong" (15:1)? Paul used similar language in 1 Corinthians in relation to those who are easily offended by the idea of consuming food sacrificed to idols (1 Cor 8:7 – 12) and in relation to his mission to Gentiles and Jews (1 Cor 9:21 – 23). It is important to note that the terms "strong" and "weak" do not indicate

6. In light of the commands to hospitality (Rom 12:13) and sharing an *agape* meal (Rom 13:10), Jewett (*Romans*, 835 – 36) thinks that "welcome" here carries the technical sense of reception into the fellowship of a congregations at its common meal.

degrees of faith or a quality of faith. A person who is weak in faith is one who's conscience is easily pricked or easily offended (see 1 Cor 8:7, "Some people are still so accustomed to idols that when they eat sacrificial food they [i.e., the weak] think of the food as having been sacrificed to a god, and since their conscience is weak, it is defiled"). We see the same phenomena in Greco-Roman moral discourse. Horace mentions a fellow poet, Fuscus Aristius, who refused to talk business on the Sabbath day in order not to affront a Jew and he describes himself as having scruples that are "weaker" (*infirmior*).[7] Cicero regarded the morally weak person as one who has an intense belief that something ought to be avoided, though in reality it need not be.[8]

As to the identity of the "strong" and the "weak," it most likely represents an ethnic-ethical distinction.[9] The "weak" are probably Jewish Christians and the "strong" are probably Gentile Christians.[10] That makes sense in light of the observations that: (1) Paul is directly addressing Gentile believers in the letter (see Rom 1:6, 13; 11:13), so the address to the "strong" (15:1) would naturally imply a Gentile audience; (2) the whole letter touches on the topic of the equality and mutuality between Christ-believing Jews and Gentiles (see 1:16; 2:9–10; 3:22, 29; 10:12; 11:25–32), and it is hard to imagine that it does not impinge itself here; (3) the matters of food, wine, observing days were quintessentially Jewish concerns (see Gal 4:10; Col 2:6), and when combined with the language of "unclean" and "clean" (Rom 14:14, 20) we can presuppose a setting about the boundary markers of covenantal loyalty indicative of the post-Maccabean Jewish Diaspora; and (4) ancillary support comes from 1 Corinthians, where Paul seems to identify the "weak" with Jewish persons when talking about his mission to Jews and Gentiles (1 Cor 9:22).

However, we probably should be flexible on this identification. Paul is a Jewish Christian and he can identify himself as having a perspective on unclean food the same as the "strong" (Rom 14:14). And we can easily imagine former God-fearers or proselytes still highly sensitive to anything that smacks of idolatry, given the embarrassing history of idolatry in their own religious biography (much like a former alcoholic being highly sensitive to all forms of alcohol). F. F. Bruce wrote: "Among the house-churches of Rome,

7. Horace, *Satires* 1.9.65–72.

8. Cicero, *Tuscan Disputations* 4.26.

9. Cf. survey of opinions in Cranfield, *Romans*, 2:690–95 and Reasoner, *The Strong and the Weak*, 1–23.

10. See esp. Dunn, *Romans*, 2:800–801; Moo, *Romans*, 829–31; Esler, *Romans*, 341–44. Contra Nanos (*Mystery of Romans*, 103–39), who thinks that the "weak" were non-Christ-believing Jews. See the responses to Nanos by Robert J. Gagnon, "Why the 'Weak' at Rome Cannot be Non-Christian Jews," *CBQ* 62 (2000): 64–82 and Witherington, *Romans*, 330–33. I have to say that Karl Barth (*Romans*, 508) reaches heights of theological hilarity when he claims that the modern equivalent of the weak in faith includes Baptists, open-air preachers, and vegetarians.

then, we should probably envisage a broad spectrum of varieties in outlook and practice between the firm Jewish retention of the ancestral customs and Gentile remoteness from these customs. Some Jewish Christians might be found on the liberal side of the half-way mark between the two extremes and some Gentile Christians on the 'legalist' side."[11]

Keep in mind as well that out of the twenty-six persons to whom Paul sends greetings in Romans 16:1 – 16, at least five are Jewish, including Andronicus, Junia, Herodian, Prisca, and Aquila, plus Rufus and his mother, Mary, are probably of Jewish origins too. In all, some 20 to 30 percent of the people whom Paul mentions in his list of persons are presumably of Jewish origins. Also, we cannot assume that the congregations were divided by ethnicity into separate Jewish and Gentile house churches. Some house churches may have been ethnically homogenous; others may have been ethnically mixed. I surmise that Gentiles were probably in the majority among the Roman house churches. In the end, it makes for a complex environment where divisive debates over Torah observance were possible.[12] In essence, the danger was that the "weak" would insist that God's people were marked out by abstentions and observances that others regarded as insignificant. Or else the "strong" put their private freedom and knowledge of matters to be held with indifference ahead of mutuality and treated the weak with disdain.[13]

It is useful to remember that Paul never demanded that Jewish Christians cease to be Jewish or that Torah observance had to be entirely phased out of their lives and devotion. He was simply adamant that the Torah not be forcibly foisted on Gentiles as a means of securing salvation or establishing corporate identity.

Paul's approach was followed by Justin Martyr in his dialogue with Trypho the Jew in the mid-second century. Justin said to Trypho, "in my opinion," Jewish believers can still keep the Torah if they so wished, as long as they do not try to force Gentiles into thinking that they can be saved by observing such rites. Trypho seized on the qualifier "in my opinion" and asked if there were other Gentile Christians who did not tolerate Jewish Christians as Justin did. Justin had to admit that "there are some Christians who boldly refuse

11. Bruce, *Romans*, 236 – 37. Cf. similarly Dunn, *Romans*, 2:802; Moo, *Romans*, 831; Wright, "Romans," 10:731; Bryan, *Preface to Romans*, 211; Reasoner, *The Strong and the Weak*, 138, 214; Watson, *Paul, Judaism, and the Gentiles*, 175, 184; Longenecker, *Introducing Romans*, 144 – 45; Michele Murray, *Playing a Jewish Game: Gentile Christian Judaizers in the First and Second Centuries* (Waterloo: Wilfrid Laurier University Press, 2004), 29 – 100.

12. Very helpful and succinct is Reidar Hvalvik, "Jewish Believers and Jewish Influence in the Roman Church until the Early Second Century," in *Jewish Believers in Jesus: The Early Centuries* (ed. O. Skarsaune and R. Hvalvik; Peabody, MA: Hendrickson, 2007), 190 – 96.

13. Talbert, *Romans*, 315.

to have conversations or meals with such [Jewish Christian] persons. I don't agree with such Christians." When it comes to Jewish Christians, Justin said, "we should receive them and associate with them in every way as kinsmen and brothers." Evidently Justin knew of Gentile Christians who refused to converse or eat with Jewish Christians and Jewish Christians who tried to entice Gentile Christians to keep the Torah and "refuse to share with them this same common life."[14] An analogous context of contested views of Torah between Jewish and Gentile Christians might be what Paul is addressing in Romans 14–15.

Back to 14:1, Paul does not want the strong to court controversy by "quarreling over disputable matters" in a manner that might inveigh against the weak. Paul was certainly resolute in his defense of the gospel, and we see that in Romans with his call for believers to remain faithful to the teaching they have received (6:17; 16:17).

However, there is no interest on Paul's part in establishing a school of tradition to provide casuistic law for every possible moral and ritual conundrum. Paul refuses to adjudicate on the rightness or wrongness of contested topics since he regards it as a matter of personal liberty. Paul does not call for uniformity on every practice, and he can accept differences of opinion on matters that might be regarded as being of secondary importance. The issues of food, wine, and sacred days are obviously secondary for him. Origen summed up Paul like so: "To eat or not to eat and to drink or not drink wine is neither bad nor good itself, he teaches; it is neutral and indifferent."[15] Paul, by taking such a position on "disputable matters," tries to inoculate the churches from creating an atmosphere of factious rivalry and intellectual competition.[16]

Paul next delineates an example of matters that might cause divisions and judgmentalism: "One person's faith allows them to eat anything, but another, whose faith is weak, eats only vegetables" (v. 2). The word "only" is not present in the Greek, but in light of v. 21, "it is good not to eat meat," a full-blown vegetarianism is obviously implied. Here we have to note that the reason for vegetarianism was not for health reasons but motivated mostly for preservation of purity.[17] The Torah includes prohibition of consuming certain animals and prescribes that blood should be properly drained from an animal before cooking it (see Lev 7:26–27; 11:1–23; 17:12–14; Deut 12:23–25; 14:3–21). Observance of the food laws became a test case for loyalty to the covenant (see 1 Macc 1:62–63). It was not just the food itself; the fact that meat was handled by Gentiles in a market might have been enough to make

14. Justin Martyr, *Dialogue with Trypho* 46.1–47.4.

15. Cited in Burns, *Romans*, 351.

16. Esler, *Conflict and Identities*, 352; Jewett, *Romans*, 836.

17. On pagan reasons for vegetarianism, see Talbert, *Romans*, 314; Keener, *Romans*, 161.

scrupulous Jews wary of consuming it. This is why Jews living in pagan cities often avoided meats.[18]

Josephus records how some Jewish priests taken prisoner to Rome chose to eat only figs and nuts.[19] Even in Judea the insurgent leader Judas Maccabees ate only "what grew wild to avoid contracting defilement" during his guerilla campaign against the Syrians (2 Macc 5:27). Eusebius reports that James the brother of the Lord abstained from "wine, beer, and meat" as a symbol of his piety.[20] In the eyes of Gentiles, Jewish abstention from certain foods and from Gentile company was one of the most characteristic features of Jewish social life.[21] Thus, the best way to avoid eating anything "unclean" (*koinos*) was to abstain from meat altogether.

Furthermore, in the context of a pagan environment like Rome, the vast majority of the meat available would have been pork. Also, meat was not an everyday commodity for the masses, but was expensive and was often associated with ritual meals in temples, and was often dedicated to a pagan deity. Bruce Winter has argued that after Claudius's expulsion of the Jews from Rome, the officials who controlled the meat market may have withdrawn the provision of appropriate meats for Jews, further forcing them to revert to vegetarianism.[22] Perhaps even after the return of the Jews under Nero, the few Jewish butchers may have been unwilling to sell meat to Jewish Christians, ostracizing them further from the web of Jewish social life.[23]

Looking behind the scenes, while most of the Gentile Christians in Rome felt no qualms about eating meat purchased in the market when it had almost certainly been offered in sacrifice to an idol, there were evidently some believers for whom such a thing was simply unthinkable. They were scrupulous about vegetarianism because they were serious about their religion.[24] If you were raised to abhor idolatry and even the food associated with it, or if you were at one time a Gentile adherent to Jewish ways who had imbibed revulsion toward idolatry, you might hesitate before relinquishing your long-held disgust toward idol food. One might naturally think that if the Messiah was the goal of the Torah, how can the Torah's proscription of certain foods itself be set aside so easily?[25]

---

18. Cf. Dan 1:3–16; 10:3; Tob 1:10–12; Jdt 12:2, 19; *Jos Asen* 7.1; 8.5.
19. Josephus, *Life* 14.
20. Eusebius, *Eccl. Hist.* 2.23.5.
21. Cf. Plutarch, *Questiones Convivales* 4.5; Tacitus, *Hist.* 4.2; 5.2; Juvenal, *Sat.* 14.98.
22. Bruce W. Winter, "Roman Law and Society in Romans 12–15," in *Rome in the Bible and the Early Church* (ed. P. Oakes; Grand Rapids: Baker, 2002), 90–91.
23. Cf. Witherington, *Romans*, 335.
24. Keck, *Romans*, 337.
25. Wright, "Romans," 10:735.

In this context, Paul elaborates how those with different convictions should treat each other: "The one who eats everything must not treat with contempt the one who does not, and the one who does not eat everything must not judge the one who does, for God has accepted them" (v. 3). Paul targets the more liberally minded believers who treat conservatives as tolerable but worthy of contempt and also the conservative minded who treat the freer liberals as intolerable and beyond the bounds of acceptable conduct.[26] In practice those who are confident in their freedom to eat all things should not "despise" (*exoutheneō*) those who feel compelled to abstain from meat. Likewise, those who are sensitive to such matters must not "judge" (*krinō*) those who feel at liberty to eat. The strong and the weak are commanded not to be contemptuous or condescending toward each other. Any type of mutual disdain is impossible because "God has accepted them."[27] As a result, it is wrongful to harbor animosity against one whom God has accepted since it would imply that God's acceptance of that person is misjudged. According to Dunn, the strong and the weak must not fall into the "trap of dictating to God and setting up their own judgment in place of God's."[28]

The incongruity of despising one whom God accepts is underscored in a rhetorical question: "Who are you to judge someone else's servant? To their own master, servants stand or fall. And they will stand, for the Lord is able to make them stand" (v. 4). Paul returns to his diatribal style to stress that God's view is the one that counts and that view should determine their attitudes toward each other. The Greek word *oiketēs* designates a domestic household slave, which builds on Paul's view of Christians as slaves of Jesus Christ (see 1:1; 6:16–17, 20). The validity or invalidity of a person's conviction in matters of meat is not for them to determine. Each person belongs to God, who is "their own master," and God has the right to judge his slaves according to how he sees just. One slave cannot peer into an adjacent room at another slave, disagree with their conduct, and pass judgment on him or her because that is the master's prerogative.

The fate of respective slaves is described as either "stand" or "fall," which function as metaphors for vindication and condemnation respectively. While it is theoretically possible that a person might "stand" or "fall," Paul remains convinced that each person will stand because "the Lord is able to make them stand." Here "stand" (*histēmi*) is theologically cognate to "justify" and

26. Dunn, *Romans*, 2:803.

27. The Greek more literally has "him" (*auton*), though several translation render it "them" (see NIV, CEB, NRSV) to rightly clarify that the acceptance applies to those who eat or do not eat.

28. Dunn, *Romans*, 2:813.

"accept." Paul believes that both the strong and the weak are equally recipients of divine approval, which cannot be undermined by human judgments.

Paul adds to the topic of vegetarianism the observance of sacred days to make the same point that human judgments on such matters do not necessarily reflect divine judgments over the person: "One person considers one day more sacred than another; another considers every day alike. Each of them should be fully convinced in their own mind" (v. 5). The idea of "sacred days" (lit., "day alongside day" [*hēmeran par' hēmeran*])[29] most probably pertains to the observance of the Sabbath and Jewish festivals like Passover and Pentecost. The Sabbath was rooted in creation (Gen 2:2–3), commanded in the Decalogue (Exod 20:8–11; Deut 5:12–14), part of Israel's covenantal framework (Exod 31:16–17), expected of proselytes (Isa 56:6), and recognized by Gentiles as a distinctive habit of the Jewish people.[30]

At the same time, one wonders if some of the Roman believers were keeping Roman holidays too or holding them to some significance. The situation is that one person observes these solemn occasions, while another considers all days to be of equal sanctity. Notice that Paul does not render judgment for or against observing the days; he is entirely neutral on whether it is right or wrong or beneficial or meaningless. He argues instead that each person "should be fully convinced in their own mind" about what they do and why they do it. The Greek word for "fully convinced" is *plērophoreō*, which has a connotation of coming to a decisive verdict on something.[31] All believers are to be "fully convinced" in their own minds about the rightness of their observance or nonobservance of sacred days. Thus, on the matters of dispute, they should follow their consciences and trust the instinct of their convictions.

Paul then brings these two issues together and views them through the lens of thanksgiving: "Whoever regards one day as special does so to the Lord. Whoever eats meat does so to the Lord, for they give thanks to God; and whoever abstains does so to the Lord and gives thanks to God" (v. 6). It is interesting that Jewish authors regarded eating unclean food and violating the Sabbath as the chief emblems of Jews who have been unfaithful to the covenant.[32] No doubt Paul would demur in light of his view of the covenant's fulfillment in the Messiah. What matters is not the actual conviction one arrives at, but the orientation that one applies to the topic. Paul calls on the

---

29. The force of the preposition *para* is comparative and indicates a preference for one day over another.

30. Seneca, *Epistles* 95.47; Tacitus, *Histories* 5.4.

31. BDAG 827.

32. Josephus, *Ant.* 11.346; 4 Macc 4:26; CD 6.17–18; Col 2:16; cf. Juvenal, *Sat.* 14.96–100.

believers to exercise their convictions on such matters with a *kyriocentric* point of view. Whether it is observing sacred days or not, whether it is eating meat or abstaining, what counts is that it is done with respect to "the Lord"[33] and in the context of "thanksgiving to God." If one is genuinely thankful to God in what one does or does not do, and if one seeks to honor the Lord by their decision, then the rightness of their action is beyond question.

Paul explains the point this way: "For none of us lives for ourselves alone, and none of us dies for ourselves alone. If we live, we live for the Lord; and if we die, we die for the Lord. So, whether we live or die, we belong to the Lord" (vv. 7–8). Believers do not live or die for themselves, but for the Lord who saved them (see 1 Cor 6:19–20: "You are not your own; you were bought at a price. Therefore honor God with your bodies"). Paul builds on that with a series of conditional clauses to the effect that their lives are so completely oriented toward the Lord that in life or in death they are living under his sovereign headship. Amidst the uncertainties of living and dying, one thing does remain certain, "we belong to God." This idea of belonging is a fitting way of summarizing what salvation means: believers are redeemed by Jesus' blood (Rom 3:24–25), united to the Messiah in his death and resurrection (4:25; 6:5; 7:4), indwelt by the Spirit (8:9), and adopted as sons of God (8:15, 23).

This belonging has a purpose: "For this very reason, Christ died and returned to life so that he might be the Lord of both the dead and the living" (v. 9). It was to this end that the Messiah died and rose,[34] that in him God would establish his supremacy over every realm, the living and the dead, this world and the one to come. In the grand purposes of God in redemptive history, Jesus is elected to be the new Adam and the true Israel who establishes God's kingship in heaven, on earth, and under the earth (see Eph 1:10; Phil 2:10; Rev 5:13).

It is recognition of this point that should provide some sobering perspective on how to treat disputable matters of sirloin steak and Sabbath days. If Jesus reigns, he reigns over vegetables and on Yom Kippur. What is required of believers is not to squabble over the rightness or wrongness of miniscule matters, but to live out their convictions in such a way as to make clear that Jesus has preeminence. Paul's objective is to relativize the disputes about food and days within a grand perspective of God's purposes set forth in Messiah Jesus.[35] As Eugene Peterson elegantly paraphrases: "That's why Jesus lived and died

33. Here the dative *kuriō* is probably a dative of agency or instrument. See Porter, *Idioms*, 98–99; Wallace, *Greek Grammar beyond the Basics*, 163–66.

34. The verb *ezēsen* is an ingressive aorist meaning "came to live" rather than "lived."

35. Dunn, *Romans*, 2:808.

and then lived again: so that he could be our Master across the entire range of life and death, and free us from the petty tyrannies of each other" (MSG).[36]

In vv. 10 – 12, Paul emphasizes that judging each other on disputable matters is simply wrong because the right to judge belongs to God alone. Paul addresses his imaginary interlocutors, both the strong and the weak, with the words: "You, then, why do you judge your brother or sister? Or why do you treat them with contempt? For we will all stand before God's judgment seat" (v. 10). Paul repeats the substance of v. 3 that the strong must not "despise" the weak and the weak must not "judge" the strong. One reason is that they are "brothers and sisters" and each has a place in the Messiah's family. A second reason is that each one will appear before "God's judgment seat." The *bēma* was basically the judge's bench where magistrates and governors publicly heard cases and delivered verdicts (see Acts 18:12, 16 – 17; 25:6, 10, 17). Elsewhere Paul says that we shall all appear before the "judgment seat of Christ" (2 Cor 5:10), indicative of the view that Jesus is the one who implements the divine judgment (see John 5:27; Acts 10:42; 17:31; Rom 2:16; 2 Tim 4:1).[37] Dunn is correct that Paul sees "no essential difference" between the *bēma* of God or Jesus.[38]

On matters of secondary or tertiary importance, believers should refrain from denigrating remarks and instead defer to divine judgment. God is the one who will judge the behavior of his subjects. Paul backs that up with a citation of Isaiah 45:23: " 'As surely as I live,' says the Lord, 'every knee will bow before me; every tongue will acknowledge God' " (v. 11).[39] The universal scope ("every knee") of judgment and salvation from this Isaianic text sets the stage for the climactic vision in Romans 15:7 – 13 about Gentile participation in the people of God as praisers of God.[40] The citation underscores that God is the one who will dish out the rewards as he sees fit — a judgment that even applies to believers so the point that "each of us will give an account of ourselves to God" (v. 12). This final judgment is the occasion when the fruit of believers' lives with their choices and convictions will be given either praise or disapproval. For believers, the final judgment is not an investigation as to whether they are a Christian, but an evaluation of how they were a Christian.[41]

36. Cf. Jewett (*Romans*, 849): "If Christ rules over everything from life to death, he certainly is the final arbiter in matters of calendar and diet. This eliminates the final shred of credibility on the part of either the weak or the powerful in their attempts to lord it over each other."

37. Some manuscript witnesses have "judgment seat of Christ," probably assimilating Rom 14:10 with 2 Cor 5:10.

38. Dunn, *Romans*, 2:809.

39. Paul cites the same text in Phil 2:10 – 11 and applies it to Jesus in an instance of clear "christological monotheism," where Jesus is a central part of the divine identity.

40. Jewett, *Romans*, 852.

41. Dunn, *Romans*, 2:809.

According to Morris,"A reminder of the judgment we all face is a fitting conclusion to this stage of the discussion. The fact that each will render account for himself leaves no room for despising and judging others. The verdict on them is for God, not us [humans]."[42]

If we were to summarize vv. 1 – 12, we could say that Paul is bent on stressing that Jesus is Lord of the weak (e.g., teetotaling Sabbatarian vegan Jews) and the strong (e.g., wine-sipping, Saturday-shopping, bacon-munching Gentiles). If God has justified them, they cannot condemn each other. If God has raised them up, they cannot put each other down. If they belong to the Lord, they belong to each other. If everyone calls him "Lord," they must call each other "brothers and sisters." If God has accepted them, they must accept each other. If they share the same faith, they share food together. As N. T. Wright puts it, "justification by faith" entails "fellowship by faith." This is what justification by faith looks like when it sits down at the table of Christian community.[43]

### Black and White Advice for Grey Areas of Life (14:13 – 23)

Paul moves to offer up some practical advice as to what one can actually do or not do to demonstrate the lordship of Jesus over disputable matters.

Paul draws the inference: "Therefore let us stop passing judgment on one another. Instead, make up your mind not to put any stumbling block or obstacle in the way of a brother or sister" (v. 13). The inference is transitional in that it sums up vv. 1 – 12 while looking ahead to vv. 13 – 23.[44] The word "judge" (*krinō*) is crucial, and our English translations do not bring out the play on words in the Greek. Paul wants the Roman believers to stop passing judgment (*krinōmen*) on each other, "but rather judge this" (*alla touto krinate mallon*) in the sense of "determine" or "make up your mind." Paul cheekily remarks that if they are really into judging, they should judge not to put any stumbling block in the way of a brother or sister. This idea of placing a "stumbling block" or "obstacle" in someone's way pertains to that which is done for the purpose of creating offense or manufacturing a disturbance toward another believer (see Isa 8:14 in Rom 9:32 – 33).[45] To use a military engineering metaphor, this stumbling block or obstacle represents an ethical embuggerance designed to impede progress and bring someone to ruin.

Paul then offers an aside about his own view on the matters of food and purity: "I am convinced, being fully persuaded in the Lord Jesus, that nothing

42. Morris, *Romans*, 484.
43. Wright, "Romans," 10:733.
44. Käsemann, *Romans*, 374; Moo, *Romans*, 850.
45. The Greek words *proskomma* and *skandalon* are effectively synonymous.

is unclean in itself" (v. 14a). Paul is "convinced" and "persuaded" about the nonapplicability of Old Testament food laws to believers — a view he has reached *en kuriō Iēsou*, where the dative could be either locative (i.e., "in the Lord Jesus") or instrumental (i.e., "by the Lord Jesus"). While most commentators favor the locative sense, the instrumental commends itself since 14:14 looks like a representation of the Jesus tradition, where Jesus taught that the food laws are of only relative importance compared to morality (see Mark 7:1–23/Matt 15:1–20; cf. Acts 10:15, 28; 11:9; Titus 1:15).[46]

Mark's editorial commentary on Jesus' words, "In saying this, Jesus declared all foods clean" (Mark 7:19c), is strikingly similar to Paul's declaration in Romans 14:14 to the point that it looks like Mark has adopted the Pauline perspective on the food laws in relation to Gentile believers.[47] Clearly, then, Paul believes he is following a trajectory begun by Jesus on the topic by insisting that the clean and unclean distinctions are no longer demanded of believers even if some believers still choose to follow them.[48] The same conclusion was reached by Peter after his vision at Caesarea and through his meeting with the centurion Cornelius (see Acts 10:1–11:18), where he learned, "Do not call anything impure that God has made clean" (11:9).

Paul's interjection of his own view is as succinct as it is shocking. The Old Testament food laws of *kashrut* provided details about unclean foods that were to be avoided by Torah-observant Jews (see Lev 11; Deut 14). Food that was ritually unclean was known as *koinos* or "unclean" as Paul calls it here, the opposite of "clean" or *katharos* in v. 20.[49] The Old Testament food laws expressed a particular understanding of Israel's special status as God's holy people and their separateness from the nations. The division between clean (edible) and unclean (inedible) foods corresponded to the division between holy Israel and the Gentile nations.[50] Generally speaking, Jews in Palestine and in the Diaspora tried to keep these food laws. The practice was widely known, and the satirist Juvenal mocked Jewish abstention from pork, saying about the Jews: "They see no difference between eating swine's flesh, from

46. Jesus and the Old Testament food laws requires a much larger treatment; for a brief take on the issues see Michael F. Bird, "Jesus the Law-Breaker," in *Who Do My Opponents Say That I Am? An Investigation of the Accusations against the Historical Jesus* (eds. J. B. Modica and S. McKnight; LHJS; London: T&T Clark, 2008), 3–26.

47. The connection on Paul and Mark requires a larger treatment too; for an initial heads-up, see Michael F. Bird, "Mark: Interpreter of Peter and Disciple of Paul," in *Paul and the Gospels: Christologies, Conflicts, and Convergences* (eds. M. F. Bird and J. Willitts; LNTS 411; London: T&T Clark, 2011), 30–61.

48. Cf. Thompson, *Clothed with Christ*, 185–99.

49. Cf. 1 Macc 1:47, 62; Mark 7:2, 5; Acts 10:14, 28; 11:8; Josephus, *Ant.* 11.346.

50. Cf. Gordon J. Wenham, "The Theology of Unclean Food," *EvQ* 53 (1981): 11.

which their father abstained, and human flesh."[51] The food laws were a distinctive part of Jewish daily life. According to E. P. Sanders:

> If we bring together the facts that pious groups in Palestine had some special food laws and interpreted all the laws strictly, and that the food laws of Lev. 11 were observed in the Diaspora, where it was more difficult to keep them than in Palestine, we must conclude that the biblical food laws were in general kept very strictly throughout Jewish Palestine. In terms of day-in and day-out Jewish practice, both in Palestine and in the Diaspora, the food laws stood out, along with observance of the sabbath, as being a central and defining aspect of Judaism.[52]

Yet Paul declares ever so nonchalantly that no food is actually, truly, genuinely, intrinsically unclean "in itself." Controversial as Paul's view might be, it is the inevitable conclusion reached from the premises that the Messiah fulfills the Torah and is the goal of the Torah.

That, however, is not the end of the matter. As we've already seen, the Torah retains its prophetic function and constitutes a type of wisdom for Christian living, even while believers no longer live under its jurisdiction. Since many will no doubt still feel an attachment to the Torah's commands, Paul adds: "But if anyone regards something as unclean, then for that person it is unclean" (v. 14b). So no food is really unclean, except he adds, unless one sincerely believes it to be unclean. In which case, for that a person, the food can be "reckoned" (*logizomai*) as being "unclean." While an ancient Jew might be shocked at Paul's nullification of the *kashrut* laws, we might find ourselves equally scandalized at the blatant subjectivity that Paul applies to the topic, as if one can believe whatever one likes about food laws.

We might grind our teeth as if Paul has become a postmodern ethical relativist who believes that it is possible to say in all honesty, "That's true for you, but not for me."[53] Although Paul clearly sides with the strong that all food is "clean," even so, he provides liberty to the weak to live according to their conscience and custom when it comes to the food laws. He'll end this section in vv. 22–23 on the same point, that people should act with consistency toward conscience and leave the matter between themselves and God rather than make it a stumbling block toward others.

Paul returns to his exhortation with a reminder to act in love toward others: "If your brother or sister is distressed because of what you eat, you are no

---

51. Juvenal, *Sat.* 14.98–99.

52. E. P. Sanders, *Jewish Law from Jesus to the Mishnah* (London: SCM, 1990), 27.

53. On which, see Paul Copan, *True for You But Not for Me: Overcoming Objections to the Christian Faith* (Minneapolis: Bethany, 2009).

longer acting in love" (v. 15a). Love, we saw earlier, was at the heart of Paul's ethical vision (see 12:9–10; 13:8–10). If someone acts in such a way as to grieve a fellow believer over the matter of food, then their behavior is the opposite of "acting in love." Such behavior is self-righteous and self-serving, precisely what they were told not to be (see 12:4, 10). The strong may enjoy their freedom from the Torah when it comes to food, but they are not to rub it in the faces of the weak with a view to denigrating their sensitive consciences. So Paul adds the command: "Do not by your eating destroy someone for whom Christ died" (v. 15b).

Perhaps one of the greatest lessons that this text has for us is that when it comes to secondary matters, Paul shows that it is more important to be loving than to be proven right. There is no gain to be made in proving that one's theology of *kashrut* laws or the Sabbath is theologically superior if it means fostering division and denigrating the convictions of another. You might win the argument or impress like-minded peers, but you lose a brother or sister for whom the Messiah died. And if the Messiah is for them, crucified for them, to wash away their sins and yours, how can you seek to bring them to spiritual ruin? Paul does not insist that the strong have to agree with the weak, but he does insist that they constrain the exercise of their freedom to promote love, peace, and unity. For the Christians in Rome, where their faith is exercised in a context of hostility and daily uncertainty, they do not have the luxury of dividing over miniscule matters about morsels of meat, since far more is at stake than steak.

Paul returns to the second person plural form of address: "Therefore do not let what you know is good be spoken of as evil" (v. 16). The prohibition in this verse is a conclusion that Paul draws from vv. 14–15.[54] The "good" in question is most likely knowledge of freedom from the Old Testament food laws. Good as that freedom is, if the strong abuse it, or brandish it with arrogance, they risk the prospect that their freedom will be reviled by the weak. This freedom will be "spoken of as evil" (see NIV, ESV, NRSV) or "criticized as wrong" (CEB), or, "blasphemed" (*blasphēmeō*). They might cajole the weak into making human insults against a divine gift. According to Moo: "Paul is warning the 'strong' Christians that their insistence on exercising their freedom in ceremonial matters in the name of Christ can lead those who are spiritually harmed by their behavior to revile the legitimate freedom that Christ has won for them."[55]

In vv. 17–18 Paul provides two explanatory sentences elaborating on the reasons for this perspective on treating each other with love on disputable

54. Moo, *Romans*, 855.
55. Ibid., 856.

matters. First, negatively, he says: "For the kingdom of God is not a matter of eating and drinking, but of righteousness, peace and joy in the Holy Spirit" (v. 17). Paul rarely mentions the "kingdom of God," and when he does he ordinarily has in mind the future state that God's people are yet to enter (see 1 Cor 4:20; 6:9–10; 15:24, 50; Gal 5:21; Eph 5:5; Col 1:12–13; 4:11; 1 Thess 2:12; 2 Thess 1:5; 2 Tim 4:1, 18). Here, though, Paul emphasizes the realized or present dimension of the kingdom of God. The kingdom is manifested in their midst by the Holy Spirit, who bestows on them the blessings of righteousness, joy, and peace. Brian Vickers comments, "By placing personal freedom, here in the form of eating and drinking, above the good of others, they are forgetting how they received the kingdom and what should mark those who belong to it."[56] When one realizes what the kingdom is and how the kingdom is expressed among them, petty squabbles over meat and sacred days appear comparatively pointless and even pitiful.

Second, positively, he says: "because anyone who serves Christ in this way is pleasing to God and receives human approval" (v. 18). Paul suggests that adopting this mode of behavior is an act of service toward the Messiah since it is a service toward his people. In serving their king they should imbibe a kingdom perspective on how to treat other kingdom people. More to the point, this behavior will result in a twofold blessing. Those who conduct themselves in this way of love and restraint toward others will not only please God, but will also meet with human approval. They will be good servants who receive not only divine praise, but are esteemed by the rest of the church family. If the Roman believers consider themselves to be slaves bound to Messiah Jesus, then they are bound to act in such a way as to promote righteousness, peace, and joy.

Paul provides a summary of his main point in v. 19 and its application in vv. 20–21. The main assertion is: "Let us therefore make every effort to do what leads to peace and to mutual edification" (v. 19). I have to confess that this is my favorite verse in Romans and how I wish it would be read out thrice at the beginning of every diaconate, eldership, session, wardens, presbytery, association, and synod meeting of Christians. The believers in Rome, despite their diversity, despite the complexity of the relationship between Christ-believing Jews and Gentiles over the last several years, and despite their personal grievances and wounds, they are to pursue peace and mutual upbuilding. The things that make for peaceful relationships, harmony, and consensus, those are the things they are to doggedly chase after. Instead of destroying God's work in his servants, they are to build each other up,

56. Brian Vickers, "The Kingdom of God in Paul's Gospel," *SBJT* 12 (2008): 61.

like adding another spiral to a beautiful cathedral. Paul wants a cessation of hostilities and a combined effort to create an atmosphere of mutual support.

The way this works out in practice is that the strong are to value fellowship more than food: "Do not destroy the work of God for the sake of food. All food is clean, but it is wrong for a person to eat anything that causes someone else to stumble" (v. 20). Food was central to Christian fellowship. Sharing food and participating in common meals was one of the most distinctive features of Christian life. Remember that when Jesus wanted his disciples to understand the meaning of his approaching death, he did not give them a sermon or a lecture; rather, he gave them a meal to explain what his death was about.[57] Food is important because of its symbolism as much as its sustenance, and it brings the church together.

The Passover meal itself symbolized the exodus, God's great act of deliverance for Israel. When Paul says "for the sake of food," he means "for perspectives about food." No belief about food is worth throwing a wrecking ball through Christian fellowship. Their fellow believers, the weak, are identified as the "work of God," which probably refers to the Christian community. So the strong cannot attack the weak because they are the Lord's servants (v. 4), Jesus died and rose for them (vv. 9, 15), and they are the work of God, the church (v. 20). The mutual upbuilding they are to pursue (v. 19) is built on the foundation of God's work in creating a new people (v. 20). Dunn says: "To belong to God's building means living out one's life as part of that building, mutually dependent on God's grace and mutually interdependent on the interlocking relationships by which the building exists and grows."[58] On the tail of that, Paul can again affirm what he said in v. 14 that "all food is clean." There are no food taboos at their table. They are free to eat anything found in the marketplace and to enjoy food because, as Paul says elsewhere, "the earth is Lord's, and everything in it" (see 1 Cor 10:24–26; cf. Ps 24:1). However, what is "wrong" or "bad" is that one's choice of eating causes another believer to "stumble" or "trip up."

The strong should not use their freedom to offend, but relinquish it where necessary to avoid division: "It is better not to eat meat or drink wine or to do anything else that will cause your brother or sister to fall" (v. 21). While it is "wrong" (*kakos*) to cause another to stumble, it is "good" (*kalos*) to avoid meat and wine if it will prevent a fellow believer from stumbling. We have already discussed the reasons for avoiding meat, but concerning wine the reasons for avoidance could be various. Although avoiding drunkenness by

57. Cf. N. T. Wright, *The Meal Jesus Gave Us: Understanding Holy Communion* (London: SPCK, 2002).

58. Dunn, *Romans*, 2:833.

excessive consumption of wine was well-known (see Prov 23:20; 1 Tim 3:8; Titus 2:3; Sir 31:25, 29), the Jewish tradition could also celebrate the joy and health benefits associated with wine (see 1 Tim 5:23; Wis 2:7; Sir 31:26–27; 2 Macc 15:39). More likely, the avoidance of wine is due to its association with idolatry as wine could be poured out for libations to pagan deities (see Add Esth 4:17, "your servant has not eaten at Haman's table, and I have not honored the king's feast or drunk the wine of libations").

In the same way that v. 20 repeats v. 14a that all foods are clean, so too vv. 22–23 repeat the substance of v. 14b that one must remain true to their beliefs whatever those beliefs are about food and purity. Stated positively, the principle Paul reiterates is: "So whatever you believe about these things keep between yourself and God. Blessed is the one who does not condemn himself by what he approves" (v. 22). It is not so much a matter of what one believes about meat, sacred days, or wine; it's a matter of consistency with conscience. Liberty and sensitivity are both fine as long as they arise out of faith.

The subsequent beatitude that Paul makes is that a person is happy if they can live in such a way as their principles match their practice without fear of incurring self-condemnation. Stated negatively, the implication is: "But whoever has doubts is condemned if they eat, because their eating is not from faith; and everything that does not come from faith is sin" (v. 23). For a person to go ahead and eat meat, if they are unsure or haunted by doubt, is sinful. For if their action comes not from faith, but from something else like fear of shame from the strong, then faith is no longer determining their course of action. Doubt or indecision is not itself wrong; it is only wrong "if" it causes the one who wavers to go ahead and eat. Paul is extolling faith as something to be unalloyed from doubt and hesistation.[59] The strong must avoid putting any stumbling block in front of the weak, while the weak must protect their conscience as they recognize the freedom of the strong on matters of food and drink. By such respect for each other, they respect the Lord who died for them, who reigns over them, and will one day even judge them.

### Throw Down the Welcome Mat (15:1–6)

I like to think of Romans 15:1–13 as Paul's graduating address for readers going through the "Christ College" of 12:1–15:13. Paul proceeds to provide a summary of his teaching about how the strong should treat the weak (15:1–6) and roots his exhortation in the Messiah's own service and the testimony of the prophet Isaiah about the Gentiles sharing in Israel's worship (15:7–13).

59. Keck, *Romans*, 347.

"We who are strong ought to bear with the failings of the weak and not to please ourselves" (v. 1). By using the first person plural "we," Paul identifies himself with the strong and their freedom from Torah observance (see 14:14, 20). Yet he places on the "strong"[60] an obligation (lit., an indebtedness) to carry the failings of the weak and not to please themselves. Carrying another's burden (see Gal 6:2) is how they pay the debt of love that believers owe to each other (Rom 13:8). Love of this order is more than mere toleration; it means indulging the weaks' tender consciences even at the expense of their own preferences. On top of that, to "not please themselves" means accommodating the requests of others rather than prioritizing one's own predilections.

In addition, Paul says, "Each of us should please our neighbors for their good, to build them up" (v. 2). By employing the adjective "each of us" Paul includes the strong and the weak in the purview of this command. For both camps, pleasing others, deferring to their needs, and seeking their benefit are ways of loving one's neighbor (13:9 – 10) and are ways that the church is built up (14:19).

Paul's exhortation is not a compromise, but christologically centered: "For even Christ did not please himself but, as it is written: 'The insults of those who insult you have fallen on me' " (v. 3). The conjunctive "for" (*gar*) shows that Paul's plea to the strong angles around the Messiah story. The strong should not think that giving in to the weak is incompatible with their apparent strength for even the Messiah did not seek to please himself.[61] Their tolerance is not a capitulation to error but a recapitulation of the Messiah's own self-giving service. For, Paul explains, even the Messiah did "not please himself" in the sense that he did not consider his status as excusing himself from the task of serving, i.e., "[he] did not consider equality with God something to be used to his own advantage" (Phil 2:6).

Paul then lodges a sharp contrast signified with "but" and goes on to describe the Messiah's self-giving service by a citation of Psalm 69:9: "The insults of those who insult you have fallen on me." The key here is that the Messiah is regarded as the speaker of the psalm. He is the suffering righteous one who is mocked and despised by his antagonists and patiently waits for his vindication from God. Paul taps into the gospel story that Jesus did not shirk from the shame and horror of his crucifixion in order to achieve atonement for God's people (see Mark 15:29 – 32). In the same way, if the weak are insulting the strong or even speaking evil of their good freedom (see Rom

60. Paul calls the "strong," literally "the powerful ones" (*oi dynatoi*) — a designation that in its Roman context signifies socioeconomic, political, and even numerical superiority (see Reasoner, *The Strong and the Weak*, 218 – 20).

61. Moo, *Romans*, 868.

14:16), they are not to respond in kind. The strong should not shrink back from the need to show patience even to the argumentative weak members. The Messiah's own example should lead them to be self-giving, not to be retaliatory or repay insult for insult.

Reflecting on Psalm 69 leads Paul to offer a somewhat excursive thought[62] on the function of Scripture itself: "For everything that was written in the past was written to teach us, so that through the endurance taught in the Scriptures and the encouragement they provide we might have hope" (v. 4). Israel's sacred texts were composed in order to provide instruction to the people, instruction that would imbibe them with endurance and encouragement and would culminate in a sense of hope. This is no random eulogizing of Scripture. We must remember, as Esler states, "What is at stake is not merely the interpretation of the past but, as clearly here, the role of memories in understanding the present and envisioning the future. Israelite scriptures were battlefields for rival groups bent on securing the victory that would preserve their respective identities."[63] Scripture, then, is a major source of hope that drives and sustains the Pauline vision for a united people of Jews and Gentiles with a shared messianic identity and common experience of the Spirit.

The themes of endurance and encouragement provide a segue into Paul's prayer wish for the Roman believers: "May the God who gives endurance and encouragement give you the same attitude of mind toward each other that Christ Jesus had, so that with one mind and one voice you may glorify the God and Father of our Lord Jesus Christ" (vv. 5–6). This is the first prayer that Paul has made for the Romans since 1:9–12. The prayer is simultaneously a direct intercession before God and an indirect exhortation to the Roman community. At the core of Paul's prayer is that unity would be restored and they would think the same on such things (much like Rom 12:16; 2 Cor 13:11; Phil 2:2–4; 4:2). He is not calling for uniformity, for the believers to think exactly the same thing about disputable matters; rather, even with their differences of opinion, he wants them to have a common perspective and purpose.[64]

Paul wants more than an agreed list of ideas; he wants them to have a mind among each other that is *kata Christon Iēsoun* ("according to Messiah Jesus"). This is a mind that is patterned after the Messiah and pursues the vision of God's people appropriate for those under the Messiah. The result of this messianic mind is two things: first, consensus and concord where it matters (*homothymadon*, lit., "one mindedness," a favorite term of Luke,

---

62. Schreiner calls v. 4 "a parenthesis in the argument" (*Romans*, 748).

63. Esler, *Conflict and Identity in Romans*, 353.

64. Moo, *Romans*, 871.

see Acts 1:14; 4:24; 8:6; 15:25; 19:29); second, worship, coming together with "one voice" to glorify the God and Father of their Lord Jesus. Unity is not prized for itself but has as its ultimate end the glory of God. Only when the Roman churches are visibly united and singing with one voice will God be glorified in a way worthy of him. It is little statements like these, so often passed over, that allow us to peer down into the tectonic plates of the theology of Romans. God brings Israel's story to its climax through the Messiah, and in the Messiah, God makes out of Jews and Gentiles a holy and obedient people to praise his glory.

### Small Squabbles in Light of the Big Story (15:7 – 13)

The final paragraph, 15:7 – 13, says Wright, "transforms into a coda of praise and celebration without any loss of theological poise."[65] Paul rounds off the entire section by repeating 14:1 with a further plea to accept one another just as the Messiah himself accepted them (15:7), then declaring that the Messiah is the one through whom God's promises to the patriarchs are fulfilled (15:8), resulting in the inclusion of Gentiles in God's people as Scripture foresaw (15:9 – 12), and concluding with a prayer wish for more abundant spiritual fruit among these Gentile believers (15:13).

Paul buttresses his plea to the strong by summing up several various themes from across the letter like God's faithfulness to Israel, the Messiah's resurrection, the inclusion of Gentiles in God's people, as well as hope, joy, peace, faith, and the Holy Spirit. Paul places the local conflict in Rome against the panoramic backdrop of redemptive history in order to prompt them to obedience and to enjoin them to a united worship. In sum, Paul provides a celebration of the Messiah's work on behalf of the nations, a work that is first and foremost for Israel, as it fulfills the promises given to the patriarchs, by consecrating Gentiles to share in God's people just as the Torah, Prophets, and Writings declared.[66] Thus, in 15:7 – 13 we apprehend at last the climax of the entire letter.[67]

"Accept one another, then, just as Christ accepted you, in order to bring praise to God" (v. 7). The NIV lessens the inferential nature of the verse by translating the coordinating conjunction *dio* as "then" rather than the more forceful "therefore" (better is the ESV, NASB, NLT with "therefore, welcome/accept each other"). The transition is important as Paul intends to gather up

65. Wright, "Romans," 10:746.

66. Cf. Moo, *Romans*, 874; Wright, "Romans," 10:746.

67. Cf. Wright, *Climax of the Covenant*, 235; Fitzmyer, *Romans*, 705 – 6; Schreiner, *Romans*, 704; Dumbrell, *Romans*, 21; Wendy Dabourne, *Purpose and Cause in Pauline Exegesis: Romans 1.16 – 4.25 and a New Approach to the Letters* (SNTSMS 104; Cambridge: Cambridge University Press, 1999), 72; Wagner, *Heralds of the Good News*, 307.

several threads of his exhortation to the strong and the weak. Just like v. 3, the Messiah's own action here is the basis and model for the Roman believers.[68] They are to welcome each other in the same way (*kathōs*) that the Messiah welcomed them (see Col 3:13 in relation to forgiving each other just as the Lord forgave them).

Notice as well the doxological end of this welcome. When Gentile believers deliberately flex in their freedom in order to extend familial bonds to Jewish believers, by this welcoming act they give praise to God (15:7). In addition, if mutual acceptance is the key idea throughout 14:1–15:13, then regard for "one another" is the primary instrument for achieving it. Paul mentions no less than nine times what they must do for one another, including belonging (12:5), devotion (12:10), give honor (12:10), harmony (12:16), love (13:10), refuse to pass judgment (14:13), build up (14:19), unity of mind (15:5), and acceptance (15:7). The most powerful sign that they are the renewed and consecrated people of God on whom salvation has come is the mutuality and unity evident within a network of multiethnic house churches.

The unity of Jews and Gentiles in the church is the culmination of the unfolding redemptive-historical drama where salvation comes to Gentiles only as it comes to and through the Jews with the gospel: "For I tell you that Christ has become[69] a servant of the Jews on behalf of God's truth, so that the promises made to the patriarchs might be confirmed and, moreover, that the Gentiles might glorify God for his mercy" (vv. 8–9). Paul slips back into the first person singular with "I tell you" to make an authoritative pronouncement, this time about the Messiah, similar to his other messianic formulations in the letter (see 1:3–4; 9:4–5). The net point is that God, by bringing Israel's covenantal history to its appointed climax in the Messiah, has opened the way for the Gentiles to join his renewed people.

It is not the case that salvation is for Jews and Gentiles and the Jews just got the first bite of the apple before it was finally offered to Gentiles. No, it was that the promises were cocooned around Israel; thus it must be to and through Israel that salvation is revealed. We might say that salvation is for the Jew first *so that* it can be for the Gentile second. The Messiah became a servant — indeed *the* Servant of whom Isaiah spoke[70] — in order to make

68. Wright, "Romans," 10:746.

69. Several commentators over interpret the significance of the perfect tense-form of *gegenēsthai* to signify the continued service of Jesus to the Jews (e.g., Dunn, *Romans*, 2:847; Moo, *Romans*, 877; Keck, *Romans*, 355), when the word is more likely accenting the state of service that Christ entered into.

70. True, Paul uses the word *diakonos* rather than Isaiah's word *pais* for "servant." However, *pais* has connotations of "child," which is inexact for the meaning here, and the whole texture of Romans is pervaded by Isaianic imagery that would not be lost on scripturally informed listeners.

good[71] what God had promised the patriarchs. What is at stake is no less than "God's truth," his fidelity to what he said he would do in giving Abraham descendants as numerous as the stars.[72] To that end, the Messiah's work was directed at Israel, the "circumcision," because of the particular place Israel held in God's plan to rescue the world and to make Abraham's promises an eschatological reality (see Matt 10:5–6; 15:24; Mark 7:24–30; John 4:22–26).

The two succeeding purpose clauses in vv. 8c–9a should be taken as parallel and consequential:[73] (1) to confirm God's promises to the patriarchs is precisely the theological platform on which Paul based the whole scope of Romans 4. God had always intended to create a worldwide Abrahamic family, through Israel, the kingdom of priests and light to the nations, a role fulfilled by the Messiah. Rescuing Gentiles was not an afterthought but part of the unswerving divine purpose for the whole world, where the messianic servant redeemed Jews and Gentiles and made them covenant partners in the renewed people of God.

(2) The second purpose was to bring Gentiles to the point where they would praise God for his mercy. The result of the Messiah's ministry, and even that of his apostle to the Gentiles, is that Gentile idolaters become true God worshipers. They celebrate an experience of "mercy," entering into divine kindness and favor (see Rom 9:16, 18, 23; 11:30–32; 12:2). According to Wright, "This is the doxological correlate of justification by faith: the gathering of Gentiles into the one people of God, not by works of Torah but simply by faith in God's saving action in the Messiah, results in praise."[74]

Assuming this entire scheme— Messiah, patriarchs, Gentiles, mercy, praise, etc.—it would be utterly unthinkable for the believers in Rome to prosecute any prejudice against their Christian brothers and sisters. Gentile Christians should not despise Jewish Christians for they are the ones to whom the Messiah came to serve. Jewish Christians should not judge Gentile Christians for he has brought them into God's mercy to be praisers of God's glory. The Messiah accepts each group and God approves of them as his servants. In response, they must show acceptance of each other. Paul thus brings together the many themes of the letter: justification by faith for Jew and Gentile, the redemptive-historical story fulfilled by the Messiah, divine mercy, mutuality,

71. Wagner is correct that "confirm" here has the sense not only of "reaffirming," but also "realizing" the divine promises (*Heralds of the Good News*, 309).

72. In the LXX, the Greek *alētheia* ("truth") often translates the Hebrew *'emet* ("fidelity"), like at Exod 34:6. On "God's truth" as "God's covenant faithfulness," see Cranfield, *Romans*, 2:741; Käsemann, *Romans*, 385; Dunn, *Romans*, 2:857; Schreiner, *Romans*, 754; Wright, "Romans," 10:746–48.

73. Cf. Moo, *Romans*, 876; Wright, "Romans," 10:747.

74. Wright, "Romans," 10:747.

and a united people of God devoted to each other as they engage in a common worship.

Paul closes this section off with a collection of four biblical citations drawn from the Pentateuch (Deut 32:43), Writings (Ps 18:49/2 Sam 22:50; Ps 117:1), and Prophets (Isa 11:10). Just like Romans 3:10 and 11:8, Paul commences with "as it is written" to introduce his catena of citations. The repeated refrain "and again" between citations means the texts are regarded as making the same point.[75] The common denominator in the texts is the word "Gentiles," but together they form a redemptive-historical mosaic that weaves together the narratives threads Paul has expounded across Romans, including God, Messiah, Israel, Gentiles, mercy, and glory. The selection of scriptural texts is concrete proof that the gospel was "promised beforehand through his prophets in the Holy Scriptures" (1:4).[76] But it is more than that, for it reminds us that "Paul's gospel was a *Jewish* message for the *non-Jewish* world ... he believed the God of Israel to be the God of the whole world and Israel's Messiah to be the world's true lord."[77]

First is Psalm 18:49 (cf. 2 Sam 22:50), "Therefore I will praise you among the Gentiles; I will sing the praises of your name" (v. 9c). Here the Messiah is depicted as the one who prays the psalm, experiencing the pattern of suffering and vindication, and at the end he leads the Gentiles in a chorus of praise for the salvation and mercy shown to "his king ... his Messiah, to David and his seed forever" (Ps 17:51 LXX [pers. trans.]). What is remarkable about Paul's "messianic exegesis" here is that he focuses on the Messiah's mission to the Gentiles. The Gentiles obey the Messiah as King and follow him in worship. Psalm 18 becomes an intertextual way of tying together the themes of Messiah, mercy, and Gentiles in vv. 7–12.[78]

Second, Paul returns to Deuteronomy 32 with, "Rejoice, you Gentiles, with his people" (v. 10). Paul follows the LXX rather than Hebrew text on Deuteronomy 32:43 to showcase the idea of Gentiles sharing in God's dramatic rescue of the Jewish nation by atonement for their sins and judgment on their enemies. The text fits perfectly with surrounding texts as it invites Gentiles to rejoice with Israel for the salvation that God has wrought for the entire world.[79] What the Old Testament called on Gentiles to do, namely, to

---

75. Kruse, *Romans*, 533.

76. Hays, *Echoes of Scripture*, 71.

77. Wright, *Paul and the Faithfulness of God*, 2:1498.

78. Hays, *Echoes of Scripture*, 70–73; Wagner, *Heralds of the Good News*, 311–13. Ambrosiaster (Bray, *Romans*, 110) says, "This is the voice of Christ, which predicted what would happen in the future, that his name would be preached among the Gentiles, who would confess God and give him the glory for the gift they had received."

79. Wagner, *Heralds of the Good News*, 316.

join Israel in the worship of God, they now do and are able to do through God's mercy to them in the gospel.[80]

Third, Paul reverts back to the Psalter, "Praise the Lord, all you Gentiles; let all the peoples extol him" with Psalm 117:1 (v. 11). This is a short psalm, only two verses, and is a classic example of the kerygmatic nature of Israel's worship in calling the nations to praise Israel's God. Viewed this way, mission is an implication of monotheism, since Israel's God was the Creator God, not merely a tribal deity or a personification of nature. As the Creator God, he was therefore worthy of the worship of the entire human race who had otherwise suppressed knowledge of their Creator and buried their minds in the dark soils of idolatry. The LXX version also adds reference to God's "mercy" and "truth" in Psalm 117:2, which resonate nicely with Romans 15:8–9.

Fourth, Paul's last citation is from "Isaiah," the only author named in the catena, and constitutes his "anchor" for the series.[81] Paul quotes from Isaiah 11:10: "The Root of Jesse will spring up, one who will arise to rule over the nations; in him the Gentiles will hope" (v. 12). The "Root of Jesse" is a messianic title (see Rev 5:5; 22:16) and this Messiah rises to reign, which naturally makes us think of the Messiah's resurrection (Rom 1:4) and enthronement (8:34). The wider Isaianic context pertains to God's purpose to rescue Israel by preserving a remnant and rallying the nations around it, and to bring this renewed community into a new world order. Paul's citation of Isaiah means that the Isaianic hope for national restoration and the renewal of creation takes place through the Messiah, who does not militarily subjugate Gentiles, but incorporates them into God's kingdom. We might add that this is probably the most politically incendiary text of the whole letter as Israel's Messiah is destined to reign over the nations and become a beacon of hope for them—precisely what the political propaganda and imperial priesthood claimed for Rome and the emperor.

Paul finishes off with a prayer wish: "May the God of hope fill you with all joy and peace as you trust in him, so that you may overflow with hope by the power of the Holy Spirit" (v. 13). Paul is cued by the mention of hope in v. 12 to launch into a prayer about hope in v. 13. Hope has been a recurring theme in Paul's exhortations throughout the letter. The reason is, perhaps, that a constant and common hope of an assured future is what they need to sustain them. Hope is the anticipation of future salvation (8:24), a hope of glory (5:5), amidst the futility and afflictions of this age (8:20; 12:12). The sign that hope in faith has taken root is the effusion of joy and peace that bubbles up in the believer by the Holy Spirit (14:17; 15:13).

80. Moo, *Romans*, 878.

81. Wagner, *Heralds of the Good News*, 317.

Imagine a group of Gentile Christians in Rome, perhaps a mixture of slaves and artisans, sitting at the back of a leather-worker's shop one night, huddled around a candle, singing a hymn, recounting their day, and sharing what little food they had. One of the slaves is a scribe and is able to read from a notebook a few verses from Psalm 69. Then in walks Herodion, a Jewish freedman, who had returned to Rome from Alexandria some weeks ago. Herodion turns to Rufus, the leader of the house church, and says "*charein kai eirēnē*" ("greetings and peace"). Rufus has not seen Herodion for six years and when they had last met there had been a ferocious debate about drinking wine. Herodion had visited Rufus's shop to explain why drinking pagan wine was wrong; it was defiled by its use in libations, so God-worshipers must avoid it or risk God's judgment. Rufus wasn't convinced and Herodion stormed off cursing Rufus and his pagan drink.

Now, however, Rufus looks at Herodion; he looks weak and malnourished. Perhaps his master has cast him out for his Christian faith. Everyone in the group looks at Rufus to see what he will do. Rufus rises, kisses Herodian on the cheek, sits him down, and gives him some bread and a few turnips and pours him a cup of water. He looks at Herodion and says, "*phagete, gar tou autou kuriou esmen*" ("Eat! For we all belong to the same Lord"). That is why Paul wrote Romans.[82]

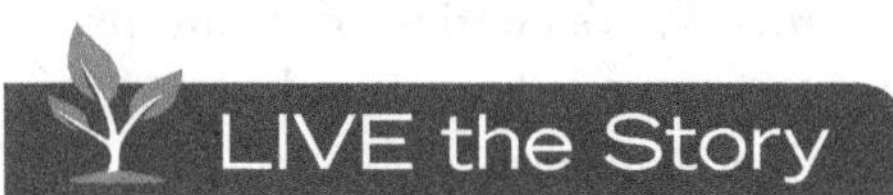


In 14:1–15:13 we find one of the most eminently practical and yet theologically profound exhortations in all of Paul's letters. If, as N. T. Wright has argued, the image of the church as the united people of God is the most lasting theological heirloom Paul has left to us, this is where Paul shows how that unity works itself out in community life. The church is the multiethnic people who confess Jesus as Lord, praise God as Father, and accept each other as brothers and sisters despite having different ideas about how to live faithfully in a pagan environment. What looms large here is the lordship of Jesus and some sage advice for dealing with disputable matters among believers.

### Christianity as Kyristanity

Paul uses the word *kyrios* ("Lord") some twelve times across 14:1–15:13. In some instances it is ambiguous as to whether "Lord" refers to Jesus or to God

82. For some helpful suggestions on teaching Romans to a Bible study group or to a seminary class, see Lareta Halteman Finger, "Getting Along When We Don't Agree: Using Simulation and Controversy to Help Students and Lay Persons Interpret Romans," in *Celebrating Romans: Template for Pauline Theology* (ed. S. E. McGinn; FS Robert Jewett; Grand Rapids: Eerdmans, 2004), 222–39.

the Father (esp. 14:4, 6, 11; 15:11), but it is crystal clear most of the time that Jesus is the one designated as "Lord" (esp. 14:8–9, 14; 15:6). By doing this, Paul is clearly situating Jesus within the divine identity, so that the "Lord" of Israel is revealed as the Lord Jesus Christ (see 10:13, 16).[83] Kirk says that "the resurrected Christ, ruling the world and the people of God on God's behalf, has transformed Paul's vision of where God's people look for their rule, as he applies to Jesus language and roles ascribed to God in the Old Testament."[84]

However, repeated reference to Jesus as Lord is more than an affirmation of Jesus' deity since Paul intends Jesus' lordship to be understood as more than an idea, but an eschatological event that imposes itself across the whole span of our lives. Paul really accents Jesus' lordship in 14:7–11, and if we take this passage seriously, a few important implications emerge.

(1) There are no lone wolves under the Lord, only one flock and one shepherd, seeking one common end. It is unthinkable that one could confess Jesus as Lord and yet separate himself or herself from the Lord's body. It is equally impossible to imagine that someone could profess to follow Jesus as Lord and yet live in deliberate isolation from his other servants. To follow Jesus as Lord will mean congregating with his other servants irrespective of how imperfect they look. The household slaves have no right to dictate who the master lets into his house!

(2) There is no area of our life that can be compartmentalized from the Lord's authority. Whether it is labor or leisure, private life or public life, finances or family, business or busyness, it is all lived before the Lord. The aegis of Jesus' lordship applies to every aspect of daily life from morning until evening and encompasses what we drink and what we think, what we eat and even the people we greet. We cannot quarantine certain objects, particular times, special behaviors, or certain bank accounts, and insist that these belong to us and not him. If we are truly thankful to the Lord for what he has done for us, then we owe him our everything, the shirt on our backs, the last cent in our wallet or our purse, and the very breath in our bodies. Cliché as it might sound, if we don't make him Lord of all, we secretly harbor the belief that he is not Lord at all! The challenge for us is to order our lives according to the story, symbols, and teachings of the Lord Jesus. We are to make Jesus' lordship a tangible and visible reality in how we live. We need to ensure that if professing and practicing Jesus as Lord is a crime, that there will be plenty of evidence to convict us.

(3) We must demur from judging Jesus' servants and leave the right to judge with our benevolent leader. When I was younger, I was very keen to

83. Cf. Moo, *Romans*, 840 n. 61.

84. Kirk, *Unlocking Romans*, 203.

make sure that all of my church friends and fellow parishioners had the correct theology. Whether it was election or eschatology, they usually needed some tips from me on how to set them straight, and I was rather miffed when they refused to come around to my way of thinking. I would often think of those who remained disagreeable with a certain degree of disdain if they could not see the truth as I assuredly knew it. Thankfully I am now older, and while I certainly haven't given up the importance of "first things" in Christian theology, I no longer find myself sitting in judgment of other people's theology or lack thereof. There are still some big theological hills I'm willing to die on, but fewer small hills that I'm willing to metaphorically fight over. The reason is simple: if someone calls Jesus "Lord," then it is his role and right to judge over them, not mine. Where the gospel is not threatened, where holiness is not tainted, there liberty may be given. Believers cannot judge each other over petty matters or condemn each other on secondary issues since that usurps the preogratives of the Lord as it is Jesus who will judge the living and the dead (2:16; 14:10).

(4) We need to have tongues wagging busily with confession and knees dirty with bowing before the lordship of Jesus. It should be clear that the lordship of Jesus is not something merely to be affirmed or assented as if it were an abstract proposition for intellectual reflection. We have a mission to proclaim the lordship of Jesus and to worship him precisely as Lord. The identity of Jesus as Lord should be central to our preaching. Yes, Jesus is Savior, Healer, and Deliverer; that is all true and should be sung from the rooftops and broadcast over the airways. But above all, Jesus is the Boss of bosses, King of kings, Master of masters, and Lord of Lords. The story of the gospel is that the one who was from the beginning Lord became a servant, so that those lost in sin might know him as Savior and love him as Lord.

At the end of the day, we must remember that Christianity is not about being nice to people. It is about being subversive people who are subversive because they are unflinchingly subservient to the kingdom, cause, and message of the Lord Jesus Christ. People who won't bend the knee to the lords of this age. People who by their actions as much as their words tell forth the love of the Lord. People who keep pointing to the Lord who offers salvation for the repentant and will usher in justice for the world. We need to live lives of such radiance that our neighbors will become curious about our *kyrios*.

Naturally this will lead us into praise, singing, and praying to Jesus as Lord. Churches will become the place where the name of Jesus is honored and esteemed as the one who loves us and leads us into everlasting glory. As Charles Spurgeon preached:

> The more you know of Jesus as your Savior, saving you from sin, the more will you recognize him also as your Lord. No one rebels against Christ because he believes in him; but, because we believe in him, he becomes our Lord, and we learn to obey him. That is the spirit I long to have reigning in all our hearts, the spirit of devout, worshipful reverence towards "Jesus our Lord."[85]

(5) A large part of our lives is to show forth the preeminence of Christ's lordship by pursuing unity with each other. It is surely significant that Paul emphasizes the lordship of Jesus in the part of the letter that speaks the most clearly to the unity of the church. Jesus is Lord of both Jews and Greeks and so Lord of the strong and the weak (10:12). That is why the church is constituted as one people under one Lord. The underlying premise is that confessing Jesus as Lord is the single criterion for being a Christian (10:9–11). If all believers call Jesus "Lord," they all relate to him as his fellow servants and are called to embrace each other in fellowship. Quite clearly for Paul, maintaining unity is not just a matter of preventing petty tiffs, but is an essential element of the church's witness to the Lord by speaking about the Lord with a united voice. As Wright comments, "If the church divides along lines related to ethnic or tribal loyalty, it is still living in the world of Caesar."[86]

This task of pursuing unity as an ongoing imperative of Jesus' lordship is something that I think evangelicals have traditionally been weak on. Many devoted Christian folk think of unity as a kind of take-it-leave-it option. We can hang about with like-minded people, who like the same theology as us, who appreciate the same worship as us, and get excited about the same social causes as us, but we can ignore those we don't naturally gravite to. In reality, however, we really need to try to build bridges with those churches that we often don't have an affinity with or those whom we don't naturally relate to because their worship is louder or too liturgical, because their preaching is too flowery or too theological, or because their leaders went to different seminaries or to no seminary at all. Yet if a united church is a sign of Jesus' lordship, then we can hardly be quite so half-hearted about pursuing unity on some level with other Christian assemblies. Charles Spurgeon put it well:

> This term, "Jesus our Lord," seems to draw a circle round all the elect of God, the whole host of the redeemed out of every nation, and kindred, and tribe, and tongue, and people in every land and every age. It seems to remind me of a kind of clanship which exists among all believers. Just as the old Highland clansmen, when they saw the head of the clan, all felt

85. Charles Spurgeon, "Jesus our Lord," Sermon #2606. www.spurgeon.org/sermons/2806.htm.
86. Wright, "Romans," 10:739.

> intense enthusiasm at the very sight of him, for he was the great center and meeting place for all the divers families in the clan, and with him leading them they rushed forward to victory or death with the utmost enthusiasm, so, when I look you in the face, beloved, we may differ very greatly in station, in ability, and in a thousand things, but your Lord is my Lord, so we are brothers and sisters in him, and we clasp hands around him, and say, "Jesus our Lord."[87]

I remember once thinking about what is the central message of the Christian faith. How could you sum it up in one catch phrase or one bumper sticker? Around that time I walking through my old neighborhood where a Pentecostal church had a sign posted up in some bushland adjacent to its property facing a small road junction. It said, "Jesus Reigns!" I have to say, I think that is it. That is New Testament theology in a nutshell. That is what our evangelism and ethics are about. Jesus reigns, Jesus is Lord, Jesus will be by might what he is by right, Jesus will establish his kingdom over the whole earth, yes, Jesus is Lord! After that, everything else, disputable matters and theological shibboleths, sports and movies, political debates and pumpkin pie—everything pales into insignificance when compared to the lordship of Jesus. Once we know that Jesus Christ is Lord, everything else, comparatively speaking, is about as important as knowing the reproductive habits of plankton.

### Don't Major on the Minors

You could be forgiven for wondering what is the deal with meat that Paul and his Jewish Christian buddies are so hung up about. Who cares if some pagan butcher prays to Jupiter before he hands on your McRome burger with Caesar salad on the side? Big whoopeedoo! Well, a thing that elicits a response of "Who cares?" from one person can draw a response of "Holy cow!" from another. It is vital to remember that in every generation, there are often small gestures or certain items that remind us about the deadly struggles we've had for survival and the painful divisions we've had to go through.

While meat was symbolic for the Jewish contest against idolatry, in other times the issues have been different. For instance, in sixteenth-century England, the dividing issue among Protestant churches was over the ministers' attire. The deeply divisive "vestrian controversy" was about whether ministers could or should wear vestments like a surplice, alb, cope, and chasuble. One's view of the preacher's attire determined who was "in" and who was "out" of certain factions. The debate led to persecutions, imprisonments, and a monumental tract war.

87. Spurgeon, "Jesus our Lord."

An immediate outcome was the Puritan split from the Church of England into the Presbyterian churches. To this day, my own institution, Ridley College, prohibits invited speakers from wearing certain forms of clerical attire, a lingering consequent of the vestrian controversy all those centuries ago. We might respond, "Who cares if the preacher wears a chicken suit, a monastic robe, or a three-piece Armani suit? As long as the guy or gal is clothed, preaches the word, no problemo?" Well, for the Puritans, vestments were "gan problema" as they were symbolic for the continuing influence of clericalism in England, and the vestrian controversy evoked the larger story of their struggle with the influence of Roman Catholicism. So little things, like boiled meat or a bishop's mitre, can stir up heated debates and cause folks to fire huge theological artillery at each other.

Debates, fellowship, and theology force us to identify the issues that are worth dividing over and which are not. Which hills should we be prepared to die on and which disagreements can we happily let fly through to the catcher? What we need to develop is a theological triage in relation to: (1) views *essential* to the faith; (2) views *important* to the faith and order of a church, but not necessary for salvation; and (3) views that may be treated with *indifference*, a matter of conscience, often called *adiaphora*.[88] Now for me, personally, I would put in the *essential* category things like the Trinity, the gospel, and salvation by faith alone, things without which no one can be a Christian. In the *important* category one might include church government and baptism, things that shape the visible operation and theological ethos of a church, but no one is gonna burn in hell if you do not agree with them. In the *third* category I would put drinking alcohol, schemes of eschatology, and Bible translations. The triage works well if everyone agrees on what issues go in which categories. But when they don't agree on what is a major issue and a minor issue, there can be unpleasant difficulties, to put it mildly. For example, during the vestrian controversy, part of the debate was over whether vestments were an essential matter or merely *adiaphora*.[89]

The problem is that some churches deny that such a thing as *adiaphora* exists as all matters are subject to some regulative principle.[90] Then there are others who misuse the concept of *adiaphora* to allow what Scripture expressly forbids. For instance, I once attended a Bible study where a member tried to convince us that abstaining from alcohol was an essential element of the faith.

88. Cf. Albert Mohler, "A Call for Theological Triage and Christian Maturity," 12 July 2015. www.albertmohler.com/2005/07/12/a-call-for-theological-triage-and-christian-maturity/.

89. Cf. Bernard Verkamp, *The Indifferent Mean: Adiaphorism in the English Reformation to 1554* (Athens, OH: Ohio University Press, 1977).

90. Cf. Käsemann, *Romans*, 375–76.

I've also met clergy who think that trusting in Christ alone for salvation is an optional extra for those who like the ambience of Anglican liturgy.

There are indeed weighty matters to be held of "first importance" as Paul says because they pertain to things necessary for salvation (1 Cor 15:3). Jude said that we are "to contend for the faith that was once for all entrusted to God's holy people" (Jude 3). Contending for the faith does not require, however, being contentious about all things. Matters that are to be considered *adiaphora* are those that may be treated with indifference as they are inconsequential. The Stoic philosopher Epictetus said: "Now the virtues and everything that shares in them are good, while vices ... are evil, but what falls in between these ... are indifferent."[91] Paul clearly regards eating meat, observing sacred days, and drinking wine as *adiaphora*. Many of the church fathers agreed, like Origen, who said:

> Eating meat and drinking wine are matters of indifference in themselves. Even wicked people may abstain from those things, and some idol worshippers in fact do so, for reasons which are actually evil. Likewise quite a few heretics enjoin similar practices. The only reason abstinence of this kind is good is that it may help to avoid offending a brother.[92]

In applying 14:1 – 15:13 we should ask about what issues divide us today between the weak and the strong. What is our "meat" and "sacred days" that some cling to for dear life and others shrug their shoulders at with blasé disinterest? What are the disputable matters that we should be teaching people to regard as *adiaphora*? I think two good examples of disputable matters for Christians today, especially in a multicultural context, would be *halal* food and food offered to ancestors.

I have a friend, Bruce, who is a prison chaplain. During his time as a chaplain, he's led a number of young men to Christ, men from a variety of backgrounds, usually steeped in crime and violence. A number of these new coverts have vigorously protested about being made to consume *halal* food while in prison. A substantial number of Muslim men are also in prison, so the meat served in the prison cafeteria is usually *halal*, killed and prepared according to Muslim custom. Many of the Christians in the prison have strong feelings about the issue as to whether a believer should eat food prepared according to the customs of another religion. Some feel like they are being made to observe Islamic customs by eating the meat, whereas other Christians are completely unphased by the origins of the meat and eat it without question. If you were a prison chaplain, trying to mediate a dispute between professing Christians

91. Epictetus, *Dis.* 2.19.13 (cited in Talbert, *Romans*, 312).
92. Cited in Gerald Bray, *Romans*, 350.

in that context and on this subject, what would you say to them about *halal* food, and what would be the basis of your remarks?

To give another example, I have another friend, Elise, who is from Korea. She became a Christian while studying at an Australian University. Her background was in a mixture of Buddhism and ancestor veneration. Much of the Bible's teaching on idolatry really convicted her about her past religious practices, however mechanical and meaningless those rituals were for her. On returning to Korea, she refused to share any meal where part of the food was going to be used as an offering to the ancestors in their family shrine. It caused a huge argument in her family, trying to shame her for her disrespect, and it led to a severing of her relationship with her mother. What would you tell Elise? Would it not be better to honor her mother as the Bible commands, keep her conscience intact by avoiding ancestor food, or else come up with some kind of compromise?

My favorite story about food and boundaries come from Thomas R. Browning in his account of what happened when he and a bunch of seminary students visited a Hari Krishnah temple. Browning was both amused and grieved at the rank idolatry at the Hari Krishnah temple. On the way out, the seminarans were given a paper cup full of homemade Hari Krishna candy. Browning noticed that just outside the door was a huge pile of the candy on the ground. His fellow seminarians had no sooner walked out the door than dumped the candy at their feet. What happened next was truly memorable:

> I knew, of course, immediately what had happened. Almost to a man, my seminary brothers had determined they were not going to eat any of the candy made by these pagan idolaters. They were not going to take a chance on being contaminated by Krishna candy. They were not about to let one of those blue skinned manikins get any sort of foothold down in their soul. And I have to tell you, I was, I was torn about what to do with my own little paper cup, with my own little piece of handmade, homemade Krishna candy. I was not quite as set in my ways then as I am now. The men were looking back to see what the guys coming out were going to do, so I just stopped and stepped aside and turned and looked back too when Prof. Blue came out with a giant glob of Krishna candy in his mouth. He looked sort of like a hamster with a cheek bulging with candy. He even walked over to where the guys had thrown down their candy, I had a feeling he had done this before, and sort of looked through what they had thrown down to see if anything was salvageable. I think he actually bent down and picked up a piece or two and then on his way back to the car asked first one guy and then the next, "Hey, are you gonna

> eat that ... and if you are not ... how about ... uh ... handing it over?" I stood there for a moment and finally made my own personal decision about what to do with my piece of candy.[93]

Notice that the seminarians were "weak" on the matter of Krishna candy, while the professor was "strong." The students were sensitive about eating it, while the professor had no qualms. These are the type of disputes that arise when we have a concern to protect the integrity of our faith from food tarnished with paganism. In my mind, the visit to the temple was a good training exercise for people going on the mission field or into ministry in a multicultural context, because this is the type of situation that forces them to think how to discern and decide about contentious matters like these.

The issues of course do not have to be about food and idolatry. Other disputable matters can also foster division. I can give you instances where I would be considered a "strong" believer and where I might be a considered a "weak" believer. To begin with, I enjoy a nice glass of wine with my meal, steak, pasta, or even crackers with cheese. A cold and frosty beer on a summer's day is also refreshing. Let me add that I was raised in a home with alcohol abuse and I even engaged in binge drinking while I was a young man in the army. So I know quite well the perils of alcohol consumption. Even so, I do not see any complete biblical ban against alcohol. So I'm a "strong" believer in that my convictions incline me toward the freedom to drink responsibly. Now I have some Baptist friends who, for many reasons, choose not to drink. They can be a bit touchy on the subject, so I try to do the Romans 14:19 thing by not drinking in front of them or discussing fine wines in their presence.

Nevertheless, I am not always one of the strong, since my teetotaling Baptist friends also put on a great Halloween party. They dress up in funny costumes with make-up, drink tropical punch, play games, and eat lots of candy. Personally this weirds me out because I've always regarded Halloween as a pagan festival, macabre, dark, and even demonic. I don't let my kids go trick or treating because we worship Jesus, not Voldemort or cute teenage vampires. Why would a good Christian even want to celebrate Halloween? It baffles me and horrifies me! Deep down, I know my Baptist friends are not worshiping demons, it's just costumes and candy. But for me, it's the vibe of the whole thing; it sends my spiritual radar crazy. I know that on this topic I'm in the minority, and it's a minor issue so I don't judge them for it. So here I'm a "weak" believer somewhat sensitive to Halloween celebrations.

---

93. Thomas R. Browning, "Lesson 13: Eating Meat Sacrificed to Idols ... 1 Corinthians 8," www.posttenebraslux.com/adobe%20pdf%20files/1%20corinthians/Lesson%2013_1%20Corinthians%208.pdf. 2007.

All these examples go to show that dealing with disputable matters requires constructing a theological triage, upholding gospel freedoms, and finding ways to respect each other's consciences. There will be some issues on which we are "strong" and others on which we are "weak." Most of the issues that are disputed are usually minor and not worth fighting over. The reason is, as Doug Moo puts it, "Divisions in the church over nonessentials diverts precious time and energy from its basic mission: the proclamation of the gospel and the glorifying of God."[94] In an age of rampant secularism and the rise of militant Islam, we have bigger things to do than argue about piddly perspectives on alcohol and Halloween. That would be like holding a diaconate meeting to argue about the proper size of liturgical candles while ISIS hordes are climbing over the walls of our city ready to kill and plunder. We need theological and pastoral priorities.

A large amount of responsibility falls on the shoulders of the strong, those mature in the faith, who rightly know their freedom, to exercise that freedom without causing the more scrupulous to stumble, or to label the more conservative as "whingers" or "fundies." It is also incumbent on the weak, those rightly concerned with preserving the integrity of the faith, not to be judgmental, or factious, and to refuse to label others as either worldly or liberal. Instead, everyone is to recognize that we all have freedom to disagree over nonessentials. That often goes against our natural instinct, which is to think that since we are right, we can treat others as if they have no right to their position. I love how Peter Adam puts it:

> If I had been writing Romans [14], I would have told those who were weak in faith, and still kept special days, to sort themselves out, and to know that they are justified by grace through faith, not by keeping special days of Jewish practice. Paul, on the other hand, told the strong in faith to accept the weak in faith, and the weak in faith to accept the strong in faith. Both the strong and the weak are answerable to God, not to each other. So we must allow people to act differently in matters that don't contradict the gospel.[95]

In terms of practice, Paul does not give the weak the power of veto over the strong. He does not ask the strong to forfeit their freedom. Rather, Paul urges the strong to be loving in the exercise of their freedom, to use it to build up, not to tear down.[96] Similarly, Paul does not give the strong the right to roll roughshod over the consciences of the weak in the name of progress. He

94. Moo, *Romans*, 872.

95. Peter Adam, *Gospel Trials in 1662: To Stay or to Go?* (London: Latimer Trust, 2012), 56.

96. Cf. Dunn, *Romans*, 2:842; Keck, *Romans*, 346–47, contra Talbert, *Romans*, 319.

does not demand that the weak surrender what they regard as sacred. Rather, Paul wants the weak to keep their judgments between themselves and God lest they usurp God's authority to judge his servants.

## Helpful Principles

On approaching disputable matters, we have to be realistic. It is hard to strike a balance that will please everyone. We have to balance liberty and love, protecting consciences while striving for consensus, and do it without lurching toward either license or legalism in the process. In the end, I would say that Romans 14 contains several helpful principles that we should apply to the disputable matters that might arise in our churches.[97]

***Learn to Differentiate between Areas of Conviction and Areas of Command.*** I think this is one of the hardest things that we can learn how to do. What are the beliefs and practices that require conformity and are the areas that allow flexibility? I hope we all agree that believing in the Trinity is mandatory and abstaining from adultery is necessary. But what about the doctrine of election or belief that Christians should not go on dates without a chaperone? Are those beliefs the basis for fellowship or purely a matter of conscience?

Generally speaking, I think the big ticket items of our faith are found in the Apostles' Creed and Nicene Creed, since they have historically been symbols and signs of the apostolic faith. Those are the subjects that all churches should require consensus and comprise a basis for fellowship. Churches with a particular confessional bent or a set of denominational distinctives may also require ministers and adherents to subscribe to a wider body of teachings as well in order to preserve their distinctive way of reading Scripture and their unique way of being the church. In addition, there is a fairly recognizable common core of beliefs about what is considered holy living and righteous conduct that is incumbent on followers of Jesus. However, beyond the major creeds, denominational distinctives, and basic ethics, we should be hesitant to prescribe a theology or a set of behaviors for persons, because the result can be a legalistic construction that places more authority of human tradition than on the freedom of the Spirit.

***Don't Major on Minor Doctrines or Minor on Major Doctrines.*** We need to develop a triage of beliefs and place those beliefs into the categories of primary, secondary, and tertiary beliefs. Major beliefs are those that all Christians should agree on. These are the "mere Christianity" doctrines about

97. Bird, *Bird's-Eye View of Paul*, 154.

God, Jesus, the Holy Spirit, salvation by grace through faith, and eternal life. Without them we can scarcely be called Christians.

Then there are secondary beliefs, which are those beliefs that determine the texture of our theology and have ramifications for the nature of our church. These beliefs include baptism, the nature of the Lord's Supper, eschatology, and church government. This is the kind of stuff that can be significant, but nobody is going to run anybody out of town over it.

Then there are teriary beliefs, matters of conscience and conviction, matters that we leave to the freedom of individuals and families to decide for themselves without judging them. Among tertiary beliefs are those like whether a Christian should drink alcohol, approaches to homeschooling, or what Bible translation we should use. What you should remember is that if you major on minor things, you'll end up as a cranky fundamentalist and cling to human-centered teachings that will choke the gospel of grace. What you should also remember is that if you minor on major things, you'll end up as a raving liberal, venerating teachings that are contrary to Scripture and permitting a pattern of life that is worldly in the worst possible sense. There is an old German proverb that speaks to this: The most important thing is to make sure the most important thing remains the most important thing.

Withhold judgment where the gospel is not threatened and where holiness is not compromised. If the gospel is at the center of our faith, guarding the integrity of the gospel will be a major task for the construction and application of Christian doctrine. Similarly, if the church is called to be holy, we must pursue holiness through committed discipleship and even the application of church discipline. However, where the gospel is not threatened and where holiness is not compromised, our automatic response should be to encourage freedom of conscience.

***Exercise Your Convictions to Build Others Up, Not to Tear Them Down.*** When it comes to tertiary matters, matters of conscience and freedom, we have to exercise our convictions to build each other up. If you feel that you have freedom to drink alcohol responsibly at home or in public, don't flaunt it or shove it in the face of someone who is sensitive about it. Similarly, if you feel the need to abstain from alcohol, do so to God's glory, but don't take it on yourself to try to make people feel guilty if they choose to enjoy the fruit of the vine or some amber ale. It is okay to have different convictions about such things. The real test of maturity and the real measure of the love for one another is how we express our convictions with those who do not share them.

I have friends and students, some of whom I wish were just as conservative as me, and others whom I wish were just as free as me. However, whether they are as conservative or as free as I am, there is no disputable matter that I'm prepared to injure them over in order to clone them after my own convictions. Usually the best way to influence people for the best is not by judging them, but by letting them judge the godliness of your own example.

***Do Not Exchange Freedom in Christ for Slavery to Human Tradition.*** While we should do our best not to offend those who do not share our sense of freedom about disputable matters like drinking alcohol or watching certain television shows, still, we must be prepared to assert our freedom in Christ against those who would try to take it away. The way of Christ is the way of freedom and the Holy Spirit is the spirit of freedom. If a group of people within a church try to begin to impose their own convictions on tertiary matters on others, especially those who are vulnerable to being bullied, then those who are mature have a responsibility to graciously oppose them. Just as Paul opposed Peter for not walking according to the truth of the gospel when he separated from Gentiles during table fellowship (see Gal 2:11 – 14), so too we have to stand up to some people when Christian freedom is under threat. We cannot exchange freedom in Christ for slavery to human tradition.

***In All Times Act in Love and Carry Each Other's Burdens.*** When it comes to getting along on tertiary topics and disputable matters, love should be our guiding rule. If we love each other, we want the best for each other. If we love each other, we will not hurt each other over matters of food, drink, and entertainment. If we love each other, we will surely prefer to be wronged ourselves than to wrong others. If we love each other, we will be compelled to think of others ahead of ourselves. If we love each other, we will value the freedom of our friends more than the resolve of our own convictions on minor matters. If we love each other and want the best for each other, we'll learn that hugs are more likely to influence someone for good than hurtful comments. Whenever the topic is tertiary, love should be primary.

I believe that following the above checklist is how we can "make every effort to do what leads to peace and to mutual edification" (Rom 14:19). The underlying principle, as many have said before, is "in the essentials unity, in the nonessentials liberty, but in all things charity."[98] We need to make it so in the church today and tomorrow as well.

98. I have heard this saying attributed variously to Augustine, Richard Baxter, John Wesley, and Billy Graham.

CHAPTER 28

# Romans 15:14–33

## LISTEN to the Story

[14]I myself am convinced, my brothers and sisters, that you yourselves
are full of goodness, filled with knowledge and competent to instruct one
another. [15]Yet I have written you quite boldly on some points to remind
you of them again, because of the grace God gave me [16]to be a minister of
Christ Jesus to the Gentiles. He gave me the priestly duty of proclaiming
the gospel of God, so that the Gentiles might become an offering
acceptable to God, sanctified by the Holy Spirit.

[17]Therefore I glory in Christ Jesus in my service to God. [18]I will
not venture to speak of anything except what Christ has accomplished
through me in leading the Gentiles to obey God by what I have said and
done— [19]by the power of signs and wonders, through the power of the
Spirit of God. So from Jerusalem all the way around to Illyricum, I have
fully proclaimed the gospel of Christ. [20]It has always been my ambition
to preach the gospel where Christ was not known, so that I would not be
building on someone else's foundation. [21]Rather, as it is written:

> "Those who were not told about him will see,
> and those who have not heard will understand."

[22]This is why I have often been hindered from coming to you.

[23]But now that there is no more place for me to work in these regions,
and since I have been longing for many years to visit you, [24]I plan to
do so when I go to Spain. I hope to see you while passing through and
to have you assist me on my journey there, after I have enjoyed your
company for a while. [25]Now, however, I am on my way to Jerusalem in
the service of the Lord's people there. [26]For Macedonia and Achaia were
pleased to make a contribution for the poor among the Lord's people in
Jerusalem. [27]They were pleased to do it, and indeed they owe it to them.
For if the Gentiles have shared in the Jews' spiritual blessings, they owe
it to the Jews to share with them their material blessings. [28]So after I
have completed this task and have made sure that they have received this
contribution, I will go to Spain and visit you on the way. [29]I know that

when I come to you, I will come in the full measure of the blessing of Christ.

[30]I urge you, brothers and sisters, by our Lord Jesus Christ and by the love of the Spirit, to join me in my struggle by praying to God for me. [31]Pray that I may be kept safe from the unbelievers in Judea and that the contribution I take to Jerusalem may be favorably received by the Lord's people there, [32]so that I may come to you with joy, by God's will, and in your company be refreshed. [33]The God of peace be with you all. Amen.

*Listening to the texts in the story:* Isaiah 52:15; 61:6; 66:19–20.

I like to think of the final major section of Romans 15:14–16:27 as a missionary forum where Paul presents a report on his missionary activities (15:14–33), greets fellow missionaries and their congregations (16:1–16), before offering a final note (16:17–20), giving his final greetings (16:21–24), and closing with a doxology (16:25–27). After the intense and even taxing argumentation in the preceding chapters, one might anticipate Paul lightening the mood with some gentle and cordial remarks about how nice it would be to get together some time. Yet there is little drop in the intensity as Paul keeps pressing on about the mission of God, the mission of the apostles, and the mission of the church. It's all about mission, mission, mission! This point goes to show that Romans is theology written from the frantic frontline of the mission field, not in the serene surroundings of a seminary professor's office.

We see in 15:14–33 one of the longest explanations Paul gives about his apostolic labors. We have a window, however small, into Paul's conception of his mission in its geographical and theological sweep. Paul identifies himself as a key protagaonist in the biblical story. He is—in the Isaianic sense—a survivor of exile, a priest, who goes on a preaching circuit to tell the furtherest islands and nations that the time has come for them to join Israel in worship of the one true God (see Isa 66:19–20). Paul announces also his plans to visit a church that he neither founded nor previously visited, but where several of his fellow coworkers now reside. It becomes apparent here that much of the letter is really preparing the ground work for that visit and tacitly assuming their support for his mission to Spain. It is in 1:8–15 and 15:14–33 that we get the closest indication as to what the purpose of Paul's letter really is. And we have to say that it becomes clear that Romans is partly at least a fundraising letter.

Paul's goal is to inform the Romans of his missionary work to date and how it relates to his plans to travel to Jerusalem, Rome, and Spain. (1) Paul affirms his confidence in the Roman believers and describes his service in the

| Similar Themes between Romans 1:8–15 and 15:14–33 | | |
|---|---|---|
| 1:8 | Thanksgiving/Blessing | 15:33 |
| 1:8 | Paul's commendation of the Romans | 15:14 |
| 1:9 | Prayer | 15:30–32 |
| 1:9, 15 | Paul's evangelical task | 15:16, 19–20 |
| 1:11–12 | Paul's desire for mutual benefit | 15:23–24, 28–29 |
| 1:13a | Hindrances in visiting Rome | 15:22 |
| 1:13b | Paul's ministry to Gentiles | 15:15–21 |
| 1:14 | Indebtedness | 15:25–27 |

gospel (vv. 14–21); (2) Paul explains why he has not yet visited the Romans and why he hopes go to Spain (vv. 22–29); and (3) Paul makes a prayer request for his visit to Jerusalem before he goes to Spain (vv. 30–33).

### Paul's Missionary Map (15:14–21)

No sooner has Paul prayed for the Romans to be infused by the Holy Spirit with joy, peace, and hope than he lunges ahead to commend them and to explain his missionary endeavors to them.

"I myself am convinced, my brothers and sisters, that you yourselves are full of goodness, filled with knowledge and competent to instruct one another" (v. 14). Just like 1:5, 14, Paul again is sensitive to the fact that he is writing to a church that he neither planted nor pastored, hence the apologetic tone of his commendation in vv. 14–15.[1] Paul's commendation focuses on their moral qualities ("full of goodness"), their spiritual insight ("filled with knowledge"), and their didactic abilities ("competent to instruct one another"). This is not frivolous flattery, but a rhetorical move common in ancient letters where a writer extols the qualities of the readers in order to elicit their support for his request (see esp. Phlm 21). Paul's confidence in their abilities is to be met with their compliance to his requests.

The compliments are not necessarily mere hyperbole or sheer vanity. The reason they are "full of goodness" is because they are "filled with knowledge" and therefore have a comprehensive understanding of the Christian faith, including God's saving purposes.[2] They have corporately achieved a point

1. Moo, *Romans*, 887.
2. Dunn, *Romans*, 2:858; Moo, *Romans*, 888.

of maturity whereby they are now competent to dedicate themselves to one another's continuing instruction and edification. Thus Paul does not think in writing to the Romans that he was starting from scratch or working with a blank slate. Much of what he has said to them should be revision rather than anything particularly new.

Paul has alluded throughout the letter to what are probably shared hymnic and confessional formulas that the Romans should well know (see Rom 1:3–4; 4:25; 10:9–10). Paul noted that they have received a certain body of teaching already (6:17). He even extolled their faith as something reported and celebrated among other Christian groups in the east (1:8; cf. 16:19). Paul is trying to show them the various implications of the gospel in the hope that the way he expounds their common faith will win them over to the specifically Pauline way of doing missionary business. To that end, he is trying to infuse more gospel into their theology and daily life, defending himself against rumors and misunderstandings, repairing some fault lines among the Roman networks, and hopefully winning over their support for his trip to Spain. Assuming all goes well, they are the perfect partners for the next phase of his apostolic work in the west—hence their need to understand where he was coming from.

Irrespective of their moral, spiritual, and didactic qualities, Paul confesses that he has been rather bold in his letter, but with good reason: "Yet I have written you quite boldly on some points to remind you of them again, because of the grace God gave me to be a minister of Christ Jesus to the Gentiles. He gave me the priestly duty of proclaiming the gospel of God, so that the Gentiles might become an offering acceptable to God, sanctified by the Holy Spirit" (vv. 15–16). Paul is mostly reminding the Romans about several things in relation to God, Messiah, righteousness, the Holy Spirit, Israel, and the future. Even so, he has been "bold" or "courageous" in what he has had to say. In particular, his diatribal side swipes "Don't you know" (Rom 6:3, 16; 7:1) and his concern that they not be "ignorant" (11:25) on certain matters are a superdirect way of saying, "You really ought to have a grip on this!" The reason why Paul has engaged in a bit of apostolic audacity is he because he does not want them to be "unaware" of his proposed itinerary (1:13) and how it relates to the divine "grace" that he has received to be an apostle (1:5; 15:15). Jewett states: "As one can see from Paul's use of this same expression in 1 Cor 3:10 and Gal 2:9, his entire existence grows out of this grace-filled call to an ecumenical ministry."[3]

3. Jewett, *Romans*, 906.

The "grace" that Paul has received is notable in a few ways. First, he is a minister (*leitourgos*) for Messiah Jesus to the Gentiles, that is, taking the message of the Messiah to the Gentiles.

Second, Paul describes this evangelistic ministry as a "priestly duty," and the verb *hierourgeō* means to perform holy service as a priest.[4] Evidently Paul's "cult" is the gospel.[5] I am convinced that what lies behind this text is probably Isaiah 61, where the Servant is anointed to "proclaim good news" (61:1) and God says of the Servant that "you will be called priests of the LORD, you will be named ministers of our God. You will feed on the wealth of nations, and in their riches you will boast."[6] The notion that Paul is identifying himself as the Isaianic Servant might seem self-inflated or grossly presumptive, yet he does it on several occasions (see Gal 1:15–26; Col 1:24)—probably because he believed, just as Romans 15:18 declares, that Jesus is at work in him (see esp. Acts 13:46–47).

Third, the goal of Paul's priestly-evangelistic ministry is expressed in cultic imagery, namely, to make Gentiles become "an offering acceptable to God, sanctified by the Holy Spirit." This is not the only time that has used cultic language to talk about himself (see Phil 2:16–17) and the obedience of Christians (see Rom 12:1–2). I think that the offering is the Gentiles themselves (see Isa 66:20), not their gifts for the Jerusalem collection, but dovetailing with 12:1, part of that offering is the worship of the Gentiles who offer God "glory" (15:9) and "obedience" (15:18).[7] The use of cultic language is deliberate as Paul believes that his life's work is built on bringing an offering to God that consists of Gentiles who are sanctified by the Spirit into an "acceptable offering." Unlike other Hellenistic Jews, Paul does not "spiritualize" the notion of sacrifice; it is more proper to say that he proceeds to transform

---

4. BDAG 471.

5. According to D. W. B. Robinson ("The Priesthood of Paul in the Gospel of Hope," in *Reconciliation and Hope* [ed. R. J. Banks; FS Leon Morris; Grand Rapids: Eerdmans, 1974], 232): "Paul cannot separate his own role from the operation of the gospel which he thus expounds to his Gentile readers in Rome. Romans is both an exposition of the gospel of hope and at the same time Paul's *apologia* for his 'priesthood' in that gospel."

6. Richard J. Gibson, "Paul as Missionary in Priestly Service of the Servant-Christ (Romans 15:16)," in *Paul as Missionary: Identity, Activity, Theology and Practice* (eds. T. J. Burke and B. T. Rosner; LNTS 420; London: T&T Clark, 2011), 55–62. Also worthy of consideration is Whittle (*Covenant Renewal*, 166), who identifies a new Moses typology in this verse: "Moses' ministry as priestly covenant mediator, consecrating Israel at the mountain, could be a background for Paul's mediation of the gospel of God and consecration of the Gentiles at the constitution of this people." See similarly Dunn, *Romans*, 2:868.

7. The genitive phrase *hē prosphora tōn ethnōn*, "the offering of the Gentiles," is not a genitive of source as in an offering *from* Gentiles, but a genitive of apposition with "the Gentiles might become an offering" (see NIV, NJB, NLT). See discussion in Robinson, "Priesthood of Paul," 231; Gupta, *Worship that Makes Sense to Paul*, 131; Whittle, *Covenant Renewal*, 167–73.

sacrifice because he identifies the church as the eschatological fulfillment of God's new covenant people.[8]

It is because of this service that Paul says, "Therefore I glory in Christ Jesus in my service to God" (v. 17). His "glory" is a boast (*kauchēsis*), not strictly in "my service to God" as the NIV renders it, but more literally "in the things to do with God" (*ta pros ton theon*). There is again a priestly connotation here since in Hebrews 2:17 we find a similar phrase used to describe Jesus as a "faithful high priest in service to God." Although Paul can elsewhere speak of his only boast being "in the Lord" or his "cross" (see 1 Cor 1:31; 2 Cor 10:17; Gal 6:14), in the next verse he explains why he can boast in the Messiah about his priestly service, namely, because of what the Messiah has achieved through him: "I will not venture to speak of anything except what Christ has accomplished through me in leading the Gentiles to obey God by what I have said and done—by the power of signs and wonders, through the power of the Spirit of God" (vv. 18–19a).

Thankfully, most translations clear up Paul's clumsy double negative (lit., "For I will *not* dare to speak about anything which the Messiah has *not* achieved through me"). This is probably a roundabout way of saying that Paul has the right to boast of these things, because they are not strictly his work, but the Messiah's work, and he is merely the vessel through whom the Messiah acts. The accent falls on divine enablement so that Paul's success in ministry is really the success of the Messiah. That ministry has been to bring "the Gentiles to obey God."

I want to press the point that getting immoral idolatrous pagans to obey God is a key theme of the letter (see Rom 1:5; 16:26). Paul was probably dogged by rumors that he was just peddling Judaism minus Moses for Gentiles. As if he was telling Gentiles that they could be part of Israel, receive covenantal blessings, and even inherit eternal life without having to adopt the rituals and regulations of the Jewish way of life. In other words, Paul's gospel was dissed for being antinomianism, as if he was promoting the idea that one just had to believe this stuff, but could feel free to keep being pagan. But nothing is further from the truth. Paul believed that the main thrust of his ministry was leading Gentiles to God through the Messiah and in the Spirit so that they would "obey" God, and so fulfill God's law (see Rom 13:8–10; Gal 5:14; 6:2).

Thus, when the Gentiles are caught by the gospel and taught to obey God, Paul says they can be brought as an offering to God. In that ministry to bring Gentiles to the obedience of faith, Paul has worked with the evangelistic word ("by word"), holy living and compassionate service ("by deed"), and even a charismatic ministry ("by the power of signs and wonders through the power

8. Dunn, *Romans*, 2:859, and esp. Peter T. O'Brien, *Consumed by Passion: Paul and the Logic of the Gospel* (Homebush West: Lancer, 1993), 31–32.

of the Spirit of God"). Paul emphasizes across his letters that his evangelistic message was accompanied by demonstrations of the Spirit's powerful work (see 1 Cor 2:4; 2 Cor 12:12; Gal 3:5; 1 Thess 1:5). We don't know for sure what these powerful deeds were, but in light of passages like Acts 14:8–18, we can imagine healings for the sick were probably prominent among them.

Paul then describes the geographical arc of his apostolic ministry: "So from Jerusalem all the way around to Illyricum, I have fully proclaimed the gospel of Christ" (v. 19b). That Paul's ministry begins with "Jerusalem" is not on account of the historical origins of the Christain faith in Jerusalem but probably because an earlier phase of Paul's ministry was mostly oriented toward his fellow Jews before he began his more concerted work to the Gentiles (see Acts 9:26–30; 26:20). From Jerusalem he embarked on several journeys through Syria, Cilicia, Asia Minor, and across the Aegean to Greece. At the end of this arc (*kuklō*, lit., "in a circle") is "Illyricum," on the Balkan coast of the Adriatic Sea, directly opposite northern Italy, and approximate to modern Albania. We do not have any report in either his epistles or in Acts of Paul ever visiting that region; however, during his time in Greece, he may have made forays to the north of Macedonia and into Illyricum at some point. Alternatively "to" (*mechri*) might mean "up to" rather than "into," and his mission work in Macedonia might be sufficient to have reached this point.[9]

Central to Paul's aim is to announce the Messiah in places where he is otherwise unknown: "It has always been my ambition to preach the gospel where Christ was not known, so that I would not be building on someone else's foundation" (v. 20). Paul sees himself as something of a pioneer, boldly going where no apostle had gone before. This is why Paul often refers to himself as a "builder" establishing a foundation for God's work in new territories (see 1 Cor 3:10–15; 2 Cor 10:15–16). He bolsters the idea with a citation of Isaiah 52:15, "Rather, as it is written: 'Those who were not told about him will see, and those who have not heard will understand' " (v. 21). In context, Isaiah 52:13–15 refers to the Isaianic Servant being announced before nations and kings, startling them, often leaving them speechless as they are forced to contemplate what God has done to and for the Servant. This, Paul says, is what he's been doing from Jerusalem around to Illyricum, getting Gentiles mesmerized and mystified by the message of the Messiah.

### All Roads Lead to Spain ... via Jerusalem and Rome! (15:22–29)

Paul began the letter noting his unfulfilled desire to come to Rome (Rom 1:10, 13), wanting to impart a spiritual gift to them (1:11), to mutually

---

9. Dunn, *Romans*, 2:864.

encourage each other (1:12), and to undertake some evangelistic work in their midst (1:13–15). Happily for Paul the next move in his missionary itinerary is Spain, and this requires going to Rome. What has thus far prevented Paul from visiting them (1:13) is the ministry he has been conducting in the regions of Palestine, Syria, Asia Minor, and Greece (15:19b). Hence his words: "This is why I have often been hindered from coming to you" (v. 22) which finally and fully explains the absence of the apostle to the Gentiles to the largest and most prominent Gentile city in the world.

The reason why he is now set to visit Rome is: "But now that there is no more place for me to work in these regions, and since I have been longing for many years to visit you, I plan to do so when I go to Spain" (vv. 23–24a). It might seem grossly exaggerated to say that "there is no more place for me to work in these regions," given the tiny number of congregations spread across the eastern Mediterranean coastland at this time. We might naturally ask after the other cites of Greece, Asia Minor, and Syria. However, we need to remember that Paul was careful to set up congregations in strategically important cities like Ephesus, Corinth, Philippi, Thessalonica, and Athens, which would naturally spread into outlying areas. For case in point, the churches in Ephesus were probably responsible for establishing house churches in Colossae, Laodicea, and Hierapolis in the Lycus Valley.[10]

If it is new missionary territory one is after, however, then Spain was definitely ripe for it. Spain might seem an odd choice given its remoteness and the fact that Latin rather than Greek was more widely spoken and it had next to no Jewish presence as far as we know.[11] Scholars have speculated that Paul's aim was to continue his mission around the northern side of the Mediterranean, ending in Spain, and then complete the circuit by preaching along the south side of the Mediterranean, passing through the Roman provinces of Mauritania, Numidia, Africa, Cyrenaica, and Egypt.[12] Paul was probably spurned on by Isaiah, who spoke of the coastlands and islands hearing about God, the Lord of Israel (see Isa 11:11; 41;1; 42:4, 10; 49:1; 51:5; 60:9), and biblical mentions of "Tarshish" in the Old Testament that refer to a sea port probably in southern Spain (see Pss 48:7; 72:10; Isa 23:1, 6, 10, 14; 60:9;

10. Jewett (*Romans*, 914) is correct: "What Paul claims is not that he has preached the gospel in every conceivable location but that he had fulfilled his specific calling to establish churches in a sufficient number of important centers to make the subsequent missionizing of their regional hinterlands by local colleagues feasible."

11. W. P. Bowers, "Jewish Communities in Spain in the Time of Paul the Apostle," *JTS* 26 (1975): 395–402; Robert K. Jewett, "Paul, Phoebe, and the Spanish Mission," in *The Social World of Formative Christianity and Judaism* (ed. P. Borgen et al.; FS H. C. Kee; Philadelphia: Fortress, 1988), 142–61.

12. Wright, "Romans," 10:775; Witherington, *Romans*, 363; Kruse, *Romans*, 545.

66:19; Ezek 27:10; 38:13; Jonah 1:2; 4:2). Several commentators have wondered if what lies behind Paul's missionary itinerary is Isaiah 66:19–20 with its reference to the survivors of exile being sent to distant regions like Tarshish as a "sign" to tell the nations that it is time to flock to Zion to come and worship God. It is impossible to say for sure, but it is certainly likely.[13]

Paul then adds a short statement but an important one: "I hope to see you while passing through and to have you assist me on my journey there, after I have enjoyed your company for a while" (v. 24b). What Paul said earlier about how he and the Romans could mutually encourage each other (1:12) is reiterated in this verse. After he has enjoyed their company, blessed them, and worked with them for a brief time, he needs their help to go to Spain. What he probably needs is a mixture of money, provisions, a Latin translator or two, and a place to retreat to should things go poorly. Paul wants Rome to be his base of operations in the west just like Antioch was for his base in the east. This will give the Romans the chance to practice genuine fellowship as it is incumbent on them to do (see 12:13), just as other Gentile congregations have done (see 15:26).

Paul next mentions, in a somewhat ominous tone, that before he can go to Spain via Rome, he first has to visit Jerusalem to deliver the collection for the saints: "Now, however, I am on my way to Jerusalem in the service of the Lord's people there" (v. 25). Paul's more immediate travel plan is to return to Jerusalem to deliver the "service" for the "Lord's people." This service was a collection for the Jerusalem believers who were having tough economic times and in hard circumstances caused by sectarian tensions in Jerusalem that Paul himself once was party to. Over a number of years, Paul had been organizing a collection for the Jerusalem saints by raising funds from the churches in Galatia, Macedonia, and Achaia (see 1 Cor 16:1–5; 2 Cor 8:1–24). Let me add that this collection was not "A Polite Bribe" as one recent documentary has alleged, as if Paul had tried to purchase a Gentile franchise on a messianic religion. The collection was Paul's fulfilling his promise to the Jerusalem apostles to "remember the poor" (Gal 2:10), which correlates precisely with the Paul of Acts, where Paul is described by Luke as saying that he came "to Jerusalem to bring my people gifts for the poor and to present offerings" (Act 24:17).

The collection was more than mere charity; it was symbolic for the reciprocal unity between Jewish and Gentiles believers who lived out the precise type of common fellowship that Paul has sketched out in Romans 3–4; 9–11; and 14:1–15:13.[14] That is why Paul says: "For Macedonia and Achaia

13. Cf. discussion in Eckhard J. Schnabel, *Early Christian Mission* (2 vols.; Downers Grove, IL: InterVarsity, 2006) 2:1294–1300.

14. Wright, "Romans," 10:756.

were pleased to make a contribution for the poor among the Lord's people in Jerusalem. They were pleased to do it, and indeed they owe it to them. For if the Gentiles have shared in the Jews' spiritual blessings, they owe it to the Jews to share with them their material blessings" (vv. 26–27). This touches on a major theme of the letter, namely, the salvation of the Gentiles comes through the Jewish Messiah and the fulfillment of the promises made to Israel (see 1:16; 4:13–16; 11:17–24; 15:7–8). The Gentile Christians are indebted to their Jewish brothers and sisters since they have come to share in their spiritual blessings, so it is only right that their natural reflex is to share their material blessings with those in physical need.

For the Gentiles to provide a monetary gift to the Jewish Christians of Jerusalem was a sign that the Gentiles regarded them as elder siblings in the one family. For the Jewish Christians to accept the gift would be a testimony that they accepted God's work among the Gentiles and recognized their membership in the family of faith.[15] The collection would be a tangible symbol that the long-awaited pilgrimage of the Gentiles was actually taking place in the messianic communities established among the nations where Gentiles had been brought to obedience, and they were sending gifts to Jerusalem as symbolic evidences of the fact (see esp. Isa 45:14; 56:6–7; 60:6–7; 66:19–20; Mic 4:1–2, 13; Tob 13:11; 1QM 12.13–15).[16]

It is after this trip that Paul intends to visit Rome: "So after I have completed this task and have made sure that they have received this contribution, I will go to Spain and visit you on the way. I know that when I come to you, I will come in the full measure of the blessing of Christ" (vv. 28–29). Paul's itinerary is clear: Jerusalem, Rome, and then Spain. Sadly, however, we know from Acts 20–28 that Paul's arrival in Rome would take years rather than months and would nearly cost him his life! Enroute to Rome, Paul suffered beatings, was nearly lynched by a mob, almost assassinated, kept in prison unfairly, and suffered shipwreck. Probably not what he had in mind when he wrote Romans 15:28, but he did get to Rome in the end.

Paul was right that he would be warmly received by the Romans, as Luke reports that when Paul arrived at the coastal town of Puetoli in Italy, "There we found some brothers and sisters who invited us to spend a week with them. And so we came to Rome. The brothers and sisters there had heard that we were coming, and they traveled as far as the Forum of Appius and the Three Taverns to meet us. At the sight of these people Paul thanked God and

15. See Schreiner, *Romans*, 776–77; Wright, "Romans," 10:756.

16. Cf. McKnight, *Light Among the Gentiles*, 47–48; Bird, *Jesus and the Origins of the Gentile Mission*, 26–29.

was encouraged" (Act 28:14–15). Paul only survived such an arduous ordeal because "the blessing of Christ" accompanied him along the way.

**Paul's Prayer Request for Himself (15:30–33)**

Paul knows he is walking into a potential lynching in Jerusalem, and I don't mean that as a metaphor. So he asks the Romans to strive and struggle in prayer for him: "I urge you, brothers and sisters, by our Lord Jesus Christ and by the love of the Spirit, to join me in my struggle by praying to God for me. Pray that I may be kept safe from the unbelievers in Judea and that the contribution I take to Jerusalem may be favorably received by the Lord's people there, so that I may come to you with joy, by God's will, and in your company be refreshed. The God of peace be with you all. Amen" (vv. 30–33). The prayer is thoroughly trinitarian, taking place *through* Lord Jesus and *through* the love of the Holy Spirit and comes *before* God.

Paul requests prayer on two fronts: first, that he will be rescued from unbelievers in Judea (i.e., unbelieving Jews), who perceived him as an apostate and a traitor both to the Torah and to God. Paul's ministry to Gentiles was affronting to many pious Jews since it involved not only fraternizing with Gentiles but was premised on the notion that they were saveable as Gentiles without Torah (see Acts 21:20–21; 1 Thess 2:15). Paul's idea that the Gentiles were an "offering to God" and his collection was the firstfruits of the eschatological pilgrimage of the Gentiles to Zion would not have won approval in Jerusalem with the increasing anti-Roman sentiment brewing as evidenced by the rise of violent groups like the *Sicarii*[17] and the fact that rejecting Roman offerings in the Jerusalem temple was the catalyst for the revolt against Rome in AD 66.[18] Such was the hatred of Paul by zealous Jews that some even plotted to kill him on his way back to Jerusalem (see Acts 20:2–3).

Second, Paul asks for prayer that the collection he will deliverer would be acceptable to the Jerusalem believers, something that cannot automatically be assumed, given the often raucous antagonism between Paul and several other Jewish Christians.

It is after he runs the gauntlet in Jerusalem, facing danger from both within and outside of the church, that Paul intends to visit Rome. He longs to come to them in joy and to be refreshed by them. With the letter's main content over, Paul finishes with a brief blessing invoking "the God of peace," which can be nothing other than "the God who gives peace" (see 2 Cor 13:11; Gal 6:16; Eph 6:23; Phil 4:7–9; 1 Thess 5:23; 2 Thess 3:16).[19]

17. Cf. Josephus *Ant.* 20.186, 204, 208–10; *War* 2.254, 425; 4.400.
18. Josephus, *War* 2.409–10.
19. Moo, *Romans*, 911.

The story behind Romans 15:14–33 is that God has made his people a kingdom of priests to preach good news to the nations and to lead them in worship of the one true God. Mission is an eschatological event whereby the Messiah mediates the message of divine mercy through his priestly servants. A godly ambition for the churches, then, is to keep our evangelical ambition fresh as we carry out our priestly and pastoral duties as heralds of the good news.

### Fulfilling the Gospel in Worship and Mission

John Piper puts it wonderfully: "Mission exists because worship doesn't."[20] Paul himself would wholeheartedly agree, because he believed that the Messiah fulfilled the promises made to the patriarchs so that "the Gentiles might glorify God for his mercy" (15:9). When Paul said that his ambition was to preach "the gospel where Christ was not named," he meant that he was going to announce the Messiah precisely where the Messiah was not worshiped.[21] When Paul said that he had "fully proclaimed the gospel" (15:19), he meant that he had fulfilled part of the plan by working to bring Gentiles out of idolatry to worship the true and living God. Mission means creating worshipers of the triune God revealed in the gospel of God. Mission means saving and sanctifying a people who confess the Lord, who call on the name of the Messiah, and who follow the leading of the Spirit.

The sum of all of our studies in Romans should also be driving toward this same missional task. As Wright says: "Just as the principal and ultimate goal of all historical work on J. S. Bach ought to be a more sensitive and intelligent performance of his music, so the principal and ultimate goal of all historical work on the New Testament ought to be a more sensitive and intelligent practice of Christian mission and discipleship."[22]

As I read this text over and over, one little word in the Greek text stands out, "ambition" (*philotimeomai*) in Romans 15:20. Paul has an ambition to preach Christ to those who do not know him. We need to add the caveat that there are obviously intrinsic dangers to having ambitions to accomplish great things. Ambition to be successful no matter what the price is not helpful or wholesome. Ambition even in a good cause should not lead us to be underhanded or manipulative in our pursuits. That said, the evangelical churches have historically been defined by their evangelical ambition. In common

---

20. John Piper, *Let the Nations Be Glad: The Supremacy of God in Missions* (Grand Rapids: Baker, 2010), 15.

21. Moo, *Romans*, 896.

22. Wright, *Paul and the Faithfulness of God*, 2:1483–84.

parlance the label "evangelical" can mean to have bucket loads of enthusiasm for something. For example, I once heard the British celebrity chef Nigella Lawson say that she was "positively evangelical" about how to cook a good Christmas dinner. I'm glad the word "evangelical" still has that connotation; we just need to live up to it. We need to keep kindling the fires of evangelical ambition in our hearts, homes, and halls so that the desire to bring men and women into the family of faith and to worship God never dies out.

I remain thankful for those great heroes of Christian mission who had a zealous evangelical ambition to make the gospel known in distant regions of the earth—persons like Pantaenus who went to India in the second century to William Taylor who went to British India in the nineteenth century. Let us not forget either the example of great figures in modern missions like the Moravian brethren, John Eliot, David Brainerd, David Livingstone, Hudson Taylor, Richard Johnson, Fanny Butler, Thomas Bray, Amy Carmichael, Gladys Aylward, and countless others. Most received little recognition in their own day. Often they knew hardship and suffering, many were expelled and mocked, and some were even martyred. Yet we remember them as heroes of the faith because of their passion for mission and for promoting the gospel. We can learn from their evangelical ambition and strive to imitate them on the missional frontiers set before us. Following Paul's example, we need to discern what is our own Jerusalem, our own Illyricum, and our own Spain where we are called to go to and preach the gospel.

Such ambitions, of course, can be fraught with all sorts of risks and uncertainties if you begin to act on them. Along the way there can be unexpected turns and sudden changes in life direction. As for me personally, on account of my teaching ministry, I've lived in three cities in the last five years stretching over two continents. I have a friend in central Asia who intended to go there to help out some churches temporarily, but instead ended up running a theological college permanently. I know of previous students of mine who embarked on what they thought was a short-term mission to a particular place only to find themselves in the same place some ten years later. The mysterious joy of missions is that we will often never know in advance what doors will open or close, what people will be brought to us or taken from us, and what triumphs and defeats we will come across. However, whatever it is we aspire to do for God, we know that we do it for a great God, who is able to use us despite ourselves, despite any trying circumstances, to further his glory and to extend his kingdom into the darkest places of the earth. In our missionary ventures we take big leaps of faith because we worship a big and faithful God.

Our ambition to serve God can lead us into all sorts of strange ventures, many of which don't seem terribly important at the time, but can later reap wonderful harvests completely unknown to us. If we are open to the Spirit's leading, many of the things that we think are insignificant can end up yielding major significance. A prayer prayed for someone, a phone call or an email to check up on a friend, a meal cooked for a grieving family, a Bible given to a teenager, or a cup of water given to a thirsty woman on a street corner. We never know what is going to come of the work we do along the way. We dedicate ourselves to service knowing that while our ambitions may not always come to fruition the way we hope they will, God's plan to use us to achieve his purposes always succeeds. Remember that for all of Paul's planning he never actually made it Spain,[23] and yet: "One of the most important lessons in Romans 15 might be put thus: God allowed Paul to dream of Spain in order that he might write Romans."[24]

### The Priestly Service of the Gospel

Paul speaks ever so chirpily of the "priestly duty/service of proclaiming the gospel." For me, this verse is the basis for a genuinely evangelical conception of ministry as priesthood. It's also been deeply formative for my own desire to enter into the Anglican priesthood, and I am currently discerning the call of God on my life to be a priestly proclaimer of the gospel in addition to being a Christian academic. The very mention of "priesthood" may well set off some big alarm bells for a good many folks. Many of my free church readers might be rather concerned that we do not take this priestly language too seriously lest we absorb it into our ideas about ministry and pastoring. The reason is that it is routinely thought that "priests" are part of that awful Catholic theology with its belief in clericalism, self-assured mediators of grace, and venerating religious paraphernalia. So it is probably best just to leave any priestly notion at the level of metaphor lest we get sucked into anything a bit too high-churchy.[25]

The problem is that metaphors matter because they represent true things. In the same way that a pastor is not literally a shepherd out in a field with sheep, neither is a priest one who stands in a literal temple offering dead animals in sacrifice. However, there is something about shepherding that makes it fitting to describe ministers as pastors. Similarly, there is something about the nature of ministry that makes it fitting to describe ministers as priests.

The other thing I have to say is that I'm not Catholic. I'm devotedly Reformed, but the Catholic theology of priesthood makes for an interesting read, especially when you grasp what Catholics actually say about priesthood

23. Though there is the claim in *1 Clement* 5.7 that he did make it there.

24. Wright, "Romans," 10:758–59.

25. Cf. Dunn, *Romans*, 2:860; Jervis, *Purpose of Romans*, 121; Moo, *Romans*, 890.

rather than rely on caricatures.[26] Catholic ideas of priesthood rest on the assertion of Thomas Aquinas who wrote on Hebrews 8:4, "Only Christ is the true priest, the others being only his ministers."[27] One of the Catholic catechism's key assertions about the priesthood would be acceptable to many other Christian traditions:

> Christ, high priest and unique mediator, has made of the Church "a kingdom, priests for his God and Father" [Rev 1:6; 5:9–10; 1 Pet 2:5, 9]. The whole community of believers is, as such, priestly. The faithful exercise their baptismal priesthood through their participation, each according to his own vocation, in Christ's mission as priest, prophet, and king.[28]

Before we disagree with conceptions of ministry as priesthood, first we have to determine what we might find agreeable.

So, in a qualified sense, I'm favorably disposed to the notion of a Christian priesthood for both the laity and clergy (I'd have to take you through Hebrews to do it properly). For not only does Paul talk clearly about a "priestly service" in the gospel, but Catholic, Orthodox, and Anglican traditions have long identified its ordained ministers as "priests." I realize that some will balk at this, but before anyone cries, "Burn the papal priestly prelate!" or "Away with Bird, give us Barabbas!" please indulge me for a moment. Let me ask you this: What do you call someone who engages in carpentry services? I can imagine you replying: a carpenter! What do you call someone who engages in electrical services? Obviously an electrician! And lastly, what do you call someone who engages in consulting services? Again, obviously a consultant! So what do you call someone who engages in the priestly service of proclaiming the gospel as Paul says here? Before you answer, take a deep breath, shake your first in rage, engage in momentary denial, lapse into cognitive dissonance, now breathe out, and accept that the answer is, yes, a priest! According to Paul, the proclamation of the gospel is a sacred work that can be described in priestly language.

At this point I need to define what I think a priest actually is, and a proper definition may alleviate some anxiety over usage of the word. According to the Australian Anglican ordinal, a priest is fundamentally a "pastor and teacher" who has as their chief charge to work "for God's glory and the strengthening of God's people." Part of the bishop's exhortation to priestly candidates is: "As the Lord's messenger, proclaim the gospel of Jesus Christ. Seek the lost,

26. See Catechism of the Catholic Church (*CCC*), sect. 2. chap 3, art. 6, paras. 1536–1571.
27. *CCC* para 1545.
28. *CCC* para 1546.

announce God's justice, warn and correct those in error. You are to encourage and build up the body of Christ, preaching the word of God, leading God's people in prayer, declaring God's forgiveness and blessing, and faithfully ministering the sacraments of God's grace with reverence and care."[29] Similarly, John Chrysostom said: "For me, the priesthood means to preach and to proclaim; this is the sacrifice I offer."[30]

In other words, our priestly ministry is the way we save, serve, sanctify, and edify a people through our gospel preaching and humble acts of service. When a priest/pastor/presbyter exercises that kind of ministry, God's people will be convicted, consoled, and consecrated. This priestly service in the gospel will lead to the "perfecting of the saints" and the "edifying of the body" (Eph 4:11 [KJV]).

To be honest, I'm not interested in converting readers into an Anglo-Catholic notion of priesthood. Each to their own for what name they use to describe the recipients for ordination! I've long thought that the spiritual qualities of a Christian leader are far more important than the labels used to identify them like Reverend, Father, Vicar, Pastor, Presbyter, Brother, Sister, Elder, Big Baptist Kahuna, Pressy Papa, or Snoop Pope Daddy. Yet I seriously wonder if we can avoid old factions and overrehearsed debates and appropriate the language of priestly service from Romans 15:16 when it comes to conceiving evangelical ministry. Even the most low-church of Christians can and should embrace the cultic language that Paul applies to ministry: sacrifice, service, temple, and priesthood.

Yet how does this imagery shape our conception of Christian service? Pastors may well want to see themselves as preparing their congregation as an offering to God or view their pastorate as a calling to build up the church like building a temple. Missionaries and evangelists might well consider the priestly nature of their calling to enable defiled sinners to stand before a holy God through the priestly work of Christ and reception of the Spirit of holiness. Teachers might want to be more thoroughly attuned to the need to sanctify their students by teaching them and nurturing them into holiness, peace, and joy. We can celebrate the sacred nature of our work without necessarily becoming sacerdotal about it.

If the church is corporately a kingdom of priests—something we can all agree on—we need to say what kind of priestly ministries we are conducting as a church. At the end of the day, the church is not a mediator presuming to offer access to Christ through its ministrations; rather, Christ sovereignly choses to mediate himself through his servants to make his word known to

29. *A Prayer Book for Australia* (Mulgrave, VIC: Broughton, 1995), 793.
30. Cited in Burns, *Romans*, 372.

the world. This is implication of Romans 15:18, where Paul says that it's not about what I do, it is about what the Messiah is achieving through me, so all glory be to him! The church as the body of Christ is the visible expression of Christ's presence on earth. I like what Whittle says:

> Whatever Paul's priestly service is therefore, it is salvation historical, in continuity with the patriarchs and the prophets, fulfilling the covenant promises, eschatological and climactic in the sense that Paul understands the promises to the fathers fulfilled in his ministry at the creation of this Jew and Gentile holy people. Christ has made this possible, but Paul has been commissioned to continue the work of Christ.[31]

And the same commission falls now to us too!

An underappreciated application of Paul's ministry is how servants of the gospel have the task of using their gifts, time, energies, and service to consecrate a people to God. We need to work in our churches to do our best to ensure that these folks, despite their struggles and setbacks, will prove to be blameless on the day of Christ Jesus and will be a fragrant and acceptable offering to God. Any Christian ministry, whether in a youth group or in a nursing home, is about preparing people to meet a holy God by receiving the holy gospel and living holy lives by those who are in Christ.

---

31. Whittle, *Covenant Renewal*, 159.

CHAPTER 29

# Romans 16:1 – 16

## LISTEN to the Story

[1]I commend to you our sister Phoebe, a deacon of the church in
Cenchreae. [2]I ask you to receive her in the Lord in a way worthy of his
people and to give her any help she may need from you, for she has been
the benefactor of many people, including me.

[3]Greet Priscilla and Aquila, my co-workers in Christ Jesus. [4]They
risked their lives for me. Not only I but all the churches of the Gentiles
are grateful to them.

[5]Greet also the church that meets at their house.

Greet my dear friend Epenetus, who was the first convert to Christ in the province of Asia.

[6]Greet Mary, who worked very hard for you.

[7]Greet Andronicus and Junia, my fellow Jews who have been in prison with me. They are outstanding among the apostles, and they were in Christ before I was.

[8]Greet Ampliatus, my dear friend in the Lord.

[9]Greet Urbanus, our co-worker in Christ, and my dear friend Stachys.

[10]Greet Apelles, whose fidelity to Christ has stood the test. Greet those who belong to the household of Aristobulus.

[11]Greet Herodion, my fellow Jew.

Greet those in the household of Narcissus who are in the Lord.

[12] Greet Tryphena and Tryphosa, those women who work hard in the Lord.

Greet my dear friend Persis, another woman who has worked very hard in the Lord.

[13]Greet Rufus, chosen in the Lord, and his mother, who has been a mother to me, too.

[14]Greet Asyncritus, Phlegon, Hermes, Patrobas, Hermas and the other brothers and sisters with them.

[15]Greet Philologus, Julia, Nereus and his sister, and Olympas and all the Lord's people who are with them.

[16]Greet one another with a holy kiss. All the churches of Christ send greetings.

*Listening to the texts in the story:* Luke 16:8; Acts 18:1 – 26; 1 Corintians 14:20; Justin, *Apology* 1.65.

Paul's greetings has a double purpose of commending the letter carrier Phoebe as his emissary to the Roman churches and of reinforcing the familial bonds that he enjoys with many of the Roman believers as well.

Phoebe, as we will see, was a prominent woman in the Pauline circle, and she was evidently a person of means and maturity whom Paul entrusted with delivering his letter to the Romans and conveying his wishes to them. She was, for all intents and purposes, Paul's personal apostle to the Romans. It is surely notable that 16:1 – 16 contains more personal greetings than all of Paul's other letters combined. The closest we come to it is Philemon 1 – 2 and Colossians 4:15 – 17, both written to the church in Colossae, a church that Paul did not himself found. The reason Paul names so many people is because he wants to demonstrate that he has many friends and allies in the Roman churches, encompassing both the "strong" and the "weak," and he greets them all without playing favorites. It is expected that Paul knows so many folks in Rome because of the mobility and travel of Christians across Roman roads and shipping routes. Merchants like Priscilla and Aquila had been in Corinth (Acts 18:2), and Ephesus (1 Cor 16:19; Acts 18:8), and recently they returned to Rome after Claudius's death (Rom 16:3).

The twenty-six persons greeted encompasses a mixture of friends and coworkers as well several individuals whom Paul does not directly know. The list of persons greeted is impressive for its diversity since it includes a number of persons with slave names, eight women and eighteen men, a majority of Gentiles but clearly a cohort of Jewish Christians as well, and persons associated with the prominent households of Aristobulus and Narcissus. Many scholars are of the mind that Paul mentions at least five house churches.[1] This includes:

The church in the house of Priscilla and Aquila (16:5)
Those among the house of Aristobulus (16:10)
Those among the house of Narcissus (16:11)
Asyncritus and his brothers and sisters (16:14)
Philologus and the Lord's holy people (16:15)

1. See further, Lampe, *From Paul to Valentinus*, 153 – 83.

There certainly may have been more than five house churches or meeting groups in Rome, but these are the ones we can best identify from Paul's greetings.[2]

Paul wants his patron Phoebe to receive a warm welcome from the Roman believers and perhaps wants her personally to extend his greetings to all the persons so named as part of a "charm offensive" ahead of Paul's visit. The greetings can be broken down into: (1) Paul's commendation of Phoebe to the Romans (vv. 1–2); (2) Paul's personal greetings to the five (or so) house churches in Rome (vv. 3–15); and (3) Paul's final admonition for his emissaries to be greeted with genuine affection (v. 16).

## EXPLAIN the Story

### Phoebe: Corinthian Deacon and Pauline Benefactor (16:1–2)

Paul begins his closing greetings by commending his envoy Phoebe: "I commend to you our sister Phoebe, a deacon of the church in Cenchreae" (v. 1). Letters of recommendation were important in the ancient world where any Josephus or Sallianus could present themselves claiming to be somebody (see Acts 18:27; 2 Cor 3:1–3; Col 4:10). Paul here provides a commendation of Phoebe to the believers in Rome as a bonafide messenger on his behalf. As a "sister" she is part of the family of faith and enjoys familial bonds with the Roman believers. She is from Cenchreae, the eastern seaport of Corinth, before the canal was dug between the two. Phoebe is probably a merchant, perhaps a widow, with enough financial means to travel to Rome. I doubt she traveled alone, and she probably would have had escorts accompanying her, such as slaves, freedmen, friends, or relatives.

Paul describes her as a *diakonos*, which can mean either "servant" in the more general sense (see KJV, NASB, ESV, NET, HCSB), or "deacon" in the more specific sense (see NIV, NRSV, NLT, CEB, or NJB with "deaconess"). Either option is strictly possible. We know of household leaders in Corinth including Stephanus (1 Cor 1:16; 16:15, 17) and a woman named Chloe (1 Cor 1:11), so envisaging Phoebe as a household leader and a deacon is not out of the question. The key thing to remember about a "deacon" is that it is not so much an office as an agency, and Paul identifies Phoebe as an intermediary between himself and the Roman churches.[3]

"I ask you to receive her in the Lord in a way worthy of his people and to give her any help she may need from you, for she has been the benefactor of

2. Cf. Dunn, *Romans,* 2:891; Jewett, *Romans*, 963; Lampe, *From Paul to Valentinus*, 359–60.

3. Lynn H. Cohick, *Women in the World of the Earliest Christians: Illuminating Ancient Ways of Life* (Grand Rapids: Baker, 2009), 304–5.

many people, including me" (v. 2). Paul asks that they receive Phoebe as fitting for a fellow believer and provide her with the assistance that any traveler would need, like lodgings and provisions. Paul commends her specifically as a *prostatis*, which is not as older translations rendered it merely a "helper" (see RSV, NASB) but more properly a "patron" (ESV) or "benefactor" (NRSV, NIV).[4] In the ancient world, patronage and benefaction were a vital part of social relationships, with patrons giving persons protection and provision in return for loyalty and service. Phoebe was Paul's benefactor, who provided him with resources and residence in which to carry out his ministry while in the Corinthian peninsula.[5] Clearly Phoebe was an important person in the Pauline circle. She was a household leader, financially independent, perhaps socially prominent, actively serving the Corinthian churches, and she is the one (not Timothy, Titus, or Tertius) whom Paul entrusts this important letter to be delivered to the Roman believers. There is much we can try to infer from this about Paul and women and more on that anon.

**Paul Gives His Regards (16:3–15)**

The first persons greeted by Paul are "Priscilla and Aquila" (v. 3). This Greek-speaking Jewish husband and wife team from Pontus were probably leather-workers or tentmakers just like Paul. They met Paul in Corinth after the expulsion of the Jews from Rome by Claudius, which forced them to leave Rome around AD 49/50 and move to Corinth (Acts 18:1–2). They accompanied Paul to Ephesus, where they remained while Paul continued on to Syria (Acts 18:18–19; 1 Cor 16:19). It was during their time in Ephesus that they met an Alexandrian Jew named Apollos, a new yet incomplete convert to Christian faith, and they both instructed him in the way of God more accurately (Acts 18:26). They made it back to Rome probably around AD 54/55 (Rom 16:3), and they later returned to Ephesus where Timothy was working when Paul was imprisoned in Rome sometime around AD 62/64 (2 Tim 4:19).

Paul describes the couple as "co-workers" (*synergos*) in v. 3, which is the description Paul used for ministry partners and traveling companions who were involved in evangelical work and church planting (see Rom 16:9, 21; 2 Cor 8:23; Phil 2:25; 4:3; Col 4:11; 1 Thess 3:2; Phlm 1, 24). That they "risked their lives for Paul" (v. 4)—lit., "laid down their necks," a colloquialism for risking execution[6]—is the greatest compliment that Paul can pay them. They put their necks on the line for him. Their fellowship was one forged in the face of danger, though sadly we do not know precisely how, where, or when. Paul can even say

4. BDAG 885.
5. See Cohick, *Women*, 305–6.
6. BDAG 1042.

that "all the churches of the Gentiles are grateful to them" given their work in Rome, Corinth, and Ephesus. No wonder that Paul greets their house church first (v. 5a). This couple is Paul's firm foot on the ground in Rome.

Greeting is also extended to "Epenetus," who is described as "the first convert to Christ in the province of Asia" (v. 5b). Epenetus is described, lit., as the "firstfruits" (*aparchē*), and he was presumably among the first of Paul's converts in Ephesus just as Stephanus and his household were the "firstfruits" of Achaia (1 Cor 16:15; cf. 2 Thess 2:13). Greeting is given to "Mary," a popular Jewish name, and she "worked very hard for you," implying her work in Rome for others in some regard (v. 6) was much like Tryphena and Tryphosa in v. 12.

We enter more contentious territory when we get to the next couple greeted by Paul: "Greet Andronicus and Junia, my fellow Jews who have been in prison with me. They are outstanding among the apostles, and they were in Christ before I was" (v. 7). An initial problem is the gender of the person named beside Andronicus, namely, Junia(s). The name in Greek reads *Iounian*, and it could be either masculine ("Junias," a shortened version of "Junianus") or feminine ("Junia"), depending on how the Greek is accented (male = Ἰουνιᾶν; female = Ἰουνίαν).[7] The problem is that there were no accents in the original autographs or even in the early earliest manuscripts! There are also over 250 examples of the feminine version "Junia" in Greek and Latin inscriptions from Rome alone and not a single instance of "Junias" has been found.[8] The acute accent, and thus feminine rendering, is by far the most well attested in extant witnesses, and patristic commentators are virtually unanimous in identifying the person as a woman.[9]

This did not stop several medieval scribes applying a circumflex accent and thus rendering it masculine — a move followed by several modern Greek editions like Stephanus, Tischendorf, von Sonden, and early editions of Nestle-Aland. This decision influenced Greek dictionaries (see BAGD 380) and translators who opted for "Greet Andronicus and Junias ... they are men of note among the apostles" (RSV; cf. NJB, NEB, NASB). Many commentators have simply assumed that the person identified had to be a male apostle and never broached the alternative.[10] However, there is a tsunami

7. The most recent editions of the Greek New Testament, the NA[28], UBS[5], and SBLGNT, all opt for the feminine Ἰουνιάν, as do the older editions like Tregelles and Westcott-Hort. See further Eldon Epp, *Junia: The First Woman Apostle* (Minneapolis: Fortress, 2005) or in brief Metzger, *TCGNT*, 475–76, and Kruse, *Romans*, 563–65.

8. Lampe, *From Paul to Valentinus*, 176.

9. Cf. Fitzmyer, *Romans*, 737–38.

10. Cf. e.g., Murray, *Romans*, 2:229. Cf. Dunn (*Romans*, 2:894), who says the "assumption that it must be a male is a striking indictment of male presumption regarding the character and structure of earliest Christianity."

of textual and patristic evidence for "Junia" that proves overwhelming. Despite some naughty scribes, biased translators, lazy lexicographers, and dogmatic commentators, the text speaks about a woman named "Junia." Jewett goes so far as to call the masculine "Junias" a "figment of chauvinistic imagination."[11]

Andronicus and Junia are described in several significant ways. (1) They are Paul's *syngenēs*, which could mean that they are Paul's "relatives" (NRSV, CEB) or "kinsmen" (KJV, RSV, ESV, NASB, NJB). But later the same word is used for "Herodion" (v. 11) and "Lucius, Jason, and Sosipater" (v. 21), so that *syngenēs* probably implies a common ethnicity and can be translated as "fellow Jews" (see NIV, NLT).

(2) They are Paul's "fellow prisoners" (*synaichmalōtos*), a term used elsewhere only to describe Aristarchus (Col 4:10) and Epaphras (Phlm 23). They shared in a forced confinement with Paul, though again, the occasion and circumstances are unknown to us.

(3) Recently disputed is what relationship Andronicus and Junia had to the apostles. Most English translations say that they are "outstanding/prominent among the apostles" (NRSV, NIV, CEB, NASB), as if to be counted as members of the apostolic college. Alternatively, others opt for "well known to the apostles" (ESV, NET), as if they are merely acknowledged by the apostles. This debate focuses on whether the adjective *episēmos* is comparative (i.e., "prominent") or elative (i.e., "well-known"). The ensuing discussion is somewhat technical, but my lexical and exegetical instincts clearly favor the comparative sense.[12] The couple are apostles who are well-known for their apostolic ministry. That said, I doubt that Andronicus and Junia were big "A" apostles in the sense that they were called and commissioned directly by the risen Lord since we have no evidence for such a commission.[13] Therefore, it is more likely that they were little "a" apostles in the sense of delegates sent out from a church much in the same way that Titus was an "apostle" of the Asian churches (2 Cor 8:23) and Epaphraditus was an "apostle" of the Philippian church (Phil 2:25).[14] According to Ben Witherington, "it would appear that Paul means that Andronicus and Junia were engaged in evangelism and church planting as itinerants. That Paul says they are outstanding may imply

11. Jewett, *Romans*, 962.

12. See Michael H. Burer and Dan B. Wallace, "Was Junia Really an Apostle? A Re-examination of Rom 16.7," *NTS* 47 (2001): 76–91; Richard Bauckham, *Gospel Women: Studies of the Named Women in the Gospels* (Grand Rapids: Eerdmans, 2002), 172–80; Linda Belleville, "*Iounian ... episēmoi en tois apostolois*: A Re-examination of Romans 16.7 in Light of Primary Source Materials," *NTS* 51 (2005): 231–49; Epp, *Junia*, 69–78; Kruse, *Romans*, 565–67.

13. Origen identified them as one of the seventy-two sent out by Jesus in Luke 10:1 (Burns, *Romans*, 385).

14. On *apostolos* as missionary in the early church, see *Did.* 11.3–6; Hermas, *Vis* 13.1; *Sim* 92.4; 93.5; 102.2 (see Stuhlmacher, *Romans*, 249).

that their work had borne fruit, prompting the recognition of the Church in various places."[15]

(4) That the couple was "in Christ before I was" testifies to their conversion early on, before Paul's conversion ca. AD 33, and this perhaps makes them part of the Greek-speaking wing of the Jerusalem church in its earliest days (see Acts 6:1). Eldon Epp offers a somewhat aggravated albeit apt conclusion: "It remains a fact that there was a woman apostle, explicitly so named, in the earliest generation of Christianity, and contemporary Christians—laypeople and clergy—must (and eventually will) face up to it."[16]

Paul then greets Ampliatus, Urbanus, Stachys, and Apelles (vv. 8–10a). The first three are personally known to Paul as either a "dear friend" or "co-worker." Apelles might be known indirectly to Paul, yet Paul commends him as one approved or tested in Christ. The mention of "the household of Aristobulus" in v. 10b has led to speculation as to whether this refers to Aristobulus, the grandson of Herod the Great and the rival brother of Herod Agrippa I.[17] Aristobulus himself died in AD 48/49; however, his household probably continued and his name remained associated with it. If there was such a prominent Jewish household in Rome, it makes sense that Paul next greets "Herodion," another "fellow Jew" (v. 11a). He was perhaps a freedman, a former Herodian slave who was sold to the imperial household. Evidence for a "Synagogue of the Herodians" in Rome suggests that there might have been more than one former Herodian slave in Rome.[18]

Greetings extended to the "household of Narcissus" (v. 11b) is interesting because Narcissus is the name of a famous mid-first-century Roman freedman who came to prominence under Claudius, until he was forced into suicide after Claudius's death by jealous rivals. If this is the same Narcissus, as many believe, then Christians in his household would have been in a rather delicate position.[19]

Paul also greets a cohort of women in vv. 12–13. First, "Tryphena and Tryphosa" as well as "Persis," who are described as working hard in the Lord. These women are known for their dedication and service to the tasks that they perform. In addition, there is "Rufus"; though a common name, we are left wondering if this is the same Rufus who was the son of Simon of Cyrene whom Mark takes time to mention (Mark 15:21). Paul mention's Rufus's

---

15. Ben Witherington, *Women and the Genesis of Christianity* (Cambridge: Cambridge University Press, 1990), 188.

16. Epp, *Junia*, 81.

17. Josephus, *War* 2.221; *Ant* 20.9, 12.

18. Cf. Lampe, *From Paul to Valentinus*, 177–78.

19. Wright, "Romans," 10:763.

"mother," not by name, extolling her because she had metaphorically "been a mother to me, too."

The people listed toward the end of the greetings probably denote two distinct households: (1) one consisting of "Asyncritus, Phlegon, Hermes, Patrobas, Hermas" in addition to "the other brothers and sisters with them" (v. 14); (2) the other household comprising "Philologus, Julia, Nereus and his sister, and Olympas," who are together with "all the Lord's people." One feels that Paul is going through his mental rolodex and trying to greet as many people in Rome as he can humanly remember. In any case, the greetings show that fellowship and reciprocation is rooted in a common conception of the gospel.[20]

### Kissing Christians (16:16)

Paul closes his greetings with an exhortation: "Greet one another with a holy kiss. All the churches of Christ send greetings" (v. 16). Greeting with a kiss is not just a European thing; it was commonplace in some quarters of the ancient world.[21] Paul's letters often mention greeting with a "holy kiss" (1 Cor 16:20; 2 Cor 13:2; 1 Thess 5:26; cf. 1 Pet 5:14). By the time of Justin Martyr in the mid-second century, the holy kiss was part of the liturgy: "At the conclusion of the prayers we greet one another with a kiss. Then, bread and a chalice containing wine mixed with water are presented [for a eucharistic meal]."[22] Chrysostom acclaims the practice because "this kiss mollifies and equalizes everyone, banishing grievances and jealousy. Paul not only directs them to kiss one another in this way, but he also sends them the kiss of greeting from all the churches."[23] Christian affection is meant to be demonstrative and wholesome. Finally, Paul ends with greetings from the various churches that he represents as the apostle to the Gentiles.

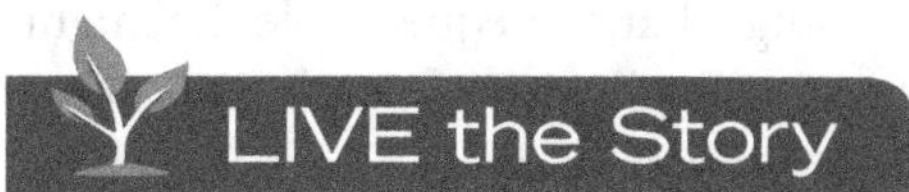


Looking for application and searching for grand biblical narratives in a list of greetings is no easy task. However, the text points us to consider the role of women among Paul's ministry partners and the importance of showing physical affection to our brothers and sisters in the Lord. In short, it points to the equality within the church and the emotional attachment we should display toward one another.

20. Murray, *Romans*, 2:232; Schreiner, *Romans*, 798.
21. See Kruse, *Romans*, 573–74.
22. Justin, *Apology* 1.65.
23. Cited in Burns, *Romans*, 386.

**Women as Partners in Mission**

Several women are named and their work noted by Paul including:

Phoebe: deacon, benefactor (vv. 1–2).
Priscilla: co-worker, church planter, teacher, fellow-prisoner (vv. 3–5).
Mary: works hard for others (v. 6).
Junia: missionary-apostle (v. 7).
Tryphena, Tryphosa, and Persis: women who work hard in the Lord (v. 12).
Mother of Rufus: mothering care for others (v. 13).[24]

Irrespective of whether one identifies as conservative or progressive on the issue of women in ministry, we all have to agree that women are certainly prominent in Paul's greetings to the Roman churches and women had a key part in the ministries of the earliest churches. Schreiner says that this text shows that while specific details are not given, these women "were vitally involved in ministry."[25] While the word for "work" (*kopiaō*) does not necessarily imply a leadership position per se, it still points to women playing a significant role in the Roman churches.[26] In fact, according to Chyrsostom, "the women of that time were more zealous than lions, sharing with the apostles in their labor of preaching."[27]

I have to confess that it was a close reading of Romans 16:1–16 that led me to a complete turnaround on my views concerning the roles of women in the church. Various women are praised in Paul's little greeting card for their service and labors. The fact that Junia is specifically identified as an apostle here is no small thing. Not only that, but it was reading about and reflecting on Phoebe—in particular her place in the Pauline circle, the reason why Paul chose her to deliver this letter, and imagining what subsequent role she might have played in the Roman churches ahead of Paul's visit—that left me completely gob smacked and led me to affirm the role of women in the teaching ministries of the church.

About Phoebe, from the outset we have to say that when Paul sent her to Rome, he probably had more in mind for her than helping out with their flower arrangements and slaving in the kitchen to make potluck dinners. N. T. Wright says that when it came to delivering this letter to the Romans that Paul "entrusted that letter to a 'deacon' called Phoebe whose work was taking

24. See further Susan Mathew, *Women in the Greetings of Romans 16.1–16: A Study of Mutuality and Women's Ministry in the Letter to the Romans* (LNTS 471; London: Bloomsbury, 2013).
25. Schreiner, *Romans*, 794.
26. Dunn, *Romans*, 2:894.
27. Cited in Burns, *Romans*, 285–89.

her to Rome. The letter-bearer would normally be the one to read it out to the recipients and explain its contents. The first expositor of Paul's greatest letter was an ordained traveling businesswoman."[28] Along the same line, when teaching through Romans 16:1–2, I habitually enjoy goading students into working out the implications of this text. Normally the scenario goes something like this:

"So then folks, if Phoebe is a deacon, Paul's benefactor, and if he trusted her to take this very important letter to the Romans, then Phoebe must have been a woman of great abilities and good character in Paul's mind. Do you agree?"

Heads nod in agreement.

"Okay, and if the Romans had any questions about the letter like 'What is the righteousness of God?' or 'Who is this wretched man that Paul refers to about halfway through?' who do you think would be the first person that they would ask?"

Eyes are now wide open; some mouths are gaping; others look a bit irritated.

Then I provocatively add, "Could it be that the first person to publicly read and teach about Romans was a woman? If so, what does that tell you about women and teaching roles in the early church?"[29]

Let me add that this is not the only text we have to address in developing a theology and practice of gender and ministry. However, I think it should be crystal clear that Romans 16:1–16 shows how much Paul highly regards women for their work in laboring for the Lord in a mixture of ministries including leadership, teaching, prayer, hospitality, and various other forms of service. According to Ben Witherington, we "see here a picture of a vibrant, multifaceted

28. N. T. Wright, "Women Bishops: It's about the Bible, Not Fake Ideas of Progress," *The Times*. 23 Nov 2012. www.virtueonline.org/women-bishops-its-about-bible-not-progress-tom-wright-updated-retort.

29. Michael F. Bird, *Bourgeois Babes, Bossy Wives, and Bobby Haircuts* (Grand Rapids: Zondervan, 2014), 20–21. I should point out that I am trying to speculate within reason about what Phoebe did, whether it was read the letter to various house churches, expound it, answer questions about it, or meet with leaders to discuss it. She may have just handed it on to Priscilla and Aquila and then headed back to Rome the next day. No one knows for sure. However, given Paul's commendation of her, I can't help but think that she had some kind of on-going task in ensuring that Paul's letter was disseminated and understood, whatever she or her colleagues had to do to achieve that end. See discussion in Alan Chapple, "Getting Romans to the Right Romans: Phoebe and the Delivery of Paul's Letter," *TynBul* 62 (2011): 195–214 (Phoebe gave the letter to Priscilla/Aquila, who made copies; they convened a meeting of all the house churches where the letter was read, and copies of letter were later distributed); Peter M. Head, "Named Letter-Carriers among the Oxyrhynchus Papyri," *JSNT* 31 (2009): 279–99 (Phoebe, as a letter-carrier, probably didn't read the letter to the recipients, but orally supplemented and expanded its contents to them); and Jewett, *Romans*, 943 (Phoebe's task was to convey and interpret the letter as well as carry out the business entailed in the letter).

church at the heart of the empire using the gifts and graces of both men and women to further the spread of the Gospel and the Church."[30] Therefore, the ministry that women do in our churches should be celebrated, honored, and esteemed, just as Paul does. We can take our cue from John Chrysostom, who wrote about Junia: "O how great is the devotion of this woman that she should be counted worthy of the appellation of apostle!"[31] Another church father, Origen, could infer: "This passage teaches that there were women ordained in the church's ministry by the apostles' authority.... Not only that—they ought to be ordained into the ministry, because they helped in many ways and by their good services deserved the praise even of the apostle."[32]

When it comes to developing ministry teams, especially in church planting, we would be wise to follow Paul's example and incorporate women into key roles, especially when our field of ministry is either highly difficult or boldly ambitious. Remember that it is women who are most likely to reach other women with the gospel. Remember that when you give women a voice, they will not only speak for themselves, but also for others like children and the elderly. Remember that when you empower women in a community, it will have ramifications on all sorts of areas ranging from domestic violence to family cohesion.[33]

### The Succor of Simple Greetings

I don't know about you but I don't get kissed a lot when I greet fellow parishioners at church. However, there are a lot of cultures and congregations that

---

30. Witherington, *Women*, 189.

31. Chrysostom, *Hom. Rom.* 31.

32. Cited in Bray, *Romans*, 369.

33. 33. Schreiner (*Romans*, 797; cf. Murray, *Romans*, 2:228; Moo, *Romans*, 927) says: "One should scarcely conclude from the reference to Junia and the other women coworkers named here that women exercised authority over men contrary to the Pauline admonition in 1 Tim. 2:12. We see evidence that women functioned as early Christian missionaries, and it may have been the case that they concentrated especially on other women, given the patriarchal nature of the Greco-Roman world. The Pauline pattern prescribed in 1 Tim. 2:11–15 was the apostolic pattern in the early Christian mission, and the vibrant ministry of Christian women did not contradict the admonitions delivered in 1 Tim. 2." This sounds to me like Schreiner is trying to reassure readers that although women were clearly active in ministry, they would never be permitted to teach a man. But this assumes that neither Paul nor anyone else could have allowed women to do anything that is proscribed by contemporary complementarian scruples. An assumption that is contestable. Did Phoebe refuse to instruct enquirers about Paul's letter because she was a woman despite the fact that that is precisely what letter carriers were supposed to do? Did not Priscilla and Aquila *both* instruct Apollos in the way of God and presumably others in their house church? Was Junia really restricted in her missionary work to working only with women? Was Junia not imprisoned for anything she said? I am aware of the danger of inferring too much about women from Romans 16:1–16, but I am also aware of the danger of denying what is a plain and obvious consequent of the text: women did ministry and it involved talking to men. See also Witherington, *Romans*, 390; Talbert, *Romans*, 340–42.

do, especially in Europe and South America. I remember once when a friend from church introduced me to a beautiful young lady from Argentina. I got about halfway through saying, "G'day, nice to meet you" when she ever so casually just leaned over and kissed me on both cheeks, leaving me feeling a little embarrassed and dumbstruck, with my friend laughing in hysterics at the spectacle. Believe it or not, gorgeous ladies do not ordinarily come up and kiss me. I am not a particularly handsome man. Ever since I was a small child, my mother kept telling me that I had a face for radio. The longevity of my marriage is anchored in making sure my wife never visits an optometrist ("Yes honey, everyone sees things blurry up close, it's perfectly normal").

While kissing might not be the most culturally appropriate way of greeting people, we can easily contextualize it. Some good paraphrases are offered with "holy embraces all around" (MSG) or "give each other a hearty handshake all round" (J. B. Phillips). If anything, maybe we should be like dogs, when you see someone you know, greet them with gusto and enthusiasm, let your excitement be physically evident and emotionally energetic. In a network of churches, including both the indigenous and immigrant varieties, where there are ethnic boundaries, disputed matters, and long-held suspicions, Paul calls these vulnerable churches to renew the bonds of affection for each other, by sharing a holy gospel and a holy kiss.

CHAPTER 30

# Romans 16:17 – 24

## LISTEN to the Story

[17]I urge you, brothers and sisters, to watch out for those who cause divisions and put obstacles in your way that are contrary to the teaching you have learned. Keep away from them. [18]For such people are not serving our Lord Christ, but their own appetites. By smooth talk and flattery they deceive the minds of naive people. [19]Everyone has heard about your obedience, so I rejoice because of you; but I want you to be wise about what is good, and innocent about what is evil.

[20]The God of peace will soon crush Satan under your feet.

The grace of our Lord Jesus be with you.

[21]Timothy, my co-worker, sends his greetings to you, as do Lucius, Jason and Sosipater, my fellow Jews.

[22]I, Tertius, who wrote down this letter, greet you in the Lord.

[23]Gaius, whose hospitality I and the whole church here enjoy, sends you his greetings.

Erastus, who is the city's director of public works, and our brother Quartus send you their greetings.

[24][May the grace of our Lord Jesus Christ be with all of you. Amen].[1]

*Listening to the texts in the story:* Matthew 7:15 – 20; Revelation 20:10.

Just when we think that Paul is done and dusted and about to say "Chow for now" or "See you in Ostia," he feels the need to squeeze in a few more remarks in his closing greetings to help guide the Roman believers. He does so maybe because as he is thinking and praying about this cluster of house churches that he feels a "sudden stab of anxiety" and wonders if they could fall prey to predatory wolves (see Acts 28:29 – 31).[2] The section has two basic parts: (1) final miscellaneous exhortations (vv. 17 – 20a); and (2) final greetings in the Messiah (vv. 20b – 23).

1. Several medieval manuscripts add v. 24, "The grace of our Lord Jesus Christ *be* with you all. Amen." The textual witnesses for this reading are so poor that most Greek editions and English translations simply omit it altogether. In any event, it merely repeats the closing words of v. 20.

2. Wright, "Romans," 10:764.

The ideas presented in vv. 17–20 might seem intrusive, and some have supposed they were a later interpolation.[3] In counterpoint I would claim that these verses are mostly supplemental to themes already raised in the letter—themes like the danger of someone advocating erroneous views about Torah and righteousness (Rom 3:21–4:25), the importance of obedience (1:5; 6:17), and the future victory of God in the Messiah over evil (8:33–39). Paul offers here a type of parting postscript, which adds a few final touches to his theological mosaic using the combined resources of ancestral wisdom, apocalyptic hope, the Jesus tradition, and bitter experiences with adversaries in newly planted churches. Thereafter, the closing greeting includes not only Paul's current cohort of coworkers (v. 21), but also his scribe Tertius (v. 22) and three socially prominent Corinthians: Gaius, Erastus, and Quartus (v. 23). It is important to remember that Paul's colleagues listed here include Jewish and Gentile believers; thus, Paul's immediate circle embodies the unity-in-diversity which the gospel of Jesus the Messiah creates between different ethnicities and social classes. Not only that, but through such greetings Paul strives to build relations not only between himself and the Roman churches, but also between the Roman and Corinthian churches.

## Just Three Things to Remember (16:17–20a)

"I urge you, brothers and sisters, to watch out for those who cause divisions and put obstacles in your way that are contrary to the teaching you have learned. Keep away from them" (v. 17). Paul provides a final exhortation signaled by "I urge you" (*parakalō*), much as he has done earlier (see 12:1, 8; 15:30). Paul warns of false teachers who are known for creating divisions and do so by putting an obstacle or trap in people's path to prevent them from holding to the "teaching you have learned." Even if not everyone in Rome is 100 percent on side with the Pauline articulation of the gospel and its implications, we have no reasons to suspect that any anti-Pauline Jewish Christians have entered Rome and penetrated the house churches there.[4] If they had, then presumably Paul would have had more to say on such a topic.

3. Cf. e.g., Byrne, *Romans*, 456; Jewett, *Romans*, 986–88.

4. Though some scholars do detect the presence of Pauline opponents in Rome, like Campbell, *Deliverance of God*, 499, 525; Stanley E. Porter, "Did Paul Have Opponents in Rome and What Were They Opposing?" in *Paul and His Opponents* (ed. S. E. Porter; PS 2; Leiden: Brill, 2005), 147–68; Peter Stuhlmacher, "The Purpose of Romans," in *The Romans Debate* (ed. K. P. Donfried; Peabody, MA: Hendrickson, 1991), 239.

While many of the claims that Paul makes in the letter assume a polemical Jewish Christian setting,[5] that is probably derived from Paul's own context rather than that indicative of the Romans' own situation. We must bear in mind that during the course of his mission, Paul had to fight a number of running battles against "opponents" of several different shapes and sizes. The most militant was a faction connected with the Jerusalem church who insisted that Paul's converts be circumcised and be made to keep the Torah as a condition for entry into the people of God and thus for salvation (see Acts 15:1–5; Gal 2:11–14; 3:1–5; 5:1–5; 6:12–13; Phil 1:15–18; 3:2). Paul calls these folks "false believers" (Gal 2:4), "agitators" (Gal 5:12), "those dogs, those evildoers, those mutilators of the flesh" (Phil 3:2), and "false apostles, deceitful workers" (2 Cor 11:13). Paul is worried that such a faction, who often followed him around, might have Rome in its sights next. Paul hopes that the Romans would not be tricked into abandoning the "teaching" that they have learned thus far (see Rom 6:17). Paul is concerned because, as he wrote elsewhere, false teaching of this kind intends to stop them obeying the truth (Gal 5:7). They should be alert to it lest they end up adhering to a "different gospel" (Gal 1:6–7) or receiving a "different Jesus" (2 Cor 11:4) other than the one they received. Paul has one bit of advice should such persons appear on the scene: "Keep away from them." In other words, avoid them like the plague.

Paul does not hold back as he proceeds to describe the unsavory nature of such intruders and their strategy: "For such people are not serving our Lord Christ, but their own appetites. By smooth talk and flattery they deceive the minds of naive people" (v. 18). Paul's language here reflects what he says about his opponents elsewhere like creating dissension (Gal 5:20), serving their own stomachs (Phil 3:19), using flattering speech, (Col 2:4; Eph 5:6), and seductive teaching (2 Thess 2:3). It pertains to those who use religion as a means for self-promotion.[6] Paul does not want the Romans to be seduced or sucked in by any charlatan using pomp to promote a non-gospel, a half-gospel, or an anti-gospel.

Paul is hopeful that the Roman churches won't of course get snookered by such intruders. Just as he opened the letter celebrating the report of their faith(fulness) throughout the world (Rom 1:8), so now he celebrates that "everyone has heard about your obedience" (16:19). Paul is elated by the Romans, and such joy anticipates their obedience also to the pattern of teaching now delivered to them through this letter as well. Paul adds a proverbial remark that instead of being beguiled by such teachers, "I want you to be wise

---

5. Correctly Campbell, *Deliverance of God*, 602.

6. Schreiner, *Romans*, 803.

about what is good, and innocent about what is evil" (v. 19c-d; see esp. Matt 10:16, "Be as shrewd as snakes and as innocent as doves").[7] There is play on words going on here. Paul said in v. 18 that people who are "naïve" (*akakos*) get fooled by false teachers, so now in v. 19 he wants them to aware of all that is "evil" (*kakos*). The chief thought is discerning evil without getting caught up in evil.

On the subject of evil, Christians look ahead to the day when evil incarnate will be destroyed: "The God of peace will soon crush Satan under your feet" (v. 20a). The hope for Satan to be crushed underfoot is extant in several Jewish apocalypses.[8] This verse is a reminder for them not to focus just on local squabbles and the sociopolitical affairs of the day, but to see a spiritual battle going on around them—a battle that will be won by God because it has already been won by the Messiah on his cross.

## Grace and Greetings (16:20b–23)

By this point we might think that Paul's closing greeting is longer than *The Sound of Music's* amusing song, "So Long, Farewell." Lest we think that Paul is going on and on, he really does get around to finishing the final greetings that began at 16:1. We see the beginning of the ending of the end with his blessing for the Romans, "The grace of our Lord Jesus be with you" (v. 20b). Just like Paul's other closing benedictions, Paul wishes his audiences a continuing blessing in God's favor and embrace (see 1 Cor 16:23; 2 Cor 13:14; Gal 6:18; Phil 4:23; 1 Thess 5:28; 2 Thess 3:18; 2 Tim 4:22; Phlm 25).

Paul mentions also, "Timothy, my co-worker, sends his greetings to you, as do Lucius, Jason and Sosipater, my fellow Jews" (v. 21). Timothy was Paul's handpicked younger colleague (see Acts 16:1–3) and is usually mentioned at the beginning of Paul's letters (see Phil 1:1; Col 1:1; 1 Thess 1:1; 2 Thess 1:1; Phlm 1) and only in Romans 16:21 is he named at the end of a letter. Named beside them are three other individuals whom we do not hear about elsewhere, unless the "Jason" is the "Jason" of Thessalonica from Acts 17:6–9 (unlikely) and "Sosipater" is identical to the Berean "Sopater" of Acts 20:4 (possibly). Paul names them as "fellow Jews" to emphasize that his Torah-free mission to the Gentiles includes a team of other Jewish Christians like himself (see Col 4:11).

The scribe who probably took down Paul's dictation adds his own greeting: "I, Tertius, who wrote down this letter, greet you in the Lord" (v. 22). Tertius was a Roman name, and he may have been a slave, freedman, or relative to one of the wealthier persons in the church, who has been provided with

7. On the virtue of shrewdness of naiveté in Jewish tradition, see Prov 1:4, 22; 8:5; 14:15; 21:11; Wis 4:12.

8. *Jub.* 5.6; 10.7–11; *1 En.* 10.4; 13.1–2; 1QM 17.5–6; 18.1.

an education and writing materials to act as a scribe, and put at Paul's disposal. The poor chap probably deserved a medal for being able to keep up with Paul in taking down the letter!

The final greetings are extended from three individuals who are probably the more prominent persons in the Corinthian churches: "Gaius, whose hospitality I and the whole church here enjoy, sends you his greetings. Erastus, who is the city's director of public works, and our brother Quartus send you their greetings" (v. 23). Paul had baptized Gaius (1 Cor 1:14; cf. Acts 18:7), who hosted a house church, and Paul was evidently staying with him (a person probably to be differentiated from the Gaius from Derbe in Acts 19:29, 20:4). The Erastus named here is probably a Pauline traveling companion known from elsewhere (see Acts 19:22; 2 Tim 4:20). We know of a prominent Corinthian citizen named Erastus from an inscription in the city and it is probably the same Erastus whom Paul mentions now.[9] Erastus, as an *oikonomos*, the equivalent of a Roman *aedile*, was probably responsible for public constructions and the city's finances during the course of his one-year term in office. What this list of names signals is that the Christian churches appear to have embraced a fairly widespread social diversity including slaves, freedmen, merchants, artisans, and socially advanced classes. No doubt it was more numerous on the bottom end of the social stratification and perhaps women too were well represented.

Furthermore, the greetings from Paul's associates shows that no church is an island. The churches of Rome and Corinth not only become aware of each other's existence but even share in each other's story and struggles by the exchange of communications like Paul's letter here. In fact, a couple of decades later, Clement of Rome would write to the Corinthians around AD 95/96 to try and heal a painful division in the Corinthians churches. Thus the situation came full circle. Paul wrote from the Corinthian peninsula partly to heal divisions in Rome, then later a leader in Rome wrote to the Corinthian churches to heal their divisions. This is further proof of the development of mutual interest and reciprocal regard for each other among the earliest churches.

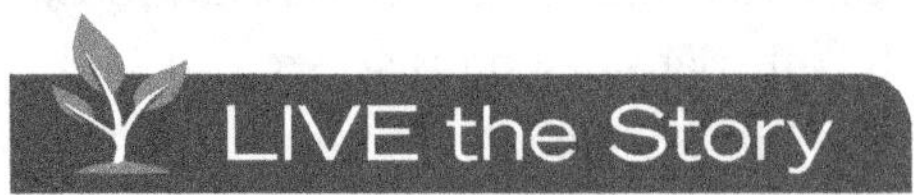

## LIVE the Story

On living the story of Romans 16:17–23, we have to be like our forefathers in the faith and actively preserve the integrity of our belief in a world that is constantly challenging us about it. If we hold to our precious faith, then,

9. The inscription reads: "Erastus laid the pavement [nineteen square meters] at his own expense in return for his aedileship." See discussion in Kruse, *Romans*, 585–87.

just like the Romans, we know that other like-minded churches rejoice in our obedience, and we can look ahead confidently to the day when the devil and his minions are finally defeated, and God's people are cosmically vindicated.

### False Teaching

I don't know if you remember the detective show *Columbo*, where Detective Columbo (i.e., Peter Falk) was known for making penetrating observations about a crime scene and poking holes in a criminal's story. Every episode Columbo would interview a suspect and just when the suspect's alibi seemed to check out, Columbo would pause and say, "Oh yeah, just one more thing . . ." and then ask a question that completely unraveled the suspect's entire story. Here, Paul pulls a Columbo by adding just one more thing that provides some insight into the Roman situation. The one thing is that Paul wants them to be wary of false teachers entering their ranks and promulgating a false gospel. I like how Eugene Peterson paraphrases vv. 17–19: "One final word of counsel, friends. Keep a sharp eye out for those who take bits and pieces of the teaching that you learned and then use them to make trouble. Give these people a wide berth. They have no intention of living for our Master Christ. They're only in this for what they can get out of it, and aren't above using pious sweet talk to dupe unsuspecting innocents" (MSG).

In my experience of churches in the UK, USA, and Australia, most evangelical churches do not get easily fooled by big and obvious heresies like denying the deity of Christ or denying the humanity of Jesus (that said, I've just come back from morning tea where a student told me that a friend who led her to Christ has recently joined a messianic group that denies the Trinity). More often than not, the danger is teaching that is vague and mushy, watered down, without substance, and has the theological depth of a car park puddle. You end up with a sermon diet that has the spiritual nutrition value equivalent to living exclusively on McNuggets.

On other occasions the danger is trendiness, wanting to be liked and loved by the masses, to be spoken of positively in the media, which puts pressure on pastors as much as parishioners to downplay certain aspects of the faith like sin, atonement, judgment, and hell. Here preaching becomes akin to pandering at the pool of popularity.

And then there are occasions where a teacher thinks that he or she has attained some new spiritual insight that somehow licenses them to deny the historic faith so that they can emphasize this new facet of the faith that they've uncovered for us. So, we need to get rid of that toxic idea of hell and judgment because I've discovered that God's grace is so radically inclusive that nobody ever misses out. Or else, we need to get away from the atonement as a transaction about sin, and instead emphasize what I've come to learn that Jesus heals the world's sicknesses. Fresh readings of Scripture are fine; so too is a new engagement with old questions, but don't get fooled by someone excavating ancient dung and calling it a diamond.

Here's my point. False teaching starts as shallow, tries to be trendy, and pursues innovation without boundaries, and before you know it, you're standing in a church where the Nicene Creed is either mocked or meaningless. That's what happened in many mainline churches, when the leadership — who should have known better — let in wolves among the flock. They did it perhaps naively because the wolf went to the right seminary, knew the right people, had a good heart, possessed a nice bag of cute sermon illustrations, he or she was well intentioned, was loved by the elderly, was adored by the youth, and had the right connections. The results, however, are always catastrophic. In fact, not long ago a friend of mine was complaining to me that a leader in her own denomination told her that Christianity was just a myth that provided meaning to the lives of many folks and clergy were merely custodians of the myth. Preaching was like telling fairy tales to children to keep them calm during a storm. More recently, I've had a student assigned as a pastoral assistant to a church where the senior minister is openly nontrinitarian and has denied almost every Christian doctrine that can be named.

Let me add that this is not just a problem for the Western churches. Even churches in the global south and parts of North Asia, which have experienced huge numerical growth, frequently have significant doctrinal problems. The results often include syncretism with existing religions, grasping onto popular movements like the prosperity gospel, and leaders promoting erroneous and erratic views in their teaching. This is partly due to a lack of access to theological education and mentoring. Such a situation is not aided by the fact that in developing countries among Africa and Asia that you can also find an elitist class of theologians who have imbibed Western liberalism and simply transferred it into their own setting. A missionary friend of mine once shared the story of finding a more fiercely held Ivy-League-divinity-school-type theology in Indonesia than he had experienced at either Harvard or Yale. The result is often a huge disjunction between the educated liberals and the grass roots believers in the villages and cities.[10]

---

10. See Simon Chan, *Grassroots Asian Theology: Thinking the Faith from the Ground Up* (Downers Grove, IL: InterVarsity, 2014).

## Checklist for Recognizing Counterfeit Christianity

When it comes to recognizing a counterfeit Christianity or a false teacher, Colin Smith offers a good checklist to consult:[11]

*Different Source*—Where does the message come from?

*Different Message*—What is the substance of the message?

*Different Position*—In what position will the message leave you?

*Different Character*—What kind of people does the message produce?

*Different Appeal*—Why should you listen to the message?

*Different Fruit*—What result does the message have in people's lives?

*Different End*—Where does the message ultimately lead you?

Let me emphasize, I'm not sanctioning witch hunts to cleanse out clergy or seminarians who are doctrinally suspect because they do not hold "conservative" views. I've learned that what is regarded as "conservative" varies from place to place. Remember our theological triage from Romans 14 about the essentials, secondary matters, and tertiary elements of the faith. We need unity on the majors, but don't major on the minors. That said, in every age we need to be vigilant and alert to incrementally approaching doctrinal revisions that will cannibalize our teaching, pervert our practice, wreck our spirituality, and ruin our witness. Paul's advice in v. 17 is wise and sure: To be forewarned is to be forearmed, and if the preacher is dodgy, then get out of Dodge!

11. Colin Smith, "7 Traits of False Teachers," *The Gospel Coalition*. 18 March 2013. http://www.thegospelcoalition.org/article/7-traits-of-false-teachers. Cited 15 Oct 2014.

CHAPTER 31

# Romans 16:25 – 27

## LISTEN to the Story

[25] Now to him who is able to establish you in accordance with my
gospel, the message I proclaim about Jesus Christ, in keeping with the
revelation of the mystery hidden for long ages past, [26] but now revealed
and made known through the prophetic writings by the command of the
eternal God, so that all the Gentiles might come to the obedience that
comes from faith — [27] to the only wise God be glory forever through Jesus
Christ! Amen.

*Listening to the texts in the story:* Ephesians 3:3 – 9; Colossians 1:26 – 27.

The closing doxology is one of the most sublime pieces of theological prose ever composed. It reprises and amplifies the earlier doxology in Romans 11:33 – 36 by celebrating God's glory as the climax to the redemptive history embodied in gospel. It is appropriate for Paul to end the letter on this note. The biblical story began with Adam falling into sin and all of humanity thereafter failing to give glory to God because they themselves have fallen short of the glory of God (see Rom 1:23; 3:23). Thankfully, the rest of the story is about the reversal of this dire state since salvation is about humanity giving glory to God and sharing in the hope of glory (see Rom 4:20; 5:2; 8:17 – 18, 21, 30). The story of Romans is then a microcosm of the biblical story since Paul takes us from glory lost to glory regained. Viewed this way, the doxology represents a virtual hermeneutical key for reading Romans, summing up the themes of God, glory, Messiah, and revelation.[1]

At the risk of getting technical, we also have to note that the doxology is arguably the most acute text-critical problem in Romans. That is because in some manuscripts it appears after 14:23 (in the majority of manuscript witnesses), in another one after 15:33 (in 𝔓[46], our earliest text of Romans), appearing after 16:23/24 (in important manuscripts like Vaticanus, Sinaiticus,

1. Keck, *Romans*, 384.

and Beza), twice in some witnesses after both 14:23 and 16:23 (like Alexandrinus), and entirely omitted from a few other manuscripts (some medieval witnesses). The doxology should probably be in there, but for whatever reason, its placement got mixed up in the transmission of the text. We follow tradition in placing it after 16:23/24.[2] In any case, the text-critical issues should not distract us from basking in Paul's theocentric and triumphant note of praise to the God of the gospel. As Wright says, "After a book like this, written by a strongly monotheistic Jew, a doxology is just what we should expect."[3] So while the doxology might be textually awkward, it is certainly an apt ending.[4]

## EXPLAIN the Story

### Wise God, Wonderful Gospel, and Worshipful Gentiles (16:25–27)

"Now to him who is able to establish you in accordance with my gospel, the message I proclaim about Jesus Christ, in keeping with the revelation of the mystery hidden for long ages past" (v. 25). The opening is abbreviated and we are to mentally insert the "glory" of v. 27 as the item that is attributable "to him" in v. 25, yielding "Glory be to him who is able ..." (see CEB, NLT). What God is able to do is "establish," "confirm," or "strengthen" the Roman believers (*stērizō*).[5] Paul used the same word to describe how he longs to see them to impart some spiritual gift to them in order to strengthen them (Rom 1:11).

In the interim, Paul believes that narrating his account of the gospel to them in this letter will yield a spiritual blessing, because "my gospel" (see 2:16) is the mechanism by which they will be more firmly established in the faith.[6] Paul teaches that God does not establish them in mere conformity to the gospel, but the gospel is the mechanism by which this strengthening takes place. The point is that Paul's gospel is the source of their strengthening.[7]

2. Cf. Metzger, *TCGNT*, 470–71 and Larry Hurtado, "The Doxology at the End of Romans," in *New Testament Textual Criticism* (ed. E. J. Epp and G. D. Fee; FS B. Metzger; Oxford: Clarendon, 1981), 185–99.

3. Wright, "Romans," 10:768.

4. See I. Howard Marshall, "Romans 16:25–27—An Apt Conclusion," in *Romans and the People of God* (ed. Sven K. Soderlund and N. T. Wright; FS Gordon D. Fee; Grand Rapids: Eerdmans, 1999), 170–84.

5. BDAG 945.

6. That Paul emphasizes "my gospel" is not to be taken to imply that his gospel represented some kind of radical innovation which differed markedly from what the other apostles preached. Paul's defense of the gospel is premised on the notion that it is the same as what others preached (1 Cor 15:1, 3, 11), even if others failed to live up to it consistently (Gal 2:11–15). What is genuinely unique to Paul is the hermeneutical paradigm that he used to "prove" the gospel and to tease out its implications. Dunn (*Romans*, 2:914) puts it well: "Paul's gospel is the proclamation of Jesus Christ common to all Christian missionaries."

7. Dunn, *Romans*, 2:914; Moo, *Romans*, 938; Schreiner, *Romans*, 811.

This gospel is further expressed as "the message I proclaim/preach about Jesus Christ." The gospel is not a system of ethics, a cultural program, or a spiritual mantra. The gospel is the proclamation of news about the death and resurrection of the Messiah and God's reconciliation of the world through him. The third clause of v. 25, "in keeping with the revelation of the mystery hidden for long ages past" is probably subordinate to the "gospel" and defines the gospel as part of a redemptive-historical mystery that was previously hidden. Such language corresponds with 1:17, where Paul said that God's righteousness was "revealed" in the gospel.

Where did this idea of "mystery" come from? The word "mystery" (*mystērion*) has prompted also sorts to speculations about Paul's relationship to Hellenistic mystery religions and Jewish apocalypticism. We are best to see Paul here identifying something of God's eternal purposes, both intimated and yet hidden, which bursts into world history to bring peace and justice. The essence of that mystery is that God had always intended to bring Gentiles into the people of God and their membership would be proven precisely by their obedience (see 1 Cor 2:7; Eph 3:3–9; Col 1:26–27).[8]

"But now revealed and made known through the prophetic writings by the command of the eternal God, so that all the Gentiles might come to the obedience that comes from faith" (v. 26). The "but now" is the eschatological "now" (see Rom 3:21), God's invasive action to repossess the world for himself, to put the world to rights, by transforming a people by the power of his own righteousness. Paul believes that the royal announcement about Jesus the Messiah is the unveiling of the long concealed "mystery." Salvation, consisting of the commonwealth of redeemed Jews and Gentiles, turns out to be in the end the crazy, messy, unexpected, and ridiculous plan that the prophets said God had always intended to do. Paul can thus claim that the arrival of the gospel of the Messiah and the obedience of Gentiles that it fosters means that God's once-hidden mystery has indeed come to fruition. The revelation happens at God's own "command," not any particular historical command, but the sovereign intention of the divine will to be the God who saves in Jesus Christ. Salvation is unveiled in God's way in God's timing and not imposed on him by external circumstances. The God who does this is "the only wise God." His wisdom is his wise plan for salvation (see Rom 11:33). To him surely belongs "glory forever through Jesus Christ!" To top that off, Paul ends with "Amen!" (v. 27), to which we might respond with our own "Amen indeed!"

---

8. See Markus Bockmuehl, *Revelation and Mystery in Ancient Judaism and Pauline Christianity* (WUNT 2.36; Tübingen: Mohr Siebeck, 1990); and more recently Greg K. Beale and Benjamin L. Gladd, *Hidden But Now Revealed: A Biblical Theology of Mystery* (Downers Grove, IL: InterVarsity, 2014).

## LIVE the Story

The ideal reader of Romans will be attentive both to the several significant theological themes in Romans as well as various applications that emerge from a close reading of the letter. Such a reader will be one who believes in Jesus as the source of righteousness, does not entrust their salvation and identity to works of the law, is conscious of belonging to the Abrahamic family of faith, enjoys peace with God, has a steadfast hope for glory, remembers and reflects on their baptism, strives to put sin to death while living to righteousness, celebrates the death of the old self, is led by the Spirit and not the flesh, confesses Jesus as Lord, prays for Israel's salvation, shuns evil by clinging to love, pursues the things that make for peace, and is eager to greet fellow believers. In other words, living Romans means transforming our theology and altering our practices to fit with Paul's gospel agenda for the churches to come to the obedience of faith. A faith of which the most visible signs are our mutual love for others and a continued commitment to gospel mission as we corporately continue to praise God the Father and glory in Jesus Christ.

Quite obviously, then, an appropriation of Romans demands acts of praise. Praise has been central to the letter since anthems of worship have been interjected at key points of the letter (see 1:25; 11:22–26; 15:7–13). Romans is a letter that compels us toward worship of God the Father and the Lord Jesus Christ. So I think the application to Romans 16:25–27 is fairly straight forward. This is a passage to be read and reflected upon, to mark and mediate upon, to savor and sing. On the singing side, Isaac Watts comes to our aid with his majestic hymn, "To God Only Wise":

To God the only wise,
Our Savior and our King,
Let all the saints below the skies
Their humble praises bring.
'Tis His almighty love,
His counsel, and His care,
Preserves us safe from sin and death,
And every hurtful snare.
He will present our souls,
Unblemished and complete,
Before the glory of His face,
With joys divinely great.
Then all the chosen seed
Shall meet around the throne,

Shall bless the conduct of His grace,
And make His wonders known.
To our Redeemer, God,
Wisdom and power belongs,
Immortal crowns of majesty,
And everlasting songs.

And there ends the lesson of Paul's letter to the Romans; a story to be read, explained, and lived with all the passion and power that God's Spirit gives us. In the words of William Tyndale:

> Forasmuch as this epistle is the principal and most excellent part of the New Testament, and most pure [gospel] ... and also a light and a way unto the whole scripture, I think it meet that every Christian man not only know it by rote but also exercise himself therein evermore continually as with the daily bread of the soul. No man verily can read it too oft or study it too well: for the more it is studied the easier it is, the more it is searched the more precious things are found in it, so great treasure of spiritual things lieth hid therein.[9]

9. Cited in Bruce, *Romans*, 9.

# Scripture Index


**Genesis**

1–3 . . . 52, 231
1:28 . . . 72
2–3 . . . 236
2:2–3 . . . 471
2:15–17 . . . 236
3 . . . 174, 185
3:13 . . . 236, 240
3:15 . . . 112
3:19 . . . 236
6–10 . . . 52
6 . . . 72
8 . . . 72
12 . . . 145
12–15 . . . 112
12:1–3 . . . 364
12:1–2 . . . 313
12:2–3 . . . 72
13:16 . . . 336
15–17 . . . 147
15 . . . 144, 145
15:1–5 . . . 313
15:5–6 . . . 138, 139, 364, 366
15:6 . . . 138, 139, 140, 141, 145, 146, 147, 148, 149, 150, 151
17 . . . 145
17:1–27 . . . 313
17:1–16 . . . 138
17:2 . . . 72
17:5 . . . 149
17:9–14 . . . 81, 146
17:11 . . . 146, 147
17:20 . . . 326
17:21 . . . 326
17:23–26 . . . 139
18 . . . 327
18:10–14 . . . 322
18:10 . . . 327
21 . . . 327
21:12 . . . 322, 326
21:20 . . . 326
22 . . . 144, 145
22:12–16 . . . 290
22:12 . . . 293, 327
22:16–18 . . . 72
25–28 . . . 328
25:21–23 . . . 322
25:23 . . . 328, 329
26:5 . . . 143
28:14 . . . 336
32:12 . . . 336
49:10 . . . 112

**Exodus**

1:8–22 . . . 331
4:10 . . . 370, 422
4:21 . . . 322
4:22 . . . 255, 266, 304, 310, 312
4:24–26 . . . 146
6:6 . . . 116
7:3 . . . 322
9:12 . . . 322
13:3, 13 . . . 216
14–15 . . . 193, 208
14:4 . . . 322
16:7, 10 . . . 312
16:10 . . . 304
17 . . . 322
19:5–6 . . . 13, 42, 71, 72, 79, 80, 87
19:6 . . . 213
20:2 . . . 217
20:4–5 . . . 52
20:8–11 . . . 471
20:9–10 . . . 453
20:13–17 . . . 453
20:13–15, 19 . . . 451
20:17 . . . 231, 236, 239
21:8 . . . 117
21:24 . . . 435
21:28–30 . . . 117
22:21 . . . 399
23:9 . . . 399
24:16 . . . 312
25:17–22 . . . 117
31:16–17 . . . 471
32 . . . 56, 331
32:13 . . . 72
32:30–34 . . . 312
32:31–32 . . . 304
33:18–23 . . . 312
33:19 . . . 322, 330
34:6 . . . 291
40:34–35 . . . 312

**Leviticus**
1:1–2:16 . . . 411
5:6–8. . . . 255
6:25 . . . 260
7:26–27. . . . 468
9:6, 23 . . . 312
11. . . . 475
11:1–23. . . . 468
11:44–51. . . . 213
12:3 . . . 81, 146
16–17 . . . 109
16:13–15. . . . 117
17:11 . . . 112, 118
17:12–14. . . . 468
18:1–5. . . . 353
18:5 . . . 77, 231, 240, 345, 346, 352, 353, 354, 356, 357
18:6–30. . . . 353
18:19 . . . 430
18:22 . . . 52, 59
19:2. . . . 213
19:18 . . . 435, 451, 453, 454
20:13 . . . 59
20:26 . . . 213
24:20 . . . 435

**Numbers**
1:18 . . . 291
6:16 . . . 260
15:17–21. . . . 377
15:19–21. . . . 387
22. . . . 371
24:11–13. . . . 349
32:23 . . . 102

**Deuteronomy**
4:7–8. . . . 356
4:16–17. . . . 56
5:6 . . . 217
5:12–14. . . . 471
5:15 . . . 453
5:17–21. . . . 453
5:18 . . . 236
5:21 . . . 239
6:4–5. . . . 430
7:6 . . . 213
7:8 . . . 216
7:9 . . . 43, 92, 155, 291
8:2 . . . 423
8:14 . . . 216
8:17 . . . 354
9. . . . 72
9:4 . . . 345, 352, 354, 356
10:5–6. . . . 352
10:16 . . . 71, 81, 82
10:18 . . . 399
12:23–25. . . . 468
13:5, 10 . . . 216
14. . . . 475
14:1–2. . . . 312
14:1 . . . 255, 304
14:2 . . . 213
14:3–21. . . . 468
18:15 . . . 112
19:21 . . . 435
24:1–4. . . . 220, 222
24:14–21. . . . 399
26:19 . . . 213
27–31 . . . 97, 185
28:1–3. . . . 240
28:9 . . . 213
28:15–68. . . . 240
29:4 . . . 377, 383
30–32 . . . 364
30. . . . 352, 353, 355, 357, 365
30:1–11. . . . 357
30:2–5. . . . 355
30:6–9. . . . 355
30:6 . . . 82
30:10 . . . 355
30:11 . . . 355
30:12–14. . . . 345, 346, 347, 352, 354, 355, 356, 357, 368
30:13 . . . 356
30:14, 17 . . . 355
30:16–18. . . . 355
30:16 . . . 299
30:19–20. . . . 355
30:19 . . . 213
31:10–11. . . . 313
32. . . . 365, 486
32:4 . . . 43, 322
32:19–25. . . . 363
32:21 . . . 345, 347, 363, 384
32:35 . . . 429, 435
32:39 . . . 150
32:43 . . . 412, 463, 486

**Joshua**
24:17 . . . 217

**Judges**
2:8 . . . 18
5:11 . . . 43
6:8 . . . 217

**1 Samuel**
1:3 . . . 313
2:6 . . . 150
12:7 . . . 43

12:22 . . . . . 381
18:25–27. . . . . 146

**2 Samuel**
7:5 . . . . . 18
7:11–14. . . . . 112
21:2 . . . . . 349
22:50 . . . . . 463, 486

**1 Kings**
17:35–36. . . . . 313
19. . . . . 381, 382
19:10, 14 . . . . . 381
19:18 . . . . . 382
21:20, 27 . . . . . 242

**2 Kings**
17:17 . . . . . 242
18:12 . . . . . 18

**1 Chronicles**
16:13 . . . . . 310
28:9 . . . . . 281
29:15 . . . . . 287

**Ezra**
3:21–22. . . . . 174
7:6, 10 . . . . . 313
7:18–19. . . . . 174

**Nehemiah**
8:1 . . . . . 313
9:17 . . . . . 291

**Esther**
8:17 . . . . . 146

**Job**
1–2 . . . . . 294
4:8 . . . . . 102
7:6 . . . . . 286
41:11 . . . . . 406, 408

**Psalms**
1:2 . . . . . 243
2. . . . . 72, 367
5–9 . . . . . 98
5. . . . . 92
9:11 . . . . . 393
10. . . . . 92
10:7 . . . . . 98
14. . . . . 92
14:1–3. . . . . 98
17. . . . . 236
17:51 . . . . . 486
18:8, 12 . . . . . 429, 436
18:27 . . . . . 423
18:49 . . . . . 26, 463, 486
19. . . . . 52
19:4 . . . . . 345, 346
19:7 . . . . . 243
22:5 . . . . . 161
23. . . . . 367
24:1 . . . . . 479
25:10 . . . . . 43
26:3 . . . . . 43
27:6 . . . . . 411
32. . . . . 138
32:2 . . . . . 140, 145
36. . . . . 92
36:1 . . . . . 98
36:7 . . . . . 299
40:8 . . . . . 243
40:10–11. . . . . 43
42:9–10. . . . . 300
44:9–25. . . . . 296
44:21 . . . . . 274, 281
44:22 . . . . . 290, 296
50:6 . . . . . 95
50:14, 25 . . . . . 411
50:20 . . . . . 393
51. . . . . 13, 92, 96
51:4 . . . . . 95, 96
51:14 . . . . . 43, 54, 96
51:17 . . . . . 413
53:1–3. . . . . 98
57:9 . . . . . 36
59. . . . . 92
59:16 . . . . . 279, 299
62:12 . . . . . 71, 75, 76
65:13 . . . . . 277
67:2–4. . . . . 36
69. . . . . 236, 482, 488
69:9 . . . . . 463, 481
69:22–23. . . . . 377, 383
71:15–16. . . . . 43
78:5 . . . . . 313
86:15 . . . . . 291
89. . . . . 72
89:3 . . . . . 310
89:5–18. . . . . 54
89:28, 51 . . . . . 43
90:14 . . . . . 299, 381
96:8 . . . . . 411
96:10 . . . . . 36
96:13 . . . . . 276
98. . . . . 35, 52, 109
98:1–9. . . . . 54
98:1–3. . . . . 36
98:2 . . . . . 43

103:8 . . . 291
106. . . . 52
106:20 . . . 56
107:22 . . . 411
110. . . . 367
110:1 . . . 290
110:5 . . . 75
110:9 . . . 116
111:5–10. . . . 43
116. . . . 92
116:11 . . . 95
116:17 . . . 411
117:1 . . . 463, 486
117:1, 11 . . . 487
117:2 . . . 487
118. . . . 367
119. . . . 172, 236
120:4 . . . 429, 436
130, 133. . . . 236
139:23 . . . 281
140. . . . 92
140:3 . . . 98
140:10 . . . 429, 436
143. . . . 92
143:1–3. . . . 54
143:1 . . . 43
143:2 . . . 78
145:8 . . . 291
147. . . . 92

**Proverbs**
1:1 . . . 92
1:4, 22 . . . 533
1:16 . . . 98
3:7 . . . 433
3:34 . . . 422
8:5 . . . 533
8:15–16. . . . 444
14:15 . . . 533
20:22 . . . 435
21:11 . . . 533
23:20 . . . 480
24:12 . . . 71, 75, 76
24:29 . . . 435
25:21–22. . . . 429, 435, 436

**Ecclesiastes**
7:20 . . . 92, 98

**Isaiah**
1:2 . . . 266
1:9 . . . 322, 336
2:2–4. . . . 72, 336
6:5–8. . . . 370
6:8 . . . 374
8:14 . . . 345, 348, 474
10. . . . 508
10:22–23. . . . 336
10:23 . . . 322
11:1–5. . . . 112
11:1 . . . 18
11:3–5. . . . 54
11:5 . . . 43
11:10 . . . 171, 464, 486, 487
11:11 . . . 508
13:13 . . . 75
14. . . . 508
16:5 . . . 43
19:21 . . . 313
24–27 . . . 274, 278
24:4 . . . 277
27:9 . . . 377, 392, 393
28:16 . . . 345, 346, 348, 359, 366
29. . . . 332
29:10 . . . 377, 383
29:16 . . . 322, 331
31:33 . . . 392
32:17 . . . 161
35:2 . . . 312
40–66 . . . 185
40. . . . 58
40:5 . . . 212
40:8 . . . 324
40:9 . . . 20
40:13 . . . 406
41:1 . . . 508
41:2–4. . . . 354
41:8 . . . 13
41:9 . . . 19
42:1 . . . 310
42:4 . . . 508
42:6–7. . . . 72
42:6 . . . 19, 42, 87
42:9 . . . 80
44. . . . 58
44:1–4. . . . 255, 256, 257
44:1 . . . 13
45. . . . 332
45:1 . . . 443, 444
45:9 . . . 322, 331
45:14 . . . 510
45:23 . . . 463, 473
46:13 . . . 43
48:12 . . . 19
49–50 . . . 231, 236
49:6 . . . 42, 72, 87
49:9 . . . 80, 332
50:1 . . . 242
50:4–9. . . . 290

50:8 . . . 294
51–52 . . . 117
51. . . 13
51:5–8. . . 114
52–53 . . . 361
52. . . 365
52:1–10. . . 17, 18
52:5 . . . 71, 81
52:7 . . . 20, 81, 345, 346, 362, 371
52:13–53:12 . . . 361
52:13–15. . . 507
52:15 . . . 502
53. . . 109, 112, 365
53:1 . . . 345, 362
53:5, 11–12. . . 151
53:11–12. . . 138
53:11 . . . 295
53:12 . . . 290, 293
54:10 . . . 162
54:17 . . . 301
55:9 . . . 407
55:11 . . . 324, 370
55:12 . . . 276
56:1 . . . 43
56:6–7. . . 510
56:6 . . . 471
59:7–8. . . 92, 98
59:20–21. . . 377
59:20 . . . 392, 393
59:21 . . . 256
60. . . 310
60:6–7. . . 510
60:9 . . . 508
61. . . 505
61:6 . . . 502
63:16 . . . 312
64:8 . . . 312
65–66 . . . 274, 278
65:1–2. . . 345, 347
65:1 . . . 363, 364
65:2 . . . 364
65:17 . . . 278
66:18 . . . 312
66:19–20. . . 36, 502, 509, 510
66:19 . . . 35, 508
66:20 . . . 505
66:22 . . . 278

**Jeremiah**

2:11 . . . 56
4:4 . . . 82
4:28 . . . 277
6:10 . . . 82
7:4, 20 . . . 96
9:25–26. . . 82
11:16–19. . . 377
11:16–17. . . 387
12:4 . . . 277
17:10 . . . 281
18:1–6. . . 322
18:6–10. . . 332
23:5 . . . 18, 112
27:4–7. . . 444
29:1–23. . . 441
31. . . 71, 112
31:9 . . . 312
31:31–34. . . 79
31:33–34. . . 377
31:33 . . . 211, 393
31:34 . . . 257
34:13 . . . 217
38:4 . . . 443
50:25 . . . 322

**Ezekiel**

1:28 . . . 312
11:19 . . . 211, 256
16. . . 72
16:60–63. . . 257
18:31 . . . 211, 256
20:42–44. . . 257
27:10 . . . 508
27:26 . . . 162
34. . . 112
34:23–24. . . 18
35:25 . . . 162
36–39 . . . 255
36–37 . . . 267
36. . . 71
36:24–38. . . 257
36:24–28. . . 79
36:26–27. . . 13, 310
36:26 . . . 211, 256
37. . . 386
37:1–28. . . 310
37:14 . . . 13
37:24–25. . . 18
38:13 . . . 509
39:25–29. . . 257
39:29 . . . 256
42:13 . . . 261
44:7 . . . 82
44:9 . . . 82

**Daniel**

1:3–16. . . 469
2. . . 72
2:21, 39–38. . . 444
3:28–30. . . 443
4:17, 33–37. . . 444

4:17 . . . 441
5:11 . . . 449
5:18–21 . . . 444
5:21 . . . 441
6:10 . . . 348
7:27 . . . 183
9 . . . 72
9:2–19 . . . 54
9:16 . . . 114
10:3 . . . 469
10:12 . . . 423
12:1–2 . . . 310

**Hosea**
1:10 . . . 266, 322, 335, 364
2 . . . 112
2:23 . . . 322, 335, 364
11:1 . . . 266, 304, 312
13:14 . . . 386
14:6 . . . 387

**Joel**
2:13 . . . 291
2:27–28 . . . 13
2:28–29 . . . 256
2:28 . . . 161
2:32 . . . 345, 361
3:17 . . . 393

**Amos**
1–3 . . . 73
3:2 . . . 310
3:7 . . . 18
5:15 . . . 429, 439
9:11–12 . . . 336

**Jonah**
1:2 . . . 509
4:2 . . . 291, 509

**Micah**
4:1–4 . . . 72, 336
4:1–2, 13 . . . 510
5:1–2 . . . 112
5:2 . . . 18
6:4 . . . 217
7:9 . . . 43

**Nahum**
1:3 . . . 291
1:5 . . . 345

**Habakkuk**
2:4 . . . 35, 40, 44, 354, 366, 393

**Zephaniah**
1:14–15, 18 . . . 75
2:2 . . . 75

**Zechariah**
1:6 . . . 18
3 . . . 294
8:8 . . . 43
8:21–23 . . . 72, 336
9:9–13 . . . 112
12:10 . . . 274, 281

**Malachi**
1:2–3 . . . 322, 329
1:6 . . . 312
2:5 . . . 162
2:10 . . . 312

**Matthew**
3:9 . . . 325
5:17 . . . 112
5:38–39 . . . 435
5:43 . . . 454
5:44 . . . 432
5:48 . . . xiii
7:3–5 . . . 85
7:12 . . . 112
7:15–20 . . . 530
8:11–12 . . . 42
10:5–6 . . . 42, 485
11:13 . . . 112
12:36–37 . . . 77
15:1–20 . . . 475
15:1–6 . . . 480–81
15:24 . . . 42, 485
19:19 . . . 454
19:28 . . . 183
20:25–28 . . . 423
20:28 . . . 116
22:39 . . . 454
22:40 . . . 112
23 . . . 85
23:12 . . . 423
24:14 . . . 21, 42
24:42–44 . . . 454
25:31–46 . . . 77, 295
26:28 . . . 118
27:52–53 . . . 24
28:19–20 . . . 27, 32, 42

**Mark**
1:1–15 . . . 17
1:9–11 . . . 193, 208
1:14 . . . 20
3:13–16 . . . 24
4:38 . . . 300
7:1–23 . . . 475
7:2, 5 . . . 475

7:19 . . . . . 475
7:24–30. . . . . 485
9:50 . . . . . 429, 435
10:38–39. . . . . 193, 196, 208
10:45, 116 . . . . . xx
12:28–34. . . . . 457
12:28–33. . . . . 430
13:33–37. . . . . 454
14:36 . . . . . 255, 268
15:21 . . . . . 525
15:29–32. . . . . 481
26:45 . . . . . 454

**Luke**
2:1–4. . . . . 21
3:8 . . . . . 325
4:23 . . . . . 84, 104
6:27–28. . . . . 432
9:23, 28 . . . . . 50
10:2 . . . . . 373
11:20 . . . . . 21
12:35–36. . . . . 454
12:50 . . . . . 196
16:16 . . . . . 112
18:1–26. . . . . 519
21:28 . . . . . 116
21:36 . . . . . 454
23:40–42, 43. . . . . 129

**John**
1:45 . . . . . 112
3:16 . . . . . 148, 354
4:22–26. . . . . 485
5:22, 29 . . . . . 295
5:27 . . . . . 473
5:28–29. . . . . 77
8:36 . . . . . 218
11:24 . . . . . 386
13:31–35. . . . . 457
13:34–35. . . . . 457
14:26 . . . . . 263
15:26 . . . . . 263
16:2 . . . . . 313

**Acts**
1:8 . . . . . 374
1:14 . . . . . 483
2:10–11. . . . . 1
2:36 . . . . . 23, 152
2:38 . . . . . 263
3:17 . . . . . 350
4:2 . . . . . 24
4:24 . . . . . 483
5:29 . . . . . 450
6:1 . . . . . 524
6:9–15. . . . . 2
7:8 . . . . . 139, 146
7:26 . . . . . 167
8:6 . . . . . 483
10:1–11:18 . . . . . 475
10:14, 17, 30 . . . . . 475
10:28 . . . . . 100
10:42 . . . . . 23, 473
11:8, 9 . . . . . 475
13. . . . . 315
13:1–3. . . . . 19
13:16 . . . . . 312
13:32–33. . . . . 21, 316, 368
13:33 . . . . . 23
13:38–39. . . . . 125, 199
13:39 . . . . . 193, 208
13:45, 52 . . . . . 2
13:46–47. . . . . 505
13:48 . . . . . 339, 391
13:50–51. . . . . 381
14:1 . . . . . 316
14:2 . . . . . 381
14:2, 5 . . . . . 2
14:8–18. . . . . 507
14:19 . . . . . 2, 315
14:22 . . . . . 268
15:1–5. . . . . 532
15:1–2. . . . . 41
15:1 . . . . . 146
15:8 . . . . . 281
15:25 . . . . . 483
16:3–5. . . . . 27
16:9 . . . . . 374
16:14 . . . . . 362
17:1–2, 10. . . . . 316
17:4–5. . . . . 315
17:5–9. . . . . 381
17:6–9. . . . . 533
17:7 . . . . . 21
17:30 . . . . . 119
17:31 . . . . . 23, 295, 473
18:1–2. . . . . 521
18:2 . . . . . 1, 5, 442, 519
18:2, 17 . . . . . 2
18:6–8. . . . . 381
18:6 . . . . . 316
18:7 . . . . . 534
18:8 . . . . . 519
18:12 . . . . . 5
18:12, 18–17. . . . . 473
18:18–19. . . . . 521
18:19 . . . . . 316
18:27 . . . . . 520
19:8 . . . . . 316, 381

19:22 . . . 26, 534
19:29 . . . 483, 534
20–28 . . . 510
20:1–5 . . . 26
20:2–3 . . . 27, 511
20:3 . . . 315
20:4 . . . 533, 534
20:16 . . . 317
20:20–21 . . . 3, 38, 97, 215
21:26 . . . 317
21:28 . . . 38
22:3 . . . 349
22:16 . . . 359, 360
22:17–21 . . . 317
22:21 . . . 19, 315
23:1, 16 . . . 446
23:6 . . . 24
23:12 . . . 315
24:5–9 . . . 315
24:14 . . . 112
24:17 . . . 509
25:6, 10, 19 . . . 473
25:11 . . . 443
26:5 . . . 182
26:16–18 . . . 19
26:20 . . . 400, 507
26:24 . . . 48
27–28 . . . 315
28:14–15 . . . 38, 510
28:17 . . . 3, 38, 195
28:23 . . . 112
28:29–31 . . . 530

**Romans**

1–11 . . . 339, 411, 413
1–8 . . . 8, 25, 214, 305, 307, 310, 379
1–5 . . . 227
1–4 . . . 6, 11, 12, 17, 151, 161, 185, 193
1–3 . . . 43, 98, 99
1:1–17 . . . 27
1:1–15 . . . 6
1:1–7 . . . 17–32
1:1–4 . . . 20
1:1 . . . 18–19, 267
1:1, 5 . . . 361
1:2–4 . . . 21–22
1:2 . . . 10, 356
1:3–4 . . . 2, 14, 22, 23, 152, 308, 356, 359, 484, 504
1:3 . . . 20, 138
1:4 . . . 41, 226, 263, 401, 487
1:5–6, 13 . . . 2
1:5 . . . 24–24, 40, 261, 362, 411, 423, 504, 506, 531
1:6–7 . . . 26–25
1:6, 13 . . . 466
1:7 . . . 414
1:8–17 . . . 35–49
1:8–15 . . . 503
1:8 . . . 2, 11, 36–36, 211, 503, 532
1:9 . . . 10, 20, 503
1:9–15 . . . 38–38
1:9–12 . . . 482
1:10, 13 . . . 507
1:11–12 . . . 503
1:11 . . . 10, 507, 539
1:12 . . . 508, 509
1:13–16 . . . 361
1:13–15 . . . 508
1:13 . . . 4, 10, 26, 223, 388, 503, 504, 508
1:14 . . . 23, 452, 503
1:15 . . . 503
1:16–17 . . . 40–43, 110, 393
1:16–9:33 . . . 350
1:16 . . . 10, 11, 28, 41, 43, 51, 73, 316, 343, 359, 361, 379, 384, 466, 510
1:17 . . . 10, 13, 25, 43, 44, 96, 111,136, 258, 540
1:18–8:39 . . . 309
1:18–4:25 . . . 176
1:18–3:20 . . . 97, 93, 98, 109, 115, 241, 360
1:18–32 . . . 13, 52–67, 71, 73, 74, 331, 337, 415
1:18–31 . . . 394
1:18–30 . . . 93
1:18–15 . . . 503
1:18 . . . 43, 53–54, 138, 443
1:18, 27 . . . 99
1:18, 31 . . . 96, 99
1:19–23 . . . 55–55
1:20 . . . 41, 73
1:20, 31 . . . 99
1:21–23 . . . 56
1:21, 25, 32 . . . 99
1:21, 26 . . . 99, 103, 211
1:21, 24, 30, 31–30, 33 . . . 99
1:23 . . . 81, 115, 150, 288, 538
1:24–28 . . . 59
1:24–25 . . . 57–56
1:24 . . . 102, 415
1:25 . . . 53, 99, 314
1:26–28 . . . 58–59, 99
1:26–27 . . . 57, 58, 69, 213
1:28 . . . 413
1:28–32 . . . 61–63
1:28–31 . . . 74, 430
1:29 . . . 99

1:29, 32 . . . . . 99
1:30 . . . . . 99
1:31 . . . . . 99
1:32 . . . . . 262
2. . . . . . 87
2:1–7:6 . . . . . 238
2:1–3:20 . . . . . 13, 124
2:1–3:8 . . . . . 97
2:1–29. . . . . 24, 70–88, 382
2:1–16. . . . . 74, 415
2:1–11, 19–24 . . . . . 235
2:1–6. . . . . 74
2:1–5. . . . . 73–75
2:1–5, 19, 23. . . . . 99
2:1 . . . . . 73, 99
2:2–3, 5. . . . . 43
2:2–3, 5–16 . . . . . 109
2:3–4. . . . . 23
2:4 . . . . . 43, 99, 119, 338
2:5 . . . . . 55, 211, 331
2:5, 15 . . . . . 99
2:6–11. . . . . 75–76
2.7–11. . . . . 444
2:7 . . . . . 81, 214, 264
2.7, 10 . . . . . 288
2:8 . . . . . 96, 99
2:9–10. . . . . 466
2:9 . . . . . 73, 95, 97
2:10 . . . . . 115
2:12–16. . . . . 76–77
2:12 . . . . . 102, 223
2:13–16. . . . . 74, 77, 79
2:13–14. . . . . 77
2:13 . . . . . 116, 151, 283
2:14–15. . . . . 235
2:14–15, 27–29 . . . . . 78, 79
2:15–16. . . . . 247
2:15 . . . . . 100, 446
2:15, 31 . . . . . 211
2:16–24. . . . . 94
2:16 . . . . . 10, 13, 50, 54, 77, 110, 281, 294, 473, 490, 539
2:17–24. . . . . 79–81
2:17 . . . . . 350
2:17, 25 . . . . . 121
2:19–20. . . . . 89
2:19 . . . . . 87
2:21–25. . . . . 351
2:21–23. . . . . 74
2:22, 25, 26 . . . . . 99
2:23–24. . . . . 81
2:25–29. . . . . 13, 78, 81–83, 94, 124, 225, 261, 263, 307, 326
2:26 . . . . . 144
2:27 . . . . . 73
2:29 . . . . . 308
3–8 . . . . . 384
3–4 . . . . . 509
3. . . . . . 95, 246
3:1–20. . . . . 91–106, 92, 93, 96, 101, 103, 108, 259
3:1–9. . . . . 121, 307, 325
3:1–5. . . . . 13
3:1–4. . . . . 94–95
3:1–2. . . . . 312
3:1 . . . . . 94, 95, 195, 210
3:1, 9 . . . . . 97
3:2 . . . . . 42, 76, 94, 259, 313, 424
3:3–5. . . . . 330
3:3 . . . . . 43, 95, 99, 114, 151, 378
3:4 . . . . . 99
3:5–9. . . . . 96–98
3:5–8. . . . . 10, 96
3:5 . . . . . 43, 55, 77, 95, 96, 141, 211, 347
3:5, 10 . . . . . 99
3:6, 19–20. . . . . 109
3:7–8. . . . . 3, 25
3:7 . . . . . 43, 95
3:7, 13–15. . . . . 99
3:8 . . . . . 38, 41, 99, 195, 307
3:9 . . . . . 95, 98, 102
3:9, 20 . . . . . 233, 351
3:10–18. . . . . 98
3:10 . . . . . 486
3:11 . . . . . 99
3:11, 20 . . . . . 99
3:19–20. . . . . 98–99,109, 115, 185
3:19 . . . . . 223, 337
3:19, 30 . . . . . 260
3:20 . . . . . 78, 102, 116, 180, 221, 239, 308, 329, 334, 353, 382
3:20, 26, 28, 30, 32 . . . . . 283
3:20, 29–28. . . . . 328
3:20, 30 . . . . . 259
3:21–5:11 . . . . . 244, 330
3:21–4:25 . . . . . 110, 122, 162, 317, 334, 531
3:21–31. . . . . 109–34, 126, 139
3:21–30. . . . . 233
3:21–26. . . . . 35, 99, 110, 114, 118, 119, 125, 258, 348
3:21–22. . . . . 122, 138
3:21 . . . . . 10, 96, 110–10, 123, 138, 211, 245, 258, 259, 288, 352, 356, 382, 453, 540
3:21, 30 . . . . . 139
3:21, 33 . . . . . 308
3:22–25. . . . . 2
3:22–24. . . . . 151

3:22 . . . . . . . . . . . . . . . 42, 113, 114, 308, 347
3:22, 29 . . . . . . . . . . . . . . . . . . . . . . . . . . 139
3:22, 31 . . . . . . . . . . . . . . . . . . . . . . 139, 466
3:22, 31–30. . . . . . . . . . . . . . . . . . . . . . . . 360
3:22a . . . . . . . . . . . . . . . . . . . . . . . . 112–13
3:22b–23. . . . . . . . . . . . . . . . . . . . . . . . . 115
3:23 . . . . . . . . . . . . . . . . . . 67, 102, 139, 538
3:24–25. . . . . . . . . . . 115–19, 152, 415, 472
3:24–25a. . . . . . . . . . . . . . . . . . . . . . . 115–17
3:24 . . . . . . . . . . . . . . . . . . . . . . . . . 117, 270
3:24, 28, 30 . . . . . . . . . . . . . . . . . . . . . . . 116
3:24, 28, 30, 32 . . . . . . . . . . . . . . . . . . . . 294
3:25b–26. . . . . . . . . . . . . . . . . . . . . . 119–20
3:25 . . . . . . . . . . . . . . . . . . . . . . . . . 166, 261
3:26, 32 . . . . . . . . . . . . . . . . . . . . . . . . . . . 44
3:27–4:25 . . . . . . . . . . . . . . . . . . . . . . . . 123
3:27–38. . . . . . . . . . . . . . . . . . . . . . . . . . 100
3:27–31. . . . . . . . 14, 110, 120–24, 141, 348
3:27–29. . . . . . . . . . . . . . . . . . . . . . . . . . 140
3:27 . . . . . . . . . . . . . . . . . . . . . . . . . . . . 259
3:28 . . . . . . . . . . . . . . . . . . . . . . . . . . . . 100
3:29 . . . . . . . . . . . . . . . . . . . . . . . . . 343, 379
3:30 . . . . . . . . . . . . . . . . . . . . . 116, 151, 379
3:31 . . . . . . . . . . . . . . . . . . . . . . 10, 123, 139
4. . . . . . . . . . . . 138, 142, 152, 153, 158, 184
4:1–25. . . . . . 13, 25, 110, 137–58, 308, 347
4:1–16. . . . . . . . . . . . . . . . . . . . . . . . . . . 323
4:1–8, 27. . . . . . . . . . . . . . . . . . . . . . . . . 294
4:1–8. . . . . . . . . . . . . . . . . . . . . . . . . . . . 149
4:1–3. . . . . . . . . . . . . . . . . . . . . . . . . 140–42
4:1 . . . . . . . . . . . . . . . 141, 195, 210, 292, 347
4:2–8. . . . . . . . . . . . . . . . . . . . . . . . . . . . 382
4:2, 4 . . . . . . . . . . . . . . . . . . . . . . . . . . . . 283
4:2 . . . . . . . . . . . . . . . . . . . . . . . . . . . . . 388
4:3, 9, 19–18, 24–23 . . . . . . . . . . . . . . . . 123
4:4–6, 8–12, 26 . . . . . . . . . . . . . . . . . . . . 144
4:4–6. . . . . . . . . . . . . . . . . . . . . . . . . 328, 338
4:4–5. . . . . . . . . . . . . . . . 142–43, 183, 214
4:4 . . . . . . . . . . . . . . . . . . . . . . . . . . . . . 338
4:4, 16 . . . . . . . . . . . . . . . . . . . . . . . . . . . 139
4.5 . . . . . . . . . . . . . . . . . . . . . . . . . . 165, 426
4:5, 11–24. . . . . . . . . . . . . . . . . . . . . . . . . 25
4:5, 11 . . . . . . . . . . . . . . . . . . . . . . . . . . . 139
4:6–8. . . . . . . . . . . . . . . . . . . . . . . . . . . . 145
4:6 . . . . . . . . . . . . . . . . . . . . . . . . . . . . . 139
4:6, 24 . . . . . . . . . . . . . . . . . . . . . . . . . . . . 42
4:8 . . . . . . . . . . . . . . . . . . . . . . . . . . . . . 119
4:9–22. . . . . . . . . . . . . . . . . . . . . . . . . . . 141
4:9–17. . . . . . . . . . . . . . . . . . . . . . . . . 14, 348
4:9–10. . . . . . . . . . . . . . . . . . . . . . . . . 145–45
4:11–17. . . . . . . . . . . . . . . . . . . . . . . . . . 308
4:11–16. . . . . . . . . . . . . . . . . . . . . . . . . . 343
4:11–12. . . . . . . . . . . . . . . . . . . . . . . 147–48
4:11–12, 18. . . . . . . . . . . . . . . . . . . . . . . 139
4:12–18. . . . . . . . . . . . . . . . . . . . . . . . . . . 94
4:12–15. . . . . . . . . . . . . . . . . . . . . . . . . . 259
4:12 . . . . . . . . . . . . . . . . . . . . . . . . . . 114, 379
4:13–16. . . . . . . . . . . . . . . . . . . 148–49, 510
4:13–15. . . . . . . . . . . . . . . . . . . . . . . . . . 236
4:13–14. . . . . . . . . . . . . . . . . . . . . . . . . . 351
4:13 . . . . . . . . . . . . . . . . . . . . . . 279, 280, 327
4:14–16. . . . . . . . . . . . . . . . . . . . . . . . . . 233
4:14 . . . . . . . . . . . . . . . . . . . . . . . . . . . . 139
4:14, 18 . . . . . . . . . . . . . . . . . . . . . . . . . . 353
4:15 . . . . . . . . . . . . . . . 55, 180, 185, 233, 351
4:16 . . . . . . . . . . . . . . . . . . . . . . . . 44, 148, 382
4:17–18. . . . . . . . . . . . . . . . . . . . . . . . . . . 36
4:17 . . . . . . . . . . . . . . . . . . . . . . . . . . 149–50
4:18–22. . . . . . . . . . . . . . . . . . . . . . . . 150–51
4:18–21. . . . . . . . . . . . . . . . . . . . . . . . . . 154
4:18–20. . . . . . . . . . . . . . . . . . . . . . . . . . 151
4:18 . . . . . . . . . . . . . . . . . . . . . . . . . . . . 171
4:20 . . . . . . . . . . . . . . . . . . . . . . 150, 288, 538
4:21 . . . . . . . . . . . . . . . . . . . . . . . . . . . . . 41
4:23–24. . . . . . . . . . . . . . . . . . . . . . . . . . 151
4:24–25. . . . . . . . . . . . . . . . . . . . . . . . . . 226
4:24 . . . . . . . . . . . . . . . . . . . . . . . . . . . . . 69
4:25 . . . . . . . . 2, 116, 151–52 164, 294, 294, 359 470, 504
4:25a . . . . . . . . . . . . . . . . . . . . . . . . . . . . 295
4:25b . . . . . . . . . . . . . . . . . . . . . . . . . . . . 295
4:4–8. . . . . . . . . . . . . . . . . . . . . . . . . . . . 348
5–8 . . . . . . . . 6, 12, 161, 175, 221, 257, 265, 278, 298
5–7 . . . . . . . . . . . . . . . . . . . . . . . . . 255, 258
5–6 . . . . . . . . . . . . . . . . . . . . . . . . . . . 10, 212
5. . . . . . . . . . . . . . . . . . . . . . . . . . . . 188, 193
5:1–11. . . . 161–71, 175, 255, 256, 292, 310
5:1–2. . . . . . . . . . . . . . . . . . . . . . . . . 162–64
5:1 . . . . . . . . 41, 44, 116, 151, 163, 258, 264, 294, 347, 366
5:1, 9 . . . . . . . . . . . . . . . . . . . . . . . . . 283, 292
5:2–3. . . . . . . . . . . . . . . . . . . . . . . . . . . . 432
5:2 . . . . . . . . . . . . . . . . . . . 168, 283, 308, 538
5:2, 11 . . . . . . . . . . . . . . . . . . . . . . . . . . . 388
5:2, 15, 19, 22–21. . . . . . . . . . . . . . . . . . 382
5:3–5. . . . . . . . . . . . . . . . . . . . . . . 164–65, 275
5:3 . . . . . . . . . . . . . . . . . . . . . . . . . . 288, 292
5:5–17. . . . . . . . . . . . . . . . . . . . . . . . . . . 214
5:5–7. . . . . . . . . . . . . . . . . . . . . . . . . . . . 102
5:5 . . . . . . . . 41, 211, 213, 222, 299, 300, 457
5:5, 8 . . . . . . . . . . . . . . . . . . . . . . . . . 293, 451
5:6–8. . . . . . . . . . . . . . . . . . . . . . . 165–66, 295
5:6, 10 . . . . . . . . . . . . . . . . . . . . . . . . . . . 293
5:8–11. . . . . . . . . . . . . . . . . . . . . . . . . . . . 11
5:8–10. . . . . . . . . . . . . . . . . . . . . . . . 294, 338
5:8–9. . . . . . . . . . . . . . . . . . . . . . . . . 294, 487
5:8 . . . . . . . . . . . . . . . . . . . . . . 172, 173, 291

5:9–11. . . . . . . . . . . . . . . . . . . . . . . . 166–68
5:9–10. . . . . . . . . . . . . . . . . . . . . . . . . . . .166
5:9 . . . . . . . . . . . . . . . . . . . .55, 152, 258, 293
5:9, 18 . . . . . . . . . . . . . . . . . . . . . . . . . . .294
5:10–11. . . . . . . . . . . . . . . . . . . . . . . . . . .167
5:10 . . . . . . . . . . . . . . . . . . . . . . . . . .293, 386
5:11 . . . . . . . . . . . . . . . . . . . . . . . . . . . . .293
5:12–21. . . . .13, 53, 71, 114, 161, 174–190, 195, 225, 241, 255, 259, 329
5:12 . . . . . . . . . . . . . . . . . . . . . . . . . 176–78
5:12, 18, 21 . . . . . . . . . . . . . . . . . . . . . . .102
5:13–14. . . . . . . . . . . . . . . . . . . . . . . . 180–79
5:13 . . . . . . . . . . . . . . . . . . . . .102, 236, 260
5:14–33. . . . . . . . . . . . . . . . . . . . . . . . . . .512
5:15–33. . . . . . . . . . . . . . . . . . . . . . . . . . .403
5:15–16. . . . . . . . . . . . . . . . . . . . . . . 181–82
5:16, 20 . . . . . . . . . . . . . . . . . . . . . . .182, 258
5:17 . . . . . . . . . . . . . . . . . . . .25, 42, 183, 264
5:18–19. . . . . . . . . . . . . . . . . . . 149, 183–84
5:18 . . . . . . . . . . . . . . . . . . . . . .264, 310, 379
5:20–21. . . . . . .184–86, 208, 209, 220, 221, 224, 241, 255, 382
5:20 . . . . . . . . . .221, 225, 233, 260, 337, 351
5:21 . . . . . . . . . . . . . .194, 214, 245, 258, 264
6–8 . . . . . . . . . . . . . . . . . . . . . . . . . . . . . .24
6. . . . . . . . . . . . . . . . .191, 193, 194, 220, 489
6:1–8:39 . . . . . . . . . . . . . . . . . . . . . . . . . .162
6:1–8:17 . . . . . . . . . . . . . . . . . . . . . .176, 194
6:1–7:6 . . . . . . . . . . . . . . . . . . . . . . . .234, 261
6:1–23. . . . .10, 194, 220, 222, 253, 255, 256
6:1–14. . . . . . . . . . . . . . . . . . . 193–205, 208
6:1–2. . . . . . . . . . . . . . . 24, 25, 38, 195–251
6:1 . . . . . . . . . . . . . . . . .3, 141, 292, 307, 347
6:2 . . . . . . . . . . . . . . . . . . . . . . . .97, 210, 221
6:2–14. . . . . . . . . . . . . . . . . . . . . . . . . . . .210
6:3–15. . . . . . . . . . . . . . . . . . . . . . . . 521–22
6:3–7. . . . . . . . . . . . . . . . . . . . . . . . . . 196–98
6:3–4. . . . . . . . . . . . . . . . . . . . . . . . . . . . .204
6:3, 16 . . . . . . . . . . . . . . . . . . . . . . . . . . . .504
6:4–7. . . . . . . . . . . . . . . . . . . . . . . . . . . . .197
6:4–6. . . . . . . . . . . . . . . . . . . . . . . . . . . . .268
6:4 . . . . . . . . . . . . . . . . . . . . . .226, 264, 288
6:4, 9 . . . . . . . . . . . . . . . . . . . . . . . . . . . . .226
6:5 . . . . . . . . . . . . . . . . . . . . . . . . . . . . . . .472
6:6–8. . . . . . . . . . . . . . . . . . . . . . . . . . . . .223
6:6–7, 19–20, 24 . . . . . . . . . . . . . . . . . . . .234
6:6 . . . . . . . . . . . . . . . . . . . . . . . . . . . . . . .414
6:6, 16–17, 22. . . . . . . . . . . . . . . . . . . . . .267
6:7, 18, 24 . . . . . . . . . . . . . . . . . . . . . .221, 267
6:8–11. . . . . . . . . . . . . . . . . . . . . . . . . 200–99
6:8 . . . . . . . . . . . . . . . . . . . . . . . . . . . . . . .221
6:11, 13 . . . . . . . . . . . . . . . . . . . . . . . . . . .205
6:12–14. . . . . . . . . . . . . . . . . . . . . . . 201–203
6:12–13. . . . . . . . . . . . . . . . . . . . . . . . . . .456
6:12 . . . . . . . . . . . . . . . . . . . . . . . . . . . . . .198
6:13 . . . . . . . . . . . . . . . . . . . . . . . . . . . . . .198
6:13, 21 . . . . . . . . . . . . . . . . . . . . . . . .413, 414
6:14–23. . . . . . . . . . . . . . . . . . . . . . . . . . .233
6:14–15. . . . . . . . . . .221, 225, 234, 245, 352
6:14 . . . . . . . . . . . . . .208, 209, 221, 259, 453
6:15–23. . . . . . . . . . . . . . . . . . . 208–17, 215
6:15–22. . . . . . . . . . . . . . . . . . . . . . . . . . .214
6:15 . . . . . . . . . . . . . . . . . . . . . 202, 209–10
6:16–21. . . . . . . . . . . . . . . . . . . . . . . . . . .225
6:16 . . . . . . . . . . . . . . . . . . . . . . . . . . . .25, 210
6:17–18. . . . . . . . . . . . . . . . . . . . . . 210–209
6:17 . . . . . .2, 24, 40, 412, 468, 504, 531, 532
6:18–19. . . . . . . . . . . . . . . . . . . . . . . . . . .267
6:19 . . . . . . . . . . . . . . 77, 211–12, 258, 414
6:20–22. . . . . . . . . . . . . . . . . . . . . . . . 212–14
6:20–21. . . . . . . . . . . . . . . . . . . . . . . . . . .394
6:21 . . . . . . . . . . . . . . . . . . . . . . . . . . . .41, 237
6:22–23. . . . . . . . . . . . . . . . . . . . . . . . . . .264
6:22 . . . . . . . . . . . . . . . . . . . . . . . .111, 199, 267
6:23 . . . . . . . . . . . . . .102, 104, 182, 214, 338
7–8 . . . . . . . . . . . . . . . . . . . . . . . . . . . . . . .220
7. . . . . . . . . . . . . . . . . . . . . . . . .220, 245, 246
7:1–25. . . . . . . . . . . . . . . . . . . . . . . . . . . .259
7:1–6. . . . . . . . .158, 199, 209, 220–27, 222, 255, 352
7:1–3. . . . . . . . . . . . . . . . . . . . . . . . . . 222–23
7:1 . . . . . . . . . . . . . . . . . . . . . .3, 221, 237, 504
7:4–6. . . . . . . . . . . . . . . . . . . . . . . . . . . . .222
7:4 . . . . . . . . . . . . . . . 221, 223–22, 226, 472
7:5–6. . . . . . . . . . . . . . . . . . . . . . 224–26, 256
7:5 . . . . . . . . . . . . . . .221, 232, 233, 256, 271
7:6 . . .111, 221, 234, 256, 258, 259, 267, 416
7:7–8:17 . . . . . . . . . . . . . . . . . . . . . . . . . . .224
7:7–25. . . . . . .220, 221, 224, 225, 230–251, 255, 256, 257, 259, 308, 337, 402
7:7–8. . . . . . . . . 180, 202, 238–39, 260, 351
7:7 . . . . . . . . . . . . . . . . . . . .141, 307, 329, 347
7:7–13. . . . . . . . . . . . . . . . . . . . . . . . . . . .125
7:7–12. . . . . . . . . . . . . . . . . . . . . . . . .232, 241
7:7–9. . . . . . . . . . . . . . . . . . . . . . . . . . . . .185
7:8–10. . . . . . . . . . . . . . . . . . . . . . . . . . . .236
7:9–11. . . . . . . . . . . . . . . . . . . . . 236, 239–40
7:9 . . . . . . . . . . . . . . . . . . . . . . . . . . . . . . .236
7:10 . . . . . . . . . . . . . . . . . . . . . . . . . . . . . .259
7:11 . . . . . . . . . . . . . . . . . . . . . . . . . . . . . .236
7:12 . . . . . . . . . . . . . . . . . . . . . . . . . . . .10, 240
7:13 . . . . . . . . . . . . . . . . . . . . . . . . . . . . . .241
7:14–25. . . . . . . . . . . . . . . . . . . . . . . . .232, 253
7:14–23. . . . . . . . . . . . . . . . . . . . . . . . . 241–43
7:14 . . . . . . . . . . . . . . . . . . . . . . . .98, 234, 259
7:14, 27 . . . . . . . . . . . . . . . . . . . . . . . . . . .267
7:21–23. . . . . . . . . . . . . . . . . . . . . . . . . . .122
7:21, 25 . . . . . . . . . . . . . . . . . . . . . . . . . . .259

7:21, 25–25 . . . 122
7:21, 25, 27 . . . 259
7:22 . . . 231
7:22, 27 . . . 234
7:24–25 . . . 243–51
7:24 . . . 198, 231
7:25 . . . 338
8–9 . . . 343
8 . . . 55, 78, 167, 256, 295, 310
8:1–39 . . . 265, 290–301
8:1–30 . . . 292, 298
8:1–27 . . . 13
8:1–17 . . . 198, 224, 225, 234, 254–71, 275
8:1–13 . . . 98
8:1–11 . . . 79, 221, 222, 253
8:1–4 . . . 257–60
8:1 . . . 41, 184, 256, 258, 294, 295
8:1, 30 . . . 116
8:2–17 . . . 24
8:2 . . . 122, 234, 241, 259
8:3 . . . 14, 120, 166, 259, 295, 316, 329, 334, 351
8:3, 32 . . . 338
8:4–5, 12–13 . . . 415
8:4 . . . 79, 123, 125, 234, 259, 352, 453
8:5–13 . . . 271
8:5–8 . . . 262–63
8:6 . . . 264
8:7 . . . 259, 416
8:9–11 . . . 234, 263–64
8:9 . . . 222, 271, 472
8:10–13 . . . 253
8:10–11 . . . 310
8:10, 32 . . . 294
8:11 . . . 197, 263, 279
8:12–13 . . . 264–65, 456
8:12 . . . 272, 452
8:13 . . . 234, 389
8:14–39 . . . 163
8:14–17 . . . 158, 265–66, 308, 310
8:14 . . . 266
8:15 . . . 234, 267, 268, 280, 281
8:15, 25 . . . 267, 472
8:16–17, 21 . . . 336
8:17–18, 23 . . . 283
8:17–18, 23, 32 . . . 538
8:17 . . . 288, 294, 296, 310
8:17, 32 . . . 295
8:18–39 . . . 310, 389
8:18–30 . . . 274–87, 308
8:18–22 . . . 276–77
8:18 . . . 288, 354, 382
8:20 . . . 171, 487
8:21 . . . 288
8:23–25 . . . 279–80
8:23 . . . 41, 116
8:24–27 . . . 432
8:24–25 . . . 171
8:24 . . . 487
8:26–27 . . . 280–81
8:26 . . . 212
8:27 . . . 295, 416
8:28–30 . . . 281–82, 310
8:28–29 . . . 292
8:28 . . . 26
8:29 . . . 268, 381, 416
8:30 . . . 163, 268
8:30, 35 . . . 116, 151
8:31–39 . . . 290–301, 335, 291
8:31–34 . . . 293
8:31–32 . . . 292–94
8:31 . . . 141, 347
8:32 . . . 260, 283, 300, 310, 379
8:32, 37 . . . 316
8:33–34 . . . 258, 294–95
8:33 . . . 308
8:34 . . . 166, 264, 293, 302
8:35–39 . . . 279, 299
8:35–37 . . . 292, 295–97
8:35, 41 . . . 293
8:38–39 . . . 297–98
8:39 . . . 296, 304, 451
9–15 . . . 9
9–11 . . . 3, 8, 11, 12, 92, 95, 116, 142, 151, 161, 282, 304–309, 315, 323, 338, 340, 341, 361, 366, 380, 392, 393, 396, 406, 509
9–10 . . . 365, 378, 379, 380, 382
9:1–11:36 . . . 115
9:1–9 . . . 324
9:1–5 . . . 3, 13, 95, 304–318, 318, 321, 322, 362
9:1–4a . . . 311–12
9:1 . . . 446
9:3 . . . 308, 381
9:4–5 . . . 10, 42, 76, 96, 379, 484
9:4b–5 . . . 312–13
9:4 . . . 267, 288
9:4, 31 . . . 259
9:5 . . . 14, 314, 316, 338, 354
9:6–11:32 . . . 321, 322
9:6–10:21 . . . 13, 332
9:6–29 . . . 311, 321–41, 345, 347, 382
9:6–13 . . . 94
9:6–9 . . . 324–25
9:6 . . . 10, 95, 325, 364, 370, 379, 380, 391

9:6a . . . 323
9:6a, 29, 33 . . . 392
9:7–8. . . . 142, 336
9:7, 11–13. . . . 323
9:8 . . . 82, 312, 332
9:8, 24–29. . . . 323
9:9–18. . . . 378
9:9–13. . . . 379
9:9 . . . 378
9:9b . . . 391
9:10–18. . . . 324
9:10–18, 228. . . . 328
9:10–13. . . . 327–28, 382
9:11–12. . . . 382
9:11–12, 18. . . . 323
9:11 . . . 282, 380, 388, 395
9:12 . . . 328
9:12, 33–32. . . . 353
9:12, 34 . . . 380
9:14–18. . . . 330–32
9:14 . . . 95, 347, 381
9:14, 32 . . . 141, 292
9:15–18. . . . 337, 379
9:15–16. . . . 413
9:15 . . . 338
9:15, 18, 20 . . . 380
9:16, 1, 25 . . . 485
9:17–18. . . . 383
9:17 . . . 339
9:17, 24 . . . 41
9:18 . . . 380, 413
9:19–21. . . . 332–33
9:19 . . . 95
9:20–21. . . . 24
9:21 . . . 378
9:22–23. . . . 333–35, 338, 390
9:22 . . . 55, 378
9:23 . . . 288, 334, 335
9:24–29. . . . 335–37, 343, 392
9:24 . . . 335, 382
9:25–26. . . . 364
9:27–29. . . . 380
9:27 . . . 95, 382
9:29 . . . 326, 382
9:30–10:21 . . . 95, 311, 344–73, 378, 381
9:30–10:4 . . . 240, 382
9:30–33. . . . 122, 309, 347–49, 364
9:30–32. . . . 382
9:30 . . . 346, 352
9:30, 34 . . . 25, 42, 44
9:30, 35 . . . 393
9:31–33. . . . 329
9:31–32. . . . 352
9:31 . . . 311
9:32–33. . . . 311, 328, 380, 474
9:32 . . . 350, 393
9:32, 35 . . . 346
9:33–10:4 . . . 10
9:33 . . . 41, 346, 359, 368
10. . . . 375
10:1–21. . . . 364
10:1–11. . . . 359
10:1–4. . . . 14, 347, 349–50
10:1 . . . 311, 380, 384, 394
10:1, 9, 10, 13 . . . 346
10:1, 21 . . . 390
10:3–6. . . . 42
10:3–4. . . . 378
10:3 . . . 13, 95, 329, 352, 353
10:4–6. . . . 25
10:4–5. . . . 259
10:4 . . . 13, 14, 22, 123, 318, 338, 352, 368, 379, 403
10:4, 5–8, 17. . . . 346
10:4, 6, 8, 9–10, 14, 19. . . . 346
10:4, 6–8, 9–11, 14, 19 . . . 393
10:4, 11 . . . 360
10:4, 11, 12, 13 . . . 346
10:5–8. . . . 347, 352–56, 368
10:5–6. . . . 10, 122, 123
10:5 . . . 350
10:6–8. . . . 354, 356, 358
10:6 . . . 44
10:6, 8–11, 19. . . . 383
10:9–13. . . . 347, 358–59
10:9–12. . . . 23
10:9–11. . . . 2, 211, 384, 491
10:9–10. . . . 25, 116, 151, 504
10:9 . . . 69
10:10 . . . 151
10:11–13. . . . 343, 346
10:11 . . . 41, 346, 359
10:12–13. . . . 346
10:12 . . . 42, 95, 308, 346, 466, 491
10:13 . . . 314, 368
10:13, 18 . . . 489
10:14–21. . . . 11, 347, 361, 365, 392
10:14–17. . . . 361–62, 408
10:14–15. . . . 372, 374
10:15–16. . . . 346
10:15 . . . 346, 368
10:16–21. . . . 337
10:16–19. . . . 346
10:16 . . . 25
10:16, 21 . . . 378
10:16, 21, 23 . . . 378, 394
10:16, 23 . . . 380
10:17 . . . 41, 365, 369

10:18–21 . . . 309, 361, 363–65
10:18–19 . . . 346
10:19 . . . 346, 347, 361, 380, 394
10:19, 23 . . . 392
10:20–21 . . . 347
10:21 . . . 346, 378
11–12a . . . 454
11 . . . 11, 311, 334, 380, 393, 402, 403, 489
11:1–32 . . . 346, 361, 376–403
11:1–5 . . . 380–82
11:1–2 . . . 95, 308
11:1 . . . 308, 311, 312, 315, 326, 365, 380
11:2 . . . 282
11:2, 7, 11 . . . 392
11:4 . . . 382
11:5–6 . . . 380
11:5 . . . 95, 380, 392
11:6 . . . 328
11:7–10 . . . 382–83
11:7–8 . . . 380
11:7 . . . 391, 392
11:8 . . . 378, 486
11:9 . . . 475
11:10 . . . 448
11:11–15 . . . 383–84, 394
11:11 . . . 311, 381, 390
11:11, 14–15, 30–31 . . . 361
11:11, 14 . . . 363, 380
11:12–13 . . . 380
11:13–33 . . . 11
11:13–31 . . . 7
11:13 . . . 2, 26, 361, 400, 466
11:14 . . . 171, 307, 312
11:14, 30–32 . . . 379
11:16–24 . . . 386–88
11:17–24 . . . 396, 510
11:18–25 . . . 361
11:18–20 . . . 378
11:18, 21 . . . 365
11:20–23 . . . 394
11:20 . . . 383
11:20, 25 . . . 393
11:25–32 . . . 10, 42, 323, 390–93, 466
11:25–26 . . . 361, 403
11:25 . . . 38, 380, 383, 504
11:26–27 . . . 379
11:26 . . . 308, 310, 335, 380
11:28 . . . 94, 309, 334, 337, 378, 380
11:28–32 . . . 361
11:28–29 . . . 379
11:29 . . . 13
11:30–32 . . . 485
11:30–31 . . . 338, 380
11:31–32 . . . 380, 413
11:31 . . . 378
11:32 . . . 329, 334, 338, 339, 379
11:33–36 . . . 46, 311, 365, 406–408, 538
11:33 . . . 407, 540
11:34–35 . . . 408, 409
11:36 . . . 288, 314, 408
12–15 . . . 5, 8, 305, 307, 412, 413, 469
12–13 . . . 11, 412
12 . . . 23, 411
12:1–15:13 . . . 12, 298, 411, 412, 424, 480
12:1–13:14 . . . 456
12:1–2 . . . 411–19, 417, 422, 451, 505
12:1 . . . 213, 305, 339, 412–13
12:2 . . . 415–15, 485
12:3–8 . . . 422–26
12:3 . . . 422, 423–25
12:4–8 . . . 422, 425–26
12:4 . . . 426
12:4, 10 . . . 477
12:5 . . . 226, 434, 484
12:6 . . . 39, 424
12:9–21 . . . 418, 429–38
12:9–16 . . . 430–32
12:9–10 . . . 436, 477
12:9 . . . 436, 452, 457
12:9, 17, 23 . . . 444
12:10 . . . 452, 457, 484
12:11 . . . 23
12:12 . . . 171, 488
12:13 . . . 509
12:14–13:7 . . . 430
12:16 . . . 482, 484
12:17–21 . . . 434–36, 443
12:17b . . . 41
12:19 . . . 23, 55, 453
13 . . . 41, 454
13:1–7 . . . 29, 430, 441–48
13:1–5 . . . 443
13:1 . . . 443–44
13:2–3a . . . 444–45
13:3–4 . . . 444, 445
13:3b–4 . . . 445–46
13:4 . . . 435, 439
13:5–7 . . . 446–45
13:6–7 . . . 5
13:8–14 . . . 451–58
13:8–10 . . . 10, 79, 123, 125, 308, 431, 452–54, 457, 477, 507
13:8 . . . 481
13:8, 10 . . . 259, 352
13:9–10 . . . 481
13:9 . . . 317
13:10 . . . 47, 457, 465, 484

13:11–12a. . . . . . . . . . . . . . . . . . . . . 454–55
13:11 . . . . . . . . . . . . . . . . . . . . . . . . . . . . . .41
13:12b–14. . . . . . . . . . . . . . . . . . . . . 455–56
13:12 . . . . . . . . . . . . . . . . . . . . . . . . . . . .456
13:13–14. . . . . . . . . . . . . . . . . . . . . . . . .455
13:14 . . . . . . . . . . .23, 69, 202, 224, 234, 272
13:32–33. . . . . . . . . . . . . . . . . . . . . . . . . .14
14–15 . . . . . . . . . . . . 3, 6, 8, 31, 87, 424 466
14. . . . . . . . . . . . . . . . . . . . . .7, 10, 489, 497
14:1–23. . . . . . . . . . . . . . . . . . . . . .308, 316
14:1–15:13 . . . 4, 9, 10, 40, 412, 433, 461–98, 464, 465, 484, 488, 494, 509
14:1–12. . . . . . . . . . . . . . . . . . . . . . 465–72
14:1–2. . . . . . . . . . . . . . . . . . . . . . .212, 465
14:2 . . . . . . . . . . . . . . . . . . . . . . . . . . . . .385
14:4–11. . . . . . . . . . . . . . . . . . . . . . . . . . .23
14:4 . . . . . . . . . . . . . . . . . . . . . . . . . . . . .489
14:7–11. . . . . . . . . . . . . . . . . . . . . . . . . .489
14:8–9. . . . . . . . . . . . . . . . . . . . . . . . . . .489
14:9–10. . . . . . . . . . . . . . . . . . . . . . . . . . .11
14:9 . . . . . . . . . . . . . . . . . . . . . . . . . . . . . .23
14:10 . . . . . . . . . . . . . . . . . . .50, 54, 295, 490
14:13–23. . . . . . . . . . . . . . . . . . 474–78, 484
14:14 . . . . . . . . . . . . . . . . . . . . .297, 466, 475
14:14, 22 . . . . . . . . . . . . . . . . . . . . . .466, 481
14:15 . . . . . . . . . . . . . . . . . . . . . . . . . . . .452
14:16 . . . . . . . . . . . . . . . . . . . . . . . .10, 11, 482
14:17 . . . . . . . . . . . . . . . . . . . . .213, 414, 488
14:19 . . . . . . . . . . . . . . . xvii, 9, 317, 484, 500
14:23 . . . . . . . . . . . . . . . . . . . . .102, 538, 539
15–16 . . . . . . . . . . . . . . . . . . . . . . . . . . . . .10
15:1–13. . . . . . . . . . . . . . . . . . . . . . . . . .480
15:1–6. . . . . . . . . . . . . . . . . . . . 465, 480–81
15:1 . . . . . . . . . . . . . . . . . . . .9, 212, 465, 466
15:4 . . . . . . . . . . . . . . . . . . . . . . . . . . . . .171
15:5 . . . . . . . . . . . . . . . . . . . . . . . . . .433, 484
15:5, 24 . . . . . . . . . . . . . . . . . . . . . . . . . . .391
15:6–7. . . . . . . . . . . . . . . . . . . . . . . . . . . . .11
15:6 . . . . . . . . . . . . . . . . . . . .23, 25, 145, 489
15:7–13. . . . . . . . 13, 465, 473, 480, 483–86
15:7–12. . . . . . . . . . . . . . . . . . . . . . . . . .464
15:7–8. . . . . . . . . . . . . . . . . . . . . . . . . .89, 510
15:7 . . . . .9, 69, 288, 385, 412, 465, 483, 484
15:8–12. . . . . . . . . . . . . . . . . . . . . . . . .10, 94
15:8–9. . . . . . . . . . . . . . . . . . . . . . .42, 131, 307
15:8–9, 12. . . . . . . . . . . . . . . . . . . . . . . .14, 23
15:8–9, 29. . . . . . . . . . . . . . . . . . . . . . . . . .11
15:8 . . . . . . . . . . . . . . . . . . . . . .260, 313, 483
15:9–12. . . . . . . . . . . . . . . . . . . . . . . . . .483
15:9 . . . . . . . . . . . . . . . . . . . . . . .26, 339, 505
15:10 . . . . . . . . . . . . . . . . . . . . . . . . . . . . .10
15:11 . . . . . . . . . . . . . . . . . . . . . . . . . . . .489
15:12 . . . . . . . . . . . . . . . . . . . . . . . . . .171, 448
15:13 . . . . . . . . . . . . . .39, 213, 414, 483, 488
15:13, 18 . . . . . . . . . . . . . . . . . . . . . . . . . .222
15:14–33. . . . . . . . . . . . . 501–515, 502, 503
15:14–21. . . . . . . . . . . . . . . . . . . . . . 503–505
15:14–16:27 . . . . . . . . . . . . . . . . . .6, 12, 502
15:14–15. . . . . . . . . . . . . . . . . . . . . . . . . . . .3
15:14 . . . . . . . . . . . . . . . . . . . . . . .40, 211, 297
15:15–23. . . . . . . . . . . . . . . . . . . . . . . . . . . .4
15:15–21. . . . . . . . . . . . . . . . . . . . . . . . .32, 503
15:15–16. . . . . . . . . . . . . . . . . . . . . . . .2, 24, 26
15:15 . . . . . . . . . . . . . . . . . . . . . . . . .2, 10, 504
15:16 . . . . . . . . . . . . . . . . . . . . .19, 39, 414, 516
15:16, 20 . . . . . . . . . . . . . . . . . . . . . . . . . . .25
15:16, 21–20. . . . . . . . . . . . . . . . . . . . . . . .503
15:17–24. . . . . . . . . . . . . . . . . . . . . . . . . . .36
15:17–23. . . . . . . . . . . . . . . . . . . . . . . . . . .38
15:17–21. . . . . . . . . . . . . . . . . . . . . . . . . . .41
15:18 . . . . . . . . . . . . . .40, 361, 411, 505, 517
15:19 . . . . . . . . . . . . . . . . . . .28, 41, 400, 512
15:19b . . . . . . . . . . . . . . . . . . . . . . . . . . . .508
15:20 . . . . . . . . . . . . . . . . . . . . . . . . . . .40, 512
15:22–29. . . . . . . . . . . . . . . . . . . . . . 508–10
15:22–24. . . . . . . . . . . . . . . . . . . . . . . . . . . .3
15:22–23. . . . . . . . . . . . . . . . . . . . . . . . . . . .4
15:22 . . . . . . . . . . . . . . . . . . . . . . . . . . . . .503
15:23–24. . . . . . . . . . . . . . . . . . . . . . . . . .503
15:24–32. . . . . . . . . . . . . . . . . . . . . . . . . . .40
15:24–28. . . . . . . . . . . . . . . . . . . . . . . . . . . .7
15:24–25. . . . . . . . . . . . . . . . . . . . . . . . . . .10
15:24, 30 . . . . . . . . . . . . . . . . . . . . . . . . . . . .4
15:24, 30, 32 . . . . . . . . . . . . . . . . . . . . . .4, 363
15:25–32. . . . . . . . . . . . . . . . . . . . . . . . . . . .5
15:25–27. . . . . . . . . . . . . . . . . . . . . . . . . .503
15:26 . . . . . . . . . . . . . . . . . . . . . . . . . . . . .509
15:28–29. . . . . . . . . . . . . . . . . . . . . . . . . .503
15:28–29, 34. . . . . . . . . . . . . . . . . . . . . . . .3, 4
15:28 . . . . . . . . . . . . . . . . . . . . . . . . . . . . .510
15:29 . . . . . . . . . . . . . . . . . . . . . . . . . . . . . .39
15:30–33. . . . . . . . . . . . . . . . . . . . . . . . . .511
15:30–32. . . . . . . . . . . . . . . . . . . . . . . . .41, 503
15:30 . . . . . . . . . . . . . . . . . . . . . . . . . .222, 531
15:31 . . . . . . . . . . . . . . . . . . . . . .293, 294, 381
15:33 . . . . . . . . . . . . . . . . . . . . . . . . . .503, 538
16. . . . . . . . . . . . . . . . . . . . . . . . . . . . . .10, 327
16:1–23. . . . . . . . . . . . . . . . . . . . . . . . . . . .47
16:1–16. . . . . . . . . . . . . . .9, 467, 502 516–27
16:1–2. . . . . . . . . . . . . . . . . . . . 520–21, 527
16:1 . . . . . . . . . . . . . . . . . . . . . . . . . . . . . . .4
16:3–16. . . . . . . . . . . . . . . . . . . . . . . . .2, 3, 463
16:3–15. . . . . . . . . . . . . . . . . . . . . . . . 521–23
16:3–5. . . . . . . . . . . . . . . . . . . . . . . . . . . . . .3
16:3 . . . . . . . . . . . . . . . . . . . . . . . . . . . . . .519
16:5 . . . . . . . . . . . . . . . . . . . . . . . . . . .387, 519
16:6–15. . . . . . . . . . . . . . . . . . . . . . . . . . . . .2
16:6 . . . . . . . . . . . . . . . . . . . . . . . . . . . . . . .3

16:7 . . . 3, 19, 442
16:10 . . . 3
16:11–12. . . . 2
16:11 . . . 3, 519
16:14 . . . 519
16:15 . . . 519
16:16 . . . 525
16:17–24. . . . 530–35
16:17–23. . . . 534
16:17–20. . . . 502
16:17–20a. . . . 531–33
16:17 . . . 25, 468
16:19 . . . 2, 25, 36, 532
16:20b–23. . . . 533–34
16:20 . . . 297
16:21–24. . . . 502
16:21–23. . . . 26
16:23 . . . 445, 538, 539
16:24 . . . 538, 539
16:25–27. . . . 42, 502, 539–40, 541
16:25 . . . 10, 390
16:26 . . . 25, 40, 261, 362, 411, 506
16:27 . . . 25, 288, 341, 406

**1 Corinthians**

1:1–2, 26. . . . 26
1:2 . . . 360
1:2, 30 . . . 213
1:4 . . . 38
1:5 . . . 360
1:7 . . . 39
1:8 . . . 455
1:9 . . . 155
1:11 . . . 520
1:14 . . . 534
1:16 . . . 520
1:18–32. . . . 61, 63
1:18 . . . 41
1:20 . . . 415
1:22–24. . . . 40
1:23 . . . 41, 48
1:26–27. . . . 61, 69
1:26 . . . 263
1:27–29. . . . 50
1:28–32. . . . 60
1:30 . . . 42, 116, 152
1:31 . . . 506
2:1 . . . 422
2:1, 7 . . . 390
2:4 . . . 507
2:5 . . . 370
2:6–8. . . . 415
2:7 . . . 282, 540
2:8 . . . 442
2:9 . . . 504
2:12, 18 . . . 416
3:1 . . . 234, 242
3:10–15. . . . 77, 507
3:10 . . . 504
3:16–17. . . . 213
3:18 . . . 183, 415
3:23 . . . 67
4:9–13. . . . 362
4:12 . . . 381
4:20 . . . 478
5:5 . . . 455
5:7 . . . 261
5:15–16. . . . 180
6:9–11. . . . 67
6:9–10. . . . 478
6:9 . . . 59
6:10 . . . 459
6:11 . . . 263
6:18 . . . 459
6:19–20. . . . 215, 417, 472
6:20 . . . 116, 117
7:1–40. . . . 60
7:7 . . . 39
7:9 . . . 82
7:11 . . . 167
7:13–14. . . . 387
7:19 . . . 147, 308
7:22–23. . . . 18
8–10 . . . 464
8. . . . 6, 7, 496
8:6 . . . 20
8:7–12. . . . 465
8:7 . . . 466
8:7, 10 . . . 9
8:7, 10, 12 . . . 446
9. . . . 39
9:1 . . . 19
9:5 . . . 387
9:12 . . . 20, 28
9:16–23. . . . 40
9:20–23. . . . 400
9:20–22. . . . 385
9:20–21. . . . 25, 223
9:20 . . . 195
9:20, 24 . . . 316
9:21–23. . . . 465
9:21 . . . 262
9:22 . . . 466
10. . . . 306
10:1–23. . . . 464
10:1–12. . . . 342
10:1 . . . 38, 390
10:2 . . . 193

10:11 . . . 316
10:22 . . . 40, 208
10:24–33. . . 464
10:24–26. . . 479
10:32 . . . 317
11:1–16. . . 60
11:7 . . . 20
11:17–34. . . 433
11:28 . . . 387
12. . . 425
12:1–31. . . 422
12:1 . . . 38
12:3 . . . 359
12:4, 28–31. . . 39
12:7–10, 30. . . 425
12:12–31. . . 425
12:26 . . . 433
12:27 . . . 226
12:28 . . . 24
13:1–13. . . 452
13:1–10, 13. . . 431
14. . . 464
14:2, 20–21. . . 464
14:5–6. . . 464
14:17, 23 . . . 464
14:20 . . . 519
14:25 . . . 54, 281
15:1–8. . . 17
15:1–5. . . 20
15:1, 3, 11 . . . 539
15:3–5. . . 21, 151
15:3 . . . 294, 494
15:8–9. . . 19
15:8 . . . 387
15:10 . . . 19, 24
15:12–21. . . 175
15:17 . . . 152
15:20–58. . . 455
15:20, 25 . . . 24, 111
15:21–22, 58. . . 71
15:22–24. . . 386
15:22 . . . 175
15:24, 52 . . . 478
15:28 . . . 302
15:35–58. . . 264
15:43 . . . 289
15:49 . . . 283
15:55–56. . . 297
15:56 . . . 175, 180, 185, 220, 221, 241, 259
15:57 . . . 297
16:1–5. . . 509
16:8 . . . 317
16:15 . . . 387, 522
16:15, 19 . . . 520
16:19 . . . 519
16:19, 23 . . . 521
16:20 . . . 525
16:23 . . . 533

**2 Corinthians**

1:3 . . . 314
1:5 . . . 268, 296
1:8 . . . 38
1:14 . . . 455
1:20 . . . 14, 21, 316, 368
1:22–23. . . 264
1:22 . . . 279
2:12 . . . 20, 28
3. . . 78, 225, 306
3:1–3. . . 520
3:6 . . . 220, 221, 225
3:9 . . . 258
3:11 . . . 291
3:17–18. . . 281, 416
3:17 . . . 256
3:18 . . . 217
4:4 . . . 20, 283, 415
4:5 . . . 359
4:7–15. . . 296
4:9 . . . 381
4:12 . . . 432
4:16–5:5 . . . 264
4:16 . . . 411
4:17 . . . 268, 274, 275, 277, 289
5:1–10. . . 454
5:2–4. . . 274
5:2, 4 . . . 280
5:4 . . . 178
5:5 . . . 279
5:10 . . . 77, 295, 473
5:11–21. . . 161
5:14–15. . . 310
5:14 . . . 295, 297
5:15 . . . 151
5:18–21. . . 167, 385
5:19 . . . 119, 372
5:20 . . . 167
5:21 . . . 20, 35, 120, 261
6:2 . . . 111, 373
6:7 . . . 455
8:1–24. . . 509
8:9 . . . 360
8:23 . . . 19, 521, 523
9:13 . . . 20, 25, 28
10:1 . . . 423
10:3–4. . . 455
10:8 . . . 27
10:10 . . . 422

10:14 . . . . . . . . . . 20, 28
10:15–16. . . . . . . . . . 507
10:17 . . . . . . . . . . 506
11:2 . . . . . . . . . . 312, 326
11:3 . . . . . . . . . . 177, 240
11:4 . . . . . . . . . . 532
11:13 . . . . . . . . . . 317, 532
11:22 . . . . . . . . . . 315, 381
11:23–29. . . . . . . . . . 296
11:23–28. . . . . . . . . . 362
11:23 . . . . . . . . . . 315, 442
11:24–26. . . . . . . . . . 381
11:31 . . . . . . . . . . 314
12:10 . . . . . . . . . . 296
12:12 . . . . . . . . . . 507
13:2 . . . . . . . . . . 525
13:5 . . . . . . . . . . 270
13:10 . . . . . . . . . . 27
13:11 . . . . . . . . . . 433, 482, 511
13:14 . . . . . . . . . . 213, 263, 533

**Galatians**

1:1 . . . . . . . . . . 19
1:4 . . . . . . . . . . 294, 349
1:5 . . . . . . . . . . 406
1:6–7. . . . . . . . . . 532
1:7 . . . . . . . . . . 28
1:10 . . . . . . . . . . 18
1:12 . . . . . . . . . . 20
1:13–14. . . . . . . . . . 385
1:14 . . . . . . . . . . 234
1:15–26. . . . . . . . . . 505
1:15–16. . . . . . . . . . 19, 24, 400
1:15 . . . . . . . . . . 19
1:40 . . . . . . . . . . 415
2:1–3:39 . . . . . . . . . . 317
2:4–5. . . . . . . . . . 41
2:8 . . . . . . . . . . 400
2:10 . . . . . . . . . . 509
2:11–15. . . . . . . . . . 539
2:11–14. . . . . . . . . . 85, 100, 500, 532
2:15–3:29 . . . . . . . . . . 232
2:15–16. . . . . . . . . . 125
2:16 . . . . . . . . . . 100, 113
2:16, 22 . . . . . . . . . . 113
2:17–19. . . . . . . . . . 220
2:17, 25 . . . . . . . . . . 388
2:19–20. . . . . . . . . . 193, 198, 208
2:19 . . . . . . . . . . 204, 221, 223
2:20 . . . . . . . . . . 196, 224, 264, 295, 297, 299, 300, 417
2:21 . . . . . . . . . . 78, 318, 403
3:1–5. . . . . . . . . . 532
3:2, 5, 10 . . . . . . . . . . 100
3:5 . . . . . . . . . . 507
3:6–18. . . . . . . . . . 139
3:6–14. . . . . . . . . . 125, 242
3:6–13. . . . . . . . . . 240
3:8 . . . . . . . . . . 21
3:10–14. . . . . . . . . . 195
3:11–12. . . . . . . . . . 354
3:11–12, 25–24 . . . . . . . . . . 122
3:11 . . . . . . . . . . 44
3:12 . . . . . . . . . . 354
3:13 . . . . . . . . . . 261
3:14 . . . . . . . . . . 260
3:16, 23 . . . . . . . . . . 313
3:17 . . . . . . . . . . 236
3:21 . . . . . . . . . . 185
3:22 . . . . . . . . . . 113, 394
3:23 . . . . . . . . . . 354
3:27 . . . . . . . . . . 388, 456
3:28–29. . . . . . . . . . 308, 434
3:29 . . . . . . . . . . 326
4:1–7. . . . . . . . . . 255, 266
4:4–5. . . . . . . . . . 260
4:4–5, 23. . . . . . . . . . 195
4:4 . . . . . . . . . . 165, 260
4:4, 21 . . . . . . . . . . 223
4:5 . . . . . . . . . . 267
4:6–7. . . . . . . . . . 268
4:8–9. . . . . . . . . . 350
4:10 . . . . . . . . . . 466
4:16 . . . . . . . . . . 268
4:19 . . . . . . . . . . 264
4:21–31. . . . . . . . . . 368
4:26 . . . . . . . . . . 393
4:28 . . . . . . . . . . 323
5–6 . . . . . . . . . . 225
5. . . . . . . . . . 454
5:1–12. . . . . . . . . . 41
5:1–5. . . . . . . . . . 532
5:1 . . . . . . . . . . 215
5:6 . . . . . . . . . . 147, 310
5:7 . . . . . . . . . . 532
5:10 . . . . . . . . . . 297
5:11 . . . . . . . . . . 381
5:13–14. . . . . . . . . . 431
5:13 . . . . . . . . . . 215
5:13, 18–18. . . . . . . . . . 234
5:14 . . . . . . . . . . 262, 453, 454, 507
5:16–17. . . . . . . . . . 253
5:16 . . . . . . . . . . 262
5:18 . . . . . . . . . . 195, 223
5:20 . . . . . . . . . . 532
5:21 . . . . . . . . . . 478
5:25 . . . . . . . . . . 197
6:2 . . . . . . . . . . 262, 418, 481, 507

6:7–8. . . . . 77
6:8 . . . . . 12
6:12–13. . . . . 532
6:13 . . . . . 82
6:14 . . . . . 204, 506
6:15 . . . . . 147, 308
6:16 . . . . . 30, 392, 511
6:18 . . . . . 533

**Ephesians**

1–3 . . . . . 199
1:3–14. . . . . 339
1:3 . . . . . 214
1:5 . . . . . 267
1:5, 11 . . . . . 182
1:7 . . . . . 117, 118, 360
1:7, 14 . . . . . 116
1:9 . . . . . 390
1:10 . . . . . 472
1:11 . . . . . 182
1:12 . . . . . 182
1:13–14. . . . . 264
1:13 . . . . . 28
1:14 . . . . . 279
1:16–19. . . . . 38
1:16 . . . . . 38
2:1–3. . . . . 263
2:3 . . . . . 66
2:4–5. . . . . 66
2:5 . . . . . 64
2.7 . . . . . 360
2:8–10. . . . . 128
2:8–9. . . . . 78, 116, 199
2:11–3:12 . . . . . 306
2:12 . . . . . 287, 313
2:13 . . . . . 111
2:14–17. . . . . 167
2:16 . . . . . 425
2:18 . . . . . 168
3:3–9. . . . . 390, 538, 540
3:6 . . . . . 217
3:8 . . . . . 360
3:11 . . . . . 182
3:12 . . . . . 113, 168
3:17–18. . . . . 297
3:17 . . . . . 264
3:18 . . . . . 296
3:21 . . . . . 406
4–6 . . . . . 199
4:4, 25 . . . . . 425
4:11–13. . . . . 24
4:11 . . . . . 425, 516
4:22 . . . . . 198
4:30 . . . . . 116
5:2 . . . . . 295, 297, 299
5:5 . . . . . 478
5:6 . . . . . 199, 532
5:8–16. . . . . 454
5:23–24. . . . . 226
5:29 . . . . . 425
6:6 . . . . . 18
6:11–17. . . . . 455
6:15 . . . . . 375
6:19 . . . . . 390
6:23 . . . . . 511

**Philippians**

1:1 . . . . . 18
1:4 . . . . . 38
1:6, 10 . . . . . 455
1:6, 25 . . . . . 297
1:9–11. . . . . 38
1:12 . . . . . 28
1:15–18. . . . . 532
1:16 . . . . . 28
1:17 . . . . . 20
1:18 . . . . . 47
1:19 . . . . . 263
1:20–24. . . . . 454
1:27 . . . . . 28
1:28 . . . . . 458
1:29 . . . . . 268, 296
2:2–4. . . . . 482
2:2 . . . . . 433
2:3 . . . . . 422, 423, 431, 449
2:5–11. . . . . 14, 114
2:6–11. . . . . xiii
2:6 . . . . . 481
2:7–8. . . . . 260
2:8 . . . . . 33, 423
2:9–11. . . . . 33
2:10 . . . . . 472
2:11 . . . . . 359
2:12–13. . . . . 27, 33, 219
2:16–17. . . . . 505
2:16 . . . . . 455
2:17 . . . . . 413
2:24 . . . . . 297
2:25 . . . . . 19, 521, 523
3. . . . . 155
3:1 . . . . . 316
3:2 . . . . . 532
3:3–9. . . . . 315
3:3 . . . . . 82, 83, 323, 392
3:5–9. . . . . 381
3:6–7. . . . . 353
3:6 . . . . . 349
3:8 . . . . . 234, 449
3:9 . . . . . 35, 113, 122

3:10–11 . . . 386
3:10 . . . 268, 296
3:12 . . . 178
3:20–21 . . . 455
3:20 . . . 393
3:21 . . . 264, 283
4:2 . . . 416, 433, 482
4:3 . . . 521
4:7–9 . . . 511
4:7 . . . 449
4:10 . . . 178
4:16 . . . 393
4:18 . . . 414
4:19 . . . 360
4:20 . . . 406
4:23 . . . 533

**Colossians**

1:3 . . . 38
1:9–11 . . . 38
1:12–13 . . . 478
1:14 . . . 116
1:15–20 . . . 14
1:15, 20 . . . 283
1:15 . . . 283
1:18 . . . 24
1:20–22 . . . 167
1:22 . . . 111, 385
1:23 . . . 287, 363, 389
1:24 . . . 296, 505
1:26–27 . . . 390, 538, 540
1:27 . . . 163, 264, 283, 360
2 . . . 225
2:2 . . . 390
2:4 . . . 532
2:6 . . . 466
2:11–13 . . . 198
2:11–12 . . . 82
2:11 . . . 147
2:14–15 . . . 297
2:23 . . . 185, 417
3:5–11 . . . 265
3:9 . . . 198
3:11–12 . . . 308
3:11 . . . 147
3:12 . . . 303, 423, 456, 459
3:13 . . . 484
3:15 . . . 425
3:25 . . . 77
4:3 . . . 390
4:10 . . . 520, 523
4:11 . . . 478, 521, 533
4:15–17 . . . 519

**1 Thessalonians**

1:2 . . . 38
1:4–5 . . . 283
1:4 . . . 303
1:5 . . . 507
1:10 . . . 393, 455
2:2, 8–9 . . . 20
2:12 . . . 478
2:13–14 . . . 283
2:13 . . . 41
2:14–16 . . . 316
2:15 . . . 41, 381, 511
2:16 . . . 471
2:19 . . . 163
3:2 . . . 20, 28, 521
4:1–5:10 . . . 455
4:3–4, 7 . . . 213
4:5 . . . 350
4:9–10 . . . 452
4:9 . . . 431
4:13 . . . 38, 390
4:14 . . . 151, 386
4:17 . . . 264
5:1–11 . . . 454
5:2 . . . 455
5:4–6 . . . 455
5:8 . . . 458
5:13 . . . 452
5:15 . . . 434
5:23 . . . 511
5:26 . . . 525
5:28 . . . 533

**2 Thessalonians**

1:1 . . . 533
1:3 . . . 38
1:5 . . . 478
1:7–8 . . . 362
1:7 . . . 393
1:8 . . . 20, 350
2:2 . . . 455
2:3 . . . 532
2:13 . . . 387, 522
3:4 . . . 297
3:16 . . . 511
3:18 . . . 533

**1 Timothy**

1:10 . . . 59
1:11 . . . 20
1:13 . . . 350
2:4 . . . 373
2:6 . . . 116
2:7 . . . 400
2:14 . . . 240

3:8 . . . . 480
3:16 . . . . 33, 152, 363
4:14 . . . . 39
4:18 . . . . 406
5:10 . . . . 432
5:23 . . . . 480
6:10–11. . . . . 459
6:11 . . . . 459

**2 Timothy**
1:5 . . . . 297
1:6 . . . . 39
2:3 . . . . 296
2:8 . . . . 20
2:14 . . . . 177
2:15 . . . . 171
2:22 . . . . 459
4:1, 18 . . . . 478
4:1 . . . . 295, 473
4:14 . . . . 77
4:20 . . . . 4, 534
4:22 . . . . 533

**Titus**
1:1 . . . . 18
1:15 . . . . 475
2:3 . . . . 480
2:10 . . . . 289
2:12 . . . . 415
2:13–14. . . . . 218
2:13 . . . . 163, 314
2:14 . . . . 116
3:1 . . . . 443
3:5 . . . . 116

**Philemon**
1–2 . . . . 519
1. . . . . 533
4. . . . . 38
6. . . . . 38
17. . . . . 167
21. . . . . 297, 503
23. . . . . 523
25. . . . . 533

**Hebrews**
1:3 . . . . 283
1:5 . . . . 23
1:6 . . . . 283
3:1 . . . . 19
3:6 . . . . 155
3:6, 14 . . . . 389
7:25 . . . . 295
8:4 . . . . 515
9:1, 6 . . . . 313
9:15 . . . . 116, 117
9:22 . . . . 118
9:24 . . . . 295
10:32–34. . . . . 433
10:38 . . . . 44
11:1 . . . . 153
11:23 . . . . 450
11:39–40. . . . . 153
12:22 . . . . 393
12:23 . . . . 283
13:1 . . . . 431
13:2 . . . . 432
13:15 . . . . 413
13:16 . . . . 418

**James**
1:21 . . . . 362
2:8–9. . . . . 431
2:14–26. . . . . 3, 76, 77
2:15–16. . . . . 418
2:18 . . . . 454
3:13 . . . . 423
4:6 . . . . 422, 423
4:6, 10 . . . . 423

**1 Peter**
1:3 . . . . 314
1:11 . . . . 263
1:18 . . . . 116
1:22 . . . . 431, 457
2:5 . . . . 413
2:5, 9 . . . . 515
2:13–14. . . . . 443
2:14–15. . . . . 445
3:8 . . . . 423
3:9 . . . . 432, 434
4:9 . . . . 432
4:14 . . . . 283
4:17 . . . . 362
5:5–6. . . . . 423
5:5 . . . . 422
5:14 . . . . 525

**2 Peter**
1:7 . . . . 431
2:2 . . . . 415
3:13 . . . . 278
3:17 . . . . 182

**1 John**
2:1 . . . . 295
2:7–11. . . . . 431
3:1 . . . . 299
3:10–18. . . . . 431
4:7–12, 20–21 . . . . 431
4:8 . . . . 291

**3 John**

8. . . . . . . . . . . . . . . . . . . . . . . . . . . . . . . . . .432

**Jude**

. . . . . . . . . . . . . . . . . . . . . . . . . . . . . . . . . . . .

3. . . . . . . . . . . . . . . . . . . . . . . . . . . . . . . . . .494

**Revelation**

1:5 . . . . . . . . . . . . . . . . . . . . . . .24, 155, 283

1:6 . . . . . . . . . . . . . . . . . . . . . . . . . . . . . . .515

3:12 . . . . . . . . . . . . . . . . . . . . . . . . . . . . . .393

5:5 . . . . . . . . . . . . . . . . . . . . . . . . . . . . . . .487

5:9–10. . . . . . . . . . . . . . . . . . . . . . . . . . . . .515

5:10 . . . . . . . . . . . . . . . . . . . . . . . . . . . . . .183

5:13 . . . . . . . . . . . . . . . . . . . . . . . . . . . . . .472

6:17 . . . . . . . . . . . . . . . . . . . . . . . . . . . . . . .75

19:7 . . . . . . . . . . . . . . . . . . . . . . . . . . . . . .226

20:4–6. . . . . . . . . . . . . . . . . . . . . . . . .183, 386

20:10 . . . . . . . . . . . . . . . . . . . . . . . . . . . . .530

20:11–15. . . . . . . . . . . . . . . . . . . . . . . . . . . .77

21–22 . . . . . . . . . . . . . . . . . . . . . . . . . . . . .170

21–22, 9 . . . . . . . . . . . . . . . . . . . . . . . . . . .226

21:1 . . . . . . . . . . . . . . . . . . . . . . . . . . . . . .278

21:2 . . . . . . . . . . . . . . . . . . . . . . . . . . . . . .393

21:3 . . . . . . . . . . . . . . . . . . . . . . . . . . . . . .276

21:11, 25 . . . . . . . . . . . . . . . . . . . . . . . . . .288

22:16 . . . . . . . . . . . . . . . . . . . . . . . . . . . . .487

22:17 . . . . . . . . . . . . . . . . . . . . . . . . . . . . .226

# Extrabiblical Literature Index


**Tobit**

1:10–12. . . . . 469
13:11 . . . . . 510

**Judith**

12:2 . . . . . 469
14:10 . . . . . 146

**Wisdom of Solomon**

2:6 . . . . . 277
2:7 . . . . . 480
2:23–24. . . . . 19, 175
2:24 . . . . . 177
4:12 . . . . . 533
4:15 . . . . . 325
6:1–11. . . . . 441
10–11 . . . . . 74
12–16 . . . . . 74
12:12 . . . . . 322
12:21 . . . . . 313
13–15 . . . . . 52, 58
14:12 . . . . . 57
14:27 . . . . . 57
15. . . . . 82
15:1–7. . . . . 332
15:1–5. . . . . 71, 80
15:7 . . . . . 322
16:5–6. . . . . 74
16:24 . . . . . 277
18:4 . . . . . 80
18:22 . . . . . 313
19:6 . . . . . 277
19:22 . . . . . 325

**Sirach**

10:4–5. . . . . 441
10:4 . . . . . 444
14:17 . . . . . 177
15:15 . . . . . 353
15:24 . . . . . 177
17:11 . . . . . 353
17:17 . . . . . 325
24:6–8. . . . . 325
26:29 . . . . . 199
28:1 . . . . . 435
28:10 . . . . . 435
31:25, 29 . . . . . 480
31:26–27. . . . . 480
33:7 . . . . . 449
35:1–5. . . . . 413
44:12, 18 . . . . . 313
44:19–21. . . . . 138
44:19 . . . . . 143
44:20 . . . . . 143
44:21 . . . . . 143
45:5 . . . . . 353
45:5, 19 . . . . . 313
45:23–24. . . . . 349

**1 Maccabees**

1:47, 62 . . . . . 475
1:53 . . . . . 326
1:62–63. . . . . 468
2:24–27, 50, 54, 58. . . . . 349
2:51–52. . . . . 138
2:52 . . . . . 143
7:9 . . . . . 326

**2 Maccabees**

2:17–18. . . . . 148
4:2 . . . . . 349
5:27 . . . . . 469
6:13–16. . . . . 117
7:18, 32–33, 37–38 . . . . . 117
7:37–38. . . . . 118
7:38–39. . . . . 109
8:15 . . . . . 313
14:38 . . . . . 349
15:9 . . . . . 112
15:39 . . . . . 480

**2 Esdras**

6:58 . . . . . 349

**4 Maccabees**

2:15–16. . . . . 231
4:26 . . . . . 471
5:25 . . . . . 72
6:17–29. . . . . 109
6:27–29. . . . . 109, 117
6:28–29. . . . . 118
9:20 . . . . . 117
10:8 . . . . . 117
17:20–22. . . . . 109

17:21–22 . . . . . . . . . . 117
18:10 . . . . . . . . . . 112

## DEAD SEA SCROLLS AND RELATED TEXTS

### Cairo Genizah Copy of the Damascus Document

3.2–3 . . . . . . . . . . 143
3.19–20 . . . . . . . . . . 72
6.17–18 . . . . . . . . . . 471
16.4–6 . . . . . . . . . . 146

## PHILO

### *On the Life of Abraham*

70 . . . . . . . . . . 145
133–36 . . . . . . . . . . 60
135–36 . . . . . . . . . . 59
273 . . . . . . . . . . 143

*On the Cherubim*
31 . . . . . . . . . . 145

*Who Is the Heir?*
279 . . . . . . . . . . 387

*Allegorical Interpretation*
3:88 . . . . . . . . . . 329

*On the Migration of Abraham*
46, 113–14, 201 . . . . . . . . . . 326
82 . . . . . . . . . . 146

*On the Life of Moses*
2.108 . . . . . . . . . . 415

*On the Change*

*Of Names*
76 . . . . . . . . . . 145

*On Planting*
160 . . . . . . . . . . 455

*On the Posterity of Cain*
13–21 . . . . . . . . . . 326
84–85 . . . . . . . . . . 355

*On Rewards and Punishments*
44 . . . . . . . . . . 326

*On the Sacrifices Of Cain and Abel*
32 . . . . . . . . . . 62
54–57 . . . . . . . . . . 120
88 . . . . . . . . . . 415
161 . . . . . . . . . . 145

*On Dreams*
2.25 . . . . . . . . . . 146

*On the Special Laws*
1.2–8 . . . . . . . . . . 146
1.201, 272, 277, 287, 290 . . . . . . . . . . 415
1.9–10 . . . . . . . . . . 146
2.50 . . . . . . . . . . 59
3.38 . . . . . . . . . . 60

## JOSEPHUS

### *The Life*

14 . . . . . . . . . . 469

*Against Apion*
2.25, 199 . . . . . . . . . . 59
2.199 . . . . . . . . . . 60
2.273 . . . . . . . . . . 60

*Jewish Antiquities*
1.155 . . . . . . . . . . 145
6.124 . . . . . . . . . . 118
8.112 . . . . . . . . . . 118
10.59 . . . . . . . . . . 118
11.346 . . . . . . . . . . 471, 475
12.27 . . . . . . . . . . 117
12.271 . . . . . . . . . . 349
18.9, 23 . . . . . . . . . . 442
18.23 . . . . . . . . . . 442
18.141 . . . . . . . . . . 94
20.9, 12 . . . . . . . . . . 524
20.100 . . . . . . . . . . 94
20.186, 204, 208–10 . . . . . . . . . . 511

*Jewish War*
2.118 . . . . . . . . . . 442
2.221 . . . . . . . . . . 524
2.254, 425 . . . . . . . . . . 511
2.409–10 . . . . . . . . . . 511
4.400 . . . . . . . . . . 511
4.618 . . . . . . . . . . 21
4.656–7 . . . . . . . . . . 21
5.385 . . . . . . . . . . 118

## MISHNAH AND RELATED LITERATURE

### 'Abot

1.17 . . . . . . . . . . 76
3.7 . . . . . . . . . . 353

### Nedarim

3.11 . . . . . . . . . . 143, 146

**Qiddushin**
4.14 . . . . . 143

**Sanhedrin**
10.1 . . . . . 82, 325

**Shabbat**
19.3 . . . . . 146

**OTHER RABBINIC WORKS**

**Genesis Rabbah**
12.6 . . . . . 115

**APOSTOLIC FATHERS**

**1 Clement**
5.7 . . . . . 514
21.7 . . . . . 431
25.2 . . . . . 1
33.1, 47.5 . . . . . 431
48.1 . . . . . 431
49.4–6 . . . . . 431
50.1–3 . . . . . 431
53.5 . . . . . 431
54.1 . . . . . 431
62.2 . . . . . 431
63.3 . . . . . 1
65.1 . . . . . 1

**Didache**
1.3 . . . . . 431
2.7 . . . . . 431

**Ignatius, to the Ephesians**
15.1 . . . . . 207

**Ignatius, to the Romans**
3.2 . . . . . 207

**CLASSICAL AND ANCIENT CHRISTIAN WRITINGS**

**Augustine**
*Enchiridion on Faith, Hope, and Love*
3.11 . . . . . 282

*The Spirit and the Letter*
6, 8, 20, 24–25 . . . . . 225

**Cicero**
*Tuscan Disputations*
4.26 . . . . . 466

**Epictetus**
*Dissertationes*
1.16.20–21 . . . . . 415
2.9.2 . . . . . 415
2.19.13 . . . . . 494
2.26.4 . . . . . 237

**Eusebius**
*Ecclesiastical History*
2.23.5 . . . . . 469

**Horace**
*Satirae*
1.9.65–72 . . . . . 466

**Irenaeus**
*Against Heresies*
3.1.1 . . . . . 29
3.4.1–2 . . . . . 29

**John Chrysostom**
*Homiliae in Epistulam Ad Romanos*
1 . . . . . 27
2 . . . . . 40
7 . . . . . 121
9 . . . . . 168
10 . . . . . 179, 197, 201
16 . . . . . 329
19 . . . . . 387
31 . . . . . 528

**Justin**
*Dialogue with Trypho*
10 . . . . . 100
46.1–47.4 . . . . . 468
135 . . . . . 325
140 . . . . . 325

*First Apology*
1.4 . . . . . 1
1.65 . . . . . 519, 525

**JUVENAL**
*Satirae*
6.306–13 . . . . . 59
14.96–100 . . . . . 471
14.98–99 . . . . . 476
14.98 . . . . . 469

**Origen**
*Commentarii in Romanos*
6:11 . . . . . 206

**Ovid**
*Metamorphosis*
9.758 . . . . . . . . . . . . . . . . . . . . . . . . . . . . .60

**Pindar**
*Pythian Odes*
2.72 . . . . . . . . . . . . . . . . . . . . . . . . . . . . .204

**Plato**
*Laws*
1.2 . . . . . . . . . . . . . . . . . . . . . . . . . . . . . .60

*Symposium*
217–19 . . . . . . . . . . . . . . . . . . . . . . . . . . .59

**Plutarch**
*Questiones Convivales*
4.5 . . . . . . . . . . . . . . . . . . . . . . . . . . . . . .469

**Seneca**
*De Clementia*
1.4 . . . . . . . . . . . . . . . . . . . . . . . . . . . . . .445

*Epistulae Morales*
4.6 . . . . . . . . . . . . . . . . . . . . . . . . . . . . . .172
6.1 . . . . . . . . . . . . . . . . . . . . . . . . . . . . . .416
94.48 . . . . . . . . . . . . . . . . . . . . . . . . . . . .416
95.47 . . . . . . . . . . . . . . . . . . . . . . . . . . . .471

**Suetonius**
*Divus Claudius*
25.2 . . . . . . . . . . . . . . . . . . . . . . . . . . . . . .1

*Nero*
10. . . . . . . . . . . . . . . . . . . . . . . . . . . . . . . .5
44.1 . . . . . . . . . . . . . . . . . . . . . . . . . . . . .446

*Vespasianus*
4.5 . . . . . . . . . . . . . . . . . . . . . . . . . . . . . .448

**Tacitus**
*Agricola*
30. . . . . . . . . . . . . . . . . . . . . . . . . . . . . . .416

*Annales*
13.50–51. . . . . . . . . . . . . . . . . . . . . . . . . . .5
13.50 . . . . . . . . . . . . . . . . . . . . . . . . . . . .446
15.44 . . . . . . . . . . . . . . . . . . . . . . . . . . . . . .1

*Historiae*
4.2 . . . . . . . . . . . . . . . . . . . . . . . . . . . . . .469
5.1 . . . . . . . . . . . . . . . . . . . . . . . . . . . . . .388
5.2 . . . . . . . . . . . . . . . . . . . . . . . . . . . . . .469
5.4 . . . . . . . . . . . . . . . . . . . . . . . . . . . . . .471
5.5 . . . . . . . . . . . . . . . . . . . . . . . . . . . . . .100
5.13 . . . . . . . . . . . . . . . . . . . . . . . . . . . . .448

**TERTULLIAN**
*Aplogeticus*
3. . . . . . . . . . . . . . . . . . . . . . . . . . . . . . . . .1
39.7 . . . . . . . . . . . . . . . . . . . . . . . . . . . . .431

**VIRGIL**
*Eclogae*
10.69 . . . . . . . . . . . . . . . . . . . . . . . . . . . .301

**Xenophon**
*Memorabilia*
2.1.32. . . . . . . . . . . . . . . . . . . . . . . . . . . . .59

# Subject Index


*Abba*, 255, 267, 268, 273, 281
Abraham
  faith of, 138–40, 150–51, 153–54, 157
  father by flesh or faith, 145, 147–49
  in Jewish tradition, 144–46, 149–51
  Paul on, 114, 137–47, 147–51, 160, 214, 259–60
Adam, 71–72, 189, 255, 394
Adam/Christ typology, 175–76, 181–89, 214
*adelphoi*, 312
*adiaphora*, 493, 494
*aedile*, 534
*agape*, 430, 437
Ahab, King, 381
*aidios dynamis*, 56
*akakos*, 533
*akatharsia*, 212
*akrasia*, 237
alcohol consumption, 499–500
*alētheia*, 485
*alla touto krinate mallon*, 474
*allēlōn*, 431
Ambrosiaster, 238
*ametamelētos*, 394
Ampliatus, 518, 524
*anakainōsis*, 416
*anastaseôs nekrôn*, 24
*anathema*, 312
Andria, Solomon, 86
Andronicus, 5, 19, 467, 518, 522, 523, 542
*anomia*, 212
*anthrōpion legō*, 77
antinomianism, 5, 17, 97, 125, 270, 506
anti-Semitism, 397–400
*aparchē*, 522
*apatheia*, 433
Apelles, 524, 538
*apokalypsis*, 277
*apokalyptō*, 54
Apollos, 521, 528
apologetics, explanation of, 28
apologia for Torah, Paul's. *See* Paul
apostle, definition of, 19
Apostle's Creed, 29, 518
apostleship, bestowing of, 26–27
apostolic calling of Paul. *See* Paul
*apostolos*, 19, 523
*Aqedah* tradition, 293
Aquila, 3, 4, 5, 306, 392, 467, 518, 519, 521, 527, 541
Aquinas, Thomas, 233, 295, 515
*ara nyn*, 258
Aristobulus, 4, 5, 518, 519, 524
atonement
  achievement of, 117–18
  God as subject and object of, 119
Augustine, 100, 132, 178, 179, 225, 231, 232, 233, 234, 245, 282, 455, 464, 500
Aurelius, Marcus, 406
*axia*, 276
baptism, 28, 195–205
Barnabas, 19, 306, 392
*blasphēmeo*, 477
boasting, 121–23, 140, 142, 167, 388
Bunyan, John, 246
Calgacus, 416
Calvin, John, xv, 8, 56, 64, 77, 100, 116, 160, 233, 245, 335, 337, 368
Cenchreae, church in, 6
Chadwick, Florence, 170
*charisma pneumatikon*, 39, 424
Chloe, 227, 520
Christology, definition of, 28
Christonomous, 216
Christos, 114–15
Christosis, 275
*christotelic* hermeneutic, 22
Chrysostom, John, 27, 40, 168, 179, 418, 516, 525, 526, 528
church, modern
  anti–government options, 449–50
  attendance, xi
  avoiding divisiveness, 439–40, 492–98
  avoiding wrongful teachings, 420–21, 498–99, 536–38
  behavior goals of, 159–60, 417–18, 422–28, 459–60, 498–501, 512–17
  clergy and, 514–17
  definition of, 23
  evangelism, 31
  mission, 28, 47, 90, 512–14
  multicultural, 135–36

multinational, 45–46
partnership among, 46–47
public justice and, xi
women in, xi, 526–28
Cicero, 84, 466
circumcision, 71, 81, 91, 94, 121, 124, 137, 141, 145–46, 379
citadel, the, 17
Clement of Rome, 534
Codex Sinaiticus, 191, 350, 538
Codex Vaticanus, 538
*conplexio*, 163
Corinthians, 37, 256, 262, 283, 417, 433, 452, 531, 519, 534
Chrysostom, John, 27, 60, 121, 168, 179, 197, 201, 232, 317, 418, 516, 525, 528
creation, 277–79
Creator, 56, 277–79
Cyrus, 443
dating, 4–7
David, 17, 18, 22, 23, 30, 95, 383
*dedikaōitai apo tēs hamartias,* 199
Dever, Mark, 160
*diakonos,* 484, 520
*dianomou pisteôs,* 122
*dia ta paraptōmata hēmōn,* 152
*dia tēn dikaiōsin hēmōn,* 152
differenus from other letters, 7–10
*dikaiōma tou nomou,* 262
*dikaiōma,* 262
*dikaiomenoi,* 116
*dikaioō,* 120, 199
*dikaios,* 120
*dikaiosynē,* 258, 264
*dikaiosynē theou,* 42, 111
divisiveness, avoidance of, 461–98, 530–32
divorce, xi
*dokimazō,* 416
*dokimç,* 170
*douleias tēs phthoras,* 278
*doulos,* 18
*dysangelion,* 309
Edict of Claudius, 3, 4, 5, 11, 13, 433, 441, 469, 519, 521, 524
*ēgerthē,* 152
*ek pisteōs,* 44
election, 340–42, 393
*en autois,* 55, 389
*encomium,* 452
*endeixin tēs dikaiosynēs autou,* 19, 119
Epaphroditus, 19, 523
Epenetus, 522
Ephesus, 48, 508, 519, 521, 522
Epictetus, 423, 494
*episēmos,* 523
Erastus, 6, 445, 531, 534
ethnocentric nominism, 121
*euangelion,* 20, 21, 309
*eulogētos,* 314
Eusebius, 469
evil. *See* sin
exodus, 116–17, 126, 216–18
*exōmen,* 163
*exornatio,* 110
expiation. *See* sin
*ezēsen,* 472
faith. *See also* righteousness
as confession, 358–61
dichotomy with obedience, 34, 142
explanation of, 153–56
God's righteousness revealed in, 120–21
justification by, 133, 135, 138, 162, 163, 167, 463
law of, 122–25
merit and, 119, 145
moral effort vs., 218–19
obedience in, 25–26, 32–34
oneself and, 157–59, 366–69, 407–410
preaching and, 369–75, 407–410
salvation and, 44, 112–113
transformation, 415–21, 422–27
urgency for, 458–59
works vs., 120–23, 125, 137, 145–46
faith in Jesus, debate over interpretation, 112–14
food, 470–71, 475–77
Gaius, 530, 531, 534
Gallio (proconsul), 7
Gentiles, Jews and, 4–5, 6, 8, 10–14, 17, 19, 26–27, 35, 41, 42, 109–10
*gezerah shewah,* 140
glorification, 163
God, 123–25, 411–12
gospel
content, 22
importance of, 27–32, 36, 41
shame and, 48–51
gospelizing, importance of, 39, 463
grace
apostolic, 24–25
law vs. grace, 122–25, 209–210, 221, 233
Luther on, 126–28, 130, 136
misunderstandings about, 128–29
of God, 120–21, 126–28, 142, 182–83
oneself and, 128–36, 168–69, 173
Pelagius on, 132
promise and, 148
religion vs., 130, 133–34

righteousness by, 139, 256
salvation by, 116, 215–18
gracism, 135
greetings, 510–25, 528–29, 523–35
*halakhah*, 100, 197
hamartiology, definition, 102–103
*hēmarton*, 115
Herodian, 467, 488, 524
*heurēskenai*, 140
*hierourgeo*, 505
*hilastērion*, debate over, 117–18
*histēmi*, *470*
holy kiss, 525
Holy Spirit, 15, 16, 25, 163, 165, 222, 271, 273, 280–81, 298, 301, 302, 304, 311, 410, 414, 417, 462, 463, 478, 483, 487, 499, 500, 501, 503, 504, 505, 511
homophobia, 66–69
homosexuality, 52, 60–69
*homothymadon*, 482
Horace, 466
*horizô*, 23
*hōsautōs*, 280
*hōsper*, 394
*houtōs*, 392, 394
*huios*, 266, 277
*huiothesia*, *267*
*humilitas*, 423
*hypernikaô*, 296
*hyperphronein*, 423
"I" in Romans 7:7–25, meaning of, 231–38, 242–47–53
idolatry, 57–58, 61, 62–63, 74
*inclusio*, 151, 167, 465
*infirmior*, 466
*insula*, 6, 126
Irenaeus, 29
*iustitia*, 43
Jacob and Esau, 327–30
Jason, 523, 529, 533, 553
Jerusalem prayer request, 510–12
Jesus
faithfulness of, 114, 164
obedience of, 114
portrayals of, 30
sacrifice of, 117–19
union with, 193–95, 366–69
Jews. *See also* law of Moses
Adamic covenant and, 71–72
advantage of, 93–94
chosen people, 80–81, 91, 94
dietary laws, 100, 476–77
disobedience to God's commands, 89
eight privileges of Israelites, 312–13
elected by God, 325–28, 379
exclusivism and, 120–21
failure of, 344–61, 378–86
God's promises to, 162, 259, 279, 305, 313, 379
God's rebuking of, 92
hypocrisy of, 79–89, 120–21, 436–37
importance of Christianity to, 15–16, 21, 33, 41, 42, 54, 304–20, 342–43
Jesus and, 317–20, 335–36, 374
Messiah and, 7, 322–43, 399–405
patriarchs, 16, 313
Sabbath, 100
salvation of, 89, 217, 380, 386–97
Jews for Jesus, 404
Jews and Gentiles, 4–6, 10–14, 17, 19, 26–27, 35, 41, 42
Jews/ Gentiles equality re, 74–76, 93, 94, 98
Judaism, three pillars of, 79, 92
Judgement, 470–88, 495–500
justice, 54–55, 93
Old Testament and, 93, 99–100
salvation and, 110–111
vengeance and 435–36
Junia, 5, 19, 467, 522, 523, 526, 528
justification, 110–11, 115–16, 120–24, 132, 142–45, 151–52, 347–50
of Abraham, 142–46
Barth on, 133
Jews and, 347–49
racial acceptance and, 134–35
ungodly persons and, 142–45, 162
Juvenal, 59, 475
*kakos*, 389, 479, 533
*kalos*, 435, 479
*kashrut*, 475, 476
*katalasso*, 167
*kata sarka*, 141, 313
*kateirgasato*, 239
*katharos*, 475
*kathōs*, 484
*kauchēsis*, 506
*klçtos*, 19, 26
*koinonia*, 135
*koinos*, 469, 475
*kopiaô*, 526
*krinô*, 474
*krinômen*, 474
*ktisis*, 277
*kuriō*, 472
*kyrios*, 359, 488
law of Moses
inadequacy of, 98–101, 119–20
Paul's direction to uphold, 125, 240–41

*legô,* 380
*leitourgos,* 505
*Lex Rex,* 450
"light" imagery, 455–56
Lincoln, Abraham, 436
*lingua franca,* 46
Locke, John, 132
*logia tou theou,* 94
*logikos,* 415
*logizomai,* 140, 144, 276
love of God, 290–303
Lucius, 523, 530, 533
Luther, Martin, xvi, 8, 123, 126–28, 130, 136, 245
Maccabees, Judas, 469
Marcion of Sinope, 30, 49, 63, 240, 378
Marcus Aurelius, 406
marriage metaphor. *See* Paul
Martyr, Justin, 467–68, 525
Mary (Rufus' mother), 467, 522, 526
*mataiotēs,* 278
*mē genoito,* 95, 238, 241, 381
Melanchthon, Philip, 8
*mellei logizesthai,* 151
*menō,* 328
Messiah, 16, 18, 21–24, 42, 111, 112, 124, 314
*metron pisteôs,* 424
midrash, 140, 151
Milton, John, 186–88
*missio dei,* 89
monetary gifts, 9–10, 509–10, 520–21
Moses, 18, 48, 78, 112, 122, 124, 148, 174, 180, 181, 185, 215, 227, 246, 247, 248, 312, 321, 330, 331, 334, 344, 345, 352, 353, 358, 370, 383, 422, 451, 506
Muratorian Canon, 8
*mystērion,* 540
Narcissus, 518, 519, 524
nature of, Letter of Romans, 8, 11, 13–14
Nebuchadnezzar, 443, 444
Nero, 5, 448
new exodus allusions, 18, 21
Nicene Creed, 498, 536
*nomos,* 122, 259
*nova obedientia,* 33
*oiketēs, 470*
*oikonomos,* 534
olive tree analogy. *See* Paul
opening verses, Letter of Romans, 18
*opheilo,* 452
Origen, Adamantius, 56, 178, 233, 431, 442, 458, 468, 494, 528
original sin, 102, 189–91
Pantaenus, 513
*paraenesis,* 429
*parakalō,* 413, 531
*para physin,* 60
*paredōken,* 57
*paredothē,* 152
*Parousia,* 378, 454
*pasa pseuchē,* 444
*pasa sarx,* 99, 100
Paul
  ambition of, 512–13
  apologia for Torah, 232–33
  apostolic calling, 19, 40, 89
  apostolic ministry, 47, 463–65, 414, 502–510
  background, 18–20, 315–17
  gospel pioneer, 507
  imprisonment, 413
  "light imagery," 455–56
  marriage metaphor, 220–29
  olive tree analogy, 9, 161, 386–90, 396
  priestly duty, 504–5
  salvation images, 41, 115–16, 149, 158–59
  slavery metaphor regarding sin, 212
  speech to Athenians, 119
Pelagius, 100, 131, 132, 179, 214, 231
Petronius, Gaius, 455
penal substitution, 120
*pephanerōtai,* 111
*peri hamartias,* 260
persecution of Christians, 448–49
Persis, 518, 524, 526
Peter, 85
*philadelphia,* 431
Philo, 58, 62, 80, 143, 325, 355, 443
*philostorgos,* 431
*philotimeomai,* 512
Phoebe, 6, 7, 244, 432, 519, 520, 521, 526, 527
*phronein,* 423
*physikos,* 60
*pietas,* 116
Pindar, 204
Piper, John, 160
*pisteōs Iēsou Christou,* debate over, 112–14
*pisteuō,* 94
*pistis,* 113, 424
*pistis Christou,* 113
Plato, 59, 237, 423
*ple{dec65}rophoreô,* 471
Plutarch, 444,
*pneumatikos,* 241
Polycarp, Bishop of Smyrna, 49
predestination, 323–37

priest, description of, 515–16
*princeps,* 456
Priscilla, 3, 4, 5, 306, 392, 467, 518, 519, 521, 526
*proēgoumenoi,* 431
promise to Jews, 148–49
propitiation. *See* sin
*propositio,* 40, 110
*prosagōgē,* 168
*proslambanomai,* 465
*prosopopiia,* 233
*prostatis,* 521
*prosthesis,* 282
*protoevangelium,* 112
purpose
- of his work, 8–14, 485–87, 502, 506
- of Paul's Rome visit, 507–10

Quartus, 531
Race, 133–36
reconciliation, 160–65, 174–76
redemption, 115, 164–65
- non–Christians and, 251
- oneself and, 172–73, 188–89
- salvation and, 116–17, 254–64, 281–84
- Torah and, 117

*regula fidei,* xii, 29, 30
resurrection, 23
revenge culture, 434–40
righteousness. *See also* grace
- Abraham's, 137–39, 142–44
- deeds and, 77–79
- faith and, 25, 44, 139, 304–20, 349–51
- Gentiles and, 109–10, 125–26
- Jewish law and, 43, 72–73, 79, 92, 98–100, 108–13, 117, 120–24, 139, 194, 221, 233, 255, 259, 329–30, 346–51, 353–54, 454
- language of, 120
- Luther on, 126–28
- of God, 40–45, 53–54, 95, 111–16, 119–20, 126
- process of, 144–45
- slavery to, 212–13, 218–19, 470
- two ways to live and, 211–15, 264–65

Roman church history, 3–6, 21–24
- factions, 5–6, 10–11, 13, 17

Roman converts, 36–40
Roman marriage law, 220, 222–27
Rufus, 6, 62, 185, 467, 488, 524, 526
sacraments, 28
sacred days, 471–72
sacrifice
- God's purpose, 119–20
- method of, 118, 412–15
- penal substitution, 120

*šâliah,* 19
salvation. *See also* grace; Jews; redemption
- extending to all, 36, 41, 42, 251
- Luke and, 129–30
- meaning, 472
- misunderstandings about, 128–29
- obedience and, 28, 30, 33
- oneself and, 252–54, 284–89

*sarx,* 224, 260
Saul, 422
Seneca, 75, 171, 237, 445
sexual misconduct, 57–63, 455
- Old Testament and, 59–60, 71

shame, 209, 213
*Shekinah,* 312
Sicarii, the, 511
similarities to other letters, 8–9
sin. *See also* original sin
- Christ dying for, 20, 31, 165–66
- consequences of, 99–100, 102–103, 180–81, 241–42
- described by authors, 178–79
- desperation and, 248–49
- enumerated, 99
- eradication of, 533
- evil and, 52–57, 105–107, 250, 436, 439
- expiation, 118–19
- God overlooking, 119–20
- grace and, 184–85, 208–214
- hypocrisy, 25, 72, 75, 79–89
- immorality 61–63
- impurity and, 212
- Jews and Gentiles equality re, 73–74, 93–94, 98, 102, 115, 131–32
- judgment and, 73–75, 99
- law and, 180–81, 209–210, 221–27, 233, 238–39, 246
- modern descriptions for, 102
- oneself and, 106–108, 191–92, 203–207, 239–40, 249–51
- preaching about, 104–106, 108
- pride, 433
- process of, 53–56, 177–79
- propitiation, 118–19
- revenge, 429–39
- slavery to, 209–212, 215–19, 242, 244, 250, 257
- superiority complex, 86–87
- transgressions, 181–84
- wages of, 214–15

slavery, 4, 59–60
slavery to sin. *See* sin
*sola fide,* 33, 123

*sōphronein,* 423
Sosipater, 523, 533
*sôtçria,* 41
Spain plan, 6, 9, 12, 403, 463, 502, 504, 508–9
spirit and flesh, 262–68
Stachys, 524
Stephanus, 520, 522
story in, Letter of Romans, 14–27, 539–42
strong welcome weak, 465–67, 479–80
submitting to government, 442–49
Suetonius, 3, 4, 448
suffering, 164
Sun–Tzu, 439
superiority complex. *See* sin
*superstitio,* 442
*symposia,* 60, 455
*synaichmalōtos,* 523
*synantilambanomai,* 280
*syneidēsis,* 446
*synergos,* 521
*syngenēs,* 312, 523
*synkrisis,* 175
*syschēmatizesthe,* 415
Tacitus, 448
*tapeinophrosynē,* 423
*ta pros ton theon,* 506
taxes, 9
*telos,* 356
Ten Commandments, 236, 239, 247, 317, 453, 471
Tertius, 304, 531, 533
Tertullian, 431
theocentrism, 20
theological depth, xvi
*theos,* 20
*theotēs,* 56
*thysia,* 413
Timothy, 521, 534
*tines,* 389
*Ti oun eroumen,* 141
wrongful behaviors avoidance, 497–500

# Author Index


Adam, Peter, 497
Allman, Jim, 172
Anderson, David, 135
Barclay, John, 182, 338
Barth, Karl, xvi, 66, 133, 154–55, 337, 369
Barth, Markus, 133
Bates, Matthew W., 353
Beker, J.C., 8
Bell, Bob, 64
Bell, Richard H., 403
Bellarmine, Cardinal Robert, 269
Bisk, Tsvi, 319
Bligh, J., 205
Blocher, Henri, 180
Blomberg, Craig L., ii
Bock, Darrell L., i, 400
Bonhoeffer, Dietrich, 34, 216, 450
Bornkamm, Günther, 8–9
Brondos, David, 261
Brown, Abnew, 427
Browning, Thomas R., 495
Bruce, F. F., 466
Cameron, David, 420–21
Campbell, Constantine, 194
Campbell, Douglas, 8
Camus, Albert, 172
Carson, D. A., 107, 421
Charles, Simeon, 427
Chester, Stephen, 245
Chesterton, G. K., 189
Corkill, Craig, 171
Craig, Lloyd, 249
Dickson, John, 423–24
Dodd, C. H., 63, 118
Douglass, Judy, ii
Dror, Moshe, 319
Dunn, James D. G., xv, 9, 178, 212, 219, 304, 389, 473, 479
Durant, Will, 449
Eastman, Susan, 395
Edwards, Jonathan, 65
Emerson, Matthew, 133
Epp, Eldon, 524
Esler, Philip Francis, 482
Fitzmyer, Joseph A., 256
Francis, Samuel Trevor, 299
Garland, David, 85
Gagnon, Robert A., 60
Geddie, John, 90
Glover, T. R., 448
Goodrich, John, 242
Grieb, Katherine, 65
Gupta, Nijay, 415
Harrison, James, 116
Hays, Richard, 136, 141, 306, 353
Horton, Michael, 130
Hultgren, Arland J., 407
Hybels, Bill, 271
Jenson, Peter, 28
Jewett, Robert K., xv, 523
Jobes, Karen, 300
Johnson, Luke Timothy, xv, 9, 220, 430
Jowett, Benjamin, 132–33
Käsemann, Ernst, 23, 242, 288, 442
Keck, Leander, xv, 298, 442, 453
Keener, Craig, i, 439–40
Kierkegaard, Søren, 437
Kirk, J.R. Daniel, 489
Koester, Helmut, 318
Kruppenbach, Fritz, 371–72
Lampe, Peter, 4
Law, Peter, 374
Lawson, Nigella, 513
Lewis, C. S., 108, 247
Lincicum, David, 353
Lincoln, Andrew, 315
Lipstadt, Debra, 397
Lloyd, Craig, 249, 250
Mann, Alan, 105
Marshall, I. Howard, 389
Machen, J. Gresham, 135
McKnight, Scot, 437
Mendelsohn, Bob, 404
Menninger, Karl A., 102
Moltmann, Jürgen, 287
Moo, Douglas J., xv, 57, 97, 164, 212, 275, 279, 348, 396, 408, 439, 497
Morris, Leon, xv, 118, 383, 474
Nietzsche, Friedrich, 439
Oakes, Peter, 11, 214, 395
Ortberg, John, i
Pannenberg, Wolfhart, 319

Perkins, William 282
Peterson, Eugene, 312, 333, 472, 535
Phillips, J. B., 529
Piper, John, 340, 512
Poirier, Jack, 424
Porter, Stanley, 167, 449
Reasoner, Mark, 41
Rosner, Brian, 111, 453–54
Rutherford, Samuel, 450
Rutledge, Fleming, 101, 160
Sacks, Rabbi Jonathan, 88
Sanders, E. P., 401, 476
Schaeffer, Francis, 457
Schreiner, Tom, xv, 12, 55, 446, 526
Seifrid, Mark A., 79, 120, 146
Simeon, Charles, 427
Smith, Christian, 133
Solzhenitsyn, Aleksandr, 106
Sprinkle, Preston M., 61
Spurgeon, Charles, 33, 490–92
Stanley, Andy, ii
Stott, John, 450
Talbert, Charles, xv, 417
Tannehill, Robert, 194
Thielman, Frank, i
Thoreau, Henry David, 248
Torrance, Alan, 302
Travis, Stephen, 65
Venning, Ralph, 103
Vickers, Brian, 478
Volf, Miroslav, 319, 435
von Soden, Hermann, 522
von Tischendorf, Constantin, 522
Wagner, J. R., 304, 406
Warfield, B. B., 135
Waters, Guy, 353
Watson, Francis, 44, 114
Watts, Isaac, 541
Wesley, Charles, 218
Wesley, John, 246, 250
White, Robert, 279
Whittle, Sarah, 414, 517
Wiefel, Wolfgang, 10–11
Wilson, E. O., 205
Winter, Bruce, 469
Winter, Sean, 373
Witherington, Ben, 523, 527–28
Wright, N. T., xv, 25, 60, 127, 172, 175, 197, 217, 261, 320, 330, 353, 364, 374, 402, 419–20, 447, 455, 488, 512, 526, 539